Land, Community, and the State in the Caucasus

Land, Community, and the State in the Caucasus

Kabardino-Balkaria from Tsarist Conquest to Post-Soviet Politics

Ian Lanzillotti

BLOOMSBURY ACADEMIC
LONDON • NEW YORK • OXFORD • NEW DELHI • SYDNEY

BLOOMSBURY ACADEMIC
Bloomsbury Publishing Plc
50 Bedford Square, London, WC1B 3DP, UK
1385 Broadway, New York, NY 10018, USA
29 Earlsfort Terrace, Dublin 2, Ireland

BLOOMSBURY, BLOOMSBURY ACADEMIC and the Diana logo are trademarks of
Bloomsbury Publishing Plc

First published in Great Britain 2022
Paperback edition published in 2023

Copyright © Ian Lanzillotti, 2022

Ian Lanzillotti has asserted his right under the Copyright, Designs and
Patents Act, 1988, to be identified as Author of this work.

Cover image: © Azamat Shomakhov.

All rights reserved. No part of this publication may be reproduced or transmitted
in any form or by any means, electronic or mechanical, including photocopying,
recording, or any information storage or retrieval system, without prior
permission in writing from the publishers.

Bloomsbury Publishing Plc does not have any control over, or responsibility for, any
third-party websites referred to or in this book. All internet addresses given in this
book were correct at the time of going to press. The author and publisher regret any
inconvenience caused if addresses have changed or sites have ceased to exist,
but can accept no responsibility for any such changes.

Every effort has been made to trace copyright holders and to obtain their permissions
for the use of copyright material. The publisher apologizes for any errors or omissions
and would be grateful if notified of any corrections that should be incorporated in
future reprints or editions of this book.

A catalogue record for this book is available from the British Library.

Library of Congress Cataloging-in-Publication Data
Names: Lanzillotti, Ian, author.
Title: Land, community, and the state in the Caucasus : Kabardino-Balkaria from tsarist
conquest to post-Soviet politics / Ian Lanzillotti.
Other titles: Kabardino-Balkaria from tsarist conquest to post-Soviet politics
Description: London ; New York : Bloomsbury Academic, 2021. |
Includes bibliographical references and index.
Identifiers: LCCN 2021015219 (print) | LCCN 2021015220 (ebook) | ISBN9781350137448 (hbk) |
ISBN 9781350137455 (ePDF) | ISBN 9781350137462 (eBook)
Subjects: LCSH: Kabardino-Balkariia (Russia)–History–20th century. | Kabardino-Balkariia
(Russia)–History–19th century. | Kabardino-Balkariia (Russia)–Ethnic relations–History–20th
century. | Kabardino-Balkariia (Russia)–Ethnic relations–History–19th century. | Balkar (Turkic
people)–Land tenure–Caucasus. | Kabardians–Land tenure–Caucasus. | Caucasus–Politics
and government–20th century. | Caucasus–Politics and government–19th century.
Classification: LCC DK511.K12 L36 2021 (print) | LCC DK511.K12 (ebook) | DDC 947.5/2—dc23
LC record available at https://lccn.loc.gov/2021015219
LC ebook record available at https://lccn.loc.gov/2021015220

ISBN: HB: 978-1-3501-3744-8
PB: 978-1-3502-6763-3
ePDF: 978-1-3501-3745-5
eBook: 978-1-3501-3746-2

Typeset by Deanta Global Publishing Services, Chennai, India

To find out more about our authors and books visit www.bloomsbury.com and
sign up for our newsletters.

To my parents for their love and encouragement

Contents

List of Maps	viii
Acknowledgments	ix
Glossary	xi
Introduction	1
1 Land, Community, and Conquest in the Central Caucasus, 1763–1825	29
2 The Caucasus War and the Disorder of Intercommunal Relations in the Central Caucasus, 1825–61	59
3 Colonization, Intercommunal Relations, and Imperial Integration: Kabarda and Its Neighbors from Reform to Revolution, 1861–1917	77
4 From Princely Fiefdoms to Soviet Nations: Border Delimitation, Intercommunal Conflict, and National Identity, 1918–28	121
5 From KBASSR to KASSR to KBASSR: Intercommunal Relations, Nationalities Policy, and the Deportation, Return, and Reintegration of the Balkars, 1944–66	169
6 Intercommunal Relations and Ethnic Politics in the Post-Soviet Caucasus: Kabardino-Balkaria and Its Neighbors	213
Conclusion	237
Notes	241
Bibliography	287
Index	305

Maps

1. Ethno-linguistic makeup of the Northwest and Central Caucasus on the eve of tsarist conquest — 16
2. Map of Kabarda compiled by the cartographer Stepan Chichagov in 1744 — 30
3. Kabarda and its neighbors *c.* 1842 — 74
4. Nalchik Okrug in its 1917 borders showing territory transferred to Karachai, North Ossetia, and Ingushetia by VTsIK decrees in 1922 and 1924 — 163
5. Administrative structure of the Soviet Caucasus, 1936–8 — 172
6. The post-Soviet Caucasus — 214

Acknowledgments

This book would not have been possible without the wisdom, hospitality, and support of many wonderful people and organizations. I am deeply grateful to the faculty of the Department of History at Ohio State University, especially Nicholas Breyfogle, Theodora Dragostinova, David Hoffmann, and Scott Levi. From my time in Columbus, I thank my dear friends Liz Kimble, William Newby, Mark Sokolsky, and Brian Whitacre. I also thank the following scholars whose feedback, insights, and passion for the study of the Caucasus have benefited this book and enhanced my understanding of the region: Irina Babich, Vladimir Bobrovnikov, Julie Fairbanks, Krista Goff, David Jishkariani, Jeronim Perović, Ron Suny, and Lidia Zhigunova. From my time at Indiana University, I am especially grateful for the insights and feedback of William Fierman and Ed Lazzerini. This book benefitted greatly from the cartographic expertise of Sike Dutzmann of the at the Leibniz Institute of Geography. I am also grateful to Arthur Tsutsiev and Georgii Derluguian for the vital historical and sociological research on the North Caucasus and for allowing me to the use the map that appears as figure 1 in this book. I am grateful to Golfo Alexopoulos, Oksana Lutsyshyna, and Victor Peppard for sparking my interest in the study of Eurasia.

I benefited from the hospitality, friendship, and knowledge of so many people during my research trips to Russia. I would especially like to thank Victoria Banionyte and Sofia Kodzova and the Baikulovs in St. Petersburg; Asiiat Gegieva, Elena Shaulova and family, Anton Shishkin, and Alim Zhgulov in Moscow. My thanks also go to all the Caucasianists of the Russian Academy of Sciences' Institute of Ethnology and Anthropology for their hospitality.

My deepest thanks go to my gracious hosts and good friends in Kabardino-Balkaria: the Shomakhovs and the Zhigunovs. Many thanks go to Sufian Zhemukhov, an amazing mentor, colleague, and friend who has taught me so much about Circassian culture and identity. Elleonora Maremukhova, a great friend and language teacher, introduced me to the beauty and complexities of *adygabza*. I thank the Baikulovs and Natoks in Adygeia and the Torshkhoevs in Ingushetia for their hospitality. I am grateful for the support and wisdom of Timur Aloev, Barasbi Bgazhnokov, Amarbi Karmov, and Madina Khakuasheva at the Institute for Humanities Studies in Nalchik. I also thank Osman Zhansitov and Galina Kalmykova for their friendship and hospitality. I am grateful to Martin Emkuzhev for his hospitality and for taking me to Khasaut. I am thankful for Safarbi Beituganov's encyclopedic knowledge of the region's history and for his hospitality. I am also grateful to the staff and archivists at the Central State Archive of the Kabardino-Balkar Republic and the Center for the Documentation of the Recent History of the Kabardino-Balkar Republic.

I could not have conducted the research for this project without generous support from Fulbright-Hays; the American Philosophical Society; and, at Ohio State

University, from the Department of History, the Graduate School, the Mershon Center for International Security Studies, and the Office of International Affairs.

Most of all, I am grateful to my family. To my parents, Tom and Brenda, for encouraging me to take my passions seriously and for always believing in me; to Eli for his wonder and joy; to Allison for keeping me inspired, loved, and focused during the writing process; to Heath for being my best friend and for always making me laugh; to Rachel for her wisdom; to Mia and Sophie for their love and support; to my grandparents, for their encouragement, love, and the coat that kept me warm through Russian winters; and to Murray and Linda for their support and love.

Glossary

AO — Autonomous region (*avtonomnaia oblast'*). An ethnically defined administrative-territorial unit of relatively low status on the Soviet Union's administrative hierarchy. AOs were usually subordinate to a larger region (*krai*) or republic.

ASSR — Autonomous Soviet Socialist Republic (*Avtonomnaia Sovetskaia Sotsialisticheskaia Respublika*). An ethnically defined administrative-territorial unit with an intermediate status above an AO but below that of a union republic (SSR).

aul — A Caucasus mountain village.

GPU — State Political Directorate (*Gosudarstvennoe politicheskoe upravlenie*). The Soviet secret police of the RSFSR from 1922 to 1923. Replaced by the OGPU, the All-Union State Political Directorate, after the creation of the Soviet Union.

inogorodnie — Literally people of a foreign city. In the North Caucasus, it referred to recent settlers from outside of the region, typically Russians and other Slavs.

ispolkom — An abbreviation for Executive committee (*Ispolniteln'yi komitet*). An elected organ of the Soviet government that existed at the district, regional, and all-union levels.

NKVD — People's Commissariat for Internal Affairs (*Narodnyi kommissariat vnutrennykh del*). Soviet secret police from 1934 to 1943.

oblast' — The most common administrative-territorial unit in Russia since the late-tsarist period. The equivalent of a region.

obkom — Regional committee (*Oblastnoi komitet*) of the Communist Party.

okrug — A district. Lower-level administrative-territorial unit subordinate to oblasts or republics. It would be replaced by the raion from the mid-1920s on.

pristav — Superintendent of a *pristavstvo*, a late nineteenth and early nineteenth-century administrative unit for Russia's Muslim-populated imperial borderlands.

raikom — A district-level committee (*raionyi komitet*) of the Communist Party.

revkom — Civil war–era local governments established by the Bolsheviks upon coming to power.

RSFSR	Russian Soviet Federative Socialist Republic (*Rossiiskaia Sovetskaia Federativnaia Sotsialisticheskaia Respublika*).
stanitsa	Plural *stanitsy*. A fortified Cossack settlement.
TsK	Central Committee (*Tsentral'nyi komitet*) of the Communist Party of the Soviet Union.
VTsIK	All-Russian Central Executive Committee (*Vserossiiskii tsentral'nyi ispolnitel'nyi komitet*). Nominally the chief legislative body of the Russian Soviet Federative Socialist Republic (RSFSR) from 1917 to 1937.

Introduction

On a cold autumn morning in 2010, shortly after arriving in Moscow to conduct archival research, I noticed an unusual sight by the tourist traps outside the Kremlin. Just past the Lenin, Stalin, and Ivan the Terrible impersonators sat a group of white-bearded mountaineers clad in the mangy, thick wool burkas and hats (*papakhi*) traditionally worn by shepherds of the Caucasus highlands. Upon closer examination, it became clear that these striking men, straight out of a Tolstoy short story or Lermontov poem, were not encamped on Manezh Square to earn a living, at least not directly. Rather, these were real mountaineers, carrying out a hunger strike in the heart of Russian power, in order to bring attention to their community's economic problems. They were Balkars, a national minority indigenous to the mountains of the semiautonomous Kabardino-Balkar Republic in the center of Russia's volatile, multiethnic North Caucasus region. They were conducting a hunger strike in protest of recent land reforms that they felt deprived them of historically Balkar pasture land vital to their cattle-breeding economy.[1] While most news reports and sound bites on the North Caucasus focus on recent problems of Islamic radicalism, terrorism, and ethnic separatism, the Balkars' protest brought attention to a much older problem: the land question. Competition over the scarce land resources of this densely populated mountain region has been the region's most enduring source of conflict and tension.

In the 1990s, Dzhokhar Dudaev, the late president of the separatist Chechen Republic of Ichkeria, called Kabardino-Balkaria "the sleeping beauty of the Caucasus."[2] Dudaev predicted that if the North Caucasus region's nationalist-cum-Islamist insurgency spread to Kabardino-Balkaria, Russia's rule over its restive North Caucasian borderland could be effectively challenged. The belief was, as goes Kabardino-Balkaria, so goes the rest of the North Caucasus. Despite tensions between Kabardians and Balkars, and, between 2005 and 2012, a low-level Islamist insurgency unrelated to Kabardian-Balkar relations, the "sleeping beauty" never awoke. Everyday relations among Kabardians, Balkars, and Russians remain peaceful; the ability of ethno-political entrepreneurs to mobilize their co-ethnics in a sustained way has remained relatively weak since the de-escalation of tensions in the mid-1990s; and Kabardino-Balkaria remains tightly under Moscow's control.

I arrived in Moscow that autumn to conduct research on the effects of Soviet nationality policies on interethnic relations and national identities in Kabardino-Balkaria. I wanted to understand why this republic, despite its tensions, had witnessed relative peace during the roughly two decades since the collapse of the Soviet Union, a period marked by conflict, usually framed in ethnic terms, throughout much of the Caucasus region. Though I suspected that land relations would be a part of my study, my serendipitous encounter with the Balkar demonstrators near Red Square indicated that questions of access to land could be *the* key to understanding intercommunal relations and state policies in the region. Indeed, as I approached the Soviet period chronologically and began examining archival materials from the Civil War years and their chaotic aftermath, land disputes, within and among nascent national communities, stood out as the most important social and political phenomena in the Central Caucasus. My search for the reasons for the intense conflict and ethnonational mobilization around the land question in the early 1920s and today took me steadily further back in time. I realized that to identify the structures and patterns of governance and intercommunal relations in the region during the Soviet years, it would be necessary to understand Central Caucasian society on the eve of the Russian conquest and how it changed and adapted to Russian rule over the *longue durée*.

Themes and Arguments

This book explores three primary themes: intercommunal relations, the expansion and evolution of imperial rule and governance, and the causes of peace and violence. To explore these topics, this study places central attention on the socioeconomic relations that developed around land use and ownership in the Central Caucasus, a region of extraordinary ethno-confessional diversity. In order to explore the deep roots of contemporary issues of governance, intercommunal relations, and conflict in the Caucasus region, this book analyzes these issues and their interaction with patterns of land use and ownership over two centuries, from the extension of Russian rule in the late eighteenth century through the collapse of the Soviet Union in 1991. This periodization allows for a comparative exploration of these themes over different regimes: the precolonial Kabardian princely confederation, the tsarist state, the Soviet Union, and post-Soviet Russia. Based on this approach, this study reaches several conclusions about the nature of Kabardian-Balkar relations and, more generally, imperial governance and the role of the tsarist and Soviet states in shaping intercommunal relations and identities in the North Caucasus.

Causes of Intercommunal Peace and Conflict

This study finds that the ultimately peaceful relationship between Kabardians and Balkars has its roots in the symbiotic, though unequal, system of intercommunal relations that existed in the Central Caucasus prior to the Russian conquest in the late eighteenth and early nineteenth centuries and that continued in evolving and modified forms through the nineteenth and twentieth centuries. This symbiosis was based on each community occupying complimentary ecological niches. From the sixteenth through eighteenth centuries, the Circassian princely confederation of Kabarda, controlling the vital arable farmland and seasonal pastures in the plains, was one of the most powerful states in the North Caucasus. Elites from neighboring transhumant mountaineer (*gortsy*) communities—today's Balkars, Karachai, Ossetians, and Ingush—collected tribute from their villagers and paid part of it to Kabardian princes to obtain for their community the right to graze cattle on Kabarda's lowland fiefdoms in the autumn and spring. Moreover, given the limitations of mountain terrace farming, mountaineers depended on grain from Kabarda for their survival. For their part, Kabardians relied on their mountaineer neighbors for animal products (regionally, Balkars kept the greatest number of sheep and cattle per capita) and refuge during invasions from external enemies.[3]

Horizontal social bonds and shared confessional identities held this symbiosis together. In particular, the elite princely and noble families of the Central Caucasus, though culturally and linguistically diverse, were tied together through intermarriage and fictive kinship. These familial ties between Kabardian and mountaineer elites ensured the stability of the region's social hierarchy and provided vital socioeconomic benefits to the families involved. Even where familial ties were absent, the tributary relationship between mountaineer nobleman and Kabardian prince reinforced the status of both members within their own communities. When this system of intercommunal relations came under attack from Orthodox Russia, the mountaineers' and Kabardians' common adherence to Sunni Islam became another important link that bound these communities together. Horizontal ties among the region's elites, though undergoing dramatic changes under tsarist rule, lasted through 1917.

During the tsarist period, class or estate categories and confessional affiliations usually had far greater meaning in society than ethnic or national ones. While the tsarist state sometimes identified loyal groups and allocated rights and responsibilities on the basis of ethnic categories, it more often determined these questions according to confessional group, estate status, or civil rank.[4] After 1917, the Bolsheviks' class warfare combined with a thoroughgoing institutionalization and territorialization of ethnicity gave ethnic categories unprecedented social significance and ended the cross-communal ties among the region's traditional elites. In deporting the Balkars and seven other nationalities during the Second World War on charges of collective treason, Stalin's genocidal policies paradoxically consolidated the sense of ethnic consciousness among these communities. After 1945, the meaning of ethnicity in the North Caucasus varied by community. The communities that the Soviet state deemed disloyal based on their ascribed nationality suffered thirteen years of exile under brutal conditions and, for many, decades of discrimination after their return to the Caucasus in the late-1950s. By contrast, other national minorities whose ascribed nationalities did not carry such negative consequences and connotations enjoyed heightened levels of social mobility, especially within their ethnically defined administrative units.

The Kabardian-Balkar symbiosis (based on economic, political, social, and familial ties) has meant that, at critical points, the choice of most Balkars and Kabardians has been for compromise rather than violence. Moreover, the imperial state, in its tsarist, Soviet, and post-Soviet forms, played an important role as a mediator of conflict between Kabardian and Balkar communities and particularly between their elites. Imperial administrators understood that, given the interdependent nature of land tenure among these communities, the state's goal of maintaining stability and order could best be achieved through the preservation of an integrated Kabardino-Balkar economic and administrative system. However beneficial close economic and political ties with Kabardians may have been for Balkars, over the *longue durée* this relationship has never been based on equality or parity of political and economic power. Over the two centuries examined in this study, rare moments of breakdown of peace and accord between Kabardians and Balkars were the results of the collapse of established state structures and centers of power. These moments of political change created windows of opportunity for Balkar elites to renegotiate and enhance their political, social, and economic positions, and the position of the people whom they claimed to represent, vis-à-vis their numerically larger Kabardian neighbors. These Balkar attempts to revise their unequal relationship with their Kabardian neighbors, which nearly caused the political and economic separation of the two communities in the early 1920s and again in the 1990s, led to elevated tensions and, sometimes, conflict. These moments of tension abated relatively quickly because state officials, Kabardian and Balkar elites, and ordinary villagers, realizing the potential for violence and economic disruption, came out in favor of compromise and the maintenance of the long-standing interconnected system in which the people lived.

As much as the state acted as a mediator of conflicts and, after conquest, strove to preserve order and peace in its new lands, this study finds that state policies were often the cause of intercommunal conflict. I demonstrate that state policies aimed at achieving both state-security goals and ideological goals fueled intercommunal tensions. Policies of resettlement and deportation disrupted historic land use and ownership regimes and, by shifting the demographic balance, disrupted intercommunal symbioses and led to violence in the North Caucasus. In contrast to communities in other parts of the region, however, Kabardian and Balkar communities, given their demographic patterns, did *not* experience the same acute land pressures as a result of Russian colonization and were thus able to expand their symbiosis to include Cossacks, Russian peasants, and other settler communities. The imposition of national categories onto the region's peoples and the delimitation of ethno-national borders demonstrates how the state's ideological projects exacerbated intercommunal conflicts. For example, from 1918 to 1926, the Bolsheviks' class warfare and introduction of the national principle led to the ethnicization of intercommunal conflict in the Central Caucasus. The national principle and its instrumentalization by local elites exacerbated tensions by turning feuds between villages over land allotments into conflicts between nations over their national territories.

This book also demonstrates the importance of social and economic aspects of Soviet modernization[5]—urbanization, the expansion of schooling, the spread mass literacy, social mobility, and bureaucratization—as factors influencing intercommunal conflict over the twentieth century. Indeed, after the conclusion of the fraught process of national border delimitation by the mid-1920s and the collectivization of agriculture in the 1930s, land, though still key to explaining the enduring Kabardian-Balkar symbiosis, ceased to be a major cause of intercommunal tension in Soviet Kabardino-Balkaria. As such, the focus of the final two chapters, which cover the period from the 1930s through the collapse of the Soviet Union, is on how Kabardians and Balkars experienced Soviet developmentalist policies rather than issues of land tenure. One of the reasons why Kabardian and Balkar ethno-political entrepreneurs were unsuccessful in sustaining their mobilizations and convincing their co-ethnics to take up arms for the creation of separate territories was the relative absence of socioeconomic inequalities between Kabardians and Balkars. With the notable exception of the period of deportation and exile that the Balkars suffered through from 1944 to 1956, the state made little distinction between Kabardians and Balkars in the application of its modernizing policies. Moreover, after the Balkars' return from exile, the Kabardian-led local authorities endeavored to mitigate the negative socioeconomic consequences of deportation and exile. The generally positive attitudes toward the Balkars' return on the part of the local population also facilitated the peaceful and ultimately successful reintegration of the region's Balkar minority. By the end of the Soviet period, Kabardian and Balkar communities demonstrated few differences in their levels of social and economic modernization. The case of Kabardino-Balkaria stands in marked contrast to other parts of the region where violence or at least seemingly intractable ethno-political tensions coincide with long histories of socio-economic stratification along ethnic lines.

Strategies for Imperial Governance and Their Impact

This book demonstrates the impact of the imperial state on intercommunal relations and probes the nature of imperial governance in the Central Caucasus. Russian rule had both destructive and creative effects on intercommunal relations. Russia's strategies and tactics for imperial conquest, control, and governance weakened some preexisting relationships, strengthened others, and, through colonization and resettlement, created new ones. For most mountaineers, the emergence of a new focus of power in Russia ended the Kabarda-centered system of intercommunal relations. Kabardian-Balkar relations were an exception to this rule. As a result of demographic, ecological, and geopolitical factors, tsarist and Soviet rule solidified and intensified Kabardian-Balkar interdependence.

Over the *longue durée*, tsarist and Soviet policies led to the replacement of the Kabarda-centered system of intercommunal relations in the Central Caucasus with a smaller symbiotic system consisting of Kabardian, Balkar, and Cossack communities, which, by the turn of the twentieth century, also included peasant settlers from Central Russia and other European regions. In an effort to weaken Kabarda as part of Russia's assertion of control over the Central Caucasus, tsarist officials attempted to end the Kabardian elites' tributary relations with neighboring mountaineer communities. Officials provided economic incentives and military support to mountaineers in order to convince them to accept Russian rule and reject Kabardian princely dominance. But as long as Kabardian elites controlled the land that the mountaineers needed for survival, these divide-and-conquer tactics met with little success. Only with the destruction and depopulation of Kabarda at the hands of tsarist armies and the plague, and the redistribution of plains land to mountaineer communities, did most mountaineers' dependence on Kabardian lands and resultant tributary relations with Kabardian princes end. However, given their proximity to the Kabardian heartland, the five mountaineer societies of Balkar, Khulam, Bezengi, Chegem, and Urusbii—today's Balkars—continued to depend on Kabardian plains land and summer mountain pastures long after Kabarda's cataclysmic decline.

Not seeing any strategic advantage in ending the symbiotic relationship between Kabardian and Balkar communities, tsarist and later Soviet administrators recognized Kabarda and the five mountaineer societies as an integrated economic system and pursued polices that further linked these communities together. Tsarist colonial policies created new types of relationships by promoting the settlement of the Central Caucasus by Cossacks, Russian peasants, and other communities whom officials viewed as loyal to the state and more culturally and economically advanced than the region's native peoples. In most cases, peasant migration to the Central Caucasus from Central Russia and Europe destabilized land and intercommunal relations. But, in contrast to most other parts of the region, the symbiotic system of relations in the remaining Kabardian lands adapted to the presence of these new communities because each community came to occupy their own mutually beneficial social and economic niche.

This book demonstrates how the tsarist and Soviet states created and used ethnonational categories as tools of imperial governance and social engineering in the Central Caucasus. Based on the idea that "ethnically" homogeneous territories are easier to govern, the tsarist state in the late imperial period introduced ethnicity as a category for grouping communities and drawing administrative borders.[6] This ethnicization of communities and territories transformed intercommunal relations in the Central Caucasus. Population resettlements and administrative-territorial transformations based on state perceptions of ethnicity made interactions across different cultural-linguistic communal boundaries less frequent. In assigning the communities of the Central Caucasus distinct ethnic status categories and dealing with them according to these statuses (in addition to the more important confessional and estate statuses), tsarist policies made ethnicity a meaningful category in Central Caucasian society. By the 1920s, the Civil War-era destruction of the empire's nobilities and the Soviet state's championing of the national principle—that the rights of Soviet peoples should be secured by granting them national autonomy within their own ethno-territorial units—paradoxically gave the category of ethnicity greater importance than social status in the lives of ordinary people in the Central Caucasus and elsewhere in Eurasia.[7] The social leveling of the Civil War years, culminating in the expropriation of noble landholdings and the equalization of land tenure within communities, meant that land inequalities shifted from class to communal lines (i.e., the greatest social tensions stemmed from plains communities, such as Kabardians and Cossacks, having more land than mountaineer communities, such as Balkars and Ossetians, rather than from individual members within these communities monopolizing land). In their bids to secure central state support, local elites of land-poor mountaineer communities in the Central Caucasus tried to demonstrate to Moscow that, after the expropriation of noble landholdings, class fell neatly along communal or, in language understood by the Soviet state, "national" lines.

In appealing to the Soviet state for support and instrumentalizing state-imposed identity categories to their advantage, both land-poor communities and those threatened by land-poor communities mastered the languages of nationality and class—they learned to "speak national" and to "speak Bolshevik."[8] By mastering these new languages, the peasants and shepherds who wrote petitions and often traveled thousands of miles to plead their cases in Moscow, embarked on a process of becoming *active* and *integrated* members of the Soviet state in addition to members of their newly promulgated nations. The instrumentalization of ethno-national and class categories during the formation of Soviet autonomies in the Central Caucasus during the early-to-mid-1920s demonstrates what Francine Hirsch calls "double assimilation": "assimilation . . . into nationality categories and, simultaneously, the assimilation of those nationally categorized groups into the Soviet state."[9]

In the case of Kabardino-Balkaria, in addition to fostering national and Soviet identifications, the Soviet state created and promoted an intermediate, supranational, Kabardino-Balkar identity (even though not a stated or conscious goal at the outset). Created in 1922 as a means of ensuring the economic well-being and cooperation of Kabardian and Balkar communities and resolving land disputes between these communities, Kabardino-Balkaria became a unitary AO for the newly promulgated Kabardian and Balkar nations. Rather than a federative relationship between two ethno-territorial units, the land and other natural resources of Kabardino-Balkaria became, at least in principle, the common property of the people of Kabardino-Balkaria, rather than that of specific national communities. In official speeches and mass media, the term "Kabardino-Balkar people"—instead of the Kabardian and Balkar peoples—came into increasing use as the Soviet period progressed. Citizens of Kabardino-Balkaria would have an extra possible layer in their (ethnic, national, cultural, and territorial) identities: their passport nationality (i.e., Kabardian, Balkar, Russian, etc.); Kabardino-Balkar identity; and a larger Soviet identity. These layers of identity were not mutually exclusive and could exist simultaneously. As Eric Hobsbawm reminds us, "[m]en and women did not choose collective identification as they chose shoes, knowing they could only put on one pair at a time. They had, and still have, several attachments and loyalties simultaneously."[10] The collapse of the Soviet Union reflected the failure of the latter of these three identity projects. In the early 1990s, Kabardian and Balkar separatism and irredentism seemed to indicate the failure of the Kabardino-Balkar project as well. Yet, the continued peaceful coexistence of Kabardians and Balkars in a common republic today shows that this identity category has, for a variety of reasons, continued to offer coherence and meaning both to state officials in their efforts to govern and to the people of the region in their daily lives.[11]

In analyzing how the state (be it tsarist, Soviet, or post-Soviet) approached its communities in the Central Caucasus, I have found Nicholas Breyfogle's typology of Russian state attitudes toward its multiethnic and multiconfessional empire useful. Often at one and the same time but in pursuit of different goals, Russia approached its empire in the Caucasus in three different ways depending on the context: as a "bureaucrat-policeman," "landscaper," and "referee."[12] The meaning of and relationship among these three roles can be seen in what I term "Russia's security dilemma in the North Caucasus": policies aimed at securing one part of the Caucasus often subverted imperial rule in other parts of the region and generally impeded other state objectives. In behaving as a "bureaucrat-policeman state" concerned with "prevent[ing] . . . unrest, opposition and the disruption of order and stability in general," the tsarist and Soviet states in the North Caucasus could not adequately perform their other roles of "human landscaper"—a social engineer molding loyal and legible populations—and "referee"—an adjudicator of the "demands of subjects for mediation and mitigation" in order to "ensure their desired outcomes and forward their policy goals."[13] For example, in deporting and resettling populations out of concerns for state security, the state created new intercommunal tensions that deteriorated security and impeded effective administration. Indeed, the legacies of Stalin-era deportations of nationalities from the North Caucasus, including the Balkars, fueled much of the intercommunal tension and ethno-nationalist mobilization that spread through the North Caucasus during the tumultuous early post-Soviet years.

This book also demonstrates the enduring importance of local elites in imperial governance and control and the multiethnic nature of tsarist and Soviet officialdom. As with most empires, the Russian Empire, the Soviet Union, and the Russian Federation depended upon native elites as sources of the essential local knowledge and sociopolitical legitimacy that they needed to police, govern, and transform their diverse communities.[14] Moreover, local elites became vital intermediaries between the imperial center and local communities. The role of native leaders underscores the ways in which the imperial state's relationship with the Central Caucasus was not simply one of a metropole dominating its periphery. Caucasian elites—particularly from favored communities like Georgians, Armenians, and Kabardians—had pathways to upward mobility and positions of influence within the state administration. The empire created webs of connections that facilitated a reciprocal relationship between center and periphery, with both Russians and non-Russians leaving their mark on each other and their regions.

Methodology and Contributions

Ethnicity, Groupness, and Conflict

Unless dealing with the evocation of ethnicity by officials and local elites and the consequences of such use of ethnic frameworks, I avoid using the terms "ethnicity" and "ethnic" when describing everyday life and social relations (hence "intercommunal relations" instead of "interethnic relations"). I reject the internal homogeneity implied by the concepts of "ethnic group" and "ethnic community" and share Rogers Brubaker's view that such concepts based on "groupness" mistakenly "treat ethnic groups, nations, and races as substantial entities to which interests and agency can be attributed."[15]

This book finds that, among the communities of the Central Caucasus, a sense of groupness crystalized around ethnicity at specific moments, especially from the early twentieth century on. This is not to say that ethnic or national consciousness did not exist among the peoples of the region. Indeed, nationality policies and social engineering projects in the twentieth century increased the importance of ethnicity as a category and lens through which Kabardians and Balkars experienced the world. But high levels of groupness, "moments of intensely felt collective solidarity,"[16] crystalized around ethnicity twice, both during periods of state collapse in the early 1920s and early 1990s as ethno-political entrepreneurs framed social and political conflicts in ethnic terms in order to improve their positions. This sense of groupness around ethnicity subsided as the Kabardian and Balkar ethno-political elites reached compromises because the costs of conflict for nonelites—violence and the disruption of symbiotic lifeways—outweighed the benefits and because central policymakers favored the preservation of the Kabardian-Balkar administrative-territorial union as a framework for effective governance.

In the Kabardino-Balkar case, on the level of individual interactions, what James Fearon and David Laitin term "spiral equilibrium" has been a particularly effective informal mechanism supporting cooperation across ethnic lines.[17] Spiral equilibrium is when "individuals cooperate in interethnic interactions for fear of losing future payoffs should they defect and cause a larger breakdown of intergroup relations." The grave collective consequences of an individual violation of norms of intercommunal cooperation—economic collapse and violence—outweigh the benefits derived by the individual from acts of opportunism. In order for a spiral equilibrium to develop, intercommunal relations must be frequent, otherwise "the threat of a breakdown of . . . relations is not compelling enough to induce individual members to cooperate."[18] The high frequency of everyday interactions between Kabardians and Balkars helps explain why a spiral equilibrium developed in the Kabardino-Balkar case but not in other cases in the North Caucasus.

Most of the violence that I describe in this book was, at least at the outset, intercommunal, rather than interethnic, in nature. In the 1920s and 1990s, ethnopolitical entrepreneurs ethnicized land conflicts between villages by framing them in ethnic terms in order to maintain, gain, or increase their power. When elites ethnically frame a violent incident that, at its roots, had little to do with ethnicity, the incident is often interpreted as interethnic violence. This ex post facto ethnicization of violence can lead to a further escalation of violence, now on the basis of ethnicity rather than whatever the original incident had been about (land, cattle, money, family honor). Most importantly for ethno-political entrepreneurs, ethnically framed violence can produce a sense of groupness around the category of ethnicity.[19] Ethnicity, then, "is not the ultimate, irreducible source of violent conflict in such cases." Rather, as Brubaker and Laitin argue, "the 'ethnic' quality of ethnic violence . . . emerges through after-the-fact interpretative claims." The framing of conflict as ethnic "feed[s] back into the conflict in such a way as to generate (by furnishing advance legitimation for) future violence."[20] Fearon and Laitin take this line of reasoning further and argue that violence is a key component of the social construction of ethnicity as a group identity category. They find that, when ethnically framed, "violence has the effect . . . of constructing group identities in more antagonistic and rigid ways."[21] The violence that plagued relations between Kabardians and their neighbors in the first half of the 1920s demonstrates how ethnic framing of conflict creates ethnic conflict and a sense of groupness around ethnicity.

Despite the ultimately productive move away from the "tendency to take discrete, bounded groups as basic constituents of social life . . . and units of social analysis"[22] toward more micro-level methodologies, I find that group-level approaches still offer important insights into ethnic processes—they provide essential context for understanding the crystallization of groupness around ethnicity and the causes of conflict. The classic modernist works on nations and nationalism which view differences in levels of economic development and social mobility ("modernization") across cultural groups as indicators of higher levels of conflict are particularly helpful in understanding the types of situations which have increased the likelihood of intercommunal conflict in the North Caucasus.²³ From the late imperial period, and then more intensely from the 1930s on, as processes associated with social and economic modernization began to transform the societies of the North Caucasus, Kabardians and Balkars generally experienced these processes in similar ways. This relatively even modernization experienced by Kabardians and Balkars stands in contrast to other more conflict-prone parts of Caucasia like Chechnya. The Balkars' deportation and exile to Central Asia marks an exception to this similarity in experiences between Kabardians and Balkars. But with the Balkars' return in the late 1950s, the Kabardian and Russian communities of Kabardino-Balkaria, and the local leadership, were keen to integrate the Balkars back into the social fabric of the republic and reconstitute the historic symbiosis. This book finds that differences in modernization across groups help to explain the broad context of conflict once it has become ethnicized, but modernization theories do not explain the outbreak of intercommunal violence and its development into "ethnic conflict." These phenomena are best explained at the micro level by looking at everyday interactions and the actions of ethno-political entrepreneurs.

In Kabardino-Balkaria, there was no clear distinction between Kabardians and Balkars based on perceived "advanced" or "backward" traits or a strong sense that one group had proved far more capable of working within the colonial system than the other. Based on Donald Horowitz's psychological theory of ethnic conflict, this lack of contrasting positive and negative perceptions of Kabardians and Balkars in Kabardino-Balkaria also helps explain the relatively low incidence of conflict between the two communities. Focusing on group emotions and perceptions in colonial and postcolonial situations, Horowitz avers that stereotypes about "advanced" and "backwards" groups—developed because some groups fared better under colonialism and were able to benefit from the opportunities brought by the colonial administration, while others remained relatively marginalized—became sources of ethnic conflict.²⁴

Imagining Nations

This book emphasizes how the policies of the modernizing tsarist and Soviet states and the discursive work of native intellectuals and political entrepreneurs helped create and reimagine national communities in the Central Caucasus.²⁵ In particular, I pinpoint the beginnings of nation-making processes in the late imperial period. Beginning in the 1860s, tsarist administrators divided the region into administrative units according to their perceptions of ethnic categories. Next, the administration pursued the ethnic homogenization of these new ethnically defined administrative units. Finally, the late imperial period witnessed the birth of national intelligentsias in the North Caucasus. While the major works on Soviet nationalities policy emphasize how, especially among the smaller peoples of the empire, the Soviet state created national forms and categories almost ex nihilo,²⁶ this book finds continuities in the tsarist and Soviet states' use of ethnic frameworks in governing and administering their non-Russian minorities. To be sure, ethnophile Soviet policymakers would take the ethnicizing tendencies of their tsarist predecessors to new heights and do so for different ideological goals.

This study also finds continuities in Soviet nationalities policy across the Soviet period. During the more than seventy years of its existence, the Soviet state pursued policies of nativization (*korenizatsiia*)—the use of titular languages in administration and education in national republics and regions; the creation of national intelligentsias; and the promotion of members of titular indigenous nationalities to positions at all levels in industry, administration, and the Communist Party. The periodic elevation in importance of statist and security policies that were antithetical to the goals of nativization—from the promotion of Russian-language schooling to ethnic cleansing—mask the ways in which nativization policies continued. In contrast to the major studies of Soviet nationality policies that argue that the Soviet state stopped giving nativization high priority after the mid-1930s, my research confirms Peter Blitstein's finding that the late-Stalin years, from about 1948 to 1953, was a time of renewed emphasis on nativization.[27] The promotion of nativization policies during the postwar, late-Stalin years had significant impacts on ethnic processes throughout the remainder of the Soviet period, especially during the Soviet collapse. Ultimately, by taking a longer periodization than most other studies of Soviet nationalities policies, this study identifies important continuities across traditional historiographical divides. Going beyond Blitstein's periodization (1936–53) and looking at nationalities policy after Stalin's death, I show that nativization continued, though it was overshadowed by opposing statist policies, throughout the Soviet era. Indeed, the successful socioeconomic reintegration of the Balkars in the late 1950s and early 1960s was, in part, a product of a robust Balkarization campaign.

Jeremy Smith has recently offered several important criticisms of the way that scholars have applied the term "nationalities policy" to the Soviet Union.[28] While they do not merit jettisoning the term as Smith suggests, they do necessitate important caveats when employing it as this book does. First, after about the early 1930s, the Soviet state did not have a "centrally determined and directed policy" toward national minorities that developed in clearly identifiable stages as it did for other policy areas such as national security and the economy.[29] There was, however, a relatively stable set of principles regarding the status of non-Russian nationalities—for example, that titular nationalities should have certain linguistic and cultural rights in their national homelands and that an ethnically stratified social structure in which the titular nationalities are disadvantaged is unacceptable. In the post-Stalin era, local Soviet officials could use these principles to support their goals in areas such as education, language, and cultural development.[30] For Smith, this stability of principles indicates the absence of a policy.[31] Second, there was also far greater variability in the experiences of the Soviet Union's non-Russian peoples than the term "nationalities policy" implies. The experiences of the national minorities of the Soviet Union and outcomes of national disputes often had more to do with the interaction of the local leaders and central policymakers or local dynamics among various interest groups and constituencies than with the top-down application of a strict set of policies.[32] This examination of Kabardino-Balkaria reflects these aspects of the experience of national minorities in the post-Stalin era. The ethnically Kabardian leadership of Kabardino-Balkaria made the reintegration of the Balkars a goal, and they drew on core principles of the Soviet nationalities policy to lobby for specific fiscal policies and funding from Moscow to achieve it. Perhaps of greater importance to the reintegration of the Balkars, though, were earlier dynamics of intercommunal relations, specifically the land-based symbiosis among Kabardians and Balkars.

North Caucasus Historiography: Beyond Religion, Borders, and National Histories

Given the central role of Islam in the extant scholarship on and popular depictions of the North Caucasus, discussion of Islam and its impact on intercommunal relations and Russian imperial governance may seem conspicuously sparse in this study.[33] However, unlike Chechnya and Dagestan, which are the regions of the North Caucasus that have attracted the most attention from scholars and journalists, in areas to the west like Kabardino-Balkaria, Islam has not historically played as strong of a role in structuring intercommunal and land relations and mobilizing resistance to Russian rule. By offering a historical narrative of the North Caucasus that does not focus on the Northeast Caucasus, my study provides a more nuanced understanding of the region by demonstrating that Islam did not always and everywhere play a central role in the history of the North Caucasus and its engagement with the Russian state. This is not to say that religion and interconfessional relations were of no importance to intercommunal relations in Kabardino-Balkaria and the Central Caucasus more generally. My study recognizes the historical contexts in which Islam played an important role in intercommunal relations. For example, before the Soviet era, common adherence to Islam was one of many bonds that preserved the long-standing influence of Kabarda's nobles over neighboring mountaineer communities. This was particularly the case with the Ossetian communities which, by the late nineteenth century, were divided between a Christian majority and a Muslim minority. Kabardian noble influence was significantly stronger among Muslim Ossetian communities bordering Kabarda than among Christian communities closer to the Russian administrative center of Vladikavkaz. The impact of Islam on intercommunal relations among Kabardians and their neighbors is a recurring, though not central, theme in this book's first three chapters.

This book emphasizes the fluidity of interactions across frontiers and borders, particularly during the tsarist period, and the dynamic social processes of the empire. Russia's long-standing relationships with the communities of the North Caucasus have, more often than not, been based on cooperation, coexistence, and cultural exchange. However, much of the Western scholarship on the North Caucasus focuses on conquest and resistance to Russian rule and its tragic consequences, with the Sufi Sheikh Imam Shamil's long successful imamate in Chechnya and Dagestan and the recent Chechen Wars being the most prominent examples.[34] To be sure, the results of the many armed conflicts between North Caucasian communities and the Russian state can explain much about the fate of the region's peoples. But while the results of armed conflicts and deportations fuel the rhetoric of Caucasian ethno-national entrepreneurs, the history of resistance to Russian rule is just one side of the complex history of relations between the region's native peoples and the Russian state.³⁵ Instead of looking at the military and political history of the relationship between the peoples of the North Caucasus and Russia, recently historians have fruitfully explored the complex social, economic, and cultural interrelations between Russians and other settlers on the one hand and the region's peoples on the other.³⁶ With its emphasis on intercommunal relations, the present study builds on this recent scholarship, but it avoids dichotomizing the relationship between "natives" and "settlers." Rather, it demonstrates the webs of economic, social and political relations that linked together the communities of the Central Caucasus and how the colonization of the region by Russians and other settlers affected relations between and among numerous different communities.

The modern ethno-territorial borders imposed on the map of the North Caucasus in the twentieth century have become discursive barriers to how we write about the region's history. While the weakness of Western historiography on the North Caucasus is its disproportionate focus on conflict and resistance during the Caucasus War of 1817–64, the more voluminous Soviet and Russian historiography on the North Caucasus, with notable exceptions, anachronistically take modern administrative-territorial units as their units of analysis for periods when these formations did not exist. This regional or national-territorial approach is common throughout Eurasia. In the case of the North Caucasus, it has led to mono-ethnic histories of a multiethnic region and, thus, misrepresentations of social life in the region. As Aleksei Miller points out, the major problem with national historical narratives such as those that dominate the historiography on the North Caucasus is that they "combin[e the nation's history] with the story of how this or that territory 'rightfully' belongs to it," making them "teleological, rooted in ideology, and poorly adapted to exposing the logic of the empire's dynamic process, since these are treated as . . . merely the background and context for the development of the nation."³⁷ Even in cases where the national territory under study is multi-titular, for example Kabardino-Balkaria or neighboring Karachai-Cherkessia, historical studies give very limited information about the interactions of these titular nationalities and deal with them in separate sections, as if they lived in complete isolation from one another. These works provide even less information on interactions between the titular nationalities and communities outside the borders of the ethnically defined administrative unit.³⁸

Despite having "Kabardino-Balkaria" in its title, this book, heeding Aleksei Miller's calls for "a situational approach" to the study of Russia's multiethnic empire,³⁹ attempts to take a web of relationships, one structured in part by space (e.g., mountains and plains), rather than a place or region, as its unit of analysis. The "situation" is Kabardians' symbiotic, though unequal, relationship with their neighbors and the effect of state power on this relationship and on the transformation of the societies of the Central Caucasus. This study's situation changes according to "the empire's dynamic processes."⁴⁰ Kabardians are at the center of my situational analysis because this study begins by examining the Kabarda-centered system of intercommunal relations that covered most of the Central Caucasus from roughly the sixteenth through late eighteenth centuries. Beginning with the Kabarda-centered system is important because the legacies and remnants of this system continued to play an important role in social life and politics in the Central Caucasus throughout the roughly two centuries covered in this study. Over time, Kabarda—its elites and its land—ceased to play a determinative role in the lives of many of its neighboring communities. Accordingly, by the 1930s, the communities in the situation had gradually diminished to include primarily those who resided within the borders of the Kabardino-Balkar Autonomous Soviet Socialist Republic: Kabardians, Balkars, and Russians. This is not to say that borders ended Kabardians' relationships with cross-border communities. But, of the original participants in the land-based economic symbiosis, only the people we now know as Balkars remained inextricably linked with their Kabardian neighbors in their everyday lives through the nineteenth and twentieth centuries. Given that their zone of compact settlement was and remains surrounded by Kabardian villages, the lives of local Slavs (primarily Russian settlers and Cossacks) are also tied to their Kabardian neighbors.

People and Place

Over the more than two centuries covered in this book, a sense of cohesion and unity of purpose and action rarely existed among the North Caucasian peoples who are now known as Kabardians, Balkars, Karachais, Ossetians, Ingush, and Chechens. Moreover, the names of these nationalities are often relatively recent creations—just as these nations themselves are—and, in some cases, members of these nationalities have their own autonyms that are distinct from ethnonyms ascribed to them by outsiders and which they sometimes use when referring to themselves to outsiders. Kabardians, who retain a distinct identity shaped by history and geography but also identify as members of the larger Circassian nation, refer to themselves in their native language as *Adyga*, the same ethnonym used by the wider Circassian community. When interacting with members of other ethnicities, Kabardians refer to themselves either as "Kabardians" (*kabardintsy*) or as "Circassians" (*adygi* or *cherkesy*). For the sake of specificity, I use Kabardians when referring to the Circassians of Kabarda/Kabardino-Balkaria. To the extent that Balkars had a common ethnonym before Balkar became widely used starting in the early twentieth century, it was *Taulu*, meaning mountaineer in their kipchak-turkic tongue. This served to distinguish Balkars from their lowland Kabardian neighbors. Before the twentieth century, Russian officials and writers referred to Balkars as "the five mountaineer societies contiguous with Greater Kabarda" (*piat' gorskikh obshchestv sopredel'nykh s bolshoi Kabardoi*), "the five mountaineer societies of Kabarda" (*piat' gorskikh obshchestv Kabardy*), or "mountaineer Tatars" (*gorskie tatary*). By the early twentieth century, Balkar intellectuals began using the name of the largest of their community's five societies—Balkar (*Malkar* in the Balkar language)—as their preferred ethnonym.[41] Unless referring to a specific one of the five mountaineer societies—Balkar, Khulam, Bezengi, Chegem, Urusbi—I use Balkar throughout. Kabardians, as plains and foothills dwellers, traditionally referred to their highland neighbors as mountaineers (*k"ushchkh'ekher*), rather than using modern ethnonyms such as Balkar, Ossetian, or Ingush. Russians have traditionally referred to the native peoples of the North Caucasus, including the Kabardians, collectively as mountaineers (*gortsy*).

The North Caucasus refers to the region, roughly the size of England and Wales combined, bordering the Greater Caucasus mountain range and the Georgian and

Azeri lands in the south, the Black Sea to the west, and the Caspian Sea to the east. The region's northern limits are less precisely defined and have historically been more of a frontier than a natural border. For the purposes of this study, I use a geo-ecological definition of the North Caucasus based on its defining natural feature—the mountains—and the peoples whose lives they affected. The region extends as far north as the zones of settlement of peoples who interacted with the mountain zone. I therefore delimit the North Caucasus in the north by the beginning of the zone where nomadic-pastoral Kalmyk and Nogai steppe communities resided before the demographic transformation of the Steppe by Russian colonization (see Map 1).

The territorial focus of the beginning of this book is the Central Caucasus—the region, roughly the size of the Netherlands, over which the princely confederation of Kabarda projected varying degrees of political, social, and economic power between the sixteenth and eighteenth centuries. I use an adaptation of historian Rustam Begeulov's definition of the Central Caucasus—the Russian Federation's Republics of Kabardino-Balkaria, North Ossetia, Ingushetia, the eastern half of Karachai-Cherkessia and the southern-most portions of Stavropol Krai.[42] At its southern limits, the Central Caucasus is situated roughly between Europe's highest mountain, Mount Elbrus (18,510 feet), in the southwest and Mount Kazbek in the southeast (16,516 feet). Central Caucasia's shortest side is its natural southern border along the Caucasus range, which stretches about 130 miles between these two mountains. The Central Caucasus is bounded by the right bank of the upper Kuban River in the west, the Kuma and Podkumok rivers in the northwest, the Kura River in the north, the Terek in the northeast and east, and the Sunzha River in the east.

The present-day Kabardino-Balkar Republic is located toward the middle of the Central Caucasus region. Within a small territory (4,800 square miles) just under the size of Montenegro, Kabardino-Balkaria includes a diversity of ecological zones. Moving southwest across the republic, the Terek plains of Lesser Kabarda, in the northeast corner, are hot, humid, and prone to drought. The fertile and naturally well-watered plains closer to the center of the republic have a continental climate. Farther to the south and west, as the elevation begins to rise to 5,250 feet above sea level, the foothills zone, composing 16 percent of Kabardino-Balkaria's territory, is covered in lush forests and has a more moderate climate. Finally, the mountain zone, in the south and west, with an extreme continental climate, makes up just over half of Kabardino-Balkaria's territory. This mountain zone generally consists of two parts: (1) the subalpine and alpine mountain pastures and surrounding valleys and ridges, covered with tall grass on its rolling hills in the short summer season and barren and often snow-covered during the long winter season, extends from approximately 5,250 to 10,000 feet above sea level; and (2) the arctic zone (rising beyond 10,000 feet above sea level), with its rocky ridges, is mostly snow-covered year-round.[43]

As they did throughout much of Eurasia, the invasions of the Mongols and Tamerlane in the thirteenth and fourteenth centuries fundamentally transformed the cultural, demographic, and political landscape of the North Caucasus. The major cultural-linguistic communities before the Mongols, such as those of the Cumans (Polovtsians) and Alans, either fled the North Caucasus or took refuge in its isolated mountain valleys with the collapse of their polities. The descendants of those who

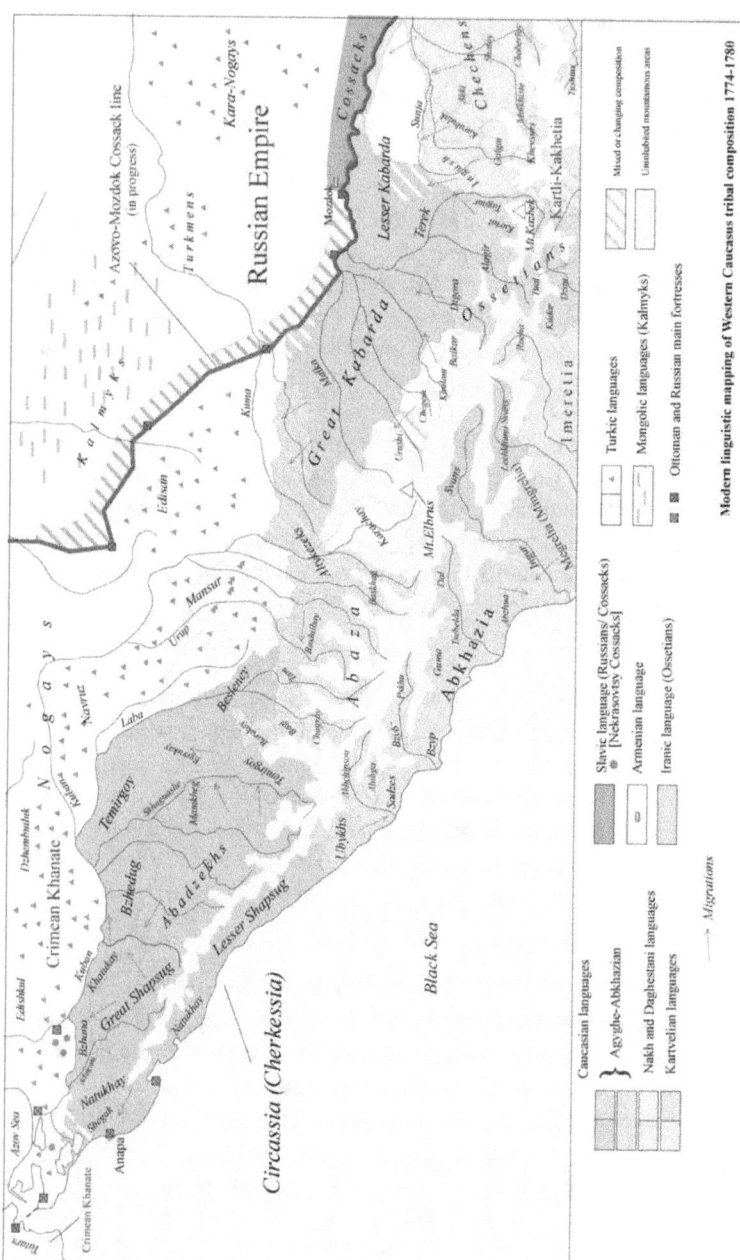

Map 1 Ethno-linguistic makeup of the Northwest and Central Caucasus on the eve of tsarist conquest. © Reproduced with the kind permission of Arthur Tsutsiev and Georgi Derluguian.

lived through the Mongol conquest, now mountain dwellers, became the progenitors (though not the only ones) of new cultural-linguistic communities—today's Karachais, Balkars, and Ossetians. Meanwhile, a new tribal confederation, that of the Adyga or Circassians, defined initially by its ability to withstand Mongol invasions, emerged in the far western end of Caucasia along the Black Sea coast. As the Kipchak Khanate weakened in the fifteenth century, legend has it that Inal, an Egyptian Mamluk ruler perhaps of proto-Circassian descent, fled Egypt and forged a confederation of several Circassian tribes. This new unity gave Circassia an expansionist impulse. Indeed, in the fifteenth century the Circassians migrated east, asserting control over lands east of the right bank of the Kuban and, subsequently, the foothills and plains of the Central Caucasus along the rivers Malka and Terek up to the latter's confluence with the Sunzha. According to oral tradition, Inal divided his patrimony among his four sons. The easternmost of these Circassian territories became known as Kabarda (*Kabardei*). This new princely state replaced the Kipchak Khanate as the suzerain[44] of the surrounding mountaineer societies that relied on the plains to their north, now controlled by Kabarda, for their survival.[45]

Numerous legends surround the origins of the name Kabarda. Some claim that Kabard was the son who received princely title to Inal's easternmost domains. Others aver that the term "Kabarda" comes from Kabard Tambiev, a high-noble (*tliakotlesh*) who broke away from the Bolotokov Circassian princes of the Black Sea coast and founded his own princely state in the Central Caucasus. Still others claim that the term "Kabarda" comes from the Georgian for "on the other side," a reference to Kabarda's position vis-à-vis Georgia and the Caucasus mountains. Finally, others claim that the term "Kabarda" comes from the name of a river or a place in the Crimea, from whence, according to the various iterations of this legend, the Kabardian people came. This same legend, which originates from Kabardian princes, claims that the Kabardians arrived in the Crimea from Arabia.[46] Whatever the origins of the name, it is clear that among Circassians, the territory known as *Kabardei* was originally limited to the area controlled by the Kazy Princes. Beginning in the sixteenth century, Russian sources called this princedom, which extended from at least the upper Malka River in the west up to the Terek in the east, "Greater Kabarda." The other smaller Circassian princedoms to the east which were loosely confederated with Greater Kabarda were *Dzhylakhstanei* (controlled by the Akhlov and Mudarov princes) and *Talostanei* (controlled by the Sholokhov princes). By the late sixteenth century, foreign sources began referring to this territory as Lesser Kabarda. At present, Kabardians refer to Lesser Kabarda as *Dzhylakhstanei*, after the larger of its two historic princedoms.[47]

Kabarda was often rife with internecine strife throughout its existence. Kabarda's ruling princely families often feuded over regional dominance and territory. In the late sixteenth century, these conflicts led to a near-permanent political split, yielding Greater Kabarda in the west and Lesser Kabarda in the east. The Terek River south of its confluence with the Malka was the natural border between the two Kabardas.[48] As Kabarda suffered repeated invasions from the Crimean Khan's armies in the mid-sixteenth century, Prince Temriuk Idarov hoped to shore up Kabarda's defensive capabilities by centralizing power in this loose confederation into his hands and seeking military allies. He secured a military alliance with Russia, solidified through an oath of allegiance and the marriage of his daughter, Guashanei (baptized Maria), to Muscovite tsar, Ivan IV "the Terrible." This alliance, marking the beginning of Russia's involvement in the North Caucasus, allowed Kabarda to fend off the Crimean threat.[49] However, Kabarda's fiercely independent princes met Temriuk's centralizing efforts with resistance. Some of the other princely families, especially the Kaitukins, defiantly oriented their domains toward the Crimean Khanate and its protector, the Ottoman Sultan. In a sign of the failure of Temriuk's centralizing efforts, each of the Kabardian princedoms conducted its own foreign policy. Nevertheless, a pattern became clear by the end of the sixteenth century: in the east, the princes of Lesser Kabarda, closer in proximity to Russia's outpost on the Terek (Terskii Gorod), allied themselves with Russia, while the princes of Greater Kabarda in the west were fickle in their allegiances, vacillating between Ottoman-Crimean and Russian protection.

The balance of power both within and between Lesser and Greater Kabarda shifted frequently from the late sixteenth through late eighteenth centuries. By about 1600, Kazy Psheapshokov's princedom in Greater Kabarda had supplanted that of Lesser Kabarda's Idarovs, as the dominant Kabardian polity. Under Kazy's successors, Aleguka and Khatokshoko, this princedom—Kazy Kabarda—continued its primacy, commanding the allegiance of neighboring Abaza, Karachai, Balkar, and Nogai communities and maintaining friendly relations with both the Crimean Khanate and Russia. Indeed, it is likely that only Russian military aid saved the Lesser-Kabardian princes from falling under the control of Kazy Kabarda. Following the death of Khatokshoko Kazyev in 1670, Kazy Kabarda declined and the princes of Greater Kabarda increasingly came into conflict with one another.

Weakened by internal power struggles from the 1670s through the 1730s, Kabarda became a site of frequent invasions by the forces of the Crimean Khan who sought to extend his control into the Caucasus. Indeed, Kabarda repeatedly suffered brutal occupations by Crimean forces during this period. Despite uniting under the Atazhukin princes to form a successful anti-Crimean coalition in the early eighteenth century, internecine conflict among the princely families of Greater Kabarda prevented Kabardian forces from capitalizing on their military victories. By the mid-eighteenth century, Greater Kabarda's four princely families divided into two mutually hostile parties: the pro-Russian Baksan Party and the pro-Crimean Kashkatau Party, named after their geographic locations within Greater Kabarda. The Atazhukin and Misostov princes led the Baksan Party and the Kaitukins and Bekmurzins led the Kashkatau Party. Meanwhile, pro-Russian Lesser Kabarda, controlled by the Mudarovs and Tausultanovs, grew increasingly weak over the first half of the eighteenth century as a result of raiding by the armies of Greater Kabarda.[50]

Kabarda exhibited a complex social hierarchy based on ties of mutual obligations. At the top were the princes or *pshi* (*murza*). Each prince lorded over his own domain. He enjoyed the rights to declare war and make peace and to act as ultimate judge and jury over his vassal princes and serfs. Members of the noble *uork* (*uzden*) class were vassals of princes. Skilled in military arts, they formed a prince's retinue and his loyal military commanders during periods of conflict. In exchange for their service, princes rewarded their *uorks* with large estates, consisting of several villages (*k"uazha* in Kabardian and *aul* or *kabak* in Russian and Turkic languages) and serfs. The *uork* noble class had a hierarchy of its own. The highest noble classes were the *tliakotlesh* (the Tambiev, Kudenetov, and Anzorov families) and *dizhenugo*. These two classes of nobles had the greatest amount of freedom vis-à-vis their princes: they could move their fiefdoms; they commanded the same level of respect and fealty as the princes; and they played a large advisory role in domestic and foreign policy. The numerically larger lesser nobility, the *shautlukhus uorks*, formed the military might of the Kabardian princedoms, and they served both the princes and the high nobles. Princes singled out members of this class who demonstrated exceptional bravery in battle to serve in their retinues and personal guards; these elevated lower nobles were known as *beslen'uorks*. The Kabardian peasantry was divided into several subclasses of varying degrees of feudal dependence. The most numerous was the *tlkhukotl'* class. These peasants were personally free and worked their own land, but they paid feudal dues (a portion of their harvest) and performed labor for the nobility. The *pshitl'* serf class worked the land of the lords. Finally, slaves or *unauts*, often non-Circassian prisoners of war, were at the bottom of the Kabardian social hierarchy. An *unaut* usually served as a household servant.[51]

The Kabardian economy was based primarily on transhumance—the driving of livestock (cattle and sheep) to pastures in different ecological zones according to seasonal weather patterns—and horse breeding. Before the tsarist conquest, the Kabardian princes controlled the best mountain pastures of the Central Caucasus between Mount Elbrus and the upper Malka and Kuma rivers (the trans-Malka pastures). During the spring and summer months, Kabardians drove their flocks and herds to these alpine meadows; in the colder months, they utilized winter pastures on the plains. Kabardian horses were prized for their speed and agility, and Kabardians supplied the armies of the surrounding empires with horses.

Unlike the surrounding mountaineer societies, which were primarily livestock focused, Kabardians also occupied land on the fertile plains, on which they engaged in extensive, though not intensive, agricultural production. Kabardians practiced long-fallow and slash-and-burn monocrop agriculture until the nineteenth century. After farming a given area for a few years, Kabardian peasants would move to another area once the soil had become exhausted. Kabardians sold their grain at nearby market towns. Indeed, Kabarda was a primary source of grain for the surrounding mountaineer societies and, in times of drought and famine, other neighboring regions. Invading armies strategically attacked one of Kabarda's key sources of power by burning crop fields. The Kabardians' dominant crop was millet, which they used to feed themselves and, sometimes, their livestock.[52] Millet-based products, such as *p'aste*—a thick, soft, and cake-like bread—remain staples of the Kabardian diet.[53]

In contrast to the surrounding mountaineers who constructed their settlements out of stone as permanent fixtures of the surrounding, crag-laden, mountain landscape, the lowland Kabardians' primary building material was straw. Kabardians built their dwellings from this weaker material because the princes and nobles of Kabarda frequently moved their villages in response to a host of socioeconomic and geopolitical factors. First, given the predominance of slash-and-burn agriculture, Kabardians often moved their settlements to be closer to their new grain supplies after a particular field became exhausted. Second, the Kabardian shepherds' division of their year between highland and lowland pastures meant that they needed mobile dwellings. Third, in terms of geopolitics, Kabarda's position on the open plains meant that it was vulnerable to invasions from neighboring empires and nomadic steppe peoples. Thus, during these outside invasions, Kabardians sought protection by moving their villages into the mountains. A reflection of the Kabardian-mountaineer symbiosis, the Kabardian elites relied on mountaineer elites to give them and their dependents refuge during these periods of outside invasion. Kabardian lords also often moved their villages in response to internal conflicts with neighboring princes and nobles. Finally, Kabardian lords might move their settlements closer to neighboring communities to better assert their authority over them. Given the mobility of Kabardian settlements, Kabardian villages were named after their ruling family.[54] Nevertheless, most resettlements occurred within a specific and delineated territory recognized by the elites of the Central Caucasus as the fiefdom of a given princely family.[55]

A diversity of cultural-linguistic communities surrounded Kabarda. To the northwest, Abaza societies resided along the upper Urup, Zelenchuk, and Kuban rivers. Kabardian princes recurrently controlled the territory inhabited by the Tapanta Abazas (also known as Altykeseks), the easternmost Abaza society, and maps and descriptions often include these Abaza within the borders of Greater Kabarda.[56] In the autumn and spring, the Abaza relied on the pastures of the Kabardians to the east and the Beslenei Circassians to the west.[57] Abazas speak a Northwest Caucasian language, distantly related to Kabardian (Eastern Circassian), but most closely resembling the Abkhaz language. The Kipchak-Turkic-speaking Karachai resided in the mountains to the southwest of Greater Kabarda, in the valleys of the upper Kuban and Teberda rivers. Once residing in the Baksan Valley of Greater Kabarda, in the mid-seventeenth century, the Karachais migrated westward across the mountains in what was likely the result of a conflict with Kazy Kabarda's princes.[58]

Speaking the same language as the Karachais, the five mountaineer societies of Balkar, Khulam, Bezengi, Chegem, and Urusbi—the Balkars—lived immediately to the south and southwest of the Greater Kabardian heartland, in the Cherek, Chegem, and Baksan valleys.[59] These societies were most closely tied with Kabarda because the mountains kept them relatively isolated from other communities. East of the Balkars, along Kabarda's mountainous southern border were the Ossetians, mountaineer societies speaking an Iranian language. From west to east, there were five Ossetian mountaineer societies bordering Kabarda, each named after their principal valley of residence: the Digorans, Alagirs, Nars, Kurtats, and Tagaurs. Speaking Northeast-Caucasian Nakh languages, the Chechens and Ingush bordered Kabarda along its far eastern and southeastern border. Finally, from the mid-sixteenth century, groups of ethnically mixed though predominantly Slavic-speaking Cossacks resided in fortified villages (*stanitsy*) scattered along the Terek River to the northeast of Kabarda.

The mountaineer societies neighboring Kabarda had a far less stratified social structure. The primary social unit in the mountains was the village society rather than the fiefdom as in Kabarda. Councils of clan elders, elected at village assemblies, provided the leadership of the village societies in the mountains. Nineteenth-century European observers, judging the Caucasian societies in terms of their own societies, labeled these mountaineer societies "democratic" and the more socially stratified states, such as Kabarda, as "aristocratic."⁶⁰ Over the seventeenth and eighteenth centuries, however, those societies most influenced by Kabarda, through both geographic proximity and socioeconomic ties, began to take on characteristics of Kabarda's feudal system. Moreover, when mountaineer communities resettled to Kabardian lands, such as the Tapanta Abaza and the Digora Ossetians, Kabardian princes accorded their leaders the same status and privileges as the Kabardian *uork*.⁶¹

Kabardian princes collected tribute (*iasak*) from some of their highland neighbors. The standard payment from these tributary mountaineer societies consisted of one sheep per household per year, additional payments in kind from the entire village (horses, cows, bulls), and a hostage (*amanat*). Most mountaineer societies made their payments to a particular Kabardian suzerain-prince.⁶² However, the right to collect tribute from various mountaineer societies often figured in the incessant quarrels between the princes of Kabarda, and tributary rights over individual mountaineer societies could shift from one prince to another. The size of tribute payments was directly proportionate to the strength of a given prince. Moreover, during periods of conflict within Kabarda, tributary mountaineer societies seized upon the resultant weakness of their suzerains and resisted Kabardian dominance with varying degrees of success. For example, in the 1740s, as the power of Lesser Kabarda waned as a result of raids from Greater Kabarda, many Ingush mountaineers successfully resisted Kabardian dominance and settled the plains of Lesser Kabarda between the rivers Kambileevka and Sunzha.⁶³

Sources from the mid-sixteenth through early nineteenth centuries help explain how Kabarda's geographic position allowed its princes to gain political and economic dominance over its neighboring mountaineer peoples. The need for vital natural resources (pasturage, grain, and salt), access to trade routes, and protection from enemies were key reasons for the mountaineer societies' dependence upon Kabarda's elites.

The need for lowland pasturage led to an economic dependence of the mountaineer societies upon Kabarda. North Caucasia's mountaineer societies practiced transhumance. Kabarda's neighbors could only graze cattle in their highland homelands during the warmest months of the year, from approximately May through October, when the mountains were covered with grass. Biannually, during late autumn and early spring, when feed no longer grew in the mountains, the mountaineers drove their cattle down to Kabarda to graze in the foothills and plains along the Terek, Malka, and Kuma rivers. In his *Travels in Russia and Caucasia: 1770-1773*, the Baltic German naturalist-explorer, Johann Anton Güldenstädt, noted, "Kabardians are more powerful, and the Bazians [i.e., Balkars] drive their cattle on Kabardian land during the winter and therefore must submit to them."⁶⁴

While fully utilizing the limited agricultural potential of the mountains—through terrace farming and cultivating durable crops such as barley—the mountaineer societies had grain reserves for no more than three months on average.⁶⁵ The mountaineers, therefore, also depended on Kabarda for much of their grain. In a 1768 report to Catherine II, Astrakhan Governor Nikita Beketov explained, "the Ossetians have long been beholden to Kabardian lords. As a result of the lack of good land in their mountains and the need to obtain grain and hay from low-lying areas that the Kabardians have asserted control over, they pay them tribute."⁶⁶

Controlling the region's major salt deposits, Kabarda also was a primary supplier of salt for the mountaineers whose cattle-breeding economy demanded large quantities of the mineral for the health of their livestock, preserving meats, and curing hides. According to Güldenstädt, "with the help of this essential commodity Kabardians not only make great profit from their neighbors, they also use salt as a means to keep these peoples in submission and obedience."[67]

Its strategic location and the strength of its armies gave Kabarda additional advantages over its neighbors. First, Kabardian princes and nobles often placed their residences and estates at the exits of the mountain valleys and placed toll posts along the major trade routes of the Central Caucasus, including the main mountain crossing into Georgia along the Dar'ial Gorge.[68] Thus, in order for the mountaineers to trade at the major Russian, Ottoman, and Kumyk market towns, and reach the outside world in general, they needed to pass through Kabarda. In times of conflict with Kabarda, mountaineer communities sometimes were forced to make dangerous treks south across mountain passes into Georgia for essential provisions. Kabardian princes and nobles collected tolls from mountaineers for safe passage across their territory. For example, in their frequent appeals to the tsarist administration for help, Ossetian elders complained that "the lords of Greater and Lesser Kabarda, especially the Akhlovs and Mudarovs of Lesser Kabarda, pressure our travelers." They requested that Russia help them by ensuring their "free passage between their homes and Mozdok and Kizliar [i.e., Russian towns]."[69]

The communities tied together in this Kabarda-centered system rarely came into *major* conflict with each other. They more frequently combined forces to fend off external threats. To be sure, Kabardians could pose a threat to mountaineer communities who did not render tribute, and tribute payments could be onerous. Outside invasion, competition for scarce natural resources (especially land), and the mountainous terrain led to high levels of brigandage and intercommunal conflict in Caucasia. However, in the face of these destabilizing factors, Kabarda represented a source of stability in the region. Kabardian princes, with their large armies, provided their mountaineer tributaries with protection from internal and external enemies.[70] Moreover, Kabardian protection allowed individual clans and families to attain and hold on to power within their societies. Klaproth's description of the Karachais bears witness to the high value placed upon Kabardian protection. According to Klaproth:

> As the friendship of the Kabardian princes is estimated very highly by them, each family strives to obtain the favor of one of the most powerful, that it may secure a protector and mediator in unforeseen misfortunes or attacks. No one will then venture to do any member of it an injury . . . nay it frequently happens that mean families acquire power and consequence solely through their friendship with Kabardian princes.[71]

Kabarda was also a defensive line between the mountaineer societies and imperial invaders. In particular, a strong Kabarda safeguarded the mountaineers from the raiding of the armies of the Crimean Khan, his Nogai allies, and other nomadic steppe peoples.[72]

As is often the case with neighboring communities that occupy complimentary ecological niches, symbiotic relations developed between Kabardians and their mountaineer neighbors. To be sure, Kabardians, especially their strong landed nobility, benefited most from this relationship. Nevertheless, the benefits derived from this system of relations by both Kabarda and its mountaineer tributaries help explain its persistence well into the nineteenth century, despite the tsarist state's bids to end Kabarda's influence over its neighbors.

While the mountaineer peoples depended on the foothills and plains pastures during late autumn and early spring, many Kabardian communities needed the alpine meadows of their neighbors for the grazing of their cattle in the summer months. Klaproth explains, for example, that "in the summer . . . Kabardians are forced to drive their herds from the plains, where everything is dried up and mosquitoes torment the cattle, to the mountains of Digora. This connects both peoples and they live in good accord because they both depend on each other."[73]

Vigorous trade relations existed between Kabardian and mountaineer communities. Mountaineers traded their animal products (cheese, milk, meat, wool) for Kabardian grain and salt.[74] A disruption in friendly relations between these groups often meant a lack of access to essential provisions for both groups.

At the top of the social hierarchy, feudal-like relations were mutually beneficial for Kabardian princes and their mountaineer vassals. Kabardian princes often competed for the prestige and economic benefits of collecting tribute from mountaineer elites, while the latter gained political and economic protection from the leaders of rival clans and unruly peasants through their relations with powerful Kabardian princes.[75] Fictive kinship also bound Kabardians and mountaineers together. The widespread practice of *atalyk*—the exchange of children between elite families as a way of forging patronage networks—further reinforced these symbiotic relations. In a useful analogy, Rustam Begeulov, a historian of pre-tsarist social and political relations in the Central Caucasus, compares "*emchak*" rights gained through *atalyk* to dual citizenship. An individual raised outside of his society of birth as an *atalyk* enjoyed the rights and obligations of membership in both societies. For many mountaineer families, there were great benefits to *atalyk*. They could receive the right to use land allotments from the family of their adopted child. Intermarriage was common, especially at the elite level. Indeed, virtually all the leading mountaineer clans were linked to Kabardian princely and noble families through marriage ties.[76] Fictive and blood relations between the societies of the Central Caucasus was especially important for obtaining military aid during major battles. For example, when the nomadic Kalmyks attacked the Kabardians in 1644, several thousand warriors from the surrounding mountaineer societies came to their aid.[77]

Finally, common adherence to Islam was an important unifying force in Central Caucasia's system of intercommunal relations. Most of the region's indigenous communities had adopted Sunni Islam, however superficially, by the beginning of the nineteenth century. The Ossetian mountain valleys, which included a mix of Christian and Muslim villages, were an exception. Beginning in the sixteenth century, Islam first spread to the elites of Kabarda mainly through the influence of Ottoman and Crimean missionaries. Trade relations with Ottoman port cities on the Black Sea, particularly Azov, Gelendzhik, and Anapa, created an incentive for Kabardian elites (and other Circassian elites in the Northwest Caucasus) to adopt Islam. The close ties between Kabardian elites and those of neighboring communities, in addition to the activity of Ottoman missionaries, facilitated the spread of the *Hanafi* school of Islamic jurisprudence (*fiqh*) to mountaineer communities in the Central Caucasus. Up to about the late eighteenth and early nineteenth centuries, the societies of the Central Caucasus generally featured a superficially Islamized elite stratum and a peasant majority who still mainly adhered to traditional folk religions with scattered elements of Christianity and Islam.[78]

Adherence to Islamic norms and sharia law began to spread throughout the societies of the Central Caucasus in the late eighteenth and early nineteenth centuries as a unifying measure in response to Russian colonization. In the face of Russian tactics for colonial conquest, Islam became an important tie that bound the diverse communities of the Central Caucasus together. Nevertheless, though nominally Sunni Muslims, a syncretic Islam combining pre-Islamic customs with Islamic rites and practices developed in the societies of the Central Caucasus. Finally, unlike the Northeast Caucasus (Chechnya and Dagestan), Sufism, with the possible late exception of the Ingush (who are culturally and linguistically related to the Chechens), never played a significant role among the peoples of the Central Caucasus.[79]

Structure of the Book

Chapter 1 tells the story of the first phase of Russia's conquest of the North Caucasus from 1763 through 1825, and it makes two general arguments. First, it argues that Russian officials shifted between opposing extremes in their policies toward Kabarda in an effort to extend Russian rule over as much territory as possible. With the Ottoman Empire's concession of Kabarda to the Russian Empire in the 1774 Treaty of Küçük Kaynarca,[80] Russia endeavored to maximize the size of this territorial acquisition by supporting a broad definition of Kabarda's domains and its claims of suzerainty over neighboring mountaineer peoples. With the Sublime Porte's acceptance of Russia's version of Kabarda's borders, Russian policymakers began to actively support mountaineer societies in their efforts to break free of their land-based vassalage to Kabarda's nobility. These were the same mountaineer societies that Russian policymakers had claimed were part of Kabarda during the war a few years earlier. In pursuing these opposing policies, Russia consistently took advantage of requests from local leaders for protection against neighboring communities and empires threatening their access to and control of land. Russia used these "invitations to empire" to easily insinuate itself into the political affairs of the region and, with much greater effort, gradually assert its full control over local societies.[81] Second, this chapter argues that the destruction of the Kabarda-centered system of intercommunal relations was a result of combined military and epidemiological onslaughts during the first quarter of the nineteenth century. Despite tsarist efforts to use divide-and-rule tactics to break up this system by attracting mountaineer communities to switch sides and come under Russian protection, social and economic ties between

Kabardian and mountaineer elites proved remarkably resilient in the face of tsarist conquest.

Chapter 2 examines the period from the conclusion of Russia's conquest of Kabarda in the 1820s to the end of the Caucasus War in the early 1860s. During this period, Russia's security dilemma in the North Caucasus comes into sharp relief. After tsarist conquest, Kabardian society was in a deep crisis—its population had declined by as much as 90 percent, it was unclear who owned what land, and Kabardian peasants and tributary elites from neighboring societies were casting off the suzerainty of Kabarda's princes and nobles. Many within the colonial administration wanted to fix the problems that Russia's conquest had wrought upon Kabarda and begin weaving its worn-torn society into the administrative, cultural, and economic fabric of the empire. Of far greater importance for the military-colonial administration at the time, however, were security concerns associated with ongoing conflict in the Northwest and the Northeast Caucasus. In pursuing policies aimed at shoring up regional security—particularly ethnic cleansing and resettlements—tsarist officials subverted imperial integration and impeded the establishment an effective administration in the Kabardian lands.

With the conclusion of the Caucasus War between 1859 and 1864, the tsarist administration in the Caucasus set about reorganizing the administration of the region, transforming social and economic relations, and generally pursuing goals that, for the first time, went beyond immediate security concerns. Chapter 3 examines the main events that structured social and intercommunal transformations in the North Caucasus in the late imperial period: first, the peasant and land reforms—the abolition of serfdom and the reexamination and codification of land rights among the region's manifold societies—and, second, state policies and modernization processes that encouraged European and Russian colonization of the region. The chapter begins with an examination of the fraught process of reforming land relations and the social structure in Kabarda and its neighboring mountaineer societies as part of the empire-wide Great Reforms. The different approaches to these reforms that officials in the region took demonstrate the disparate ideological currents within tsarist officialdom and highlight the roles and goals of different state representatives in the region. Debates among officials over the proper reform course for the Central Caucasus ended with the triumph of a conservative policy aimed at shoring up the local native nobilities as bulwarks of support for the tsarist regime.

The reforms of the 1860s failed to solve land problems in the North Caucasus. Rather, they exacerbated existing tensions by giving the best lands to mountaineer elites, former feudal lords, and members of the Russian imperial elite, leaving the region's peasantry with a grossly inadequate amount of farmland and pastures. Moreover, the beginnings of modernization in the Russian Empire led to a sharp increase in Russian colonization, which further exacerbated land disputes and intercommunal conflict. During the Russian Revolution and Civil War years, these tensions exploded into violent ethnicized conflict as ethno-political entrepreneurs exploited them for their political goals.

Chapter 4 focuses on the period of socioeconomic and political collapse and reconfiguration between 1918 and 1928. Conflicts during this period often began as land disputes between neighboring villages and had little to do with ethnicity. This chapter demonstrates that in cases where these intercommunal disputes involved culturally and linguistically distinct villages, the Soviet state's championing of the national principle and delimiting of ethno-national borders transformed and intensified these disputes into ethno-national conflicts involving two peoples rather than two villages. I argue that the new connections and opportunities created through border-making led individuals to identify with national communities. Villagers learned that they could derive important benefits by claiming membership in a national community— they could gain important support for their cause of securing more land. The mass mobilization surrounding border and land disputes between Kabarda and its neighbors also demonstrate "double assimilation": assimilation into newly promulgated national communities and assimilation into the supranational Soviet state.[82]

Most importantly, the early 1920s witnessed the birth of Kabardino-Balkaria as a unitary autonomous region. In a compromise aimed at preventing bloodshed between Kabardians and Balkars, the ethno-political elites of the two communities agreed that because of the intertwined and interdependent nature of Kabardian and Balkar land and economic relations, the two communities should remain united in a common Kabardino-Balkar AO. To ensure the stable functioning of this new multiethnic autonomous administrative unit, Kabardian, Balkar and Russian elites worked out an informal power-sharing agreement that remains in place to this day.

During the waves of ethnic cleansing that swept through Eastern Europe during the Second World War, the Stalinist state deported the Balkars from the North Caucasus to Central Asia on false charges of mass treason. The Balkars, along with about a half-dozen other nationalities from the Soviet Union's southern borderlands, spent the next thirteen years living in internal exile as "punished peoples" without full civil rights in Kazakhstan and Kyrgyzstan.[83] The Balkar deportations are the central event around which Chapter 5 is structured. This chapter seeks to understand the links between ethnic processes and the deportations and how the deportations, in turn, affected intercommunal relations and ethno-national identities. To determine whether local ethno-political factors played a meaningful role in the deportation, the first section of this chapter explores intercommunal relations and Soviet nationality policies in Kabardino-Balkaria during the decade and a half leading up to the deportations. Next, this chapter examines Kabardino-Balkaria's experience during the war, focusing particularly on the six-month Nazi occupation and its aftermath. While some Balkars fought against Soviet power (just as some of their Kabardian neighbors did), this was common throughout Nazi-occupied Soviet territories, and groups of active anti-Soviet collaborators represented small minorities in most regions, including the mountains of Balkaria. Moreover, wartime Soviet policies exacerbated resistance to Soviet rule. I argue that the deportation of the Balkars was a product of Stalinist xenophobia, paranoia, and the growing use of ethnic cleansing to pursue state-security goals. Chapter 5 also examines Soviet nationalities policies during late-Stalinism, a critical but understudied period, focusing particularly on the contrasting experiences of Kabardians and Balkars.

The final chapter examines ethno-political mobilization in Kabardino-Balkaria and neighboring national republics during and immediately following the collapse of the Soviet Union. This chapter offers conclusions, based on long- and medium-term patterns and processes, as to why tensions between Kabardians and Balkars did not descend into interethnic violence and the ethno-political situation in Kabardino-Balkaria stabilized while neighboring regions witnessed unrelenting ethno-political deadlock at best and violent conflict at worst. I demonstrate how the long-standing history of cooperation, compromise, and economic symbiosis between Kabardians and Balkars and the general lack of socioeconomic disparity between the two peoples impeded the attempts of ethno-political entrepreneurs among the republic's Balkar minority to mobilize mass support for Balkar separatism. I conclude by considering how, after the deescalating of Kabardian-Balkar tensions by the mid-1990s, ethno-political conflict moved from the streets to the halls of academia and has been particularly pronounced in debates over the history of the region.

1

Land, Community, and Conquest in the Central Caucasus, 1763–1825

In 1744, the tsarist state dispatched Moscow cartographer Stepan Chichagov to the North Caucasus to compile a map of Kabarda. The fieldwork for this map and other concurrent Russian missions to Kabarda reflect the region's increased strategic significance for the Russian Empire in the mid-eighteenth century. A long-standing ally in Russia's struggle with the Crimean Khanate, Kabarda's importance for Russia increased after 1739 when the Treaty of Belgrade, which ended the Russo-Ottoman War of 1735–9, recognized Kabarda's independence and made it a "buffer zone" between Russia and the Ottoman Empire. Compiled at the peak of Kabarda's power, Chichagov's map (see Map 2) is one of the most complete descriptions of the territory controlled by Kabarda's princes and nobles.[1] The upper reaches of the Kuma River form Kabarda's western frontier. The Podkumok and upper Kura rivers form Greater Kabarda's frontier in the northwest, and the Terek River forms Lesser Kabarda's northeastern frontier. The Lesser-Kabardian villages in the Sunzha River basin are Kabarda's eastern frontier. The mountains form Kabarda's natural boundary in the south. According to these borders, which were fluid frontier zones until the mid-nineteenth century, Kabarda occupied the foothills and plains of the Central Caucasus. Unlike their neighbors' mountain valleys, these lands were rich in pasturage and salt deposits and were well suited for agriculture. This fertile, productive land allowed Kabarda's princes to dominate their highland neighbors economically and politically.

Two decades after Chichagov drafted his map, the tsarist state launched a process of imperial conquest that would—through colonization, emigration, deportations, warfare, and disease—result by 1822 in the destruction of the world depicted by Chichagov. Occurring between the 1770s and 1820s, these massive territorial changes that accompanied the Russian conquest of Kabarda were the products of the first stages of Russia's conquest of the North Caucasus. Chichagov presented an "ethno-territorial" picture of the North Caucasus that is vastly different from that of contemporary maps. Much of eighteenth-century Kabarda now belongs to neighboring communities. The plains south of the Terek River basin, once the heartland of Lesser Kabarda, are now core Ossetian territories. The frontiers of Lesser Kabarda extended eastward into the lands of contemporary Ingushetia. The northern frontiers of precolonial Kabarda are now the spa-resort towns of the overwhelmingly Russian Stavropol Province. In the

Map 2 Map of Kabarda compiled by the cartographer Stepan Chichagov in 1744. *Source: Kabardino-Russkie otnosheniia*, vol. 2, 114–15. © Out of copyright.

west, at the height of their power, Kabardian princes laid claim to what is now the northeast quarter of the Karachai-Cherkes Republic.²

This chapter tells the story of this important, yet often overlooked, early phase in Russian empire-building and social engineering in the North Caucasus. Integral to this process of imperial expansion was a shift from Kabardian to Russian control in the Central Caucasus. Taking place from the 1760s to the 1820s, this power shift profoundly transformed intercommunal and land relations in the Central Caucasus and contributed, perhaps more than any other period, to the formation of the region's current ethno-demographic makeup.

During these years, the tsarist state sought to weaken Kabarda by destroying and reconfiguring the long-established system of intercommunal relations in the Central Caucasus. While Kabarda's princes sat comfortably atop Central Caucasia's multiethnic social hierarchy, the region's system of intercommunal relations was symbiotic, and all the communities involved derived important benefits through their participation in it. The mutually beneficial nature of these relations explains their persistence, among many of Central Caucasia's communities, despite the tsarist state's best efforts to end Kabarda's influence over its neighbors. Even after the 1820s, despite the collapse of the Kabarda-centered system of intercommunal relations, Kabardians continued to influence their neighbors in important ways.

Nevertheless, Russian colonialism fundamentally transformed intercommunal relations in the Central Caucasus. Old enmities between Kabardians and landless mountaineers dissipated, while others continued to simmer. Russian culture began to supplant the influence of Kabardian culture among some of the region's mountaineer communities. New antagonisms emerged as the land interests of Russian colonizers sent to maintain Russia's hold on the region clashed with those of the region's native population. Religious affiliations became more important in the relationships among different communities. Finally, by the end of this period, Russia overtook Kabarda as the central political, economic, and cultural force in the region. Russian officials replaced Kabardian princes as the main arbiters of disputes among the region's different communities.

The transformation of intercommunal relations in the Central Caucasus was both a strategy for and consequence of Russian conquest and colonization. From its early efforts to press its claims on Kabarda after 1774 through General Aleksei Ermolov's brutal pacification of Kabarda in the early 1820s, the tsarist state consciously strove to end the Kabardian princes' political and economic power over their neighbors. Moreover, the forces of the Russian Empire worked in conjunction with disease and land pressures in the mountains to severely reduce Kabarda's territory and decimate its population. The change in tsarist policy toward Kabarda from the sixteenth to the eighteenth centuries was tremendous. From their earliest engagements with the Caucasus, Russian policymakers, grasping the links between land and power in the region, recognized Kabarda as a key polity in the region. Indeed, in addition to controlling neighboring peoples, Kabarda also controlled the major mountain passes and trade routes across the Caucasus. Muscovite and early-imperial Russia saw Kabarda as a military ally in a common struggle with the Crimean Khanate and sought to strengthen the power of loyal Kabardian princes.[3] By the 1760s, however, concerted efforts at weakening the power of Kabarda lay at the heart of the tsarist state's plans for imperial control in the Caucasus.

The problems that tsarist officials encountered in trying to end Kabardian elites' power over neighboring communities remind us that, despite the wide use of "ethnicity" as a category of analysis in discourse on the region, social status was often more important than ethnic group solidarities in determining allegiances and identities in the eighteenth-century Caucasus. Attempts by Russian generals to compel neighboring elites to join them in putting down Kabardian elite-led resistance, or at least cease offering refuge to restive Kabardians, often faltered. The tsarist authorities in the Central Caucasus had greater success in subverting regional power structures by encouraging peasants to rebel against their feudal lords with whom they usually shared a common culture and language than by attempting to stoke conflict between different cultural-linguistic communities.

Russian Policy Toward Kabarda and Its Tributaries Societies Until 1774

For all its benefits, the cross-cultural symbiosis among the peoples of the Central Caucasus was often not well accepted by those who were subordinate to the Kabardian princes. Russian officials did their best to make use of these intercommunal tensions to further the interests of their empire. During moments of Kabardian weakness due to infighting among Kabarda's princely parties, individual mountaineer societies periodically challenged Kabardian princely power by refusing to render tribute for land use and by fending off resultant Kabardian punitive raids. Mountaineer societies farthest away from Greater Kabarda—the stronger of the two Kabardas—and those with social structures most different from Kabarda's were most successful at challenging Kabardian power. For example, as Lesser Kabarda declined vis-à-vis Greater Kabarda in the eighteenth century, the Ingush societies to the southeast of Lesser Kabarda rejected their previous tributary relations with Kabarda's princes.[4]

Russian officials saw the possibility of exploiting the inequalities between Kabarda and its neighbors long before they began to do so. In 1650, the Muscovite state sent an embassy to the Western Georgian Kingdom of Imeretia, an important ally in its struggle against an expanding Ottoman Empire. The Muscovite ambassadors relied on the princes of Kabarda for safe passage to Georgia. At the time, Kabarda was Russia's most important ally in the North Caucasus given its suzerainty over surrounding mountaineer societies and control over the strategic military-trade routes across the Caucasus range. While in Kabarda, the ambassadors met with representatives of some of Kabarda's tributary mountaineer societies, including Balkars and Ossetians. The accounts of these meetings provide some of the earliest sources on the economic and sociopolitical relations between Kabarda and its neighbors. In particular, the Muscovite representatives met with delegates from Digora, the Ossetian society closest to and most heavily influenced by Kabarda. The Digorans described the relationship between Digora and Kabarda: "for protection they pay tribute [*iasak*] to the [Kabardian] Cherkasskii princes Aleguka and Khodozhduka and the noble Zazaruka Anzorov, in the amount of 10 cows or bulls, one hostage [*iasyr*], and one good horse from each village [*kabak*], and one sheep . . . a bushel of wheat, and a bushel of millet from each household."[5] In this first of many mountaineer appeals for Russian support in throwing off Kabardian suzerainty, the Digorans made clear that "if your ruler allows for the construction of a town and the placement of soldiers near the mountains, then the Digorans and all mountaineer peoples will be your ruler's servants. And the tribute we now give to the Kabardian princes we will begin to give to the sovereign of Moscow."[6]

Just as nineteenth-century Estonians and Latvians saw the Russian state as an ally in their efforts to end their subordination to the Baltic Germans,[7] from the mid-eighteenth century through the first quarter of the nineteenth century, some mountaineer communities in the Central Caucasus saw the Russian state as an ally in their struggle with the Kabardian nobility. The expanding Russian presence in the region, especially in the form of Cossack *stanitsy* (fortified settlements) along the Terek River, encouraged mountaineer appeals for protection. Despite Russia's repeated rejection of their appeals, until the 1820s mountaineer elites continued to petition the tsarist administration for help in ending the Kabardian nobility's economic dominance over their societies.

These appeals steadily increased in the eighteenth century. As Kabarda's power reached its apogee in the mid-eighteenth century, Kabardian princes increased their tribute demands on the mountaineer societies. Forces loyal to Kabardian nobles raided mountaineer villages to collect the increased tribute by force and bring communities back under their economic and political control.[8] At the same time, however, one of the major benefits of Kabardian supremacy in the Central Caucasus, protection from external enemies, steadily diminished as the ability of the Crimean Khanate to conduct devastating raids on the mountaineers weakened.[9] Moreover, Ossetian and Ingush mountaineer societies experienced Malthusian pressures as the limited agricultural and pasture resources of their mountain valleys could no longer sustain their growing populations. This land shortage in the mountains forced many mountaineers to resettle to the plains. In the 1740s, most Ingush resettlers asserted their control over plains land from the weak princes of Lesser Kabarda. By contrast, most Ossetian mountaineers who resettled to the plains settled on Kabardian fiefdoms, further increasing the economic control of Kabarda's princes and nobles over these communities.[10]

Throughout the 1750s and 1760s, petitioners asked tsarist officials in Kizliar and Astrakhan to bring their people under Russian rule (*poddanstvo*) and extend their military settlements into Kabardian territory to protect mountaineers wishing to resettle to the plains. They even sent delegations to St. Petersburg. In their petitions to Russian officials, mountaineers highlighted their lack of land. Ossetian petitioners requesting land on the Kabardian plains, complained to the tsarist government: "we live in the mountains in very cramped conditions . . . we suffer great deprivations and some of our low people [serfs] do not have the least bit of arable land where they can sow wheat and millet for their subsistence nor can they keep enough cattle."[11]

In the mid-eighteenth century, larger geopolitical concerns precluded Russia's acceptance of invitations to rule over the mountaineer societies of the Central Caucasus. In response to mountaineer appeals for Russian protection, the tsarist leadership instructed its administrators in the Caucasus to do little more than "reassure" (*obnadezhivat'*) the mountaineers of Russia's good intentions.[12]

As long as the Ottoman Empire retained its regional influence, the Russian state was not in a position to risk its strategic relationship with Kabarda for the sake of smaller gains in the hitherto little-known mountain regions. Kabarda continued to be an important ally and counterweight to Ottoman power in the Caucasus, and Russia was bound by the Treaty of Belgrade. The Russian administration understood that the Ottoman Empire would see Russian claims of sovereignty over Kabardian vassals and the dispatching of soldiers to Kabardian lands as interference in the affairs of independent Kabarda. This would be a violation of the Treaty, which specifically stated that the "Turks and Tatars of the Sublime Porte must not enter or interfere with [Greater and Lesser Kabarda] and they will likewise be left in peace by the All-Russian Empire."[13] Thus, given Kabarda's claims to Ossetian and other neighboring mountaineer societies, the College of Foreign Affairs concluded that "leading [the Ossetians] to an oath of allegiance prematurely could evoke some suspicion [*ombrazh*] of harmful intentions from their neighboring powers such as the Persians and Turks."[14]

Under certain conditions, the Russian Empire's long-term plans for the region also led it to assist Kabardian princes in maintaining their dominance over their neighbors. Russian policymakers understood that a successful future war against the Ottoman Empire would reverse the Treaty of Belgrade's ruling on Kabarda's independence and allow for the annexation of this North Caucasian princely confederation. According to this long-term plan, by deferring the immediate extension of Russian rule over the mountaineers of the Central Caucasus for the larger prize of Kabarda, Russia would later be able to lay claim to both Kabarda and its tributaries. Such noninterference would also prevent Russia from needlessly upsetting the Kabardian nobility at a time when it needed to maintain their support or neutrality and focus its attention on conducting a successful campaign against the Ottoman Empire. In the interim, it was in Russia's interests to keep Kabarda strong, enable Kabardian princes to maintain their dominance over their neighbors, and even assist them in extending their dominion over other Caucasian tribes. The more lands and peoples under Kabardian suzerainty at the time of the next peace treaty with the Ottoman Empire, the more lands and peoples would come under Russian rule with the expected annexation of Kabarda.[15]

Nevertheless, even without direct Russian support, some mountaineer societies managed to shed their dependence on Kabarda's princes and colonize plains lands previously controlled by Kabarda. In particular, in the 1750s and 1760s, Vainakh communities (specifically, the ancestors of today's Ingush), desperately seeking relief from their land hunger in the mountains, forced the Lesser-Kabardian population out of the Sunzha River basin.[16] Weakened by attacks from the stronger Greater Kabarda in the late seventeenth and first half of the eighteenth centuries, the Lesser-Kabardian nobles gradually lost their ability to control parts of their territory and collect tribute from their neighbors.[17]

Ossetian communities, facing the same land pressures as Ingush highlanders, also began to resettle to the plains. However, until the 1820s, Ossetian resettlement was largely limited to the noble *badiliat* class of landowners and their serfs from Digora (western) Ossetia. The less extensive migration of Ossetians compared with that of the Ingush was a result of Kabarda's stronger hold over the Ossetian societies than the Ingush. This was the case because the strongest princes and nobles of Kabarda were located closer to the Ossetians than to the Ingush. Indeed, in the mid-eighteenth century, the lords of Greater Kabarda moved their domains to the exits of Ossetia's mountain valleys to shore up their ability to collect tribute from Ossetian communities.[18]

Thus, while Ingush migrants from the mountains managed to assert control over Kabardian lands, Ossetians could only avail themselves of lands in Kabarda by entering the service of Kabarda's princes. The only group at liberty to take on these added feudal obligations was Digora Ossetia's noble class, the *badiliat*. Therefore, between the 1740s and 1770s three *badiliat* families—the Karadzhaevs, Kubatievs, and Tuganovs—encouraged by invitations from Kabarda's princes, moved with their serfs from Digora to the foothills of Lesser Kabarda. Settling on princely domains of Kabarda, these Digora-Ossetian nobles entered Kabarda's social hierarchy at the level of high nobles (*dizhenugo* and *tlekotlesh*). While always tributaries of Kabardian princes, these Ossetians who migrated to the foothills became princely vassals. However, class affinities between the Kabardian and Ossetian nobilities meant that while giving up their former vestiges of independence, these Ossetian nobles could now count on assistance from the Kabardian feudal elites in their efforts to maintain control over their serfs during a period of socioeconomic flux.[19] Aside from the Digorans, who had especially close ties with Kabarda, most Ossetian communities were only willing to resettle to the plains with Russian military support, which, in the eighteenth century, was not an option.[20]

If, given their need to preserve friendly relations with Kabarda and avoid provoking conflict with the Ottoman Empire, Russia's leaders were not interested in accepting mountaineer invitations to extend its empire in the Central Caucasus, they were interested in increasing Russia's regional presence through other means. By promoting Orthodox missionary activity among Central Caucasia's religiously syncretic mountaineer communities and extending its frontier outposts, Russia hoped to become a counterweight to Ottoman influence in the region before the renewal of open conflict with the Ottoman Empire.[21]

In 1744, the Russian Senate formed a Spiritual Commission for the North Caucasus (also known as the Ossetian Spiritual Commission). This institution, which was staffed by Georgians to bypass the prohibition against Russian involvement in the internal affairs of Kabarda and its tributary societies,[22] marks the beginning of Russia's use of missionary activity as an insidious form of empire-building in the Central Caucasus. Russia justified its missionary activities in the region—as it would continue to do a century later—by citing the presence of relics of Christianity in the region (e.g., the ruins of Byzantine Churches) and the perceived lack of firm religious convictions among the mountaineers.[23] As Michael Khodarkovsky reminds us, "religion and state sovereignty were not and could not be clearly separated, [and] the major powers in the region often laid claims to lands and peoples on the basis of their common religion."[24] In the North Caucasus, where folk religions remained dominant into the eighteenth century,[25] the Ottoman Empire promoted the spread of Islam while the Russian Empire sponsored Orthodox Christian missionary activity. In this imperial competition, both empires saw religious affiliation as a chief indicator of political loyalty. Both sought to expand their influence in the region by acting as the protectors of their respective co-religionists. Both empires could use religious conversion as a means to increase their influence in the region without violating the Treaty of Belgrade because Article Eight of the Treaty specified that neither of the powers had the right to protest if any of the Kabardians or other mountaineer peoples decided to "change faiths" and enter into the service of Russia or the Ottoman Empire.[26] The primary targets for conversion were the Ingush and Ossetian communities along Kabarda's eastern frontier because they were closest to the Russian border. While the Spiritual Commission hoped to bring about mass conversions, initially it focused its efforts on the elites within the mountaineer societies. It set up churches and schools for the children of the elites. Indeed, in a 1771 rescript to Astrakhan Governor Ivan Jacobi, Catherine II characteristically argued that "in the case of the Ossetians and Ingush and other mountaineers, there is no better means to make them true Christians who are loyal to our side than the enlightenment of their youth."[27]

These efforts at conversion among Ossetians and Ingush met with mixed results. Between 1745 and 1792, the Spiritual Commission converted 8,199 Ossetians and Ingush to Orthodoxy.[28] While these are seemingly sizable numbers, many of these conversions were in name only and most "converts" continued to practice their traditional religions. Many baptized mountaineers were poor peasants who converted for material incentives: five rubles or the equivalent in canvas and tax breaks and trade incentives in Russian market towns. According to one witness, mountaineers "willingly allow themselves to be baptized; some repeat this several times in order to receive the seven yards of rough canvas that they give out for this; however, after their baptism, as proof of their Christianity, all they are able to do is make the sign of the cross and eat pork [as a sign that they were not Muslims]."[29]

Given its fundamental importance to political, socioeconomic, and intercommunal relations in the Central Caucasus, land played *the* central role in the matter of mountaineer conversions to Russian Orthodoxy. The main impetus for Ossetian and Ingush conversion to Orthodoxy was the hope of many land-poor mountaineer communities that by converting to the Russian Orthodoxy the tsarist administration would assist them in resettling to the plains and protect them from Kabardian incursions. Before the mid-1760s, however, Russia could not offer this type of assistance because of the Treaty of Belgrade and a reluctance to start another war with the Ottoman Empire.[30]

However, Russia's construction of the fortress Mozdok in 1762 and the opening of a religious school for mountaineers here in 1764, on an uninhabited territory on the frontiers of Lesser Kabarda, provided a solution to many of the constraints that Russia faced in the region. Mozdok offered a base from which Russia could expand its influence and promote missionary activity among the mountaineers of the Central Caucasus. More importantly, it provided a viable place for resettlement for mountaineers wishing to adopt Orthodoxy and become Russian subjects. The fortunes of the Spiritual Commission and its missionary activities increased significantly with the establishment of Mozdok.[31]

Russia's establishment of Fort Mozdok set off a chain of events that deeply altered Russia's political relations with the communities of the region and led to transformations of the cultural-linguistic boundaries of the Central Caucasus. While Russia had previously rejected requests to extend its presence into the region, in 1759, the Russian administration took a calculated risk in accepting an "invitation to empire" from Kurgoko Konchokin, a Lesser-Kabardian prince threatened by raids from the stronger princes of Greater Kabarda. Konchokin appealed to the commandant at Kizliar, Russia's main fortress town in the North Caucasus located in present-day Dagestan. He requested permission to embrace the Russian Orthodox faith and resettle with his retainers and dependents across the Terek to lands under Russian protection. That the tsarist administration facilitated the baptism of Konchokin and accepted him as a Russian subject is not surprising; it was long-standing practice for loyal Kabardian nobles to enter Russian service. What was unusual was the decision to allow an entire Kabardian princely family to convert and become Russian subjects. More unusual still was the decision to allow Konchokin and his family to resettle under Russian protection across the Terek River along the northeast frontiers of Lesser Kabarda. These lands were not settled at this point, but they were used sporadically by Kabardians for pasturage and forestry.[32] Given Russia's imprecise borders in the region, this area, known as Mozdok (Kabardian for "dense forest"), had emerged as a point of contention between the lords of Greater Kabarda and the Russia administration already in the 1740s when the latter established a guard-post (*karaul*) here to protect its Lesser-Kabardian clients from Greater Kabardian raids. In 1744, the princes of Greater Kabarda appealed to the Russian administration for the removal of this *karaul* because it "was constructed in a place where we chop timber and graze our cattle."[33] Even more risky, however, was Russia's construction, at Konchokin's request, of a fortress town on this land in 1762. In addition to upsetting the Greater Kabardian nobility, this move could be interpreted by the Ottoman Empire as interference in the internal affairs of Kabarda and a violation of the Treaty of Belgrade.[34]

After the establishment of Mozdok, the Russian College of Foreign Affairs issued a plan for the settlement of the town with baptized mountaineers and other Christian peoples of the Caucasus (Georgians and Armenians). From its new base at Mozdok, the Ossetian Spiritual Commission began to more actively agitate for conversion and resettlement among the landless mountaineer communities. From this point on, the Spiritual Commission's efforts met with more success. In addition to the 700 Kabardians who resettled near Mozdok with Kurgoko Konchokin in 1759, by 1765, two years after its establishment, over 500 Ossetians and 200 Kabardians had resettled to Mozdok.[35]

Given the incentives for resettlement—tax breaks and free land—and the mountaineers' land hunger, Russian policymakers expected massive mountaineer resettlement to Mozdok. In 1768, Russia's College of Foreign Affairs noted with disappointment, "all of this, however, against the most likely expectations, did not happen."[36] Frustrated with the pace of mountaineer resettlement, by 1769 the tsarist government looked to supplement mountaineer resettlement by settling Cossacks to Mozdok and its environs.[37]

The initial lack of mountaineer resettlement to Mozdok stemmed from the divergent aims of the Russian administration and most baptized mountaineers. The Russian administration viewed baptism and resettlement as a transfer to Russian subjecthood, whereas the mountaineers who adopted Christianity wanted an independent existence on the plains.[38] Given mountaineer concerns over retaining their freedom, the only Christian converts willing to resettle to Mozdok were those with no freedom to lose—serfs. Indeed, fugitive serfs from the societies of the Central Caucasus with the most highly developed feudal systems and where Islam had relatively strong roots—Kabarda and Digora Ossetia—formed the main contingent of resettlers to Mozdok. These runaway serfs were taking advantage of a 1743 *ukaz* stating that "newly baptized converts [*novokreshchennye*] from the Mohammedan faith would be forever freed from servitude of infidel landlords [*pomeshchikov inovernykh*] . . . [and]resettled to live among other newly baptized . . . but if their landlords by their own wishes also take holy baptism, they will be returned to their control."[39] Because the Russian administration equated conversion with becoming Russian subjects, most Kabardian and Digoran lords refused to give up their independence by converting. For these lords, the loss of serfs was a significant economic blow.

The flight of serfs from Kabardian and Digoran noble estates became the first major rift between the lords of Kabarda and the tsarist state. Through the rest of the 1760s Kabardian lords took a series of measures to combat the exodus of serfs to the Russian side. First, they repeatedly petitioned the tsarist administration to close Mozdok Fortress and return their serfs. In 1764, the lords of Greater Kabarda sent a delegation to Saint Petersburg with a petition calling for the destruction of the fortress. The delegation argued that Russia had illegally constructed the fortress on Kabardian land. However, Count Nikita Panin—Catherine II's chief policy advisor at the time—instructed his assistant charged with receiving Kaituko Kaisynov, the leader of the Kabardian delegation, "to use money to persuade the Kabardian lord to provide a petition that would justify [Russia's] rights [to Mozdok] in the reasoning of the Porte and Crimean Khan." This plan worked. On September, 13, 1764, Kaisynov signed a document stating that "the Kabardians have no rights to the area of Mozdok and they cannot graze their cattle within 30 versts [20 miles] of the area."[40] With the failure of diplomacy, and after a few unsuccessful clashes with Russian Cossack forces in 1767, the Kabardian landlords began to move their settlements farther away from Mozdok and set up frontier posts to prevent their serfs from fleeing across the Russian side. If they could not persuade Russia to abandon Mozdok, then the Kabardian landlords saw an armed attack against the Russian fort as their last resort.[41] Understanding the superiority of tsarist forces, the Kabardian landlords also appealed to Russia's enemies, the Ottoman Empire and the Crimean Khanate, for support. As early as 1764, Ottoman representatives had exchanged diplomatic notes with the Russian ambassador protesting the construction of Mozdok and other recent Russian maneuvers in Caucasia as a violation of the Treaty of Belgrade. Russia, however, was able to prove, using Kaisynov's statement, that Mozdok lay outside of Kabardian territory.[42] In 1767, several princes from Greater and Lesser Kabarda fled with their retinues to Crimean-controlled territory across the Kuban River.[43] It was only in 1774, at the height of another Russo-Ottoman War, that the aggrieved Kabardian landlords were able to count on the support of Ottoman and Crimean forces in a planned attack against Mozdok and other Cossack fortifications along the Russian frontier.

Kabarda and the Critical Juncture of the Russo-Ottoman War of 1768-74

A Kabardian uprising during the Russo-Ottoman War of 1768 marked the beginning of over a half century of intermittent conflict between Russia and Kabarda. This period of conflict would only reach a conclusion with the conquest of Kabarda between 1818 and 1825—at which point the geopolitical, communal, and social fates of Kabarda and the mountaineer communities were forever changed. The first clashes between Kabardian and Russian forces occurred in the summer of 1769. Several Kabardian princes and their retinues refused to swear oaths of loyalty to Russia when war broke out with the Ottoman Empire in late 1768, and they began conducting raids on Russian fortifications near Kabarda. In July 1769, Russian forces handily defeated the anti-Russian Kabardian forces whose numbers amounted to little over 200, compelling them to swear new oaths of allegiance to Russia.[44]

The majority of Kabarda's elites, however, initially sided with Russia during this Russo-Ottoman conflict. Numerous factors explain Kabarda's loyalty to Russia at the beginning of the 1768-74 war. First, despite recent differences over Mozdok and fugitive serfs, Kabarda had historically benefited from Russian protection and military aid. Second, Russia was an important trading partner for the Kabardians who hoped to retain their access to Russian markets. Third, Russia was more powerful, and, judging by its success in the last Russo-Ottoman conflict, it seemed the likely victor in this one. Fourth, many Kabardian princely and noble families had dynastic ties of service to the Russian state. Fifth, the Russian and Ottoman practice of taking hostages (*amanaty*) from elite Kabardian families ensured Kabarda's neutrality. Finally, a deep-seated antagonism between the Kabardian princes and the Crimean Khan (the Ottoman vassal and representative of Ottoman power in the North Caucasus), stemming from Kabarda's repeated resistance to Crimean invasions and particularly the brutal 1708 defeat and slaughter of Crimean forces on Mount Kanzhal, hampered the forging of a Kabardian-Ottoman alliance.[45]

Despite the Kabardian princes' proclivity toward maintaining friendly relations with their powerful neighbor, the actions of tsarist administrators in the Caucasus during the war pushed the majority of Kabarda's elites toward the Ottoman side. For example, as soon as war broke out, the Cossack forces of Nikolai Potapov, Commandant of Kizliar, seized over 20,000 heads of cattle from the Kabardians as a guarantee of Kabarda's loyalty to Russia.[46] As the Russo-Ottoman War progressed, it became increasingly clear to Kabarda's elite that a Russian victory in the war would mean the end of their independence and the curtailment of their power, both over their own dependent population and over their tributary neighbors.

When Russian forces entered Kabarda to "protect" it from Ottoman invasion in 1769, the Russian Empire nullified the Belgrade Treaty and began to treat Kabarda as its protectorate rather than an independent state. The appointment of Dmitrii Toganov as *pristav* (superintendent) of Kabarda marked the beginning of Russia's gradual assertion of administrative control over Kabarda's internal affairs. *Pristavs* performed functions similar to the British Residents in the princely states of the British Raj under "indirect rule."[47] While Kabarda's Grand Prince or *Wāli* served at the pleasure of the Russian administration as the ruler of Kabarda, real central power in Kabarda, to the extent that it existed, emanated from the *pristav*. However, prior to Russia bringing Kabarda's princely class to submission in the 1820s, political power in Kabarda remained atomized among individual princes, many of whom refused to obey the orders of the Grand Prince or the *pristav*.[48]

On August 17, 1771, Empress Catherine II issued a Charter (*Gramota*) to the Kabardian people. Aimed at satisfying some of the grievances of the Kabardian lords, this document further alienated many of them. The Charter addressed the Kabardian lords' concerns over the loss of their serfs. It promised that the state would compensate Kabardian lords for those serfs who had already fled across the Russian frontier and adopted Christianity. It also guaranteed that "all native Kabardian serfs who run away in future [would] be returned back." However, this document failed to satisfy the Kabardian princes' chief demand, namely the removal of the Russian fortress from Mozdok. Catherine II's Charter insisted, "Her Imperial Majesty will never agree to the destruction of the village that we constructed in the vicinity of Mozdok." In addition, the document further angered the Kabardian elite by addressing "the Kabardian lords, princes, and all the people" as "Our [i.e., Russian] subjects." Finally, by chastising all the Kabardians for the rebellious activity of a minority of their princes, and by claiming that "the prosperity of the [Kabardian] people and the means to a comfortable life are the result of the indulgences and kindness We have shown them," Catherine adopted a patronizing and self-aggrandizing tone vis-à-vis the Kabardians.[49]

The last straw for the Kabardian elite came in November 1772, after the Russian Army defeated the Crimean Khanate and forced the new pro-Russian khan to sign a peace treaty at Karasu. In addition to making the Crimean Khanate an independent state under Russian protection, the Karasu Treaty also ceded Kabarda, an independent state since the 1739 Treaty of Belgrade, to Russia. This was done without the presence or consultation of any Kabardian representatives.[50] The Ottoman Empire, however, was still at war with Russia. It refused to recognize the Karasu Treaty and backed its own rival claimant the position of Crimean Khan, Devlet-Girei. As Kabarda's independence appeared increasingly doomed, the Ottoman government became more desperate to attract the support of the mountaineers of the North Caucasus to their side. Upon ascending to the throne in January 1774, the new Ottoman Sultan, Abdul Hamid, dispatched emissaries to the region to shore up the support of the predominantly Muslim population in a holy war against the Russian infidels. Ottoman representatives visited the Kabardian and Kumyk princes, who together counted as their vassals and tributaries much of the North Caucasus' mountaineer population east of the Kuban River. By the summer of 1774, when Kabarda's princes welcomed large contingents of Ottoman and other anti-Russian forces into their domains, it became clear that the Ottoman agitation had achieved its goal. From Kabarda, Devlet-Gerei and his combined Turkish, Crimean, Kabardian, and mountaineer allies staged attacks on the Russian fortresses, including Mozdok. Indeed, when pro-Russian Kabardian princes, Dzhankhot Tatarkhanov and Devlet Kasaev, called upon Russian forces to liberate Kabarda from Ottoman occupation, General Johann Friedrich von Medem, Military Commander of Russia's Mozdok Fortified Line, turned his troops back after learning that most of the Kabardian princes had sided with Devlet-Gerei and the Ottoman forces.[51]

Fighting on the Caucasian front took on a dynamic distinct from the rest of the war. Local communities, upset by Russian expansion but previously too weak vis-à-vis Russia to act on these grievances, used the war and the extra force provided by the Ottoman Empire as an opportunity to attack Russian power in the region and exact their revenge. Indeed, despite the signing of Küçük Kaynarca Peace Treaty on July 11, 1774, which officially ended the war in Russia's favor, fighting between pro-Ottoman and tsarist forces continued in Kabarda until the end of August.[52] Fighting continued partly because, according to the Ottoman reading of the Küçük Kaynarca Treaty, Kabarda did not become part of the Russian Empire. Instead, as the Ottoman administration understood it, Kabarda remained an independent state that was now an ally of the Ottoman Empire. Article 21 of the Treaty of Küçük Kaynarca stated, "[B]oth Kabardas, that is Greater and Lesser, which are neighbors of the Tatars, have strong ties with the Crimean Khan; therefore their annexation to the Imperial Russian Court should be left to the will of the Crimean Khan."[53] According to the official tsarist reading, this article made Kabarda part of the Russian Empire because the Crimean Khan had already ceded Kabarda to the Russian Empire in the Karasu Agreement of 1772. However, the Ottoman Empire, never having recognized the Karasu Agreement, consequently, also did not recognize Russia's claims to Kabarda. It was left to Russia to press its claims on Kabarda by force, which it successfully did in August 1774. Ottoman representatives would continue to insist on Kabarda's independence for years to come.⁵⁴

The Russo-Ottoman War of 1768–74 and Russia's attendant annexation of Kabarda strained relations between Kabarda and its neighbors. After the war, Russia's rulers were now ready to extend their dominion over Kabarda's eastern highland neighbors. No longer hindered by the conditions of the Belgrade Treaty, Russia began to actively interfere in the political affairs of the Central Caucasus and make special efforts to attract the support of new groups. If Russia had previously denied sporadic Ossetian and Ingush petitions to come under Russian protection, now the extension of Russian rule over these communities was of far greater interest to Russian policymakers because they occupied an increasingly strategic position along the northern frontiers of Georgia. Moreover, Russia's desire to secure the Caucasus Mountains from Ottoman influence during the war also increased Russia's interest in these Ossetian and Ingush mountaineer societies. At the same time, the Kabardian lords increasingly tried to reinforce or reintroduce their dominion over Ossetian and Ingush societies, launching raids to collect tribute from these recalcitrant groups. This straining of Kabardian-mountaineer relations resulted in Ossetian and Ingush mountaineer communities swearing oaths of allegiance to Russia during the war.⁵⁵ While many elites within these Ossetian and Ingush communities would later attempt to throw off Russian rule because it impeded their retention of control over their serfs, the tsarist state began to regard these communities as Russian subjects and their territories as part of the Empire; officials cited these oaths as evidence of this relationship.⁵⁶ For the purposes of international diplomacy, Russia based its claims to Ossetian societies on its annexation of Kabarda. Astrakhan governor, Petr Krechetnikov, writing to Catherine II after Küçük Kaynarca, explained, "Greater and Lesser Kabarda remain in the definite sovereignty of your Imperial Majesty, and because the latter regard the Ossetians . . . as their subjects, then [Kabarda] together with [the Ossetians] belong to us."⁵⁷

Toward the end of the war, antagonistic actions of tsarist officials toward Kabardian elites caused relations between Russia and Kabarda to deteriorate further. In 1773, General von Medem attempted to stop Kabarda's princes from raiding Ingush villages. In response to von Medem's order for Kabardian princes to cease their raids, the Kabardian elites replied that "the Ingush had long ago been conquered by them" and that "they had always taken tribute according to custom." The Kabardian princes threatened to "leave the protection of H[er] I[mperial] M[ajesty]" if Russia did not cease interfering in Kabarda's affairs; however, if Russia ceased to provide protection to the Ingush, the princes promised "to reconcile with the Ingush . . . [and] be unswervingly loyal." General von Medem maintained a pro-Ingush position; he detained twelve Kabardians and planned to use force to protect the Ingush societies. However, not wishing to further anger the Kabardian elites and set them against Russia during a war, the court in St. Petersburg ordered General von Medem "not to protect the Ingush from the Kabardians and not to provoke them [the Kabardians] further because the Ingush themselves admitted that they had been their tributaries."⁵⁸

Russo-Kabardian Tensions and the Politics of Land in the Late Eighteenth Century

In the long term, Russia's victory over the Ottoman Empire in 1774 was a harbinger of great change for Kabarda's powerful position in the region. Russia could now pursue its objectives of expansion in the Central Caucasus without hindrance or fear of provoking an untimely war with the Ottoman Empire. It was only a matter of time before Russia's imperial ambitions in the region would provoke Kabarda into a full-on revolt—a move which, given Russia's strength, would lead to Kabarda's demise.

While significantly altering Russia's geopolitical position on its southern frontier, in the short term, the Russo-Ottoman War of 1768–74 only moderately affected the relationship between Kabardians and their neighbors. Hoping to prevent a general Kabardian uprising during the war, Russia avoided actions that would provoke the Kabardian princes into open conflict. Despite the fact that many Kabardian princes allowed Ottoman forces to operate on their domains and even provided assistance in Ottoman raids on Russian forts, Russo-Kabardian conflict at the end of the war had not yet reached mass proportions. While extending Russian rule over Kabarda's southeastern neighbors—the Ossetians and Ingush—Russia refrained from providing these communities with the assistance that had led them to join Russia in the first place. Russia did not protect them from Kabardian princes' efforts to forcibly collect tribute, nor did Russia assist communities wishing to resettle to the plains of Kabarda. In other words, Kabarda's princes and nobles were allowed, for the time being, to continue to collect tribute from their mountaineer neighbors. Kabarda's princes also retained control of the most sought-after land in the Central Caucasus.

After 1774, official tsarist policy toward Kabarda's neighbors depended on location. The tsarist state refrained from interfering with the Karachais and other communities to the west of Kabarda's frontiers because this area was still in the Ottoman sphere of influence. The Russian administration did not interfere with Kabarda's relationship with the Balkars on its southern frontiers because these societies did not reside in a strategically important territory. In the Ossetian and Ingush societies to the east, Russia continued to promote missionary activity and encourage resettlement across the Russian line. But, despite promising protection to the mountaineer societies that swore allegiance to Russia during the war, after 1774, the tsarist administration was reluctant to interfere militarily by providing this protection for fear of stoking tensions with Kabarda. For example, regarding the Tagaur-Ossetian nobles (*aldary*), Russian officials determined that "if they historically paid tribute to the Kabardians, they must continue to render this without hindrance so as to not disturb them."[59] When Eastern Georgia became a Russian protectorate in 1783, the situation on Kabarda's eastern frontiers began to change. With Russia's construction of the fortified Georgian Military Highway through Eastern Ossetian and Ingush mountain territories as the sole overland road to Georgia, much of the Kabardian elites' influence over these regions ended.

Russia's victory in 1774 did not mean an end to Russo-Ottoman imperial competition. The Northwest Caucasus up to the frontiers of Kabarda remained under Ottoman influence, a situation incompatible with Russia's long-term plans. In anticipation of a future war with the Ottoman Empire, Russia immediately began to shore up its expanded frontier in the North Caucasus through the construction of forts and the resettlement of Cossacks to the region. This expansion provoked Circassian communities on the other side of these new fortified lines, including Kabarda, into open warfare with Russia. In 1777, Russia launched the construction of this new fortification line. This line would extend westward from Mozdok along the northern edges of Greater Kabarda, through the steppes north of the Kuma River where it would branch off into two lines. One would lead to the Sea of Azov. The other would stretch along the right bank of the Kuban (Russia's border with Ottoman protectorates of the Northwest Caucasus) to the Taman Peninsula. The older line of fortresses and Cossack *stanitsy* completed with the construction of Mozdok in 1763 provided Russia with a fortified frontier line from Kizliar, near the Caspian Sea, along the Terek River. This new fortification line would establish an official Russian presence across all of the North Caucasus, from the Black Sea to the Caspian Sea.[60] The Azov-Mozdok Line was an economic blow to Kabarda because it cut it off from important croplands and winter pasturage on the Kuma steppes.[61]

The construction of these new forts—Ekaterinogradsk, Pavlovsk, Mar'insk, Georgievsk—finally convinced Kabarda's princes, already aggrieved by Russia and coming under increasing Ottoman influence, to enter into open conflict with Russia.[62] From the autumn of 1777, the armies of the Kabardian princes and nobility and the still-independent Circassian communities from the left bank Kuban began conducting small-scale raids on the fortresses and Cossack *stanitsy* of Russia's Caucasus Fortified Line and demanding that the construction of these new forts cease. When the tsarist administration rejected their demands, Kabarda's princes swore off their allegiance and entered a state of war with Russia. Kabarda's elites enjoyed the support of their tributary mountaineer neighbors. They also concluded alliances with Caucasian societies farther afield, such as the Chechens, Nogais, and Kuban Circassians. By the spring of 1779, the anti-Russian revolt had spread across much of the Caucasus Line and Kabardians staged coordinated attacks with their neighbors.[63] Despite some success in cutting off Russian communication between fortifications along the line, by the late autumn of 1779, the technologically superior tsarist forces defeated the Kabardian forces. On December 9, 1779, the Kabardian elite swore new oaths of loyalty to Russia.[64]

The tsarist administration harshly punished the Kabardian nobles for their revolt: they had to render crippling reparations; they had to supply the surrounding Russian military garrisons with provisions; and they agreed to relinquish their rights to serfs who fled across the Kabardian frontier to Russian territory. Most importantly, at the conclusion of this peace with Kabarda, the tsarist administration established new, abbreviated borders for Kabarda along its northern frontier with Russia's fortification line. The River Malka was the border of Greater Kabarda and the Terek the border of Lesser Kabarda. Russia forbade Kabardians from settling beyond these borders; moreover, they could not legally cross beyond these river borders without special permission from the local tsarist military administration. This border delimitation particularly hurt residents of Greater Kabarda because it cut them off from vital pastures, croplands, and salt deposits. These changes also impeded the Kabardian princes' ability to collect tribute from their Karachai neighbors beyond the Malka River.

The tsarist administration, troubled by Kabarda's ability to marshal the forces of their neighbors, set out to weaken Kabarda's influence on these communities through its peace terms—a fundamentally important step in the reconfiguration of intercommunal relations in the region. One of the clauses of the 1779 oath, for example, obligated the Kabardian princes "to not impede and under no circumstances oppress the Ossetians of the Digora, Karadzhaev, Kurtat, Alagir, and Tagaur societies, as well as the Ingush and all other Russian subjects who are receiving holy baptism and resettling to Mozdok and other places along the Line, because the Kabardians' oppression had no basis besides brute force." Moreover, the administration informed the Kabardian princes that the mountaineer societies "had never been their subjects."[65] Thus, the tsarist administration outlawed the established practice of Kabardian princes collecting protection payments, often by force, from neighboring Ingush and Ossetian societies. Indeed, the tsarist administration began to send "security" (*zalogi*) to the Ossetian societies in the form of an officer, a brigade of Cossacks, and a priest. The administration charged these security forces with protecting the Ossetians from Kabardian raids and securing safe passage for baptized Ossetians who wished to resettle to Mozdok.[66]

In expanding Russia's influence in the region, colonial administrators entered a complex web of social relations. This complexity is best illustrated by the case of the Ossetian societies. As competition over land increased in the mountains as a result of population growth in the mid-eighteenth century, so too did social conflict between the Ossetian peasantry and the Ossetian nobility who, allied with their fellow Kabardian nobles, were attempting to collect ever greater rents. Given the mutually beneficial relationship and close familial ties between Kabardian and Ossetian elites, the majority of Ossetian complaints to the tsarist administration about Kabardian oppression came from serfs. Refusing to pay increasing rents to their Ossetian lords, these serfs hoped to use Russia to break free from feudal control. By adopting Orthodox Christianity and resettling beyond Russia's Caucasus Line, Ossetian serfs gained their freedom. In the social conflicts within Ossetian society, the Orthodox missionaries of the Spiritual Commission and the Russian administration, as was common throughout the empire, often took the side of the peasantry, seeing in them a bulwark of support for the tsarist state.[67]

The response of the Ossetian lords to rebellion among their serfs illustrates the ways that class ties were often more salient than ethnic ties in the Central Caucasus. The Ossetian lords, especially those of Digora, facing large-scale serf rebellions from the 1750s on, turned to their Kabardian protectors for assistance in putting down these revolts and forcing the peasantry to submit to their lords.[68] Sharing a common hostility toward Russia and deriving mutual benefits from each other, in some areas of Ossetia, particularly in Digora where ties between the local elites and the princes of Greater Kabarda were the strongest, the old system of Kabardian-Ossetian relations continued.[69] However, the Russian alternative to Kabardian feudal rule was more attractive to the many Ossetians who hoped this new power in the region would solve their land problems and stop Kabarda from forcing tribute payments from them.

By the early 1780s, clashes with Russian armies and a creeping Russian encirclement had significantly weakened Kabarda. By this time, Kabarda lost nearly all its influence over the Ingush and some of its influence over Ossetians. Notably, Russia's acquisition of Eastern Georgia (Kartli-Kakheti) as a protectorate through the 1783 Treaty of Georgievsk increased the strategic significance of the Central Caucasus in general and the Ossetian and Ingush lands in particular. The safest and quickest route across the Caucasus range to Georgia ran through Ossetian and Ingush highlands along the Dar'ial Gorge near the upper reaches of the Terek. Facing the imperative of maintaining secure access to Georgia, Russia immediately set about the construction of a fortified road—the Georgian Military Highway—along this highland territory. The fortress Vladikavkaz—its name ("ruler of the Caucasus") a projection of Russia's new imperial status in the region—became the starting point of Russia's road to Georgia. Built in the vicinity of the Tagaur Ossetians and the Ingush in 1784, Vladikavkaz had the secondary consequence of cutting off the Kabardian princes' access to these mountaineer societies, which prevented them from using force to collect tribute. Indeed, with the increasing Russian presence here, land-poor Ingush and Ossetians peasants began to descend from the highlands and settle the foothills around Vladikavkaz.[70] Kabarda's princes looked on with increasing concern as Russia continued to construct forts along its frontiers and, thereby, cut off Kabardians from important economic resources—pasture lands, croplands, and people.[71]

Despite this weakening, the dominance of Kabarda's princes in other parts of the Central Caucasus continued unabated even after their defeat in 1779. With Ottoman-backed anti-Russian unrest in the Crimea and the neighboring Kuban region in the Northwest Caucasus in 1783, and another war with the Ottoman Empire on the horizon, Russia could ill afford a Kabardian insurrection. This was particularly the case because Kabarda could martial the support of its neighbors. As in the 1768–74 war, Russian policymakers, appreciating Kabarda's enduring strength, hoped to avoid another Kabardian revolt while pursuing Russia's imperial interests in the region. In 1783, Count Pavel Potemkin, then Russia's governor-general in the Caucasus, allowed Kabarda's princes to continue collecting tribute from those mountaineer societies that had not yet come under Russian rule—the Balkars, Karachais, and Abazas.[72] At this point, the isolated mountainous territories of the Karachais and Balkars were of little strategic value for Russia. It is precisely at this juncture in the 1780s that Karachais and Balkars first begin to show up with frequency in the Russian sources. Contacts between the local tsarist administration and the Karachai and Balkar societies increased because representatives of these societies began to visit tsarist officials to request that Russia accept their peoples as Russian subjects. Karachais and Balkars hoped that by becoming Russian subjects they could benefit from Russian protection and weaken Kabarda's suzerainty over them as the Ossetians and Ingush had. In response, Kabardian elites did their best to cut off their tributaries' access to the Russian lines.[73] Ultimately, these Karachai and Balkar efforts to come under Russian protection failed because Russia did not wish to risk another Kabardian rebellion only for the sake of ending Kabardian dominance over several small, remote mountaineer communities.

In his efforts to placate the Kabardian elite, Governor-General Potemkin also restored Kabardians' rights to their historic mountain pastures (necessary for their summer transhumance), which were located outside of Kabarda's new 1779 borders. Regaining control of this land meant that Kabardian princes continued to collect payments from neighboring peoples to the southwest—Karachais, Balkars, and Abazas—for the use of these trans-Malka pastures.[74] Kabardian communities deemed loyal by the tsarist administration received permission to resettle across the Malka, north of Kabarda's official 1779 borders.[75] Moreover, Russia continued to support Kabardian claims to suzerainty over neighboring peoples and even facilitated the resettlement of these groups to Kabardian-controlled territory. After about 1783, with the permission of the tsarist government, Kabardians began to settle Piatigor'e (Russia's famed spa region) northwest of Kabarda's eighteenth-century frontier. A center of Kabardian settlement in the sixteenth century, this region, given its position directly abutting the unruly steppe and the absence of natural defenses against Nogai and Crimean Tatar raids, lacked a permanent settled population throughout much of the eighteenth century. Instead, Kabardians used this relatively flat region to their north for croplands and pasturage when the risk of invasion was minimal.[76] With the collapse of the Crimean Khanate and Russia's annexation of the Crimean Peninsula in 1783, the Kabardians hoped to resettle the fertile area of Piatigor'e. The tsarist administration based its decision to include this region within the administrative jurisdiction of Kabarda (*kabardinskoe pristavstvo*) on more than a mere desire to appease the Kabardian elite: tsarist officials hoped to extend the borders of the empire and bring other peoples under Russian rule.[77]

Because Kabarda's borders were not precisely defined, the extent of the territory annexed to Russia through the incorporation of Kabarda in 1768–74 was unclear. In order to maximize its gains and secure Russia's hold over the strategic region of Piatigor'e, the tsarist administration resettled several Kabardian villages to the region to justify claims that this region was part of Kabarda and, by extension, part of the Russian Empire. The tsarist administration also populated Piatigor'e with Tapanta Abazas, a community that had a history of alternating between Kabardian and Crimean suzerainty and migrating to one or the other side of the Kuban River (the border between Russia and lands under Ottoman protectorate) according to geopolitical and economic circumstances.[78]

By the 1780s, in terms of Kabarda's relations with its neighbors, official tsarist policy differed depending upon location. Kabarda's neighbors to the south and west—Karachai, Balkar, and Abaza societies—either did not occupy land of strategic value to Russia or resided in territories that did not unequivocally transfer to Russia after the Treaty of Küçük Kaynarca. In these cases, it was to Russia's advantage, in the short term, to maintain Kabarda's position of dominance vis-à-vis its neighbors. On the other hand, Kabarda's neighbors to the southeast—the Ossetians and Ingush—occupied strategic locations, well within Russia's post-Küçük-Kaynarca territory, along Russia's road across the Caucasus to Georgia. It was imperative for Russia to maintain security along this route. Thus, Russia established forts and outposts along the Georgian Military Highway, effectively ending Kabarda's influence in these mountainous regions of Eastern Ossetia and Ingushetia. Russia also understood that Kabarda's continuing influence in these regions would be of considerable strategic advantage to the Kabardians in the event of another rebellion against Russia, given that it could block off Russia's access to Georgia.

Kabardian influence over Ossetians remained substantial even after Russia's official annexation of the Ossetian societies in 1774 and 1781. Despite being pushed back to the north and west by Ingush and some Ossetian societies in the mid-eighteenth century, the princes of Lesser Kabarda still controlled swaths of plains territory on the right bank of the Terek basin. Ossetians who resettled to Kabardian domains to escape their land hunger in the mountains still paid rent to the princes of Greater Kabarda. Thus, as long as they occupied this territory, Lesser Kabarda's princes, while no longer enjoying the power to conduct raids into the mountains to collect tribute, still collected payments from Ossetians when they descended to plains to graze their flocks and herds.[79]

Governor-general Potemkin's more conciliatory policies toward the Kabardian nobility paid off because when a large-scale insurrection in the Northeast Caucasus broke out under the leadership of the enigmatic Chechen, Sheikh Mansur, in 1785, most of Kabarda's princes and nobles remained loyal to Russia. Indeed, even when Russia's situation further deteriorated with the outbreak of a new Russo-Ottoman War in 1787, which featured heavy fighting in the Northwest Caucasus, Kabarda's loyalty to Russia endured. In addition to respecting and restoring much of the Kabardian elites' claims to lands and people, the tsarist administration successfully co-opted powerful Kabardian princes by providing them with Russian noble titles, military ranks, and state salaries. It would take the rise of a new generation of Kabardian elites, less wedded to Russian institutions and power structures, before another large-scale Kabardian revolt like that of 1779 could take place.[80]

Law, Islam, and Kabardian-Mountaineer Resistance to Russian Rule (1793–1822)

After securing its position in the Central Caucasus with a victory in the Russo-Ottoman War of 1787–93, Russia launched its first attempts to integrate its North Caucasian territories into the empire, beginning with Kabarda. The initial efforts at integration—through legal reforms—did not turn out as tsarist officials had hoped and instead provoked a Kabardian opposition movement that increasingly turned to Islam for ideas, goals, and social cohesion. Russia's introduction of "Tribal Courts" (*rodovye sudy*) in 1793 ended the relative peace that existed between Kabarda and Russia since 1779. A legal system based on a reified version of the existing system of customary law, rather than Islamic *sharia* law, and limited to questions of family law and minor civil and criminal offenses, the Tribal Courts were under the strict control of the Russian administration and its local *pristav*. Russian military courts tried more serious cases in Vladikavkaz. By interfering in long-standing power structures and infringing on Kabarda's internal autonomy, the introduction of the Tribal Courts provoked a renewed and, this time, prolonged, period of Russo-Kabardian conflict.[81] The Russian administration wrongly assumed that the Kabardian elites would be compliant with this transformation of Kabarda's internal administration. However, by the 1790s a new generation of elites had supplanted the older "traditionalist" leadership in Kabarda.

While the older generation based their rights to lord over Kabarda and its tributaries and their decisions to collaborate with or resist Russian rule on traditional social structures and historic dynastic alliances, this younger generation understood the importance of Islam as a unifying force in the Central Caucasus. These "Islamists," as they are described in the historical literature,[82] viewed the traditional feudal justification for Kabardian princely rule in the Central Caucasus as unviable in the long term because the Kabardian nobles were proving incapable of checking Russian influence. They sensed the impending collapse of the traditional structures of society and power in the face of Russian colonization.[83]

The turn to Islam by the younger generation of Kabardian elites was an effort to strengthen intercommunal ties and prevent the division of the peoples of the Central Caucasus into separate communities. Kabarda's Islamist leaders, particularly princes Adil'-Girei Atazhukin and Atazhuko Khamurzin, sought to resist the erosion of Kabarda's autonomy and power, and the general collapse of the Kabarda-centered system of intercommunal relations, by redefining the relationship between Kabarda and its neighbors on more equal terms. Indeed, based on the egalitarian aspects of *sharia*, which the Islamists championed over local customs (*adat* or *khabze* in Circassian), and the pragmatic need to retain the allegiance of neighboring elites through noncoercive means, the Kabardian Islamists began to treat the elites of neighboring societies as their equals rather than their vassals.[84]

Over the final decades of the eighteenth century, Sunni Islam supplanted folk religion in the Central Caucasus and Islamic norms became an important integrative force among the region's peoples.[85] As the class-based ties between Kabardian and mountaineer elites weakened as a result of the growing Russian presence, Islam became another, more powerful, supra-ethnic force binding the peoples of the region together. Kabarda's new elites began to cast their struggle against Russia as a holy war (*ghazawat*). Indeed, Islam came to many mountaineer societies, particularly Digora and the Balkar societies, through members of the Kabardian *ulama* (Islamic clergy). More generally, given the historic dominance of Kabardian culture throughout the Central Caucasus, it is unsurprising that as Kabarda Islamized under the influence of Ottoman missionaries and anti-Russian sentiment, so too did neighboring peoples. This was especially the case among neighboring elites who remained linked to Kabarda's aristocracy through marriage and fictive kinship ties.[86] By the late eighteenth century, Kabardian influence also meant Islamic influence,[87] though, to be sure, Islam never fully supplanted *adat*, and a syncretic Islam developed in the Central Caucasus.[88]

Russia's continued support of missionary activity in Ossetia added an important religio-cultural element to the Russo-Kabardian conflict over land and power. Indeed, tsarist officials understood this connection between religion and intercommunal relations and responded by continuing to emphasize conversion to Orthodoxy as a means of weakening Kabardian (and Ottoman) influence over mountaineer communities. This use of religion as means of interfering in local power structures and intercommunal relations resembles the way Russian officials promoted Orthodoxy among Estonian and Latvian peasants at the expense of the Lutheranism of the German nobles in the Baltics nearly a century later.[89]

In 1793, the Russian administration, viewing Islamic norms as an impediment to Russian rule and the empire's desire to transform the region's civilizational orientation,[90] attempted to replace *sharia* courts with Tribal Courts based on customary law. Russia would pursue similar policies among the Kazakhs of the Middle Horde nearly a century later.[91] The introduction of Tribal Courts in Kabarda had two goals: the weakening of the newly ascendant ulama in Kabarda and the general assertion of Russian control over administration and political power in Kabarda at the expense of the power of individual princes. Customary law, not *sharia*, was to serve as the basis of this new administrative-legal system.[92]

The Russian state created *adat*-based Tribal Courts in the Central Caucasus to counter Islamic influence at roughly the same time as its was creating an Islamic ecclesiastical establishment (the Orenburg Muslim Spiritual Assembly) and promoting Islamization elsewhere.[93] This seeming paradox is a product of Russian officials' different perceptions of the North Caucasus as compared to other Islamic lands in the empire. More than elsewhere, Russian officials viewed Islam in the North Caucasus as a threat to Russian rule. Sheikh Mansur's uprising, which united the region's peoples in a holy war against Russia from 1785 until Mansur's capture in 1791, and the Ottoman Empire's support of Islamic missionary activity here, fostered the perception among Russian policymakers of Islam as a threat to Russian rule. Moreover, Russia had begun Orthodox missionary activity in the region relatively recently and still hoped for mass conversions. Finally, finding evidence of Christianity's long history in the region, many Russian officials saw Islam as a deviation from the Christian roots of the region's peoples. Given that Russian rule was long established among the settled Muslim Tatars of the Volga region, officials saw Islam here less as a force for resistance and more as a means for the empire to integrate neighboring nomadic peoples with a history of resistance to Russian rule through state-sponsored Tatar-Muslim missionary activity.[94] The peoples of the Central Caucasus did not have Muslim neighbors like the Volga Tatars who were noted by Russia's leadership for their loyalty to the state and civilizational progress.

Kabardian elite society was divided in its attitude toward the Tribal Courts. The older "traditionalist" elite generally supported this new institution. The younger elites were opposed to it because it did not give precedence to Islamic law and because it further limited Kabarda's administrative autonomy. Indeed, this new system of Tribal Courts infringed on Kabarda's autonomy and customs in a variety of ways: it banned public assemblies not officially sanctioned by the tsarist authorities; it forbade Kabardians from leaving Russian territory without the permission of the Caucasus military command; it criminalized harboring individuals who had committed crimes against; and it outlawed the traditional practice of blood vengeance.[95]

Disturbances began in Kabarda almost immediately after the establishment of the Tribal Courts. In late 1794, a faction of Islamist princes launched an uprising against the Tribal Courts and called for the introduction of religious courts (*dukhovnye sudy*) based on *sharia*.[96] Throughout 1795 and part of 1796 these princes and their retinues fled to the mountains, where they received support from their Balkar and Karachai tributaries and staged attacks on Russian forts. The tsarist forces succeeded in sapping the momentum from the uprising by arresting and deporting its leaders, Atazhuko Khamurzin and Adil'-Girei Atazhukin. Nevertheless, fighting continued in Kabarda, and the authority of the Tribal Courts, and by extension that of the tsarist state, especially in Greater Kabarda, remained negligible.[97] Indeed, the greatest battles in the Russian conquest of Kabarda were yet to come.

Russia's construction of the fortress Kislovodsk on Kabarda's northwestern frontier provoked the Kabardians to launch a new uprising in 1803. The land around Kislovodsk, along the upper Podkumok River, was important for the Kabardian economy as pasturage. Moreover, the construction of a Russian fortress here made it increasingly difficult for Kabardians to travel beyond Russian-controlled territory to the unconquered Circassian and mountaineer societies, many of which were tributaries of Kabarda, across the Kuban in Ottoman protectorate territory. The tsarist administration likely had this in mind when they chose this location for their new fortress.

Tensions in Kabarda worsened in 1804 when the Kabardian elite boycotted the scheduled elections to the Tribal Courts. Instead, a coalition of Kabardian princes and nobles sent a petition to General Pavel Tsitsianov, commander-in-chief of Russian forces in the Caucasus, requesting the introduction of religious courts. In his vitriolic response "to the honorable Kabardian princes, nobles, and *effendis*" from April 4, 1804, Tsitsianov wrote:

> My blood is boiling over like a kettle and my appendages tremble with an avaricious desire to water your lands with the blood of the disobedient. I am a man of my word and I don't make promises that I can't uphold with my own blood.... On my command, bayonets and rivers of blood await you; the turbid waters of the rivers that flow through your land will be painted red by the blood of your families.[98]

In May 1804, large contingents of Russian forces under the command of Lieutenant General Grigorii Glazenap entered Kabarda with the aims of squashing the rebellion and forcing the Kabardian elites to accept the Tribal Courts.[99] The Russian presence in Kabarda only further enflamed the Kabardian rebellion. As before, the Kabardians turned to their tributary mountaineer societies for refuge and military assistance. After the first battles, the main contingent of Kabardian forces retreated to the mountains of the Chegem Balkars. From their highland redoubt in the Chegem Valley, Kabardians and their mountaineer allies consolidated forces and settled in for a long summer of fighting. The Kabardian forces managed to hold off the Russian assault, thanks to the help from their neighbors.[100] First, in addition to providing refuge, Kabarda's mountaineer tributaries provided reinforcements. Glazenap's May 14 report to Tsitsianov testifies to the strength and multiethnic composition of Kabarda's forces: "from eleven in the morning to six in the evening we fought in the valleys against a large detachment of 11,000 desperately fighting Kabardians, Chegems, Balkars, Karachai, and Ossetians."[101] Second, smaller rebellions in neighboring valleys, particularly along the Georgian Military Highway in Ossetia, diverted Russian forces from Kabarda.[102]

Despite periodic ceasefires, fighting in Kabarda continued through 1804 and into early summer of 1805. Russian forces managed to restore control over Lesser Kabarda and two of the four fiefdoms of Greater Kabarda. However, as soon as Russian troops left these "pacified" domains, the population rebeled once again after receiving news of a general insurrection throughout the Central Caucasus. In March 1805, General

Glazenap entered Kabarda again, this time with a much larger contingent of forces. In this punitive expedition, Glazenap terrorized the Kabardian population in hopes of forcing the insurgents to descend from the mountains and recognize the Tribal Courts. Glazenap's forces burned down eighty Kabardian villages and destroyed Kabarda's grain and fodder supplies.[103] If the Russian Army could not defeat the Kabardians in battle, they would starve them out of the mountains.

However, it soon became clear to the local tsarist administration that this war could not be won through force alone. Among the concessions offered to the Kabardians to end the hostilities was the introduction of religious courts. On May 9, 1805, Tsitsianov grudgingly decreed the replacement of the Tribal Courts with the *Mekhkeme*, a legal system based on *sharia* law.[104] With one of their main demands met, the Kabardian elites, beaten and broken, once again swore allegiance to the tsar and reluctantly submitted to Russian rule for the time being.

After a few years of relative calm, tensions in 1810 between Kabarda and the tsarist administration again boiled over into full-scale war. The results of this conflict were even more devastating for the Kabardian people than the last. In the midst of another Russo-Ottoman War, Ottoman emissaries, hoping to sow conflict in the Russian Caucasus, covertly entered Kabarda with false rumors of Russia's impending defeat and Russian plans to deport the Kabardians to Siberia.[105] At a meeting on the upper Malka in the autumn of 1809, Kabarda's ruling elites solidified plans to utilize their ties with their mountaineer neighbors and evacuate their villages to the Cherek, Chegem, and upper Baksan mountain valleys of the Balkars in the spring and launch another revolt against Russia. Upon entering Kabarda on April 1810, Russian forces under the command of General Sergei Bulgakov found that the Kabardian lords had already absconded to the mountains with their serfs. Rather than return to the Caucasus Line, Bulgakov unleashed his forces on the mountains to punish the Kabardians, indiscriminately raiding and burning down villages. On April 25, Bulgakov's forces combined with those of General Ivan Del Pozzo, the *Pristav* of Kabarda, to unleash even greater destruction upon Kabarda. Bulgakov's punitive expedition resulted in the destruction of 200 villages, the confiscation of 20,000 head of cattle, and thousands of dead and wounded Kabardians.[106]

The Kabardian uprisings of 1804–5 and 1810 contributed to the demographic transformation of the Kabardian lands and the Northwest Caucasus. This period witnessed the first mass resettlements of Kabardian noble families to the neighboring Kuban region, which was under Ottoman protection, to escape tsarist rule. The intercommunal ties among the region's elites facilitated this migration. Ties between Kabarda and the peoples of the left bank Kuban—Karachais, Abazas, and numerous Western Circassian communities—had always been close. Many lines of powerful Kabardian noble families sought to escape Russian rule by fleeing, with as many of their serfs as possible, to live among the peoples of the Kuban.[107]

Plague, Land, and Empire

The first quarter of the nineteenth century, a period of intense military conflict, witnessed a massive demographic transformation of Kabarda and the Central

Caucasus generally. Battlefield deaths and resettlement beyond the Russian frontier contributed to a rapid decline in Kabarda's population. But the plague epidemic that struck the Central Caucasus in the first decade of the nineteenth century was even more significant in this regard. Researchers, singling out the region's indigenous mountain gophers as the main carriers of plague, have classified the Central Caucasus a "natural foci of plague."[108] Already weakened after fighting tsarist colonial expansion for a quarter century, the plague, which began in 1803 and lingered for a decade, hit Kabarda especially hard and had far-reaching effects on the region's ethno-political relations, economy, and demographic makeup.[109]

Wiping out entire family lines and villages, the plague combined with military conquest to dramatically depopulate Kabarda during the first decade of the nineteenth century. By the 1820s, the Kabardian population was between 26,000 and 35,000. While it is impossible to offer an exact figure for the population loss and the relative impact of various factors on Kabarda's demography, historians have ventured estimates ranging from 78 percent to 90 percent.[110] In his analysis of the causal weight of different factors in Kabarda's depopulation, Historian Petr Kuz'minov attributes about 60 percent of Kabarda's depopulation to the plague and about 40 percent to nonepidemiological factors associated with imperial conquest: battlefield deaths punitive expeditions against villages, migration of Kabardians to unpacified territories, and starvation.[111]

While disease played a greater role in the devastation of Kabarda's population than the Russian military's technological superiority, plague greatly facilitated tsarist conquest. On April 16, 1811, Kabarda's *Pristav* General Del Pozzo wrote to General Aleksandr Tormasov, commander-in-chief of the Caucasus Line, "as a result of infectious disease, the Kabardians had become completely weak, having experienced a nine-fold loss of their former great strength."[112] The initial response of the leaders of Kabarda's Islamist resistance was to explain the plague as divine punishment from Allah for insufficient observance of Islamic norms and rituals, and inadequate resistance to Russian infidel rule.[113] Ironically, the leaders of this movement, Adil'-Girei Atazhukin and Iskhak Abukov, died of plague in 1807.[114] Despite such efforts to rally support for resistance, in each of the successive Kabardian rebellions, the strength of the Kabardian forces diminished while the destructive abilities of the tsarist army increased. While war fatigue and differentials in size and technology help explain this tendency, it was also clearly the result of plague's destructive effects. A Kabardian proverb of the time helps us to understand the connection between plague and military conquest: "What remained after the plague, the River Kambileevka carried off" (*"Emynem k"elar kh"umbaleim ekh'yzh"*).[115] The River Kambileevka, then the southeastern border of Kabarda, was the end point of Bulgakov's deadly 1810 punitive expedition. Indeed, General Aleksei Ermolov, the mastermind behind the brutal final conquest of Kabarda, explicitly credited the plague in facilitating his task:

> The plague was our ally against the Kabardians because, having completely destroyed the population of Lesser Kabarda and ravaged much of Greater Kabarda, the Kabardians were so weakened that they could no longer assemble large forces. Rather, they sent out small raiding parties. Had it been otherwise, our armies, stretched thin over a large territory, would have been in great danger.[116]

This interplay between disease and colonial conquest is, of course, not unique to Kabarda. The Central Caucasus in the early nineteenth century fits a global pattern of imperial expansion facilitated by disease.[117]

The economic consequences of plague—some direct effects of the plague and others the result of how Russia responded to it—were incredibly far reaching. The tsarist administration established a cordon sanitaire which cut off Kabardian and mountaineer access to the important Russian market towns along the Caucasus Line. More importantly, Russia's cordon also restricted Kabardians' access to vital pasturage, croplands, and salt lakes. The loss of these economic resources only compounded the effects of the plague and led to greater desperation on the part of a population resisting Russian rule.[118] On the most basic level, the plague depleted Kabarda's able-bodied population and decimated its labor force.[119]

The plague led to major changes to the region's ethnic frontiers by depopulating swaths of Kabarda. While the plague affected all of Kabarda, Lesser Kabarda suffered the most from the epidemic because the spring and summer brought malaria outbreaks.[120] According to a visitor's account, "the extraordinary disaster that struck Lesser Kabarda in the form of infectious disease brought it into the abyss of misery. The majority of its residents died off, most of the rest dissipated into neighboring areas, while the smallest share of them remained in their miserable hovels. The fields and vineyards remained unworked and the villages lay empty."[121] The frontiers of this part of Kabarda had already contracted during the mid-eighteenth century, when Ingush migrations caused Lesser Kabarda's princes to move their villages to the northwest, away from the Sunzha basin.[122] With the decline of Lesser Kabarda's princes in the eighteenth century, well-to-do Ossetians traded slaves for land from Kabardian princes and formed small settlements in the foothills near the entrances to their valleys.[123] At the turn of the nineteenth century, however, Ossetians had not yet settled the Terek plains—Lesser Kabarda's elites still precariously controlled this land. The plague and resultant depopulation caused Lesser Kabarda's frontiers to further contract. By 1810, the plague in Lesser Kabarda had depopulated much of the right bank of the Terek basin up to the Kurp River. Between 1810 and 1815, the tsarist administration, now controlling these lands, resettled landless Ossetians to the now-largely depopulated areas of what had been the heart of Lesser Kabarda.[124]

Ermolov and the Final Conquest of Kabarda: 1818–25

The final conquest of Kabarda came between 1818 and 1825 at the hands of Aleksei Ermolov, the tsarist general and Proconsul of the Caucasus infamous for his cruel tactics of colonial warfare and disdain for the region's indigenous societies. Ermolov achieved his conquest by uncompromising force, compulsory resettlement, and surrounding Kabarda's villages with lines of Cossack forts. These tactics isolated Kabardians from most of their neighbors, ending Central Caucasia's Kabarda-centered system of intercommunal relations, and prevented groups of "unpacified" Kabardians from absconding to the mountains.

After Russia's victory over Napoleon in 1815, Alexander I once again turned his attention to pacifying Russia's most volatile borderland and expanding Russia's Empire into the South Caucasus. To accomplish this task, Alexander turned to General Ermolov, a hero of the Napoleonic Wars with a reputation for bravery and independent-mindedness. Ermolov also exhibited a willingness to employ violence, fear, and intimidation in pursuit of Russia's interests.[125] A product of the Enlightenment, Ermolov had an intense disdain for the "irrational Asiatics" of Caucasia typical for men of his milieu. He believed that the only language that native populations of Caucasia understood was that of brute force and that Russia's only hope of introducing order was through despotic rule, which he believed was inherent to "Asiatic" societies. Ermolov adopted the persona of an "oriental despot"—he kept a harem, claimed descent from Chinggis Khan, and ruthlessly punished all who disobeyed.[126] In some parts of Caucasia, such as Kabarda, Ermolov's policies were a glowing success for Russia because they ended native resistance; in others areas, such as Chechnya, they provoked the population into a long and bloody war of resistance against tsarist rule.[127]

In 1816, Ermolov arrived in Tiflis to take up the position of commander-in-chief of the Caucasus forces. From this position, he began his infamously brutal "pacification" campaign against the mountaineers of the North Caucasus. Backed by an expanded military force of up to 50,000 soldiers, Ermolov's tactics included the destruction of rebellious *auls* (villages), resettlement and concentration of pacified *auls* to the plains, the encirclement of *auls* by new fortification lines of Cossack settlements, and scorched-earth policies that left large swaths of the Northeast Caucasus deforested.[128] If the Treaty of Küçük Kaynarca ended Kabarda's de jure independence, by 1825, Ermolov's policies ended Kabarda's de facto independence.[129]

Ermolov established five main fortresses (Baksan, Chegem, Nalchik, Cherek, and Urukh) in a line across Kabarda at the entrances to the mountain valleys. Ermolov also installed numerous smaller outposts at strategic locations. Nalchik became the center of Russian power in Kabarda.[130] By covering Kabarda with military fortresses and outposts, which encircled the Kabardians within a much smaller territory, Ermolov achieved two important objectives: he weakened Kabarda's access to and relations with its neighbors and inhibited the ability of restive Kabardian elites to provision themselves in the mountains.

The line of fortresses and outposts running across Kabarda (the Kabardian Line) cut Kabardian shepherds off from important summer mountain pastures. Moreover, the Line impeded Kabardians' access to their mountaineer neighbors, ending their elites' political influence over most neighboring communities. This attempt to prevent restive Kabardians from using the mountains to their advantage lay at the heart of Ermolov's plans. If prior to Ermolov the colonial administration sporadically sent Russian forces into Kabarda to put down insurrections in the mountains, only to return them to the Caucasus Line afterward and leave "pacified" *auls* in place, Ermolov established a permanent Russian military presence in Kabarda. Ermolov resettled Kabardian *auls* that submitted to Russian rule within this circle of Russian military fortifications.[131] For example, Ermolov resettled eighteen *auls* from the left bank of the Malka River around Piatigor'e.[132] Since tsarist diplomats and generals had solidified Russia's hold on this frontier region of Piatigor'e—thanks in no small part to the settlement of

Kabardians to this region in the 1780s—the Kabardian presence among the Cossack military population of the Caucasus Line became more of a security threat than an asset for Russia. This fortified line blockaded "unpacified" (*nemirnye*) Kabardians still in the mountains from their essential economic resources in the foothills and plains and prevented them from obtaining weapons from their neighbors. According to Ermolov, "without farmland and pasturage for their cattle to spend winter during periods of intense cold, [Kabardians] will have nothing left to do but submit to Russian power."[133] Ermolov's goal here was to disrupt preexisting land use structures and economic practices in order to force the Kabardians into submission. Moreover, this enforced isolation of the mountains prevented rebellious Kabardians from linking up forces with "unpacified" Chechen and Ingush communities to the east and Western Circassians across the Kuban. Indeed, Kabarda's elites only retained their tributary relations with the numerically small mountaineer societies of Urusbi, Chegem, Khulam, Bezengi, and Balkar closest to Kabarda (i.e., the Balkars).

The period, in the late 1820s and 1830s, immediately following the conquest of Kabarda, marked the transformation of the Lesser-Kabardian plains into the Ossetian plains. Ermolov's policies led to a shift in the cultural-linguistic frontiers of the Central Caucasus. In plagued-ravished Eastern (Lesser) Kabarda, Ermolov resettled the surviving Kabardian population, scattered among ghost villages in the Terek basin, westward onto a compact cluster of several villages, closer to the fortresses of the Caucasus Line. With this resettlement, most of the land formerly belonging to the princes and nobles of Lesser Kabarda transferred to the state. In an effort to attract Ossetian support and to further weaken ties between Ossetian mountaineers and Kabardian elites, Ermolov immediately charged colonel Skvortsov with resettling land-hungry Ossetians of the Digora, Alagir, Kurtat, and Tagaur mountaineer societies to this plains land.[134] As with Kabardian villages, the Russian military administration placed military fortifications and Cossack settlements next to these new Ossetian villages in order to establish control over them.[135] The Russian military presence in the form of Cossack *stanitsy* would also deter Kabardian incursions into these lands. Tsarist policies of resettlement caused intercommunal conflict between Kabardian elites and Ossetian mountaineers. In particular, cattle thieving and the burning of crop fields accompanied this mass Ossetian settlement of plains land previously under the control of Kabardian feudal lords.[136] However, the weakness of the Kabardian elites after the dual catastrophes of military conquest and plague limited the scope of such intercommunal conflict.

The Russian administration also tried to deconstruct the Kabarda-centered system of intercommunal relations in the Central Caucasus by ending the fictive kinship ties between the region's elite families. In August 1822, Ermolov issued a proclamation prohibiting *atalyk* between Kabardian and non-Kabardian families. This proclamation indicates a premeditated tsarist policy aimed at curbing Kabarda's influence over neighboring communities.[137] This decision was partly motived by Ermolov's awareness that the "Kabardians . . . sent their sons to the [Circassian] tribes across the Kuban, from where, after growing up, they returned to Kabarda with a harsh and irreconcilable hatred toward Christian Russia."[138] More generally, Ermolov saw *atalyk* as important link in the relationship between Kabarda and its neighbors. Ermolov's efforts at banning *atalyk* in Kabarda between members of different cultural-linguistic communities, however, were not always successful, and Ermolov's attempts to enlist the forces of Kabarda's neighbors in tsarist battles with rebellious Kabardians often came to naught.

Ermolov used extreme force and violence to intimidate the Kabardians into submission. He resorted to these tactics because he perceived Kabardians as almost universally disloyal. He also believed, as did many other Russian officials, that an overwhelming culture of violence existed among the indigenous peoples of the North Caucasus—he thought that Caucasians only really understood violence as a tool of persuasion and communication. Ermolov intensified the policy of destroying rebellious *auls* by extending it to those that housed fugitives or aided the rebels. The destruction of the mixed Kabardian and Abaza *aul* of Tramovo in May 1818 was the most infamous example of Ermolov's brutality in Kabarda. Residents of Tramovo, located in the Piatigor'e area near the fortress Konstantinogorsk, gave shelter to fugitives and allowed a band of Kabardian rebels to pass through their *aul*. In response, Ermolov ordered the "pacified" *aul* of Tramovo, which he labeled "a den of thieves and eternal plague," burnt to the ground.[139] Russian forces surrounded the village in the middle of the night and ordered its residents to disperse. Cossacks and regular soldiers set the village ablaze from four sides. Given the straw-and-wood construction of the Kabardian dwellings, the fires quickly engulfed the entire village. Cossacks looted as much of the villagers' property as possible before it was all destroyed. The military command gave the village's cattle and horses to the neighboring Russian soldiers and families of the Caucasus Line. The soldiers did not permit residents to bring any of their property with them.[140] Ermolov hoped that the destruction of Tramovo would serve as an example for other Kabardian *auls* that gave shelter to anti-Russian elements.[141]

In 1822, Ermolov eliminated the last vestiges of Kabarda's autonomy when he abolished both the position of Grand Prince of Kabarda and the *Mekhkeme*. Ermolov replaced these institutions with the Kabardian Provisional Court (*Kabardinskii vremennyi sud*) as the main legal structure for Kabarda. Despite its name, the Provisional Court, which adjudicated cases according to local traditions until 1858, proved rather more permanent. These administrative changes provoked two last desperate uprisings in Kabarda in 1822 and 1825.[142] By the late 1820s, Ermolov's plans had succeeded in Kabarda; those Kabardian nobles who refused to submit to tsarist rule had either died in battle or fled with their vassals and serfs to the rebellious tribes across the Kuban. Using the affinities between the Russian and Kabardian social structure to its advantage, the tsarist state co-opted the rest of the nobility into the tsarist state's service-nobility system, with most Kabardian nobles becoming officers in the tsarist military.[143]

The Central Caucasus After Ermolov

The half century between Russia's formal annexation of Kabarda and Ermolov's final conquest of the region in the 1820s witnessed a fundamental transformation of the system of intercommunal relations in the Central Caucasus. In the 1770s, Kabarda was the region's dominant polity, and neighboring mountaineers still relied on Kabarda for protection, pasturage, grain, and access to Russia and its markets. By the 1820s, a Russia-centered system of intercommunal relations replaced this Kabarda-centered one. Most peoples of the region now looked to Russia to provide protection from external enemies (often Kabardian princes), access to farmland and pasturage, and entry to regional markets. Those who refused these changes fled to the still-independent societies across the Kuban or joined the Islamic resistance in Chechnya and Dagestan to the east. In addition to religion, this transformation was largely tied to demographic changes caused by a combination of Russian colonialism, disease, and land pressures among the mountaineers. Whatever the relative importance of each of these factors, it is clear that the tsarist state played no small role in these transformations; indeed, it pursued policies, cautiously at first, aimed at weakening Kabarda's influence while strengthening its own.

Russian colonial administrators became the arbiters of local disputes, often over land, between the peoples of the Central Caucasus. Here the tsarist state took on a classic Russian-imperial role: referee.[144] This dynamic was spurred on as much by state officials trying to establish order as by those on the ground trying to gain an advantage. In addition to using force and violence to fundamentally reconfigure the region's social and economic structures, by actively insinuating itself into local social and political dynamics, the tsarist state began to integrate the peoples of the Central Caucasus into the Empire's administrative framework. In seeking to benefit from the new opportunities that the tsarist state offered, mountaineers and Kabardians alike associated with tsarist officials, learned the complex bureaucratic protocols and administrative hierarchies of the tsarist colonial administration, and presented themselves as loyal subjects of the tsar.[145]

The collapse of the Kabarda-centered system of intercommunal relations was both destructive and creative. It destroyed old relationships and hierarchies. Contacts between the Kabardian elite and Ossetians, Ingush, Karachai mountaineer societies were no longer as intense or as frequent. It also created new relationships, hierarchies, and enmities. Cossack colonization accompanied empire-building in the region.[146] At first, Cossacks and mountaineers occupied separate but neighboring spheres, and relations between the two groups were largely complementary and symbiotic. A clear example of the "creative" aspects of Russian imperialism,[147] Cossack culture and society in the Terek became a hybrid of Slavic and indigenous Caucasian influences.[148] However, as intensified Cossack settlement deprived native communities of scarce land in the late eighteenth and early nineteenth centuries, relations between Cossacks and natives worsened but varied across the region. The demographic losses suffered by Kabarda left its remaining population relatively well supplied with land; consequently, Kabardians and Cossack communities rarely came into direct conflict over land. In contrast, Ossetian, Ingush, and Chechen communities, suffering acute land shortages, entered into sharp land conflict with Cossacks. The tsarist administration scattered Cossack *stanitsy* among the Ossetian and Ingush communities that resettled to the former plains lands of Lesser Kabarda in the early nineteenth century. Conflict between Cossacks and mountaineers in this area would only increase as the nineteenth century wore on.[149] Divergent economic practices—the Cossacks were agriculturalists (albeit often unsuccessful ones) and the mountaineers were cattle breeders—contributed to these conflicts. Mountaineers grazing cattle on Cossack cropland became the cause of many disputes.[150] The demographic and territorial changes brought about by the collapse of the Kabarda-centered system also created new enmities among mountaineer communities. For example, during the early nineteenth century, Ossetian and Ingush communities increasingly came into conflict over lands in the foothills and plains.

By 1825, the imposition of Russian rule in the Central Caucasus overturned long-established patterns of settlement and landownership and transformed the region's Kabarda-centered system of intercommunal relations. Russian conquest modified, but would never completely dismantle, this symbiotic system. Despite the mass colonization of much of the Lesser-Kabardian plains by Ingush mountaineers in the eighteenth century and Ossetian mountaineers in the first third of the nineteenth century, and the dramatic political, economic, and demographic weakening of Kabarda, Kabardian nobles still controlled lands needed by neighboring communities of transhumant stockbreeders. In particular, the Balkars of the small isolated mountaineer societies of the Cherek, Chegem, and Baksan valleys remained locked in their valleys south of Kabarda and dependent upon Kabarda's plains pastures for their winter transhumance even after they swore allegiance to the tsar in 1827. The nature of Kabardian-Balkar relations would change along with the political situation in the region, and the end of feudalism and the collapse of the tsarist state decimated the elites of both Kabarda and Balkaria. Nonetheless, now 200 years later, the basic contours of the world created by Russia's conquest of Kabarda are still in place, and Kabardians and Balkars remain tied together politically, economically, and culturally.

2

The Caucasus War and the Disorder of Intercommunal Relations in the Central Caucasus, 1825–61

Russia's violent suppression of the last Kabardian uprisings by 1825 marked the beginning of a new phase of the history of the peoples of the Central Caucasus. Kabarda, which had long been in decline at the hands of Russian soldiers and Cossack forces, was no longer a political force in the region. Its territory, along with the rest of the Central Caucasus, was under Russian colonial rule. However, Russian rule throughout the wider North Caucasus was far from secured. In the years immediately following the conquest of Kabarda, Russia found itself mired in long and bloody wars in the Northeast and Northwest Caucasus.

The conquest of Kabarda, the lynchpin to the control of the Central Caucasus, gave Russia a stable power base as it entered a period when the rest of the North Caucasus was ablaze with anti-colonial resistance. In this context, maintaining firm control over the pacified Central Caucasus became supremely important to Russia and shaped and constrained its engagement with the peoples of the Central Caucasus. In many ways, this postconquest era was a period of indeterminacy for the peoples of the Central Caucasus. Wartime conditions prevented the tsarist state from stabilizing intercommunal relations and pursuing imperial integration in the Central Caucasus. Concern over ongoing resistance in surrounding regions led tsarist officials to undertake policies, such as deportation and resettlement, in the "pacified" Central Caucasus that, while aimed at shoring up security in the short term, had the long-term effect of destabilizing intercommunal relations and weakening social cohesion. In pursuing these policies, tsarist Russia engaged in "population politics," a political phenomenon developed in nineteenth-century Europe and with its origins in the Scientific Revolution and the Enlightenment, by which states categorized their populations into groupings, ascribed qualitative features to them, produced knowledge on these populations through emerging disciplines such as statistics and economics, and then used that knowledge to mold society through various positive or negative interventions.[1] Often these state interventions on populations took the form of deportation and resettlement. As was often the case with social engineering projects, tsarist population politics in the North Caucasus—removing "pacified" mountaineers from strategic locations and settling Cossacks in their place—had unintended and unwelcome consequences.[2] Such population politics, while perhaps increasing security in the short term, led to a deep-seated mistrust of the government on the part of uprooted indigenous communities and increased animosity among resettled mountaineer communities, plains dwellers, and Cossacks, who found themselves fighting for an ever-dwindling share of land.

The settling of Cossacks on lands in the heart of Kabarda intensified relations between Kabardians and settlers (both Cossacks and retired Russian soldiers). On the one hand, the intensification of Kabardian-settler relations meant an increase in cultural interactions—through the borrowing and adapting of aspects of each other's material culture (housing, dress, cuisine) and agricultural practices—and economic interaction through trade. On the other hand, settlement of formerly Kabardian lands meant an increase in intercommunal conflict between Kabardian peasants and Cossacks over land. However, in comparison to the Cossack-native violence going on at the time in Chechnya, Kabardian-Cossack relations were relatively amicable and more subject to legal disputes than fighting. Raids by the forces of Imam Shamil, the famed leader of the Islamist resistance to Russian rule in Chechnya and Dagestan, were much more of a threat to the Cossacks of the Georgian Military Highway than disputes with their Kabardian neighbors.[3]

The land disputes of the 1840s and 1850s examined in this chapter taught the tsarist administration that it could not work within the existing system of land relations. By the mid-nineteenth century, Russian colonization had undermined traditional land relations in Kabarda and replaced it with a hybrid system that tsarist officials did not fully understand. Given this lack of understanding, tsarist officials' attempts to make relatively small changes to this system of land relations and mediate problems within it opened a floodgate of legal and administrative disputes over land rights.

Although Kabarda was now firmly under its direct political control, Russia was unable to implement its colonial plans on Kabarda's territory—Russian peasant colonization, the expansion of surveillance over the native population, the creation of a class of loyal private landowners, and the landed emancipation of Kabarda's serfs—without creating new problems and incurring significant administrative difficulties and expenses. Perhaps more alarming, the state was unsuccessful in performing its essential function of administering the territory in a way that it deemed efficient and rational.

This chapter also examines changes and continuities in intercommunal relations in the wake of the collapse of the Kabarda-centered system. For the mountaineer communities of the Central Caucasus, the consequences of the demise of Kabarda's position of regional dominance differed depending on state policies, geographic conditions, and proximity to Kabardian lands, Russian forts, and strategic roads. The ways in which the communities of the Central Caucasus renegotiated their relationships with each other during this period from the late 1820s to the early 1860s helped determine the larger patters of intercommunal relations that would characterize life in the region through the twentieth century.

This chapter examines these problems of imperial governance, land relations, and intercommunal conflict by examining three cases: the intercommunal strife created by the resettlement of mountaineers and other non-Kabardian communities to Lesser Kabarda; the Balkars' attempts to use the window of opportunity created by the conquest of Kabarda to expand their landholdings; and competition between Kabardian and Karachai shepherds over the trans-Malka summer mountain pastures.

After tsarist conquest, the old and the new intermingled in Kabarda in a system of legal pluralism, as traditional family fiefdoms coexisted and overlapped with other types of landownership such as private property and peasant communal ownership,[4] based on Russian legal practices.[5] In Kabarda, as was often the case in other colonial situations, the colonized were able to use the legal pluralism created by the colonizers to their advantage.[6] Indeed, in her study of customary law and the integration of the Kazakhs into the Russian Empire, Virginia Martin highlights "the active role that Middle Horde Kazakhs played in negotiating meanings of imperial laws and nomadic customs within their own community, and in creating new meanings to suit their diverse legal and political needs under changing socioeconomic circumstances."[7] This mixing of landownership regimes created a situation characteristic of governance throughout much of the empire's non-Russian borderlands: a complex mixture of land tenure regimes that was highly dependent on local practices and oral agreements for its functioning.[8]

Cases like those described in this chapter convinced the Russian administration of the need to bring order to the chaotic system of land relations in the Central Caucasus by clearly establishing landownership and estate rights. In the 1840s and 1850s, the tsarist administration created the first commissions to resolve the questions of landownership arising from these disputes. While these commissions did not complete their task, they marked the beginning of a long-term land reform project in Kabarda and the Central Caucasus generally. Many of the ideas that would guide the land reforms of the 1860s in the Central Caucasus (examined in chapter three) came out of discussions on how to deal with the land disputes in Kabarda during the 1840s and 1850s.[9]

The Geopolitical Context

The final conquest of Kabarda, achieved by Ermolov at great human cost by 1825, came none too soon for Russia's colonial government, as major conflicts engulfed the rest of the North Caucasus soon thereafter. By the late 1820s, an anti-colonial resistance movement led by Naqshbandi Sufi imams erupted in highland Dagestan in the Northeast Caucasus. A small Islamic state known as the Imamate formed in the mountains of Dagestan in the late 1820s. With the rise of Shamil as the movement's charismatic leader in 1834, the Caucasian Imamate quickly spread its influence throughout the rest of Dagestan and Chechnya. Imam Shamil replaced local elites who had been amenable to cooperating with the Russians with rulers devoted or at least willing, often on threat of violence, to accept the tenets of his theocratic state.[10] Unifying the mountaineer communities of Dagestan and, later, Chechnya, on the basis of *sharia* law and strict military order and discipline, Imam Shamil led the longest resistance campaign against a European colonial power of any Muslim community in the nineteenth century.[11] The period from the founding of the Caucasian Imamate to

Shamil's surrender to the Russians in 1859 is the most well-researched periods of the Caucasian War.

This period of anti-colonial resistance in the Northeast Caucasus coincides with the long struggle of the Circassian tribes of the Northwest Caucasus beyond left bank of the Kuban to resist Russian colonization. Clashes between Cossacks and Ottoman-backed Circassian and Nogai communities had been common since the establishment of Russian control over the right-bank Kuban region (the Kuban Steppe) and the construction of the Kuban Line of fortresses at the close of the eighteenth century. The outbreak of another Russo-Ottoman War, in 1828, caused a spike in conflict in the Northwest Caucasus. More importantly, the Treaty of Adrianople, marking Russia's victory the following year, ceded the Black Sea coast along the shores of the Northwest Caucasus to Russia. Arguing that the Adrianople Treaty gave Russia possession of all Northwestern Caucasia, Russia's military commanders launched a campaign to impose its rule over the predominantly Circassian tribes of the left-bank Kuban region (the mountain valleys along the upper Kuban and its tributaries).[12] Though receiving some covert British aid and becoming a minor cause célèbre in Europe, the Circassians resisted Russian rule largely on their own for over three decades. By the time Russia had quelled the last pockets of Circassian resistance in 1864, hundreds of thousands of Circassians had left the Caucasus for the Ottoman Empire, a significant number of whom died en route. Except for a small minority of Circassians who agreed to resettle to the plains where they would be surrounded by Cossack *stanitsy*, the Northwest Caucasus lost the overwhelming majority of its Circassian population.[13] These losses were the result of emigration and death, the latter caused by Russian raids, the destruction of native *auls*, and combat on the battlefield.[14] As the case of Kabarda illustrates, the Northwest Caucasus was not the only part of the region that witnessed dramatic population losses as a result of Russian conquest. Indeed, from the capture of Shamil in 1859 to the end of the Russo-Ottoman War of 1877–8, as many as two million people from the highlands and lowlands of the North Caucasus emigrated.[15]

Russia's policies toward Kabardians and the other peoples of the Central Caucasus in the period before the conclusion of the Caucasus War in 1859–64 were dictated by wartime exigencies and security concerns. In addition to being Russia's only stronghold in the North Caucasus, Russia's only overland access to its empire in the South Caucasus lay through the Central Caucasus.[16]

The Land Question After Ermolov

The land question remained the chief concern of the region's peoples after 1825. In the short term, the conquest of Kabarda seemed to solve the land question for those mountaineer communities, especially the Ossetian societies, who were formerly confined to highland valleys and dependent on Kabarda's princes and nobles for seasonal access to plains pastures. While Ermolov's policies ended Kabarda's dominance over these mountaineer communities, resettlement to the plains of Lesser Kabarda did not provide the type of permanent land stability that the mountaineers had hoped for. The military administration repeatedly resettled these new plains villages from one location to another to make room for military settlements.[17] With each resettlement these recently landless communities from the mountains found less land at their disposal in the plains, and it became less clear which land was rightfully theirs. These continual land upheavals also engulfed the remaining Kabardian communities of Lesser Kabarda.[18]

Although significant depopulation negated many of the land pressures caused by its territorial losses, Kabarda faced a series of land problems after decades of conflict. First, the few Kabardian princes and nobles who came out of the 1820s relatively strong began to seize, by force of arms, lands of weaker families or those that had died out or fled the region as a result of war and disease. Elite families seized as much land as they could defend from their rivals and used the tsarist administration's ignorance of Kabardian landownership practices to gain legal confirmation of their property rights.[19] Second, the tsarist administration frequently gifted lands in Kabarda to the most loyal members of the Kabardian elite without regard to hereditary land rights.[20] Third, the redirecting of the Georgian Military Highway through Kabarda, farther away from the fighting in Chechnya, added new complexities to the land question in Kabarda by forcing Kabardian nobles to move their villages to make way for new fortified Cossack settlements.[21] Fourth, the mountain pastures north of the Malka River (the trans-Malka pastures), vital to the health of Kabarda's cattle- and horse-breeding economy, remained outside of Kabardian control since Ermolov deported Kabardians from all lands north of the Malka's left bank and placed the pastures under Cossack jurisdiction.[22] Kabardians hinged their hopes for economic recovery on the reclamation of these pastures; however, as we will see, the Karachais also had their eyes on these lands. Fifth, the Balkars to the south and southwest of Greater Kabarda, so isolated from the Russian administration by mountains and Kabardian princedoms, were unable to expand the land under their control during Ermolov's conquest of Kabarda. However, after the upheavals of Ermolov's reign in Kabarda, the Balkar societies, long-standing vassals of Kabarda's upper nobility, seized the moment and stopped paying Kabardian lords for the use of their plains pastures. The mountaineers' refusal to pay for the use of these lands became an additional source of tension among Kabardian and mountaineer elites and a source of administrative confusion for local tsarist officials.[23] With the conclusion of the Caucasus War in the 1860s, the Russian administration would attempt to solve these mounting land problems as part of its larger efforts to extend the abolition of serfdom to the diverse societies of the North Caucasus.

Cossack Colonization and Intercommunal Relations

The expansion of the size of the Cossack population in the Central Caucasus during the late eighteenth and first half of the nineteenth centuries transformed intercommunal relations. In many parts of the Caucasus, Cossack colonization increased intercommunal tensions over land and led to elevated conflict. In the case of Kabarda, however, after an initial period of conflict, by the 1830s, Cossack-Kabardian relations stabilized around an economic symbiosis based on relative abundant supply of land for both communities. Nevertheless, even in the relatively peaceful Kabardian lands, Cossack colonization produced bitter disputes over landownership rights.

The colonization of Kabarda by Cossacks accompanied the extension of tsarist control in the North Caucasus during the late eighteenth and early nineteenth centuries. Instrumental in facilitating the first trade and military contacts between Muscovite Russia and the peoples of the North Caucasus, Cossack communities had resided in the North Caucasus since at least the mid-sixteenth century. The Greben Cossacks, inhabiting areas near the confluence of the Sunzha and Terek rivers across from Chechen and Ingush *auls*, were composed of a diverse array of runaway Russian serfs, members of other Cossack armies who had resettled farther south, and mountaineers. Though representing Russia's economic and political interests in the Northeast Caucasus, the Greben Cossacks remained independent of the tsarist state until they were accorded state salaries and formally incorporated into the Russian military structure in the early eighteenth century. These Cossack communities retained much of their local autonomy well into the nineteenth century.[24] Moreover, the frontiers between the Cossacks and mountaineers remained porous and populations flowed freely between the two sides, resulting in a hybrid culture whereby, in the words of historian Thomas Barrett, "the North Caucasus was pulled into the empire, but at the same time the Terek Cossacks were pulled into the North Caucasus."[25] Despite close trade relations and the extensive cultural mixing characteristic of the creative forces of Russian imperialism,[26] in most parts of the Terek Valley relations between Cossacks and *gortsy* were most frequently characterized by military conflict. Both sides competed for pasturage along the Terek—a region where mountain Chechens were resettling at the same time as Cossacks were establishing their *stanitsy*—a cycle of raiding, involving cattle and horse thieving, developed between the two sides.[27] Kabarda, by contrast, remained relatively unaffected by the Cossack presence until the establishment of the first Cossack *stanitsy* on Kabardian territory in the late eighteenth century.

From the founding of Mozdok in 1763 to the construction of the Kabardian Line in 1820, the lines of Cossack and Russian military colonization around Kabarda formed its contracting northern frontier. These Cossacks and families of retired Russian soldiers were supposed to secure the North Caucasus for the tsarist empire and bring "civilization" to the region's mountaineer peoples. The harsh realities of life on this restive frontier, from frequent Kabardian raids to the difficulties of agriculture in a natural environment so different from that of Central Russia, the latter being a common problem for Russian colonizers throughout the vast southern steppes,[28] meant that these settlers were more frequently on the defensive or learning from the local economic practices of their native neighbors.[29] Compared to the mid-nineteenth century, however, contacts between Cossacks and Kabardians were limited given the quarantine separating the Caucasus Line and the *auls* of Kabarda during the years of plague in the early nineteenth century. In ordinary years, to cross the Line, a Kabardian needed to obtain a pass from the military administration and go through defumigation. During epidemic years, the trading posts and towns were closed off to native populations from infected areas.[30]

Cossack colonization of Kabarda significantly increased during Ermolov's conquest of Kabarda. By encircling the Kabardian population within fortified lines of Cossack settlement, colonization was one of the keys to the success of Ermolov's plan. In 1822, Ermolov ordered the construction of the forts at the entrances to Kabarda's river valleys leading up to the mountains. This string of fortresses, known as the Kabardian Line, was the first concentration of Cossack settlement within (rather than along) Kabarda's borders.[31] Ermolov also established the Kislovodsk Line—a series outposts between Kislovodsk on the Kuma and Kammenomostkaia on the Malka along the frontier between Kabarda, Karachai, and the Kuban Circassians.[32] The Kabardian and Kislovodsk lines connected the Kuban region west of Kabarda with Vladikavkaz, the main fortress of the Georgian Military Highway to the east. Moreover, with the establishment of Nalchik, the largest of the fortresses, in the heart of Greater Kabarda in 1822, the tsarist administration of Kabarda was, for the first time, located inside Kabarda. By the time Russian forces had violently put down the last Kabardian resistance effort in 1825, about 2,500 Russian soldiers and Cossacks had permanently settled in the fortresses of the Kabardian line.[33] This number does not include those residing on the Azov-Mozdok and Kislovodsk Lines, which delimited the northern and northwestern frontiers of Kabarda.

Cossack colonization of Kabarda continued in the 1830s with the establishment of military settlements and *stanitsy* along the Georgian Military Highway in Kabarda.[34] By the mid-1830s, with active military operations in Kabarda concluded, the Caucasus military command launched an earlier plan of Ermolov's to redirect the Georgian Military Highway, Russia's road across the mountains to its territories south of the Caucasus, through Kabarda along the left bank of the Terek. This new route for the highway would separate Greater Kabarda from Lesser Kabarda and further isolate Kabarda from Ossetia (see Map 3).[35] This isolation was a policy priority because the tsarist administration wanted to prevent a renewal of Kabardian dominance over Ossetian societies, weaken remaining Kabardian-Ossetian ties, and preclude the possibility of the two communities combining forces in future outbreaks of resistance. Finally, in 1837 and 1838, the administration shored up the defenses of the Georgian Military Highway in Kabarda by establishing several *stanitsy* and military settlements for retired soldiers at the sites of former outposts of the Kabardian Line on the Terek.[36] Approximately 400 military families had moved to these four new settlements by the end of the 1830s.[37] In the view of tsarist administrators, these settlers would also help bring Russian culture to Kabarda. While the spread of Russian culture through peasant colonization may well have been the long-term result of these new settlements, in the short term, they wreaked havoc upon land relations in Kabarda.

Diversity, Displacement, and Land Disputes in Lesser Kabarda

No region exemplified the disrupted and uncertain state of land relations in the North Caucasus better than Lesser Kabarda. From the 1820s to the 1860s, the population of Lesser Kabarda, which had dramatically decreased as a result of war and disease during the first two decades of the nineteenth century, steadily increased through the tsarist administration's numerous resettlement projects. The ethnolinguistic makeup of Lesser Kabarda became more diverse from the late 1840s on because the administration began to resettle mountaineers from strategic areas around the Georgian Military Highway and the fortress Vladikavkaz to Lesser Kabarda. These resettlements placed ethnically and religiously diverse populations within a relatively small and disease-prone region and led to a situation whereby disparate communities living side by side competed for access to a dwindling supply of land. Moreover, by issuing contradictory decrees and orders, the tsarist administration created a situation in which multiple communities could legally claim ownership rights to the same land.[38]

With the fracturing of Kabarda between Lesser Kabarda and Greater Kabarda in the late sixteenth century, Lesser Kabarda (i.e., the Kabardian lands east of the Terek and west of the Sunzha) became politically and geographically divided between two princely factions: the Tausultanis and Dzhylakhstanis. The Dzhylakhstan domains of the Mudarovs and the Akhlovs (Dzhylakhstanei) were in the eastern portion of Lesser Kabarda from the Sunzha River to the Kurp River. The Tausultan domains (Talostanei) of the Sholokhovs, located between the Terek and Lesken rivers in the west and the Kurp in the east, formed the western portion of Lesser Kabarda.[39]

In the century between 1740 and 1840, the frontiers of Lesser Kabarda moved in a northwesterly direction, contracting to a fraction of their former size. The geopolitical, social, and demographic changes occurring in the Central Caucasus from the mid-eighteenth century on (feudal rivalries, mountaineer population growth and colonization of lowland areas, and Russian colonization) weakened the Dzhylakhstan princes earliest.[40] First, Ingush societies moved north to Dzhylakhstanei land from their cramped mountains, casting off Kabardian suzerainty and settling the right bank of the Sunzha River and its tributaries.[41] Next, inter-feudal strife within Kabarda weakened the Dzhylakhstan princes.[42] Kurgoko Konchokin, the imperiled Kabardian prince who sought Russian protection through baptism in the late 1750s and founded Mozdok in 1764, came from Dzhylakhstanei. The founding of Mozdok created a platform for the expansion of Russian influence in Kabarda and the Central Caucasus generally.[43] In the late eighteenth and early nineteenth centuries, Lesser Kabarda's *auls* suffered from punitive expeditions.[44] Tsarist armies burned down Kabardian *auls* and resettled communities from the banks of the Sunzha and Kambileevka, settling Cossacks in their place. After plague laid waste to much of Lesser Kabarda in the first decade of the nineteenth century and Ermolov resettled mountaineers to the Terek plains of Lesser Kabarda in the 1820s, Ossetians, Ingush, and Cossacks had colonized almost all of historic Dzhylakhstanei. During the first quarter of the nineteenth century, most of the remaining Dzhylakhstan families moved to the right bank of the Kurp—the border between Dzhylakhstanei and Talostanei—and, in the east, only three small *auls* remained on the rivulet Psedakha.[45] Then, by 1840, Ossetians colonized the eastern frontier of Talostanei on the right bank of the Terek near Mount Zamankul.[46] By the end of the 1830s, Lesser Kabarda's territory had been halved and its population—909 households living on 17 small *auls*—was a quarter of its former size.[47]

As with much else in the region, to understand the problems of intercommunal and land relations in Lesser Kabarda in the middle of the nineteenth century, it is necessary to go back to the period of rapid demographic change and migration in the 1820s, when Ermolov's armies conquered the Central Caucasus. By the mid-1820s, Lesser Kabarda, bordering the restive Chechen lands to its east, was only secured by an old line of fortresses along the Sunzha River. Moreover, the depopulation of Lesser Kabarda through military conquest and disease made Lesser Kabarda, in the words of Ermolov, "a convenient place for brigands and thieves and gave them the possibility to break through our borders or move forward into Greater Kabarda and conduct raids there and provoke disturbances." Moreover, Ermolov believed that the security problems posed by Lesser Kabarda "would become especially troublesome with the transfer . . . of [the Georgian Military Highway] along the left bank of the Terek and the abandonment of the currently occupied redoubts of Konstantinovskii and Elisavetinskii." In 1822, with these considerations in mind, Ermolov invited Colonel Fedor Aleksandrovich Bekovich-Cherkasskii, a Kabardian prince from a family that had long been integrated into Russia's ruling elite, to resettle with his *auls* to Lesser Kabarda, and, in 1824, Ermolov provided him with the title to 265,980 acres (98,511 desiantinas)[48] of land here.[49] In 1825, the Committee of Ministers in St. Petersburg confirmed Bekovich-Cherkasskii's rights to this land.[50] Bekovich-Cherkasskii became the lord of the Kabardian *auls* located on his new lands and those of his dependents that he resettled with his family from the Kizliar region.[51] This latter category of newcomers included Kumyk, Chechen, and Kabardian serfs, who paid feudal dues to the Bekovich-Cherkasskii princes. From the mid-1820s, the population of Lesser Kabarda took on much greater ethnolinguistic diversity.[52]

Beginning with Alexander Bekovich-Cherkasskii, Peter the Great's military advisor and ill-fated explorer of Central Asia, the Bekovich-Cherkasskii princes, who traced their lineage back to Greater Kabarda's Bekmurzin princes, earned fame and fortune for their military service to tsarist state. As a reward for his participation in Peter the Great's Persian Campaign in 1722, Alexander's younger brother, Elmurza, received land around the newly built fortress of Holy Cross (*Sviataia Krest'*), and when Empresses Anna Ivanovna moved Russia's fortress in the North Caucasus further east to Kizliar in 1735, Elmurza Bekovich-Cherkasskii resettled there with his serfs and family. The government gave Elmurza a large allotment of land and serfs near Kizliar in the lands of the Kumyks, a Turkic community of present-day Dagestan in the Northeast Caucasus. Additionally, the Bekovich-Cherkasskiis owned the Cherkasskii quarter of Kizliar, where the town's Circassians and Caucasian mountaineers resided. Elmurza was instrumental in ensuring the pro-Russian orientation of his relatives in Kabarda during middle of the eighteenth century. Fedor Alexandrovich (Temir-Bulat Kaspulatovich), Elmurza's grandson, gained Ermolov's favor as his adjutant in 1816–17.[53]

In 1818, the Mudarov princely line that controlled Dzhylakhstanei (Eastern Lesser Kabarda) came to an end with the murder of Albakhsid Mudarov, providing Ermolov with a convenient solution to the security problem of Lesser Kabarda.[54] By giving these lands to Fedor Bekovich-Cherkasskii, a westernized educated member of the Kabardian elite whose loyalty to Russia was proven, Ermolov counted on the improvement of the security and general welfare of Lesser Kabarda. Ermolov hoped that Bekovich-Cherkasskii would "attract back to their former places of residence those who left Lesser Kabarda after the [plague] epidemic and settle them there in a permanent fashion" next to his *auls* from Kizliar. According to Ermolov, a repopulated Lesser Kabarda, under the control of Bekovich-Cherkasskii, "would serve in future as a trustworthy defense against brigands in Kabarda." Moreover, Ermolov continued, "the Bekovich-Cherkasskiis could be useful in gradually bringing enlightenment to the Kabardians and integrating them into the general order of the administration [of the Empire]." Finally, "colonel Bekovich-Cherkasskii and his brother, Ensign Efim Bekovich-Cherkasskii, ha[d], through their mother, inheritance rights to the Mudarov lands on which they will be settled."[55] The only hitch in Ermolov's plan was that estates could not be inherited matrilineally, and the real heirs to the Mudarov estate were Dzhylakhstaneï's other princely family, the Akhlovs. According to the laws of time, Ermolov was justified in revoking the Akhlovs' rights to these lands because the eldest Akhlov, Temriuk, was the leader of the anti-Russian movement in Lesser Kabarda before Ermolov's violent conquest.[56]

In 1822, prince Fedor Bekovich-Cherkasskii and his brother Efim established the villages of Kizliar, Kozdemir, Psedakh, and Magomet-Iurt in Lesser Kabarda.[57] The residents of these new villages were the Bekovich-Cherksskiis' serfs from the Kilziar region. Moreover, lesser nobles and their serfs, former Mudarov vassals, who had fled the region during the recent insurrections, also moved back to their former lands now under the control of the Bekovich-Cherkasskiis.

Far from creating the type of stability envisaged by Ermolov, the transfer of land to Bekovich-Cherkasskii created legal and administrative chaos in the Dzhylakhstan lands of Lesser Kabarda. In particular, this area witnessed competing claims to the Mudarov lands, unclear and contradictory decrees from the Caucasus administration over the ownership of these lands, and questions of the administrative and economic power of the Bekovich-Cherkasskiis.[58] Ermolov not only made the Bekovich-Cherkasskiis the largest feudal lords of Lesser Kabarda by far, he also appointed them as *pristavs* of Kabarda, a position that also gave them administrative control of the region. The transfer of control of the Bekovich-Cherkasskii land to Fedor's brother Efim, after the former's death in 1832, weakened the Bekovich-Cherkasskii's omnipotence in Lesser Kabarda.[59] Unlike his brother, Efrim attracted the negative attention of the Caucasus administration by abusing his powers. Efim regarded all of the former Mudarov domains as his personal fiefdom, when, by customary law, he was required to respect the feudal rights of other princes and nobles living on these lands.[60] By collecting land rents from serfs belonging to the Akhlov princes and other nobles of Dzhylakhstaneï, Efim provoked a peasant rebellion in 1837. In that year, the Caucasus administration forbade Efim from serving as *pristav* of Lesser Kabarda.[61] In 1839, Russia's commander-in-chief in the Caucasus, Evgenii Golovin, also ruled that the Bekovich-Cherkasskiis did not control all of the former Mudarov lands, because inheritance rights could not be passed matrilineally; rather, Efim had rights only to those lands on which the Bekovich-Cherkasskii *auls* were located and could not collect payments from populations outside of those lands.[62] At the same time, however, Golovin issued Efim Bekovich-Cherkasskii with a title to all 265,980 acres of the Mudarov lands originally granted to him by Ermolov.[63] For the next thirty years, this land became the subject of an intense legal dispute among the Bekovich-Cherkasskiis, the Akhlovs, and other Kabardian families claiming inheritance rights to the Mudarov lands. The state's purchase of 106,150 acres from Efim Bekovich-Cherkasskii to provide land for the Sunzha Cossack Regiment and Ossetian resettlers helped solidify the Bekovich-Cherkasskiis' claims to the remainder of their land.[64]

Lesser Kabarda took on greater ethnic diversity from the late 1840s on because the administration began to resettle potentially hostile mountaineer communities away from the strategic area around the Georgian Military Highway and the fortress Vladikavkaz to this part of Kabarda. The tsarist administration used the land freed up by these resettlements for new Cossack *stanitsy*. The Caucasus administration resettled communities to Lesser Kabarda as a temporary measure (until permanent land could be found for them) without providing them with a clear understanding of their land rights. In 1847, the military administration established the Sunzha Cossack *stanitsa* Magomet-Iurtovskaia on lands purchased from the Bekovich-Cherkasskii estate.[65] By 1848, the population of Lesser Kabarda included a Kabardian majority (fourteen villages belonging to the Bekovich-Cherkasskiis, two Akhlov villages, and seven Talostanei villages) and a diverse minority consisting of Chechens in Psedakh, Kumyks in Trulovo *aul*, Ingushes resettled to Bekovich-Cherkasskii lands from the Nazran society, and two small Ossetian villages.[66] The rights of these settlers to surrounding lands remained unclear, which led to clashes with their Kabardian neighbors. On September 19, 1857, Musa Kundukhov, then *pristav* of Lesser Kabarda,[67] reported on clashes between Lesser-Kabardians and Ossetian settlers. According to Kundukhov, "the settlers living there do not have the ability to use communal land in the same way as the Kabardians, with whom they have constant disagreements."[68]

In the early 1860s, new resettlements further increased the share of non-Kabardians in historic Lesser Kabarda. In 1861, the administration of Terek oblast resettled 80 Ingush households from the Terek plains to the *aul* of Keskem on Bekovich-Cherkasskii lands; two years later, there were 200 Ingush households on Keskem.[69] Finally, in the wake of land reforms among the Ossetians and Ingush, 1,500 households of Karabulak Ingush remained landless.[70] The administration temporarily resettled these Ingush households to Lesser Kabarda, where they formed the *aul* Ak-Barzoi.[71]

In 1865, on the eve of the serf emancipation in Kabarda, Lesser Kabarda was divided among the following communities. Talostanei—the western half of Lesser Kabarda, between the right bank of the Terek and the left bank of the Kurp—included fifteen Kabardian *auls* belonging to eleven noble families and six mixed Christian-Muslim Ossetian *auls* on Kuian Creek. Dzhylakhstanei had become even more diverse. There were fourteen Kabardian *auls*. Bekovich-Cherkasskii lands included villages of serfs and free communities.[72] The Bekovich-Cherkasskii serfs included a Kumyk majority and Kabardian and Chechen minorities. The free communities included the Chechen *aul* Psedakh and the Ingush *auls* Keskem, Sagopsh, and Ak-Barzoi. Additionally, the Ingush *auls* Chirikovo and Bezevo, though located in the neighboring Nazran (Ingush) society, had their farmland and meadowland on Bekovich-Cherkasskii lands.[73]

Disputes over land rent between the Bekovich-Cherkasskiis and the diverse communities who settled on the land they claimed grew increasingly heated in the mid-1860s as increasing numbers of settlers competed for the small amount of arable land in Dzhylakhstanei. In the late 1850s and early 1860s, as land commissions began deliberations on landownership rights in Kabarda, at least three groups staked competing claims to Lesser Kabarda's lands. The Dzhylakhstan Kabardians—Kabardian families whose ancestors resided on the Mudarov and Akhlov lands before they were transferred to the ownership of the Bekovich-Cherkasskiis—based their rights to these lands on ancient Kabardian custom and claimed that the Bekovich-Cherkasskiis only owned the lands on which their estates and serfs were located. The Bekovich-Cherkasskii princes cited numerous documents from the 1820s and 1830s in their efforts to prove that the vast majority of these lands had been gifted to them by Ermolov.[74] The Ingush of Dzhylakhstanei and the Ossetians of Talostanei claimed that the government gave them lands in Lesser Kabarda in exchange for their ancestral lands on which Cossack *stanitsy* had been established. Only the Kumyks and Chechens remained silent because they knew that they lived on Bekovich-Cherkasskii lands, and their history of paying feudal land rent to the Bekovich-Cherkasskii princes could prove this.[75] Ultimately, the government chose a solution to the land disputes and intercommunal tensions in Lesser Kabarda that involved what they hoped would be a final round of resettlements and territorial delimitations of Lesser Kabarda according to ethnic categories. This solution, described in Chapter 3, led to the last major reduction of Lesser Kabarda's territory until the Second World War, and it highlights the ways in which the identity category of ethnicity was becoming more important and more activated and instrumentalized in the colonial situation of the late imperial era.

The Politics of Pasturage: The Mountain Pastures and Colonial Policies

If the land question in Lesser Kabarda troubled the tsarist administration the most, the status of the trans-Malka and Zolka mountain pastures, situated between the upper Malka and Zolka rivers in the south and Kuma in the north, worried the Kabardian people the most. The mountain pastures, forming Kabarda's historic western and northwestern borderlands with the Karachais and Abazas, were a vast expanse of rolling hills interspersed with rivers and streams. Cool, lush, and verdant with alpine meadow grasses, and free of mosquitoes in the summer, at the peak of their prosperity, Kabardians thrived by using these summer pastures in their cattle and horse breeding. Between May and September, shepherds from all over Kabarda would spend the summer with their flocks and herds on these pastures. For the remaining eight months of the year, these highlands were barren and often snow-covered. As a result, the mountain pastures were sparsely settled.[76] Before the Russian conquest, control of the summer pastures facilitated Kabardian dominance over neighboring Abaza and Karachai communities. Crucial to Russia's conquest of Kabarda was its ability to limit and, at times, fully cut off Kabardians' access to their mountain pastures. By ending Kabarda's control over much of these pastures after the first major Kabardian revolt in 1779, and then restricting access to this land at key moments during the next forty-five years of conquest, the Russian Army was able to end Kabarda's power over neighboring communities, prevent collusion between Kabardians and hostile communities across the Kuban, physically weaken the Kabardian people during the plague, and deprive Kabardians of safe havens from tsarist armies. Ermolov's resettlement of all Kabardian *auls* located between the Kuma and Malka rivers south to the plains on the Malka's right bank and the establishment of fortification lines throughout this mountain zone was the final act in Russia's expropriation of Kabarda's mountain pastures.[77]

After Ermolov's conquest, Kabardians viewed the return of this pastureland to their permanent control as the key to their economic recovery. Of particular concern were the Zolka pastures. At lower elevation than the rest of the mountain pastures, Kabardians drove their cattle on these pastures along rolling hills between the Zolka and Etoko rivers in early summer and early autumn, when snow prevented the use of the trans-Malka pastures higher in the mountains.[78] The status of the highland mountain pastures between the Malka and Kichmalka rivers was undetermined because, while the state forbade Kabardians from residing on this land and access to it depended on permission from the administration of the Caucasus Cordon Line, the Caucasus administration never officially transferred the land to Cossack ownership. On the other hand, Ermolov gave the Zolka pastures to the Volga Cossacks of the Caucasus Line, preventing Kabardian use of this land.[79]

In 1827, immediately after Nicholas I and Field Marshall Ivan Paskevich forced Ermolov out of his position as commander-in-chief in the Caucasus, Kabardian representatives traveled to Tiflis and petitioned the Caucasus administration to reverse the losses that Kabarda had suffered during Ermolov's reign. In addition to requesting permission to continue to collect tribute from their Ossetian neighbors and demanding the dissolution of the Kabardian Temporary Court, chief among the Kabardian requests was a return of the mountain pastures and the salt lake (Tambukan) located on the northern edge of the Zolka pastures.[80] After refusing all of the Kabardians' main requests, on January 2, 1828, the commander of the armies of the Caucasus Line, General Georgi Emmanuel, approved the allotment of lake Tambukan and 2,808 acres surrounding this salt lake to the Kabardian people.[81] While this lake was an important watering ground for livestock, its importance to Kabardian shepherds was largely negated by the administration's refusal to return any of the pasturage beyond the River Malka to Kabardian ownership. Emmanuel, Paskevich, and others in the administration argued that the security imperatives that prompted Ermolov to forbid Kabardians from residing in the mountains ("beyond the Malka") still existed.[82] In particular, viceroy Paskevich argued that "it is necessary to forbid the Kabardians from settling in the upper reaches of rivers because the Karachais, Chechens, Balkars . . . and other mountaineers . . . would again fall subject to the Kabardian yoke as close neighbors who must cross through their lands; conflicts and disagreements would not cease and illegal acts would only increase again."[83] General Emmanuel dismissed the Kabardians' humanitarian concerns, stating that "Kabardians could just as easily keep their cattle in the plains as in the mountains."[84] Ignorance of transhumance livestock breeding and a desire, based on security concerns and conceptions of civilizational progress, to fully sedentarize the Kabardians into agriculturalists also lay behind the administration's refusal.

The Kabardians' access to their mountain pastures decreased as the local Cossack military administration, whose job it was to guard this land, gradually began to assume landlord rights over the Kabardian lands beyond the Malka. Cossacks began to illegally collect payments from Kabardians for use of the pastures.[85]

Kabarda's elites made repeated attempts to petition the administration for the return of the mountain pastures to their permanent ownership. Using the occasion of Emperor Nicholas I's tour of the Caucasus in 1837, they complained that "the land owned by them . . . is completely insufficient for both agriculture and pasturage and that they are suffering heavy losses." In a case of Cossacks' defending their entrenched interests, commander of the armies of the Caucasus Line, Lieutenant General Pavel Grabbe, reported to Commander-in-Chief Golovin that "the land requested by the Kabardians cuts too deeply into the domains of the Volga Cossack regiment" and that "the Malka should remain the border between unintegrated Kabarda and the Caucasus oblast." In August 1839, Golovin, finding these explanations satisfactory, ordered that the Kabardians' petition be denied and that the land be given to Cossacks.[86] Learning of this denial of their requests, in September 1840, the Kabardians lodged a new petition describing their extreme lack of land and complaining that additional land was being taken from them for military settlements around Nalchik Fortress. Golovin conceded that Kabardians should be compensated for their losses by granting them the pastures on the Zolka. However, in deference to the Cossacks' wishes, Golovin argued that "the existence of . . . *auls* inside the Cordon Line would be very inconvenient and could impede the establishment of order and peace in our borders and prevent us from populating this part of the line with Russian population."[87] Rather than permanently returning the Zolka pastures, on February 4, 1841, "in order to quiet their concerns," Golovin issued a decree "allow[ing] the Kabardians each year to use the land between the Zolka and Etoko without any payment."[88]

In 1844, during a visit to St. Petersburg to receive an honorary banner from the tsar in recognition of the Kabardian people's loyalty and service, the Kabardian delegation again petitioned Nicholas I for the return of their pastures. On January 31, 1845, Minister of War Alexander Chernyshev informed Viceroy Vorontsov that the emperor had approved the transfer to Kabardian ownership of 121,500 acres beyond the Malka River (i.e., within the Cordon Line), including the Zolka summer pastures. The new commander of the armies of the Caucasus Line, Nikolai Zavadovskii, immediately protested this decision, citing security concerns and Cossack economic interests. Zavadovskii ordered an investigation into the merit of the Kabardians' request. Fortunately for the military administration, which did not want to give this Cossack land back to Kabardians, this investigation coincided with Shamil's incursion into Kabarda. In writing to the emperor on the Kabardian land question in the summer of 1846, Viceroy Vorontsov sided with Zavadovskii and cited the disloyal behavior of many Kabardians during Shamil's recent incursion as further evidence of the folly of granting Kabardians ownership of pasture lands near the Caucasus Line.[89] The state would only grant the Kabardians temporary rights to the Zolka and mountain pastures beyond the River Malka. The status of Kabarda's pastures would remain unresolved, and no further changes would be made to their status until the late 1850s and 1860s.

The question of the mountain pastures also caused disputes between Kabardians and their Karachai neighbors to the west. The Karachais of the mountainous upper-Kuban region relied almost exclusively on stockbreeding for their survival. During the summer, many Karachai communities drove their cattle to pasture on the western part of Kabarda's trans-Malka mountain pastures, between the Kichmalka and Kuma rivers.

The status of these Karachai communities, as tributaries of Kabarda's elites, was based on the latter's control of this summer pastureland. After Russia's conquest of Kabarda, the Karachais began freely using pastures for which they formerly rendered tribute to Kabarda's princes.[90] Now both Karachais and Kabardians used the pastures at the pleasure of the Cordon Line administration. Moreover, the Karachais began to expand their use of these pastures and petition the government for permanent rights to these lands.[91]

This expansion of the Karachais' use of pastures that the Kabardian elites regarded as their historic land provoked conflict. Each community attempted to assert its rights to these pastures by driving off and stealing livestock from the other.[92] As the Caucasus War wound down after the capture of Shamil in 1859, the government replaced the wartime administrative divisions of the North Caucasus with three provinces (oblasts)—Kuban, Terek, and Dagestan. As far as the government was concerned, in separating the Karachais and Kabardians between Kuban and Terek oblasts, respectively, in 1860, it resolved the question of who had the right to use the mountain pastures.[93] According to a decree from April 20, 1851, the border would run along the Kuma River so that the vast pastures along the Kislovodsk Line fell within the jurisdiction of Terek oblast.[94] As residents of Terek oblast, Kabardians gained usage rights to these pasturelands at the expense of the Karachais, the vast majority of whom resided in Kuban oblast. Despite this seeming resolution of the Karachai-Kabardian dispute over the summer mountain pastures, tensions periodically flared between the two groups and border conflicts would break out sporadically into the late 1920s.

The Balkars: Continuity and Change in Symbiotic Relations

Given their continued isolation from Russia, persistent encirclement by Kabardians, and their relatively small population (roughly one-fifth that of Kabarda), the Balkars' historic relationship with Kabarda remained relatively stable during the period of Russian conquest in the late eighteenth and early nineteenth centuries. It was only after Ermolov's conquest in the mid-1820s that the Balkar peasants and nobles (*taubiis*) began to extend their territory and assert their economic independence at the expense of a defeated and still-suffering Kabarda. After the conquest of Kabarda, large swaths of pasturage on the Kabardian foothills and plains lay vacant and unclaimed. These were lands that Balkar shepherds had traditionally rented from Kabardian princes for cattle grazing during the autumn and spring. Given the absence of the former lords of these lands, due to death or emigration, Balkars continued to use them, now rent free, and, according to some sources, settle on these lands permanently.[95]

The Caucasus administration repeatedly denied Balkar requests for unhindered access to Kabardian land and intervention to end their status as tributaries of Kabardian elites. Despite refusing to allow the surviving Kabardian nobles to renew their tributary relations with neighboring Ossetian communities after Ermolov's conquest, the Caucasus administration did not want to further antagonize the pacified Kabardians by also ending their enduring economic dominance over their Balkar neighbors. In the late eighteenth and early nineteenth centuries, the military's policies had been

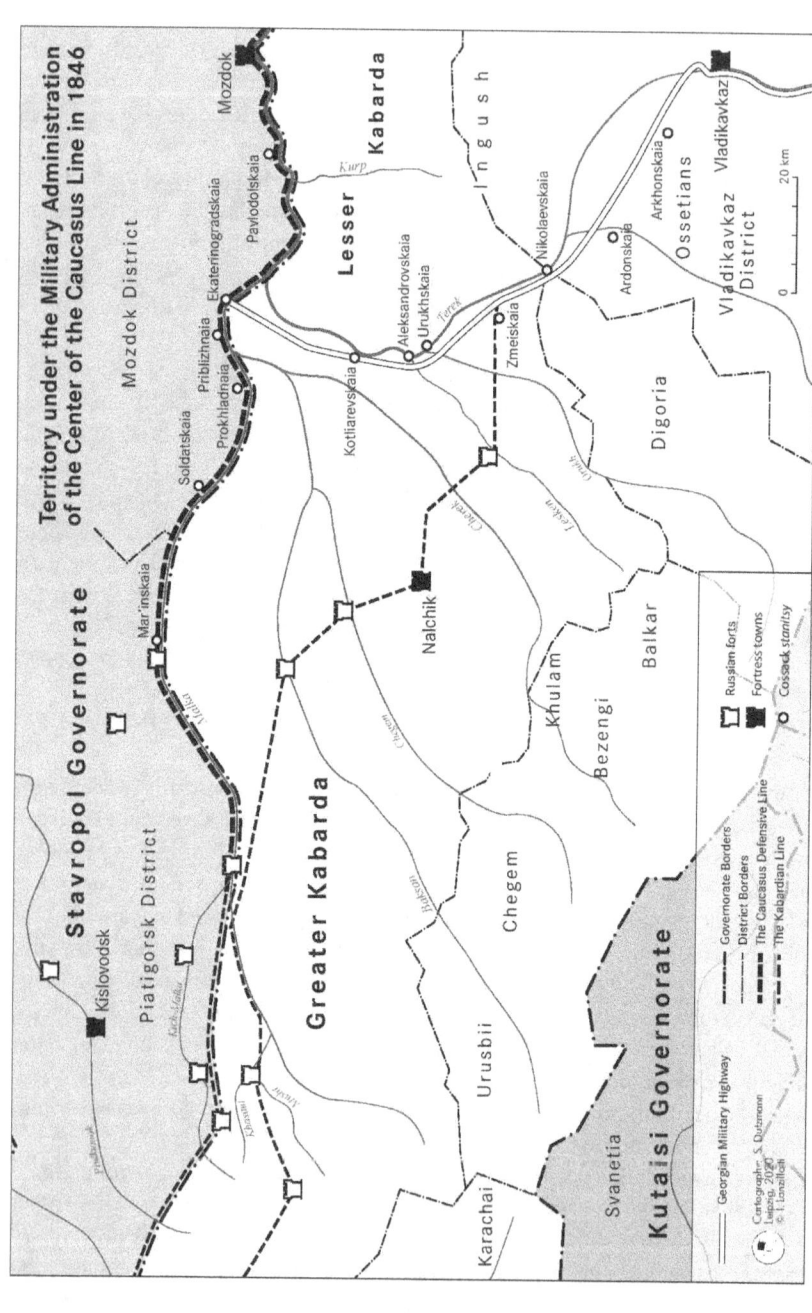

Map 3 Kabarda and its neighbors c. 1842. © Silke Dutzmann, map editor at the Leibniz Institute of Geography (Leibniz-Institut für Länderkunde) in Leipzig, Germany.

aimed at ending Kabarda's dominance over its Eastern Ossetian and Ingush neighbors. Therefore, on the one hand, the Caucasus administration did not want to see its success among Ossetian and Ingush communities reversed. In responding to a Kabardian petition calling for a return of their right to collect tribute from Ossetian communities, General Emmanuel reasoned that "the more relations the Caucasian peoples have with each other, the more unruly they become . . . therefore, I do not find a change of the current relations between Kabardians and Ossetians conducive to maintaining current conditions."[96] On the other hand, the Caucasus administration could not push policies of weakening Kabardian influence any further for fear of jeopardizing the hard-won peace in the strategic Center of the Caucasus Line.

The Caucasus administration generally supported surviving Kabardian nobles in their bids to retain their economic dominance over their Balkar neighbors. In 1850, the Kabardian high noble (*tlekotlesh*), Batyrbek Tambiev, complained to the Caucasus administration that "according to the established order those with the means to do so must give him one sheep for the use of his land and the residents of the Balkar, Urusbii, and Khulam mountaineer societies are not fulfilling this obligation."[97] The commander of the Center of the Caucasus Line, Major General Georgii Eristov ordered Major Khoruev, *pristav* of the Balkar, Khulam, Bezengi, Chegem, and Urusbii societies (i.e., Balkaria), to ensure that peasants from these societies pay the Tambiev nobles for the use of their land.[98] In 1853, having taken oaths of allegiance and become subjects of the tsar in 1827, a delegation of Balkar nobles visited Nicholas I to express their loyalty, reaffirm their noble status, and petition for ownership rights to the lands in the Kabardian foothills that they had been using. However, in another example of the state refusing to interfere in Kabardian-Balkar relations, with the Kabardian resistance pacified by this time, the tsar denied this request, citing the continued inclusion of these lands within Kabardian noble domains.[99] The Balkars joined the Russian Empire too late to profit from Kabarda's lands. With Kabarda pacified, it was no longer in the state's interest to support claims—no matter how justified—to land belonging to the now-loyal Kabardian nobility. Moreover, with major military operations ongoing in the Northeast and Northwest Caucasus, the tsarist administration could ill afford to divert troops to support Balkar claims.

Conclusions

The cases of Lesser Kabarda and the mountain pastures demonstrate how Russian security policies during the Caucasus War affected intercommunal relations in the pacified Central Caucasus. The case of Lesser Kabarda demonstrates how the tsarist state's use of population politics—the policy of resettling mountaineers to the plains—produced new land tensions between Kabardians and their neighbors. The case of the mountain pastures highlights how administrative transformations and border delimitation disrupted long-standing intercommunal land tenure arrangements and, by unintentionally favoring one community over another, caused intercommunal conflict.

The cases in this chapter also demonstrate that Russia's difficulties in administering the territory of Kabarda and adjudicating land disputes were the result of at least three factors. First, the devastating tsarist conquest wrought chaos upon the precolonial patterns of land use and landownership, and the Russian administration could not initially offer anything to replace it. Second, while sometimes deferring to Kabardian custom to determine land rights, at other times, as was the case with the mountain pastures, the tsarist military administration in the Caucasus treated land as state patrimony and dispensed with it as it saw fit. This created further confusion about the use, possession, and ownership of land. Third, the tsarist state's most frequent response to security concerns was to use resettlement as a means of maintaining security, by removing untrustworthy populations and replacing them with loyal Cossacks and other groups. This population politics produced a panoply of unintended and unwanted consequences: *inter*communal and *intra*communal tensions and, sometimes, open conflict over land; mistrust of and hostility toward the tsarist state; and added complexities to traditional patterns of land tenure. These consequences of tsarist resettlement policies impeded the colonial state's ability to pursue its other goals for the region: the integration of the Central Caucasus into the empire's administrative and legal structure; and, most importantly and urgently, the establishment of effective administration and good governance.

Given these impediments to its goals for the region, it unsurprising that thoroughgoing land reform became the tsarist administration's main priority as the Caucasus War wound down in the late 1850s and early 1860s. In the North Caucasus, as was the case throughout the empire, the serf emancipation and land reforms created more problems after the 1860s than they solved. Tsarist administrators, educated society, and the peasantry spent the last fifty years of the tsarist period in search of a solution to "the land question." Given Caucasia's ethnolinguistic diversity and social stratification, these tensions surrounding land reform and colonization sometimes led to intercommunal conflict. In the Kabardian lands and most surrounding areas of the Central Caucasus, the land reforms, while certainly affecting relations among different ethnicities, led to social contradictions that were more *intra*communal than *inter*communal. As we continue to explore the effects of tsarist policies on Kabarda and the mountaineers of the Central Caucasus and their relations with each other, it is to the fraught process of land reform and its consequences that we turn in the next chapter.

3

Colonization, Intercommunal Relations, and Imperial Integration

Kabarda and Its Neighbors from Reform to Revolution, 1861–1917

In the late imperial period, a growing impulse toward imperial integration, standardization, and various forms of Russification characterized tsarist policies throughout the empire's diverse borderlands. These policies, which were consequences of this period's push toward modernization in an autocratic and nationalizing political context, were well at work in the North Caucasus.[1] After years of violent social and political upheaval and imperial conquest, the early 1860s marked the first time that tsarist officials could move beyond immediate security concerns and toward schemes for the socioeconomic and cultural transformation of their diverse colonized communities in the North Caucasus. This chapter examines how these tsarist policies, which exhibited a tension in their shifting emphases between security and social stability on the one hand and economic modernization on the other, affected social relations within and among Kabardian, mountaineer, Cossack, and European settler communities during the late imperial period.

This turn from wartime security imperatives toward schemes for social and economic transformation of the land and peoples of the North Caucasus coincided with an empire-wide social and economic renewal known as the "Great Reforms." The centerpiece of these reforms was the abolition of serfdom. Since the reign of Catherine II, Russia's rulers understood that serfdom held back the efficiency and productivity of the Russian economy. However, Russian nobles jealously guarded their status and privileges, especially their right to own serfs, and they made it clear that they would not tolerate any changes to their status. Slowly, however, a combination of factors led to a consensus that serfdom could not continue indefinitely: the rise of liberal humanitarian ideals, the increasing disparity between the industrializing economies of Europe and Russia's sluggish agrarian economy, and the increasingly frequent peasant unrest (*volneniia*). Russia's decisive defeat at the hands of Britain and France in the Crimean War (1853–6) finally convinced Russia's new tsar, Alexander II, that immediate and far-reaching reforms were necessary to modernize the Russian economy, strengthen its military, and, ultimately, prolong the life of the empire. The cornerstone of the Great

Reforms was the emancipation of Russia's serfs and attendant land reforms. In addition to the liberation of the serfs and reconfiguration of land relations, the period of the Great Reforms witnessed crucial judicial, administrative, military, and educational reforms.²

After five years of negotiation between the nobility and various factions within the bureaucracy, in 1861, Alexander II liberated the serfs of the Russian areas of the empire. After a two-year waiting period of "temporary obligation," Russia's newly liberated peasants did not receive land outright. Instead, the three-fifths of former noble lands that they received came under the control of their village communes. The remaining two-fifths, usually the best land, went to the nobility who were also well compensated by the government for the land that went to the peasantry. In general, the peasants had less land at their disposal than they had as serfs. Moreover, the peasantry had to repay the government with interest through a series of redemption payments stretched out over forty-nine years. Considering the accrual of interest, the peasantry would end up paying many times more than the actual value of their land. Throughout European Russia, peasant villages were left with insufficient land to meet to needs of their growing populations. To solve this, by the late nineteenth century, the Russian government began to encourage peasant migration to Siberia and the empire's non-Russian borderlands, including the steppes of the North Caucasus region. The emancipation statutes of 1861 did not apply to state peasants and serfs in non-Russian parts of the empire. Alexander II called for the emancipation of other communities to follow in short order. Indeed, on the day of the proclamation of the Emancipation Manifesto, the tsar contacted the governor-general of the Caucasus, his friend Alexander Bariatinskii, to request that he commence work on emancipating Georgia's serfs. While the tsar expected the essence of the Emancipation Manifesto of 1861 to inform the emancipation of serfs in non-Russian parts of the empire, he understood that regional particularities would have to be taken into account. Thus, tsarist colonial officials worked out distinct emancipation laws for different parts of the empire.³

In the Central Caucasus, as in many other regions of late imperial Russia, the serf emancipation, attendant land reforms, and resultant peasant migrations were the catalysts for social and economic changes. By examining the peasant and land reforms in the Central Caucasus, with particular focus on Kabarda and the Balkar lands, and their long-term consequences, this chapter provides insight into the nature and functioning of tsarist imperial rule; tsarist social engineering; and the intersecting categories of class, ethnicity, and territory in the late imperial period.

During the 1860s, great interministerial debate surrounded the question of proper forms of land tenure and property rights for Kabarda and its neighbors. Some officials argued in favor of an expansion of the state domain at the expense of former Kabardian princely and noble fiefdoms and the establishment of communal land tenure for Kabardian village societies as a means of enhancing the economic conditions of the peasantry. Others called for enshrining the private property rights of Kabarda's nobility as a means of promoting the interests and fostering the loyalty of the region's ruling class, encouraging Russian colonization, and stimulating economic development.⁴ These debates in the Central Caucasus reflect empire-wide debates in the post-reform era about the best ways to promote colonization and social stability and the relative importance and compatibility of these two goals.⁵ These debates also demonstrate the ways in which both social and ethnic statuses, which often intersected, are crucial to understanding intercommunal relations and conflict in the multiethnic borderlands of late imperial Russia.

Many of the statist policies and processes for integrating the societies of the North Caucasus into the empire traditionally fall under the heading of "Russification": the imposition of Russian language, culture, social structure, and administrative-political institutions on non-Russian communities. Arguing that the term lacks specificity, scholars have problematized the concept of Russification. Depending on time, place, and the characteristics of the communities involved, a variety of often opposing processes and policies can be understood by the term "Russification."⁶ Any given form of Russification could often include non-Russifactory components and produce results that worked against other forms of Russification. Moreover, in terms of "administrative Russification," the legal and administrative norms that the tsarist state was trying to spread throughout the empire had little in common with those of the Russian village, which was still governed by customary law.⁷ The fact that non-Russians were often responsible for both devising and carrying out statist policies associated with Russification has led to a reexamination of what we mean when we describe the empire as "Russian" and its policies as "Russification."

The tsarist administration, like most colonial administrations, relied on native elites as vital intermediaries and sources of information. In Terek oblast—the administrative division that included Kabarda from 1860 on—many of the officials behind the serf emancipation and land reforms were non-Russian "people of empire" of Georgian and Armenian heritage.⁸ The tsarist state, viewing the Christian peoples south of the Caucasus, with their long histories of statehood and literacy, as more "advanced" than the mountaineer societies to the north, often relied on Georgian and Armenian elites to govern and "bring civilization" to the North Caucasus.⁹ Russia's approach to governing the North Caucasus fits a larger pattern of empires embedding their subject peoples within civilizational hierarchies and assigning representatives certain positions within the empire according to these perceived differences.¹⁰ Of course, men like Mikhail Loris-Melikov (Armenian), Grigorii Orbeliani (Georgian), and Georgii Eristov (Georgian), while retaining their ties to their native land and, importantly, for the tsarist administration, knowledge of the societies and cultures of the Caucasus, had embraced Russian educated society and high culture through access to the empire's best schools and military academies.¹¹ It was with ideas formed within the European cultural milieux of St. Petersburg and Moscow that these men of empire approached their task of reforming the social and administrative-territorial structures of the North Caucasus.

In addition to elites of South Caucasus heritage, the tsarist administration also relied on native elites from the societies of the North Caucasus. Often, these local elites, torn between the interests of their own society and the demands of imperial service, were forced to make bitter choices. At the center of this chapter is just such a man: Dmitrii Magometovich Kodzokov, a scion of the Kabardian lower nobility who, through a series of unlikely circumstances, rose to become the head of the commission in charge of land reform in Terek oblast. In many ways, however, Kodzokov was more than simply a local intermediary for the colonial regime. Kodzokov hoped to use his powerful position to implement his own vision for social reform that was formed out of his long exposure and devotion to the Slavophile ideals of his godfather and close friend, Aleksei Khomiakov. Kodzokov's story reveals the intricate webs of imperial connections that wove together Russia's multiethnic ruling elite.

The institutionalization and territorialization of ethnicity during the late imperial period discussed in this chapter played an important role in reifying ethnic categories in the North Caucasus. In its conducting of the land reforms and the attendant administrative-territorial restructuring, the tsarist state institutionalized ethnicity as a category and embedded it in its forms of governmentality, a modern form of power that functions through expert knowledge and official discourse, rather than through explicit laws, to subtly influence people's thoughts and actions.[12] In this case, the use of ethnicity as an organizing framework for governing the peoples of the Caucasus helped to make ethnicity a more salient category in the lives of the region's peoples. Austin Jersild argues that because Russian colonial administrators, like their Soviet successors, believed that all peoples should possess a historic homeland, in the late imperial period, "imperial territorial distinctions more or less corresponded to . . . a territorially defined and homogenous ethnic identity." Therefore, he continues, "by the late nineteenth century, all Russians in the Caucasus associated the mountaineers with particular cultural traditions, languages, histories, and a bounded territory."[13] However, despite the tsarist state's ethnicized approach to administration, at the end of the tsarist era, ethnic categories were far from supplanting other affiliations, such as those associated with religion, social estate, and geography.

In addition to the general belief in the existence of clearly defined ethnic homelands, as Jersild demonstrates, tsarist administrators also saw the separation of mountaineer communities into distinct administrative-territorial units as a form of security through exclusion.[14] If mountaineer communities could be separated from one another and from nonindigenous communities, the tsarist administration, it was believed, could better perform its policing functions.

Through three broad policy endeavors—(1) serf emancipation, (2) land reforms aimed at integrating the region's land tenure practices into those of the empire and allocating land to emancipated serfs, and (3) administrative-territorial transformations in the Central Caucasus—the tsarist state demolished the old system of princely fiefdoms—a system, as the label suggests, in which social estate and class differences had far more salience than ethnolinguistic differences. As we have seen, tsarist conquest had already transformed this old system of social and land relations beyond recognition, but the Great Reforms era ended them. This is not to say that the reforms of this era ended the strong supra-ethnic ties that had historically characterized Central Caucasian society. These ties remained particularly strong among the region's nobility through the end of the tsarist period. The reforms of this era undermined the region's social hierarchy and its specific system of intercommunal relations, but they did not replace them with a patchwork of ethnically defined nations. However, the territorializing of ethnicity and embedding of ethnicity in the forms of tsarist governmentality, though incomplete, laid the groundwork for later Soviet nation-building.

Administrative-territorial changes and land reforms in the late imperial era ended some intercommunal relationships while strengthening others. By placing most of the Ossetian and Ingush villages that were still located on Kabardian noble lands in 1860 outside of the administrative-territorial borders of Kabarda (and transforming these former noble estate lands into communal lands for these Ingush and Ossetian peasant societies), these transformations led to a further weakening of Kabardian influence upon Ingush and Ossetian communities. On the other hand, by placing Kabardians and Balkars within a common district, providing landless Balkars with Kabardian lands lower in the foothills, and legally enshrining the shared use of the trans-Malka mountain pastures among Kabardian and Balkar village societies, tsarist policies in the late imperial era ensured the continuance of the close economic and political relationship between these communities. Finally, a confluence of factors—the land reforms in Kabarda, the emancipation of Russia's serfs and their resultant lack of land, the construction of railways, new legislation on residency and migration—led to Terek oblast becoming a site of peasant immigration from Slavic parts of the empire by the 1880s. In Nalchik district, as the remaining territory of Kabarda and the Balkars' five mountaineer societies had become known by 1888, increased peasant migration did not exacerbate social and intercommunal tensions as it did in other regions of the North Caucasus. Rather, increased peasant migration strengthened the largely peaceful cultural and economic ties between Kabardians and Russians.

Toward a Land Reform and Serf Emancipation Project

By the 1860s, numerous factors made land reform the top priority of both the postwar North Caucasus administration and the region's war-weary population. First, the chaotic and contested state of landownership and usage made administering the region's disparate cultural-linguistic communities and adjudicating disputes between and within these communities difficult. These were critical issues because Russia, like most modern empires, justified its imperial sovereignty on its ability to bring just administration and laws to its subject peoples. Second, among the region's native communities, these same conditions bred hostility and resistance toward the tsarist administration and led to reluctance among native communities to invest in their land. Moreover, if the pacified communities of the North Caucasus, such as Kabarda, had long voiced demands for reforms that would confirm their land ownership rights and enshrine the territorial borders of their societies, these demands only grew louder with the end of active military operations. Aleksandr Bariatinskii, viceroy of the Caucasus from 1856 to 1862, recognized that "with the conclusion of the war in the Caucasus ... and [the emergence of] the ... possibility of focusing on agriculture and economic development ... the determination of rights to ownership and use of farmland became the main life goal of every mountaineer."[15] Administrators also viewed the unresolved state of the land question as one of the factors (after military conquest) promoting the exodus of Caucasians to the Ottoman Empire. Many in the Caucasus administration viewed the exodus of peoples from the Caucasus, especially long-pacified communities like Kabardians, as a public relations disaster for the empire and an economic loss.[16] Third, land reforms could promote colonization of the North Caucasus by Russian peasants after their emancipation.[17] According to tsarist officials, colonization would, in turn, promote security and the long-term goal of cultural Russification. By surveying the region's land, delimiting borders, and establishing ownership rights, a land fund could be set up for future Russian settlement.[18] Finally, given that expansion into Caucasia had been a financial drain on the Russian state, the Ministry of Finance lobbied for expeditious land reform because it would finally enable the collection of land taxes,[19] a prime concern of the "bureaucrat-policeman state."[20]

In an 1861 memorandum to Minister of War Dmitrii Miliutin, Grigol Orbeliani, newly appointed viceroy, outlined the reasons for the perceived urgency of conducting land reforms in the North Caucasus. Orbeliani argued that "a satisfactory resolution of [the land] question . . . will serve of the surest guarantee of the material wellbeing of the people and the likelihood of their imminent moral development." According to Orbeliani, the state's wartime policies of repeatedly resettling mountaineer communities to temporary lands "sowed among the population a distrust of the government, forced everyone to be in constant fear for their future, and clearly led to a situation whereby no one wants to develop their land and expend significant labor and capital on it." Orbeliani viewed the establishment of borders and ownership rights as "the necessary condition for the emergence among the people of a desire to expend capital and labor on land, and accordingly, for their complete sedentarization, for their attachment to land through material interest . . . and finally, for the emergence among them of a demand for a significant improvement of their way of life and moral development."[21]

The empire-wide serf emancipation only strengthened the impulse to conduct land reforms in the region. To avoid the socially and politically volatile consequences of creating a landless rural proletariat after the abolition of serfdom in the North Caucasus, the administration needed to find a way to emancipate the region's serfs with land.[22] Issues of land and serfs were most acute in the plains regions of the North Caucasus, such as Kabarda in the Central Caucasus and the Kumyk lands of Northern Dagestan, because these regions had the arable land needed to implement the envisaged reforms and because, not coincidentally, it was also in these regions that feudalism and serfdom were most highly developed.[23]

Between 1859 and 1861, Viceroy Bariatinskii led the first major land reform effort throughout the North Caucasus.[24] Bariatinskii formed Committees for the Investigation of Personal and Land Rights of the Mountaineers in each district (*okrug*) of Terek oblast. The Kabarda Committee began its work in November 1861. Though conducting extensive research on land and social relations, these committees never achieved the administration's goal of drafting comprehensive land reform legislation. A lack of unified leadership and common principles hindered the success of these land commissions.

Another major impediment to their success was the difficulty of determining landownership rights, as stipulated by the Caucasus administration, according to "historical documents and customary law." The use of customary law was part of a long-established practice—born out of fears of provoking unrest at the imposition of foreign Russian laws on the one hand and of strengthening of Islamic influence on the other—of promoting *adat* (*khabza* in the Kabardian case) at the expense of *sharia*. In codifying customary law, as Jersild argues, "colonial administrators attempted to create a recognizable order in the colonies."[25] But the diversity and fluidity of customs and practices of the manifold societies of the North Caucasus pointed to a level of administrative complexity at odds with the tsarist state's quest for a streamlined and standardized administrative order. Moreover, the absence of written law codes among these societies, and only scattered collections of recorded customs, further complicated the administration's efforts. Moreover, to the limited extent that texts on traditional land ownership and usage practices existed, the situation on the ground after tsarist conquest bore little resemblance to these customs. As they began to receive claims to land allotments, each committee became bogged down in the adjudication of a dizzying number of small disputes. This administrative gridlock meant that the tsarist state in the North Caucasus could not perform its usual functions of referee—a state that uses its role as mediator of disputes to integrate communities into the legal-administrative structure of the empire—or landscaper—a "gardening state" that seeks to transform its societies.[26] Indeed, the Kabardian Committee complained that "the [land] rights of lords, as a result of constant resettlement of *auls* have become so conflicted that it is impossible to allot them with land according to ancient customs."[27] The Caucasus administration dissolved the first Kabardian Land Committee in late 1862 and formed new Land Committees for the districts of Terek oblast.

Meanwhile, as these committees deliberated, a new leadership came to power in the Caucasus and established a set of common principles on which the land reforms would be based.[28] Importantly, the principles for the land reforms, formulated first by viceroy Orbeliani in a July 1861 memorandum to Minister of War Dmitrii Miliutin, abjured customary law as the legal basis for future legislation.[29] During the Caucasus War, the administration had to tread lightly around the land question and tried to work within the framework of the Kabardian feudal customs of landownership when resolving land disputes, lest it risk provoking the pacified societies to a new rebellion. After the war, the Caucasus administration decided that a more heavy-handed, top-down solution to the land question, based on its own considerations, could be achieved without great security risk.[30]

The main tenets of this postwar approach to land reforms are reflected in Orbeliani's 1861 project draft. According to his project, the government should not spend valuable resources and time determining the historic landownership rights of each family, a process fraught with complexities. Instead, the tsarist government would consider all land on the plains—the most valuable land in the region—state (*kazennaia*) land and redistribute it at its own discretion.[31] The plains of the North Caucasus, the only area suitable for large-scale agriculture, was of great importance for the economic development of the region and the empire as a whole. The tsarist authorities believed that, among other factors, the numerous territorial disputes and competing claims to landownership among native nobles and the general reluctance of most of these lords to modernize their agricultural practices inhibited the full economic exploitation of this land. The old feudal-like system of land relations would be replaced by a new one that combined private (*chastnaia*) and communal (*obshchinnaia*) land. Orbeliani suggested that the state recognize a set number of allotments as the private property (*chastnaia sobstvennost'*) of princes and nobles (and nonnobles who had rendered significant service to the state) under the condition that they give up their claims to all lands formerly belonging to them and their vassals. However, in this case, private landownership would be a privilege of the nobility, rather than a right. The state's expropriation and redistribution of Kabarda's land would obviate the difficulties of adjudicating competing claims to land. The remaining majority of the land in Kabarda would be given to the communal use of the Kabardian peasantry after their liberation.[32]

The government favored the transformation of Kabarda's land into communal property controlled by the state as a resolution to the land question in Kabarda for at least five reasons. First, it would drastically simplify the administrative work involved in conducting land reforms and facilitate the future provisioning of Kabarda's emancipated serfs with land. Second, by reapportioning land, the state could set aside land for future Russian colonization. Third, by giving the Kabardian peasantry communal land, the state could defuse social tensions between the Kabardian peasantry and noble landlords. Fourth, by also taking away the nobility's land—albeit temporarily until a new redistribution—the state could remove the last vestiges of their former power, make them entirely dependent upon the state, and take away the lynchpin of feudalism on the eve of its final destruction. Fifth, by limiting private landownership in Kabarda, the state could treat most of the remaining Kabardian territory as a tabula rasa and resettle communities within Kabarda at will so that the demographic map of Kabarda fit the state's conceptions of regional security: the consolidation of native *auls* into larger villages on the plains surrounded by Cossack *stanitsy*.[33]

The impulse to expand the state domain through land reforms in the North Caucasus was also common in other parts of the empire. The Ministry of State Domains, which Nicholas I created in the 1830s as a means to better regulate and manage the state resources and their use,[34] was interested in having lands—in North Caucasia, Transcaucasia, Turkestan, and other non-Russian regions—recognized as state lands because it could then use these lands as part of a land fund for a future state-regulated and -controlled process of Russian peasant colonization. According to Pravilova's analysis, local officials, "look[ing] down upon a society that they considered inferior," "believed that conquest endowed them with the right of ownership."[35] In Transcaucasia and Turkestan, local officials interpreted Islamic property law to suit their goals (a common practice among modern European empires) so that the legal status of the vast majority of newly annexed lands corresponded with the Russian conception of state (*kazennaia*) lands.[36] Similarly, as we will see, the Caucasus administration, ignoring the fact that Kabardian land customs did not correspond to any Russian legal categories, interpreted Kabardian customary property law so that all lands would be considered communal land. This concept of communal (*obshchinnaia*) land was more constraining for the administration than the concept of state land in Transcaucasia and Central Asia because it meant that the land belonged to the entire Kabardian people rather than the state. In other words, once recognized as Kabardian communal land, this land could *not* be used for the settlement of other communities, namely Russian peasants. But communal land did mean that the state *could* redistribute land among Kabardian village societies, and resettle communities within this territory at will, and it meant that it could avoid the complexities of determining the landownership rights of Kabarda's noble and princely families.

In early 1863, Grand Duke Mikhail Nikolaevich, Alexander II's brother, replaced Orbeliani as viceroy of the Caucasus. Remaining true to his predecessor's project, Mikhail Nikolaevich tasked the new head of Terek oblast, Mikhail Loris-Melikov, with implementing land reforms in the Central Caucasus according to Orbeliani's principles. A Russian-educated scion of one of Transcaucasia's most powerful Armenian princely families, Loris-Melikov made a name for himself through military service in the Caucasus War.[37] Loris-Melikov would become one of Alexander II's closest advisors and Russia's minister of internal affairs on the eve of the tsar's assassination in 1881, notably championing a constitutional reform package as a means of shoring up the government and counteracting the appeal of revolutionary organizations.[38] In May 1863, Loris-Melikov replaced the multiple district-level commissions with a single Commission for the Determination of Personal and Land Rights for the Residents of Terek oblast, also known as the Terek Estate-Land Commission. This Commission would operate according to most of the principles expounded by Orbeliani two years earlier.

Loris-Melikov appointed a Kabardian, Collegiate Councilor of the Viceroy Dmitrii Kodzokov, as chairman of the Commission. In choosing the Commission's leader, Loris-Melikov sought out a highly educated administrator with insider knowledge of the societies of the North Caucasus. Additionally, according to Loris-Melikov, the Commission needed to be "composed of members, practically and theoretically educated, not only in military arts and military administration, but also . . . in law, history, geography, statistics . . . political economy and agriculture."[39] Its chairman also needed to support the principles for land reform adopted by the government. In other words, he could not have any entrenched corporate interests with the native nobility that would interfere with a program of expropriating and redistributing the plains land of the nobility. Kodzokov, an exceptional figure for his time, met these criteria.

Kodzokov's mixed Kabardian and Russian upbringing and his Slavophile intellectual milieu had a formative impact on his approach to land reform in the North Caucasus. Born in 1818 in the mixed Kabardian-Abaza *aul* of Abukovo in what is now Karachai-Cherkessia, Dmitrii was known as Lukman before his conversion from Islam to Orthodoxy in 1830. Lukman was the son of Magomet Kodzokov, a member of the lower Kabardian nobility who briefly served in the Russian Army as a member of the tsar's Caucasus-Mountaineer Squadron in Saint Petersburg. In 1824, hoping to provide a better future for his son, Magomet gave up six-year-old Lukman to be raised by Maria Khomiakova, a Russian noblewoman and mother of the cofounder of the Slavophile movement, Aleksei Khomiakov. At the time, Khomiakova was taking in the waters at the burgeoning spa town of Piatigorsk, just outside the new frontiers of Kabarda.[40] With the pacification of Kabarda and the end of major military operations in the Central Caucasus, the spa towns of the Piatigor'e region began to attract a growing number of vacationers from among the empire's elites. It is unclear whether Maria Khomiakova met Magomet Kodzokov in Piatigorsk, which was becoming a center of trade for the surrounding mountaineer population, or in Abukovo during an organized excursion to the surrounding "pacified" *auls*, a common occurrence at the time.⁴¹ Kodzokov spent the next six years of his life on the Khomiakov estate outside Moscow where he was raised by an English governess. When Aleksei Khomiakov returned from the Balkan front of the Russo-Turkish War of 1828–9, he took an interest in the intellectual and spiritual development of the young Kabardian boy. In 1830, Lukman was baptized Dmitrii Stepanovich. Aleksei, Dmitrii's senior by fourteen years, became his godfather.⁴²

Kodzokov's intellectual development would play a key role in his return to the Caucasus as an adult and his later championing of communal landownership in Kabarda. Kodzokov's schooling took place in the Russian Empire's most elite institutions. In 1830, the Khomiakovs concluded Dmitrii's homeschooling and sent him to the Moscow boarding school of Professor Mikhail Pavlov where he received a classical liberal arts education. In 1834, Kodzokov entered Moscow University, where he studied in the philosophy department. As a student, Kodzokov read avidly and developed as a writer himself. Under the influence of the popular romantic Russian literature of the era in which the Caucasus figured prominently as Russia's orient, Kodzokov exhibited an increasing interest in his native Caucasus.⁴³ Indeed, his writings demonstrate that, despite his Russian upbringing, he identified with the Caucasus.⁴⁴ In 1837, Moscow University published a collection of his poetry entitled *Poems of a Young Circassian*. His entries for university essay competitions, "A Description of the Caucasus" and "Siege of the Troitskii Monastery," reflect his cultural duality. His writings won gold medals at Moscow University's annual essay contest. Other medalists included his classmates Iurii Samarin (one of the architects of Alexander II's Emancipation Statues) and Mikhail Katkov (the conservative Russian nationalist journalist).⁴⁵ Moscow University was one of the centers of intellectual life in the empire during the birth of the Westernizer-Slavophile debate in the late 1830s.

Throughout his long career in the Caucasus administration, Kodzokov's approach to reforming the native societies of the North Caucasus reveals the influence of Slavophile views on the peasant and land questions. These views were the result of Kodzokov's imbibing in the intellectual ferment of Moscow in the 1830s. Given the influence of his godfather and close friend, Aleksei Khomiakov, Kodzokov gravitated toward a Slavophile milieu that included the Aksakov and Kireevskii brothers and Dmitrii Valuev, the latter being in Kodzokov's class at Pavlov's boarding school and Moscow University. The "peasant question" was a frequent topic of conversation among Khomiakov's circle of Slavophile philosopher-friends.⁴⁶ Both Slavophiles and Westernizers were opposed to serfdom as it then existed in Russia. Unlike the Westernizers, who advocated paths of development based on Western European models and thus envisaged a future for the Russian countryside based on private property and commercial farming, Khomiakov and his followers idealized the Russian peasant commune and believed that communal land use and self-governance were essential components of Russia's unique path.⁴⁷

In 1839, after graduating from Moscow University, Kodzokov returned to the Caucasus to reconnect with his Kabardian family and, he hoped, apply his knowledge and skills in the service of the Russian administration to benefit his native land and the empire. In one of his frequent early letters from Piatigorsk to his adoptive mother in Moscow, Kodzokov declared,

> nothing could be more pleasant than to ensure the wellbeing of the people ... and, in so doing, perhaps forge a career for myself, not a brilliant one, but an original and noble one. ... It is more gratifying to receive the thanks of several thousand poor peasants, than the rank of a ... state councilor.[48]

Kodzokov settled in Piatigorsk in the home of the exiled Decembrist-*cum*-Caucasianist Vasilii Sukhorukov.[49] For the first three years after his return to the Caucasus, Kodzokov unsuccessfully attempted to find employment in the local administration near Kabarda. According to Tugan Kumykov, author of Kodzokov's biography, the Caucasus leadership was unwilling to place Kodzokov in the local administration because of his Kabardian ethnicity.[50] No matter how loyal and Russified Kodzokov was (he had forgotten most of his native Circassian language), his loyalties would always be suspect in the eyes of tsarist officials. Kodzokov spent this time of "retirement" (*otstavka*) (re)learning Circassian, studying the customs and socioeconomic conditions of the peoples of the North Caucasus, meeting with Russian and native intellectuals and writers (Mikhail Lermontov and Kabardian intellectual Shora Nogma, among others), and attempting to introduce Russian schools and new, European and Russian farming practices into Kabardian society.[51]

In the roughly two decades between his return to the Caucasus and appointment to chairman of the Terek Estate-Land Commission, Kodzokov developed negative views of the Kabardian nobles because their conservatism had repeatedly disappointed Kodzokov and thwarted his modernizing projects. Kodzokov's enmity toward the Kabardian nobility made him a perfect candidate to lead the administration's land reform efforts because they would entail ending the nobility's monopoly on land and introducing communal land use. While satisfied by his progress in his ethnographic and linguistic studies, the results of his reform efforts disappointed Kodzokov. In an 1839 letter home to the Khomiakovs, Kodzokov confessed, "I will not lose sight of the transformations in Kabarda's way of life I had so fervently taken up. ... But it is impossible to do everything anytime soon."[52] Initial attempts to open a school that would teach peasant boys basic math and Russian in his home village and a project for administrative reform in Kabarda based on customary law all came up against the conservatism of the Kabardian nobility and opposition or indifference from the tsarist administration.[53] Kodzokov's frustration with the Kabardian nobility would only grow stronger when, in later years, his attempts to introduce Western agricultural and stockbreeding practices to Kabarda failed due to the disinterest of the Kabardian nobility. His attempts to promote the construction of irrigation canals, improvements in crop rotation, and horse breeding were consistently dashed by the rigidity of Kabarda's nobles.[54] While Kodzokov used his limited resources to set up model farms, these efforts suffered from a lack of free labor (due to serfdom) and the reluctance of other nobles to assist him or learn from and adopt his practices.[55] Kodzokov experienced culture shock and frustration with Kabardian economic practices. Kodzokov wrote to Maria Khomiakova that "the local inhabitants have no understanding of their carelessness: their herds are dying; they lose horses . . . and there is nothing to say about their farming, it is just pitiful."[56] Kodzokov quickly developed an antipathy toward the Kabardian nobility that would last the remainder of his life. Indeed, this struggle against the conservative nobility to reform Kabardian society came to define Kodzokov's life from the 1860s on.

In 1845, by relocating to Tiflis, the center of the Caucasus administration, Kodzokov's efforts at securing a position finally met with success. This appointment marked the beginning of a long and successful career in the Caucasus administration. Kodzokov's success in 1845 may be no coincidence. It was in this year that Mikhail Vorontsov became viceroy of the Caucasus. In addition to his role as an enlightened modernizer bringing European culture to the Caucasus, Vorontsov is noted for his attempts to foster imperial loyalty by integrating social elites from Caucasia's diverse communities into the region's administrative apparatus. Vorontsov brought new opportunities for native Caucasians like Kodzokov to serve in and ascend the ranks of the tsarist administration.[57] Starting out in the Customs department as the assistant to the head of the Nakhichevan Customs Post, Kodzokov was quickly promoted to head clerk of the Transcaucasian Customs District. During this period, Kodzokov swiftly ascended the Table of Ranks.[58]

Kodzokov was essentially an outsider to the privileged Kabardian upper nobility. Indeed, the Kodzokovs had never been large landowners in Kabarda. Moreover, his *lower* noble status complicated the question of his entry position in the Table of Ranks. This contributed to the lack of corporate solidarity that made Kodzokov an excellent candidate to lead the administration's land reforms in Kabarda. If Kabardian princes (*pshi*) and first-level nobles (*tlekotlesh*) had little difficulty being recognized as nobles upon entering Russian service, members of the lower, second-level, nobility (*beslanuork*), like Kodzokov, often encountered difficulties in trying to prove their noble status. Kodzokov had to jump through a series of bureaucratic hoops in order to secure his place as a *Russian* nobleman.[59] Difficulties surrounding Kodzokov's noble status may also explain his hostility toward the Kabardian upper nobility, who, in his view, took their privileges for granted and were "lazy and inept."[60]

With his ascension to the rank of Collegiate Secretary in 1847, the administration promoted Kodzokov to head of the Chancellery of the Transcaucasian Quarantine and Customs District. From this position, Kodzokov attracted the favorable attention of Viceroy Vorontsov.[61] In 1848, a political crisis struck Kabarda as a result of the local administration's heavy-handed actions. These administrative abuses occurred in the wake of an incursion by Imam Shamil's insurgent forces in 1846 and amid general tensions surrounding Cossack colonization and the Kabardians' struggle to regain control of their Cossack-administered mountain pastures.[62] Vorontsov sent Kodzokov on special assignment to Kabarda to investigate numerous complaints against the excesses and abuses of Colonel Nikolai Beklemishev, head of the Center of the Caucasus Line. Beklemishev outraged Kabardian society by taking a young Kabardian woman as his mistress, impregnating her, and then attempting to marry her off to a local man for money. Kodzokov's report was responsible for the replacement of the reviled Beklemishev with Georgii Eristov. A Georgian prince known for his more conciliatory attitude toward the native population,[63] Eristov's appointment reflects both the generally frequent use of Georgians throughout the Caucasus administration and Vorontsov's practice of replacing ineffective Russian administrators with elites from Georgia and other parts of Caucasia. After serving in several other posts in various parts of the Caucasus, in 1861 Orbeliani promoted Kodzokov to senior official for Special Assignments of the viceroy of the Caucasus. Kodzokov would hold this position until his death in 1893, serving simultaneously as chair of the Terek Estate-Land and Terek-Kuban Estate Commissions from 1863 to 1888.[64]

Kodzokov's first task as chair of the Terek Estate-Land Commission was to find a way to legally justify the transfer of all Kabarda's land to the state for redistribution as what he hoped would be communal land. In the summer of 1863, Kodzokov achieved this task with the Kabardian nobility's singing of the Declaration of August 20, 1863. In this document, "representatives of the Kabardian princes, nobles (*uzdens*), freemen, and serfs (*chernyi narod*)" declared that "the land of the Kabardian people is our common property, and we wish to use it on the basis of communal ownership and according to those mutual relations under which we, Kabardians, have always lived."[65] In calling for communal landownership and denying the documented existence of noble landownership in Kabarda, the Kabardian nobles signed away their monopoly over Kabarda's land. In giving up their land rights, they, in effect, lost the basis of their noble privileges as serf owners.

Why would the Kabardian landed nobility sign a declaration that was so clearly against their interests? One answer can be found at the end of the declaration. After stating their desire for a communal system of landownership, the Kabardian representatives continued by requesting

> that the lands along the Zolka and Etoko, given back to us in 1845 for our use and necessary for our economy, be gifted to us; and also that the borders of the Kabardian lands with the mountaineers [Balkars], Ossetians, Karachai, and Cossack Cordon lands be made known . . . and that we be given a map of these borders officially approved by His Imperial Majesty.[66]

Kabardians never resigned themselves to the loss of their summer pasture lands along the Zolka and Etoko rivers. Without these pastures, Kabardians would be unable to maintain their large stockbreeding economy. Kabardians of all social estates continued to fear that the state would retake these lands, to which they had only temporary usage rights (*vremennoe pol'zovanie*) and use them for Russian settlement. Kodzokov, also recognizing the importance of these lands and, hoping to preserve them permanently for the Kabardian people, convinced Kabarda's nobles that by declaring Kabarda's land communal, they would be rewarded by the return of these pastures to Kabardian ownership. Moreover, given Kabarda's land losses to Cossacks and neighboring mountaineers during the tsarist conquest of the first quarter of the nineteenth century, Kabardians hoped to preserve the remainder of their land from future annexations by signing this declaration and obtaining an official map of Kabarda's borders. Indeed, Kabardian elites had learned from their European-Russian colonizers the power of the map as means of legitimizing claims to contested lands.[67] Finally, it must be added that Kodzokov, as a Kabardian, also wanted to prevent the further contraction of Kabarda's territory.[68]

The limited source base does not allow a definitive answer as to why the Kabardian nobility signed the Declaration of August 20, 1864. In recounting his conversations with an aged Kodzokov in the early 1880s, the Balkar intellectual Misost Abaev indicates that Kodzokov convinced Kabarda's feudal elite, who were wary of further interference in their internal affairs, that this declaration would prevent future Russian attempts to transform Kabardian society. Kodzokov's key role in removing the corrupt local official, Beklemishev, in 1848, earned him the trust and respect, at least temporarily, of all classes in Kabardian society.[69] In his memoirs, the disgraced Beklemishev recalls how

> Kabardians awaited Kodzokov's arrival with great impatience. They set up sentries on the tops of the hills far from the *auls* to report on his arrival. They came out on horseback to meet Kodzokov who, with the arrogance of an Asiatic upstart, solemnly entered Kabarda with a large retinue. . . . Long lines formed outside Kodzokov's residence in Nalchik where people crowded in [to voice their grievances] around the clock.[70]

Kumykov argues that the Kabardian elites naively believed that this declaration would give them immunity from the impending emancipation of serfs in the North Caucasus and allow them to preserve their privileges.[71] While the Kabardian nobility's belief that they could retain their privileges while giving up their ownership of land may seem utterly naive, it may have also been the case the Kabardian elite, predominately illiterate and inexperienced in the juridical norms of Russia and textual law in general, did not fully understand the implications of what they were signing. It is plausible that they believed that the Russian administration would not interfere with Kabarda's social structure and that the power of Kabardian custom would uphold relations of dependence in their society. Based on Abaev's conversations with Kodzokov, it is clear, however, that Kodzokov deceived the Kabardian princes and nobles into signing this declaration. According to Abaev, "Kodzokov worked hard on the business of getting the upper estates of Kabarda to submit this declaration and he achieved his goal by using several influential Kabardian princes and nobles who, as a result, repented their not altogether selfless act."[72] Reflecting on his actions, an aged Kodzokov admitted to Abaev that he "used every clean and unclean measure to force the Kabardian princes and nobles to voluntarily give up their property rights to their ancestral lands" because he "thought that all of the lands would transfer to the property of the Kabardian people."[73]

After achieving the communalization of Kabarda's land in August 1863, Kodzokov's Commission spent the next four years working out the remaining aspects of comprehensive land reform in Kabarda.[74] In late 1863 and early 1864, the Commission delimited borders between Kabarda and Balkaria. The Commission spent 1864 collecting data and examining the territory of Kabarda. In 1865, the Commission implemented some of its most far-reaching reforms, including the following: the establishment of rules for communal landownership; the introduction of state taxes on households of village societies; a draft on the allotment of land to Nalchik Fortress (the center of tsarist power in Kabarda), its suburbs, and the recently formed Mountain Jew colony; and the resettlement and enlargement of Kabarda's *auls*. This last action was the most consequential. In February, the Land Commission met with the head of the Kabardian district, local officials, and Kabardian delegates over the course of six days and resolved "to form 33 *auls* from the existing 97."[75] Resettled *auls* continued to exist as quarters retaining their former name within an enlarged *aul*.[76] The enlargement program had three purposes: (1) it facilitated the administration's policing tasks; (2) it simplified the task of allotting communal land to *auls*; and (3) it helped free up land for future settlement. This last point was especially true for Lesser (eastern) Kabarda, where the administration formed nine Kabardian *auls* out of the existing 19.[77] In 1866, Kodzokov's draft on the allotment of communal land among the *auls* of Kabarda awaited official approval by the viceroy. Thus, when Kodzokov received the unwelcome order "to determine how much land in . . . Kabarda could be set aside for a private-ownership land fund and in which places it would be most convenient to have this land,"[78] his land reform project for Kabarda was nearly complete.

Given his populism and his antipathy toward Kabarda's noble elites, Kodzokov considered communal landownership to be "fully in accordance with the people's character and customs and, without the slightest doubt, with the general happiness of the entire Kabardian people."[79] The Caucasian administration in Tiflis, and Viceroy Mikhail Nikolaevich in particular, developed a very different opinion on land reform in Kabarda. Most importantly, Mikhail Nikolaevich wanted to establish a system that would include private and communal land tenure as outlined in Orbeliani's 1861 project, of which Mikhail Nikolaevich was a supporter and to which Kodzokov was not privy.

In his 1861 draft project for land reform in the North Caucasus, Viceroy Orbeliani weighed the pros and cons of private and communal landownership and argued for a reform that would combine the two. Orbeliani argued that "communal [landownership] precludes the possibility of a proletariat [but] private [landownership] leads to the more complete development of agriculture." While admitting that "the upper estates . . . really were owners of the land and, because of this, all who lived on their lands owed them personal and monetary dues," Orbeliani maintained that "it is impossible to keep these rights of the upper estates in force because such a measure would not accord with our understanding of their Russian subjecthood." Nevertheless, in claiming that "it would be unjust to take away all of the aristocratic estate's former rights," Orbeliani recognized the importance of maintaining the native nobility's support. Orbeliani deemed it "necessary to reward them with . . . land allotments . . . based on full landownership rights, under the condition that they not have any further pretensions to the lands, which they formerly considered their property and, likewise, to those persons whom they considered their vassals."[80]

Another consideration that would have influenced Mikhail Nikolaevich to support the distribution of private land to the Kabardian nobility was the latter's fierce hostility to the planned emancipation of their serfs. The emancipation of serfs in the North Caucasus, implied in Orbeliani's project and being planned by Kabardian district chief Aleksandr Nurid, as to be expected, aroused the anger of the Kabardian nobility, the largest serf-owning group in the North Caucasus. The Kabardian nobility was already upset by Kodzokov's resettlement of their *auls* during the village enlargement.

About 3,000 Kabardians resettled in the Ottoman Empire in protest of the reforms between 1865 and 1866.[81] In December 1866, Kabarda's nobles issued an ultimatum to the government: "either leave us with our serfs or allow us to resettle to Turkey."[82] When the government rejected mass requests to resettle in the Ottoman Empire, the Kabardian elite began to resist openly. In February 1867, an armed detachment of 300 Kabardians, led by the most powerful Kabardian nobles in Russian military service, marched on Nalchik and restated their demands to district chief Nurid. Meanwhile, representatives of the Kabardian nobility went around Kabarda's *auls* to prepare them for an uprising. Nurid stood firm, declaring to the nobles: "just as the River Baksan cannot be made to flow backwards up the mountains, the process of emancipation cannot be stopped."[83] Nurid's timely use of nearby Cossack armies and the clear lack of support among their own peasantry forced the Kabardian nobles to stand down. However, the administration understood that they would need to placate the Kabardian nobility in some way.[84]

Viceroy Mikhail Nikolaevich explained his reasons for favoring the distribution of a significant portion of Kabarda's land to the local nobility in a draft project that he sent to Loris-Melikov in late December 1866. The viceroy's motives in revising the Kodzokov Commission's land reform project reveal two crucial aspects of the tsarist state's ideology of colonial rule. First, the viceroy was concerned that an exclusively communal system of land rights would isolate Kabarda from Russian cultural and economic influences and inhibit the imperial integration of the region because it would preclude the possibility of future Russian peasant settlement on purchased or rented land here.[85] Second, the administration generally believed that to maintain stability in this restive part of the empire, it would need to rely on the support of local elites. The land reforms and looming serf emancipation would clearly antagonize native elites in the Central Caucasus, particularly in Kabarda where a feudal-like system of land tenure was most developed. Mikhail Nikolaevich and others in his administration understood that something needed to be done to placate the stratum of society that the tsarist state would rely on to maintain control in the region. In making his case for the allotment of Kabardian princes and nobles with private land, Mikhail Nikolaevich also argued that since "the upper estate will be economically weakened by a communal system . . . justice demands that the upper estate be compensated in order to give it a means to support its social standing."[86] Indeed, the reforms of the 1860s weakened the Kabardian nobility and exacerbated tensions between Kabardian landed elites and the peasantry.

The tsarist state's approach to serf emancipation and land reform in Kabarda—balancing the need to provide peasants with land, on a communal basis so as to avoid creating a "proletariat," with the need to placate the nobility and a desire to create a basis, however weak, of private landownership—was similar to the one that the tsarist state took to the peasant and land reforms in Central Russia at the beginning of the decade. Among other considerations, the tsarist bureaucrat-policeman state approached the land and peasant questions, as it did most other things in the Caucasus and indeed the entire empire, from the standpoint of security and stability. In emancipating Russia's serfs with land in 1861, the tsarist state demonstrated that it had learned from its experiences in the Baltic region, where a landless emancipation in the 1820s led to sharp ethno-social tensions between German nobles on the one hand and

Estonian and Latvian peasants on the other. The tsarist state wanted to avoid potential social disruptions that might occur if the Kabardian lords were allowed to keep all of their land and emancipated serfs were left landless.[87] However, tsarist administrators, following popular liberal economic theory, also believed that private landownership was more economically productive than communal. They also reasoned that they should sustain and grow a loyal cadre of native elites by rewarding them for their service and sacrifices with private land allotments.

In May 1867, Loris-Melikov, despite sharing Kodzokov's negative opinion of Kabarda's princely elite,[88] followed the viceroy's orders and instructed Kodzokov and his Terek Estate-Land Commission to set aside land for private ownership in Kabarda. By this point, Kodzokov's Commission had finished most of its work on the land reform project.[89] Upon learning of the administration's plan to transfer land to Kabarda's nobility, writing in the name of the Commission, Kodzokov vehemently objected, asking, "should the interests of the masses be sacrificed to benefit a small group of people and is it profitable for the government to pit against itself entire societies for the sake of the well-being of the few?"[90] After a long invective against the Kabardian elite, Kodzokov asks, "what benefit will people with such a narrow outlook on life and such little energy for useful activities ... bring to agriculture and the economy of the country?"[91] Finally, Kodzokov asks, "What use is it to cheat [former serfs] of their land and give the lazy, incompetent upper estate the opportunity to exploit the laboring class?"[92] In a separate personal objection appended to the Commission's report, Kodzokov argued that "if we now allow private ownership on the basis of [noble] background and custom, then there was no reason to not recognize as just and legal all of the landholdings which existed earlier and which we ourselves successfully tried to destroy."[93] Kodzokov warned that the allotment of land to the nobility "would show the people that a thieving prince ... will receive land through government decree on the basis of class ... or blood rights, while someone of different background, who has spent his entire life being an diligent farmer and honest member of his society, will remain deprived of land." Lest it appear that he was opposed to the idea of private property in principle—and he may indeed *not* have been—Kodzokov ends with a historicist argument, stating that "it is still premature to have property owners in this region because of the low educational level and the dominant form of economic activity [transhumant stock breeding], which, more than anything else, influences a society's ability to develop."[94]

Kodzokov's objections were of no avail. The viceroy's only response to Kodzokov was a strict reprimand for insubordination. Word spread to the Kabardian nobility that Kodzokov was trying to stop the transfer of land to them. Kodzokov began to fear for his life after a Kabardian peasant informed him that the nobility was plotting to have him assassinated.[95] Kodzokov reluctantly complied with Loris-Melikov's orders and implemented the redistribution of land according to the viceroy's project. At the end of his life, Kodzokov lamented, "trying to be useful to the state and, in particular and in a direct way, to my people, but falling on a false path, I did much that was shameful and this torments me."[96] In terms of the land question, writing in 1911, Abaev characterized Kodzokov as "a blind tool in the hands of Loris-Melikov."[97] Given the way Mikhail Nikolaevich orchestrated policies from Tiflis, it would probably be more accurate to characterize both Kodzokov and Loris-Melikov as tools in the hands of the viceroy.

The Preconditions for Peasant Migration to the North Caucasus

After the peasant and land reforms, the next major set of policies and processes that affected intercommunal relations in the North Caucasus during the late imperial period were those that encouraged the migration of peasants to the region from Central Russia and the empire's western borderlands. In the wake of the Great Reforms, Russia's peasantry suffered a severe land hunger as a result of a population boom and the fact that the terms of the serf emancipation left the Russian peasantry with less and lower-quality land at their disposal for which they had to pay far above the market value.[98] In order to alleviate the land shortages among the peasants of Russia, the tsarist state needed to find a way to open up new lands to Russian colonization. Additionally, many within the administration hoped that Russian peasant colonization of the empire's diverse borderlands would promote the spread of order and the integration of these regions into the empire through the spread of Russian culture and "civilization" among non-Russian peoples in the Caucasus, Central Asia, and Siberia.[99] Official restrictions on peasant migration, kept in place out of concerns for maintaining social order and to protect the nobles' labor supply,[100] were major impediments to Russian peasant colonization of new lands. Even after the easing of these restrictions in the 1880s, the fact that peasants could not leave their commune without the approval of local elders continued to impede Russian peasant colonization of southern and eastern steppe lands.

From the late 1860s through the early 1900s, the tsarist state pursued policies that directly or indirectly encouraged Slavic peasant colonization in the North Caucasus. In 1868, after Russia's Cossacks had become a closed estate, Alexander II passed legislation that allowed peasants to rent and reside on Cossack land without joining the Cossacks.[101] The Terek and Kuban Cossacks, per capita, controlled more land than any other group in the North Caucasus. Indeed, Cossack landholdings far exceeded their productive capabilities, and, therefore, many Cossack *stanitsy* readily rented out excess land to peasant newcomers. Indeed, in the late imperial period, Russian peasants, not Cossacks, were the most significant agriculturalists on Cossack lands. These new peasant arrivals to Cossack lands of the post-reform period usually fell under the category of foreigners or *inogorodnie* (literally people of a foreign city) for legal and tax purposes. In an ironic historical twist, the colonial administration considered Cossacks and other permanent-resident Slavs who had been in the Caucasus since before the peasant reform as *korennye* or natives. "Native" Slavs enjoyed greater rights than the *inogorodnie*; they were included within local village societies and accorded local self-governance rights and a share of the communal lands. *Inogorodnie* faced a number of restrictions and burdens, especially in the 1880s and 1890s: they were unable to vote or speak at village assemblies; they paid taxes often greater than those of the native Slavs but did not receive the same land use rights in return; they were restricted in the number of cattle they could graze on communal pastures; and a series of legislative acts impeded their ability to gain residency status in their new locations.[102] The *inogorodnie* of the North Caucasus formed, in the words of historian Alex Marshall, "a discontented local underclass, who suffered under the exaction of special Cossack-instituted taxes."[103] In the late imperial and revolutionary Caucasus, social conflict centered just as much around the *intra*communal conflict between Slavic settlers and their Cossack landlords as it did around the *inter*communal enmity between land-rich Cossacks and land-poor mountaineers.

Economic modernization also promoted the migration of Slavic peasants and workers. The completion of the Rostov-Vladikavkaz railway in 1875 and the extension of branch lines during the late imperial period were important prerequisites to opening the North Caucasus to waves of peasant settlement. In addition to facilitating peasant migration, the Rostov-Vladikavkaz railway also brought Russian railway workers to the region. In 1888, local railway workers and Cossacks established a new village around the railway station Kotliarevskaia, which was situated just south of the *stanitsa* Prishibskaia on the corridor of Cossack land along on the Georgian Military Highway separating Greater Kabarda from Lesser Kabarda. By 1913, a new branch line connected Nalchik, Kabarda's administrative center, to Kotliarevskaia and the Russian railway grid.[104] By 1917, the Cossack *stanitsa* Prokhladnaia and the town of Mozdok, just outside the Kabardian zone of settlement, were some of the region's most important railway junctions with significant numbers of Russian railway workers. Finally, the discovery of large oil fields near Chechen and Ingush lands between the Terek and Sunzha brought significant numbers of Russian workers to the region, particularly to the burgeoning city of Groznyi.[105] The administrative center of Terek oblast, Vladikavkaz, on the upper Terek near Ossetian, Ingush, and Cossack settlements, also became an industrial city with a significant Russian worker population.[106]

It was the easing of restrictions on migration from the 1880s on that facilitated significant peasant migratory flows into Kabarda and elsewhere in the region. Facing the reality of spontaneous illegal migration caused by the Russian peasantry's land hunger, the tsarist state issued the "temporary regulations" on resettlement in 1881 and permanent resettlement law in 1889. Though cautious and blunted by bureaucratic impediments, this legislation marked a change in tsarist policy from discouraging peasant migration to fostering controlled migration as means of solving the empire-wide land question and colonizing the empire's peripheries.[107]

Relatively low land prices and rents made the North Caucasus an attractive destination for Russian peasant migrants seeking respite from their land hunger. Of all the regions of the Caucasus, Kuban oblast in the northwest, which had lost as much as 90 percent of its native Circassian population by the end of the Caucasus War, received the largest share of this immigration. Terek oblast, which included historic Kabarda, also witnessed significant peasant immigration during the late imperial period. Between 1876 and 1896 the population of the Terek region increased by 64 percent on account of peasant settlers.[108] After migrating to Terek oblast, these mainly Russian and Ukrainian peasants lived on rented Cossack lands or lands purchased or rented from private landowners.[109]

The Transformation of Land and Social Relations in Kabarda

On November 18, 1866, Kabardian and Balkar representatives of the *auls* of the Kabardian district (*okrug*) gathered in Nalchik to hear Loris-Melikov read the Viceroy's Decree of October 1 proclaiming the beginning of the emancipation of the district's dependent estates.[110] The administration gave the nobility a year and a half to conclude emancipation contracts with their serfs before the government would automatically decree their emancipation on less advantageous terms.[111] As in Central Russia, the tsarist administration created mediation courts (*posrednicheskie sudy*) for the Kabardian district's four precincts (*uchastki*) to oversee and approve emancipation contracts.[112] The terms regulating emancipation contracts in Kabarda were more favorable for the Kabardian peasantry than the 1861 terms were for the Russian peasantry. As we will see, however, the opposite was true for the mountaineers of the Caucasus, including the Balkars, who, unlike the Kabardians, were emancipated without land.[113] Most former serfs, because they could not pay their redemption payments immediately, would remain temporarily bound to their lords for no more than six years.[114] Some nobles made last-ditch efforts to resist—petitioning for the right to emigrate from Russia to the Ottoman Empire with their serfs. Sensing the impending collapse of their livelihood, the nobles conceded that, even if they could not keep their serfs, they still wanted to emigrate because "it would be easier to work for people who do not know us, then work for our own peasants."[115] Ultimately, district chief Nurid denied these requests for emigration and called 1,000 soldiers into Kabarda to reinforce his task of carrying out the emancipation.[116]

By mid-March 1867, Nurid reported to Loris-Melikov that the emancipation of the serfs had been completed.[117] In the Kabardian district, the peasant reform of 1867 resulted in the emancipation of 16,499 Kabardian serfs of all categories from a total Kabardian population of around 44,000 and 4,722 mountaineer serfs from a total mountaineer (i.e., Balkar) population of around 10,000. While the terms regulating the emancipation of serfs in Kabarda and the Balkar lands were roughly the same,[118] unlike in Kabarda, serf emancipation in the mountaineer societies was not accompanied by land reforms. Rather, the tsarist administration, in an attempt to graft the mountaineers' existing system of land tenure onto Russian law, left the legal status of many lands in the Kabardian district's mountaineer societies unclear for decades to come.

On December 28, 1869, Alexander II signed the final version of the land redistribution project into law. This project, reluctantly authored by Kodzokov, gave special allotments to princes, members of the upper nobility, lower nobles who were lords of their *auls*, and commoners who "through their service to the government obtained for themselves an honorary position."[119] Kabarda's 42 *auls* received 896,022 acres of communal farmland and plains pastures. Two hundred families of the Kabardian aristocracy received about 268,785 acres as private property. During periodic redistributions of communal lands within the *auls*, lords of the *aul* also received one-tenth of the *aul*'s land.

Much to Kodzokov's chagrin, much of Kabarda's land remained in the control of the state rather than the Kabardian peasantry. Kabarda's Zolka and trans-Malka mountain pastures, which were of such great economic importance, were left under state control. The project gave the viceroy of the Caucasus the right to determine the use of these mountain pastures and the Caucasus administration allocated them for "the use of the society of Greater Kabarda" and "for the free grazing of the herds of [their] contiguous five mountaineer societies."[120] The administration did not include the pastures within the communal land belonging to the Kabardian people for two reasons: (1) this land would be shared between Kabardians and Balkars and (2) the state hoped to generate extra revenue from this land. Minister of War Miliutin explained that

> after the division of land according to the needs of the *aul* societies and private owners, all the remaining land of Greater Kabarda should be left for the state [*za kaznoi*] so that ... those plots that remain completely unused after the final distribution of pastures to *aul* societies and private landowners could be rented out [by the state] for a set price.[121]

The administration also set aside the smaller Little Eshkakon mountain pastures to the west for communal use by the shepherds of Lesser Kabarda. This land had previously been part of the Kislovodsk Cordon Line and used by Karachai and Kabardian shepherds. The administration left Kabarda's forests for the Kabardians' communal use and created the Kabardian Forestry Department to manage them. After the administration of the Kabardian district carried out the serf emancipation in 1867, around 400 former serf families from the Balkar societies remained landless; these mountaineers received 10,800 acres in Kabarda. Finally, the state retained 102,600 acres of Bekovich-Cherkasskii land in Lesser Kabarda for future Russian settlement.[122]

The land reform project gave former Kabardian serfs access to land on a communal basis on similar terms as the Russian peasantry. Kabardian peasants became members of *aul* societies with rights to a share of their village's repartitional communal land.[123] In Kabarda, the average allotment size was between 97.2 acres and 110.7 acres per household. This was the largest allotment size of all the indigenous peoples of the North Caucasus. The large size of Kabarda's household allotments was the result of both the extensiveness of Kabarda's historic, though much-decreased, landholdings and the poor quality of land in Kabarda's village allotments.[124] According to F.P. Troino, a specialist on land relations in the late imperial North Caucasus, "more than two thirds of the land in [Kabarda's communal] allotments was hardly usable for cattle grazing, let alone agriculture—it was rocky cliffs filled with brush and bushes and completely infertile ... the best lands, first and foremost farmland and haymaking land, went to private owners."[125] Nevertheless, the size of Kabarda's allotments helped make up for their poor quality.[126]

Lesser Kabarda

According to Kodzokov's Estate-Land Commission, "because of its great significance for the resolution of the land question throughout Terek oblast, the land question among the Lesser Kabardians and all non-Russians [*inorodtsy*] residing in Lesser Kabarda, and the question of the land rights of the Bekovich-Cherkasskii princes, was given top priority by the Commission." The land question in Lesser Kabarda presented the administration with particular difficulties because the usual problems of competing claims to land, disputed borders, and lack of access to land existed within a territory whose population had become increasingly diverse in the middle of the nineteenth century. As the Caucasus administration saw it, "Lesser Kabarda ha[d] the most restive and mutually hostile population of all of the North Caucasus," both because of its "diverse population, composed of various native tribes of the Caucasus different from each other in language, religion, and historical past" and because of "the general lack of understanding of land rights."[127]

Ethnic diversity was not, however, a primary cause of tensions in Lesser Kabarda; rather, wartime tsarist policies were the cause of both the tensions among diverse communities and the diversity itself. The military administration's resettling of communities with little regard for long-term impact, the lack of defined borders or land use rights, and the administration's issuance of contradictory rulings on landownership, and not ethnic diversity per se, all led to the volatile situation in Lesser Kabarda. Indeed, intercommunal symbiosis and cooperation were essential elements of social life in the multiethnic North Caucasus. As we have seen for earlier periods, tsarist policies were the leading cause for the disruption of intercommunal symbioses in the Central Caucasus. In any event, Lesser Kabarda's diversity did not fit the tsarist administration's postwar vision for how the region should be administered.

The case of the administrative-territorial and land reforms in Lesser Kabarda demonstrates how the territorialization of ethnicity that we often ascribe to the Soviet era was already well at work by the mid-nineteenth century.[128] In the eyes of tsarist administrators, the North Caucasus was divided into numerous distinct "tribes" and, in order to properly serve the needs of each of these communities, all the members of each one should live together in a distinct administrative unit.[129] Moreover, for tsarist officials in the Caucasus, the fact that multiethnic Lesser Kabarda also happened to be a site of high intercommunal conflict reinforced the idea that "ethnic mixing" was inherently dangerous and opposed to orderly administration.[130] In his 1869 report on his Commission's work, Kodzokov reflected on the explosive situation in Lesser Kabarda:

> In 1863 and 1864 [Lesser Kabarda] had the most restive and mutually antagonistic population of all the tribes [sic] of the North Caucasus. This bleak phenomenon was caused ... more than anything else by the diversity [raznorodnost'] of the population, which was composed of different native Caucasian tribes, alien to each other in language, religion, and history, differing from each other in their ways of life and with divergent economic needs and general misunderstandings over land rights.[131]

For Kodzokov and modernizers in the tsarist state, peace and prosperity could best be met when local administrative borders coincided with ethnic borders as closely as possible. However, despite similarities between the tsarist and Soviet emphases on drawing administrative borders along ethnic lines, when compared to later Soviet nationality policies, the tsarist state's commitment to ethnicizing territory appears relatively weak.

Before applying the official land reform model—the transformation of all the former noble lands into state land and its redistribution at the sole discretion of the government as communal and private land—to Lesser Kabarda, Kodzokov's Estate-Land Commission sought to first solve the "tribal" question. Given the belief, widely held among tsarist officials and reflected in the writings of Loris-Melikov and Kodzokov,[132] that Lesser Kabarda's social tensions were a product of its ethnic diversity, this question would be solved by creating an ethnically homogenous Lesser Kabarda. Kodzokov's Commission approached the issue of Lesser Kabarda's diversity through a combination of resettlement, land buyouts, and changes in administrative borders.[133]

The large landholdings of the Bekovich-Cherkasskii princes, on which a variety of communities had settled during the second third of the nineteenth century, were the major impediment to transforming Lesser Kabarda. By the mid-1860s, the Bekovich-Cherkasskii lands had been at the center of land disputes for three decades among rival Kabardian princes and, later, Ingush and other mountaineers forced to resettle in these lands by the military administration.[134] Unlike most other Kabardian elites, the Bekovich-Cherkasskiis had well-documented rights to their lands originating from tsarist decrees rather than oral tradition.[135] The Caucasus administration could not legally appropriate these lands for redistribution by using the fiction of historic communal ownership.

During the land reforms in Lesser Kabarda, the fate of the Bekovich-Cherkasskii lands, most of which wound up in a private land fund for future Russian colonization, was another defeat for Kodzokov and a revealing example of the differences between his reform vision and that of the Caucasus colonial administration. In 1863, at the outset of his Commission's land reform work, Kodzokov reported to Loris-Melikov that the state needed to buyout the Bekovich-Cherkasskii lands in order to have the freedom of maneuver to redistribute land, resettle populations, and transform the administrative borders of Lesser Kabarda.[136] According to Kodzokov, "the only way to reform the Lesser Kabarda district lay in the detailed examination of the land rights of the Bekovich-Cherkasskii princes and ... their liquidation by one means or another, and then in the correct distribution of this land among its residents."[137]

On October 24, 1863, Kodzokov initiated appeals to the state for funds to purchase the Bekovich-Cherkasskii lands.[138] While quickly receiving approval from Loris-Melikov, the slowness of the tsarist bureaucratic machinery, and the Bekovich-Cherkasskiis' efforts to get as much money from the government as possible for their land, delayed the government's buyout of the Bekovich-Cherkasskiis for several years. However, Kodzokov convinced Fedor Bekovich-Cherkasskii to sell his land at the modest rate of 1.50 rubles per *desiatina* by threatening that those who gave them the land for free could just as easily take it back for free.[139] On January 20, 1866, the state purchased 151,718 acres from the Bekovich-Cherkasskiis for 85,152 rubles, leaving the Bekovich-Cherkasskii princes with 8,114 acres of their former domains. Kodzokov hoped that much of this land would be transferred to the residents of Lesser Kabarda as communal land. However, the administration, disappointing Kodzokov again, decided to keep much of this land for a private land fund for Russian peasant colonization.[140]

Almost immediately after reaching a settlement on the purchase of the Bekovich-Cherkasskii lands, the Estate-Land Commission took the first step in the ethnic unmixing of Lesser Kabarda. They forcibly resettled westward the remaining Kabardian population from Dzhylakhstanei lands to the left bank of the Kurp River in Talostanei, home to most of Lesser Kabarda's remaining Kabardians. Aside from three small Ossetian *auls* around Kuian Creek, Talostanei was populated by Kabardians residing in fifteen *auls* between the Terek and Kurp rivers. Dzhylakhstanei (Eastern Lesser Kabarda), which was composed of lands claimed by the Bekovich-Cherkasskii princes, included a far more diverse population: Kumyks in *auls* on the Bekovich-Cherkasskii estate; Chechens in the *aul* Psedakh and on the *auls* of the Bekovich-Cherkasskii estate; Ingush in the *auls* Keskem, Sagopsh, and Ak-Barzoi; Kabardians in Abaevo, Azapshevo, Perkhichevo, Inarokovo, Zhagishevo, Indarovo, and Pshekau on the Bekovich-Cherkasskii estate; and, finally, Ingush from two *auls* of the neighboring Nazran society also used these lands for cattle grazing. On January 27, 1866, the heads of the Kabardian district and its Lesser-Kabardian precinct (*uchastok*) met with nine Kabardian deputies to sign an official decree. According to this decree, the twenty-three Kabardian *auls* of Lesser Kabarda would be consolidated into nine enlarged, ethnically homogeneous Kabardian *auls*, all of which would be located between the Terek and Kurp, in historic Talostanei.

This resettlement of the Dzhylakhstanei Kabardians to the left bank of the Kurp marked the last major reduction of the territory of Lesser Kabarda. This resettlement matched the *aul* enlargement program being carried out in Greater Kabarda around the same time for the purposes of security and administrative ease and out of a desire to free up more land. With this decree, the administration cleared Dzhylakhstanei, once the heart of Lesser Kabarda, of its Kabardian population and freed up land for redistribution among other groups. In order to free up land for these Kabardians and to make what remained of Lesser Kabarda ethnically homogenous, the administration resettled Talostanei's three Ossetian *auls* to the Ossetian district.[141]

In a reflection of the malleability and instrumentalization of ethnic categories, many residents of the Bekovich-Cherkasskii estate were ready to accept whichever ethnicity would allow them to obtain more land and remain close to their place of residence.[142] The elders of Lesser Kabarda's *auls*, not wanting to share the communal allotments with newcomers, were reluctant to take in households from the Bekovich-Cherkasskii estate claiming Kabardian identity. Of the seventy-nine "Kabardian" households registered on the Bekovich-Cherkasskii estate, the elders of Lesser Kabarda's *auls* only accepted thirty-four and claimed that the rest were actually "Chechen defectors from the *Nadterechnoe Naibstvo*," who were trying to receive larger land allotments by claiming Kabardian ethnicity and remaining in Lesser Kabarda rather than resettling to Chechen lands.[143]

The Kodzokov Commission's efforts at ethnic homogenization were a first step toward the ethnic unmixing of the region, a process normally associated with Stalinist population politics of the 1930s and 1940s and the twentieth century more generally.[144] The Commission attached the Ingush *auls* of Lesser Kabarda to the jurisdiction of neighboring Nazran-Ingush district where the majority of their co-ethics resided.[145] The Land Commission resettled the Chechens residing as dependents on the Bekovich-Cherkasskii *aul* to the *Nadterechnoe Naibstvo* of Chechnya. "As a result of the common language and customs [of the Chechens and Ingush]," the Caucasus administration did not resettle the Chechen *aul* of Psedakh; rather, it annexed Psedakh to the Ingush district—where it remains the only majority Chechen village in Ingushetia.[146] Almost all of the Kumyk households of Lesser Kabarda, however, stayed. A total of 243 Kumyk households remained on the *aul* of their former Bekovich-Cherkasskii lords—the descendants of the Bekovich-Cherkasskii princes also lived here—as free peasants with communal land rights. Indeed, the Land Commission resettled in the Bekovich-Cherkasskii *aul* an additional forty-nine Kumyk families that were scattered among the Kabardian *auls* of Lesser Kabarda because "they could expect more peace among members of their own tribe than among the Lesser Kabardians."[147] The reforms made the Bekovich-Cherkasskii *aul* almost completely Kumyk. This *aul*, located 8 miles southwest of Mozdok on the right bank of the Terek and named Bekovichevo before the revolution (now the village of Kizliar in North Ossetia's Mozdok district), would remain administratively tied to Lesser Kabarda until the Second World War.[148]

At the time of the resettlements and redistricting, the population of Lesser Kabarda totaled about 12,000 (out of a total Kabardian population of around 44,000).[149] According to an April 19, 1866 decree, this population would receive the remaining 207,900 acres of historic Talostanei land between the right bank of the Terek and the left bank of the Kurp. The April 19 decree also gave the Lesser-Kabardian population use of the Little Eshkakon pastures west of Greater Kabarda's Zolka and trans-Malka mountain pastures, totaling 67,500 acres, for their summer transhumance. Before this land transfer, Kabardians and Karachais used these pastures jointly. The Little Eshkakon pastures would become a point of contestation between the two communities in the future.[150] Finally, the Land Commission's allotment draft for Lesser Kabarda included 10,800 acres for private ownership.[151] This last point of the April 1866 decree reflects the tsarist administration's belief that it had to prop up the Kabardian nobility as a means of maintaining order and stability. The Land Commission, under pressure from the viceroy's office, transferred nearly three times as much land to the nobles and princes of Lesser Kabarda than the decree had originally stipulated.[152]

By the mid-1860s, reacting to the social disruptions caused by the Great Reforms, the Caucasus administration prioritized order and stability over concerns for the economic well-being of the region's native communities. By 1865, as far as Mikhail Nikolaevich and the Caucasus administration in Tiflis were concerned, they had attained the desired administrative resolution to the land question in the most important plains regions of the North Caucasus: Kabarda's elite recognized Kabarda's land as communal property in exchange for promises—later broken—that they would regain inalienable control of their mountain pastures and that the state would not interfere in their internal affairs, and the Kumyk nobility agreed to give up half of their land for peasant communal ownership.[153] While the administration was still concerned with the needs of the land-poor and landless peoples of Terek oblast, new priorities for the future of the region took precedence. The Caucasus administration wanted to forge a class of loyal native elites by providing them with allotments of private land and giving them a stake in local governance. Tsarist policymakers also hoped that the (re)landed nobility would invest in their land and spur on economic growth in the North Caucasus. Even if the nobility proved unable to flourish without their serfs, the administration realized that they would sell off their lands to those who could, be they native or Russian.[154] First and foremost, the administration wanted to use the land reforms to create a land fund for future Russian colonization of the North Caucasus.

This priority of promoting Russian settlement is reflected in Loris-Melikov's December 1865 memorandum to Viceroy Mikhail Nikolaevich's assistant on the administration's plans for the Bekovich-Cherkasskii lands and Lesser Kabarda in general:

> [I]t would be a big mistake to leave such large land holdings in the hands of the Bekovich princes because the current members of this family, given their constitution, would not add anything of substance to either the material or the moral forces of the country, and it would be an extreme mistake not to buy these lands at the agreed-upon lucrative price.... The remaining free land [after the allotment of the Chechens and Ingush of the Bekovich-Cherkasskii lands] ... should be divided into ... allotments and given as rewards ... to officials serving in the local administration.... [G]iven the deep transformations that the native population of Terek oblast is going through, the introduction of Russian landowners into Lesser Kabarda, having a special significance because of their middle-class position, will ensure the security of the region more than the force of weapons.[155]

Of the 151,830 acres purchased from the Bekovich-Cherkasskiis in 1866, the Estate-Land Commission, under orders from the Caucasus administration, subsequently added 16,128 acres of former Bekovich-Cherkasskii lands on the right bank of the Kurp to Lesser Kabarda, most of which went to Lesser-Kabardian princes as private land. Of the former Bekovich-Cherkasskii lands, 43,497 acres went to the Ingush and Chechen *auls* transferred to the Nazran-Ingush district. The largest share of Bekovich-Cherkasskii land, the remaining 102,600 acres, went to a land fund for future Russian settlement.[156]

The Peasant Reform and Kabardian-Balkar Relations

By the mid-nineteenth century, of the former Kabarda-centered system of intercommunal relations, the only groups that remained dependent upon the landowning nobility of Kabarda were the five mountaineer societies of Balkar, Khulam, Bezengi, Chegem, and Urusbii—today's Balkars. To be sure, individual Ossetian, Ingush, and Karachai communities still rented Kabardian-controlled lands. But, as a whole, the Balkars still depended upon Kabardian plains for winter pasturages. Moreover, due to their lack of arable land, the Balkars depended on trade with their Kabardian neighbors for grain. The period from the serf emancipation and land reforms of the 1860s to 1917 witnessed great changes in the balance of land use and ownership between Kabardians and Balkars and, ultimately, the creation of new ethno-territorial borders between these two peoples and new social boundaries within these communities. The transformations during this period also created the foundations for the continued coexistence of Kabardians and Balkars within a common administrative-territorial unit. Given the symbiotic (though unequal) economic relations that continued to exist between Kabardians and Balkars, the delimitation of these borders was an especially contentious and delicate matter.

Three centrifugal forces pushed Balkars to leave their mountain valleys and settle the Kabardian foothills before and during the land reforms: (1) the natural desire to escape their perennial landlessness in the mountains in light of ethno-demographic and political changes in Kabarda (i.e., the decimation of Kabarda's population during the early nineteenth century and the near-total collapse of Kabardian princely authority); (2) a population explosion resulting in a near doubling of the Balkar population from 1834 to 1862; and (3) the monopolizing of lands within the five mountaineer societies by local Balkar nobles (*taubiis*) after the peasant emancipation in 1867.[157] These factors led to repeated petitions from Balkar representatives to the colonial administration requesting land allotments in Kabarda to ease their land hunger and resultant economic burdens. The tsarist administration proved relatively amenable to the Balkars' requests. In total, the Balkar societies received nearly 116,000 acres below their mountain valleys in the foothills during the post-reform period.[158]

One of the earliest tasks of Kodzokov's Estate-Land Commission was the delimitation of borders between Kabarda and its five contiguous mountaineer societies (i.e., Balkaria). No official border existed between Kabarda and its Balkar neighbors. Rather, as was the standard before the modern period,[159] natural borders, in this case the mountains—"the high snowy range,"[160] or "the black mountains"[161]—were the most commonly cited and recognized boundary separating Kabardian fiefdoms from (Balkar) mountaineer lands.[162] Therefore, since there is no clear separation between the foothills and the mountains, there existed a Kabardian-Balkar frontier rather than a political or administrative border. Kodzokov's Commission needed to establish Kabarda's borders before it could determine how much land Kabarda controlled and then set about redistributing this land among Kabardian communities. While the Caucasus administration had already delimited Greater Kabarda's northern and eastern borders with the Terek Cossacks and its western border with the Karachais of Kuban oblast, Kabarda's southern borders with the Balkar societies remained officially nonexistent as of 1863.[163]

Kodzokov's Kabardian ethnicity interfered in his ability to smoothly conduct policies concerning the Balkars. In delimiting the Kabardian-Balkar border and adjudicating the disputes that arose in the process, Kodzokov had to temper his allegiance (real or perceived) to his native Kabarda or, more precisely, the Kabardian peasantry, with his mediatory role as a tsarist official. Despite his efforts to appear neutral, in the eyes of the Balkars, Kodzokov's Kabardian ethnicity precluded his neutrality. Indeed, in their national histories from the late-tsarist period to the present, Balkar intellectuals blame Kodzokov's border delimitation for the continuing land problems of their people.[164]

Immediately after the Declaration of August 20, Kodzokov set about trying to get Kabardian and Balkar representatives to come to an agreement on their borders. On September 18, 1863, after it had become clear that Kabardians and Balkars had opposing ideas about what the border should look like, representatives of the two peoples—nearly all officers in the tsarist army—met on the neutral territory of the Ossetian *aul* of Major-General Tuganov. The goal of this meeting was "to determine the borders of Greater Kabarda ... discuss the extent to which the Balkar, Bezengi, Khulam, Chegem, and Urusbi mountain tribes are in need of lands on the plains outside of the valleys that belong to them ... [and] peacefully settle their dispute." Each group presented its version of the correct borders. The Kabardians' description of the border relegated the Balkars strictly to their mountain valleys. While disputing specific details of the Kabardian version of the border in a few places, the Balkar representatives—whose shepherds always depended upon the use of plains pastures in Kabarda in autumn and spring—claimed that "since the establishment of the Russian government in the Caucasus, the mountaineer societies have not had a defined border with Kabarda and the mountaineers have not encountered impediments to their permanent use of pastures even in locations below [i.e., in lowland areas north of] Kabardian *auls*." The representatives of the Balkar societies were arguing, not without basis, that the very idea of border delimitation went against past historical practice. Ensign Kuchuk Barasbiev, a representative from the Chegem Society, continued that "it would be ruinous for their stockbreeding economy if they are left without a place on the plains for pasturing below the [mountain] valleys occupied by the mountaineer societies."[165]

In an effort to bridge the gulf between the Kabardian and Balkar approaches to the border, Kodzokov called upon the representatives of both sides to validate their testimonies by swearing oaths on the Qur'an. Each side was willing to swear an oath; however, they could not reach an agreement as to what they were swearing to. The Kabardian delegates demanded that they swear oaths to specifically demarcated borders. The Balkars would only swear that they "controlled land below the Kabardian *auls* before the Kabardians entered this region [i.e., between the fifteenth and sixteenth centuries] and that in recent times [i.e., since the Russian conquest of Kabarda] they used these lands without payment and that they did not have a border with Kabarda."[166]

In their versions of the border, each side emphasized different aspects of the region's history and relied on different understandings of the natural borders in the region. The Kabardian representatives described a border which, prior to the Russian conquest, functioned as a barrier between the mountaineer societies and Kabarda's princely fiefdoms. But, before the modern period, borders in the Caucasus were fluid frontiers that changed frequently depending on the balance of power among different feudal lords. While the border described by the Kabardian representatives still existed in the sense that the administration and the local population generally understood where historic Kabardian territory stopped and where Balkar territory began, Balkar shepherds had, since Ermolov's conquest of Kabarda in the 1820s, taken advantage of the Kabardian elites' weakened position and disregarded this border in many places and freely used the plains below it for autumn and spring pasturage.[167] These were lands that remained unused after large numbers of Kabardian lords either died (through plague and warfare) or fled across the Kuban to unconquered Circassian societies.[168] After the 1820s, the Balkars' free use of these pastures caused conflict with Kabardian nobles attempting to reassert their land rights.[169] When Balkars refused to renew their tribute payments to the Kabardians for the use of their pastures, Kabardian lords extracted payments by force by stealing cattle.[170] The Balkars' claims that they once controlled the Kabardian plains were also not untrue. Judging by folklore, Turkic toponyms, and archeological evidence, at least some of the Balkars' progenitors likely inhabited the plains of the Central Caucasus at the time of the Mongol invasions and before the rise of Kabarda.[171]

The Kabardians' claims about the border and their historic landownership rights ultimately held greater weight for the tsarist administration than those of the Balkars. The Kabardian representatives had the advantage because, in 1852, Tsar Nicholas II set a precedent by refusing the request of the Balkar delegation to St. Petersburg to transfer what the tsar's advisors determined were Kabardian lands to Balkar ownership.[172] The tsar based his decision on ethnographic materials collected by tsarist military officials in the 1830s and 1840s, which described the territory controlled by Kabarda and its neighbors.[173] Thus, while the state had not demarcated an official border between Kabarda and the Balkaria, administrators had an approximate idea of what one should look like. Moreover, the Kabardians could describe a border based on natural and artificial markers, and they were ready to swear to these borders or have their other neighbors (i.e., the Ossetians or the Karachais) testify to them.[174]

After long arguments, in which a multiethnic cast of tsarist officials played the roles of mediators or referees shaping the resolution of the dispute to suit their purposes, the Kabardian and Balkar delegates came to an agreement. They would allow Kodzokov and an Ossetian member of his Commission, Lieutenant Mikhail Baev, to delimit the borders "according to their own judgment," under the condition that they take into consideration "that without the provision of land on the plains to the mountaineer societies, [they] will be deprived of a means to preserve [their] cattle breeding."[175]

Kodzokov's report on the border delimitation reveals his understanding of the link between land and intercommunal and class relations in the Central Caucasus. In Kodzokov's report, moreover, we see a tsarist official, a Kabardian no less, arguing, as local Soviet officials would do almost sixty years later, for the need to right past wrongs. Kodzokov pushed for social and cultural engineering in the name of historical fairness. As we have seen, Kodzokov derided Kabarda's landed nobility for their regressive role within Kabardian society. Kodzokov was also critical of the way the Kabardian landed nobles historically stifled the development of their neighbors. For example, in the introduction to his summary report of his Commission's work, Kodzokov wrote "[W]ith the conquest of Kabarda . . . the existing order changed noticeably for the better. . . . After entering Russian protection, the Ossetians, weak and completely oppressed until this time, breathed freely for the first time."[176] Kodzokov reported that a subsequent survey of the border found the Kabardians' version of the border "plausible." However, Kodzokov continued, "these borders were the result of the power and advantage over the mountaineer societies that [the Kabardian elite] once enjoyed, but with the [impending] declaration of independence of the former from the Kabardians, there is an obligation to bring the [Balkar] mountaineers from out of the insularity that has so far condemned them to the region that belongs to them [i.e., the mountains]."[177]

According to Kodzokov's report, the state was also obliged to "provide [the five mountaineer societies] with a means to develop cattle breeding—their only economic activity [sic]—in the form of pastures on the plains near the exits of the mountain valleys."[178] Kodzokov's redistribution of land along ethnic lines between Kabardians and Balkars, which was occurring around the same time as similar ethnically defined territorial changes in Lesser Kabarda, had great long-term significance. Among other issues, the settling of Balkar mountaineers on formerly Kabardian lands would make any future administrative separation of Kabardians and Balkars a fraught process. Kodzokov described the Balkars' transhumance patterns that made them dependent upon Kabarda:

> Their valleys are good places [for cattle-breeding] in summer and winter, but the mountaineers need pastures in spring through the middle of May, because grass does not grow in the mountains until then, and in autumn, because mountain frosts kill the feed. During these times of year, mountain cattle and sheep descend to the plains; therefore, the mountaineers have been, and are still, dependent upon the Kabardians.

Given the mountaineers' dependence on Kabardian land, Kodzokov concluded that "in order to protect the mountaineer societies from the arbitrary actions of their neighbors and give them a means to a stable economy, it is possible to transfer to them several allotments below the forest of the Kabardian lands." Kodzokov's project for the delimitation of the Balkar lands and Greater Kabarda went further and called for "pushing part of the borders of the Kabardian lands away from the mountain zone, in order to provide the mountaineer societies with pastures on the plains." In the delimitation of the borders between Greater Kabarda and the five mountaineer societies, the Kodzokov Commission ultimately called for 108,000 acres of former Kabardian land to be transferred to the Balkars for their economic needs.[179]

Lest one assume that Kodzokov was being totally altruistic in his apparent sympathy toward the Balkars' plight, Kodzokov also tried to use the border delimitation, in addition to the Declaration of August 20, as a bargaining chip in aid of his goal of permanently transferring control of the Zolka and trans-Malka mountain pastures from the Cossacks of the Cordon Line to the Kabardian people. In his report to Loris-Melikov on the delimitation of Kabarda's border with the five mountaineer societies, Kodzokov argued that by conceding land to land-poor Balkars, "the Kabardians should be rewarded . . . with . . . allotments from the Cordon lands [i.e., the trans-Malka and Zolka mountain pastures] which they use" and which "have always belonged to them," but "which have not been recognized as [permanent] Kabardian land."[180] The problem with Kodzokov's argument was that Balkars also historically utilized the expansive mountain pastures along Kabarda's western frontier. While it may be the case that in requesting that these pastures be recognized as Kabardian, Kodzokov was hoping to keep all of this land for the Kabardians, it is more likely that Kabardian concerns over these pasture lands had more to do with fears of the state's ability to dispose of this land at will and, as the state had in the past, cut off Kabardian access to it or potentially sell off the land.

Once again, Kodzokov's vision for land reforms did not come to fruition. In the land reform legislation, signed into law in late 1869, the tsarist administration gave Kabardians use of the trans-Malka pastures, but it did not recognize Kabardian ownership of this land. Rather, the administration gave this land the status of "state reserve land" (*kazennye zapasnye zemli*).[181] Much to Kodzokov's chagrin, the state could dispense with this land at will and, if it so chose, use this land for Russian settlement or sell it to wealthy native elites. Moreover, the Kabardians were to share the trans-

Malka and Zolka pastures with the Balkars. Ten years later in 1879, a formal agreement stipulated which parts of the trans-Malka and Zolka pastures would be used by the shepherds of each *aul* society from Kabarda and the Balkar societies.[182] This stipulation is significant because, similar to the land transfers to landless Balkars, it prefigured the continued coexistence of Kabardians and Balkars in a common administrative-territorial unit, in this case on the basis of shared communal pastures.

On May 18, 1864, Tsar Alexander II approved Kodzokov's "Project for the Delimitation of the Kabardians the Neighboring Mountaineer Societies."[183] Upon receiving the tsar's approval, Kodzokov's Commission was to immediately set about surveying, physically demarcating, and drafting a map of the border.[184]

Serf Emancipation in the Five Mountaineer Societies (Balkaria)

During the border surveying and demarcation, it came to light that the Balkars would need significantly more land to satisfy their needs. These additional land needs were the result of the peasant reform in Balkaria and, in particular, the fact that many Balkar serfs were freed without land or lost their land due to the onerous terms of their emancipation settlements. The reforms ultimately gave the Balkar nobility (*taubiis*) control of over half of all land in the mountain zone and made over 400 Balkar families, or one-fifth of the population, landless.[185]

The tsarist administration placed great emphasis on an expeditious and careful execution of land reforms in the plains of the North Caucasus. This territory was the most sought after, most prone to disputes, and held the greatest potential for economic development and Russian colonization. By contrast, the tsarist administration had no strategic plans for the development of the mountain zone. As usual, Kodzokov's priorities were different from those of Viceroy Mikhail Nikolaevich and his administration. During the lead up to the emancipation of the Balkar serfs, Kodzokov hoped to extend his plans for communal landownership to the Balkars as well. Indeed, given the land shortages in the mountains, the more equitable distribution of land that could be achieved through a communalization of land was even more urgent here than in the plains. However, the dearth of arable land meant that Balkar landowners valued their land much more than the slash-and-burn agriculturalists of Kabarda. The Balkars expended great efforts on the terrace plots, painstakingly clearing them of rocks and brush, bringing up fresh soil from the foothills, and constructing networks of irrigation canals.[186] According to late imperial sources, Kodzokov attempted to get the Balkar nobles to sign a similar declaration to the one the Kabardian nobles signed, by which they would give up their ownership rights to their lands. According to the Balkar intellectual and educator Misost Abaev, who was critical of Kodzokov and accused him exhibiting bias in favor of Kabarda, "Kodzokov, following the same goal as in Kabarda, also attempted to persuade the *taubiis* to serve up a similar declaration on the absence of landownership in the mountains, but they rejected this lie."[187] In his 1913 book, *Historical Accounts of the Kabardian People*, Vladimir Kudashev, a russified Kabardian like Kodzokov, reports that "the *taubiis*' refusal [to recognize their societies' lands as communal] was so categorical that Kodzokov decided to never visit the Balkars out of fear for his life."[188] According to Kudashev, after Kodzokov's disappointment, Loris-

Melikov called upon the Balkar deputies to meet with him in Vladikavkaz. According to the family of Izmail Urusbiev, one of the then young Balkar nobles invited to the meeting:

> The conversation between ... Loris-Melikov and Izmail ... regarding the declaration of the Balkar land as communal took place first in the former's general reception hall. Loris-Melikov ... asked Urusbiev what right he had to his land. An enraged Izmail Urusbiev pulled out his sabre, stabbed the end of it into the parquet floor, and exclaimed, "These are my rights! My ancestors conquered and controlled this land, and I will protect it with arms." ... Loris-Melikov invited Urusbiev into his office, had a long conversation with him, and, in parting, apparently said "Attaboy, hold on stronger to your rights."[189]

The Balkar nobility would continue to own their lands until the establishment of Soviet power in 1920.

As a result of the administration's lack of success and relative disinterest in getting the Balkars to turn over their land to the discretion of the state, in 1867, the tsarist administration emancipated Balkar serfs without land.[190] As a result, the *taubiis* lost their tribute-paying peasants (*karakish*) and their serfs (*iasakchis, chagars,* and *kazaks*) but kept most of their land. Tribute-paying peasants received rights to the land they had worked because tsarist officials determined that, despite their various obligations to the *taubiis*, in practice the *karakish* enjoyed inalienable land rights.[191] Nevertheless, the *taubiis* retained a degree of control over these peasants after their liberation. The *karakish* still had the following obligations vis-à-vis the *tabuiis*: they could only sell or transfer their land to members of their extended families; they had to obtain their *taubii*'s permission to conclude sales and transfers; each household paid a small tax in kind to its *taubii* overseer and performed limited seasonal corvée.[192] Unable to make their redemption payments, these Balkar peasants gave up between a third and half of their movable property and land to their former lords. The Balkar serfs (*iasakchi* and *chagars*) and household servants (*kazaks*) were freed without any land.[193]

These processes and policies led to severe land shortage among most Balkars in the post-reform period.[194] Importantly, these land shortages forced landless and land-poor Balkars to seek out land on the Kabardian foothills, which exacerbated land tensions between Kabardians and Balkars. In four of the Balkar mountaineer societies, 139 *taubii* families, or 6 percent of the population, controlled an average of 20 percent of the farmland, 43 percent of the hayfields, 30 percent of the pastures, and 33 percent of the forests. Land disparities were greater in the Urusbi society; here, the Urusbiev family considered almost all the land as their property,[195] though the local peasantry fought this in the courts.[196]

Serf emancipation in the Balkar societies demonstrates again the ways in which both ethnic and class concerns shaped the empire's approach administration and social control in the region. In deferring to the interests of the ruling class of the empire, here the *taubiis*, the tsarist administration created intra- and intercommunal tensions. In the late imperial period, social conflicts within Balkar societies between the *taubiis* and their former serfs were more intense than interethnic tensions over land between Balkar mountaineers and Kabardians. The need to provide land to the 400 Balkar families left landless after their emancipation in 1867, and problems with the suitability of the land originally transferred to the Balkars through the 1864 border project, forced Kodzokov to make significant corrections to his original border project in an effort to solve the Balkar land question. In May 1867, Loris-Melikov issued instructions to Kodzokov to "determine the number of [Balkar] families without an allotment after their emancipation . . . [and] definitively discuss the question of the establishment of borders between Kabarda and the mountaineer societies so that the area of the mountaineer societies includes enough land for the allotment of landless mountaineers."[197] The new land reform project, signed into law in December 1869, transferred 10,800 acres of land from the Kabardian communal lands to landless Balkar mountaineers. Over the course of the late imperial period, as more Balkar families lost land to the *taubiis*, the administration gradually transferred additional land, totaling about 121,500 acres, in the Kabardian foothills and near the trans-Malka pastures to the Balkars. Thousands of Balkars resettled in seven new villages located on this land beyond the Balkars' 1864 borders: Kashkhatau, Gundelen (Këndelen), Chizhok-Kabak (Nizhnii Chegem), Khabaz, Shaugen-Kabak-Bashi (Ianikoi), Nalchik-Bashi (Belaia Rechka), and Khasan'ia.[198] As a steady stream of settlers flowed out of the mountain valleys of Balkaria, these new villages on the foothills quickly became the most heavily populated Balkar villages.[199] These resettlements expanded the territory of Balkar habitation, further intensified Kabardian-Balkar relations, and more closely entwined the political-administrative futures of the two peoples.

During the last years of tsarist rule, the administration attempted to solve the Balkar land question. In 1906, the Caucasus Viceroy, Count Illarion Vorontsov-Dashkov, established a commission to draft land reform projects for the mountain zone of Terek oblast and the Karachai lands of Kuban oblast under Iakov Abramov, a lawyer from the Caucasus Military District Headquarters. Viceroy Vorontsov-Dashkov created the Abramov Commission in response to the empire-wide peasant rebellions during the Revolution of 1905 and, in particular, local spontaneous land seizures by landless mountaineers.[200] In the 1860s, the Kodzokov Commission's land reforms in the mountain zone were limited to the de facto recognition of private landownership. No official survey of the land and borders of allotments in the mountains had ever been conducted, few Balkars had deeds to their land, and land relations were regulated by oral traditions and customary law. After years of brewing land tensions in the mountains, particularly since the 1860s, during which the number of landless mountaineers steadily increased as a result of demographic increases and the terms of the serf emancipation, the Abramov Commission was the tsarist administration's first and only attempt to fully solve the land question in the mountain zone.

Between 1906 and 1907, the Abramov Commission, with its staff of land surveyors and land experts, visited every *aul* in the mountains of Terek oblast and Karachai and conducted a complete study of land tenure and the socioeconomic conditions in the region to that point.[201] In 1908, the Abramov Commission published its findings and recommendations for land reform as *The Works of the Commission for the Examination of the Current Condition of Land-use and Landownership in the Mountain Zone of Terek*

Oblast.²⁰² The Abramov Commission report revealed the great extent of land shortages in the mountain zone. The situation was particularly dire among the Balkars. With about half an acre of arable land per person, the Balkars had the smallest amount of arable land of all the region's mountaineer communities.²⁰³

The Abramov Commission concluded that the mountaineer landowning elites received too much land during the serf emancipation and that most of the land in the Balkars' mountain valleys should be redistributed to the residents of each society for their permanent communal use. Viceroy Vorontsov-Dashkov vetoed the Abramov Commission's land reform project for the mountain zone to appease the landowning mountaineer elites and because the project did not accord with the government's general agrarian policies, especially those of Prime Minister Petr Stolypin, of promoting private landownership.²⁰⁴

The land reforms and ethno-demographic changes taking place in Kabarda and the Balkar societies during the late imperial period strengthened Kabardian-Balkar social, economic, and administrative-territorial ties. The post-reform period witnessed the emergence of numerous Balkar exclaves inside Kabarda. The interspersed nature of Balkar and Kabardian territories, in addition to the continued shared use of pastures among Kabardians and Balkars, would make future ethno-national border delimitation an especially difficult task and create the preconditions for the continued coexistence of both communities within a shared administrative unit. During the last decades of tsarist rule, the development of the town of Nalchik as an economic center for both Kabardians and Balkars, and the construction in 1894 of a cart road from the Balkar society's Cherek Valley to Nalchik²⁰⁵ only strengthened economic links between Kabardians and Balkars. As the Abramov Commission's report made clear, the Balkars depended on outside sources of grain for their survival. In all five mountaineer societies, only eleven families had enough farmland to be economically self-sufficient. Balkars traveled to Nalchik to purchase from Kabardians the grain necessary for their survival. The Balkars, however, did have, by far, the greatest number of cattle per capita of all communities in the North Caucasus.²⁰⁶ Kabardians traveled to Nalchik, along far less treacherous roads, to purchase meat, dairy, wool, and other products from the Balkars.

Khasaut: An Anomaly on the Mountain Pastures

In 1865, during the consolidation of Kabarda's *auls*, Kodzokov's Estate-Land Commission decreed the formation of a mixed Karachai-Balkar-Kabardian *aul* on the river Khasaut.²⁰⁷ The formation of a mixed Kabardian-Karachai-Balkar *aul*, Khasaut, on the edges of Kabarda's summer trans-Malka mountain pastures, reflects the long history of intercommunal ties that characterized life in the Central Caucasus. It demonstrates that estate or class ties were often far more salient than ethnic status in the everyday lives of mountaineers and Kabardians. Khasaut's smaller and poorer land allotment, when compared with neighboring Kabardian *auls*, created tensions during the late imperial period. These tensions were more between Khasaut residents and the administration of Nalchik district than with their Kabardian neighbors. More importantly, there was no reason for the Karachai shepherds of Khasaut to believe that because they were Karachai they would be better off living with the rest of their Karachai brethren in Kuban oblast.

The mountains along the Upper Malka Valley, forming Kabarda's historic western frontier with the Karachais, are an area only suitable for summer cattle pasturing and horse breeding. This region's high elevation—the lowest elevation being 9,000 feet—rugged terrain, and harsh climatic conditions (it is prone to high winds, fog, blizzards, and long winters) make this land nearly useless for eight months of the year.[208] Despite these conditions, a variety of indigenous communities (Abazas, Karachais, Kabardians, and Balkars) have historically inhabited the upper Malka, albeit sporadically and sparsely. Usually, communities moved here out of necessity, for example, to escape conflict with neighboring societies or political conflict within their native society. By the eve of the land reforms in the mid-nineteenth century, the mountain pastures were home to five scattered homesteads with a total of about 100 households located on the Malka tributaries Lakhran, Khasaut, Kichmalka, and Gundelen. Most of these households settled in the upper Malka around 1855 when two noble families, the Kabardian Zhereshtievs and the Karachai Chipchikovs, fled Karachai during an anti-Russian uprising there led by Muhammad Amin, Imam Shamil's *naib* (lieutenant) in Northwestern Caucasia.[209]

The Zhereshtievs of Khasaut illustrate the intercommunal ties that held together Central Caucasia's nobility. In Greater Kabarda's feudal hierarchy, the Zhereshtievs were noble vassals (*uorks*) of the Kasaev princes. Before fleeing across the Kuban to the Karachais and Western Circassians during the Russian conquest, the Kasaevs were one of the most powerful princely families of eighteenth-century Kabarda. Between 1764 and 1780, a need for plains pastures forced the Balkars of the Khulam Society to come under the protection of the Kasaev princes. This relationship involved the Khulam Balkars giving the Kasaevs one sheep per household annually in exchange for the right to use pastures on the plains and to receive protection from Kabardian raids. To ensure this tributary relationship, the Kasaev princes assigned their Zhereshtiev vassals to the Khulam society, placing a Zhereshtiev residence near the Khulam Valley. Living among the Khulam Balkars, the Zhereshtievs intermarried with the local Balkar nobility.[210] During Kabarda's last major anti-Russian rebellion, in 1822, Ermolov accused the Zhereshtievs of "collaboration with unpacified mountaineers." In the wake of this accusation, Aslan Zhereshtiev fled with his family and serfs (both Kabardians and Balkars) to the unconquered lands across the Kuban to live among his Karachai wife's relatives. In 1828, when the Karachais took oaths of subjecthood to the tsar and submitted to Russian rule, so too did the Zhereshtievs. The Kabardian Zhereshtievs lived peacefully among the Karachais for three decades. However, in 1855, when Muhammad Amin raised the Karachais to rebellion, the Zheshtievs—Aslan's son Bekmurza and grandsons Zhenus, Iusup, and Magomet—remained loyal to Russia and requested permission to move back to Kabarda. Having forfeited their noble landholdings in Kabarda when they fled across the Kuban, the Zhereshtievs had to settle on vacant land in the mountains of the upper Malka basin.[211] The three Zhereshtiev sons each lived with their serfs on their own *auls*. A number of free Karachais joined the Zhereshtievs on their *auls*. Finally, the Karachai noble, Kurgoko Chipchikov, joined the Zhereshtievs, with whom he was related through marriage, and settled his *aul* nearby on the Lakhran River.[212] At the time of the land reforms, the upper-Malka region had a Karachai majority and Kabardian and Balkar minorities.[213]

But, at least at this point, the ethnicity of the residents of these upper-Malka mountain *auls* was not important in their everyday lives. Rather, class or estate categories were far more salient. The culturally and linguistically diverse nobility lorded over an equally diverse peasantry. Whatever their background or ancestry, most residents of these *auls* were likely bilingual in both the Karachai-Balkar and Kabardian languages. This region was already a zone of heightened intercommunal contact. During the summer months, Kabardians, Balkar, and Karachai shepherds lived together on the pastures with their herds and flocks. Residents of these upper Malka *auls* retained and continued to develop connections (usually familial) with Greater Kabarda, Karachai, and the Balkar societies.[214]

In the 1860s, two factors led the tsarist administration to resettle these scattered *auls* onto one *aul* on the Khasaut River: the program of *aul* enlargement in Kabarda and the impending delimitation and distribution of Kabarda's mountain pastures among the Kabardian and Balkar *auls*.[215] First, Kodzokov's Commission pursued a policy of *aul* enlargement in Kabarda, whereby it combined small *auls* to form larger ones. The administration conducted this enlargement of *auls* for purposes of administrative ease, enhanced policing, and facilitating colonization and economic exploitation. Second, before it could delimit borders and parcel out pasture allotments to Kabardian and Balkar villages, Kodzokov wanted to rid the mountain pastures of all permanent settlements. While the trans-Malka pastures were always an area of sparse settlement, Kodzokov envisaged a neat delimitation between the pastures, as a zone of seasonal residence for shepherds, and the plains as a zone of permanent residence. In choosing a place for the new *aul*, the Kodzokov Commission's main goal was to ensure that "that the *aul* would not be an impediment [to shepherds] on the summer pastures."[216]

In 1865, the Estate-Land Commission ordered the residents of the Zhereshtiev and Chipchikov *auls* to either form one *aul* in the upper-Malka area or return to their "home societies."[217] In April 1865, Kodzokov traveled to the upper Malka to resolve the question of these scattered *auls* on the mountain pastures. In a meeting with family heads of the upper Malka *auls*, Kodzokov gave them a week to decide upon a place to form a single, compact *aul* "for ease of administration and [their] general economic interests."[218] When they could not agree on the best location for the new *aul*, Kodzokov took it upon himself to find one. Kodzokov decided upon the Khasaut Valley "where there had historically been a large and thriving population and where timber can be obtained nearby." Most importantly for Kodzokov's land reform plans was the fact that "this location [did] not have a single Kabardian *aul* and [did] not interfere with the use of the summer pastures."[219] Loris-Melikov quickly approved the choice of Khasaut. Between 1865 and 1867, residents of the scattered *auls* of the mountain pastures resettled in Khasaut. By 1868, thirty-eight households resided in Khasaut.[220]

According to its 1867 project on the delimitation of Kabarda and the Balkar lands, approved as part of the land reform package in 1869, the Kodzokov Commission envisaged settling Khasaut with between 100 and 125 of the 400 landless Balkar families.[221] This plan proved unrealizable. Most landless Balkars, considering Khasaut's location equally inhospitable to the mountain valleys of their native societies, elected to resettle in the new villages of Kashkhatau and Gundelen that were being established on the foothills land transferred from Kabarda. In the wake of the reforms, only eight Balkar families resettled in Khasaut. By 1879, there were fifty-eight households officially registered in Khasaut: fifty households of original setters from the Zhereshtiev and Chipchikov *aul*s, and eight formerly landless Balkar families. The smaller-than-hoped-for number of settlers put the local administration in a difficult position in terms of distributing Kabarda's communal pastures. According to the 1869 land reform legislation, in anticipation of the resettlement of about 70 households, the Khasaut allotment included 27,969 acres for 108 *aul*s.[222]

By the end of the tsarist period, Khasaut had grown from a small cluster of homesteads to a large village, despite its isolated location and inhospitable terrain. Part of this increase was due to the resettlement of landless Karachais to the *aul* in the 1880s.[223] In 1907, Khasaut had about 200 households.[224] According to a 1914 census of Nalchik district (Kabarda's administrative unit from 1871 to 1917), the population of Khasaut stood at 1,739.[225] Indeed, with its large madrasa, Khasaut had become a local center for education for Karachai and Balkars.[226]

Available sources do not indicate that the fact that Khasaut was a majority Karachai *aul* included within the administrative jurisdiction of Kabarda was a major concern for the *aul*'s residents. Judging by the frequent appeals of the Khasaut residents to the Nalchik district administration to have the size of their allotment increased (the administration had not increased the Khasaut's original communal allotment size despite the arrival of new households and natural population growth), the main concern for the residents of Khasaut was land.[227] Ethnicity per se had little to do with the Khasautites' insufficient allotment. Rather, their lack of land had more to do with the peculiar history of the formation of Khasaut—a product of wartime upheavals, cross-communal class ties of mountaineer elites, and Kodzokov's desire to remove all permanent villages from the summer pastures. Those in charge of administering Karachai, Kabarda, and the region in general, were almost invariably not members of the local indigenous population and their loyalties were to the empire and its goals. In the tsarist period, the formation of ethnically defined administrative borders, while certainly reifying ethnic categories and providing a blueprint for future ethno-national delimitations, did relatively little for the instrumentalization of ethnicity. There were few material benefits—for example, in terms of access to land or education and career opportunities—to be gained by Karachai peasants if they lived under the same jurisdiction as the rest of their co-ethnics as opposed to Kabardian jurisdiction. Far from being a problem, the Karachais of Khasaut could benefit from their current administrative situation. Unlike the rest of the Karachais who lost their access to Kabarda's summer pastures in 1859 with the creation of Kuban and Terek oblasts, the Karachais of Khasaut, as residents of Terek oblast's Nalchik district, retained access to a share, however inadequate, of these pastures.

Ossetian Migration to Kabarda and the Village of Lesken

During the peasant reform in the North Caucasus, hundreds of landless Ossetian households, and often entire *aul*s, packed up their belongings and resettled from the desolate mountains of Digora (Western Ossetia) to live among their Kabardian neighbors in the foothills and plains to the north. In a reflection of the relative indifference to ethnic ties among mountaineers, the existence of Ossetian *auls* outside of their "native" districts, much like the case of Khasaut, was not a problem for the residents of these *auls*. Many of these resettlers began their flight from the mountains long before the peasant reform. The first stops for many Ossetian resettlers were the *auls* of the Kubatiev, Tuganov, and Kabanov Ossetian nobles, established on Kabardian lands many decades earlier.[228] However, after the land reforms on the Ossetian plains, the communal *aul* lands there were insufficient to provide all of the resident households with a minimum allotment. The Terek oblast administration resettled some of these landless Ossetians to lands in Kuban oblast that had been freed up with the mass exodus of Circassians to the Ottoman Empire at the end of the Caucasus War.[229] Most of these landless Ossetians, however, resettled in villages and worked lands then belonging to two Kabardian noble Kabardian families, the Anzorovs and the Kogolkins. In the last decades of the nineteenth century, about 400 Ossetian families purchased or rented land in Kabarda.[230] In particular, forty households of Ossetians from the Lezgor society (Digora) resettled from the *aul* Kabanovo, which had been dissolved during the land reforms,[231] to the *aul* of Kaisyn Anzorov on the Lesken River.[232] When Ossetians resettled from Digora on the scale of one or several households, these households usually dispersed among Kabardian households, ultimately leading to assimilation and the loss of their distinct Ossetian culture and language. However, when entire *auls* relocated, the villagers continued to live together compactly, forming distinct quarters (*kvartaly*) in their new villages, facilitating the retention of their separate identity. For example, Ossetian settlers in Kaisyn-Anzorovo (Anzorei) formed the Kabanov Ossetian Quarter.[233]

Two factors motivated this wave of resettlement: land and religion. First, the enduring land problems of the Digoran peasantry became more acute after land reforms in Ossetia transferred most of Digora's scarce arable land and pasturage to the local nobility. In order to quell intense conflict between Ossetian serfs and nobles, the wartime administration conducted land reforms here in an ad hoc manner before the Kodzokov Commission's work on the plains.[234] Later, the Kodzokov Commission's communalization of Ossetian land on the plains further exacerbated the situation by not providing *auls* with enough land to meet their residents' needs. Tsarist colonial administrators, hoping to solve the land problem for the Ossetians of Digora and transform formerly restive mountaineer peoples into peaceful agriculturalists, facilitated the resettlement of landless Digorans (and other mountaineers) onto the plains of Kabarda, just north of the mountain zone. Given the Kabardians' relatively large land allotments, as we have seen in the Balkar case, regional colonial administrators hoped that the lands of Kabarda could be used as part of the solution to neighboring Ossetians' landlessness.[235] Second, the division and resettlement of religiously mixed Ossetian villages along confessional lines accompanied serf emancipation and resettlement in Ossetia. Digora's Orthodox Christians resettled onto Christian villages, while Digora's Sunni Muslims resettled together into Islamic village societies.[236] In terms of religion, three factors ultimately directed some of the outmigration of Muslims from highland Digora toward Islamic Kabarda: the tsarist state's use of confession as a means of administering its empire;[237] the desire of Digora's Muslims to live among their brothers in faith (thereby escaping Orthodox missionary activity); and the relative amenability of Kabardians toward absorbing refugees who were fellow Muslims into their villages.[238]

It was under these conditions of territorial transformations and ethno-demographic change in the North Caucasus that a group of four extended Muslim families from the Digoran village of Lezgor, the Khaevs, formed a permanent settlement, Khaevo, along the upper reaches of the river Lesken in 1878. The Khaevs originally settled in the Kabardian *aul* of Kogolkino along with numerous other Ossetian settler-families in 1866.[239] After renting land belonging to a branch of the Kabardian Anzorov noble family, the four Khaev families obtained ownership of 432 acres along the river Lesken, using credit to purchase a portion of the 29,182 acres recently transferred to the ownership of the Anzorov and Kogolkin nobles. The Khaevs and other Ossetian settlers who joined them in their new *aul* gradually purchased more land from surrounding Kabardian nobles over the course of the late nineteenth and early twentieth centuries.[240] This new settlement of Khaevo fell within the local jurisdiction of Kabarda's Kaisyn-Anzorovo village society, ensuring close economic, political, and familial ties with neighboring Kabardians throughout the late imperial period.

During the last decades of tsarist rule and through the revolution and civil war years, Khaevo, or the village of Lesken as it was known from 1893 on, experienced waves of further Ossetian immigration from Digora. As Lesken grew, newcomers to the village settled in compact groupings according to their ancestral village.[241] Over time, the quality and quantity of land allotted to new settlers diminished. In terms of land and general socioeconomic conditions, Lesken was one of the poorest *auls* in the foothills. Most residents were subsistence agriculturalists who did not own cattle. Only the original Khaev settlers had access to Kabarda's communal pastures.[242] By 1917, many Leskenites were virtually landless and had to resort to renting land from wealthier villagers and neighboring Kabardian nobles.[243] This socioeconomic polarization within the village of Lesken matches a general pattern also found within most Kabardian villages in the late imperial period. As the tsarist military administration dissolved smaller Kabardian villages and relocated their populations onto enlarged villages, newcomers formed quarters that retained the name of their village of origin. These village divisions persisted for generations. Constant feuds over the division of village land allotments only sharpened these divisions within the village. During regular division of village allotments, one or several quarters, often those forming the original core of the village, would band together to dominate the village assembly to ensure that their quarters received the best land.[244] Sources indicate that this type of socioeconomic polarization was especially pronounced in Lesken because the village itself straddles the boundary between plains and foothills. By 1917, the village was divided into two mutually hostile quarters. The lower quarter formed from the village's original Khaevo core, and its members worked the village's arable land to north. The upper quarter, consisting of more recent arrivals, received mountainous land of lesser quality to the south. Lesken represented a microcosm of the land-based socioeconomic divisions of the late imperial North Caucasus.[245]

Intercommunal Relations and Slavic Peasant Migration in Post-Reform Russia

By the 1880s, Kabarda was experiencing a new wave of colonization that would last through the First World War. These colonizers were primarily Eastern Slavs (Ukrainians and Russians) and, to a less extent, Germans. The conclusion of the serf emancipation and the attendant delimitation and redistribution of Kabarda's lands, the construction of the Rostov-Vladikavkaz railway, and the easing of restrictions on resettlement cleared the way for intensified migration to the region.[246]

In addition to the historic disparity in landholdings between Kabarda and its mountaineer neighbors, two other factors relegated the native peasantry to landlessness or small plots of the worst land: Cossack colonization of the best plains land and the native nobility's monopoly on the limited usable land in the mountains. With the transformation of most of Kabarda's land into communal village land, the Kabardian peasantry came away from the land reforms relatively better off than their Ossetian, Balkar, Karachai, and Ingush neighbors. If all members of Kabardian village societies were guaranteed a share of the communal farmland and pastures, however poor in quality and small in size this land may have been in comparison with that of Kabarda's private landowners, among the mountaineer communities, the serf emancipations, which were conducted without land reforms, left hundreds of peasant families landless. These landless peasants turned to renting land on the plains at high rates and working as hired laborers on the region's commercial farms or working as seasonal laborers elsewhere in the empire.[247]

Nevertheless, Kabardians faced internal land disparities of their own. By the 1880s, the colonial administration had awarded Kabardian nobles, and other Kabardians who rendered significant service to the state, between 2 percent and 3 percent of Kabarda's population, with private landholdings totaling about 17 percent of Kabarda's land.[248] These private lands were equal to nearly half of Kabarda's communal *aul* allotments. Moreover, the nobility, still wielding substantial power in their *auls*, seized portions of the best communal land during the last decades of the nineteenth century, and,[249] during the first decade of the twentieth century, wealthy Kabardian horse and cattle breeders managed to assert their control over the best mountain pastures along the Zolka River.[250] Importantly, many other nobles, unable to adapt to life without free labor, quickly sold off their lands to more prosperous Kabardian elites and settlers from outside the region. Finally, non-Kabardian high-ranking tsarist officers also received large allotments in Kabarda as a reward for their service.[251]

During the debates over the nature of the land reforms in Kabarda, Kodzokov and Loris-Melikov warned that if the Kabardian nobles are allotted private land, many would rush to sell it off and, in so doing, cause their own economic demise.[252] These prophecies came true in the post-reform period. By 1914, about 79 percent of the Kabardian nobility's lands had been sold off to settlers, Russian entrepreneurs, and a small number of more successful nobles who now formed the nucleus of a burgeoning native bourgeoisie.[253] Those who purchased these lands, whether prosperous Kabardian nobles or outside investors, most frequently rented these lands out to peasants from near and far.²⁵⁴ By the 1880s, these private lands, combined with the extensive Cossack lands, became sites of large-scale Russian and Ukrainian peasant migration.²⁵⁵ This would be the first large-scale settlement of Slavic peasants to the region since the construction of the Cossack *stanitsy* and military settlements along the Georgian Military Highway in the 1830s and 1840s.

Between 1880 and 1889, the Slavic population of contemporary Kabardino-Balkaria (Nalchik Okrug and seven surrounding Cossack *stanitsy*) had expanded from around 13,000 to over 20,000. The census of 1897 recorded about 30,000 Russian and Ukrainian settlers, and by the First World War this number had reached 54,000.²⁵⁶ While forming several large villages—Novokonstantinovskoe (1885), Novopoltavskoe (1886), and Baksanskoe (1895)—these Russian and Ukrainian peasants usually established small homesteads (*khutora*), each consisting of about several dozen households from the same region. Settlers rented lands from Kabardian nobles or Cossacks, forming homesteads away from the nearest *aul* or on the outskirts of a *stanitsa*.²⁵⁷ Additionally, groups of religious dissenters also took up residence in Kabarda. Several hundred Molokans lived on a homestead rented from Prince Inaluk Anzorov in Lesser Kabarda near the *aul* of Astemirovo. Baptists resided in a homestead rented from the Atazhukin princes on the River Zolka in Greater Kabarda.²⁵⁸ The *narodnik* artist Mitrofan Alekhin, organizer of the Tolstoyan movement in Nalchik Okrug, established three communes in Kabarda.²⁵⁹ Nalchik, the former fortress and growing regional administrative center, attracted the single greatest number of settlers. By 1900, 3,337 Russians and Ukrainians formed 69 percent of Nalchik's population.²⁶⁰ In addition to Slavic settlers, Nalchik had sizeable populations of mountain Jews, Ossetians, and German colonists.

*Intra*communal conflict was more common than *inter*communal conflict in late imperial Kabarda. In late-tsarist Kabarda, unlike in neighboring parts of the North Caucasus, tensions between the marginalized *inogorodnie* and their more powerful Cossack neighbors were a more common form of social conflict than unrest between Kabardians and Slavic settlers. Rather, with wealthy Kabardian stockbreeders trying to gain private control over the best of the Kabardian communal pastures and neighboring mountaineer peoples expanding their territory to the foothills and plains of Kabarda, Kabardians were more often at odds among themselves and neighboring mountaineer peoples than with settlers from further afield.

Lesser Kabarda experienced waves of immigration during the last decades of tsarist rule. As we have seen, Lesser Kabarda had been a site of near-constant demographic transformations and ethnic mixing since the eighteenth century.

During the peasant migrations of the late imperial period, Lesser Kabarda and particularly the Kurp River Valley, always a zone of cultural-linguistic mixing, became even more heterogeneous, as migrants from near and far settled among the Lesser-Kabardian *auls*. Settlers rented small allotments from the local nobility and the state (former Bekovich-Cherkasskii lands) and crowded onto the scarce arable land along the few rivers and streams of this drought-prone region. Neighboring Ingush and Ossetians, continuing to expand into Kabarda, though on a smaller scale than before, established homesteads on rented land along the right bank of the Kurp and the smaller Kuian rivulet.²⁶¹ Meanwhile, a mix of Russians, Ukrainians, Germans, and Bulgarians established homesteads next to the Kumyks of the Bekovich-Cherkasskii *aul* on lands formerly belonging to these princes.[262]

The relatively amicable relations among natives, *inogorodnie*, and Cossacks in Kabarda stand in stark contrast to the fraught relationship among these groups elsewhere in the North Caucasus. Among Kabarda's Karachai, Ossetian, Ingush, and Chechen neighbors, relations with local Cossack villages remained strained throughout the tsarist period and early years of Soviet power. These tensions between natives and Cossacks resulted from numerous factors: (1) military campaigns and anti-colonial resistance continued in neighboring regions decades after Russia's final conquest of Kabarda; even after the official conclusion of the Caucasus War in 1864, violent rebellions continued to flare up periodically in Chechnya and Ingushetia in particular; (2) unlike the Kabardians, neighboring mountaineer peoples faced extreme land shortages because, despite gaining land at the expense of a declining Kabarda in the late eighteenth and nineteenth centuries, this was not enough to ameliorate these people's historic landlessness, and the administration never conducted land reform in the mountain zone. Moreover, these mountaineer peoples did not experience the type of depopulation witnessed in Kabarda during this period; (3) despite these land shortages and enduring land pressures, in the 1860s and 1870s the colonial administration seized much-needed land from the Chechen and Ingush for Cossack settlement as a way of defending this region from further native rebellions and integrating it into the empire; (4) these newly acquired Cossack lands along the Sunzha River remained a source of violent conflict between Terek Cossacks and Chechen and Ingush mountaineers throughout the late imperial period; (5) finally, in the wake of the great social, economic, and political upheavals caused by decades of war and, especially, the peasant reforms, destitute and declassed former nobles took to banditry and raiding (*abrechestvo*), targeting mainly Cossack *stanitsy* and settler villages.

Conclusions

At the close of tsarist rule, Viceroy Orbeliani's remark of fifty-five years earlier, that "the question of land rights is undoubtedly of the greatest importance in the life of the people,"[263] rang truer than ever. Despite the tsarist administration's efforts to create a system of land tenure that would permanently provide the region's inhabitants with access to land, the number of landless and land-poor mountaineers had only increased in the post-reform era. As in Central Russia and indeed most of the empire, the state's approach to security, based on an ideology of rule that viewed the traditional nobility as the bulwark of the imperial order, impeded the resolution of the peasant question in the North Caucasus. The ascendancy of an approach to land reform, based on the retention of large noble estates prevented an equitable redistribution of the region's land, left large portions of the highland population landless, and left peasants on the plains with inadequate communal allotments. While Kodzokov hoped that the communalization of plains land would solve the land crisis in the region, others in the tsarist administration used this policy more as a means to ease the administrative difficulties of conducting reforms and to obtain complete legal authority to dispose of land at their discretion. Not fully grasping the correlation between the land and security questions, the administration chose an approach to the latter that exacerbated the former. By economically and politically propping up native nobles and elites and neglecting the needs of the region's peasantry, the administration further inflamed conflict within the societies of the North Caucasus.

In addition to supporting the native nobility and other elites, the administration also viewed increased Cossack and Slavic peasant settlement of the region as a means to promote security and imperial integration through Russification.[264] The resultant increase in colonial migration to the North Caucasus created additional land tensions in the region. The resettlement and concentration of Ingush from the Tarskaia valley into crowded *auls* in the Nazran district to make way for new Sunzha Cossack *stanitsy* in the 1860s created an explosive situation whereby neighboring Cossacks, Ossetians, and Ingush competed for land. These tensions would cause some of the fiercest conflicts in the region during the Russian Civil War.[265] While certainly not easing land problems in Nalchik district (Kabarda and the Balkar societies), peasant migration to the plains here did not result in open intercommunal conflict. Rather, tensions remained largely *intra*communal. Slavic *inogorodnie* settlers who rented land from Cossacks demanded greater rights within local village societies; Kabardian shepherds demanded a more equitable share of their communal pastures; and Balkars called for access to farmland within their mountaineer societies. While Kabarda's diverse communities periodically came into conflict with one another over the borders of their land allotments, conflicts remained sharper within (rather than among) these communities. Indeed, the major incidences of peasant unrest and violence in Nalchik district—the Zolka and Cherek uprisings in 1913—saw Kabardian and Balkar peasants take up arms against their own elites. In the Zolka Uprising, poor Kabardian shepherds, with the help of exiled Bolshevik Sergei Kirov, staged an armed occupation of the Zolka pastures after the passage of a law allowing the monopolization of these supposedly communal pastures by wealthy Kabardian horse breeders. In the Cherek Uprising, Balkar peasants fought against the seizure of communal lands by local *taubiis*.[266]

In conducting land reforms, the Caucasus administration attempted to foster greater ethnic homogeneity among the administrative-territorial units of Terek oblast. In its reforms for Lesser Kabarda, for example, the Kodzokov Commission viewed the district's diversity—itself a product of tsarist wartime policies of resettlement—as an inherent cause of its land tensions. These views resulted in the ethnic homogenization of Lesser Kabarda through resettlement, administrative redistricting, and annexations.

But the tsarist administration did not strictly follow the principle of ethno-territorial homogenization in its land reforms. As the examples of Khasaut and Lesken demonstrate, the existence of Karachai and Ossetian *auls* outside of their "native" districts was not a problem for the administration or the residents of these *auls*. Residents of these villages had little to gain and, likely, more to lose moving to their co-ethnics or petitioning for the administration annexation of their *auls* into their "native" districts. Finally, the existence of Balkar exclaves on the Kabardian foothills, provided Balkars moved to lands designated by the state for their settlement, did not lead to serious intercommunal conflict. Rather, the Kabardian-Balkar socioeconomic symbiosis continued to thrive, though in a different form. In the early 1920s, Soviet nationality policies would give new meaning to ethno-territorial borders in this region and lead to a spike in violence, usually on interethnic grounds, not seen since the Caucasus War.

4

From Princely Fiefdoms to Soviet Nations

Border Delimitation, Intercommunal Conflict, and National Identity, 1918–28

At the beginning of the twentieth century, a confluence of crises griped the Russian Empire and shook the foundations of the tsarist autocracy. The peasantry suffered from acute land shortages. The lack of labor laws and the inadequacy of urban social infrastructure led to unrest among the empire's small but fast-growing industrial working class. Once a bulwark of support for the autocracy, the landed gentry were struggling to keep their estates, and they resented the government's policies of attracting foreign investment for industrialization at the expense of the agrarian sector. Nicholas II, a reluctant and ineffectual tsar, was never able to endear himself to the Russian people. The liberal intelligentsia became more aggressive and steadfast in their opposition to the autocracy. Populist parities promoting peasant socialism and employing the use of terror reemerged with a vengeance. Marxist parties, divided between the gradualist Mensheviks and the revolutionary Bolsheviks, saw their support base surge in Russia's industrial centers. Finally, the social problems that accompanied rapid industrialization combined with intensified forms of Russification to increase discontent within, and animosities among, the empire's non-Russian national minorities.

In 1905, the Russo-Japanese War exacerbated these tensions and sparked an abortive empire-wide revolution. The intelligentsia, peasantry, workers, soldiers, and various nationalities rose up, but they failed to coalesce into a unified revolutionary force. Concessions from the tsar, most significantly promises of a constitution and an elective legislative assembly, sapped the revolution of its momentum by late 1905.

Though the national question and ethnic tensions were not the primary causes of the Revolution of 1905, the revolution spread from the striking workers of St. Petersburg to many of the multiethnic peripheries of the empire more quickly than it did to the Russian core. Especially in the borderlands that were relatively industrialized and where there were previously existing national movements, nationalist mobilization heightened social and political conflict during the revolution. The revolutionary upheavals of 1905 became catalysts for new national movements around the empire. Given the ethnically stratified nature of landownership throughout many of the empire's borderlands, rural unrest in these areas often took the form of interethnic conflict.[1]

The North Caucasus, which remained a restive borderland prone to bouts of unrest long after the conclusion of the Caucasian War, witnessed a spike in violence during the 1905 Revolution. Much of this violence took the form of intercommunal land conflict between Cossacks, on the one hand, and Chechens and Ingush, on the other hand.[2] Unlike the South Caucasus, which saw widespread and well-organized revolutionary activity,[3] the North Caucasus, due to its lack of major industrial centers and the relative absence of revolutionary political parties there, did not experience significant political mobilizations during the 1905 Revolution. In the years between 1905 and the outbreak of the First World War, however, social-revolutionary groups became more active in the region,[4] though their influence among the Kabardians and mountaineer peoples, with the exception of the Ossetians, remained negligible.[5]

The Russian Empire needed decades of peace to pursue a path of development that could have averted another revolution. Unfortunately for the Romanov Dynasty, the Russian Army marched off to the slaughter of the First World War in 1914 lacking the industrial base needed to sustain years of total war and with its long-standing social, economic, and political problems unresolved. By February 1917, these brewing tensions boiled over under the weight of two-a-and-half years of war and severe food and fuel shortages in the cities. On International Women's Day, the women textile workers and housewives of Petrograd came out onto the streets to protest bread shortages. This set off a wave of strikes and protests that, within days, led to the loss of government control over the capital and other major cities and, soon thereafter, the abdication of Nicholas II.

After the February Revolution, the Provisional Government, Russia's internationally recognized interim authority composed of liberal Duma deputies and eventually some moderate socialists, coexisted with the Petrograd Soviet, a socialist-led council of workers and soldiers. The Soviet exercised de facto control over the empire's essential infrastructure and the military. By the spring, local soviets had formed in towns and villages throughout the empire. Meanwhile, the Provisional Government saw its support steadily erode due to its refusal to address the people's most pressing concerns: Russia's continued involvement in the First World War and the peasants' landlessness. The Provisional Government put off major reforms until a democratically elected Constituent Assembly could be convened. From April 1917, Vladimir Lenin's Bolsheviks distinguished themselves from the other socialist parties (the Mensheviks and the Socialist Revolutionaries) through their calls for noncooperation with the Provisional Government, the transfer of all state power to the soviets, immediate negotiations for a separate peace, and the redistribution of land to the peasantry. With these policies and the other socialist parties' cooperation with the unpopular Provisional Government, the Bolsheviks went from relative obscurity to become the largest party in the Petrograd Soviet and the soviets of Russia's largest urban centers by late summer. Emboldened by the Bolsheviks' surging support, Lenin began calling for a Bolshevik seizure power in the name of the soviets. On the evening of November 7–8, pro-Bolshevik Red Guards stormed the Winter Palace, the seat of the Provisional Government, and arrested its ministers. Meanwhile, at the Second All-Russian Congress of Soviets, Leon Trotsky, Bolshevik chairman of the Petrograd Soviet, declared the end of the Provisional Government and the formation of the Council of

People's Commissars as the supreme governing authority of the new Russian Soviet Republic. With the overthrow of the Provisional Government and the armed dispersal of the Constituent Assembly in January, Russia descended into years of civil war.

As news of the February Revolution made its way to the North Caucasus, the region's small native intelligentsia began to organize a political movement to represent the interests of the Caucasian mountaineers before the Provisional Government. In May 1917, mountaineer delegates from across the region met in Vladikavkaz and proclaimed the Union of United Mountaineers of the North Caucasus and Dagestan (Soiuz ob'edinennykh gortsev Severnogo Kavkaza i Dagestana). Among the movement's leaders and founding members were the wealthy Kabardian horse breeder Pshemakho Kotsev and the Balkar lawyer and military officer Basiat Shakhanov. Like most of the movements representing the empire's national minorities, the Union of Mountaineers did not call for separation from Russia. Rather, they called for participation in elections to an All-Russian Constituent Assembly and the inclusion of the mountaineer territories as an autonomous administrative unit within a democratic and federal Russian Republic.[6] Many of the leaders of the Union of Mountaineers also served in the region's civil executive committees, which had been created by the Provisional Government as the interim authority's local administrative organs.[7] The Union of Mountaineers divided between secular and Islamist factions, and, by the Second Congress of Mountaineers in August, tensions emerged over the creation of a theocracy in the mountaineer lands.[8] Simultaneously, the Cossack districts of the North Caucasus formed their own administrative organs under a new government of the Terek Cossack Host.[9]

Meanwhile, the Bolsheviks and other social-revolutionary groups slowly began to expand their influence beyond the predominantly Russian working-class strongholds of Vladikavkaz and Groznyi. Party organizers helped to establish soviets of workers, peasants, and soldiers in the larger towns, railroad junctions, and military garrisons of Terek oblast.[10] These local soviets became rival centers of the power to the civil executive committees of the Provisional Government. In response, the district civil executive committees loyal to the Union of Mountaineers attempted to suppress the activities of their Bolshevik party organizers, most of whom were Russian outsiders.[11] Over the course of 1917, the Bolsheviks, initially having only a few party members based in Vladikavkaz, saw their ranks increase in the predominantly Russian towns and urban centers of the Terek region. However, the Bolsheviks would not achieve a base of support among the mountaineers until well into 1918.[12]

With the overthrow of the Provisional Government in November 1917, the fragile stability in the region shattered and simmering social tensions boiled over. In particular, land disputes between Chechens and Ingush, on the one hand, and Cossacks, on the other, and between Ingush and Ossetians communities, led to frequent armed clashes. In response to the collapse of the Provisional Government and the dissolution of its regional and local administrative organs (the civil executive committees), the Union of Mountaineers declared its autonomy and proclaimed the Mountaineer Republic (Gorskaia Respublika) with its capital in Vladikavkaz.[13] With the goals of promoting mountaineer-Cossack intercommunal peace and combating Bolshevik influence, on December 1 the leaders of the Mountaineer Republic signed a union treaty with the leaders of the Terek Cossack Host, forming a unified Terek-Dagestan government.[14] In November and December, the Ataman of the Terek Cossacks Mikhail Karaulov declared martial law in the Terek Cossack *stanitsy* and dispatched units under his command to disband local soviets and Bolshevik party cells.[15] Unsurprisingly, the soviets of the Terek refused to recognize the authority of the Terek-Dagestan government.[16] Ultimately, the coalition government fractured along national lines and animosities between Cossacks and mountaineer communities hampered its effectiveness. Indeed, a rebel faction of Cossacks assassinated Ataman Karaulov in December for his policy of mountaineer-Cossack cooperation. By late December, full-scale civil war had broken out in the Terek region, as violence between Cossacks and mountaineers escalated and Vladikavkaz and the surrounding area descended into chaos. Even more threatening to the survival of Terek-Dagestan government, however, was the breakup of the North Caucasus Wild Division (*Dikaia diviziia*).[17] This battle-hardened cavalry division of the Russian Army formed from among the mountaineer peoples during the First World War had been the only significant armed force loyal to the Union of Mountaineers/Mountaineer Republic.[18]

In early 1918, the Bolsheviks, taking advantage of the weakness of the Terek-Dagestan government, expanded their efforts to establish Soviet power in the region and to win over the mountaineer peasantry, whose allegiances the self-appointed delegates of the Mountaineer Republic did not widely command. The Bolsheviks' support for national self-determination and, perhaps more importantly, the expropriation of privately held land and its redistribution among the peasantry helped them garner mountaineer support. At the First Congress of Soviets of Terek Oblast, held in Mozdok in late January, the delegates formed the Terek Oblast People's Soviet as the chief organ of Soviet power in the region.[19] At the same time, the new Terek Cossack leadership rejected political cooperation with the mountaineers and left the Terek-Dagestan government.[20] This split played into the Bolsheviks' hands. On March 4, at the Second Congress of Soviets of Terek Oblast in Piatigorsk, the delegates officially recognized Russia's Soviet government and declared the formation of the Terek Soviet Republic. On March 18, the pro-Bolshevik forces of the Terek Soviet Republic with the backing of loyal factions of the Terek Cossacks moved into Vladikavkaz and the Terek-Dagestan government fled to Dagestan, from which they would be expelled in May.[21] By May 11, after fleeing across the mountains to Georgia, leaders of the Terek-Dagestan government had reemerged in Ottoman-controlled Batumi, where they declared the independence of the Mountaineer Republic and obtained Ottoman recognition and promises of military aid.[22]

With the Bolsheviks enjoying little support beyond the cities in early 1918, the Terek Soviet Republic was unable to assert its authority throughout the region. At the third Terek People's Congress in April and May 1918, the Bolsheviks won Chechen and Ingush support by backing the deportation of Cossack *stanitsy* and the transfer of their land to mountaineer communities. In response to the deportations, by late summer, the Terek Cossacks with support from some Ossetian and Kabardian factions rose up in revolt and briefly occupied Vladikavkaz.[23] In the fall of 1918, the Ottoman-backed forces of the Mountaineer Republic carved out a small area of influence in the Dagestani town of Temir-Khan-Shura.[24] By early 1919, Soviet rule, already weakened by the Cossack uprising, would fall to a coalition of anti-Bolshevik forces led by General

Anton Denikin's British-backed Volunteer Army. As Denikin's forces moved into the Terek region from the Kuban, they were joined by the Terek Cossacks and other anti-Bolshevik groups. By February, Denikin's forces occupied the entire North Caucasus. Denikin's regime brought the traditional landowning elites back to power across the region, rejected autonomy for the mountaineer peoples, and meted out bloody reprisals against entire mountaineer communities whose members were suspected of harboring Bolsheviks. During this period, many mountaineer groups, including Islamist political factions, sided with the Bolsheviks. They saw cooperation with the Red Army as the best means for liberating the region from Denikin's oppressive regime, having the mountaineers' land needs met, and obtaining religious and cultural autonomy. Bolshevik forces and their allies fled to the mountains, formed partisan bands, and awaited a counteroffensive by the Red Army. The Red counteroffensive came in late 1919 and early 1920. By March 1920, Soviet power had been reestablished across the region. Over the next year, the Civil War in the North Caucasus wound down as Red Army forces put down pockets of anti-Soviet resistance.[25]

Land, Community, and Nation during the Revolution and Civil War

During the revolutions of 1917 and their chaotic aftermath, the peoples of the North Caucasus exhibited little concern for the big political questions of the day, such as Russia's future political system or the possibility of their national independence. The concerns of mountaineers, Kabardians, and *inogorodnie*, like those of Russia's peasantry in general, were firmly rooted in local issues of land rights and village power differentials. By 1918, these local concerns had become part of the larger national struggles of Russia's multiethnic peasantry over land.[26] During the Civil War years, the North Caucasus witnessed some of the war's fiercest fighting, most of which involved land disputes. This chapter examines these land disputes and related border conflicts between Kabardians and their neighbors.

While land disputes had a long and turbulent history coming into the Soviet era, there are important contrasts between the land question before and after the Russian Revolution. In particular, the Bolsheviks' inversion of privileged social and ethnic categories changed the land dynamic in important ways. The social leveling of 1918, culminating in the expropriation of noble landholdings and the equalization of land tenure within communities, meant that remaining social inequalities were more clearly divided along ethnic rather than class lines. The coincidence of this more pronounced "ethnicization" of social structure and the Bolsheviks' introduction of the national principle—the idea that the rights of Russia's peoples should be secured by granting them national autonomy within their own ethno-territorial units—provided new opportunities for land-hungry communities to improve their economic situations. Therefore, in addition to helping to create national communities in places where they had not previously existed, the Bolsheviks' delimitation of national borders provided an opportunity for mountaineer communities to use their socioeconomic status, which they specifically tied to their ethnicity, to convince Soviet officials to redistribute land held by other purportedly "kulak" peoples to their new national territories.

Amid the breakdown of political authority during Russia's Civil War years, land disputes between neighboring villages in the North Caucasus often spiraled into violence. In cases where these disputes involved culturally and linguistically distinct villages, the Bolsheviks' introduction of the national principle and delimitation of ethno-national borders, beginning in 1920, transformed and intensified these disputes into conflicts involving two nations rather than simply villages. Based on the land disputes surrounding Kabarda and its neighbors, I argue, as Peter Sahlins does for the early modern Pyrenees,[27] that the new connections and opportunities created through border delimitation—in this case, opportunities to improve the quality and quantity of land that they controlled—led individuals to identify with national communities. These land disputes also demonstrate what Francine Hirsch calls "double assimilation": "assimilation . . . into nationality categories and, simultaneously, the assimilation of those nationally categorized groups into the Soviet state."[28] By mastering the "ideological literacies" of class and nation, and learning how to "speak Bolshevik" and "speak national," the peasants and shepherds, who wrote petitions and often traveled thousands of miles to plead their cases at central party and state agencies in Moscow, embarked on a process of becoming *active* and *integrated* members of both the Soviet state their nascent national communities.[29]

During this period of revolution and conflict, the symbiotic relationship between Kabardians and Balkars nearly broke down into what would have been a protracted and violent intercommunal conflict over land and borders. In the context of the Soviet-sponsored proliferation of national autonomies in the early 1920s, Balkar ethno-political elites hoped to carve out a separate ethno-territorial autonomous unit for their people. In separating from the Kabardians, the Balkar leadership hoped to secure greater land resources for their perennially land-poor mountaineer people. However, given the interconnectedness of Kabardian and Balkar land tenure and settlement patterns—an interconnectedness that late imperial land reforms had only increased—the prospect of dividing the two peoples presaged a panoply of economic and administrative difficulties for the state and represented a threat to the Kabardians' land interests. Ultimately, Kabardian and Balkar leaders reached a compromise and agreed to share power and land, thus preserving the long-standing symbiotic relations between their communities. In 1922, this compromise resulted in the formation of Kabardino-Balkaria as a unitary ethno-territorial AO for the Kabardian and Balkar peoples, the land resources of which would be the common property of the Kabardino-Balkar people—that is, all citizens of Kabardino-Balkaria.

This chapter examines these issues of intercommunal and class relations, identity formation, and Soviet nationality policies by focusing on four case studies of land and border conflicts involving Kabarda and its neighbors: the Kabardian-Ossetian conflict over Lesken; the Kabardian-Karachai conflict over mountain pastures and the village of Khasaut; Kabardian-Balkar tensions over land and the prospect of the administrative separation of the two peoples into their own autonomous regions; and the confrontations between Kabarda and its neighbors over the territorial jurisdiction of (mainly Russian) settler villages along the Kurp River.

Land Disputes, Border Conflicts, and Nationality in the Central Caucasus

During the Civil War years, the peoples of the Central Caucasus were forced to take sides in the fighting. The indigenous landed nobility reluctantly allied with local Cossack armies in support of the White Army, while most of the region's poor peasantry tacitly supported Soviet power and the Red Army. The peasants and nobles based their decisions on which side offered them the best possibility to gain or retain land. The Bolsheviks, realizing that their base of support, the urban proletariat, was nonexistent outside of Vladikavkaz and Groznyi, obtained the support of the land-hungry native peasantry by promising to carry out (or recognizing already-completed) land redistributions in their favor at the expense of the Cossacks and nobility.[30] In addition to receiving Cossack lands, the mountaineer communities of the Central Caucasus also hoped to receive plains land from their relatively better-off Kabardian neighbors. But the pro-Bolshevik mountaineer leaders could not easily depict Kabardians as anti-Bolshevik colonial oppressors as they could with the Cossacks.

The Bolsheviks kept their promise, carrying out immediate land reforms upon coming to power in Terek oblast in March 1918. Importantly, in May 1918, the Bolsheviks set a precedent by sanctioning the deportation of Cossack *stanitsy* along the Sunzha River to free up territory for landless Ingush.[31] By November 1918, Soviet forces had violently deported three *stanitsy* and redistributed their land to land-poor Ingush. Infighting among ethno-political factions and the resistance of the Terek Cossacks impeded the full implementation of deportations and other land reform policies, and the collapse of the Terek Soviet Republic in early 1919 halted these measures altogether. While some mountaineer peoples, such as the Chechens and Ingush, never fully submitted to White-Army rule, the native peoples that did fall to General Anton Denikin's regime (Kabardians, Balkars, Ossetians) offered the Whites little active support and more frequently joined an anti-Denikin coalition of Bolshevik and Islamist forces in the mountains. By February 1920, these insurgent forces in the North Caucasus staged coordinated attacks coinciding with the advance of the Red Army. By early March, the last of the White forces had fled the Terek region.

Once the Bolsheviks and their local supporters in the North Caucasus had reestablished Soviet power in early 1920, the land-poor mountaineer peoples once again set about the daunting task of solving the land question on the basis of land socialization and equalization. This land reform program translated into the violent expropriation of the estates of nobles and princes (most of whom subsequently emigrated or perished as kulaks under Soviet rule) and the redistribution of their land among the peasantry. The peoples of Terek oblast had already begun the process of expropriating and redistributing private land before Denikin's Whites came to power, but in the areas under White rule the anti-Bolshevik authorities restored the land rights of local nobles. With the Bolshevik victory in early 1920, local soviets quickly reinstated the land reforms of 1918. Apart from the Kabardians, whose nobility held significant land allotments, the communal redistribution of lands was not nearly enough to solve the land hunger facing Karachai, Balkar, Ossetian, and Ingush communities. The native leaders of these communities—usually coming from either the small stratum of semiliterate rural day laborers or Islamic clerics educated in reformist madrasas in Istanbul and Cairo—advocated two additional methods for freeing up land for their land-starved peoples: (1) the deportation of Cossack *stanitsy* and other nonnative settlers and the resettlement of landless mountaineers onto their lands—a practice the Bolsheviks had turned to before and, as Peter Holquist has shown, one they had inherited from tsarist and pan-European "tools of wartime coercion and mobilization" but used "to pursue [their] revolutionary project";[32] and (2) the administrative annexation of territory from Kabarda and limited resettlement of Kabardian villages.[33] This latter idea was not new. However, Soviet categories of "class" and "nation" offered new opportunities for the fulfillment of irredentist claims to the territory of Kabarda.

The Ossetian, Ingush, Karachai, and Balkar representatives began their first in a long series of attempts at ameliorating their people's land problems at the expense of Kabarda in 1918, prior to the White occupation of the region. In March 1918, the Second Congress of the Peoples of the Terek passed the Law on the Socialization of Land, based on the Soviet principle that "every peasant regardless of nationality must have land."[34] In May, the Third Congress of the Peoples of the Terek formed the Emergency Land Commission of the Terek Soviet Republic to oversee the redistribution of land in the region on the basis of "the equalization of national borders."[35] This Land Commission was composed of pro-Soviet mountaineer elites and nonparty land surveyors. In addition to the deportation of the four Cossack *stanitsy* from the Sunzha region, an Emergency Land Commission proposal ratified by the Congress called for "the granting to [landless mountaineers] of lands that they had previously rented from Kabardians." Upon surveying Nalchik district, which over the course of the late imperial period had been generally accepted as the ethno-territorial borders of Kabarda, the Land Commission also called for the redistribution of large swathes of Kabardian areas of this district among Karachai, Balkar, Ossetian, and Ingush peasants. The decisions of the Emergency Land Commission caused great consternation among Kabardian leaders, and during the district-level Congress of Peoples of Nalchik District in August, they unilaterally canceled the decisions of the Land Commission.[36] Nevertheless, by October 1918, of the former privately held land and noble estates of Kabarda, the Emergency Land Commission had temporarily allotted 114,987 acres to Kabarda's neighbors.[37] However, the collapse of Soviet power in the region in early 1919 postponed a determination on the ultimate fate of these lands.

After the reestablishment of the Terek Soviet Republic in April 1920, the land question remained a major concern of local leaders, second only to the security imperatives of mopping up remnants of anti-Bolshevik resistance and eliminating the region's widespread banditry. Indeed, local Soviet officials correctly viewed the unresolved land question as the primary cause of this banditry which usually took the form of cattle and horse thieving and grain requisitions.[38]

Between 1920 and 1924, mountaineer leaders employed history and mass mobilization to turn the delimitation of national borders in their favor. Seeking to convince Soviet officials of the necessity of transferring land from Kabarda to their national territories, they produced histories depicting their people's economic destitution as the result of centuries of Kabardian oppression. Whatever the possibilities of employing ethno-history in the cause of politics, statements openly disparaging a fraternal Soviet people were politically dangerous given Soviet support for proletarian internationalism. Accordingly, most elites writing on Kabarda and the land question in the North-Central Caucasus were careful to apply a class-based, Marxist analysis to their discussions of the region's ethnically stratified socioeconomic structure. They were quick to distinguish between the exploiting class of Kabardian nobles and the Kabardian "working peasantry" (*trudovoe krest'ianstvo*).[39] However, one prominent pro-Soviet mountaineer leader, Umar Aliev, came dangerously close to what Soviet leaders could have easily labeled "bourgeois nationalism" by depicting the Kabardians in general as the historic oppressors of the Karachai people. Beyond the ideological problems of Aliev's approach, Moscow officials viewed his rhetoric as inimical to their goal of ending intercommunal strife in the region, and, consequently, they transferred him out of his native Karachai.[40] Soviet leaders of the mountaineer peoples also mobilized their populations and co-ethnics living within the borders of Kabarda/Nalchik district, rallying them to arms against Kabardians, instructing them to petition Soviet authorities, and using the discourses of nation and class to legitimize claims to lands within Kabarda.

Kabardian leaders responded by producing countermobilizations and counter-histories. They called on residents of all nationalities to submit petitions to central authorities arguing that their village and surrounding lands would be better served as part of a Kabardian national territory. In writing histories, they argued that Kabardians had suffered equally or greater than their mountaineer neighbors under tsarist rule, that the territory of Nalchik district (with the exception of the Balkars' mountain valleys) was the historical national territory of the Kabardian people, and that any significant annexations from that territory would be a violation of the Kabardians' national rights and would lead to Kabarda's economic ruin.[41]

In early 1921 the People's Commissariat of Nationality Affairs (Narkomnats) and the Caucasus Bureau of the Communist Party (*Kavbiuro*) placed Kabardians in a common autonomous republic with their land-poor mountaineer neighbors. The creation of the Mountaineer (*Gorskaia*) Autonomous Soviet Socialist Republic (GASSR) was a product of the geopolitical situation of the time. While the independent Democratic Republic of Georgia still existed, the North Caucasus was one of Soviet Russia's most strategically important and volatile international borders. Policymakers viewed the creation of a large autonomous republic north of the Georgian border as the most effective means of securing this frontier and presenting a united front against anti-Bolshevik forces from the North Caucasus then in exile in Tiflis. This new administrative framework placed Kabarda in a vulnerable position because representatives of Kabarda's landless neighbors dominated the central administration of the GASSR and were now in a position to implement their designs on Kabarda's territory. Swiftly responding to signals that a new round of annexations was about to begin, Kabarda's leaders obtained the support of People's Commissar for Nationalities Affairs Joseph Stalin, who, conveniently, was in a Nalchik sanatorium during the summer of 1921 recovering from an illness,[42] and, under the pretext of "an absence of economic ties between Kabarda and the remaining population of the GSSR," they preemptively announced the separation of Kabarda from the GASSR at the Fourth Congress of Soviets of the Kabardian district on June 13, 1921.[43] With the establishment of Soviet power in Georgia in the spring, the Mountaineer ASSR lost its chief raison d'etre. On September 1, 1921, the All-Russian Central Executive Committee (VTsIK) officially decreed the separation of the Kabardian people from the GASSR and the formation of the Kabardian AO.[44] By cutting off Karachai and Balkaria from the eastern parts of the GASSR (Ossetia, Ingushetia, and Chechnya) Kabarda's secession marked the beginning of the breakup of GASSR into smaller AOs for its constituent nationalities.[45]

Kabarda's separation from the GASSR resulted in the escalation of disputes between the newly formed Kabardian AO and its neighbors (Karachai, the GASSR, and after the dissolution of the later in July 1924, North Ossetia and Ingushetia) over the borders of this new administrative unit. These disputes centered on competing claims to jurisdiction over border villages and their coveted land allotments (pasturage, arable plots, and forests). Having failed to secure much-needed land through political lobbying, mountaineer leaders (with the exception of the Balkars who had secured a political settlement) condoned the use of force as Karachai, Ossetian, and Ingush peasants, backed by local militias, began making armed incursions into Kabarda, seizing pasturage, driving off cattle, stealing horses, raiding and occupying villages, and chasing peasants off their farmland. Kabarda's leaders, Betal Kalmykov and Nazir Katkhanov, responded by mobilizing their populations in defense of their "national" territory and "liberating" occupied villages and their allotments. Three main zones of conflict emerged, each of which corresponded to a contested border with a different community. The conflict along Kabardino-Balkaria's western border with Karachai revolved around rights to mountain pasturage along the Malka River (the trans-Malka pastures) and jurisdiction over the majority-Karachai village of Khasaut. Conflict erupted along Kabardino-Balkaria's eastern border with Ingushetia over small Ingush homesteads and their farmland located on former Bekovich-Cherkasskii land along the Kurp River. Finally, prolonged conflicts raged along Kabardino-Balkaria's southeastern border with North Ossetia around the Lesken and Urukh river valleys.

In a reflection of the "referee" role that the metropole would continue to play in the Soviet period, local leaders declared that only intervention and definitive rulings from Moscow could end these hostilities. Between 1921 and 1924, central and regional Soviet authorities formed eight land commissions charged with delimiting borders and ending the conflicts between Kabardino-Balkaria and its neighbors. Assassinations of expert witnesses, violence and intimidation of villagers by officials from the conflicting sides, and refusals to participate on the part of one of the sides (usually Kabarda) impeded these commissions' efforts.[46] Moreover, different commissions, composed of members of different Soviet state organs, often approached questions of border delimitation with different priorities and principles.[47] Some commissions— notably the one headed by I. I. Smirnov—favored ideological concerns in determining issues of borders and land, while other commissions—the Odintsov Commission, for example—privileged economic and administrative ones. Using the Odintsov Commission's recommendations, on July 21, 1924, the VTsIK passed a definitive decree on the borders of Kabardino-Balkaria, Karachai, North Ossetia, Ingushetia, and Terek governorate (*guberniia*). Nevertheless, disagreements over the interpretation of this decree and other border disputes continued to periodically flare up through 1928.[48]

The Land Question and the (Re)Unification of Kabarda and Balkaria

Among the mountaineers of the North Caucasus at the time of the Russian Revolution, the Balkars faced the greatest land hunger with about half an acre of arable land and hay fields per person. With 10.8 acres per person, the Kabardians of the plains were much better supplied with farmland and pasturage than any of the region's other indigenous communities.[49] Given this disparity, in 1917 the Balkars remained economically dependent upon land in the Kabardian foothills and plains. Balkar leaders Magomed Eneev and Iusuf Nastuev, like those of other mountaineer peoples, viewed Soviet land and nationality policies as an opportunity to ameliorate their people's landlessness at the expense of their larger neighbor, Kabarda.

Immediately after the establishment of Soviet power in the North Caucasus in early March 1918, Balkar representatives petitioned the leadership of the Terek Soviet Republic for additional pasturage, citing the failure of that year's feed crop.[50] The Terek Soviet Emergency Land Commission examined Balkar land needs and allotted Balkar communities 93 pasture plots, totaling 33,880 acres, from the Kabardian pastures for one year.[51] At the local level, the Nalchik district Soviet Land Commission decreed that, given the needs of the Balkars' transhumant stockbreeding economy, it was necessary "to give the laboring Mountaineer-Balkar population temporary use of pastures in the area of the Kabardian communal pastures and forest meadows that the Balkars had rented in 1917."[52] In other words, in accordance with Soviet legislation, the local administration canceled land rents and the Balkars retained access to lands they had historically rented from Kabardians. Some sources claim that Kabardians' use of their mountain pastures had diminished as a result of banditry in the countryside in 1917, and, therefore, the allocation of extra mountain pastures to the Balkars did not affect the Kabardian economy.[53] Increasing disputes over pastures between Kabardians and Balkars during the summer of 1918 belie this assertion. Concerned over the land disputes, Kabardian leaders used the Fourth Congress of the Peoples of Nalchik district, during August 8–12, to protest the temporary land allocations of the Emergency Land Commission by arguing that these land transfers would hurt Kabarda's economy. On August 15, with the Balkar fraction abstaining, the Congress issued an official declaration condemning the temporary transfers and deeming them null and void.[54] For their part, the Balkars sought permanent rights to these lands in the months that followed. On December 6, 1918, the Fifth Congress of the Peoples of the Terek issued a "Resolution on the Agrarian Question," which permanently gave the Balkars 65,837 acres.[55] However, the collapse of Soviet power in the region prevented Soviet authorities from implementing these land reforms.

Soon after the reestablishment of Soviet power in the North Caucasus, the Balkars and neighboring mountaineer peoples renewed their calls for land redistribution. In September 1920, the mountaineer-led Terek regional authorities issued an order calling for the transfer of 18,900 acres to land-poor Balkar families. The District Land Commission gathered 13,656 acres of former privately held land for these families with the possibility of exchanging nonarable land for portions of the allotments of the Kabardian villages Karmovo and Atazhukino-III.[56] This order further strained relations between Kabardians and Balkars.

On January 20, 1921, Kabarda and the Balkar societies joined the newly created Mountaineer ASSR as separate districts: *Kabardinskii okrug* and *Balkarskii okrug*. This development marked the first administrative separation of Kabarda and Balkaria since their incorporation into the tsarist state in the early nineteenth century. Given the ethno-demographic transformations of the late-tsarist period, particularly the intermixing of Kabardian and Balkar lands, it is unsurprising that the borders between the new Kabardian and Balkar districts became a fiercely disputed issue, further exacerbating already-tense land relations between the two communities.

The January 20, 1921, VTsIK decree "On the Formation of the Mountaineer Autonomous Soviet Socialist Republic" did not define the GASSR's internal and external borders with any precision because it envisaged future land redistribution between administrative units according to the needs of individual ethnicities. For example, the decree called for the formation of a Kabardian district from "the northern part of the former Nalchik district," a Balkar district from "the southern part of the former Nalchik district," and a Karachai district from "the western part of the former Nalchik district, the southern part of the Piatigorsk Department, and the southern part of Batalpashinsk department of Kuban oblast."[57] Clearly, much work remained, and, indeed, the conflict-plagued process of border delimitation lasted through 1926.

In January 1921, the VTsIK created a commission chaired by Central Committee member Vladimir Nevskii, the first of many centrally mandated commissions charged with delimiting borders and resolving land disputes in the North Caucasus.[58] In addition to the substantial land requests submitted to the Nevskii Commission on behalf of Kabarda's other neighbors, sources suggest that the Balkar representatives to this Land Commission hoped to enlarge Balkaria's borders by resettling Kabardian villages from the foothills to the plains.[59] Kabardians and local Cossack communities— the latter being threatened with further deportations[60]—protested what they viewed as the committee's extreme approach to the land question. Ultimately, the differences between the two sides (Kabardian/Cossack and mountaineer) paralyzed the Nevskii Commission. The same fate awaited the next commission, chaired by V.S. Muromtsev, sent in late February to solve the land question in the GASSR.[61] In a further escalation of tensions between Kabarda and Balkaria, on April 8 the Kabardian District Executive Committee issued a notice prohibiting Balkars from grazing their cattle on Kabarda's plains pastures and demanding that the Balkars "drive those cattle already being grazed back to the mountains no later than April 15."[62] The Kabardian leadership likely issued this prohibition in retaliation for recent Balkar claims to Kabardian lands. On the same day, the First Congress of Soviets of the Balkar district passed a resolution condemning the prohibition, claiming that

> this order from the Kabardian Executive Committee damns all the mountaineers' cattle to death and creates great material harm not only to Balkaria, but to the state as well. . . . In the worst case the mountaineers will be forced to leave their cattle and flee to the mountains to avoid conflict with the Kabardians.[63]

On May 21, 1921, four months after the creation of the GASSR, the Kabardian District Executive Committee resolved to begin the process of separating from the GASSR as a means of preventing further land grabs by its neighbors.[64]

Despite assurances by Stalin that the separation of Kabarda "would not mean the collapse of the Mountaineer Republic,"[65] it was clear that in losing Kabarda, the GASSR would be geographically separated from two of its remaining constituent ethnicities, the Balkars and Karachais. It was only a matter of time before separation from their administrative center would cause Balkaria and Karachai to break away. Meanwhile, during the summer of 1921, with borders still undefined and central authority far away, Kabardian, Balkar and Karachai peasants clashed repeatedly over contested allotments on the trans-Malka mountain pastures, the nebulous frontier zone so vital to Ermolov's pacification of Kabarda a century earlier.[66] These disputes happened because of misunderstandings (or rejections) of the recent land reform decrees from the Terek government and a general absence of law enforcement, particularly in the mountains. In late July, for example, the shepherds from the neighboring villages of Khabaz (Balkar) and Karmovo (Kabardian) clashed over access to the trans-Malka mountain pastures.[67] Elsewhere, shootouts occurred between Balkars of Ianikoi and Kabardians of Lechinkai over nearby hay fields.[68]

These conflicts arose from Balkars using the lands allotted to them on a temporary basis in 1918 and 1920 and the Kabardian leadership's refusal to continue to recognize these land transfers. The result was a general state of disorder on the mountain pastures, a condition that was only exacerbated by the absence of sufficient law enforcement personnel.[69] Indeed, on August 31, the day before the VTsIK issued its decree formally creating the Kabardian AO, Betal Kalmykov, the head of the Kabardian revolutionary committee (*revkom*) who would ultimately lead Kabardino-Balkaria until 1938, dispatched an interministerial telegram to Moscow requesting that Kabarda retain its prerevolutionary borders as they stood before the Terek government divided up the Kabardian summer pastures.[70] The September 1 decree merely named the villages included within the new Kabardian AO; the final settlement of the disputes over borders depended on intervention from Moscow. In late 1921, Kalmykov telegraphed Kabardino-Balkaria's liaison to the VTsIK, N. Nazarov, that "the Balkar district has raised claims to forests included within the borders of Kabarda and, moreover, the Balkars are using our forest lands and fields, which will bring a material loss to the economic development of Kabarda." Kalmykov requested that Nazarov "immediately petition the Peoples' Commissariats of Nationality Affairs and Internal Affairs to remove these fields and forests from the Balkars' use and to secure Kabarda from future [land] seizures of this kind."[71]

In early December 1921, Muromtsev, the chair of the dissolved VTsIK Land Commission from earlier that year, suggested a solution to at least some of the problems of national border delimitation and land use between Kabarda and its neighbors: the amalgamation of Kabardians and Balkars into a shared AO.[72] This idea was based on several beliefs. First, and probably most important for the Soviet state's long-term goals, was the economic imperative. Given the historic symbiosis between Kabardians and Balkars, especially in terms of interdependent economic relations, the foothills and plains of Kabarda together with the mountains of Balkaria formed an integrated economic system. More than an administrative center, the city of Nalchik formed a common economic center for both Kabardians and Balkars. Muromtsev, therefore, argued that a common administrative unit for the Kabardians and Balkars would promote the economic development of both communities. Second, Muromtsev argued that the creation of a shared AO would promote the more immediate goal of solving land disputes between Kabardians and Balkars. In its role as a "bureaucrat-policeman," the Soviet state prioritized finding a system of administration and land relations that would facilitate the establishment of order out of the chaos of the Civil War. Essentially, the amalgamation of Kabarda and Balkaria could help deescalate the Kabardian-Balkar conflict by lowering the stakes of land redistribution for Kabarda. If the lands at stake, regarded by the Kabardians (or at least their leaders) as their national land, were kept within a Kabardian-majority territorial unit and treated as the common property of all citizens of Kabardino-Balkaria, then the idea of giving up land for the use of land-poor Balkars would seem more palatable to the Kabardian leadership. If nothing else, such an arrangement would incline the Kabardian leadership toward compromise with the Balkars. Indeed, compromise is ultimately what led to a resolution, however temporary, of the Kabardian-Balkar question. On December 7, 1921, after discussing Muromtsev's suggestion, the Kabardian Executive Committee issued a nonbinding decree accepting "the possibility of the unification of Balkaria with Kabarda under conditions than can be determined by the Kabardian oblast and Balkar district congresses of soviets."[73]

With the idea of unifying Kabarda and Balkaria floating around in official circles, on December 9 the Balkar leadership, apprehensive about its ability to secure a favorable land reform settlement within a Kabardian-dominated Kabardino-Balkar AO, sent a memorandum to the Narkomnats requesting the separation of the Balkar district from the GASSR and the formation of a Balkar AO.[74] While its author is unknown, as Artur Kazharov, a specialist on Soviet nation-building in the North Caucasus, avers, someone well versed in Soviet nationalities policy and Marxist-Leninist theory composed this nuanced memorandum, likely a party worker sent from Moscow.[75]

First, this memo argued that the separation of Balkaria from Kabarda during the formation of the GASSR and the Balkars' current desire to form an AO subordinate to Moscow were dictated by the need to solve the land question between Kabarda and Balkaria. Given the seemingly irreconcilable differences between Kabardian and Balkar leaders on this issue, this task was something that could only be accomplished by the intervention of a higher authority. Initially, that authority was the GASSR; however, when Kabarda broke away, it became clear that the GASSR government could no longer secure Balkaria a favorable resolution to the land question. Therefore, the memo argued, Balkaria needed to form an AO, with equal status to that of Kabarda, so that both Kabarda and Balkaria would be directly subordinate to Moscow, the only higher authority with the power to solve the land question. Second, the memo argued that a multiethnic federation of mountaineer peoples, such as the GASSR, could only exist once "national mistrust" had been eliminated and "economic equality" had been attained between its constituent peoples. In order for this equalization to occur, the author continued, it would be necessary to "1) solve the disputed land question between the landless mountain zone and the land-abundant plains; and 2) implement the total sovietization of the mountaineers through development of native schools, government, and courts." Extending this argument to the planned unification of Kabarda and Balkaria, the author contends that, given Kabarda's historic economic and political dominance over Balkaria, which has inhibited the latter's economic and cultural development, the two peoples should not be unified until these disparities had been erased. Third, accepting the premise that Kabarda and Balkaria remain economically intertwined, the author envisaged the creation of a "permanent economic council" to foster the economic cooperation and development of the two peoples. Finally, the author argued that, through its stockbreeding economy, Balkaria had the economic basis for an independent existence.[76] This memorandum clearly piqued the interest of some in Moscow, and, on December 14, the VTsIK formed a commission to study the question of the formation of a Balkar AO.[77]

In the month between the beginning of the Balkar bid for independence from Kabarda and the January 16 VTsIK decree creating a united Kabardino-Balkar AO, both sides lobbied intensely in Moscow. While many of the sources on the negotiations are unavailable, it is possible to reconstruct the general progression of events. While the Balkar representatives, led by Magomet Eneev, continued to lobby in Moscow for the creation of a separate Balkar AO, events next door made the union of the two peoples more likely. On December 17, 1921, the VTsIK decreed the creation of a shared AO for the Karachai and Cherkes (Circassian) peoples immediately to the west of the Kabardian and Balkar lands.[78] This move, guided by the same economic and administrative principles behind the proposed Kabardian-Balkar union, set an important precedent and signaled Moscow's turn toward an official policy of combining smaller ethnicities in the interests of economic development and administrative efficiency. Moreover, on December 29, an article appeared in the regional newspaper, *Gorskaia Pravda*, which, in addition to reporting on the possible union of Kabarda and Balkaria, added that "two representatives had been appointed to the commission for the delimitation of the border of Balkaria and Kabarda."[79]

Negotiations seemed to be underway for a settlement to the border question that would either clear the way for the reunification of the Kabardian and Balkar lands or allow for the creation of a Balkar AO. During the first days of January 1922, the latter seemed to be the most likely, as the VTsIK has issued a draft resolution "On the Formation of an Autonomous Oblast for the Balkar People" that would have allotted to Balkaria much of the disputed pasture land and Balkar villages.[80] While agreeing to many of the resolution's provisions, the Kabardian leadership vociferously objected to three of its provisions: (1) the transfer of the village of Khabaz because of its location far from the Balkar national border; (2) the transfer of Nalchik's resort district of Dolinsk to Balkaria; and (3) the inclusion of forests located on Kabardian lands within the Balkar AO. Finally, this protest note called for the establishment of an authoritative committee to make a determination on the border based on a thorough examination of the territory concerned.[81] Nevertheless, on January 6, the VTsIK approved the decree on the formation of the Balkar AO.[82] Balkar autonomy, however, was short lived. Betal Kalmykov of Kabarda and Muromtsev, the VTsIK representative to the North Caucasus, prevailed upon Stalin to cancel the January 6 VTsIK decree. In addition to the economic and administrative arguments against the separation Kabarda and Balkaria, both Kalmykov and Muromtsev argued that the creation of a separate Balkar

AO would further exacerbate tensions between Kabardians and Balkars because of the interconnected nature of their land use and settlement patterns, and it would make it more difficult to solve the land question.[83] Three days later, on January 9, the Narkomnats drafted a decree canceling the January 6 decree and creating the Kabardino-Balkar AO.[84] On January 16, 1922, the presidium of the VTsIK formally issued the decree "On the Formation of the Kabardino-Balkar Autonomous Oblast."[85]

While this decree ensured that Kabarda and Balkaria would be merged de jure into one administrative unit, de facto this decree remained unimplemented throughout much of 1922. Two of the decree's provisions almost led to a breakdown of Kabardian-Balkar relations and a descent into armed conflict.

The first point of contention stemmed from a provision stating that "the exact borders of the oblast, as well as the borders of Kabarda and Balkaria [within the oblast], would be determined on the ground by a special VTsIK Commission, which will also resolve all land disputes between the sides concerned."[86] This new commission, chaired by I. Dmitriev, surveyed land, visited villages and interviewed villagers about their land use practices from March to May 1922. The commission received numerous petitions from Balkars requesting land within Kabarda. According to reports, the Kabardian side, unhappy with the commission's initial findings, tried to halt the commission's work. For example, in a May 10 telegram complaining about the Kabardian leadership's actions, the Dmitriev Commission reported to Moscow:

> Representatives of Kabarda led by Kalmykov are constantly delaying the commission's work. On the eve of a decision regarding the land disputes . . . they demonstratively left the final general meeting, voicing fears that the commission's rulings will provoke bloodshed; however, we have not issued any ruling or voiced any suggestions. . . . During our field work, Kabardian attempts at resolving land disputes through force of arms in Balkar villages were only stopped through our intervention. We ask that you call the Kabardian leaders to order and hold them responsible for the consequences of their calls to arms among the Kabardian population.[87]

Despite claims from the Kabardian leadership that the Dmitriev Commission's decision would "economically and politically destroy Kabarda,"[88] the sides reached a compromise, and, on June 22, the VTsIK passed a resolution delimiting the borders of Kabarda, Balkaria, and Karachai. Each side had some of its demands met. The Kabardian side granted many, but not all, of the Balkar land requests in exchange for having its northwest border with Karachai delimited so that Kabarda would retain its mountain pastures between the rivers Malka and Kichmalka.[89]

The second impediment to the implementation of the January 16 decree on the creation of the Kabardino-Balkar AO was a provision that called for the retention of separate Kabardian and Balkar Executive Committees and the creation of a "common unified (*obshchii ob"edinennyi*) Kabardino-Balkar Oblast Executive Committee formed on the basis of parity."[90] This provision, a concession to the Balkars, was an effort to create political equality between Kabardians and their numerically smaller Balkar neighbors within a shared administrative unit. Throughout 1922 the Kabardian leadership protested this provision as unfair and unconstitutional. On April 21, Kalmykov telegraphed Moscow arguing that "local conditions do not allow for the implementation of the decree because . . . the rights of the population of Kabarda to representation are being made equal to those of Balkaria whose population is ten times [sic] smaller."[91] Here too, the sides compromised. According to the "Conditions for the Unification of Kabarda and Balkaria," ratified on August 17, 1922, instead of dividing representation equally between Kabarda and Balkaria, representation would be split between Kabardino-Balkaria's three main nationalities: Balkars, Kabardians, and Russians. Moreover, rather than retaining separate nationally defined executive committees at the oblast level, the Kabardian Executive Committee would be replaced by the Kabardino-Balkar Executive Committee, while the Balkar Executive Committee would take on the status of a district (*okruzhnoi*) executive committee.[92] While this compromise led to the formation of a Kabardino-Balkar government based on ethnic parity, this parity was ephemeral. According to the Soviet Constitution, the number of delegates elected to local Congresses of Soviets, which formed the basis for regional executive committees, had to be based on local population size. There was no constitutional provision allowing for representation based on ethnic parity. Therefore, while the first post-unification Congress of Soviets in Kabardino-Balkaria saw the creation of an Executive Committee with fifteen Kabardian, fifteen Balkar, and fifteen Russian representatives, sources indicate that in all future cases, nationalities were represented in local government relative to their share of the population.[93]

The unification of Kabarda and Balkaria by no means solved all the problems between Kabardians and Balkars, and land disputes continued throughout the 1920s as the Soviet administration carried out sweeping land reforms. However, after 1922, when disputes arose, Kabardian and Balkar leaders treated them as land disputes between villages, rather than struggles over rights to national territory. To be sure, for the villagers involved in these disputes the issues at stake were no less important; they involved access to land resources vital to their daily existence. Previously, local ethno-political elites ethnicized these everyday issues in order to gain more land and resources for their territories. After the merger of Kabarda and Balkaria and its attendant compromises, these villagers were unable to effectively utilize the national principle and gain institutional supports to help them press their claims. Kabardian and Balkar political elites now had little to gain by calling their co-ethnics to arms, so they worked together to solve land disputes on the basis of Soviet economic-administrative principles, rather than national ones. On the other hand, Kabardian and Balkar leaders did invoke the national principle to defend the borders of Kabardino-Balkaria from annexations by neighboring ethno-national administrative units. For example, in 1927, Kabardian and Balkar representatives successfully worked together and mobilized villagers to prevent Balkar pastures along the Khaznidon River from being incorporated into the North Ossetian AO.[94]

In forming a shared national territory for the Kabardian and Balkar peoples, most of those involved—from central Soviet officials to many local native elites to Kabardian and Balkar shepherds—recognized to one degree or another the symbiosis that had developed between Kabardians and Balkars over the centuries. However unequal their relations, Kabardians and Balkars had become interdependent stakeholders in the local system of intercommunal relations based on economic complementarity, and the costs of dismantling this system appeared too high. Since the 1990s, the land imbalance between Kabardians and Balkars has led to renewed tensions and calls for separation on the part of the leaders of the Balkar national movement. However, once again, the risks involved in such a separation—intercommunal violence, economic decline, and regional destabilizaition—as perceived by local stakeholders and central authorities, have thus far prevented the breakup of Kabardino-Balkaria.

Kabardians and the Cossacks and Settlers of the Terek: Unlikely Allies

Kabardians, *inogorodnie* settlers, and Cossacks—communities with histories of mutual animosity and, sometimes, cooperation—were under threat of losing land to neighboring mountaineer communities. As part of their strategies to avoid losing land, Cossack and Kabardian leaders sought to foster and take advantage of the idea of close Kabardian-Cossack-settler relations. In promoting the idea of Kabardian-settler (whether Cossack or *inogorodnie*) friendship, the leaders of Kabarda hoped that the "bureaucrat-policeman state," with its great concern for maintaining order, would see the advantages of leaving areas of Cossack and *inogorodnie* settlement under Kabardian jurisdiction. The alternative would be placing them under the jurisdiction of mountaineer peoples with whom, according to Kabardian leaders and their Cossack and settler allies, they had troubled relations.

In confronting the rapid changes brought on by tsarist and, later, Soviet rule, the region's peoples, native and settler alike, faced choices that were more complex than those allowed by the master narratives of "friendship of peoples" and "genocidal conquest" that have dominated discourse on the North Caucasus in Russia and the West, respectively.[95] The decision taken by most of the Kabardian nobles to submit to tsarist rule in the 1820s was dictated both by their much-weakened position and by their desire to preserve some of their privileges as native elites. Whatever the cause, Kabardian elites chose sides with a heavy heart. A century later, Cossacks of the North Caucasus faced similarly difficult choices, as pro-Bolshevik native elites, touting Soviet support for national self-determination and the liberation of oppressed colonial peoples, began a process of decolonization—a process initially supported by the Bolsheviks for pragmatic and ideological reasons and one that threatened the Cossacks' economic status. The Terek Cossacks, as the former privileged colonial community, would have preferred to retain a separate autonomous status rather than be incorporated into neighboring national districts of Caucasian peoples. The choice of many Cossacks to take up arms against Soviet power was a natural response to threats upon their lives and property. In these conditions, cooperation with Kabarda, once an enemy of the Cossacks and a target of their colonization, appeared as a last hope for the Cossacks to retain some of their land. Seen in utilitarian terms, the behavior of Kabarda's nobles and the Cossacks during their respective periods of crisis is understandable—their choices were dictated by a desire to retain their land and to survive.

The *inogorodnie*—a diverse contingent of peasants who resettled to the North Caucasus during the late imperial period—found themselves in a particularly precarious position both in the late-tsarist period and during the revolution and Civil War years. Forced from their homelands by landlessness, these families sought respite in the far-off and unfamiliar North Caucasus, a region facing its own "land question." While managing to establish small homesteads on rented land, these settlers did not enjoy the rights of permanent residents, and were scorned by Cossacks and mountaineers alike.[96] When regional tensions exploded into violent conflict in 1918, the settlers were caught in the crossfire between Cossacks and mountaineers. Settlers, such as the Germans of Gnadenburg and the Russians of Raz'dolnoe, had no allegiances and no historic grievances, yet they were among the hardest hit by the violence of the Civil War in the North Caucasus.

A Draw Toward Kabarda, a Draw Toward Russia: Kabardians, Russians, and Cossacks

As we have seen, in early 1921, motivated mainly by geopolitical concerns, the Soviet leadership placed Kabarda in a common autonomous republic (the GASSR) with its mountaineer neighbors. By the summer of 1921, Kabarda began the process of breaking away from the GASSR to avert further land transfer to their neighbors. While the main reason for Kabarda's separation from the GASSR was the threat of further land grabs, the Kabardian leadership understood that Moscow would not sympathize with such an argument. Instead, Kabarda's leaders argued that Kabarda had "an economic draw [*tiagotenie*] toward neighboring Russian regions because it was through them that [European] culture had come to Kabarda."[97] In a display of Kabardian-Russian unity at the Fourth Congress of Soviets, a representative of Kabarda's Russian population declared, "We see that both the Kabardian and Russian people share the same point of view on this question and the same desire."[98] On 1 September 1921, the VTsIK officially decreed the Kabardian AO.[99]

The Terek Cossacks' initial response to being included in GASSR was similar to the Kabardians'; they sought greater autonomy. After the restoration of Soviet power in 1920, the regional authorities incorporated the Terek Cossack *stanitsy* along the Georgian Military Highway into the national districts of the surrounding Kabardian and Ossetian populations. On March 5, 1921, the Terek Cossacks called a congress in the *stanitsa* Sleptsovskaia and voiced the idea of forming an autonomous Cossack territory. On March 18, the Congress of the People of the Terek Line decreed the formation of a Cossack District Executive Committee centered in Groznyi with jurisdiction over seven *stanitsy*, three homesteads, and one settlement. In this way the Terek Cossacks hoped to end their subordination to mountaineer administrations and prevent further land annexations and deportations. On May 7, the mountaineer-led presidium of the Soviet of People's Commissars of the GASSR issued a decree forbidding the formation of a Cossack district in the republic.[100] On May 21, the Cossack Executive Committee protested that decision and appealed to Moscow, declaring that "the transfer of the *stanitsy* of the Terek Line to the national [mountaineer] executive committees is a violation of minority rights."[101] Ultimately,

Moscow upheld the GASSR leadership's decision to incorporate the Cossack *stanitsy* into the surrounding national districts.

Having failed to secure a district of their own, the Terek Cossacks of the Georgian Military Highway sought incorporation into Kabarda rather than Ossetia or Ingushetia. Realizing that they both sought to preserve what they regarded as their people's land from annexation by neighboring communities, Kabardian and Cossack leaders found common cause. The Kabardian leadership was happy to incorporate Cossack lands into the borders of Kabarda during a time when it was losing land to neighboring peoples. For their part, the Terek Cossacks viewed Kabarda as the lesser of multiple evils. Kabarda, seeking to preserve its own lands and being relatively well supplied with land to begin with, did not represent a threat to the Cossacks. The first of multiple petitions by Terek Cossacks requesting incorporation into Kabarda came from the *stanitsa* Aleksandrovskaia in January 1921. During the creation of the GASSR in early 1921, the Ossetian leadership hoped to annex all of the Cossack *stanitsy* of the former Sunzha department to Ossetia, including the three *stanitsy* along the Kabardian portion of the Georgian Military Highway, Aleksandrovskaia, Kotliarevskaia, and Prishibskaia.[102] Confronted by Ossetian raids and the prospect of ceding land to Ossetian peasants since early 1920,[103] Aleksandrovskaia unsurprisingly protested Ossetia's plans for its incorporation into the Ossetian Vladikavkaz district. Citing the long-standing social and economic ties between their *stanitsa* and the neighboring Kabardian villages and the distance to the Ossetian capital, Vladikavkaz, the Cossacks of Aleksandrovskaia and the remaining two *stanitsy* succeeded in their goal of being annexed into neighboring Kabarda rather than land-poor Ossetia. By joining the Kabardino-Balkar AO, the Cossacks of these *stanitsy* were able to retain their land and avoid further violent conflict with Ossetia.

Attempts at incorporation into Kabarda by other Cossack *stanitsy* on the borders of Kabardian settlement, such as Zmeiskaia and Soldatskaia, did not meet with the same success as the three *stanitsy* within Kabarda. On March 15, 1923, a meeting of the Zmeiskaia village assembly petitioned to separate from the Digora-Ossetian Okrug of the GASSR and join the neighboring Kabardino-Balkar AO. With the *stanitsa's* northern and western edges bordering Kabarda, the petitioners cited their geographic proximity to Kabarda and "most lively economic relations with [Kabardian] villages."[104] However, it was the Cossacks' grievances with the GASSR that provided the greatest motivation for incorporation into Kabarda. In addition to complaints about excessive taxation and requisitions and the inability of local authorities to protect villagers from raiding, the land question was a key factor in Zmeiskaia's decision to separate. The Cossack petitioners complained:

> In terms of the land question, the local Digora officials treat the *stanitsa* Zmeiskaia with complete arbitrariness despite the latter's acute land shortage. For example, 1) the annexation of 2,990 desiatins [8,073 acres] [from Zmeiskaia's allotment] which has remained mostly unworked for the last two years; 2) the forced, illegal settlement onto the *stanitsy* of 60 Ossetian families; 3) the grazing of cattle on our lands by Ossetian militiamen with the permission of Digora authorities, destroying our meadows and fields.[105]

In response to this petition, the GASSR Executive Committee argued to Moscow that "as a land-rich Cossack society,"[106] Zmeiskaia's petition for incorporation into Kabarda "has no basis, except for the Cossacks' desire to retain their lands, which during socialist land reforms would likely be subject to redistribution anyway."[107] In addition, the GASSR denied the existence of close economic ties between Zmeiskaia and Kabarda, claiming instead that geographically and economically Zmeiskaia was tied to Ossetia.[108]

In August 1923, after studying conditions on the ground, the Smirnov Land Commission, tasked by the VTsIK with resolving land disputes between Kabarda and its neighbors, sent its recommendations regarding Zmeiskaia to Moscow. The Smirnov Commission based its ruling on geographic and economic factors. Siding with the GASSR, the commission determined that the *stanitsa* is geographically and economically connected more closely with Ossetia than Kabarda and that incorporation into Kabarda would pose administrative and economic problems for Ossetia.[109] While the lands around Zmeiskaia may have once been thoroughly Kabardian, after over a century of resettlement and war, by the early twentieth century, Zmeiskaia, though located on the Ossetian-Kabardian frontier, was within the socioeconomic orbit of Ossetia rather than Kabarda. Thus, neither national nor economic arguments could save Zmeiskaia from sharing its land with its Ossetian neighbors.

The Embattled Villages of Lesser Kabarda

In delimiting the borders of national oblasts and republics, Soviet officials, depending on their background and institutional affiliation, weighed ethnographic, ideological, economic, and administrative concerns.[110] Sent to the North Caucasus in 1923, the Smirnov Commission approached questions of land reform and borders from a purely ideological perspective, privileging class concerns in its recommendations. Given the ethnically stratified social structure of the Central Caucasus between land-poor mountaineers and relatively land-rich Kabardians and Cossacks after the expropriation of local tsarist-era elites, and his agenda of social equalization, Smirnov was especially receptive to Ossetian, Ingush, and Karachai claims to Kabardian and Cossacks lands. Among other land transfers, the Smirnov Commission tentatively approved GASSR requests for the transfer of most of the remaining land of Lesser Kabarda to Ossetia and Ingushetia. Smirnov's plan, which was based on an equalization of land holdings between Kabardians and their mountaineer neighbors, called for all of Lesser Kabarda outside of the official village allotments of the region's nine Kabardian villages to be transferred to landless Ossetians and Ingush.[111]

The lands set for transfer to the GASSR included a diverse mix of settler villages on the lands of former Kabardian nobles of the Kurp region, south of Mozdok on the right bank of the Terek and east of the left bank of the Kurp River: the Kumyk village Kizliarskoe (the former Bekovich-Cherkasskii *aul*); the German colony Gnadenburg; and the mixed Ukrainian, Russian, and Bulgarian village Razdol'noe and homestead Sukhotskii. Given their location on the unprotected plains of the tumultuous borderland between the Cossacks (to north), Chechens (to the east), Ingush and Ossetians (to the south), and Kabardians (to the west), these *inogorodnie* villagers suffered greatly during the fighting of the Civil War and the mountaineer raiding that followed. As part of Lesser Kabarda during the late imperial period, these villages remained under the same jurisdiction as the rest of Lesser Kabarda after 1917.

When news reached these villages of their impending transfer to the administrative jurisdiction of the Ingush Okrug of the GASSR, each village quickly sent petitions to Moscow protesting this transfer. The heads of the local village soviets requested that they remain within the Kabardino-Balkar AO, citing the history of conflict between their village and neighboring Ingush populations, unsanctioned Ingush land seizures, and the inability of the GASSR to protect them from raids. The petitioners claimed that they had "always had good neighborly relations with Kabardians."[112] The Kabardino-Balkar leadership also protested against the transfer of these villages, along with large swathes of land elsewhere, and supported the villages' petitions to remain within the Kabardino-Balkar AO. The GASSR leadership took measures to convince the villagers to end their protests and accept their new administrative jurisdiction. For example, in a letter to the residents of Gnadenburg German colony, the head of the Council of Peoples Commissars of the GASSR, Sakhandzherei Mamsurov, addressed the villagers' concerns. Mamsurov assured the Gnadenburgers that the GASSR was now able to ensure their protection from raiding by Ingush bands; he also promised that the GASSR would not take their land; and he promised them administrative autonomy within the GASSR.[113] Mamsurov also tried to assuage the Gnadenburgers by arguing that the GASSR was better able to provide for the economic and cultural development of its citizens than Kabardino-Balkaria.[114]

In this competition for the allegiances of this culturally, linguistically, and religiously diverse cluster of villages, actions spoke louder than words. Whereas the villages had not faced conflict from their Kabardian neighbors, the relations between the settlers of Kurp region and the Cossacks to the north remained tense, and, more importantly, the villagers lived in fear of Ingush and other mountaineers to the south and east. Despite promises of protection by the mountaineer government, the villagers had been on the receiving end of many mountaineer raids, especially since the breakdown of order in 1917, and were naturally skeptical of the GASSR's ability to ensure their security. With the final breakup of the GASSR into the Ingush and North Ossetian AOs and the Sunzha (Cossack) Okrug in the summer of 1924, Moscow sent yet another commission to the North Caucasus to reexamine administrative borders in the region. This presented a new opportunity for Kabarda to regain some of the land that it had given up under the recommendations of the Smirnov Commission a year earlier; it also presented an opportunity for villagers unhappy with their administrative jurisdiction, like those of Kizliarskoe, Gnadenburg, and Razdol'noe of the Kurp region, to repetition for the administrative-territorial transfer of their villages. The chair of this new commission, S. Odintsov of the People's Commissariat of Land (*Narkomzem*), disagreed with the approach taken by the Bolshevik Smirnov during the previous Land Commission. Odintsov criticized the work of the Smirnov Commission for being too ideological and disregarding economic concerns. Therefore, while Smirnov recommended granting any and all Kabardian lands that Ossetians and Ingush had ever owned or rented, however briefly, to the GASSR to alleviate the mountaineers' landlessness, Odintsov considered how transferring a particular allotment would affect the economies of the two oblasts.

While Kabarda's neighbors still retained many of the allotments transferred to them under the rulings of the Smirnov Commission, Odintsov made significant changes to the border in favor of Kabarda and ruled out further deportations of Cossacks from the mountaineer regions of the North Caucasus.[115]

In terms of the Kurp villages of Kizliarskoe, Gnadenburg, and Razdol'noe, Odintsov recommended their reincorporation into Kabarda on the basis of national rights and economic development. In his concluding report from July 8, 1924, Odintsov explains:

> I cannot agree with the Smirnov Commission's transfer of all the settlements along the [right bank of the] Terek to the control of the GSSR first of all because this contradicts the will of the population, which categorically protests against this transfer. Regarding the village Bekovichi (Kizliarskoe) in particular, whose Kumyk population does not wish to transfer to the administrative jurisdiction of the GSSR, this would be a violation of the rights of a national minority.[116]

Moreover, Odintsov determined that transferring these settler villages would be economically damaging to both Kabarda and the villages. In determining the borders of the Kurp region, Odintsov based his determinations on economic expediency and the national principle. Odinstov only sanctioned the transfer to the GASSR of several small Ingush homesteads immediately bordering the GASSR's Ingush district, ruling that "all of the villages above the Terek [i.e., Kizliarskoe, Gnadenburg, Razdol'noe, and Sukhotskii] remain within the administrative jurisdiction of the Kabardino-Balkar AO and retain necessary land allotments according to local conditions."[117]

The relatively peaceful and symbiotic relations that developed among Balkars, Kabardians, Cossacks, and other settlers over the *longue durée* of Russian rule meant that, during the Russian Civil War and the establishment of Soviet power, relative peace reigned in Kabarda. By contrast, given the absence of symbiotic relations elsewhere in the region, ethnicized warfare, fueled by land disputes and colonial animosities, raged along its borders, periodically spilling over into Kabarda. To be sure, cultural animosities and misunderstandings fueled sporadic conflicts between Kabardians and Cossacks. However, these conflicts usually occurred between Kabardians and Cossacks or Russian populations outside the borders of Kabarda, for example when Kabardians, poorly conversant in Russian, would travel to Russian market towns to sell cattle or purchase essential goods.[118] The historic colonial-era legacies that contributed to the relative intercommunal peace in Kabarda in the 1920s lasted through the Soviet period.

The Struggle for Lesken: 1920–6

The conflict between Kabarda and North Ossetia over the status of the village of Lesken (Khaevo) stands out as one of the most divisive and enduring disputes of this period of irredentist strife. The six-year conflict over this Ossetian village located within the historic borders of Kabarda witnessed political mobilization among its polarized residents, armed clashes, persecution of villagers, and mass arrests. The land and border conflicts in Lesken provides important insights into the role of nationality in the North Caucasus and the effects of Soviet nation-building and social engineering.

During the revolution and Civil War years, Lesken remained within the borders of Kabarda as part of Nalchik Okrug. Indeed, most of Lesken's Ossetian peasants fought alongside their Kabardian and Balkar neighbors against Denikin's White Army and their local supporters, the Kabardian military aristocracy, during the Red counteroffensive in late 1919 and early 1920.[119] The unity of the people of Lesken in their struggle against White rule belied deep socioeconomic divisions within the village. In May 1920, shortly after the Red Army restored Soviet power, the poorer residents of the upper quarter successfully used the recently introduced principle of national autonomy and the emerging territorial disputes to their advantage. The residents of upper Lesken banded together and successfully petitioned the Terek oblast government to transfer Lesken to the jurisdiction of their titular nation: "Ossetia." By transferring to Ossetian jurisdiction Lesken's landless upper-quarter residents hoped to be rewarded for their support by the Ossetian administration during land redistribution. On January 2, 1921, the residents of Lesken's lower quarter, realizing that a shift to Ossetian jurisdiction meant their loss of power within the village, banded together and petitioned for (re)incorporation into the Nalchik (Kabardian) district.[120] This marked the beginning of a seemingly irreconcilable division of Lesken between supporters of Kabarda (the lower quarter) and supporters of North Ossetia (the upper quarter). This also marked the transformation of the village's internal power struggle into a border war between two North Caucasian autonomous territories.

Officially, the lower-quarter supporters based their "draw toward Kabarda" (*tiagotenie k Kabarde*) on economic and geographic ties.[121] First, they argued that the proximity and accessibility of Nalchik (Kabarda's administrative center) compared to Vladikavkaz (North Ossetia's center) made Kabardino-Balkaria better able to administer and develop Lesken. Second, having lived in Lesken for forty-five to fifty years, they claimed that important economic and familial ties had developed between Kabardians and the Ossetians of Lesken; whereas, the GASSR (i.e., North Ossetia) had "not done anything positive" for Lesken.[122] Unofficially, questions of power and village feuds provided much greater motivation for each side in the dispute. A September 1923 report from Smirnov's VTsIK Commission enumerated the following unofficial motives for some villagers' support of Kabarda: (1) that the GASSR could "in no way allot them with the amount of land they hoped to receive from the K[abardino-Balkar autonomous] oblast"; (2) that many of the "older industrious, kulak residents of Lesken had established strong economic ties [with Kabarda] in the form of homes in Nalchik"; (3) that the Karaev family, representing sixty households in the lower quarter, had blood enemies (*krovniki*) in the upper quarter; and (4) that many were drawn to Muslim Kabardians as their co-religionists, while most Ossetians were Orthodox. According to the Smirnov Commission report, this final religious motive was "the most important and extremely serious."[123] In addition to these motives was the equally important question of village land use. Lesken's original settlers, the residents of the lower quarter, did not want the village's best allotments to the north, land that they had brought under the plow half a century earlier, redistributed among the upper quarter's recent arrivals. This was a much thornier issue for the lower Leskenites to maneuver given the Soviet state's support for land equalization and class war in the village.

The motives of North Ossetia's supporters were more transparent and, ultimately, more amenable to Soviet ideology. The upper-quarter residents argued that the struggle between the upper and lower quarters was a clear-cut case of class war.[124] They argued that the supporters of Kabarda were former White Army supporters and representatives of the exploiting classes—Kulaks and members of the Muslim clergy—who had brainwashed other villagers into following them. In addition to describing numerous cases of exploitation of the Lesken poor by leaders of the lower quarter, in one of their many appeals to Moscow, the upper Lesken petitioners provided brief biographical sketches of thirty-six leaders of the lower quarter. The petitioners described these "class enemies" of the Lesken poor as "former landowners and speculators," "horse and cattle thieves," "tax evaders," "rich mullahs," and "former tsarist administrators."[125] The land-starved residents of upper Lesken demanded the immediate and equal redistribution of Lesken's entire land allotment and, citing Soviet-supported principles of national self-determination, the right to join with their co-ethnics as part of an autonomous North Ossetia.[126] While the land question was the primary factor driving the residents of upper Lesken to insist upon inclusion within North Ossetia, there is no reason to doubt the sincerity of the national component of their argument. Unlike the residents of the lower quarter, in the years before and after 1917, the recent immigrants to Lesken's upper quarter maintained close ties and continued to identify with their homeland of Digora in North Ossetia.[127]

Kabardino-Balkaria's leaders initiated attempts to reincorporate Lesken into their jurisdiction after the VTsIK issued a decree on November 2, 1922, stating that the Kabardino-Balkar AO was "to be left within its existing borders."[128] This decree was a victory for Kabarda because it represented a rejection by the central authorities of further demands by the GASSR (Ingushetia and North Ossetia) to large amounts of territory in Lesser Kabarda. However, the ambiguity of the decree's phrasing also created an opportunity for Kabardian officials to undo what they perceived as past injustices by reclaiming lands recently incorporated into neighboring autonomous regions. Kabardian leaders interpreted Kabarda's "existing borders" to mean the borders of the former Nalchik district. This interpretation allowed Kabardian leaders to reclaim villages, such as Lesken, that were formerly under Kabardian jurisdiction but not listed on the September 1, 1921 decree, "On the Separation of Kabarda from the GASSR."[129] The leaders of the GASSR, on the other hand, interpreted "existing borders" to mean precisely those borders formed by the villages listed in the September 1 decree. Kabarda's representatives retorted that the September 1 decree, rather than specifying new borders of Kabarda, separated the Kabardian district from the GASSR and elevated it to the status of an AO. Since the Kabardian and Balkar districts were officially formed out of the northern and southern halves of tsarist-era Nalchik district, the Kabardino-Balkar AO should, they argued, be understood as the former Nalchik district. As usual Moscow formed several committees to examine this dispute and clarify the borders. Ultimately, the conflicts hinged on a clarification from Moscow—the imperial referee—over the exact meaning of Kabardino-Balkaria's "existing borders."[130]

While these commissions slowly went about their work, the situation in Lesken heated up as Kabardino-Balkaria's leaders set about forcibly (re)establishing control over the border villages. On March 20, 1923, the Kabardino-Balkar Central Executive Committee (TsIK) issued "Order Number 24," officially declaring Lesken's administrative subordination to Kabardino-Balkaria's Urvan district. The next day Urvan District Executive Committee ordered the heads of the Lesken and Novyi Urukh village executive committees and their secretaries to assemble for "the removal of [GASSR] administrative documents and the dissemination of official directives."[131] In late March, the Kabardino-Balkar TsIK, anticipating resistance from supporters of the GASSR, sent in armed squadrons to Lesken and installed a new revolutionary committee in the village, forming a local governing authority that was subordinated to the authority of Kabardino-Balkaria. This marked the beginning of an anarchic period of dual power in Lesken during which two *revkoms*, one loyal to the KBAO and the other loyal to the GASSR (later North Ossetia), existed simultaneously in different quarters of the village. It remained unclear for many villagers to which *revkom* they should answer. Local supporters of Kabardino-Balkaria rallied around the *revkom* in the lower quarter, while supporters of North Ossetia rallied around the *revkom* in the upper quarter.

On August 17, 1923, the GASSR sent in a militia force to back up its claims over the village. According to reports from lower-quarter supporters of Kabarda, the GASSR militia, having temporarily expelled Kabarda's forces, surrounded the village and arrested and interrogated supporters of Kabarda who had not fled with the Kabardino-Balkar militia to neighboring Kabardian villages.[132] This clash initiated a pattern of sporadic fighting between the two armed camps, each side enjoying only temporary victories and suffering significant casualties. Central and regional authorities initially proved incapable of halting the conflict. In a secret-police report from September 22 to the second deputy chairman of the GPU, Genrikh Iagoda, the GPU's plenipotentiary for the South-East of Russia and the North Caucasus, I. Andreev, declared:

> Clashes have occurred between Kabarda and the Mountaineer Republic over the unresolved question of Lesken. There are casualties on both sides. The situation has become extremely tense. The South-East [Party] Bureau and I are taking measures [to stabilize the situation], but to no avail. Local powers are acting independently. ... Urgent actions from Moscow are needed.[133]

This anarchic situation in which attacks and counterattacks shifted power between the two sides continued until October 9, when, after suffering losses to the Urvan district militia and the Kabardino-Balkar NKVD, the GASSR reestablished its *revkom* in the village.[134] At this point, each side seems to have tacitly agreed to a temporary solution: a divided village. Between October 1923 and June 1925, two local governments in the form of *revkoms* existed in Lesken—one, in the lower quarter, wielded authority on behalf of Kabardino-Balkaria and another, in the upper quarter, governed on behalf of the GASSR/North Ossetia.[135]

While confrontations and clashes periodically occurred during this period of dual power, the two sides now sought more with words than guns. In addition to promising land to their supporters, representatives of Kabardino-Balkaria and North Ossetia sought to intimidate villagers into recognizing their power. For example, villagers' accounts describe how in 1923 government representatives from Kabardino-Balkaria threatened North Ossetia's supporters with deportation if they did not switch sides in the conflict.[136] The two village factions sent delegations to Rostov-on-Don and Moscow to lobby and argue their cases before regional and central authorities.[137] Meanwhile, the leaders of Kabardino-Balkaria and North Ossetia tried to influence the findings of commissions sent to make recommendations on Lesken and other land disputes. These tactics led to a series of contradictory decrees issued at different levels of the Soviet state apparatus. On September 14, 1923, regional party secretary Nikolai Gikalo issued a decree calling for the GASSR to disperse its *revkom* and for Lesken to be temporarily placed under Kabardino-Balkar jurisdiction. On June 21, 1924, the VTsIK decreed the permanent transfer of Lesken and its land to North Ossetia. After protesting this decree, Kabardino-Balkaria's leaders and their local supporters modified their demands and petitioned for the permanent division of Lesken between the two AOs, with the lower quarter's land allotment going to Kabardino-Balkaria. Responding to these new demands and doubting the efficacy of transferring control of Lesken entirely to North Ossetia, on October 21 the VTsIK ordered the North Caucasus Regional Executive Committee (*Kraiispolkom*) to form a commission "to examine the possibility of administratively delimiting Lesken in accordance with the desire of one or the other side." Citing the recommendations of this commission, on November 27, 1924, the North Caucasus *Kraiispolkom* divided Lesken into two parts "given the impossibility of normal cohabitation of both parts of ... Lesken within the North Ossetian AO."[138] Receiving approval at various levels of the Soviet administrative hierarchy, this latest decree initially seemed to be a permanent solution to the Lesken question. Then, unexpectedly, on February 23, 1925, the VTsIK issued a new decree cancelling all previous decrees on Lesken, transferring the village permanently back to North Ossetia, calling for immediate land reform in the village, and promising land to those who wished to resettle in Kabardino-Balkaria.[139]

Despite this latest decree of February 23, the residents of the lower quarter disregarded the directives from Moscow, retained their *revkom*, and divided their coveted land allotment exclusively among lower-quarter supporters of Kabarda. This move provoked a new round of clashes between the upper and lower quarters. With spring planting season well underway, in early May the residents of the upper quarter invaded the lower quarter's fields with hoes and plows in an attempt to forcibly implement the decree.[140] On May 15, the VTsIK, losing patience with the Lesken question, gave the North Caucasus regional authorities free reign to reexamine the question and ordered them to put an end to the Lesken question once and for all.[141] The North Caucasus *Kraiispolkom* responded vigorously to these fresh clashes. On May 28, the regional authorities confirmed the irrevocability of the February 23 decree and called for the following measures: (1) the February 23 decree was to be read aloud at a village assembly meeting by a member of the North Ossetian Central Executive Committee and the two quarters commanded to stop all conflicts over the question; (2) the GPU was ordered to arrest the "most malicious leaders who instigate the population against North Ossetia"; (3) the two *revkoms* were to be immediately disbanded and elections to a new village Soviet were to be held; (4) land redistribution was to be carried out by a special commission; (5) all villagers were ordered to not encumber efforts by lower quarters residents to resettle in Kabardino-Balkaria; (6) finally, all of these measures were to be carried out by the beginning of June.[142]

On June 20, with these decrees still unfulfilled, the North Caucasus GPU and North Ossetian militia invaded Lesken with 6 machine guns and 150 armed horsemen. Without the aid of the Kabardino-Balkar militia, which the GPU prevented from intervening, this was lower Lesken's last stand and the end of dual power in the village.[143] According to a GPU report on the operation, "after being disarmed, the population of lower Lesken subordinated themselves to North Ossetian power. Twelve activists from lower Lesken escaped into the forest. Three were wounded and one killed. . . . The problem had been liquidated. Complete calm reign[ed] in Lesken."[144] In the wake of the invasion, the North Ossetian militia arrested twenty-one pro-Kabarda local leaders and many lower Lesken residents fled to neighboring Kabardian villages for fear of reprisals.[145] Reports indicate that leaders of upper Lesken harassed the lower Leskenites remaining in the village, forcing them to sign statements disavowing their support for Kabarda.[146] One of the lower Lesken leaders who managed to escape, Dris Karaev, fled to Moscow to appeal to Aleksei Rykov, head of the Council of People's Commissars (the highest executive branch of the Soviet government). However, the GPU informed Rykov that Karaev was wanted by North Ossetia's authorities for disturbances in Lesken. Rykov had Karaev arrested and sent to prison in Vladikavkaz.[147]

In late 1925, more contradictory and unclear decrees allowed Kabardino-Balkaria's leaders and their remaining supporters among Lesken's villagers to make an abortive final attempt at securing some of the village's land. Faced with having to provide land to the 197 lower quarter households registered for resettlement to the Kabardino-Balkar AO,[148] the oblast's leaders refused to resettle their Lesken supporters within the borders of Kabardino-Balkaria "owing to the absence of free land reserves."[149] However, on October 26, new hope emerged for the lower Lesken cause when two different branches of the Soviet government issued contradictory decrees. The VTsIK in Moscow issued a decree calling for residents of lower Lesken to be resettled within the borders of the Kabardino-Balkar AO, while the North Caucasus regional government, responding to petitions from lower quarter representatives, issued a decree calling for a "commission to examine the possibility of annexing lands from the Lesken allotment to the Kabardino-Balkar AO for the resettlement of Kabarda supporters."[150] The ambiguity created by these contradictory decrees led to a situation whereby Kabardino-Balkaria's leaders argued that they would only resettle residents of lower Lesken if the Soviet government transferred bordering land allotments of Lesken (i.e., the coveted plots formerly belonging to lower Lesken) to Kabardino-Balkaria. In other words, the demands of the Kabardino-Balkar government and its Lesken supporters had not changed much. While reconciled to the fact that annexing all or part of the village to Kabardino-Balkaria was now impossible, they stood firm on the issue of their land allotment. Their goal was now to have their land annexed by Kabardino-Balkaria and to resettle their homes on this land, forming a new village, Lower Lesken.[151]

On December 7, 1925, I.T. Boiar of the People's Commissariat of Land, and chair of the most recent commission sent to Lesken, concluded that "it was definitely possible to divide Lesken's land allotment into two parts and still observe the interests of both quarters" and that "the only possible place to resettle the supporters of Kabarda would be the northern portion of the Lesken allotment."[152] This seemed to signal victory for lower Lesken and Kabardino-Balkaria. However, at the last minute, as Boiar made his way back from Lesken to Nalchik to submit his findings, an Ossetian messenger on horseback stopped the commission and presented them with a VTsIK decree from November 30. With this decree the VTsIK reaffirmed its October 26 order to resettle lower-quarter residents within the borders of Kabardino-Balkaria and overruled the North Caucasus regional government's formation of a commission on the division of Lesken's land.[153] Moscow had stripped the Boiar Commission of its authority before it had begun its work.

Despite a new round of appeals from the lower quarter's leaders, Moscow's decision was final. By the end of 1925, Kabardino-Balkaria's leaders gave up hope of retaining any of Lesken's land, and most of the original supporters of Kabarda had reluctantly resigned themselves to life in North Ossetia. The Kabardino-Balkar authorities ultimately facilitated the resettlement of only about twenty to twenty-five households.[154] While this marked the end of Lesken's internal struggle, the Lesken-Urukh region remained the scene of sporadic but violent disputes between North Ossetia and Kabardino-Balkaria over rights to forests and pasturage into 1928.[155]

Rustling Cattle on the Mountain Pastures: The Kabardian-Karachai Conflict

The prospect of land redistribution according to the needs of individual nationalities raised the Karachai people's hopes that they would regain control over a portion of the trans-Malka mountain pastures. These hopes came up against the Kabardian leadership's equally fervent desire to retain Kabarda's mountain pastures and prevent the further erosion of Kabarda's borders. This dynamic produced a cycle of Kabardian-Karachai violence with the ethnically mixed mountain *aul* of Khasaut as its focal point. At its peak in 1921, this conflict led Moscow to send Red Army peacekeeping forces to the disputed territory.

The division of the Kabardian and Karachai peoples between Terek and Kuban oblasts in 1860, and subsequent legislation giving Kabardians (and eventually Balkars) exclusive usage rights to the trans-Malka pastures, forced the Karachais, whose permanent settlements were located to the west of the pastures on the other side of the border, to rent vital pastures from Kabardians. In the centuries before Russian conquest, Kabardian princes' control of the mountain pastures enabled them to collect tribute from the Karachais, who needed access to these pastures to maintain their stockbreeding economy. Ermolov's conquest of Kabarda in the 1820s cut off its access to these pastures and allowed the Karachais to freely use its share of the mountain pastures up to the left bank of the Malka (which Kabardians were forbidden to cross). From 1845 on, Kabardians gradually reasserted their rights to the mountain pastures beyond the Malka, coming into sporadic conflict with Karachais in the process. The land reforms in the 1860s gave the Kabardians usage rights to vast mountain pastures along the Malka and Kichmalka rivers as far west as the Eshkakon River. After regaining control of the trans-Malka pastures in 1869, the Kabardians reasserted some of their economic control over their Karachai neighbors by renting out excess pasturage to Karachai shepherds. Kabardians profited by renting out pastures for which they paid a nominal ten-kopek-per-*desiatina* fee to the Kabardian Public Treasury (a tax fund for public works, infrastructure, and education initiatives) at far higher rates.[156] By 1917, about 20,000 Karachais, or almost a third of the total Karachai population, drove their cattle to rented pastures in Terek oblast's Nalchik district during the summer.[157]

The Karachais never forgot that they had once controlled the Kabardian mountain pastures, and, when the revolution broke out and talk of land reform spread to their *auls*, they saw the recovery of these pastures as the principle means to their economic rebirth. As soon as Soviet power spread to the North Caucasus, Karachai's pro-Bolshevik elites began to lobby for control of the portion of mountain pastures that their people had historically rented. On February 16, 1918, at the Second Congress of Peoples of the Terek, the first Karachai attempt to raise their land claims failed. The Congress denied the Karachais representation at the congress on procedural grounds because the Karachai people resided in Kuban, rather than Terek oblast. In late May 1918, a Karachai delegation managed to gain entrance and representation at the Third Congress of the Peoples of the Terek in Groznyi by convincing the Mandate Commission that enough Karachais resided in Terek oblast to warrant having a delegate with voting rights at the Congress.

During the Third Congress's preliminary discussions on the formation of the Emergency Land Commission—the Commission tasked with redistributing land to landless mountaineers on a temporary basis until a formal land reform could be carried out—a heated argument erupted between the Karachai delegates, who hoped to be included in the Commission, and the Kabardian delegates, who aimed to prevent this. Arguing that "the Karachais live in Kuban oblast and have baselessly staked claims to the land of the Kabardians," the Kabardian fraction protested the inclusion of Karachai representatives in the Emergency Land Commission. The Karachai delegate, Khamzat Golaev, defended the Karachai position, claiming that "the Karachai tribe once resided [in Terek oblast] until they were pushed into the mountains around Elbrus by Cossacks." Golaev also argued that since the Kabardians were sharing their land with local Russian settlers or *inogorodnie*, they should also share their land with the equally needy Karachais. Golaev pleaded with the Kabardians:

> Reach out to us, your younger brother, to avoid possible excesses. We have nowhere to turn. Remember this! If you share your land with settlers [*s inogorodnimi*], why then do you not want to share the mountain pastures with us!? If it is because we are foreigners, then why are these other foreigners not deprived of this right as well and why can we not participate in ... the Commission?!

As was frequently the result of the work of land commissions during this period, the Emergency Land Commission ended this dispute inconclusively with a call to investigate further the actual size of the Karachai population living within Terek oblast.[158] Lingering questions over the Karachais' right to representation based on their population size within Terek oblast ultimately prevented the Emergency Land Commission from examining the Karachais' land needs, and the Commission's December 5, 1918, resolution called for redistribution of Kabardian land to Balkars but not Karachais.[159] The collapse of Soviet power and the period of White-Army rule temporarily ended discussions of the Karachai-Kabardian land dispute.

In May 1920, two months after the restoration of Soviet rule, the summer transhumance to the mountain pastures brought the Karachai-Kabardian land dispute to the fore. A cycle of armed clashes and cattle thieving erupted as Karachai stockbreeders drove their cattle onto Kabardian-controlled pastures on the left bank of the Malka.[160] On May 28, the *revkom* of Terek oblast issued the order "On the Resolution of the Land Dispute between the Karachais and Kabardians," giving authority to the Terek Oblast land department to investigate the situation and issue a ruling on the disputed pasture lands.[161] On July 20, after examining the disputed land and meeting with representatives of both sides, chairman of the Terek land department and professional land surveyor, M.V. Dergachev, reported his findings to the Soviet authorities of Terek oblast. Dergachev's report did not bode well for the Kabardian leadership's goal of retaining the trans-Malka mountain pastures. Dergachev reported that the Kabardians were unable to fully utilize all their pastures, the Karachais had rented this land from Kabardians, and they needed these pastures because there were insufficient pastures for their needs in Kuban oblast. Based on these findings, Dergachev concluded that "it would be expedient to allow the Karachai to use the mountain pastures this summer season." Two factors led the Dergachev Commission to issue only a temporary ruling. First, because of limitations on its jurisdiction, the Commission was unable to fully examine the amount of land that the Karachais had within Kuban oblast and how much more they needed. Second, Dergachev understood the potential for an escalation of the conflict and sought to defer responsibility for a permanent resolution to a future commission, one with a higher-level sanction and broader mandate. Indeed, Dergachev's belief that the dispute should be resolved "extremely carefully for political reasons" was only enhanced by both sides threatening violence should the land disputes be resolved against their interests.[162]

Khasaut: The Key to the Mountain Pastures

As the Kabardian and Karachai leaders struggled for what they viewed as the preservation or reassertion of their peoples' national territories, Khasaut, the majority-Karachai village at the center of the disputed territory, became embroiled in a local dispute for access to surrounding pastures. Khasaut became an important pawn in Karachai's plans for gaining control of the mountain pastures. The Karachais of Khasaut, historically dissatisfied with the poor quality of the land that the tsarist state had assigned to them,[163] felt that the Kabardian-led local government was neglecting their interests, particularly in terms of land redistribution.[164] Seeing the expansion of Kabardian *aul* allotments on account of expropriated private land (from the Kabardian nobility), Khasaut's residents also hoped for an increase in farmland and pastures. On March 30, 1920, the Khasaut village assembly requested either land from the district's

Kabardian allotments or that "Soviet power transfer their village from the jurisdiction of Nalchik district to Piatigorsk district."[165] Tensions over Khasaut escalated after May 12, when a conflict broke out between a Kabardian patrol on the mountain pastures and a group of Khasaut villagers serving as guides for the patrol. Khasaut villagers killed several Kabardians in the incident. Rumor spread that the Kabardian militia was sending a force of 4,000 to punish Khasaut. At the same time, in the nearest village, the Kabardian *aul* Karmovo on the Malka, which was involved in a land dispute with Khasaut, rumor spread that the Karachai were sending in their militia.[166] The rumors of paramilitary mobilizations were unsubstantiated. Nevertheless, in the lead up to the formation of the Dergachev Commission, tensions over Khasaut helped fuel the already-fierce dispute between Kabarda and Karachai over the trans-Malka mountain pastures.

The Dergachev Commission's July 20 ruling gave the Karachais the right to use the trans-Malka mountain pastures for the remaining month of their summer pasture season.[167] The end of the summer transhumance brought a temporary de-escalation of the Karachai-Kabardian conflict. Meanwhile, the Karachai leadership continued to seek a means to gain permanent control over the disputed pastures.

With the formation of the GASSR in January 1921, the Karachais found themselves, for the first time, in a common administrative unit with the mountaineers of the Terek region. Knowing that much like them, the Ossetian, Balkar, and Ingush leaders hoped to gain needed land for their peoples at the expense of Kabarda, this new administrative arrangement pleased the Karachai leadership. The majority of the GASSR's leaders were sympathetic to the Karachais' plight. Initial decrees indicating the territorial division of the GASSR seemed to signal Karachai success in their efforts to annex the trans-Malka pastures. A November 1920 decree cited Khasaut in a list of villages to be included within the borders of the future Karachai district of the GASSR. In typically vague fashion, the VTsIK decree on the formation of the GASSR included "the western portion of the former Nalchik district" within the republic's newly formed Karachai district.[168]

In the summer of 1921, ethno-territorial disputes between Kabarda and most of the other constituent members of the GASSR intensified as Kabardian leaders prepared to remove Kabarda from the fledgling autonomous republic and form an AO for the Kabardian people. In addition to tensions between Kabardians and Ossetians along Kabarda's eastern border in the Lesken Valley, in the west, conflict also erupted on the mountain pastures with renewed vigor. This time, Kabardian shepherds and militiamen clashed with Karachai and Balkar shepherds and fighters, in separate incidents, as each group staked claim to pastures beyond the Malka. In early July, Karachai shepherds, backed by their militia on horseback, chased Kabardian shepherds east from the mountain pastures down to the Zolka pastures in the foothills, stealing cattle in the process. On July 19, the head of the Kabardian district militia, Mikhail Tkachenko, backed by 150 armed Kabardian horsemen, ordered the Kabardian shepherds to reoccupy the mountain pastures under their protection.[169] After pushing back the Karachais, the Kabardian militia established block posts along the mountain passes and river crossings onto the trans-Malka pastures under the pretext of "definitively closing off the mountain pastures to outlaws."[170] On August 16, after weeks of failed attempts to reach a mediated solution to the conflict, Karachai armies invaded the mountain pastures again and occupied hayfields. In order to avoid an all-out war between Kabarda and Karachai, Moscow dispatched a Red Army peacekeeping mission under the command of Nikolai Kuibyshev, commander of the Second Caucasus Corps, and supervised by Kliment Voroshilov, the then commander of the North Caucasus Military District. The Commission established a temporary cease-fire line and dispatched a Red Army unit to ensure its observance. The Red Army forbade Kabardians and Karachai to cross the established border, which would be in effect until the Muromtsev VTsIK Commission finished its work and issued a ruling on the borders between Kabarda and the GASSR.[171]

Between September 1921 and January 1922, Karachai's leaders, Umar Aliev and Islam Khubiev-Karachaily, began a forceful campaign aimed at shoring up support from central and regional officials for the Karachai position in the land dispute. In numerous articles, declarations, and official memoranda, Aliev and Karachaily launched a two-pronged attack on the Kabardian leadership's claims to all the mountain pastures.

First, Aliev and Khubiev-Karachaily crafted histories depicting the Karachais as the victims of centuries of Kabardian oppression enabled, in its most recent phase, by a close relationship between the Kabardian nobility and the tsarist administration. According to these histories, the tsarist administration gave Karachai's mountain pastures to Kabarda's princes as a reward for their loyalty. The Karachai leadership hoped to use anti-tsarist sentiment to their advantage by depicting their people as anti-colonial resistors and the Kabardians as colonial collaborators. In a September 1921 memorandum to the VTsIK, Aliev claimed: "Kabarda voluntarily joined Russia and helped it conquer other mountaineer tribes, but the Karachais resisted and were the last of the mountaineer peoples to be conquered [sic]. . . . The princes of Kabarda not only did not lose land by joining the autocracy, to the contrary, they were gifted land from other mountaineer peoples."[172] In a September 23 proclamation (*vozzvanie*) "to the laboring people of Karachai," Aliev argued that the Karachais had been under "the triple oppression of the tsarism, the Cossack whip, and Kabardian princes." Claiming that the Kabardians are up to their same old tricks, Aliev continued, "petty bourgeois Kabardian elements are in Moscow hoping that the government, which placated loyal Kabardian princes under tsarist rule against the interests of the free Karachai shepherds . . . but which is now a workers-peasant power, will still placate them."[173]

The second prong of the Karachai leadership's campaign was economic. They argued that the Kabardians were a predominantly agrarian people and therefore, unlike the stockbreeding Karachais, had no need for their vast mountain pastures, whereas the Karachais were desperate for more pasturage on which to practise their sole economic activity. According to Karachaily's January 1922 article in *Zhizn' natsional'nostei*:

> The Kabardians are a grain-growing people of the plains among whom stockbreeding never played a central economic role and despite Soviet power's cardinal slogan that the "land should go to those who work it" . . . a small group of Kabardian comrades have tried to fight for Kabarda's rights to the disputed pastures, which are completely unnecessary for the laboring Kabardian people and were never under their ownership.[174]

Karachaily continued his economic argument by claiming that only small group of Kabardian horse breeders used the mountain pastures. In his conclusion, Karachaily demanded that

> the reserve mountain pastures, totaling more than 100,000 desiatinas [270,000 acres], which are utilized by the laboring Karachai people, must be transferred once and for all to the laboring mountaineers who live and work on them. . . . The definitive . . . transfer of [the mountain pastures] . . . is necessary in the interest of saving the mountaineers' economy from ruin.[175]

The Karachai leaders' historiographic attacks on Kabardian oppression of the Karachais did not achieve the desired result. Their narratives, especially those of Umar Aliev, strayed from a class-based, Marxist-internationalist analysis of social relations in the region and came perilously close to what the central Soviet leadership called "bourgeois nationalism." Most notable in this regard is Aliev's December 1921 Report to Moscow, "On the National Antagonism between Karachai and Kabarda and the Land Question."[176] Before his appointment as chair of the Karachai *revkom*, Aliev served as the head of the Mountaineer Section of the *Narkomnats* and played a key role in the establishment of Soviet power in the North Caucasus.[177] One of the most influential and powerful native Bolsheviks from the North Caucasus, Aliev hoped to use his connections in Moscow to his advantage.

Aliev's report paints a picture of a long history of Kabardian oppression of the mountaineers of the North Caucasus, especially the Karachais. He makes numerous exaggerated claims regarding Kabarda's power over the Karachais, and, most importantly, he often does not distinguish between the feudal elites and the peasantry. In one characteristic example, Aliev writes,

> Kabardians would expel [Karachai] husbands from their homes and sleep with their wives. If a Kabardian placed his hat outside the door of any Karachai home as a sign that he was sleeping with the wife or daughter of the master of the house . . . then the latter did not have the right to enter his home until the former had picked up his hat.[178]

Rather than gaining the support of the central Soviet leadership, Aliev's report had the opposite effect. It is likely that Aliev's report convinced Soviet leaders that his continued presence in Karachai impeded the establishment of order and intercommunal peace.[179] In March 1922, several months after his report, the Central Committee transferred Aliev to party work in Southern Dagestan.[180]

The Kabardian leadership, not yet sure what effect Aliev and Khubiev-Karachaily's writings would have in Moscow, took to the pages of *Zhizn' natsional'nostei*, a forum for all-union debate on issues related to nationalities policies. A February 9 article, "Kabarda: Past and Present," sought to dispel claims that Kabardians were collaborators with and beneficiaries of tsarist rule.[181] The author, M (Zarakush Midov?), claims that "for more than 300 years the Kabardians defended their rights and freedoms, not submitting to the Tsarist regime, but repeatedly raising the banner of rebellion against oppressors who were trying to turn the freedom-loving mountaineers into subjects of the autocratic tsar and his officials."[182] On February 25, Kabardino-Balkaria's liaison to the VTsIK, Nazarov, published a response to Karachaily's claims that the trans-Malka pastures were not necessary for the Kabardian economy.[183] Nazarov took the position that Kabarda's access to the mountain pastures for horse breeding, in addition to stockbreeding, was vital to the security interests of Soviet Russia. According to Nazarov,

> Kabardian horse-breeding is not, as Karachaily claims in his article, the pastime of a few sportsmen; rather it is a highly developed sector of the national economy. For the Red Cavalry, for example, the question of a supply of thousands of excellent horses is extremely important, which is why the People's Commissariat of Land is taking the most serious measures to support the Kabardian Ashabovo horse-farm.

Nazarov also argues that Karachai's demand for more pasturage is born out of "the primitive condition of their stockbreeding" and ineffective use of their own land.[184]

If the Karachai propaganda campaign met with little success in Moscow, sources indicate that Nikolai Kuibyshev's Red Army peacekeeping forces nonetheless took Karachai's side in the dispute. In early November, Kuibyshev's forces redistributed Kabardian hayfields and baled hay on the disputed land among Karachai stockbreeders. Despite the end of pasture season and the onset of winter, the Karachais would remain on the pastures to ensure their continued control over them. On November 8, 1921, Betal Kalmykov telegraphed the Regional Party Committee in Rostov-on-Don about Kuibyshev's actions and informed them that "Kabarda is sending an armed militia to clear the territory of Kabardian oblast of Karachai invaders and to maintain order on the border."[185] The Kabardian militia sent a force of 200 to the mountain pastures.[186] A week later, on November 16, the presidium of the Second Kabardian Oblast Party Conference received a telegram describing clashes over hayfields between Karachai and Kabardians.[187] In response to this report, the conference delegates issued the following decree:

> Given that Karachai has been a den for counterrevolutionaries since 1918, where both Karachai and Kabardian bandits find refuge, steal cattle . . . and prevent the Kabardian peasantry from peacefully working their land: 1) Request that Karachai immediately remove their shepherds from Kabardian territory; 2) strengthen the police force on the border with Karachai with a special-forces detachment; 3) report to higher authorities that the Karachai Executive Committee cannot be deemed to represent the will of the Karachai working people because it has been infiltrated by counterrevolutionaries.[188]

On the same day, Stalin, having received a copy of Kalmykov's report on the actions of Kuibyshev's peacekeeping mission, telegraphed Voroshilov, commander of the North Caucasus Military District, that "Kuibyshev does not have the right to make decisions regarding land redistribution; the center has not given him such authority."[189] Despite Kalmykov's threat that Kabarda was sending in forces to retake disputed territory, according to Voroshilov's December 18 report to Stalin, it appears that only skirmishes took place in November and December.[190]

With the peacekeeping mission's neutrality compromised, the Kabardian leaders prepared a large assault aimed at expelling Karachais from the disputed lands. On January 5, 1922, Kabardian militia chief Tkachenko and Nazir Katkhanov, a Civil War hero and popular Kabardian leader, mobilized horsemen from Kabarda's *auls* and concentrated these forces in Karmovo on the outskirts of the mountain pastures. Tkachenko and Katkhanov planned to disguise these paramilitaries as a Red Army detachment and have them remove the Karachais from the disputed territory at gunpoint. Kuibyshev, learning of Kabarda's planned assault, left his headquarters in Kislovodsk to persuade Tkachenko and Katkhanov to pursue peaceful negotiations, showing them a series of orders obliging both sides to reject violence and seek a negotiated resolution of the question. Tkachenko and Katkhanov temporarily called off the attack; however, the Kabardian forces gathered in Karmovo were becoming restless and yearned to avenge the Karachais for past grievances, namely the theft of cattle.[191]

At 2:00 a.m. on the night of January 8, the Kabardian horsemen broke out of their barracks, disarmed the watchmen, and raided the safe house where Tkachenko and Katkhanov had stored a large cache of rifles and cartridges, several machines guns, and artillery pieces with crates of mortars.[192] This force of 600 heavily armed horsemen advanced upon the Karachai border in the early-morning hours. The Kabardians stole horses and took prisoners, but the Karachais fought back. There were dozens of dead and wounded on both sides. The next day Kabardian officials visited the conflict zone in an effort to end the fighting. Meanwhile, the Karachai leadership mobilized their forces for a counterattack. On January 11, in an urgent telegram to the Regional Party Bureau in Rostov-on-Don, the Kabardian Oblast Executive Committee reported that "captured Kabardian militiamen had been brutally beheaded by Karachai forces" and requested that "Karachai be ordered to cease the formation of armed detachments with the aim of attacking Kabardian villages."[193] Stalemate set in over the next several weeks. Having forced the Karachais back from the mountain pastures between the Malka and Kichmalka, the harsh winter conditions on the mountain pastures caused many sick and weary Kabardian militiamen to desert. The remaining 150 militiamen patrolled the border along the Kichmalka, enduring freezing gale force winds and snowstorms.[194] Service in the Karachai campaign became a test of loyalty to the new regime in Soviet Kabarda. The Kabardian leadership purged deserters from local party and state organs.[195] and, in future years, service in the campaign was used (in addition to service in the Civil War) to evaluate party members during regular purges.[196]

On January 25, 1922, with Kabarda and Karachai on the verge of a full-scale war as both sides mobilized additional forces, the Revolutionary Military Council (*Revvoensovet*) of the North Caucasus Military District brokered a cease-fire and an emergency meeting in Piatigorsk between representatives from Karachai and Kabarda. The *Revvoensovet* meeting, chaired by Voroshilov and fellow Civil War hero Semen Budennyi, found a temporary solution to the dispute. The *Revvoensovet* called for the creation of a neutral zone between the two AOs encompassing the disputed mountain pastures and a military-legal commission to ensure its observance. The

Red Army military-legal commission would administer this territory, regulate the use of its hayfields by Karachai and Kabardian peasants, and ensure that Karachai and Kabardian officials and militiamen remained outside of the zone.[197] This neutral zone would remain in effect until the issuance of a VTsIK Commission ruling, expected later in 1922, on the borders between Kabarda and Karachai.

As the Kabardino-Karachai conflict evolved over 1921 and early 1922, the strategic importance of the majority-Karachai village of Khasaut became increasingly clear. Given its location on the mountain pastures, whoever could establish official jurisdiction over Khasaut would control a large swath of the disputed territory. Karachai's leaders understood this first and claimed Khasaut as part of the GASSR's Karachai district. The January 20, 1921, VTsIK decree on the formation of the GASSR included Khasaut in the Karachai district without any protest from the Kabardian side. However, almost a year later, on January 11, 1922, Kabardian officials protested Karachai attempts to include Khasaut in the future Karachai-Cherkes AO (Kabarda's exit from the GASSR separated Karachai from the Mountaineer Republic territorially, forcing it to secede and form the Karachai-Cherkes AO with its neighboring trans-Kuban Circassian minority).[198] Karachai representatives included Khasaut in their list of villages to be included in the new KChAO, but protests from Kabardian representatives convinced the *Narkomnats* to append a footnote to the list reading: "all of the listed villages are approved except Khasaut, the status of which will remain open until the question is resolved by the VTsIK Dmitriev Commission."[199] The VTsIK Decree on the Formation of the Karachai-Cherkes AO, issued the following day, did not mention Khasaut.

With the neutral zone in effect, the Dmitriev VTsIK Commission used the winter and spring of 1922 to examine the question of the borders of Kabardino-Balkaria, Karachai-Cherkessia, and the GASSR. After delays caused by Kabardian protests over the Commission's approach to border delimitation with the Balkars, on May 30, 1922, the Dmitriev Commission presented its report to the VTsIK Federal Land Commission, and on June 10, 1922, the VTsIK adopted a decree demanding a final resolution on the border within two weeks.[200] In the time between the submission of the Dmitriev Commission's report and the final VTsIK decree, a Kabardian delegation led by Kalmykov traveled to Moscow to lobby for a favorable outcome. On July 19, for example, Kalmykov telegraphed Stalin that the Commission's project, which called for giving most of the pastures beyond the Malka to the Karachais and Balkars, "would destroy Kabarda economically and politically."[201] These lobbying efforts bore fruit, perhaps because of Kalmykov's close ties with Stalin. The June 22, 1922, VTsIK decree delimited the borders of the Karachai-Cherkes and Kabardino-Balkar AOs along the Kichmalka River, leaving most of the disputed mountain pastures and Khasaut within the borders of Kabardino-Balkaria.[202] The Karachai-Cherkes AO received a smaller allotment of pasturage from Kabarda between the rivers Eshkakon and Kichmalka.[203]

As we have seen, in terms of the delimitation of land between Kabardians and Balkars, the June 22 VTsIK decree represented a compromise that largely satisfied the territorial demands of Kabardian and Balkar leaders. The Karachai leadership, however, remained unsatisfied. The Karachais, now led by Kurman Kurdzhiev, continued to demand that the borders of the AO be extended to the Malka. These trans-Malka pastures were part of a larger puzzle for the Karachais. The Karachai leadership simultaneously petitioned for Cossack land around Kislovodsk from the Terek governorate (former Terek oblast less the GASSR) and the Kuban-Black-Sea governorate.²⁰⁴ Though never reaching the same level of armed conflict as the Kabardino-Karachai conflict, there were several small skirmishes between Karachai shepherds and Cossack peasants in this area.²⁰⁵

Meanwhile, despite being satisfied with the modest land transfer to Karachai in the June 22 VTsIK decree, the Kabardian side also protested the decree, demanding that Kabarda be left in its 1917 borders which extended to the Eshkakon. In protesting the VTsIK decree, the Kabardian leadership pursued what historian Artur Kazharov calls "active defense." Sensing that the Karachai leadership would not cease in its efforts to gain all of the mountain pastures between the Malka and Kichmalka for the Karachai people, the Kabardian leadership "attempt[ed] to show how much Kabarda needed the disputed land by acting as if even the mountain pastures were not enough."²⁰⁶

The Karachai leadership, similar to the Ossetian leadership in Lesken, hoped to use the Karachai ethnicity of Khasaut's residents, and their historic land grievances with Kabarda's administration and neighboring Kabardian *auls*, to achieve a reversal of the June 22 VTsIK decree. The Karachai leadership mobilized Khasaut's residents to launch a petition campaign aimed at achieving approval for the annexation of their village to the Karachai-Cherkes AO.

On June 27, 1922, shortly after the VTsIK decree placed their village back under Kabardian jurisdiction, representatives from Khasaut sent a declaration to the VTsIK presidium and to Stalin at the *Narkomnats*. This would be the first of many such petitions and declarations. Citing the Declaration of the Rights of the Peoples of Russia, the villagers requested that "the Presidium of the VTsIK immediately reexamine the decree of the VTsIK Commission on the borders between Karachai and Kabarda and include Khasaut within Karachai." To justify their request, Khasaut's representatives included a long list of grievances. In addition to noting the great distance from their village to Kabarda's administrative center, Nalchik, and the lack of concern for their landlessness on the part of the Kabardian authorities, the representatives complained that "since the revolution, still more than before, Kabarda committed among the Karachais a series of murders, attacks, and the rustling of cattle." Citing a historic "national enmity between Karachai and Kabarda," the Khasaut representatives framed their grievances in national terms. They complained that "the citizens of Khasaut [the only Karachai village in Kabarda] are an insignificant minority and Kabarda completely ignores their interests." They explained that "[Khasautites] never lost their connection with the Karachais, with whom they are connected by blood, language, customs, and way of life."²⁰⁷ Similar petitions from Khasaut residents, backed up by requests from the Karachai leadership, continued to flow into the offices of the VTsIK, *Narkomnats*, and regional party and state organs throughout 1922 and 1923.²⁰⁸

It was not difficult for Karachai leaders to mobilize the Karachais of Khasaut; they had long been dissatisfied with their land allotment in Kabarda and had repeatedly looked for ways to leave Kabardian jurisdiction in hopes of gaining more land. Whatever the Khasautites' feelings about their Karachai ethnicity, land was clearly the core issue of this dispute. Many of the Khasaut villagers' complaints, particularly in terms of access to land, were justified. Indeed, the residents of Khasaut were understandably upset that the Kabardian authorities had not expanded Khasaut's allotment on account of recently expropriated private land. However, the sincerity of the Khasautites' ethno-national argument—that Khasaut should be transferred to Karachai because its residents are ethnically Karachai and that the Karachais and Kabardians have historic and ongoing tensions—is more difficult to gauge. To be sure, relations between Khasaut and the Kabardian administration had soured in recent years. Moreover, Khasaut's majority-Karachai villagers maintained close ties with relatives in Greater Karachai and spoke Karachai. However, many of the Karachais of Khasaut were also connected to Kabarda and Kabardians. Indeed, the Zhereshtievs, the family that established Khasaut, descended from Kabardian nobility and were conscious of it. Through intermarriage and decades of cohabitation among Karachais, the Zhereshtievs of Khasaut had become culturally and linguistically Karachai, yet they still maintained close ties with their Kabardian relatives, some of whom resided in the Kabardian *aul* of Karmovo, one of the closest settlements to Khasaut. At their roots, Khasaut's conflicts with the villagers of Karmovo and the Balkar *auls* Khabaz and Gundelen had little to do with ethnicity. Rather, they reflected the historic land-based feuds that existed between many neighboring villages in this land-starved region. Moreover, Khasaut's location on the mountain pastures, which, as in the past, became notorious for lawlessness and banditry during the Civil War, only increased such conflict during this period. But the Bolsheviks' introduction of the national principle elevated the importance of ethnicity for the Karachais of Khasaut and exacerbated existing tensions by providing institutional support (i.e., a Karachai-majority AO and its organs of power) and a rhetorical framework based on nationality and class for advancing their aims.

In their search for land, the Karachai leadership and the residents of Khasaut found common cause. By speaking the languages of nation and class and appealing to Soviet support for national self-determination, Khasaut's residents could help Karachai's leaders in their goal of controlling the trans-Malka pastures on which their *aul* was located, and, in return for this favor, Karachai's leaders could allot Khasaut the additional land that they so desperately sought. In terms of "speaking national," the Khasaut petitioners consistently stressed that their national-minority status as a Karachai *aul* in Kabarda was unacceptable.[209] In terms of "speaking Bolshevik," the Khasaut representatives painted Kabardians as class enemies. The petitioners ended their long list of reasons why their *aul* should be included within Karachai's borders with the following condemnation of Kabarda: "We are sure that Kabarda, as a land of petty bourgeoisie and wealthy farmers, will not adopt a proletarian lifestyle and way of thinking anytime soon; the proletarian dreams of equal rights will not be made into reality in Kabarda in the near future."[210]

As part of their strategy for having their village transferred to Karachai, the Khasautites ignored the VTsIK decree and de facto recognized the jurisdiction of the Karachai-Cherkes AO. On December 11, 1922, the Khasaut village assembly resolved to reject Kabardian administration "until the receipt of orders from Moscow."[211] In 1922 and 1923, Khasaut paid its taxes to Karachai rather than Kabarda. Khasaut authorities did not allow Kabardian officials into their village, taking their orders instead from the Lesser Karachai District Executive Committee.[212] Tensions heightened as Kabardino-Balkaria's leaders demanded that Khasaut submit to its authority and pay taxes to the Kabardino-Balkar AO. In a telegram to the Central Committee and the VTsIK in Moscow, Kalmykov complained that "the *aul* Khasaut is located in Baksan district [of the Kabardino-Balkar AO] . . . [and] Karachai's bid to subordinate Khasaut to its authority during the tax collection campaign is another seizure of the territory of Kabarda."[213] In February 1923, Kalmykov ordered the head of the Baksan district to subordinate Khasaut to the district-level executive committee.[214] In an abortive attempt to reach a compromise with the Khasautites, on August 4, 1923, the Kabardino-Balkar TsIK adopted a resolution transferring Khasaut from Baksan district to Balkar district.[215] The Kabardian leadership hoped to address Khasaut's national concerns by placing them in a common administrative district with their Balkar co-ethnics (the Karachai and Balkar languages and lifeways are nearly identical). This compromise did not satisfy Khasaut's residents because it did not change their prospects for gaining access to a larger land allotment.

Meanwhile, between January and March 1923, the Kabardian leadership responded to Karachai's posturing by orchestrating a petition campaign of their own. The Kabardino-Balkar TsIK collected petitions from nearly all of Kabarda's villages in which the villagers recounted numerous incidents of Karachai raids and cattle thieving on the mountain pastures during their summer transhumances since 1918.[216] This Kabardian petition campaign was an effort to discredit Karachai claims to good stewardship over the mountain pastures and depict Karachais as dangerous cattle thieves rather than peaceful shepherds in need of more land. For example, in an official complaint to the Kabardino-Balkar TsIK signed by the Kezhne village assembly on January 29, the villagers summarize their situation:

> the Karachais stole from us a total 57 head of large cattle, 595 head of small cattle, and one horse . . . now our society is afraid to drive its cattle to the mountain pastures and we do not have enough land to keep our cattle on village land . . . this thieving is occurring solely on the basis of land. Having discussed this issue from all sides our society unanimously requests that the Nalchik District Executive Committee petition for the establishment of a clear border with Karachai and the Mountaineer Republic . . . so that we can quietly go about our peaceful labor without carrying rifles on our shoulders.[217]

Most of Kabarda's villages lodged similar complaints describing in detail the number of cattle stolen by the Karachais; the exact date, time, and place where the robbery occurred; and the value of the stolen property.

Despite these efforts to discredit the Karachais, the Karachai leadership's efforts to convince Soviet authorities that its shepherds desperately needed the trans-Malka mountain pastures were successful. In an abrupt turn of fortunes for Kabarda and the Kabardian leadership, on August 24, 1923, the VTsIK issued a decree calling for the temporary transfer of the trans-Malka pastures to Karachai for 1923 and 1924.[218] Shortly thereafter, the Karachai leadership gained the support of Nariman Narimanov, the Azeri Bolshevik leader who had recently been appointed co-chair of the VTsIK. In a November 6, 1923, report to the VTsIK, Narimanov argued that "the petitions of the residents of Khasaut are correct and legal. We should satisfy their requests and also reexamine the question of the Karachais' land allotment because several mistakes were made in the previous decree on this question."[219] In December 1923, the VTsIK created a new commission to reexamine the borders of KBAO and KChAO.[220] During its first meeting, on February 6, 1924, this latest VTsIK Commission decided to defer responsibility for the examination and resolution of the Kabardino-Karachai border dispute to the People's Commissariat of Land. Ultimately, the Narkomzem delegated the Kabardino-Karachai land question to the Odinstsov Commission, which, as discussed earlier, also had the responsibility of establishing the borders between Kabarda and the new North Ossetian and Ingush AOs.[221]

Unsurprisingly, the Kabardian leadership reacted strongly against the VTsIK's temporary transfer of the trans-Malka pastures to the Karachais and the reopening of the Kabardino-Karachai dispute. In August 1923, shortly after receiving the order giving the Karachais the use of the trans-Malka pastures, Kalmykov telegraphed Enukidze, Kabarda's perceived ally in the VTsIK:

> The plenum of the Kabardian Central Executive Committee is shocked and upset. We categorically protest this decree because the question of the borders of land-use with Karachai was already decided by the Presidium of the VTsIK. . . . The mountain pastures are currently covered with sheep and cattle from Kabardian villages. . . . We warn that the VTsIK Presidium's decision to permit Karachai to use our pastures will provoke unwanted, large disturbances. Therefore, we consider the VTsIK decision unfulfillable.[222]

The Kabardian leadership did not limit its response to official protests and petitions; they took matters into their own hands at the local level.

First, on February 23, 1924, the Kabardino-Balkar TsIK decreed the formation of a new, Mountain (*Nagornyi*) district in the northwest corner of the oblast. This new district included Khasaut and neighboring Kabardian *auls*, the Zolka pastures, and the disputed mountain (*nagornyi*) or trans-Malka pastures, which, according to the decree, "are of enormous economic significance for the oblast." The decree established Piatigorsk, a large economic hub outside the borders of the KBAO, as the administrative center of this new district. The ostensible reasons for the creation of the Mountain district were "to secure the economic relations between the peasantry of the northwest part of the oblast with the neighboring territory of Terek governorate and for the better administration of the vast territory of the Zolka and Mountain pastures."[223] While these official reasons are not untrue (they follow a pattern of placing the administration of predominantly rural, non-Russian administrative units in neighboring Russian cities), the creation of the Mountain district was also strategically connected with the question of jurisdiction over Khasaut and the trans-Malka pastures. First, the creation of a special district for the mountain pastures would allow the Kabardian leadership to tighten its administrative and police power over the region and counter the claims of Khasaut residents that their village was located too far away from the district administrative center. Indeed, the appointment of Kabarda's security chiefs, Khabala Beslaneev (Department of Internal Affairs) and Mikhail Tkachenko (militia), to head up the administration of the new district, attests to the security significance placed on this new district.²²⁴ Second, the Mountain district had a rhetorical and symbolic importance. Now a district of Kabardino-Balkaria carried the name (*nagornyi*) of the disputed territory. Also, now if this territory were transferred to Karachai, Kabarda would lose almost an entire district, rather than a small portion of one.

Drought struck the plains of Kabarda in 1924, making the dispute over the trans-Malka pastures, in the drought-free mountain zone, even more urgent for the Kabardian leadership. The Kabardino-Balkar administration planned to retake the trans-Malka pastures from Karachai in May 1924, in time for the summer transhumance. The leadership of the Kabardino-Balkar AO argued that Karachai's year of use of these pastures (decreed in August 1923) ended in May. Knowing that the Karachai leadership intended to keep its shepherds on the mountain pastures until the end of August, the Kabardian leadership proceeded to petition Moscow to end Karachai's use of the pastures while simultaneously concentrating paramilitary forces in the Mountain district in preparation for renewed conflict. On June 18, the VTsIK issued a clarification stating, much to the chagrin of the Kabardino-Balkar leadership, that the Karachais could use the pastures until August 1.²²⁵ On July 11, after Kabardino-Balkaria's cattle had exhausted the Zolka pastures in the foothills, Mountain district head Beslaneev sent armed detachments to the trans-Malka pastures and forced out Karachai shepherds from the grass-rich pastures between the Malka and Kichmalka. Beslaneev allotted hayfields to Kabardian villages.²²⁶ On July 14, the Kabardino-Balkar TsIK ordered hay-collecting machines sent to the mountain pastures, mobilized groups of villagers from all over Kabarda to collect hay, and established block posts on the border with Karachai, ordering border guards to "under no circumstance let Karachai enter the borders of Kabarda."²²⁷

On July 21, as the Kabardians finished their swift operation to remove as much hay as possible from the mountain pastures, the VTsIK issued a final resolution on the borders between the Kabardino-Balkar AO and its neighbors based on the findings of the Odintsov Commission. The VTsIK decreed the transfer of Khasaut with its surrounding land allotment to the Karachai-Cherkes AO. Additionally, in order to link Khasaut with the rest of Karachai, the KChAO received all the land between Khasaut and the old Karachai border. The July 21 VTsIK resolution was "final and not subject to reexamination," and it bound the Karachai side to resist making any further territorial claims against Kabarda. This resolution satisfied the Kabardian side because, despite losing Khasaut, most of the trans-Malka mountain pastures remained within Kabardino-Balkaria's borders. After July 21, the Kabardino-Balkar leadership considered the battle for Khasaut over. In a decree to the chair of the Mountain district *revkom*, Kalmykov gave orders "to always try to avoid provoking tensions with the Khasautites, and liquidate any misunderstandings peacefully [and] show that we will live in peace and friendship with our laboring neighbors."²²⁸

Conclusions

Between 1918 and the final 1924 VTsIK decree on the borders of Kabardino-Balkaria and its neighbors, land-poor mountaineer communities received nearly 330,000 acres

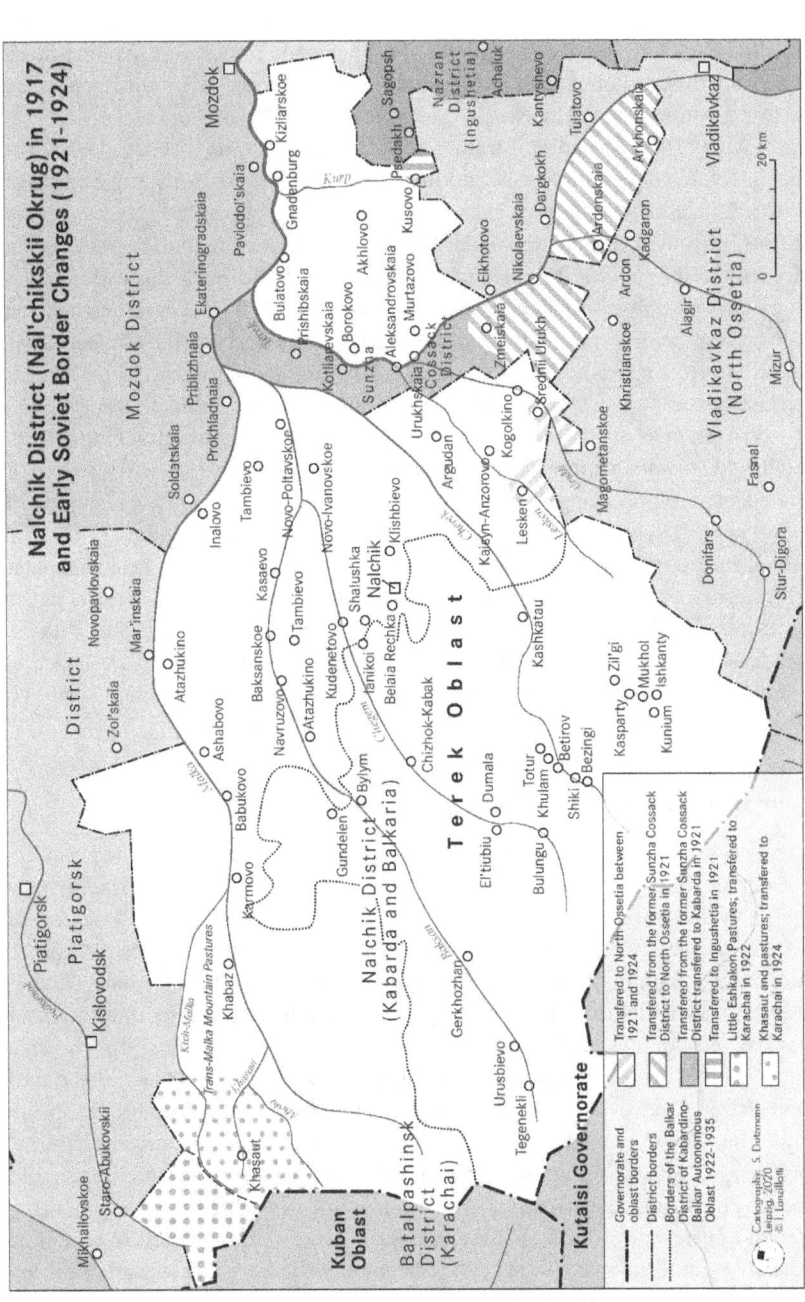

Map 4 Nalchik Okrug in its 1917 borders showing territory transferred to Karachai, North Ossetia, and Ingushetia by VTsIK decrees in 1922 and 1924. © Silke Dutzmann, map editor at the Leibniz Institute of Geography (Leibniz-Institut für Länderkunde) in Leipzig, Germany.

of lands previously controlled by Kabarda. Karachai received a total of 248,813 acres from the communal mountain pastures and tsarist-era private lands. In the Urukh-Lesken Valley, the state transferred 17,120 acres, including the Ossetian villages Lesken and Srednyi Urukh, to North Ossetia. In the Kurp region of Lesser Kabarda, Ingushetia received two Ingush homesteads, Kusovo and Indievo, and the Ukrainian Kievskii homestead, totaling 7,449 acres. Finally, the Balkars received 56,592 acres (see Map 4).[229]

By the late 1920s, Soviet administrators decided future questions over borders swiftly and behind closed doors in Moscow and Rostov-on-Don (the administrative center of the North-Caucasus Region from 1924 to 1934). For example, in 1932 the leadership of North Caucasus region made the decision to transfer the predominantly Cossack district around the *stanitsa* Prokhladnaia to Kabardino-Balkaria.[230] This decision was based on administrative concerns (the district's loss of several villages to neighboring Russian regions made it too small to exist as a separate district) and the *stanitsa*'s close economic ties to Kabardino-Balkaria's Malka district.[231] While Kabardino-Balkaria's leadership voiced support for the transfer of this territory, regional authorities in Rostov-on-Don determined the fate of Prokhladnyi district with minimal input from local officials, let alone petitions from villagers.[232]

The collectivization of agriculture and stockbreeding in the 1930s (discussed in the next chapter), which placed the state in control of the Soviet Union agricultural resources, further militated against intercommunal land conflict and helped explain this shift from a populist to an administrative approach to border adjustments in the region. After collectivization, there was little point in Kabardians, Ossetians, Balkars, or Karachais fighting for land that they did not control. Indeed, in Kabardino-Balkaria, land largely ceased to be a driver of intercommunal tension and conflict through the Soviet period.

Border Delimitation, Land Disputes, and Soviet Nations

The conflicts surrounding Lesken, Khasaut, the Kurp villages, and the Cossack *stanitsy* do not demonstrate the type of "divide-and-rule" policies that scholars traditionally attributed to the Bolsheviks during the formation of the Soviet Union.[233] Indeed, as scholars have demonstrated for other parts of the Soviet Union,[234] it is difficult to identify a single guiding principle behind the delimitation of borders here. Rather, the administrative statuses of these villages were determined by the interaction of ideological, economic, ethnographic, and administrative principles. To cite one example, the 1924 commission chaired by Odintsev of the People's Commissariat of Land criticized the work of the 1923 VTsIK Commission headed by the Bolshevik Smirnov for being too ideological and disregarding state economic concerns. According to Odintsov, "the foundation for the resolution of the [land] question should not be an equalizing redistribution of the land of one oblast between neighboring oblasts [as Smirnov advocated], but the transfer of territory on the basis of economic expediency as understood by the state."[235] Therefore, in the Lesken case, while Smirnov recommended granting any Kabardian lands that the village's residents had ever owned or rented, however briefly, to North Ossetia as part of Lesken's village allotment, Odintsov considered how transferring a particular plot would affect the economies of the two oblasts. Indeed, Odintsov ruled against transferring forest allotments near Leksen to residents because doing so would put the nearby Argudan lumber mill out of commission.[236] While we can see the opposing goals of ideology and economic development at work in the approaches of these two commissions, each expert commission was clearly under pressure from Moscow ("the bureaucrat-policeman") to permanently resolve the Lesken question so that stable Soviet administration could be installed in the village. In Lesken, as with other cases in the North Caucasus, and as was often the case in Russian imperial governance, Moscow's main priority was to push for order.[237]

The delimitation of ethno-territorial borders between Kabarda and its neighbors illustrates the "participatory aspect of double assimilation," the important role that modern states play in forging identity categories, and the strength of these categories in shaping modern societies.[238] Conflicts over land which blended into political disputes over national boundaries in the 1920s served as immediate and effective lessons in the importance of national and class identifications and categories in the modernizing Soviet state. Learning how to speak national and speak Bolshevik provided "social legitimacy" for the peoples of the Central Caucasus.[239] These new literacies also transformed the peoples of the Central Caucasus. By mastering the modern discourses of national rights and self-determination on the one hand, and class struggle and social equality on the other, the peasants and shepherds who wrote petitions and often traveled thousands of miles to plead their cases at central party and state agencies in Moscow, embarked on a process of becoming *active* and *integrated* members of the Soviet state in addition to members of their newly promulgated nations.

The North Caucasus figures little in the major studies of the Soviet state's fraught delimitation of national borders and most discussions focus on conflict between mountaineers and Cossacks.[240] Given the master narrative of Cossack-mountaineer violence in Caucasus historiography, this latter tendency is understandable. Indeed, the prevalence of Cossack-mountaineer violence, ultimately resulting in the deportation of *stanitsy* from the Sunzha region in 1918 and 1920, led Terry Martin to place the North Caucasus in the same category as Kazakhstan in his typology of ethnic conflict resulting from border delimitation.[241] There are striking similarities between the North Caucasus and Kazakh cases. Both regions had experienced recent and extensive Russian colonization at the expense of native landholdings during the late-tsarist era and, in the aftermath of the Civil War, the native elites of both regions called for "the equalization of native and European landholdings."[242] In both cases, the establishment of national autonomy and the land question intersected to produce a wave of native-settler violence culminating in partially successful attempts to deport nonnative groups from the region. However, in the North Caucasus, unlike in the Kazakh case, historic, land-based, socioeconomic tensions among the numerous mountaineer nationalities led to fierce conflict among the region's ethnically mixed indigenous communities. Given the high incidence of border conflict among mountaineer nationalities, the North Caucasus also resembled Martin's "Uzbek variant" of ethnic conflict characteristic of the rest of Central Asia, where, in the absence of substantial non-Russian national minorities, "the formation of national republics [or oblasts] not only increased ethnic conflict, but also turned local disputes, often with a clan or regional aspect, into national ones." In Central Asia as in the North Caucasus, "any ethnic conflict immediately drew the interest of that ethnic group's 'home' republic." Border disputes in both regions "illustrate the role played by government actors—at the local, republican, and all-union levels—in exacerbating ethnic conflict."[243]

The processes of colonization and imperial integration in the North Caucasus described in the previous chapters were part of a transitional period during which the broad contours for later, Soviet-sponsored, nation-building were formed. From the late eighteenth through the nineteenth centuries, the rough boundaries of the contemporary national territories of the North Caucasus began to take shape as a result of tsarist colonial policies, population resettlement, and early experiments with social engineering. More importantly, in the nineteenth century, new colonial-era administrative units, formed with an adherence to ethnic borders, albeit loose and vaguely defined, replaced premodern social, political, and economic structures that were often multiethnic, decentralized, and rarely included entire cultural-linguistic communities. The Soviet state used these tsarist-era administrative formations as the basis for national delimitation in the North Caucasus. However, tsarist-era administrative units only loosely cohered to ethnic boundaries, often giving precedence to natural boundaries and administrative expedience. This sporadic tsarist disregard for ethnic homogenization frequently resulted in ethnic exclaves like Lesken and Khasaut along frontier territories. Far from being artificial or inherently problematic, these villages formed out of the natural interactions of place, social status, and ethnicity. These areas often created great difficulties for the ethnicizing Soviet state.

In determining the status of Lesken, Khasaut, the Kurp villages, and the Cossack *stanitsy*, finding a workable resolution to seemingly intractable disputes was the Soviet state's primary consideration. As the arbiter of local disputes throughout a vast and unruly empire, the Soviet state took on an enduring Russian imperial role: referee. This dynamic was, of course, spurred on as much by state officials trying to establish order as by those on the ground (upper and lower Leskenites, for example) trying to gain an advantage. This reactive role, whereby the state responded to or was forced into local political dynamics and initiatives, has been well documented throughout the tsarist period, but Soviet studies have tended to emphasize the state as a "landscaper" intervening in and "gardening" society according to its ideological goals.[244] The conflicts that accompanied border delimitation in the North Caucasus indicate that we should also pay attention to the reactive, mediator role of the state in the Soviet period.

These tsarist-Soviet continuities should not be taken too far. Ideology was more important to the functioning of the Soviet state than it was for tsarist state. Imperial Russia tolerated ethnically mixed administrative divisions and even fostered them when it suited its plans. The formation of territorial divisions based on ethnographic principles in the tsarist period reflects the relatively westernized mentalities of tsarist administrators who viewed Caucasian society through the lens of ethnicity and believed that ethnically homogeneous administrative borders would provide the best means to effectively administer the region and maintain order. At the same time, many of these westernized administrators were native sons of the Caucasus and also brought local visions to bear on the administration. By contrast, the Soviet division of the North Caucasus along national lines reflected a self-conscious and hotly debated ideological program of "state-sponsored evolutionism," whereby the Soviet state would guide its diverse peoples, all at varying stages of historical development, along a teleological Marxist-Leninist timeline from a prenational, to national, to supranational phase coinciding with the construction of a Communist society.[245] According to Bolshevik ideology, then, the existence of ethnically Ossetian and Karachai *auls* on the "wrong" sides of the Kabardino-Balkar/North-Ossetia and Kabardino-Balkar/Karachai border was not to be tolerated, for their persistence would inhibit the Soviet state's ability to transform its citizenry, in this case into members of modern nations and eventually members of a supranational Soviet people. That said, ethno-national delimitation and attendant border conflicts were not always adjudicated on ideological principles alone. The Soviet state was often very concerned about the immediate economic consequences of border changes. Moreover, the Soviet state, like its tsarist predecessor, was a "bureaucrat-policeman state" concerned with maintaining order and stability. These "administrative" concerns weighed heavily on the Soviet state's decisions in the various border conflicts discussed in this chapter. For example, the decision to keep Kabardians and Balkars together in a single ethno-territorial unit reflected both economic and administrative concerns.

In creating a shared, dual-titular, national homeland for the Kabardians and Balkars, the Soviet state created a new type of identity category. In the compromise that prevented the separation of Kabardians and Balkars, the Kabardian leadership agreed to grant the Balkar people access to the land needed for their economic needs. This land was not considered a transfer to another ethno-territorial unit in the same way as the land annexed to Karachai, Ingushetia, and North Ossetia. The Balkars' land would remain part of a united Kabardino-Balkar AO (later republic). While the Balkars had the use of these needed pasture lands, they would not be firmly enshrined by national borders as Balkar land. That is, rather than a Kabardino-Balkaria consisting of two clearly delineated Kabardian and Balkar regions, the creation and subsequent historical development of Kabardino-Balkaria was an attempt to forge a dual-titular autonomous administrative unit, the territory of which would be considered, at least officially, the common property of all the peoples of Kabardino-Balkaria. Indeed, the term "Kabardino-Balkar people" came into increasing official use as the Soviet period progressed. Ultimately, while it may not have been a stated and conscious goal at the outset, the project of Kabardino-Balkaria became an attempt to forge a supranational Kabardino-Balkar identity. Soviet citizens of Kabardino-Balkaria would have an extra possible layer in their (ethnic, national, cultural and territorial) identities: their passport nationality, Kabardino-Balkar identity, and a larger Soviet identity.

These processes of nation-building at work in the North Caucasus of the 1920s bear striking resemblances to earlier processes described by Peter Sahlins in his study of another mountainous borderland, the Cerdanya, the border region between France and Spain in the Pyrenees in the seventeenth and eighteenth centuries. Sahlins argues that it was not so much the efforts at national integration on the part of modernizing nation-states that turned Cerdanyans into Spaniards or Frenchmen, but rather "the evocation of national identities . . . by the village communities of the Cerdanya [after national border delimitation] was grounded in local economic interests, and in a local sense of place."[246] According to Sahlins, "disputes among villages divided by the [national] boundary became vehicles for the development and expression of national identities in the Cerdanya."[247] Similar processes were at work in this early modern borderland as in the Lesken-Urukh Valley and the trans-Malka mountain pastures of the early twentieth-century Central Caucasus: the delimitation of the borders connected communities to different polities and transformed the sense of belonging and identity of the local inhabitants. In the Soviet case, as exemplified here by the cases of Lesken and Khasaut, we have this process of the transformation of identities through new connections to certain governing entities (local/ethno-national and Soviet) and also the more ideological drive of dividing people by perceived nations. Therefore, while the national discourse introduced by the Bolsheviks may have been unique to the modern period, viewed comparatively, the processes that resulted in the formation of national identity, in addition to being "constructed" products of a modernizing interventionist state, are also the less intentional offspring of state-building projects not unique to the nineteenth and twentieth centuries.

How did interactions change between residents of Lesken and Khasaut, on the one hand, and, neighboring Kabardian, Balkar, Karachai, and Ossetian communities, on the other, as a result of the triumph of the national principle under Soviet rule? To what extent did the national principle triumph on the ground? Did the delimitation of borders and the institutionalization of nationality represent a fundamental rupture in the lived experience of ethnicity? Given the available source base, it is difficult to answer these questions of "everyday ethnicity" with certainty.[248] Nevertheless, it is possible to hazard tentative conclusions.

Soviet policies caused intercommunal tension by providing opportunities for the instrumentalization of nationality. The stories of Lesken and Khasaut are important reminders that, at their roots, conflicts in such regions have historically been fought over access to scarce land resources rather than national rights. These disputes could be *inter*communal or *intra*communal. Where they were intercommunal, the introduction of the national principle propelled land disputes into conflicts over national self-determination, and, in this way, the ethnicizing Soviet state created "ethnic" violence. Arguments of national self-determination helped those involved find institutional leverage for what were originally conflicts driven by local, nonnational, concerns. Transformed by the national principle, these conflicts became more violent and prolonged, involving far more people and institutions than they otherwise would have. For example, during the same period, conflicts regularly erupted between and within ethnically Kabardian villages over similar issues of land rights. However, these conflicts rarely turned as violent and took on such high stakes as the struggles over Lesken and Khasaut. The relative mildness of these conflicts arose not because the passions of the conflicting sides were weaker, but because, with the absence of a national border in the immediate vicinity, these villages were unable to utilize the national principle and gain institutional support to help them press their claims. Ultimately, Soviet officials did not seek to create interethnic conflict through the drawing of borders in the North Caucasus. However, by delimiting these borders and determining access to land according to nationality, Soviet policymakers inadvertently created new social fractures. The resultant reconfigurations of territory and belonging have been the cause of much conflict throughout the region.

5

From KBASSR to KASSR to KBASSR

Intercommunal Relations, Nationalities Policy, and the Deportation, Return, and Reintegration of the Balkars, 1944–66

Early in the morning of March 8, 1944, over a year after Soviet troops had liberated the Central Caucasus from Nazi occupation, NKVD troops flooded into the slumbering mountain valleys of the Kabardino-Balkar Autonomous Soviet Socialist Republic.[1] Soldiers stormed into Balkar homes, informed the unsuspecting residents of their impending deportation on charges of mass treason during the occupation, and instructed families to board the waiting Studebaker trucks in twenty minutes with no more than 500 kilograms of their possessions. Soldiers shot or arrested those who resisted. Trucks transported their human cargo to the nearest train station and the Soviet security services loaded 37,713 Balkars—nearly the entire Balkar population not serving in the Red Army—onto cattle cars bound for Soviet Central Asia. A total of 37,103 Balkars reached their final destinations on the barren steppes of Kazakhstan and Kirgizia. During brief stops, the Balkars hurriedly buried the bodies of children and elderly who had died along the way.[2] As the war came to an end, rather than receiving a hero's welcome in their homeland, demobilized Balkar soldiers received orders to join their families in exile. After their deportation, the Balkars no longer had an official homeland in the Soviet Union. Soviet authorities renamed the Kabardino-Balkar ASSR the Kabardian ASSR and, henceforth, no mention of the Balkars—their history or their very existence—could be made in official publications.

The expulsion of the Balkars from the North Caucasus was one of about a half-dozen other mass deportations of entire Soviet nationalities to Central Asia and Siberia during the Second World War.[3] In late 1956, Nikita Khrushchev allowed most of the "punished peoples," including the Balkars, to return home after thirteen years of exile and, in early 1957, the Soviet government restored their autonomous administrative units. For most involved, however, the terror of deportation and exile did not end in 1957; their return marked the beginning of a new struggle for full rehabilitation. This struggle continued into the post-Soviet period, and the legacies of Stalin-era deportations continue to inform ethno-political discourses in the Caucasus, the Crimea, and elsewhere. The idea and practice of rehabilitation, as it developed by the end of the Soviet period, was multifaceted: (1) political rehabilitation: the attainment of an official apology from the state condemning Stalin's ethnic deportations, the cancelation of all Stalin-era decrees and legislation on the "punished peoples," the ethno-territorial restoration of their homelands as they existed on the eve of deportation, and the full right of return; (2) socioeconomic rehabilitation: programs designed to compensate for and alleviate the deleterious social and economic effects caused by deportation and exile; (3) finally, cultural rehabilitation: state programs for the rebirth and revitalization of the languages and cultures of the deported peoples and the banning and criminalization of publications defaming the punished peoples as traitors.[4]

The deportation, return, and rehabilitation of the Balkars raise numerous questions about the historic relationship between Balkars and Kabardians, these two communities' relationship to their land, and the relationship between both communities and the Soviet state. In exploring these questions, this chapter uses the Balkar deportations as a lens to examine larger questions of intercommunal relations, Soviet nationalities policies, and ethnic cleansing from the 1930s to the 1960s. Why did the Stalinist state deport the Balkars and not the Kabardians? Was there a connection between intercommunal relations and the deportations? Did Kabardians play a role in the deportation, and did they stand to gain through the removal of the Balkars? What role did land play in the deportations, and how did the Balkar deportation affect land relations in the region? How did postwar Soviet nationalities policies affect Kabardians and the exiled Balkars? To what extent did the former symbiosis among the communities of Kabardino-Balkaria, and between Kabardians and Balkars in particular, reappear after the Balkars' return from exile?

For all its significance, the Balkar deportation was part of a larger, complex web of intercommunal relations, state policies, and violence that developed from the early 1930s to the late 1960s. The chapter begins with a discussion of how Kabardians and Balkars experienced the Stalinist policies of the 1930s—nativization, collectivization, industrialization, and the terror—in similar ways. With the radical shift in structures of landownership and use brought on by collectivization, the land question that had been at the core of intercommunal relations was fundamentally changed, and it was no longer a driver of intercommunal conflict. Afterward, top-down state policies rather than historic tensions over land drove intercommunal politics in Kabardino-Balkaria. These politics revolved around disparities in levels of socioeconomic and cultural modernization rather than disparities in land tenure. Soviet policies toward national minorities and land, often inadvertently, reduced tensions between Kabardino-Balkaria's non-Russian communities. To the extent that intercommunal tensions surfaced publicly in the 1930s, they were now most often between Russians, on the one hand, and Kabardians and Balkars, on the other, and they reflected shifts in Moscow's policies rather than long-standing grievances over land.

This chapter also explores the goals, experiences, and outcomes of postwar Soviet nationalities policy. The divergent fates of the Kabardian and Balkar peoples during the late-Stalin years reflect the opposing extremes of nationalities policy during this critical period. From the late 1940s on, Kabardians received unprecedented state support for education, national culture, and social mobility. More than in the prewar years, in the postwar years the Kabardian people experienced the beginnings of rapid modernization. Meanwhile, their former Balkar neighbors lived in exile from their homelands, deprived of civil rights. This experience stunted the demographic, economic, and cultural development of the Balkar people, and its legacies continue to shape Balkar identity.

By finding important continuities where others have seen rupture, this chapter offers a new perspective on Soviet nationalities policy. Historical research in the post-Soviet decades has led to a deeper understanding of the USSR as the world's first ethno-federal state and an empire that created nations and practiced a variant of affirmative action toward its minority communities. The lynchpin of Soviet nationalities policy was nativization (*korenizatsiia*): the promotion of the use of titular languages in administration and education in national republics and regions; the creation of national intelligentsias; and the elevation of members of titular indigenous nationalities to positions at all levels in industry, administration, and the Communist Party. This chapter examines the sustained nativization campaigns conducted in Kabardino-Balkaria from the late 1940s through the early 1960s. In contrast to studies of Soviet nationality policies that argue that the Soviet state stopped giving nativization high priority after the mid-1930s,[5] this chapter confirms Peter Blitstein's finding that the late-Stalin years, from about 1948 to 1953, were a time of renewed emphasis on nativization.[6] It was precisely the nativization campaign in the Kabardian ASSR, launched in 1948 in response to a lack of native cadres in the republic's postwar leadership structures, that signaled an increase in Moscow's prioritization of nativization throughout the Russian Soviet Federal Socialist Republic (RSFSR).

The case of the Kabardian ASSR demonstrates how the pursuit of nativization policies during these late-Stalin years had a significant impact on ethnic processes throughout the remainder of the Soviet period. To be sure, it was not until after Stalin's death that the Soviet state made its greatest push to bring technological modernity to its semicolonial peripheries, including the national autonomies of the North Caucasus,[7] just as post-colonial states in Africa and Asia began their modernization drives.[8] But while the full force of Soviet developmentalism (the focusing of state policies on social and economic modernization) would not be felt in the region until the large industrial projects of the 1960s and 1970s, the preceding nativization campaign initiated key social and cultural transformations among Kabardians and established a nativized worksite as a priority that would endure across the succeeding decades of Soviet economic development. The presence of native scholars, engineers, technical experts, and administrators made possible by the late Stalin-era nativization drive ensured that the Khrushchev and early Brezhnev–era developmentalist push in Kabardino-Balkaria would in part be carried out by and, if the insights of Artemy Kalinovsky's study of post-Stalinist modernization in Tajikistan can be applied to the Kabardino-Balkar case, shaped and promoted by native experts and politicians.[9] While there would be an enduring deficit of native experts trained on the most up-to-date technology,[10] the push to increase native representation in industry and management and to establish new norms for hiring during this nativization campaign meant that, going forward, Kabardians and Balkars would find employment in Kabardino-Balkaria's new industrial enterprises in large numbers.[11]

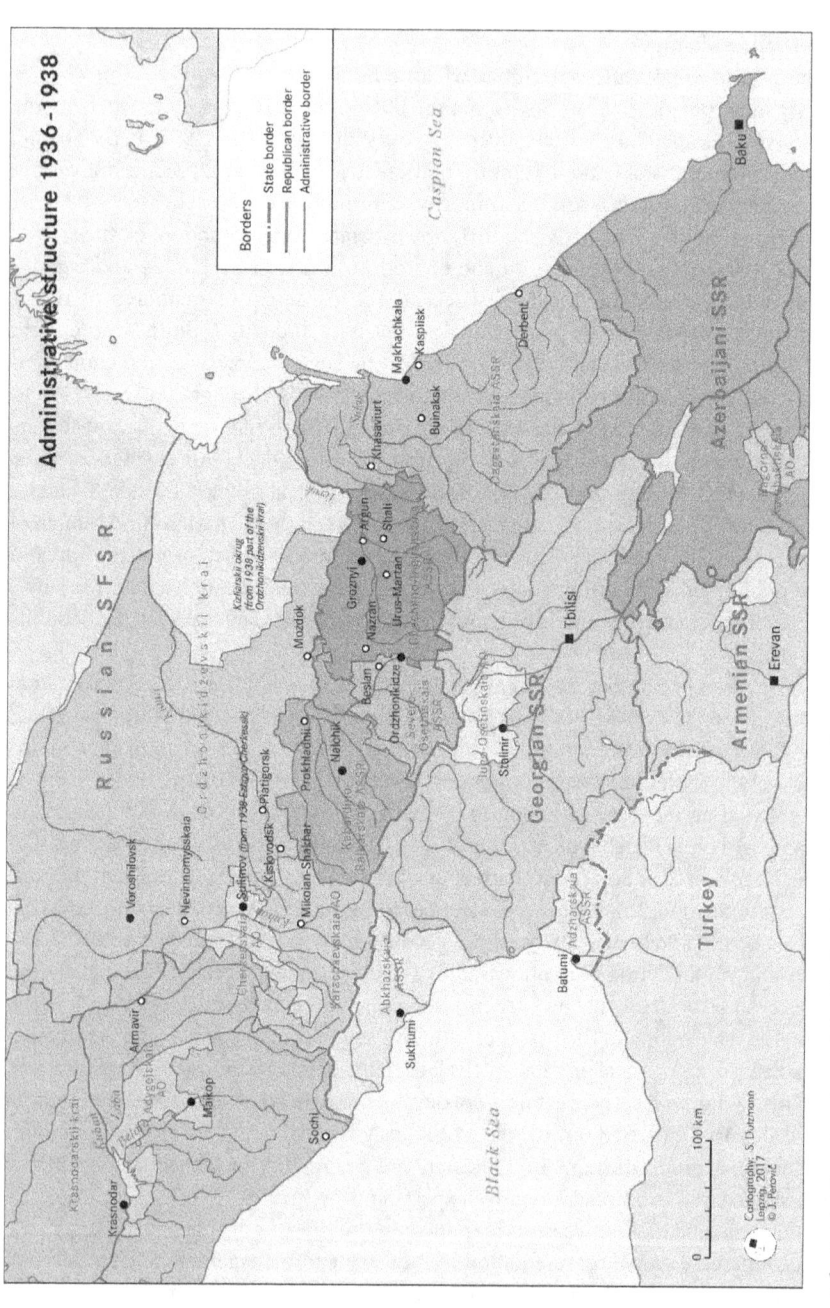

Map 5 Administrative structure of the Soviet Caucasus, 1936–8 from *From Conquest to Deportation: The North Caucasus Under Russian Rule* (New York: 2018). © Reproduced with the kind permission of Jeronim Perović.

Finally, this chapter examines the socioeconomic reintegration of the Balkars after their return to the North Caucasus beginning in 1957. By pursuing "affirmative action" policies aimed at leveling disparities in education and employment levels between Kabardians and Balkars, local state organs endeavored to ameliorate the deleterious socioeconomic effects of deportation and exile on the Balkar people. I argue that the expansion of nativization policies among Kabardians during the decade preceding the Balkars' return—and the attendant development of an educational and economic infrastructure geared toward the specific needs and conditions of a non-Russian republic—facilitated the Balkars' reintegration. These factors distinguish the Balkars' experience from that of other deported peoples. This chapter also demonstrates the importance of the long-standing Kabardian-Balkar symbiosis as one of the factors that promoted the Balkars' relatively seamless reintegration. For many in Kabardino-Balkaria, particularly Kabardians, many of whom were connected to Balkars through extended family ties and long-standing friendships, the deportation of the Balkars was a difficult and unwelcome personal loss rather than an opportunity for personal economic gain. Local communities—Kabardians, Russians, and others—enthusiastically greeted the return of their former neighbors and provided assistance to returning Balkar families.

Kabardians and Balkars Under Stalinism

Conflict between Kabardian and Balkar communities over land rights steadily diminished in frequency and intensity after the unification of the Kabardians and Balkars into a shared AO in 1922. The compromise resolution to the ethno-political conflict between the Kabardian and Balkar national leaderships meant that rather than both sides mobilizing their co-ethnics, they instead worked together to resolve disputes peacefully.[12] Tensions also diminished because the political compromise that resulted in the formation of Kabardino-Balkaria was based in part on the idea that the land resources in the KBAO would be shared among its peoples according to need rather than nationality. Pasturage use became more a question of the allocation of a common resource rather than one of national rights. In the first half of the 1930s, the most important questions for the Balkars became how and when collectivization would affect their stockbreeding economy and way of life. When forced collectivization finally reached the Balkars, several years after the collectivization of Kabardian agriculture, they demonstrated little active resistance to Soviet policies.

During the Civil War and early 1920s, local concerns, particularly over access to land, had major impacts on the implementation and consequences of larger Soviet state policies. Beginning around 1928, and coinciding with Stalin's industrialization and collectivization drives, the concerns of the central Soviet authorities in Moscow—related to social engineering, modernization, and security—became primary movers of events. This primacy of central policies and ideological imperatives is borne out in the application of nationalities policy and collectivization, the scope of Stalinist repression, and administrative-territorial changes in Kabardino-Balkaria. This shift to centralized decision-making had a crucial impact on intercommunal relations and, particularly, on the relative peace between Kabardians and Balkars during Stalinism. A comparison of the history of Kabardino-Balkaria before and after the late 1920s indicates that there was greater conflict when issues were locally driven, but when issues were decided centrally, the resultant conflicts were not between Kabardian and Balkars but rather between the local nationalities and Russians and the central administration. In the 1930s, Kabardino-Balkaria witnessed resistance to and conflict with Soviet power—though this resistance was relatively weak in comparison with other parts of the North Caucasus[13]—but not conflict between Kabardians and Balkars.

By the late 1920s, border conflicts between Kabardino-Balkaria and neighboring national-territorial units had also diminished, and, when they did arise, local leaders worked to defuse them.[14] Several factors contributed to this. The now Stalinist Soviet state had made it clear that the window of opportunity for border revisions had closed.[15] Before the predominance of Stalin, local Soviet leaders had been able to use the various and often competing power centers and figures of influence with the Communist Party and Soviet state to shape the delimitation of borders. With the rise of the Stalinist dictatorship, political factions were no longer available for local leaders to instrumentalize. Finally, with Soviet power well entrenched, local Soviet leaders had become largely expendable. Understanding this and that outbreaks of interethnic conflict would make them appear unable to maintain stability in their territories in the eyes of the Stalinist leadership, local Soviet leaders refrained from stoking intercommunal tensions.

Nationalities Policy in 1930s Kabardino-Balkaria

During the 1930s, the main hotbeds of intercommunal tensions in Kabardino-Balkaria were the region's growing number of industrial worksites. While Kabardino-Balkaria remains a predominantly agrarian region, its industrial sector expanded dramatically in the decade after Stalin began his industrialization drive in 1928. By 1939, Kabardino-Balkaria had seventy-three new industrial enterprises. Two-thirds of these enterprises were in food production and light industry, though the region's mining industry, which would develop more fully after the Second World War, began to grow during the 1930s.[16] The vast majority of Kabardino-Balkaria's industrial workers were Russians. Only 12.4 percent of Kabardians and 2.1 percent of Balkars were employed in industry and related fields by 1939.[17] Indeed, intercommunal tensions at the industrial worksite revolved around Russians and "nationals" (Kabardians and Balkars) whom the Soviet authorities were trying to attract into jobs in industry. This rise in tensions between non-Russians (usually members of titular nationalities) and Russians at the Soviet Union's growing industrial worksites fits the pattern that scholars of Soviet nationalities policy have described for this period.[18] According to Martin's analysis of what he terms the "Greatest Danger Principle," in the late 1920s and first half of the 1930s, Stalin's belief that Russian nationalism ("great-power chauvinism") was a greater danger than non-Russian, minority nationalism ("bourgeois nationalism") undergirded Soviet nationalities policy.[19] By the mid-1930s, responding to increasing geopolitical tensions and the related rehabilitation of the Russians as the leading Soviet nationality, Stalin revised this formula and launched a campaign against bourgeois nationalism.[20] This is not to say that tensions between Kabardians and Balkars did not exist during this period. However, part of the reason why Kabardian-Balkar tensions are largely absent from the historical record was that local party leaders, following signals from Moscow, were more concerned with unmasking "great-power chauvinists" and "local nationalists" than highlighting tensions between indigenous titular nationalities.

This shift in nationality policies is evidenced by articles in local newspapers. In the early 1930s, articles singled out Russians for exhibiting "great-power chauvinism." Often these ethnically framed tensions involved Russian workers reacting negatively to nativization of industry—affirmative-action-style policies that gave preference in hiring in local industry to titular "nationals" at the expense of Russians and other nontitular groups. Accusations of "great-power chauvinism," as Martin points out, were part of "a rhetoric of abuse that could be (and was) hurled at any Russian ... who was felt to be behaving in a colonial manner."[21] In the second half of the 1930s, on the other hand, and particularly after Stalin's speech at the Seventeenth Party Congress in January 1934, where he clarified that "the greatest danger is that deviation against which one ceases to battle and which therefore grows into a danger to the state,"[22] charges of bourgeois nationalism gradually grew more frequent in the local press, reaching a peak in late 1937.

On November 28, 1931, the newspaper for *Baksan-Stroi*, the construction site of the Baksan Hydroelectric Dam, featured an article on problems of intercommunal relations and nationalities policy entitled "Firmly Follow the Party's Leninist Nationalities Policy in the Unceasing Struggle with Great-Power Chauvinism— the principal danger—and local nationalism." The article rebuked Russian workers for "the rudest manifestations of great-power chauvinism" (*grubeishie proiavleniia veliko-derzhavnnogo shovinizma*). According to the article, the head of one of the construction site's warehouses, Litvinenko, a party member, was fired for shouting obscenities at Kabardian workers and declaring, "I cannot work with these illiterate Kabardian dummies." The reporter, Nechiporenko, criticized the local party cell for not expelling Litvinenko from the party. Apparently, this was not Litvenenko's first violation of Soviet nationalities policy. Nechiporenko asks, "Why did Litvinenko's systematic persecution of Communist nationals [i.e., national minorities] for almost half a year go unnoticed by the local Party cell?" Nechiporenko also called out the head of the dam's public utilities department, Iaroshchuk, for "ignoring nationals who come to him with questions" and rebuked Iaroshchuk's assistant, Shchur, "who cannot speak to nationals without cursing at them."[23]

In addition to being Kabardino-Balkaria's largest industrial project of the 1930s with hundreds of Kabardians and Balkars laboring on the project alongside several thousand Russians, the Baksan Hydroelectric Dam was one of the most important sites of interethnic contact and nativization in 1930s Kabardino-Balkaria. This was a site where "nationals," as non-Russians were referred, would be exposed to the "more advanced culture" of the Russian proletariat, where a native proletariat would be created, and where Kabardians and Balkars would gain the skills necessary for promotion into leading positions in industrial management and party leadership.[24] Despite the robust propaganda campaign against "great-power chauvinists" and the general ideological importance placed on the dam as "a forge ... hammering out a national proletariat,"[25] the construction site had great difficulty retaining Kabardian and Balkar workers. Over 78 percent of the Kabardian and Balkar workers at the Baksan Dam left between 1933 and 1934;[26] they would often leave this construction site, and other industrial projects, after several months as a result of the hostile attitudes of Russian workers and poor working conditions.[27] The hostile attitudes of some Russian workers toward Kabardian and Balkar workers were partially a result of nationals receiving preference in hiring despite often lacking industrial experience and skills and partially a result of cultural prejudices.

Similar articles criticizing the attitudes of Russian workers toward their new Kabardian and Balkar colleagues abound in *Leninskii put'*, Kabardino-Balkaria's central newspaper. The most common form of abuse meted out to Kabardian and Balkar workers by Russians was the rubbing of pork fat on lips or the forced consumption of pork. In traditionally Islamic parts of the Soviet Union, this was a frequent form of symbolic violence designed to humiliate and underscore Russian dominance in the industrial workplace.[28] A July 21 1932 article rebukes the director of the Malka Machine and Tractor Station for doing nothing to stop Russian workers from abusing Kabardians by rubbing pork lard on their bread in the cafeteria.[29] Similarly, a September 17 report from a Komsomol member called for the firing of Soldatov, a senior worker at a local flour factory, for rubbing pork on the mouth of Balkarov, a Kabardian worker. Soldatov, a Russian, suspected the national was not really eating his pork ration, but selling it on the black market.[30] Martin's observations that both "crude affirmative action" and "the ethnic mixing of previously segregated populations . . . br[ought] an upsurge in ethnic conflict,"[31] apply to the situation in Kabardino-Balkaria. To be sure, Kabardians and Balkars had a long history of symbiotic relations with Cossack and Russian peasants. But they had little experience working with and for Russian workers. The industrial workplace was a new site of intercommunal mixing in Kabardino-Balkaria.

A gradual shift in emphasis from struggling against Russian nationalism ("great-power chauvinism") toward combating non-Russian nationalisms ("bourgeois nationalism") and toward a less-mechanical implementation of *korenizatsiia* took place in the mid-1930s. The July 17 1934 issue of *Sotsialisticheskaia Kabardino-Balkariia* (as *Leninskii put'* was renamed after Stalin declared the triumph of socialism earlier that year) included the first open critique of supposed nationalist tendencies and crude implementation of *korenizatsiia* in Kabardino-Balkaria. The newspaper published a speech by Kabardino-Balkar party secretary and Civil War–era hero, Betal Kalmykov, warning of the dangers of nationalism and improper implementation of *korenizatsiia*. In particular, Kalmykov singled out the editing house of the newspaper. There were some employees at the newspaper, according to Kalmykov, "who reason in the following way: 'why isn't Kabarda just for Kabardians' and 'why isn't Balkaria just for Balkars?'" Kalmykov accused nationals of scheming among themselves to replace Russians with natives. "It often begins," Kalmykov continued, "with individual conversations, then it turns into a general program of local nationalism, then they will openly declare—'Kabarda for Kabardians, Balkaria for Balkars' and make other anti-Party and anti-Soviet declarations." Kalmykov clarified the implications of this rebuke: "This in no way means that we should not conduct *korenizatsiia*, but the heart of *korenizatsiia* should be proletarian internationalism." Kalmykov finished with a warning that "class vigilance should be directed not only toward the class enemy . . . it should be directed just as much toward local nationalism."³² The publication of this speech did not signal an immediate shift, but by 1937, however, the tables had turned, and the local press had orders to unmask bourgeois nationalists. Indeed, the editor of *Sotsialisticheskaia Kabardino-Balkaria*, Grigorii Petrov, was fired by Central Committee (TsK) decree in 1937 for "not wishing to actively struggle against bourgeois nationalists."³³ Going forward, the local press pursued a vigorous campaign attacking Kabardians and Balkars for bourgeois nationalism.

Petrov's ouster by TsK decree raises a question: Why would Stalin and the Central Committee in Moscow concern themselves with and issue decrees on the content and staff of a local newspaper in Kabardino-Balkaria? The answer to this question lies in the most infamous case of "bourgeois nationalism" and intercommunal tension in 1930s Kabardino-Balkaria: the Sarmakovo affair.

On March 4, 1937, a special *Pravda* correspondent sent a report from Piatigorsk to Moscow on his investigation of rumors, apparently ignored by the local press, that local authorities in the Kabardian village Sarmakovo had expelled all non-Kabardians from the village. The unnamed *Pravda* correspondent's investigations confirmed that the authorities in Kabardino-Balkaria's mountain district had ordered the deportation of Russians and Roma ("tsygane") from the Kabardian village as part of efforts to remove Russians from the district.³⁴ The local militia ignored the affair. While the Kabardino-Balkar newspapers remained silent, *Pravda* published two articles on the Sarmakovo affair.³⁵ After describing the local authorities' efforts at deporting Russians from Sarmakovo, the *Pravda* reporter ended the first article, published on March 5, with a message to the Kabardino-Balkar leadership: "'Pravda' calls the attention of the Kabardino-Balkar Oblast Committee (Obkom) of the VKP(b) to these incidences of bourgeois nationalism, which are unheard of under Soviet conditions."³⁶ Embarrassed and likely frightened at being called out in the pages of *Pravda*, the Kabardino-Balkar leadership launched an immediate investigation. The author of the next article, from March 11, was Kabardino-Balkar First Secretary Kalmykov.³⁷ He provided further details on the affair: those marked for deportation had recently arrived in Sarmakovo from other districts and represented a variety of nonnative nationalities; and the deportations were only prevented at the last minute by the local NKVD. Kalmykov also provided the text of a decree removing those involved from their posts and from the Party. Kalmykov explained:

> This upsetting incident of bourgeois nationalism became possible only because the Party organization of the Mountain district and its secretary Bekishev weakened their struggle with local nationalism, forgetting comrade Stalin's admonition at the Seventeenth Party Congress that "the greatest danger is that deviation against which one ceases to battle."³⁸

The Sarmakovo affair led to a campaign against bourgeois nationalists in the Kabardino-Balkar press. In late 1937, as the purges struck national intelligentsias throughout the Soviet Union, *Sotsialisticheskaia Kabardino*-Balkariia featured numerous articles uncovering bourgeois nationalists and rebuking local officials for their liberal attitude toward known bourgeois nationalists.[39] An article on the firing of the editor of *Sotsialisticheskaia Kabardino-Balkariia* explained that "Petrov demonstrated rotten liberalism and political short-sightedness in the struggle against bourgeois nationalists . . . [He] covered up the sabotage of enemies of the people and delayed or ignored the investigation of workers' letters unmasking bourgeois nationalists."[40]

These campaigns against supposed "bourgeois nationalists," and the regular purges of Kabardino-Balkaria's party apparatus and attendant unmasking of secret "counter-revolutionary" groups, targeted Kabardian and Balkar officials in proportion to each nationality's share of the population.[41] Indeed, in 1927, Kalmykov, a Kabardian, directed the first "counter-revolutionary" purge campaign within the Kabardino-Balkar Party organization exclusively against Kabardians.[42] Throughout the purges, only two of about a dozen major campaigns targeted high-placed Balkar leaders, the "Gemuevshchina" (Ako Gemuev) in 1931 and the "Ul'bashevshchina" (Kellet Ul'bashev) in 1935.[43] Frequent purges affected local Party cells throughout Kabardino-Balkaria equally.

There is no evidence to suggest that this policy of proportional repression was a conscious policy, but it shows that the purge did not discriminate among Kabardino-Balkaria's two titular nationalities. Indeed, the Kabardino-Balkar government, party, and security organs applied both repressive "hard-line" policies (purges of national intelligentsias) and more benign "soft-line" policies (nativization[44]) to the communities of Kabardino-Balkaria in relative proportion to their share of the population.[45]

If we take differences in modernization levels in multiethnic societies as a cause of conflict,[46] then the balanced application of nativizaiton policies to both titular nationalities likely promoted intercommunal stability in Kabardino-Balkaria. In its relatively balanced application to Kabardians and Balkars, nativization in 1930s Kabardino-Balkaria vindicated the power-sharing agreement reached between the Kabardian and Balkar leaderships during the administrative unification of the two peoples in 1922.

To be sure, the absence of conflict between Kabardians and Balkars during this period may be an illusion created by the ideological lens of the Soviet press and the party that controlled it. When attacking deviations from the party line, the Kabardino-Balkar Party organization reacted to ideological signals from above. These signals included exhortations to fight against bourgeois nationalism and great-power chauvinism. Highlighting conflict between Kabardians and Balkars would not demonstrate obedience to the party line. Rather, it would attract unwanted attention from Moscow and demonstrate the Kabardino-Balkar leadership's ineffectiveness at maintaining the tenets of intercommunal cooperation upon which Kabardino-Balkaria was founded. Nevertheless, not only does conflict between Kabardians and Balkars not figure in newspaper reports, the archived minutes of meetings of the Kabardino-Balkar Party Committee (Obkom) and district committees (raikoms) also do not reveal significant tensions or conflicts between Kabardians and Balkars between 1928 and 1941.

Collectivization, Repression, and Resistance

By 1929, Stalin initiated his so-called "great break" (*velikii perelom*): an about-face from the mixed economy of the New Economic Policy (1921–8) to a full assertion of state control over all spheres of the economy and a massive concentration of the country's economic resources toward industrialization. With the First Five-Year Plan, one of the center pieces of this "great break," the Stalinist state set unrealistically high targets for industrial growth and then called on workers to fulfill the plan in four years instead of five. The plan was designed to push Russia's industrial workforce to its limits. To finance this industrialization drive, the Soviet government needed access to the country's most valuable economic resource: grain. To achieve this and assert control over the countryside, Stalin introduced "total collectivization" (*sploshnaia kolletivizatsiia*) as part of a "socialist offensive" in the countryside. This involved the forced transformation of the country's peasantry into rural proletarians and the destruction of the traditional power structures and way of life in the countryside. The strips of land farmed by families would be combined into kolkhozes (collective farms). The state would also transfer livestock and farming implements to the kolkhozes. Peasants would no longer control their land and farm for their own families. Rather, they would work on collective farms as employees. Chairs of kolkhozes would divide the farming tasks among the peasants who would receive part of the harvest as payment for their labor. They calculated these payments through a system of "labor-days." Importantly, most of the harvest went to the state. The Stalinist state then sold much of this grain abroad to raise capital for the ambitious industrial projects of the First Five-Year Plan.

To further break up social solidarities in the countryside, the state fomented class war by forcibly removing "kulaks," more prosperous peasants, from villages. The Soviet state security organs arrested over a million alleged "kulaks," and hundreds of thousands were deported to labor camps or executed as enemies of the people. There was no standard definition of a "kulak," and, frequently, they were simply those members of a village who were slightly better off than more impoverished peasants. For example, in Kabardino-Balkaria, the Soviet authorities regarded those who sold produce from their gardens at the market as "kulaks."[47]

An assault on traditional culture accompanied these transformations of the social and economic structures of the countryside. Attacks on religion were a key feature of this acceleration of the Bolsheviks' ongoing cultural revolution. The state launched propaganda campaigns against the observance of religious rituals and holidays, closed remaining churches and mosques, and, frequently, arrested members of the clergy. During this period, the Soviet state endeavored to root out practices that it deemed backward and to impose Western cultural norms. In the name of women's liberation, party activists in Kabardino-Balkaria worked to promote women's employment outside the home and engagement in Soviet communal activities. They also worked to combat negative attitudes toward the use of childcare facilities, the wearing of winter coats by women, the payment of bride price (*kalym*), and sending girls to school.[48]

Throughout the Soviet Union, chaos engulfed the countryside in 1929 and 1930 as peasants violently resisted the Soviet state's collectivization drive. Resistance took on many forms, including the slaughter of livestock and the destruction of farm machinery, the refusal to carry out kolkhoz directives, and, less frequently, direct armed resistance. In the North Caucasus, regions that had traditionally been most steadfast in their resistance to Russian rule, most notably Chechnya, witnessed the greatest levels of resistance to collectivization. After initial waves of resistance, however, peasants throughout the Soviet Union gave in to the enormous pressure and resigned themselves to life on the kolkhozes. Throughout the Soviet Union, the collectivization of agriculture had priority over the collectivization of stockbreeding. As such, while collectivization concluded in the plains regions of Kabardino-Balkaria in 1932, collectivization did not conclude in the transhumant stockbreeding Balkar communities until 1937.[49]

While collectivization was a massive change in land tenure practices within the communities of the North Caucasus, it did not have a noticeable impact on intercommunal relations. Because collectivization did not involve the transfer of land from one people to another but, rather, from individuals and local communities to the state, aggrieved communities directed their opposition toward the state rather than a specific national group. If anything, this may have further diminished the likelihood of intercommunal land disputes.

Among other causes, it is generally accepted that the deportation of the Chechens during the Second World War was a form of population politics used to deal with an ethnicity that demonstrated particularly strong resistance, through frequent armed uprisings and sustained support of insurgent groups, to Soviet social and cultural transformations.[50] This policy of deportation to remove an overtly restive population was not the case with Kabardians and Balkars. Compared with their Chechen neighbors, Kabardians, and, more importantly, given our efforts to understand the reasons for their deportation, Balkars offered less overt resistance toward Soviet policies, such as collectivization, the repression of the Islamic clergy, and the closure of religious schools and mosques. Moreover, in Kabardino-Balkaria, it was Kabardians, a group *not deported* during the Second World War, rather than Balkars, who figured in most incidences of violent resistance and "banditry" in the late 1920s and early 1930s.[51]

Balkars played but a minor role in the Kabardian-led Baksan Uprising of 1928, the largest rebellion against Soviet rule in Kabardino-Balkaria. When violence erupted in the summer of 1928, tensions had been brewing over Soviet economic and religious policies. Predominantly Kabardian villagers in the Baksan district were upset at compulsory grain requisitions, the beginnings of collectivization, the closure of mosques and Islamic schools, and the repression of respected members of the local clergy.[52]

The locus of resistance during the summer of 1928 was Baksan district, the heartland of Greater Kabarda. Baksan had a strong tradition of Islamic education, and the recently repressed leaders of the so-called *sharia* movement came from this region.[53] The use of forced labor on a canal construction project during the middle of the summer harvest triggered the uprising. On the evening of June 9, the head of the Baksan district executive committee (*ispolkom*) and local militia arrested seven villagers from Kyzburun 2 for refusing to work on the canal. At six the following morning, the adult population of Kyzburun 2 marched to the town of Baksan, the district administrative center, where the seven villagers were detained. Joined by disgruntled villagers from surrounding Kabardian *auls*, a large crowd surrounded the *ispolkom* offices. Calling for "sharia law and the elimination of Communists," the crowd stormed the building, raiding a weapons cache and freeing the seven prisoners.[54] A four-day standoff between the rebellious Kabardian villagers, temporarily in control of the town of Baksan, and Soviet security services followed. On June 14, the government sent Red Army divisions to Baksan to put down the uprising.[55] Soviet security services punished 118 people for participation in the Baksan Uprising: the OGPU executed 20 people on the spot, a further 11 were sentenced to death and later executed, and the remainder served Gulag sentences.[56] Though gradually attracting the support of some surrounding Balkar *auls* and Cossack *stanitsy*, the rebellion remained a predominately Kabardian affair. Of the four major cases of armed resistance in Kabardino-Balkaria during the late 1920s and early 1930s, only one occurred in the Balkar district.[57]

To be sure, collectivization, the repression of Islam, and attacks on tradition evoked an equally negative reaction among many Balkars as among Kabardians. However, one of the reasons for the lower incidence of *violent mass resistance* among Balkars was that the collectivization of stockbreeding in Kabardino-Balkaria occurred four to five years after the collectivization of agriculture in the oblast. It was not until 1934 that Soviet authorities forcibly collectivized the sheep and cattle of the stockbreeding Balkar families, long after the Kabardian plains had been fully collectivized and Soviet security forces had brutally put down associated resistance. News of resistance in neighboring regions, such as Terek district and Ingushetia, helped fuel Kabardian resistance to collectivization. By the time the Balkars faced collectivization, neighboring plains regions had been pacified, and there appeared to be little hope for the isolated Balkars to conduct a successful resistance movement. Acts of passive resistance—the mass selling off and slaughter of livestock—rather than overt attacks on Soviet power came to characterize the struggle to collectivize the Balkars' mountain valleys. The Balkars gave up their cattle and joined collectivized brigades (*artely*) of shepherds only reluctantly, and when an opportunity to reverse collectivization arose during the Nazi occupation, the Balkars redistributed their cattle among households with great enthusiasm.[58] But in the 1930s, the Balkars remained comparatively docile before Soviet power, and there is no reason to conclude that they had garnered a reputation, as the Chechens had, for being especially resistant to Soviet rule.

Administrative-Territorial Transformations and Kabardian-Balkar Relations

The 1930s witnessed a series of transformations of Kabardino-Balkaria's internal administrative borders and, in 1936, the passing of the new Stalin Constitution was accompanied by the promotion of a number of AOs, including Kabardino-Balkaria, to the nominally higher administrative status of Autonomous Soviet Socialist Republic (ASSR) (see Map 5). These transformations reflect administrative and ideological concerns of the Stalinist regime rather than local ethnic politics. In the post-Soviet period, however, some Balkar ethno-political entrepreneurs, advocating the separation of Balkaria from Kabardino-Balkaria, have claimed that some of the border changes during this period were part of an effort by the Kabardian leadership to weaken the

Balkars' territorial sovereignty and their ability to defend their national interests. According to a March 1993 article by the Working Group of the National Council of the Balkar People (NSBN), the administrative structure of Kabardino-Balkaria as codified in the 1937 Constitution of the Kabardino-Balkar ASSR "established a unitary nation-state structure for the republic." This unitary status, the authors continue, "disregarded the fact that from its inception Kabardino-Balkaria was formed from two constituent parts—Balkaria and Kabarda—and [the constitution] did not provide a mechanism for these constituent territories to defend their interests."[59]

The NSBN may be correct in arguing that Kabardino-Balkaria's administrative structure did not provide the Balkars with a means to effectively represent and defend their interests. However, as we have seen, its claim that Kabardino-Balkaria was formed through the union of two coequal national territories is not accurate. From its inception, there was no legislation enshrining the territorial integrity of a distinct Balkar territory and preventing changes to its administrative borders. Balkaria—the areas of compact Balkar settlement—entered the newly formed Kabardino-Balkar AO with the status of a district equal to the oblast's other districts.[60] Partly as an effort to overcome the complexities of the land question (i.e., the fact that Kabardian and Balkar shepherds used pastures scattered throughout the republic), the Soviet state applied national autonomy to Kabardino-Balkaria as a whole but not to its constituent districts. For example, the trans-Malka mountain pastures of the Kabardian-majority Mountain (later Zolka) district were shared, as they historically had been, among all shepherds of Kabardino-Balkaria according to need rather than nationality. For purposes of administrative efficiency (particularly in terms of implementing nativization), and as a result of historic patterns of settlement, the districts of Kabardino-Balkaria roughly corresponded to zones of compact Kabardian, Balkar, and Russian settlements. During the first decade and a half of Soviet rule, some of these districts temporarily held the names of their majority nationality: Balkar district (1922–35), Lesser-Kabardian district (1921–35), and Cossack district (1925–8). But the names and borders of these districts changed frequently throughout the Soviet period. If each district was not officially tied to a single nationality, each village provided cultural infrastructure for its majority nationality. For example, Balkar-majority villages in Kabardian-majority districts offered schooling in the Balkar language.

The changes to Kabardino-Balkaria's administrative-territorial structure during the 1930s were in line with larger all-union trends and policies. In 1935, the government dissolved the Balkar district replacing it with three smaller ones: Chegem, Cherek, and Elbrus. In 1938, the government separated the Khulam and Bezengi societies from Cherek district, the most populous of the Balkar districts, to form the Khulam-Bezengi district. That same year the Balkar village of Tashly-Tala and the Balkar settlement attached to the Lesken light factory were transferred to the newly formed Lesken district, which had a Kabardian majority. These administrative changes were all part of an all-union policy of *razukrupnenie raionov*: the dividing up of districts into smaller units. The ultimate goal of this policy was to bring state and party institutions closer to the people and to allow for the establishment of tighter control over village life by central and republican Soviet authorities.[61] The administrative-territorial changes associated with *razukrupnenie* affected each of Kabardino-Balkaria's communities equally—the Kabardino-Balkar leadership, based on directives from Moscow, divided up both Kabardian-majority and Balkar-majority districts into smaller units and broke up larger villages into smaller ones.[62] More importantly, the division of the Balkar District into smaller districts did not violate the original conditions on which the Balkars entered into a shared AO with the Kabardians. Finally, these new districts still contained overwhelming Balkar majorities.

Kabardino-Balkaria Under Nazi Occupation: The Collapse of the Soviet Order

The causes of the temporary rupture in intercommunal relations in Kabardino-Balkaria brought on by the deportation of the Balkars lie in events and processes during the Second World War and the evolution of Soviet population politics and ethnic cleansing.[63] Geopolitical concerns, magnified by Stalin's paranoia, interacted with long-standing practices of state violence to produce ethnic cleansing. This interaction led Soviet security services to respond to the development of local anti-Soviet insurgencies during the war among peoples whom the Stalinist regime already viewed as untrustworthy by deporting entire nationalities.

The Development of Soviet Ethnic Cleansing

The turn to mass deportation during the Second World War was not new. Before the Soviet era, tsarist officials practiced ethnic deportations and resettlement as a form of population politics aimed at reengineering the demographic makeup of their empire based on security and economic concerns. Military-colonial officials sought to secure their imperial peripheries by removing communities deemed "undesirable" or "unreliable" and replacing them with "trustworthy" elements, usually the core population of the Empire.[64] Notably, this type of population politics led to attempted genocide in the Northwest Caucasus. In the 1860s, tsarist military officials ethnically cleansed the Northwest Caucasus of about 90 percent of its long-resisting Circassian population, through the destruction of *auls* and deadly forced expulsion to the Ottoman Empire. Tsarist officials replaced the indigenous Circassian population with a loyal Russian core element and other loyal communities that could easily adapt to the region's ecological conditions in order to more effectively tap its economic potential, namely Greeks and Armenians.[65]

The tsarist state practiced mass ethnic deportations during the First World War. The Russian military, suspicious of the loyalties of diaspora nationalities whose compatriots resided in neighboring states with whom Russia was at war, deported about one million of these minorities—particularly Germans, Jews, Poles from the Western borderlands and Muslim groups from the South Caucasus—to the interior of the empire.[66] Soviet Russia would turn to the same tactics of deporting "enemy nations" used by its tsarist predecessor, but with a totality and absence of restraint characteristic of the modern interventionist states of the twentieth century.

With the possible exception of the Civil War–era deportations of Cossacks from the Don, Terek, and Kazakh steppe regions,[67] the Soviet Union's population politics of deportation initially targeted groups based on social class rather than ethnicity. By deporting *relatively* prosperous peasant families in villages across Russia, the population politics of dekulakization in the early 1930s focused on removing "socially alien elements" from the countryside throughout the Soviet Union.[68]

By the mid-1930s, geopolitical tensions between the Soviet Union and its neighbors produced a spike in "Soviet xenophobia" and ultimately led the Soviet state to shift the targets of its deportations from class enemies to enemy nations. In the early 1930s, Soviet population politics began to take on an ethnic emphasis when Soviet security organs targeted *specific ethnicities* for increased dekulakization measures.[69] By the mid-1930s, however, Soviet xenophobia led to outright ethnic cleansing of border regions. Soviet ethnic cleansing began with the deportation to Kazakhstan of Poles and Germans from border regions of the Ukrainian SSR in early 1936.[70] Next, in 1937, as tensions mounted between the Soviet Union and Japan, NKVD forces deported the entire Korean population of the Soviet Far East to Central Asia.[71] The deportation to Kazakhstan of Persians from Azerbaijan's borderland with Iran followed in 1938.[72]

This move to deport entire ethnicities from border regions entailed the triumph Soviet xenophobia over of what Martin calls the "Piedmont Principle": the belief that Soviet national autonomy for diaspora nationalities (in the form of national village soviets and districts) and state support for their cultures would allow the Soviet Union to serve as a national center—as Piedmont did during Italian unification—around which the rest of a given nation would rally. The Soviet Union would, its leaders hoped, serve as a motor for the future unification, under a Soviet or at least pro-Soviet framework, of territorially divided national communities. The goal of the "ethnophilia" exhibited by Soviet nationality policies in border regions was the projection of a positive image of the Soviet Union abroad, particularly among communities just across the Soviet border, in hopes of extending Soviet influence and paving the way for possible territorial expansion.[73] By the mid-1930s, the Stalinist regime had gone from seeing diaspora communities and "cross-border ethnic ties" as tools for the projection of Soviet influence abroad to seeing them as tools for foreign states to infiltrate the Soviet Union for nefarious purposes.[74] The perception among the Soviet leadership that the Soviet Union had failed in its efforts to project its influence across its borders, first and foremost in Polish-controlled Western Ukraine (Galicia), led to the abandonment of the Piedmont Principle amid growing fears of foreign infiltration throughout the Soviet borderlands.[75]

Soviet xenophobia only increased with the outbreak of the Second World War as perceived "enemy nations" became real ones; deportations increased accordingly.[76] Not trusting the allegiances of representatives of nationalities whose titular states the Soviet Union was at war with or occupying—Finns, Germans, Lithuanians, Estonians, and Latvians—Soviet security organs subjected these nationalities to varying degrees of mass deportation. Among the Baltic peoples, "anti-Soviet" and "socially alien" elements and their families faced deportation as the Stalinist regime struggled to root out resistance in and apply collectivization to its newly annexed territories.[77] In 1940 and 1941, the NKVD cleansed its northwestern border regions with Finland of most of its non-Russian populations.[78] The Stalinist regime dissolved the Soviet-German autonomous territories including the ASSR of the Volga Germans, and security organs deported the entire Soviet-German population to Siberia and Central Asia.[79] Indeed, in October 1941, 5,803 Germans became Kabardino-Balkaria's first wartime victims of ethnic deportation.[80] In 1944, as tension rose between Turkey and the Soviet Union, the NKVD deported entire diaspora communities of Kurds, Meskhetian Turks, and Hemshins (Armenian Muslims) from Georgia.[81]

During the war, the Stalinist regime grew increasingly suspicious of nationalities that had demonstrated notable resistance to Soviet cultural and economic transformations in the 1920s and 1930s. In general, the non-Russians of the Soviet peripheries, especially Islamic peoples, including Caucasian mountaineers, exhibited greater resistance to collectivization and Soviet assaults on religion than the Russian core.[82] Stalin's growing mistrust of non-Russian minorities during the war, especially if they were Muslim, is evidenced by the Red Army's exclusion in the summer of 1942 of Caucasus mountaineer peoples from conscription. In October 1943, the Red Army stopped conscripting all "local nationalities" from the Caucasus and Central Asia. These were the very nationalities whose loyalties the tsarist state also viewed with suspicion and, accordingly, exempted from military service.[83] The Red Army offered no official explanation for its ending of conscription of these nationalities. Unofficially, the Stalinist leadership viewed these non-Slavic Soviet nationalities as "hostile and unreliable elements."[84]

Why the Balkars?

For all the Stalinist regime's increased mistrust of local nationalities along the empire's peripheries, there is a vast difference between ending conscription of representatives of various "untrustworthy" (*neblagonadezhnye*) nationalities and deporting entire nationalities on false charges of collective treason. For most of the "punished peoples" of the Soviet Union, several other factors would align to seal their fates. First, the front— and thus the borders of Soviet control—would approach their autonomous territories and most of these territories would then come under Nazi occupation. Second, fears of a Turkish invasion of the Soviet Union would cause the Stalinist regime to view most of these peoples—given their ethnolinguistic and religious ties with Turkey—as potential fifth columns.[85] Both factors likely played a role in the deportation of the Balkars.

On April 8, 1944, one month after the mass deportation of the Balkars to Central Asia, the presidium of the Supreme Soviet of the USSR post facto decreed the deportation of the Balkars. The official explanation for the deportation was the high incidence of collaboration with the Nazi occupiers during the war. According to the decree, the Balkars were being deported

> in connection with the fact that, during the period of occupation of the territory of the Kabardino-Balkar ASSR by the Germano-fascist invaders, many Balkars betrayed their motherland, entered into armed detachments organized by the Germans, conducted diversionary actions against Red Army divisions, helped the fascist occupiers in the capacity of guides on the Caucasian passes, and, after the expulsion of the enemies armies from the territory of the Caucasus by the Red Army, entered into German-organized bands for the struggle against Soviet power.[86]

As Khadzhi-Murat Sabanchiev, the leading historian of the Balkar deportation, argues, "at a time when the vast majority of the male population of fighting age was serving at the front it is absurd to accuse the Balkars of mass treason." Therefore, he continues, "collaboration is not...the reason for the deportation but an excuse for the deportation."[87]

Based on available material, it is impossible to be completely certain of the driving reasons behind the brutal mass deportations of the Balkars and other peoples (Karachais, Ingush, Chechens, Crimean Tatars, and Kalmyks) on charges of mass treason during the Second World War; but the perceptions of the Soviet leadership, particularly Stalin and NKVD chief Lavrentii Beria, provide a more convincing explanation for the deportations than the official one. In particular, extreme Soviet xenophobia during the Second World War and a long-standing suspicion of the loyalties of restive borderlands communities in the Caucasus and elsewhere led Soviet policymakers to view some nationalities as threats to Soviet state security. The Stalinist bureaucrat-policeman state used techniques of population politics to combat these perceived threats.

By 1944, a confluence of factors led the Stalinist leadership to view the Balkars as a security threat. First, they were "untrustworthy" because they were Caucasian mountaineers. From the 1930s through the Second World War, of all the native regions of the North Caucasus, only Chechnya witnessed a relatively broad-based insurgency. In other republics of the North Caucasus, there were only small groups of insurgents.[88] Nevertheless, long-standing popular perceptions of mountaineers as fiercely anti-Russian (given their resistance to tsarist rule), the *marginally* higher rate of anti-Soviet resistance in the region generally, and the severe problems of controlling Chechnya, led the Soviet state, which had begun to associate itself with the Russian nation at an unprecedented level during the war, to lump mountaineer nationalities together as "untrustworthy elements."[89] In a self-fulfilling prophecy, the fact that Kabardino-Balkaria fell to the German armies only reinforced the "untrustworthiness" of its mountaineer population.

The geography of the Balkars' mountain valleys also impacted the fate of the Balkar people. Particularly concerning for the Soviet leadership was the German occupation of the strategic mountain passes leading across the Caucasus range into Georgia. Should the Germans have crossed the mountains, they would have had a relatively open path to the Baku oil fields. After an alpinist detachment of the German Army scaled Mount Elbrus in late August, the passes into Georgia seemingly lay open to Nazi invasion. It was only at great human cost that, during the autumn of 1942, the Red Army was able to halt the German Army's advance across the mountains into the South Caucasus.[90] Rather than accept the blame for not protecting the Elbrus region, Soviet military and political officials passed the blame onto the peoples inhabiting the mountain regions in the vicinity of the passes: the culturally and linguistically related Karachais and Balkars. As we have seen, Stalin and Beria accused them of guiding the fascist armies along the perilous mountain passes and conducting diversion in the Soviet rear.[91] Sabanchiev argues that the Germans' occupation of the mountain passes was a result of their greater preparation compared with the Red Army. First, the German Army was able to occupy the mountain passes around Mount Elbrus because their assault group included a special detachment of mountain climbers who had traveled to the Elbrus region before the war under the guise of a civilian alpinist expedition. These alpinists brought back detailed maps for use by the German Army during a future assault on the Caucasus.[92] Second, the Red Army initially sent an inadequate number of forces to defend the mountains.[93]

The mountains also offered Red Army deserters and active anti-Soviet resistors alike—the NKVD did not distinguish between the two categories—refuge from Soviet security forces. Therefore, while Kabardians and Balkars resisted Soviet rule or simply deserted during the war in roughly equal measure, the crags and caves of their mountain valleys enabled Balkars to evade capture by the NKVD for much longer than Kabardians.[94] For this reason, and others discussed later in the chapter, local NKVD reports on the security situation in Kabardino-Balkar emphasized the problems in Balkar regions.

Rising fears of Turkish invasion of the Caucasus and Crimea, initially sparked by an escalation of pan-Turkist rhetoric in the Turkish press and Turkey's 1941 friendship pact with Germany, led the Stalinist regime to view the Turkic peoples of the Soviet Union with increased suspicion, especially those, like the Balkars, residing in southern regions closest to the front and to Turkey.[95] Meanwhile, the anti-Soviet leaders of Turkey's large Caucasian émigré community began making plans for returning to the Caucasus after a German invasion. Finally, Turkey's concentration of troops on its Soviet border in the summer of 1942 and the simultaneous German advance in the North Caucasus magnified Stalin's fears of Turkish invasion and paranoia about the Turkic peoples of the Crimea and the Caucasus as potential fifth columns.[96] According to G. Takoev, former North Ossetian NKVD chief who defected during the war, "the General Staff of the USSR came to the . . . conclusion that in the case of war in the south, the peoples of the Caucasus could become a problem for the military machine in this sensitive place and, therefore, it would be strategically appropriate to take timely 'special' measures."[97]

Balkar historians argue that local dynamics—having more to do with the wartime shortcomings of the republic's leadership than with problems of intercommunal relations—also played a role in the deportation of the Balkars. According to this interpretation, Zuber Kumekhov, the young Kabardian leader of Kabardino-Balkaria's party organization, provided compromising material on the Balkars, such as reports that exaggerated the extent of Balkar resistance and Nazi collaboration, in an effort to deflect the blame for what the Stalinist leadership viewed as his failures during the German invasion and occupation of Kabardino-Balkaria.[98]

On June 22, 1941, when Hitler's invasion brought the Soviet Union into the Second World War, Kabardino-Balkaria's leadership consisted of younger *vydvizhentsy* (promoted workers) who had risen through the ranks of the local party organization in the 1930s. Kabardino-Balkaria's young leadership proved unable to cope with the tasks of the party organization during wartime. The NKVD had purged nearly the entire Kabardian and Balkar leadership of the 1920s between 1934 and 1938.[99] After overseeing the destruction of rivals, former comrades-in-arms, and the remaining pre-Stalinist intelligentsia, Kabardino-Balkar First Secretary Kalmykov also fell victim to the purges as an "enemy of the people" in 1938.[100] After a brief interlude of leadership by a Moscow-appointed Russian, in 1939, the party chose a Kabardian, Zuber Kumekhov, then only twenty-nine years old, to fill Kabardino-Balkaria's highest leadership position.[101]

Kumekhov was the exemplar of a Kabardian *vydvizhenets*: a worker who ascended the ranks to a leadership position as a result of his social background. The sixteenth of seventeen children in a poor peasant family, with his mother dying of illness and his father executed by the White Army for supporting the Bolsheviks, Kumekhov became an orphan at the age of nine. He worked as a shepherd for his *aul*'s communal flocks until the mid-1920s, when he joined the first cohort of young Kabardians and Balkars to study and live in Nalchik's Lenin Educational Village.[102] Controversial at the time, this new communist boarding school was designed to indoctrinate and train new Soviet cadres from the local nationalities and, importantly, break the hold of national customs over the younger generation by removing them from their *auls*.[103] Kumekhov continued his education as part of the first class to enter Nalchik's new Pedagogical Technical School. After finishing his higher education in 1932, Kumekhov went on to serve in a series of important administrative posts in Kabardino-Balkaria, including as head of the Department of Education for his home district of Urvan, chairman of a kolkhoz, party secretary of the Dokshukino Alcohol Factory and, in late 1937, party secretary of Lesken district.[104] In 1939, after less than seven years of party and state service, Kumekhov found himself in charge of the Kabardino-Balkar ASSR on the eve of the Second World War.

The chief challenges that Kumekhov and the young Kabardino-Balkar leadership confronted during the war included the mobilization of Kabardino-Balkaria's material resources for the war effort; the organization and equipping of a volunteer cavalry; the defense of Kabardino-Balkaria's capital; the evacuation of key party and state personnel, heavy industry, and other valuable material from the republic in the event of occupation; and the coordination of partisan resistance. Initially, Kumekhov and Kabardino-Balkaria's leaders coped well with the first of these tasks. Kabardino-Balkaria mobilized great material and human resources for the front. They oversaw the quick retooling of local factories to produce armaments and military supplies. Kabardino-Balkaria provided substantial grain and meat provisions for the front.[105] Finally, the initial mobilization of those under military service obligation was a success. After the halt in conscription of indigenous groups from the North Caucasus, the republic's leaders, under orders from the State Committee of Defense (GKO), found no shortage of volunteers for a Kabardino-Balkar National Calvary Division. The 3,500 Kabardian and Balkar volunteers of the 115th Kabardino-Balkar Cavalry fought bravely under difficult conditions. The Red Army sent this division's Kabardian and Balkar horsemen to fight against the main contingent of German armored tank detachments on the southern front. After helping to slow the German advance in the Don region, the 115th Kabardino-Balkar Cavalry suffered crippling defeat on the Sal'sk Steppes in August 1942.[106]

In mid-August 1942, as German and Romanian armies advanced on the North Caucasus, conditions in Kabardino-Balkaria deteriorated rapidly and the local leadership proved incapable of dealing with the herculean tasks placed upon it. First, most of the 700 surviving volunteers of the 115th Cavalry, now leaderless and badly beaten, decided to return home, considering their mission fulfilled and not wanting to be broken up and reassigned among different Red Army divisions. Fearing punishment, these former cavalrymen decided to wait out the war as fugitives in the mountains of Kabardino-Balkaria, a minority joined armed resistance groups.[107] With the appearance of these deserters in the mountains in August, the number of "bandits" in local NKVD reports to Beria increased exponentially because the security organs did not differentiate between deserters and active members of armed groups. This seeming increase in "banditry" reflected poorly upon Kumekhov and the party leadership. Second, Kumekhov made the decision to evacuate Kabardino-Balkaria's industry, agricultural equipment, and cattle too late, and, consequently, the fascist armies took control of a significant number of tractors, cattle, horses, and functioning factories.[108] Third, 43 percent of the republic's party members and candidates remained on occupied territory.[109] The occupation authorities forced party members, under threat of execution, to relinquish their party allegiance and serve in the occupation administration. Many party members were among the 3,000 people who fled westward from Kabardino-Balkaria in January 1943 with the Germans in hopes of evading retribution for their collaboration.[110] Fourth, the defense of the capital, Nalchik, which the party placed in the hands of Kumekhov, collapsed in late October 1942. Finally, Kumekhov did not do enough, according to a July 1943 Party Control Commission report and his postwar critics,[111] to organize an effective and sufficiently large partisan movement in Kabardino-Balkaria.[112]

To be sure, the tasks that the GKO delegated to Kumekhov and the Kabardino-Balkar leadership would have been difficult for even the most capable and tested party leaders and administrators. Nevertheless, Sabanchiev posits that by exaggerating the size and actions of the anti-Soviet resistance in the mountains during and after the Nazi occupation, Kumekhov attempted to deflect blame for these perceived failures and create a perception that his working conditions were worse than they actually were.[113]

Even before the deportations, alarmist reports on anti-Soviet resistance from Kumekhov and the local NKVD had tragic consequences for the Balkars as the Soviet security organs responded to the exaggerated threat with absolute destructive force. In responding to reports of Balkar resistance, the Soviet security organs adopted policies of ethnic cleansing similar to those used by colonial empires in the nineteenth and early twentieth centuries.[114] Indeed, policies of destroying and relocating rebellious villages were the very ones that tsarist armies in the Caucasus used a century earlier, and ones that Soviet security forces had been using to root out resistance in Chechnya since the mid-1920s.[115]

The violence perpetrated by NKVD forces upon peaceful civilians in the Cherek Valley between November 27 and December 4, 1942, on the eve of the relatively brief (month-long) Nazi occupation here, exemplifies these destructive practices. During an Obkom meeting in October 1942, Kumekhov claimed that there were "more than 600 armed bandits."[116] There were really about 150–200 people of various nationalities—Balkars, Kabardians, Georgians, and Ossetians—whom the NKVD labeled "bandits" hiding out in the Cherek Valley. The majority of these "bandits" were deserters evading prosecution.[117] After the only major clashes between deserters-*cum*-insurgents and Soviet forces in the Cherek Valley, which occurred from November

21 through November 23 as the 37th army retreated deeper into the valley from the German advance into the Balkar districts of the KBASSR, hundreds of NKVD soldiers conducted a brutal punitive expedition in the valley. As a result of the NKVD's execution of civilians in the area, the until-then-mostly-peaceful deserters resorted to insurgent tactics, including a raid on the district executive committee.[118] Unable to root out the insurgents, NKVD forces sealed off five villages and began taking hostages in order to pressure the elusive bandits to lay down their arms. Over the course of four days, NKVD forces, fearing that the impending arrival of the Germans would prevent the total elimination of the insurgents, burned down three villages and executed 1,500 women, children, and elderly men.[119] There was one small clash involving Balkar insurgents responding to the murder of their families, which resulted in the death of three insurgents and seven Soviet soldiers.[120] Before abandoning the region to the advancing German forces, NKVD forces piled the corpses of the murdered villagers in a building and burned it down. Captain Fedor Nakin, commander of the mission, summarized the results of his punitive expedition:

> During the period from 27.11.42 through 30.11.42 five villages have been destroyed: Upper Balkaria, Salty [Sautu], Kumiun, Upper Cheget and Glashevo. Of these the first three were burned down. Fifteen hundred people were killed, according to the testimony of hostages this included 90 bandits, 400 people (men) capable of carrying arms, and the remainder were women and children.[121]

As in similar cases of Soviet wartime atrocities, most infamously Katyn, the Soviet state covered up NKVD culpability in the Cherek massacre and blamed the German occupation forces. Immediately after the breakup of the USSR, a special commission of the Supreme Soviet of the Kabardino-Balkar Republic established the NKVD's responsibility for the Cherek massacre.[122]

NKVD Culpability for the Balkar Deportation and the Role of Kumekhov

The NKVD conceived of, planned, and implemented the mass deportation of the Balkars from Kabardino-Balkaria, then about 16 percent of the republic's population, as part of the Stalinist regime's targeting of nationalities that it deemed unreliable. The deportation of the Balkars and others was a product of Stalin's growing xenophobia and paranoia about foreign infiltration and potential fifth columns within non-Russian populations.

According to Sabanchiev's interpretation, during the thirteen months between the end of the Nazi occupation and the Balkar deportations in March 1944, the interests of local NKVD chief Konstantin Bziava and First Secretary Kumekhov aligned; both signed their names to damning reports to Beria, which were likely ordered by Beria, on banditry and treason in the Balkar districts. Kumekhov was able to target the Balkar districts for two reasons. First, the number of fugitive deserters and active insurgents was indeed greater in Balkar districts because their mountainous environment attracted those hiding from or actively resisting Soviet power.[123] Second, the Balkars had few of their own representatives among Kabardino-Balkaria's ruling elite;[124] the Balkar *nomenklatura*, always relatively small given the Balkars' minority share of the population, had either fallen victim to Stalinist repression before the war or were called up to the front during the war. Sources suggest that Bziava, under orders from Beria, was interested in organizing the deportation of the Balkars.[125] In June 1943, Beria, a Mingrelian Georgian, appointed Bziava, a loyal Mingrelian comrade from the Georgian NKVD, as new Kabardino-Balkar NKVD chief. Immediately upon his arrival in Kabardino-Balkaria, Bziava issued a report to Beria falsely criticizing his predecessor for intentionally underestimating the size of the insurgency in the republic and in the Balkar districts in particular.[126] This spike in alarmist rhetoric about the scope of the Balkar resistance coming from a loyal Beria appointee at exactly the time when Beria was preparing the deportation of other nationalities (the Karachais, Ingush, and Chechens) suggests a premeditated NKVD plan for the eventual deportation of the Balkars.

In an accusatory February 23 1944 report to Beria, "On the Condition of the Balkar Districts of the Kabardino-Balkar ASSR," local NKVD and NKGB chiefs Bziava and Filatov and First Secretary Kumekhov cited the events leading up to the Cherek massacre as evidence of the Balkars' guilt.[127] After citing statistics on Balkar "bandit" attacks, they asserted that "the fascist-German armies were received positively by the majority of the population in Balkaria."[128] Given the brutalities committed by the NKVD immediately preceding the arrival of the German Army, which of course were omitted from the report, it is unsurprising that the local population would have welcomed Nazi forces as liberators.

This report is of great importance in the chain of events that culminated in the Balkar deportations because it would form the evidentiary basis for the Balkars' deportation on charges of mass treason. The role of the Kabardian Kumekhov in compiling this report has been the subject of recent disputes between Kabardian and Balkar historians.[129] Ultimately, there is general agreement among scholars that, for Kumekhov, deportation was the unintended consequence of the reports to which he signed his name. The report provided the justification for Beria to order the deportation, and Beria's request to Stalin for approval of the Balkar deportations made specific references to the content of the report. After describing the topography and natural resources of the Balkar regions, surveying the history of the formation of Kabardino-Balkaria, briefly highlighting some of the Balkars' contributions toward the Soviet war effort, and offering a longer account of Balkar resistance to Soviet rule from 1929 to the present, Bziava, Filatov, and Kumekhov conclude: "Based on the above, we consider it necessary to decide the question of the possible resettlement of the Balkars beyond the borders of the KBASSR."[130] This was not the first suggestion of using population politics to solve the exaggerated security problems in the Balkar districts. In April 1943, Zhanakait Zalikhanov, the Balkar head of the Cherek district, suggested to Kumekhov the resettlement of the population of the Cherek Valley to the plains of Kabardino-Balkaria as a means of definitively rooting out the "bandit element" and improving the Balkars' material conditions.[131] But this report to Beria, written less than two weeks before the deportation, is the first documented mention of the deportation of the entire Balkar population from the KBASSR.

On March 1, 1944, Beria sent 21,000 NKVD soldiers to Kabardino-Balkaria's capital Nalchik. One week later, these forces conducted the deportation of the republic's entire Balkar population. These soldiers were experienced. They had helped carry out the deportations of other nationalities during the preceding six months. On March 2, Beria visited Kabardino-Balkaria to examine the republic's industrial recovery and oversee final preparations for the deportations. He left the command of the Balkar operation in the hands of Major General Ivan Piiashev. On March 5, Piiashev sent his troops to positions in the republic's mountainous Balkar districts. These troops sealed off the passes between the valleys. The unsuspecting Balkar villagers greeted the soldiers hospitably. The soldiers informed residents that they had come for rest and relaxation before returning to the front. On March 7, the day before the deportation, Bziava, Filatov, Kumekhov, and Piiashev informed the heads of the Balkar districts of the impending deportation and ordered them to hand over their dossiers and other official party documents.[132] Balkar NKVD agents and militia were ordered to hand over their badges and weapons.[133] At two in the morning on March 8, the NKVD forces sealed off the Balkar villages, erected checkpoints, and cut off radio and telephone connections. At five in the morning, the soldiers stormed into Balkar homes, informed the residents (mainly women, children, and elderly men) that they were being deported for treason, and gave them between fifteen minutes and a half hour to pack their belongings. All day on March 8, NKVD forces drove Studebakers packed with Balkars down from the valleys to the train station in Nalchik, where they loaded the entire Balkar population not serving at the front onto cattle cars.[134] On March 11, Beria reported to Stalin: "the operation involving the deportation of the Balkars from the Kabardino-Balkar ASSR was concluded on March 9. 37,103 Balkars were loaded into echelons and sent to new places of settlement in the Kazakh and Kirgiz SSRs."[135]

Kabardino-Balkaria witnessed a series of administrative-territorial transformations in the wake of the deportation, many of which reflected the republic's new ethno-demographic realities. On April 8, 1944, the presidium of the USSR's Supreme Soviet issued a decree "On the Resettlement of the Balkars Residing in the Kabardino-Balkar ASSR and the Renaming of the Kabardino-Balkar ASSR to the Kabardian ASSR."[136] In addition to changing the name of the republic, which was part of a larger Stalinist policy of removing all official mention of the Balkars, this decree transferred territory from the former Kabardino-Balkar ASSR to neighboring republics. The Georgian SSR, the homeland of Beria and Stalin, received portions of the region surrounding Mount Elbrus, including the strategic passes across the Caucasus range that had fallen to the Nazis. This territory became part of the Upper Svaneti district of the Georgian SSR. The decree transferred most of the Kurp district (Eastern Lesser Kabarda), once the home of the German colony of Gnadenburg, to the North Ossetian ASSR. Home to Slavic peasants who settled Lesser Kabarda in the late-tsarist period and the Kumyks of Kizliarskoe, the five villages near the confluence of the Kurp and Terek became part of North Ossetia in order to connect Mozdok, newly transferred to that republic's jurisdiction, with the rest of North Ossetia. Other decrees transformed Kabarda's internal borders and renamed the few Balkar villages that the republic's authorities elected to repopulate.[137] The Kabardian authorities dissolved the Balkar districts of Khulam-Bezengi and Cherek, replacing them with a new Soviet (*sovetskii*) district, which now included a number of Kabardian villages. The remaining two Balkar districts, Chegem and Elbrus, kept their names, but their borders also were changed to include Kabardian villages.[138] A dizzying number of other decrees followed in an effort to maintain the population balance among the republic's districts.[139]

Kabardian Responses to the Balkar Deportations

Sadness, confusion, and anger characterized the Kabardian popular response to the Balkar deportations, as many Kabardians watched the NKVD forcibly remove their friends, coworkers, and relatives from their homeland.[140] To be sure, there were those who sought to profit from the Balkars' departure by pillaging the depopulated Balkar villages in search of valuables.[141] However, evidence of Kabardian grief at the deportations and Kabardians trying to offer assistance to the desperate Balkars is far more plentiful.[142] Most often, such help took the form of Kabardians providing the departing Balkars, who did not have enough time to adequately pack, with food and other provisions for the road.[143] In one particularly sad incident, as a guarded train of cattle cars filled with Balkars waited to depart from the station outside the Kabardian village of Nartan, hundreds of villagers rushed to the train in order to give provisions to the Balkars. Siuttun Atakuev, a Balkar deportee, recalls:

> Balkar families arrived one after another. They were mostly elderly and women with their children. The residents of Nartan tried to give them some extra provisions, but the soldiers pushed them back, hitting them with rifle butts. The noise was unimaginable. Everyone was screaming, crying, trying to find their relatives in the crowd.[144]

Local officials responded to the Balkar deportations with dismay and finger-pointing. Local Kabardian and Russian officials could not openly criticize the central Soviet leadership's decision to deport the Balkars. They did, however, view the deportations as an economic blow to their republic and an unwelcome disruption of a long-standing symbiotic relationship. In a rare moment of candor following the deportations, at an Obkom meeting, People's Commissar of Land for the Kabardian ASSR, Zhankhot Khuzhokov, declared that "the deportation of the Balkars from the territory of our Republic at such a difficult moment for our motherland is an enormous detriment for our country, for our Party organization, for the regional Party Committee, and for all the people of our Republic."[145]

Local Kabardian officials, taking their lead from Moscow, which was quick to understand that the deportations were being received negatively by the local population, found a politically safe way to criticize Kumekhov for allowing the deportations to happen without criticizing Stalin and Beria's population politics. They faulted Kumekhov for not doing enough to tackle the ostensible cause of the deportation—banditry and collaborationism—through political means. This attack on the local leadership helped to bolster the Stalinist regime's justification of the deportations while allowing local officials to express their dismay at the deportations. At a meeting of the Plenum of the Kabardian Obkom, organized to facilitate Kumekhov's ouster one month after the deportations, Kabardian and Russian Party members offered criticism of the first secretary's wartime management of the republic. The barrage of criticism began with Kruglikov, a political organizer sent to the Kabardian ASSR from the Central Committee (TsK) in Moscow:

> the resettlement of the Balkars . . . an act of great political importance . . . speaks . . . first and foremost to the [low] level of past [political] work. . . . In connection with these events it is necessary to significantly heighten and strengthen the quality of political work both among the . . . population; it is necessary to correctly explain this event.[146]

Criticism of the local party leadership's role in the Balkar deportations continued over the next three years. At the Twelfth Oblast Party Conference in December 1946, Party Secretary Kazmakhov noted:

> The deportation of the Balkars was not the result of . . . the Germans' arrival here and groups of Balkars bandits. . . . It became possible because ideological work in our republic—work on nurturing a spirit of Leninist-Stalinist friendship of peoples—did not meet the demands of the critical moment for our country.[147]

The deportation of the Balkars negatively impacted the republic's economy. A steep decline in sheep and cattle stock, which had only just begun to recover after the wartime destruction, accompanied the deportation of the Balkars, and the Kabardian ASSR was never able to fully make up this economic loss. Official plans from Moscow called for the repopulation and economic utilization of former Balkar lands. The government of the Kabardian ASSR decided against repopulating the Balkars' mountain villages because of "the absence of necessary conditions (lack of arable land and the high-mountain location) for normal economic development."[148] Local Kabardian and Russian populations had no desire to become mountaineers and take the Balkars' place in the republic's cattle-breeding economy. The local government repopulated only four of the thirty-three former Balkar kolkhozes. Kabardians from neighboring villages moved to the Balkar villages of Gundelen, Kashkhatau, and Gerpegezh, and Belaia Rechka, outside Nalchik, became a kolkhoz for invalids of the war. The government repopulated these villages because they were located in more desirable locations. These were mainly villages in the foothills that the Balkars established in the late-tsarist era after the land reforms. The land in these villages was better than in the mountains, and they were closer to and better connected with the republic's population centers. The Georgian SSR resettled several dozen Svan-Georgian families in the former Balkar villages Elbrus and Upper Baksan near Mount Elbrus, territory transferred to the Georgian SSR. Finally, the Kabardian government sanctioned the use of allotments from the foothills Balkar villages Khasan'ia and Lower Chegem as garden plots for employees of state enterprises. On the eve of the Balkars' return in 1957, only 7.5 percent of former Balkar farmland and pasturage was in use.[149] In contrast to the other deported peoples of the Caucasus, especially the Chechens and Ingush, the vast majority of former Balkar villages lay empty, and in shambles, waiting to be rebuilt by their former residents.

One reason why few Kabardians volunteered to resettle in neighboring Balkar villages, despite government incentives to do so, was that Kabardians did not believe that the Balkar deportations were permanent.[150] Many expected the eventual return of the Balkars to their homes and villages. Indeed, there are reports of Kabardians maintaining the homes of their Balkar friends. In a 2003 essay competition for school children in Kabardino-Balkaria on the theme "how events in the twentieth century are reflected in people's fates," a young Kabardian girl from Zaiukovo reported on a story told to her by her grandmother about how she experienced the deportation of her Balkar friends as a young girl. After the deportations, this then-young Kabardian girl would visit the neighboring Balkar village of Gundelen every spring for thirteen years to repaint her best friend's home in anticipation of her and her family's return. In her essay, the schoolgirl explains further, "my grandmother did not know then that she was preserving this empty house not only for her friend. She was also looking after the future family nest of her youngest daughter, because when [this Balkar family] returned, my aunt married the son of my grandmother's friend."[151]

The Kabardian ASSR and Balkars in Exile: Two Extremes of Soviet Nationalities Policy

The divergent fates of the Kabardians and Balkars during the period of the Balkar exile from 1944 to 1957 reflect the contradictions of Soviet nationalities policy. On the one hand, late Stalinism marked the height of Soviet repression of some national minorities. The brutal deportations of entire ethnicities led to their temporary disappearance from Soviet society, and, after the return of these ethnicities, the deportees' traumatic experience of exile would remain etched in their consciousness for decades to come.[152] On the other hand, the Kabardian case suggests that this era marked a high point for Soviet developmentalist policies aimed at forging "socialist nations" out of the Soviet Union's manifold ethnicities and moving them along a Marxist-Leninist timeline of historical development by means of affirmative action-style policies.[153] Nativization, though always present in the Soviet Union, would never again receive the high priority and attention from central authorities that it received during the Stalin years.[154] In particular, after de-emphasizing nativization during the late 1930s and the Second World War, during the final years of his life, Stalin placed renewed emphasis on this policy. The experience of the Kabardian ASSR from 1948 to 1953 exemplifies this late 1940s shift in Soviet nationalities policy. During this period, the Kabardian ASSR witnessed the maturation of its national intelligentsia, an accelerated promotion of titular nationals (in industry, education, culture, and the party and state administration), and the expansion of the use of titular languages in administration. Therefore, while Kabardians experienced the full effects of Soviet developmentalism through nativization, the Balkars, deprived of their right to exist as an official nationality, experienced socioeconomic and cultural discrimination and decline as a result of Soviet policies.

The case of nationalities policy in the Kabardian ASSR accords with Blitstein's view that, from the late 1930s on, the Stalinist state pursued two contradictory policies—nativization and Russification—because Soviet ideology held contradictory views on the role of ethno-national difference in "overcoming backwardness." On the one hand, from the standpoint of Marxist-Leninist ideas about historical development, the perceived "backwardness" of non-Russians relative to Russians "meant emphasizing the fact that they were different from Russians," that they constituted distinct socialist nations. On the other hand, "from the standpoint of statist uniformity, this fact of ethnic difference was a form of backwardness that was necessary to overcome" through a common Soviet culture based on the Russian language and culture.[155] At different moments, the Stalinist regime emphasized one or the other approach to "overcoming backwardness." In the immediate postwar years, Stalinist nationalities policy shifted toward a renewed emphasis on nativization.

Officials in the Kabardian ASSR began to pay greater attention to questions of nativization after May 1948, in the wake of Central Committee criticisms of the republic's handling of Soviet nationalities policy. While the postwar years witnessed a general reemphasizing of nativization, particularly the training of national cadres, the 1948 critique of the Kabardian ASSR had implications beyond the North Caucasus. It set off a larger campaign to investigate shortcomings in conducting nationalities policy around the RSFSR. However, a robust campaign to ensure the immediate correction of these shortcomings foundered as a result of changes in Central Committee leadership in late 1948.[156] Nevertheless, this return to nativization as a policy priority gradually bore fruit, and, by the last years of Stalin's reign, nativization efforts had met with success in achieving their developmentalist goals.

In January 1948, the Central Committee (TsK) of the party sent Dmitrii Protopopov to the Kabardian ASSR to report on conditions in the republic as part of a usual all-union inspection campaign. Protopopov sent back a critical report on "shortcomings" in the spheres of agriculture, education, and "the implementation of nationalities policy." He placed the blame for these problems on the republic's Party chief Nikolai Mazin, a Russian appointed after Kumekhov's ouster. Protopopov directed his harshest invective at Mazin's handling of nativization. Protopopov reported that in the republic's poorly performing native schools, the Kabardian language was the language of instruction only through the fourth grade and that Kabardians, and the Kabardian language, had little representation in the economy and administration in the republic. Protopopov's report also criticized Mazin's antagonistic attitude toward the Kabardian population. In particular, Protopopov characterized Mazin's public comments about supposed widespread Kabardian disloyalty during the war as a "serious mistake."[157] In May 1948, the TsK sent another inspector, Mikhail Fonin, to the Kabardian ASSR to verify Protopopov's reports and confront the local party leadership on its shortcomings. Speaking at a plenary session of the Kabardian Obkom on May 12, Fonin attacked Mazin for incorrectly implementing Soviet nationalities policy. Fonin criticized Mazin, for "not doing enough to create a native intelligentsia."[158] Fonin read out an April 7 TsK decree, "On the Work of the Obkom of the Kabardian ASSR," censuring Mazin for his inactivity in the development of a Kabardian intelligentsia. According to the decree, "despite the fact that 50 percent of the Kabardian Republic's population is of the native nationality, the republic's native intelligentsia can be counted on one's hands . . . and the number of national cadres is not increasing in the . . . Republic."[159] Fonin described the disproportionately low share of Kabardians among the republic's intelligentsia:

> There are only seven Kabardian teachers with higher education. For every fifteen teachers with higher education there is one Kabardian. For every 50 doctors only one is Kabardian . . . very few Kabardians work in republican, oblast, and district organizations. There are very few officials of the local native nationality in the Presidium of the Supreme Soviet and the Obkoms of the Party and Komsolmol. Moreover, in a number of the republic's districts there are no Kabardians in Party and Soviet organs whatsoever.[160]

The problems of a small or nonexistent national intelligentsia that Fonin highlights were not unique to the Kabardian ASSR.

The problems for which the TsK criticized the Kabardian ASSR leadership illustrate the ways in which the results of the nativization campaigns of the 1920s and 1930s, particularly in the "Soviet east," fell short of their desired goals. These shortcomings were the results of factors common to many Soviet ethno-territorial units. First, despite impressive increases in literacy and primary schooling, there was never enough funding to meet the demands for secondary and higher schooling necessary for the creation of a sizable native intelligentsia. The use of native-language instruction in primary schools and increasing fees and entrance standards for higher education, where education was conducted exclusively in Russian, impeded the transition of nationals to higher schooling.[161] Second, the shift from Latin to Cyrillic scripts for Soviet languages (applied to Kabardian and Balkar in 1936) meant losing the already-inadequate supply of native-language textbooks and other literature and retraining those with literacy in Latin script.[162] Third, the small number of nationals who received higher schooling often did not work in their specialization. Rather, as Martin points out, they "were diverted into more visible leadership positions."[163] On the other hand, to meet the ambitious nativization quotas for the hiring of titular nationals, party and state organs employed large numbers of titular nationals in menial jobs. This type of "mechanical nativization" created a "hole in the middle," whereby titular nationals were relatively well represented at the top and bottom of the employment hierarchy but not in the technical jobs in the middle. Fourth, the purges of the 1930s, especially the targeting of the so-called "bourgeois nationalists" after September 1937, decimated minority national intelligentsias.[164] Finally, the Second World War dealt a blow to prewar nationalities policy successes: many educational institutions were repurposed for the war effort; much of the republic's native-language literature and many of its schools were destroyed during the war; wartime production priorities precluded printing new textbooks and construction of new schools; mobilizations and Nazi occupation interrupted the training of national cadres; and many members of the native intelligentsia perished in the war.[165]

In the postwar years, the Soviet state redoubled its nationalities policy initiatives and began to make significant progress in forging national intelligentsias, nativizing administration and industry, and expanding schooling in the non-Russian republics. Unlike in the 1930s, when the party emphasized "mechanical nativization" over other aspects of nativization in the Soviet east,[166] in the late 1940s the party, while not abandoning quotas, pursued linguistic nativization and the formation of a native intelligentsia to a far greater degree. Declaring that the "main task" for the Kabardian Party was "the creation of cadres of the non-Russian intelligentsia and the strengthening of ideological work among non-Russian cadres," the TsK decree "On the Work of the Obkom of the Kabardian ASSR" called on the republic's Obkom to "correct the mistakes and distortions of nationalities policy."[167] In particular, the Central Committee issued the following tasks to the Kabardian Obkom: the introduction of native-language education through the seventh grade; the introduction of the Kabardian language in local administration; and the expansion of the number of Kabardians in political and administrative positions.[168] After hearing Fonin's criticisms, the Kabardian Obkom issued decrees reflecting the TsK's demands. Despite efforts to expiate himself and address the Central Committee's criticisms on his neglect of Soviet nationalities policy, the April 7 TsK decree, "On the Work of the Obkom of the Kabardian ASSR," ruined Mazin's political career. In 1949, Moscow replaced First Secretary Mazin "for not ensuring the Bolshevik training [*vospitanie*] of the republic's party *aktiv*" with Vasilii Babich, another Russian outsider.[169]

In June 1948, the republic's Council of Ministers issued a flurry of nativization decrees.[170] The goals of these decrees included: the introduction of Kabardian as the language of instruction for grades five to seven; the transfer of the work of republican, district, village, and kolkhoz administrations into the Kabardian language (with the exception of Russian districts and villages); and the training and promotion of Kabardians into industry and administrative positions. The Council of Ministers and the Kabardian Obkom put pressure on the districts to ensure the implementation of these decrees and to report back on their progress.

The Kabardian ASSR government placed greatest urgency on the transfer of administrative work from Russian to Kabardian because, as the Central Committee pointed out, the Constitution of the Kabardian ASSR stipulated that "in order to serve the workers of the Kabardian ASSR in their native language, administrative work in the Kabardian ASSR is conducted in the Kabardian language in districts, villages, and settlements with a majority Kabardian population."[171] The Council of Ministers decree explained the importance of conducting administrative work in the native language:

> In the Kabardian ASSR administrative work in village and in republican organizations and departments [is] . . . conducted in the Russian language and this is a violation of Article 24 of the Constitution of the Kabardian ASSR and a violation of the most important principle of Leninist-Stalinist nationality policy. The conducting of administrative work in the Russian language has led to some of the directives of the Party and the government being poorly understood by the native population and has impeded the ability of the native population to appeal to Soviet organs in the Kabardian ASSR.[172]

Among a host of measures aimed at ensuring nativization, the Council of Ministers tasked the republic's district executive committees (*ispolkoms*) with organizing Kabardian literacy study circles for local officials. District authorities mandated "one-hundred-percent attendance" at these circles and set deadlines for literacy acquisition for all Kabardian officials and recommended that non-Kabardians attend these study circles as well.[173] The Council of Ministers charged the Kabardian National Publishing House with printing official forms, stamps, and letterhead in the Kabardian language for all village, district, and republican organs, which were now all obliged to answer complaints and letters from Kabardians exclusively in Kabardian. The Council of Ministers requested that Moscow provide the republic with 100 new Kabardian-script typewriters to meet the demands of nativizing the republic's administration. The majority of the Kabardian villages of the republic were ordered to immediately transfer their administrative work from Russian to Kabardian because, according to the Council of Ministers, "a study of the number of officials literate in the Kabardian language established that in 43 of the 62 Kabardian villages and in most Kabardian kolkhozes, officials are sufficiently literate in the Kabardian language." Indeed, the decree notes that nativization should not be too difficult because "in a series of village soviets and kolkhozes . . . the minutes of meetings are already taken in Kabardian."[174] The remaining Kabardian villages were given until the end of 1948 to transfer their administrative work into Kabardian.

The minutes of district executive committee (*raiispolkom*) and district party committee (raikom) meetings reveal that these linguistic-administrative nativization efforts met with several impediments on the ground. Kabardian literacy classes were not being attended regularly or, in some cases, had not been formed at all. For example, a decree from the Mountain district *ispolkom* complained that "the organization of classes for the mastery of Kabardian literacy among workers is moving unacceptably slowly."[175] Similarly, the Kuba district *ispolkom* reported that "Kabardian literacy classes for senior administrators of village soviets and kolkhozes have not been organized and managers are not working on Kabardian literacy independently despite the fact many have poor literacy skills or none at all."[176] Village administrators were also not informing residents of the official nativization of administrative work. The Chegem district *ispolkom* , for example, reported that officials had not informed local residents that they should submit official paperwork in Kabardian.[177] Finally, village soviets were often the only local administrative bodies capable of achieving immediate nativization because Kabardians, and hence those literate in Kabardian were underrepresented in more specialized or technical local administrative organs, particularly the courts, the prosecutor's office, district *ispolkoms* , and their subdepartments.[178]

District governments ostensibly responded to these impediments to linguistic-administrative nativization with great vigor and persistence. *Raikoms* and *ispolkoms* stepped up pressure on local administrators to attend Kabardian literacy courses, inform residents of the switch to Kabardian language as the language of administration, and publish local newspapers in Kabardian. *Raiispolkoms* and *raikoms* also set quotas for the training and promotion of literate Kabardians into senior positions in local administration and established commissions to oversee the implementation of nativization.[179]

The republic's leadership, following orders from the Central Committee, also put pressure on the Russian-dominated central bureaucracy and upper leadership of the Kabardian ASSR to nativize. Shortly before his ouster, party chief Mazin mandated that all republic-level organs "issue replies in Kabardian to all complaints and declarations that are submitted in Kabardian." In order to implement this type of linguistic-administrative nativization at the republican level, Mazin decreed that

> in the apparatus of every republican organ . . . there should be workers who are literate in Kabardian. Mastery of Kabardian literacy for senior and ordinary Kabardian officials who work in the state apparatus should be required. . . . Moreover, it is extremely necessary that senior officials with no Kabardian fluency [i.e., Russians and other non-Kabardians] also study Kabardian literacy.[180]

With Kabardians occupying only 36 percent of the Kabardian ASSR's leadership positions, the republic's leadership also called for the promotion of Kabardians in order to achieve the nativization of the republican administration. The difficulty in promoting Kabardians to leadership positions, as Mazin indicated in a party meeting, was that "a reserve of [Kabardian] cadres for promotion had not been created."[181] The republic's leadership correctly linked the solution of the cadre problem with efforts to improve and expand secondary and higher education for Kabardians.

The leadership of the Kabardian ASSR also made significant efforts to ensure the introduction of Kabardian language for secondary grades five through seven. According to a May 28 report from Mazin, an additional 235 Kabardian teachers were needed to meet the demands for the expansion of Kabardian-language schools. This amounted to an approximately 150 percent increase. Eighteen textbooks would also have to be translated into Kabardian and published. Mazin called for the shift to Kabardian-language instruction from the fifth grade to begin about fifteen months later, in the 1950–1 school year. The government allocated funding for the expansion of the local Pedagogical Institute, increased Kabardian-language publishing, and ordered a census of all trained Kabardian teachers working outside of their field for possible reassignment back into education.[182]

Given the TsK's criticisms of the small size of the native intelligentsia, the Kabardian ASSR leadership began to place greater emphasis on the training of "national cadres" who would eventually fill the ranks of an expanded Kabardian intelligentsia. The representation of Kabardians in higher education was very low. As Mazin pointed out at a meeting of the Obkom, "there are 559 students in the Kabardian Pedagogical Institute and only 56 are Kabardian."[183] To lay the groundwork for the creation of a Kabardian intelligentsia, the republican government emphasized expanding secondary education though the tenth grade so that more Kabardian students could enter higher education.[184]

The 1948 nativization campaign in the Kabardian ASSR emphasized bringing native workers into the industrial sector. The industrialization of the Soviet Union's ethnic-minority communities was a major part of the Soviet developmentalist vision, and, by the late 1940s, the state had achieved only modest progress in this modernization project among Kabardians and most other nonindustrial minorities. In 1948, Kabardians accounted for only 9.7 percent of the Kabardian ASSR's industrial workforce. Most of these Kabardian workers were occupied in menial jobs.[185] The lack of skilled laborers, low level of technical education among Kabardians, and concentration of industry around the overwhelmingly Russian city of Nalchik contributed to the small number of Kabardians in industry. In the postwar period, just as in the 1930s, hostile attitudes of Russian factory directors, foremen, and workers toward Kabardians also impeded the growth of a Kabardian industrial working class.[186]

The Kabardian Obkom spurred on the nativization of industry in several ways. It set quotas for the number of Kabardians that each industrial enterprise was to hire and train for various positions along the employment hierarchy.[187] The party mandated that the factory training schools (FZOs) attached to the republic's major industrial enterprises achieve at least 50 percent Kabardian enrollment.[188] Some industries sent Kabardian workers on training courses in Moscow and Leningrad.[189] The Kabardian Obkom required industrial enterprises to prepare a "reserve" of current Kabardian employees for quick promotion.[190] The republic's meat processing and packing plant and its chocolate factory sent Kabardian workers to study at Moscow's Food Industry Institute.[191] In an effort to attract and retain Kabardian workers, industrial enterprises were required to provide Kabardian workers with material incentives, including priority access to housing, fuel, and garden allotments.[192] Industrial enterprises were required to form Kabardian literacy circles for managers and technical personnel.[193] The Kabardian Obkom required each of the republic's industrial enterprises to submit regular reports on their nativization efforts. The short-term results of this nativization campaign resembled the mechanical nativization of the 1930s: more Kabardians entered industries, but in lower-level positions.[194] However, in the long term, over the 1950s, as the party maintained its pressure on industrial enterprises, Kabardian representation gradually increased at all levels in the industrial sector.[195]

While many of the more ambitious nativization plans—getting significant numbers of Russian officials to attend Kabardian-language classes and achieving full nativization of administrative work by the beginning of 1949—went unfulfilled, the nativization campaign quickly yielded desired results. During raikom meetings and conferences throughout 1949 and 1950, party leaders reported gradual progress (in addition to impediments) toward the nativization of administrative work in their districts.[196] They achieved this progress in part by continuing to pressure officials to attend literacy courses.[197] Nevertheless, there were certain skilled positions (e.g., accountants and prosecutors) that could not be filled by people literate in Kabardian because there were few Kabardians trained in these professions.[198] The nativization of such positions depended on the success of long-term programs aimed at creating a Kabardian intelligentsia. The Ministry of Education of the Kabardian ASSR fulfilled its duty to transfer secondary education into Kabardian. The fifth-grade class of 1949–50 became the first secondary school class to be taught in Kabardian. By the 1950–1 school year, Kabardians made up over half of the republic's tenth-grade students, up from less than one-third in 1948.[199] This expansion in secondary schooling meant that more Kabardians had the requisite training to enter higher education. The 1951 graduating class of the Kabardian Pedagogical Institute included eight times more Kabardians than the graduating class of 1945.[200] In 1948, just under one-tenth of the students at the

Kabardian Pedagogical Institute were Kabardian; already by 1951, Kabardians made up over one-third of the student body.[201] By the early 1950s, the number of Kabardian teachers with higher education had doubled and, by 1956, there were 304 Kabardian teachers with higher education, a fivefold increase from 1950.[202] The Kabardian ASSR's industrial sector took on more permanent Kabardian employees in both menial and, by 1950, technical and management positions.[203] If in 1948 Kabardians made up 9.7 percent of the republic's industrial workforce, by 1950 they made up 17.2 percent.[204] The local party apparatus also made progress in nativizing its leadership positions. If on January 1, 1948, Kabardians filled 36 percent of the leadership positions within the party apparatus, by December 1, 1950, they were employed 46 percent of these positions.[205]

Terry Martin argues that a type of "silent *korenizatsiia*" emerged by the late 1930s that would "characterize Soviet policy for the rest of the Stalin years."[206] As the Kabardian case shows, the de-emphasizing of nativization and attacks on "bourgeois nationalists" that accompanied the xenophobia of the late 1930s were not dominant features of Soviet policy for the rest of the Stalin years. Moreover, when the Central Committee shifted its focus to nativization again in the late 1940s, discussion of nativization was not confined to party and state organs. Rather, nativization was widely discussed in public, particularly in local newspapers. The Kabardian nativization campaign of the late 1940s and early 1950s was hardly silent. Throughout this period, the pages of *Kabardinskaia pravda* are replete with articles exhorting citizens to "strengthen work on the growth of national cadres," "tirelessly develop national cadres for industry," "carefully cultivate national cadres for industry," "train national cadres for agriculture," "overcome the backwardness of Kabardian theatre," and "improve the training of Kabardian teachers in every possible way."[207] *Kabardinskaia pravda* featured articles explaining the importance of the shift to Kabardian language in local administration, explaining the relative significance of native- and Russian-language instruction, and highlighting the achievements of the young Kabardian national intelligentsia.[208]

In the 1950s, *Kabardinskaia pravda* began to feature an unprecedented number of scholarly articles by young Kabardian academics on Kabarda's national history and culture.[209] These articles reflect an important long-term achievement of the nativization campaign: the creation of a native Kabardian academic establishment. After the April 1948 TsK decree, the republican government began to allocate greater funds and pay more attention to the Kabardian Scientific Research Institute (KNII),[210] opening new departments, increasing the number of researchers, and emphasizing the need for more Kabardian representation among the Institute's faculty. In the late 1940s and early 1950s, the first groups of Kabardians earned their *Kandidatskaia* degrees (roughly the equivalent of PhDs) at the Soviet Academy of Sciences and major universities in Moscow, Leningrad, and Tbilisi. These young scholars returned to the Kabardian ASSR and entered the faculties and departments at the Kabardian Research Institute and the Pedagogical Institute.[211]

The renewed emphasis on nativization after 1948 combined with the Soviet Union's general postwar developmentalism (increased industrialization, urbanization, and expansion of and improvements in schooling) produced important changes to the structure of Kabardian society. By the late 1950s, the size of the Kabardian intelligentsia had increased exponentially. In the ten years from 1948 to 1958, the number of Kabardian doctors, veterinarians, geologists, trained teachers, agronomists, and other members of the intelligentsia went from numbering in the tens to the hundreds. While the size of the republic's ethnically Russian intelligentsia and industrial workforce still dwarfed that of the Kabardians and the Kabardian population remained overwhelmingly rural, the Kabardians had taken a major step toward Soviet modernization during the late 1940s and 1950s. Importantly, the Kabardian leadership's efforts to develop infrastructure for further modernization and nativization, of which the opening of a state university in Nalchik in 1957 was its crowning achievement, had been established during these years.[212]

The Late-Stalin-Era Balkar Experience: A Nation in Exile

The Balkars' experiences during the thirteen years of their exile from the North Caucasus were diametrically opposed to those of the Kabardians. While the Kabardians experienced a form of Soviet modernization tailored to the conditions of an agrarian national-minority region, the Balkars experienced severe demographic, cultural, and socioeconomic decline as a result of deportation and exile. Deprived of their national autonomy and its benefits, the Balkars were absent during these important years of increased nativization and socioeconomic modernization.

Deportation was a demographic blow to the Balkar people that would take decades to overcome. Given the cramped, unhygienic conditions and dearth of basic provisions during the eighteen-day journey from the North Caucasus to Central Asia, 307 Balkars died en route to their places of resettlement.[213] The Stalinist regime deported the Balkars from the temperate mountains of the Caucasus to the extreme continental steppe zones of Kazakhstan and Kirgizia. The difficulties of adapting to these environmental changes led to an initial sharp rise in mortality and decline in birthrate among the Balkars.[214] The lack of basic provisions and housing for Balkars and heightened demands for physical labor imposed on them in their places of special settlement (*spetsposelenie*) also contributed to the significant population decline among Balkars during the first four years of their exile.[215] On the eve of their deportation, the total Balkar population stood around 38,300. Nine months later the total Balkar population stood around 33,000. The Balkar population continued to decline until late 1948, when it reached a low of 31,700.[216] It was only in 1949 that the birthrate of the Balkars and other deported peoples began to exceed the death rate. The Balkar population only reached its pre-deportation levels by the time of their return from exile in 1957. By 1959, the Balkar population stood at 42,400, roughly the equivalent of the pre–Second World War Balkar population.[217]

The Stalinist regime deprived the deported peoples of many of their rights, stunting their socioeconomic and cultural development. Officially, according to the Sovnarkom Decree, "On the Legal Position of Special Settlers," the only restrictions placed on representatives of the deported peoples were that they did not enjoy freedom of movement and were subject to a curfew.[218] "Special settlers" (*spetsposelentsy*) could not travel more than 3 kilometers outside of their place of residence without official permission. Given that schooling in the special-settler villages was usually limited to the primary level, travel restrictions meant that opportunities for education beyond the fourth grade were often closed off to Balkar children. Travel restrictions also meant that Balkars usually were unable to find employment in their fields of expertise.[219] In addition to these official restrictions, the NKVD commandants who oversaw the administration of the special settlements received the following list of instructions regarding how they were to treat their special-settler residents:

- Do not accept into the party.
- Do not accept into higher education institutions.
- Only employ as unskilled laborers.
- Do not promote to positions of authority.
- Do not assign community agitation work.
- Do not give them any awards or medals.
- Do not encourage any initiative.
- Do not conscript into the army.[220]

This list hung on the wall of each commandant's office, visible to all. Finally, with the dissolution of their national autonomy, the Balkars and other deported peoples lost their cultural rights. Balkars could no longer receive education in their native language or study Balkar in an official capacity. All Balkar language publishing ceased. Scholars could not study or write on Balkar history and culture. Balkar national music, dance, theater, and literature could not exist in any official capacity.[221]

In addition to the official mechanisms that cut Balkars off from their national culture, the general dislocation and destruction of the deportations produced a cultural rupture among the Balkars. Much of the Balkars' inventory of national handicrafts and heirlooms—from ceramic and metal housewares, to weapons, to national costumes— was lost or destroyed during and after the deportations. The Balkars transmitted their national customs, legends and other forms of folklore orally within families from one generation to the next. The death of many elderly Balkars during and shortly following the deportation, and, to a lesser extent, the division of families across different areas of special settlement, led to a break in the line of transmission of these important components of Balkar culture.[222]

Soon after Stalin's death in 1953, the Soviet leadership initiated a relaxation of the most repressive features of the Stalinist regime. The regime released prisoners from the Gulag system in large numbers and, regarding the special-settler communities, issued decrees removing the most onerous restrictions on the special settlers. These decrees raised hopes for many that they would soon be allowed to return to their homelands. These documents played an important role in the improvement of the lives of the special settlers in their places of residence. From 1954 on, as the state eased travel restrictions on special settlers, the Balkars enjoyed vast improvements in their employment and schooling opportunities. In 1955, the Balkars and the other special-settler communities began to receive passports and youths were drafted into the army.[223] Encouraged by signals of liberalization from Moscow, Balkar representatives, including the celebrated poet and war hero Kaisyn Kuliev, launched a petition campaign to achieve the full restoration of their people's cultural, territorial, and political rights. The leadership of the Kabardian ASSR indicated its support to Moscow in favor of the Balkars' petitions to return to the republic.[224] The Balkars' dream of returning to their homeland became a reality with the start of Nikita Khrushchev's de-Stalinization campaign in 1956.

Nikita Khrushchev hoped to rejuvenate the Soviet experiment in part by drawing on popular enthusiasm and restored faith in the construction of a just and prosperous communist society. He saw that Stalin's repressive rule had the effects of stifling initiative and fostering a mentality of fear and subservience. To mitigate these effects, Khrushchev initiated a campaign of de-Stalinization based on a repudiation of Stalin's cult of personality and the repression of innocent Soviet citizens during the Great Terror and entire peoples during the Second World War. Indeed, in his secret speech at the Twentieth Party Congress in February 1956, which marked the official start of de-Stalinization, Khrushchev specifically condemned the deportations of entire nationalities.

Return to the North Caucasus and the Politics of Reintegration

During their thirteen-year exile, the "special settlers" harnessed the idea of returning to their historic homeland and reconstituting their national existence. Indeed, the experience of exile, particularly the sense of difference fostered by their position as minorities and newcomers to the foreign environment of Central Asia, the stigmatizing restrictions on movement and employment, and segregation from the rest of the population, produced a strong sense of national consciousness among the "punished peoples," despite their lack of access to native-language education and other aspects of national autonomy.[225] Moreover, the mixing of mountaineer populations broke down geographic barriers that had traditionally impeded national consolidation among the peoples of the North Caucasus.

The first waves of Chechens, Ingush, Karachais, and Balkars began to return to the North Caucasus after Khrushchev's secret speech at the Twentieth Party Congress in February 1956. It was not instantly clear whether the Soviet government would reestablish the national autonomies that had been dissolved during the war or even sanction the return of the "punished peoples" to their homelands. In the wake of the Twentieth Party Congress, a series of decrees removed restrictions on residence and movement from the deported peoples; however, these decrees explicitly forbade former special settlers from returning to their historic homelands. The peoples of the North Caucasus forced the Soviet leadership's hand by coupling elite-led letter-writing and petition campaigns with the mass return of tens of thousands of families.[226] On November 24, 1956, the Central Committee issued a decree, "On the Reestablishment of the National Autonomy of the Kalmyk, Karachai, Balkar, Chechen and Ingush Peoples."[227] It called for the renaming of the Kabardian ASSR back to the Kabardino-Balkar ASSR, and Moscow directed the KASSR government to include Balkar representatives before new elections.[228] On January 9, 1957, the presidium of the Supreme Soviet of the USSR published an Ukaz, "On the Transformation of the Kabardian ASSR."[229] The Supreme Soviet of the Kabardino-Balkar ASSR's adoption of the law, "On the Transformation of the Kabardian ASSR into the Kabardino-Balkar ASSR," on March 28, 1957, concluded the legislative process of reestablishing the autonomy of the Balkar people.[230]

The Soviet government took measures at the central and regional levels to facilitate the return and reintegration of the "punished peoples." These measures were more effective in reintegrating the Balkars than any of the other deported nationalities. Among numerous factors that contributed to this outcome, two were central: the Balkars' valleys had not witnessed mass colonization;[231] and, aside from brief tensions during the early-Soviet delimitation of borders, the Balkars had maintained friendly and largely symbiotic relations with their Kabardian neighbors prior to their deportation. The Council of Ministers of the RSFSR and the governments of the reestablished autonomous territories issued decrees allocating funds, building materials, seed, cattle, and other supplies to "resettler families" and reconstituted collective farms. The leadership of the newly reformed Kabardino-Balkar ASSR played an important role in facilitating the return and reintegration of the Balkars. The ethnically Kabardian leaders of the Kabardian ASSR, Timbora Mal'bakhov (first secretary of the Regional Party Committee) and Aslanbi Akhokhov (chair of the Council of Ministers), successfully lobbied the Central Committee of the Communist Party in Moscow for specific policies and funding to better facilitate the return and reintegration of the Balkars.[232] The local government decreed the reconstruction of essential infrastructure for the reestablished villages. The state exempted returnees from taxes and agricultural procurement obligations. The Council of Ministers provided long-term credit to returning families.[233]

In Kabardino-Balkaria and elsewhere, government aid for resettlement of deported peoples was often inadequate, especially during the first years of return. In this regard, Kabardino-Balkaria's failures are typical of those faced by other regions of return. Misappropriation of funds was by far the most pervasive problem plaguing reconstruction efforts.[234] Despite the heavily censored Soviet press, *Kabardino-Balkarskaia pravda* reported extensively on problems of misuse and misappropriation of reconstruction funds. For example, an article from January 7, 1958, "Urgent Tasks of Balkar Kolkhozes," reported that "of the 19.5 million rubles allocated for the construction of homes, only 7 million were spent on housing. For example, the kolkhoz . . . in the village of Tashly-Tala received only 17,000 rubles of the 650,000 rubles it was supposed to receive."[235] Though not mentioned here, but likely clear to readers, members of the Soviet *nomenklatura* (administrative and Party elite) embezzled much of this funding as it made its way down the chain of command.[236]

The misappropriation of funds severely impeded housing construction. While articles such as "Widen the Scope of Housing Construction in Balkar Kolkhozes" and "Increase the Pace of Construction in Balkar Kolkhozes" also mention insufficient housing stock, officials in Nalchik hid the full extent of the state's inability to meet the housing needs of the returning Balkars.[237] Indeed, the housing shortage caused the Kabardino-Balkar government to freeze Balkar resettlement in June 1957 for the rest of the year out of "fear that most Balkar families will not have housing by winter."[238]

While housing was the most pressing issue, other factors impeded reintegration. Most importantly, the failure to purchase the planned amount of cattle meant that the cattle-breeding Balkar returnees could not be employed according to plan. In addition to lack of housing and unemployment, other problems stemming from inadequate funding and misappropriation, such as insufficient infrastructure (roads, schools, hospitals, and bathhouses) and a lack of basic consumer goods, continued to hamper reintegration efforts through 1958.[239]

Given the corruption and irresponsiveness to consumer demand of the Soviet-planned economy, the problems of funding and supply that plagued Balkar reconstruction efforts should not come as a surprise. All returning peoples faced similar sets of problems. These structural economic problems slowed down the reconstruction efforts, but in no way precluded their success.

Indeed, by 1967, that is, within ten years of their return, in terms of socioeconomic status and political representation, the Balkars occupied a position vis-à-vis the other peoples of Kabardino-Balkaria similar to the one they had before their deportation. By 1967, the debts incurred by the Balkars during resettlement had been written off, reconstruction—of housing, infrastructure and the Balkar economy—had been achieved, and, most importantly, in terms of standard of living, levels of schooling, and employment, differences between Kabardians and Balkars were minimal. The pre-deportation practices of power-sharing—for example, the practice of reserving positions within the regional government for Balkars—continued after the Balkars' return. From 1957 on, beginning with the appointment of Chomai Uianaev as chairman of the presidium of the Supreme Soviet of the Kabardino-Balkar ASSR, a Balkar consistently occupied the republic's second most powerful leadership position.[240] Going forward, for better or worse, Soviet modernization processes transformed Balkar society in the last three decades of Soviet rule.

Whatever statistics may tell us, it is important to balance our assessment with a sense of Balkar subjectivity. The experience of exile, the collective humiliation of being unjustly labeled traitors, and the permanent loss of ancestral homes and property live on in the historical memory of the Balkars and continues to shape their sense of identity.

A comparison of the Balkar's return and reintegration with those of other "punished peoples" reveals the important roles of that earlier patterns of intercommunal relations and late Stalin-era transformations played in structuring intercommunal relations in the North Caucasus during the post-1957 period. The reintegration of the other deported North Caucasian peoples—the Chechens, Ingush, and Karachais—was fraught with difficulties that the Balkars did not experience. These problems stemmed from ethno-demographic transformations, administrative-territorial changes, and the reemergence of historic intercommunal animosities.

After the deportations, rather than let depopulated lands lay vacant, Soviet officials in Moscow tried to boost the economic productivity of the dissolved autonomous regions by settling them with representatives of neighboring ethnicities, Russians, and other nationalities from farther afield. These ethno-demographic changes between 1944 and 1956 meant that the "punished peoples" often returned to ancestral villages and towns now occupied by settler populations reluctant to give up their homes and jobs to the returning mountaineer peoples and unenthusiastic about sharing power and resources. These demographic changes created tensions between the returnees and settlers, from time to time boiling over into violent conflict (e.g., riots and intercommunal violence in Groznyi in the summer of 1958), and they prevented the returnees' reintegration into society. Tensions were most acute between the returning native population and settlers in the reconstituted Checheno-Ingush ASSR. The Soviet state resettled tens of thousands of Russians in Chechnya (renamed Groznyi oblast) largely to further develop the region's oil industry. These Russians did not leave the region when Chechens began to return, and nonnatives continued to occupy most top-level managerial and administrative positions. Consequently, Chechens and Ingush remained at the bottom of the region's socioeconomic hierarchy throughout the remainder of the Soviet period.[241]

Administrative-territorial transformations after the deportations also reawakened historic animosities and created new impediments to reintegration. After the deportations, Stalin transferred territory from the dissolved autonomous regions to neighboring regions and republics. The Soviet state did not restore any of the three of the dissolved North Caucasus autonomous territories exactly as they existed before the deportations. Kabardino-Balkaria did not regain land in the Kurp district that the state transferred to North Ossetia, and the former Balkar-majority districts were not restored in the same form as before. The state did not restore the Karachai AO. Rather it combined Karachais with the neighboring Cherkes people to form the Karachai-Cherkes AO.[242] The formation of this new AO led to tensions because the Karachais did not return to an administrative unit in which they controlled the allocation of resources and administrative appointments. They now had to share power with a multiethnic population of Cherkeses, Russians, Nogais, and Abazas. Indeed, a previous attempt at creating a dual-titular Karachai-Cherkes AO, between 1922 and 1926, failed as a result of tensions between the constituent ethnicities.[243] Territorial-administrative transformations were most problematic in Checheno-Ingushetia. In particular, the Ingush part of the Checheno-Ingush ASSR lost a sixth of its territory to North Ossetia, most notably Prigorodnyi district outside Vladikavkaz, and returning Ingush clashed with Ossetian settlers. The Ossetian-Ingush conflict was not new, but administrative-territorial changes reignited tensions. The Ingush in North Ossetia felt themselves a discriminated minority for the remainder of the Soviet period.[244] Finally, the Soviet government forbade Chechens from reestablishing many of their former mountain *auls*, deeming them economically unviable. The government exacerbated intercommunal tensions by resettling these Chechens to Cossack villages.[245]

Part of the explanation for why the reintegration of the Balkars was more successful than that of the Karachais, Ingush, and Chechens can be chalked up to numbers. At approximately 42,000, the Balkars were numerically smaller than the other three groups (there were about 80,000 Karachais, 105,000 Ingush, 415,000 Chechens), and their small numbers made return and reintegration a simpler task.

Long-term patterns of peaceful intercommunal contact and more recent developments in the Kabardian ASSR also help explain why reintegration was more successful here. In contrast to continuing Ossetian-Ingush, Russo-Chechen, and

Karachai-Cherkes tensions, after the land redistribution and power-sharing agreements between Kabardians and Balkars that accompanied the formation of the Kabardino-Balkar AO in 1922, these two communities coexisted in relative harmony during the first decades of Soviet rule. As we have seen, relatively peaceful, symbiotic relations had been characteristic of Kabardian-Balkar relations over the longue-dureé. Reports indicate that most Kabardians and local Russians were enthusiastic about the Balkars' return. Old friends and relatives ceremoniously met the returning Balkars at Nalchik train station in 1956, 1957, and 1958.[246]

Articles and official reports demonstrate that neighboring Kabardian villages and kolkhozes donated cattle, seeds, farming implements, construction materials, and labor to the Balkar reconstruction efforts.[247] Indeed, during the reconstruction of Balkar villages, Kabardians welcomed Balkars into their homes, and a significant number of Balkar families permanently settled in Kabardian villages.[248] Throughout 1957 and 1958, local district administrations organized official "Days of Friendship" (*dni druzhby*) for Kabardian and Balkar kolkhozniki. According to a November 1958 Report from the Kabardino-Balkar Obkom to the TsK, "during these meetings, Kabardian kolkhozes brought gifts of cattle, grain, and agricultural tools to Balkar kolkhozes."[249]

Arguably more important to the Balkars' reintegration than the historic relationship between Kabardians and Balkars, which was not always tension-free, were the events of 1944–56 and official policies toward Balkar returnees. Although official plans called for the settlement and economic exploitation of former Balkar lands, after the deportations the local government did not repopulate most Balkar villages, and their farmland and pastures awaited the Balkars' return.[250] In contrast to the other deported peoples of the Caucasus, especially the Chechens and Ingush, the former Balkar villages lay empty, and in shambles, waiting to be rebuilt by their former residents. Moreover, while some disagreements arose between returning Balkars and Kabardian resettlers (over rights to land and houses), Kabardians were amenable to returning to their ancestral villages nearby.[251] For example, after Balkars began to return, the Kabardians who had settled the Balkar village of Gundelen, having received state support to rebuild their homes, returned to their neighboring home village of Zaiukovo in a matter of months.[252]

In most respects, the Balkars returned to the territorial and political status quo ante. In terms of external borders, the Soviet government reestablished the Kabardino-Balkar ASSR in much the same form as it existed before. The republic's government made limited changes to the size, number, and ethnic composition of districts (*raiony*), including the Balkars ones. While the republic's government conducted this redistricting of post-deportation borders for economic reasons, it had the unintended consequence of ending the Balkars' majority in two out of three of their districts of compact settlement. Relative to the problems facing the Karachais, Ingush, and Chechens, the issue of districts seems not to have been a major issue at the time.

Finally, during the Balkars' absence, the Kabardian ASSR underwent a renewed nativization campaign in which the state devoted significant resources to training native Kabardian cadres to fill upper- and middle-level positions, previously occupied by Russians, in industrial and agricultural management, administration, and education. The development of a nativized higher education infrastructure accompanied this nativization campaign. The opening of Kabardino-Balkar State University in 1957, the same year as the official start of the Balkar return, capped off this ten-year process. These new institutions and infrastructure allowed the Kabardino-Balkar government to conduct a rapid and effective Balkarization campaign. This campaign included the training of new Balkar cadres, the nativization of the administration and economy of Balkar districts, and the closing of the educational gap between Balkars and the rest of the population of Kabardino-Balkaria.[253] By the mid-1960s, the Balkars' reintegration into Kabardino-Balkaria was complete.

Conclusions

There is no basis to claim that the deportation of the Balkars was the product of long-standing tensions between the Kabardian majority and Balkar minority over national rights to land and political representation. After the settlement of the Kabardino-Balkar land question and the attendant easing of tensions between the two neighboring peoples, the focus of state policies in Kabardino-Balkaria moved from issues of *inter-* and *intra*communal competition over land to questions of socioeconomic modernization and cultural transformation. Before 1944, local, regional, and central authorities applied state policies—whether "soft-line" policies like nativization or "hard-line" policies like NKVD repression of national elites as "bourgeois nationalists"—evenly to both Kabardians and Balkars.[254] Policymakers did not differentiate between Kabardians and Balkars; they were both treated as "nationals," that is, non-Russians. Finally, the forced collectivization of agriculture and stockbreeding during the first half of the 1930s, which ultimately shifted land control from the people to the state, and the attendant crushing of resistance to these policies, further eroded the potential for mass mobilization around questions of land.

The deportation of entire nationalities on baseless charges of collective treason during the Second World War was the columniation and most complete expression of the Soviet state's long-standing practices of population politics and state violence. During the first fifteen years of Soviet rule, Soviet population politics focused on removing representatives of real or politically constructed social groups from their social environments. With the growth of Soviet xenophobia in the mid-1930s, Soviet officials refocused their population politics on nationalities deemed disloyal to the state. The Second World War and Nazi occupation expanded the scope of Stalinist xenophobia and paranoia. The wartime collaboration of a minority from among the soon-to-be deported nationalities provided the Stalinist regime with an excuse to cleanse strategically important borderlands of suspect national minorities.[255] A confluence of factors, having much to do with geography and perceived geopolitical threats—and nothing to do with Kabardian-Balkar relations—came together to cause the deportation of the Balkars.

Many Kabardians reacted to these deportations, which often separated them from close colleagues, friends, and family members, with sadness and dismay. The deportation of the Balkars was not only a rupture in intercommunal relations but was also an ecological rupture. The deportation meant the collapse of a long-developing symbiotic system based on Kabardians and Balkars occupying complementary ecological niches. Vast swathes of mountain pasturage, which formerly brimmed with sheep and cattle each summer, lay vacant as a result of the deportations. Consumption of meat and dairy products by the local Kabardian and Russian populations declined during the Balkars' absence. The mountain zones of the Kabardian ASSR lay vacant and the Balkar *auls* became ghost villages.

Many Kabardians looked forward to the return of the Balkars and the restoration of the socioeconomic symbiosis with their neighbors that, though not without major transformations and adaptations, had characterized life in their corner of the Caucasus for centuries. Indeed, when the Balkars began to return to their homeland in the late 1950s, Kabardians and other local communities were quick to help reintegrate the Balkars back into the social and economic life of the republic. The expansion of the Kabardian ASSR's cultural, educational, and economic infrastructure during the nativization campaigns of the late-Stalin years combined with the generally welcoming attitude of the local population contributed to the Balkars' relatively quick and smooth reintegration. Indeed, when compared with the return and reintegration of other deported nationalities, the Balkar case, though not without its problems, stands out as the most successful. As I argue in the final chapter, during the Soviet collapse and the early post-Soviet years, this successful Balkar reintegration helped preserve relative intercommunal peace and blunt the appeal of separatism in Kabardino-Balkaria.

6

Intercommunal Relations and Ethnic Politics in the Post-Soviet Caucasus

Kabardino-Balkaria and Its Neighbors

For five and half years, from the summer of 1991 until late 1996, as the Soviet state collapsed and the Russian Federation gradually reestablished the power of the central government, Kabardino-Balkaria experienced waves of ethno-nationalist mobilization and intercommunal tension. Just as in the political breakdown of the early twentieth century, Moscow's lack of solid authority in the early 1990s led to ethno-nationalist mobilization and conflict throughout the North Caucasus. Conflict in Kabardino-Balkaria during this period proved less intractable than ethnicized conflicts in other parts of the North Caucasus. In late November 1996, with Kabardino-Balkaria on the brink of violent disintegration along ethno-national lines, the leader of the Balkar national movement, who had recently proclaimed the formation of the Republic of Balkaria and called for the formation of armed self-defense units, came on local state television and called for the preservation of Kabardino-Balkar unity and offered to dissolve his separatist government.[1]

Drawing on the patterns and structures of Kabardian-Balkar relations that we have traced over the previous five chapters, this chapter analyzes the medium- and long-term historical factors behind the preservation of intercommunal peace among Kabardians, Balkars, and other communities of Kabardino-Balkaria during the period of heightened tensions and ethno-national mobilization in the early 1990s. In particular, this chapter argues that long-standing patterns of intercommunal symbiosis and interdependence between Kabardians and Balkars and the related absence of a disparity in levels of modernization played primary roles in the peaceful outcome of ethno-political tensions. In order to demonstrate the effects of these long- and medium-term factors, this chapter compares Kabardino-Balkaria's experience with other, less-stable areas of the North Caucasus during this period: Karachai-Cherkessia, North Ossetia's Prigorodnyi district, and Chechnya.

The first sections of this chapter describe the events surrounding the ethno-national mobilizations and political conflicts in the North Caucasus during the 1990s. Next, it examines medium-term factors associated with the reintegration and rehabilitation of the "punished peoples" that influenced the trajectory of intercommunal relations in Kabardino-Balkaria and our three other cases during the early post-Soviet years. The Balkars, Karachais, Chechens, and Ingush did not return to a historical *tabula rasa*; long-term historical patterns and structures of social interaction and intercommunal relations had much to do with the success or failure of the reintegration and rehabilitation of the punished peoples. The Soviet collapse, as with the shattering of the tsarist empire, provided a window of opportunity for ethno-political entrepreneurs to mobilize their co-ethnics around issues of land. Demands for the readjustment of national borders or the elevation of the political status of national territories were at the heart of many of these mobilizations. To be sure, land played a different role in the ethno-political mobilizations of the 1990s than it did in the early 1920s because of the pervasiveness of modern ethnic nationalism and ethnic identity politics during the Soviet collapse. In the 1990s, deeply felt and more abstract associations of nations with specific territories often played a more salient role than the desire of villagers to expand access to land as was the case in the early 1920s. Ultimately, historic patterns of intercommunal relations and medium-term factors related to the reintegration and ethnic stratification of social structures had a significant influence on whether the ethno-political entrepreneurs were able to sustain these mass mobilizations and whether they descended into violence. This chapter draws on the forms of political and socioeconomic interaction that we have seen develop between Kabardians and Balkars over the *longue durée* in order to identify

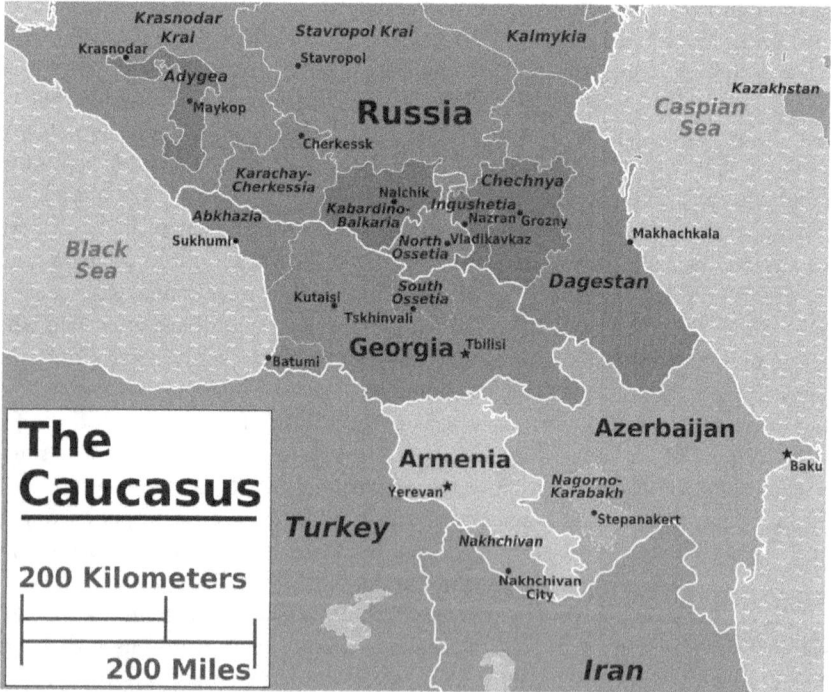

Map 6 The post-Soviet Caucasus. © Wikimedia Commons (public domain).

the long-term factors that contributed to the peaceful resolution of Kabardian-Balkar tensions in the 1990s.

The conclusion of this chapter examines the continuation of these tensions in the nonviolent but highly fraught sphere of ethno-cultural politics. After the de-escalation of intercommunal tensions and the co-opting of nationalist elites in Kabardino-Balkaria, many of the remaining Kabardian and Balkar oppositional figures went from the streets back to the academy to continue their work as national patriots in the cultural sphere. A peaceful outlet for the expression interethnic animosities and nationalism, the existence of the more formal parts of this cultural sphere (universities, research institutes, and journals) was, in large measure, a result of the late Stalin-era nativization efforts discussed in the previous chapter. The 1990s and 2000s witnessed a dramatic expansion of the forums for ethno-cultural expression as new national movements published journals and newspapers and, eventually, launched numerous websites and online discussion forums. Within this sphere, the writing of history became an important means for the expression of national grievances and contestation. These history wars revolved around competing interpretations of the history of land relations and borders, topics that have been central to this book, and the related issue of the ethnogenesis of the region's ethnicities.

Ethno-National Mobilization, Intercommunal Tensions, and Resolutions

Kabardino-Balkaria

During the waning months of the Soviet Union and the first five years of post-Soviet Russia, nationalist mobilization and tensions seemed to be pushing Kabardino-Balkaria to the brink of a violent division along ethnic lines. These tensions came as a surprise to observers of the region. A 1986 ethno-sociological survey of Kabardino-Balkaria reported no tensions between the republic's principal communities. Rather, this perestroika-era work focused on the positive ties binding Kabardians and Balkars to each other. It noted, for example, that one of every five Kabardians and Balkars were connected to the other nationality through familial ties and that 68.4 percent of Kabardians had Balkar friends and 81.9 percent of Balkars had Kabardian friends.[2] Despite these friendly relations, Kabardino-Balkaria was poised to become another in a growing list of conflict zones that had emerged throughout the Caucasus region since the late 1980s.

The waves of nationalist mobilization that swept through the USSR during perestroika arrived in the North Caucasus relatively late.[3] But once nationalist mobilization gripped Kabardians and Balkars, their national movements quickly moved through Miroslav Hroch's stages of development for national movements.[4] In "Phase A" of the development of the Kabardian and Balkar national movements, the Kabardian "Adyge Khasa" (Circassian Council) and the Balkar "Nyg"ysh" (village square) and, later, "Tëre (Council) began in 1989 as small associations of "patriots,"[5] often scholars, who, through the liberalization of glasnost (openness), began to exhibit "a passionate concern . . . for the study of the language, culture, [and] history of the[ir] oppressed nationality."[6] The Balkar national movement coalesced around the commemoration of the forty-fifth anniversary of the deportation of the Balkar people on March 8, 1989. The Kabardian national movement coalesced around the broader Circassian national movement's May 21 commemoration of the 125th anniversary of the end of the Caucasus War, a conflict that many Circassians view as having led to a genocide against their people.[7]

These events of cultural celebration and historical commemoration pushed the nascent national movements from Hroch's Phase A to Phase B of mass "patriotic agitation" and "fermentation . . . of national consciousness."[8] During this phase, the Kabardian and Balkar movements broadened their programs to include the consolidation of ties with their co-ethnics in other republics of the North Caucasus. For the Kabardians, this meant forging a pan-Circassian nation. For the Balkars, this expansion of national consciousness entailed the promotion of a Karachai-Balkar nation. One of the reasons why this mobilization happened so quickly was that key tenets of Soviet nationalities policy—nativization and territorialized nationality—had already fostered ethnic nationality as one of the multiple layers of identity for Soviet citizens.[9] Also, many of the Kabardian and Balkar patriots who led their respective movements from Phase A to Phase B had, thanks again to Soviet nationalities policy, long been employed locally in scholarly fields devoted to the study of their people's culture and history.[10] The liberalization of Mikhail Gorbachev's policies of glasnost and perestroika provided them with the opportunity to move from the halls of the local research institute and university to the streets for patriotic agitation.[11]

By 1991, political developments surrounding perestroika and the Soviet collapse—democratic elections, the local *nomenklatura's* support of the August "putsch," and the war in Abkhazia[12]—broadened popular support for the Kabardian and Balkar national movements, provided the Kabardian and Balkar "patriots" an opportunity to contest the power of their *nomenklaturas*,[13] and pushed them from Phase B to Phase C. They became "mass national movements" with political goals.[14]

Throughout twentieth-century Eurasian history—from the City Duma conflicts in the Western borderlands after 1905, to Georgian-Armenian political deadlock in Tbilisi in 1905 and 1918, to the escalation of violence in Nagorno-Karabakh in the late 1980s—movements toward participatory government and democracy in multiethnic regions often exacerbated intercommunal tensions.[15] Similarly, the Balkar national movement's turn from cultural agitation to political mobilization and, eventually, separatism, came as a result of Balkar candidates' inability, because of their people's minority status (they were about 10 percent of the republic's population), to compete in democratic elections to Russia's Supreme Soviet in 1990.[16] Previously, one of Kabardino-Balkaria's three representatives to the Supreme Soviet of the RSFSR was reserved for a Balkar.[17] As a means of achieving their people's representation in the Russian Parliament and avoiding a local political system that, under new "democratic" conditions, they feared would be increasingly run by and for its Kabardian majority, by late 1990 the Balkar national leadership of Tëre issued a number of political demands: "the reestablishment of political and economic parity" among the republic's nationalities; the declaration of a sovereign Balkaria; and the establishment of a federation based on two sovereign ethno-territorial units (Kabarda and Balkaria).[18] The national leadership of the

Kabardian majority in Adyge Khasa, in opposition to the Balkar national platform, offered a draft declaration on state sovereignty that would retain Kabardino-Balkaria's status as a unitary republic.[19] The counter-elites of the Kabardian national movement and the Soviet-era *nomenklatura* alike viewed the declaration of Balkar territorial sovereignty as the first step toward Kabardino-Balkaria's breakup. It seemed clear to all that a breakup would involve territorial disputes.[20]

In late 1991, tensions between the Kabardian and Balkar national movements escalated. When the republic's leadership failed to reach a compromise acceptable to both sides, on November 17, 1991, Tëre convoked the First Congress of the Balkar People to determine the Balkars' political future. After a vote, the Congress declared Balkar sovereignty and decreed the formation of the Republic of Balkaria as a constituent part of the RSFSR.[21] The Congress formed the National Council of the Balkar People (NSBN), headed by General Sufian Beppaev, former commander of Soviet armed forces in the South Caucasus, as the "highest organ of power of the Balkar people."[22] Beppaev, whom the Russian press depicted as the next Dzhokhar Dudaev (the Soviet general who led Chechnya's independence movement),[23] declared a Balkar boycott of the upcoming elections for Kabardino-Balkaria's first president.[24] The NSBN quickly organized a Balkar referendum on the question of Balkar sovereignty and the formation of the Republic of Balkaria. After high voter turnout at the referendum, by the end of 1991, the NSBN reported that 98 percent of the Balkar population voted "yes" when asked: "Do you support the declaration of national sovereignty of the Balkar people and the formation of the Republic of Balkaria as a constituent part of the RSFSR?"[25] In response, on January 10, 1992, Adyge Khasa countered by calling a Congress of the Kabardian People which resolved "to re-establish the sovereignty of the Kabardian Republic within the borders of the historic territory of the Kabardian people."[26] The long-term plan of the leaders of the Kabardian and Balkar national movements was to unite their republics with their co-ethnics in other neighboring republics—to create a Karachai-Balkar republic and a pan-Circassian republic that would include the territories of the Kabardians, Cherkeses, Adygeis, and Shapsugs (a small community near the Black Sea coast).[27]

The prospect of creating separate republics for the Kabardian and Balkar peoples based on their "historic territories" posed a potentially explosive problem: as in the past, again in the early 1990s, there was wide disagreement over what these historic borders were. On November 19, 1992, Kabardino-Balkaria's Supreme Soviet recognized the decisions of the Kabardians' and Balkars' respective congresses to form separate republics, and its presidium formed a commission to assist in the implementation of the legislation necessary to formalize the split.[28] Meanwhile, Kabardino-Balkaria's organs of state power would continue to exercise sole jurisdiction over the republic's territory. Regarding the question of the borders of these planned republics, the SKN and the NSBN each formed their own "expert groups," composed of Kabardian and Balkar historians, to study and report on the historic borders of the two nations. Each "expert group" reported contradictory findings. The Kabardians reported that, in 1863, the Kodzokov Commission clearly delimited a Kabardian-Balkar border. To meet the continuing land needs of the Balkar people, as we have seen, the local administration repeatedly allotted land to the Balkars beyond their 1863 borders. The historian Khasan Dumanov, head of the Kabardian expert commission, argued that any territorial delimitation between Kabarda and Balkaria should reflect the 1863 borders.[29] The Balkars argued that Kodzokov's project was never officially approved and that it did not reflect the historic borders of the two peoples but rather reflected the "national" sympathies of its Kabardian author.[30] Appealing to the more distant past, the Balkar expert group argued that Balkars occupied the territory of Kabardino-Balkaria long before the arrival of Kabardians in the late fifteenth century and that Kabardian colonization pushed the Balkars into the mountains. The Balkar elites wanted the borders of their republic to include the four Balkar districts as they existed on the eve of the deportation (January 1, 1944) and the three Balkar villages lying outside these districts.[31] From 1992 through 1994, Kabardian and Balkar scholars engaged in heated debates over the history of Kabardian-Balkar land relations, often taking to the pages of the republic's newspapers.[32]

As national intellectuals debated their people's historic borders, and the lack of consensus and potential for violent ethno-territorial conflict became increasingly clear, the Kabardino-Balkar government took measures to prevent the breakup of the republic. A stabilized Kabardino-Balkar political establishment, formed from an unofficial coalition of the Soviet-era *nomenklatura* (led by President Valerii Kokov) and co-opted Kabardian counter-elites, began to find ways to co-opt the Balkar national leadership and preserve Kabardino-Balkaria.[33] In this context, co-optation meant offering national activists positions in government. On July 21, 1994, the Kabardino-Balkar Parliament resolved that, given that the decree of the former Supreme Soviet of the Kabardino-Balkar SSR (in 1991, Kabardino-Balkaria's legislature elevated the republic's status by promoting it from an ASSR to SSR) contradicted the Constitutions of the Russian Federation and the Kabardino-Balkar Republic, the decrees on the formation of separate Kabardian and Balkar Republics had "lost their force."[34] In its next step to sap Balkar separatism of its force, the Kabardino-Balkar government conducted a survey of 91.5 percent of eligible Balkar voters asking whether they were in favor of "preserving a united Kabardino-Balkar Republic." With 95.7 percent coming out in favor of preserving the union, the results of the survey were almost as unequivocal as those of NSBN's Balkar referendum in favor of separation less than three years earlier.[35] Part of the combination of factors that contributed to this shift in Balkar public opinion between 1991 and 1994 was a desire to avoid the violence that had befallen nearby Ingushetia, Chechnya, South Ossetia, and Abkhazia as a result of the escalation of intercommunal tensions into ethnicized conflicts in the intervening years. Moreover, given that the results of both polls demonstrated over 90 percent support for opposing questions, the accuracy of these polls is highly suspect. On November 18, 1994, the Parliament of the Kabardino-Balkar Republic recognized the results of the survey as the will of the Balkar people.[36] On the basis of this decree, the Parliament banned those organizations whose activity was directed toward the transformation of the republic's ethno-territorial structure or had pretensions to state power on the territory of the republic, namely the First Congress of the Balkar People and the NSBN.[37]

For the next two years, tensions remained high between the Kabardino-Balkar Republic and the outlawed NSBN. Beppaev, NSBN's leader, ignored the Kabardino-Balkar government's ultimatum to dissolve the separatist Balkar government or register it as a "community organization" disavowing politics. The intransigence of Beppaev's position regarding the NSBN led to the defection of more moderate Balkar national elites, many of whom were subsequently given positions in government and co-opted into the new *nomenklatura*. The NSBN lost some legitimacy in the eyes of its constituents by arbitrarily replacing these elected representatives with other Balkar elites loyal to Beppaev's separatist goals.[38]

The Balkar separatist movement and the standoff between the NSBN and the Kabardino-Balkar government peaked in late 1996. On November 17, Beppaev reconvened the Congress of the Balkar People. The Congress confirmed its 1991 decision to create the Republic of Balkaria. The Congress formed a State Council to serve as the government of the Republic of Balkaria and created Balkar self-defense units. The Congress declared that only the orders and decrees of the Republic of Balkaria's organs of power were to be recognized on Balkar territory and that Balkars who do not abide by the decisions of the these organs of power or who speak on an official capacity for the Balkar people without authorization would be strictly punished. The Kabardino-Balkar government responded by having Georgii Cherkesov, Kabardino-Balkaria's ethnically Balkar prime minister (this number two position in the republic remains unofficially reserved for Balkars), conduct emergency meetings of the governing councils of the republic's Balkar villages on November 18 and 19. At the conclusion of each of these meetings, the representatives of the Balkar village councils declared the decisions of the recent Congress of the Balkar People "illegal" and "unconstitutional."[39] Meanwhile, the Kabardino-Balkar Parliament decreed the unconstitutionality of the recent decision of the Congress of the Balkar People and the state prosecutor of the Kabardino-Balkar Republic began legal action against the NSBN. On November 21, Kabardino-Balkaria's Balkar fraction of parliamentarians and representatives of the Balkar village councils issued a joint resolution supporting the Parliament's decree and stating that "only legally elected organs of power can act in the name of the people of KBR."[40]

With his powerbase subverted, Beppaev, as the head of the NSBN, stood at the crossroads of open conflict or retreat. Choosing the latter, on November 28, Beppaev appeared on state television and gave a repentant address to people of the republic and called for a cessation of the NSBN's activity. Among the reasons for his decision, Beppaev cited "forces in Kabardino-Balkaria and outside its borders (including in Moscow) interested in creating a hotbed of tension in the North Caucasus." Importantly, he also claimed that the government of Kabardino-Balkaria had already "solved many questions related to the rehabilitation of the Balkar people" and that President Kokov had promised further measures in the near future.[41] Finally, he claimed that Balkars had received a sufficient share of leadership positions in the republic.[42] Shortly after this appeal, President Kokov co-opted Beppaev, making him head of his Presidential Commission for Human Rights and the Rehabilitation of Victims of Political Repression.[43]

Karachai-Cherkessia, Ingushetia, and Chechnya

The history of Karachai-Cherkessia during the first half of the 1990s closely resembles that of Kabardino-Balkaria. The republic's titular nationalities clashed over questions of political representation and experienced national revivals and ethno-political mobilization. Just as in Kabardino-Balkaria, the leaders of Karachai-Cherkessia's national movements declared national sovereignty and proclaimed republics for the nations they claimed to represent. Indeed, as declarations of independence among the republic's national communities peaked in late 1994, President Yeltsin sent federal forces into the republic's capital of Cherkessk to maintain intercommunal peace.[44] Unlike Kabardino-Balkaria, however, the late 1990s did not bring a stabilization of intercommunal relations to Karachai-Cherkessia. During the period from 1999 through 2004, acute elite-level political contestation among and within the republic's Karachai, Cherkes, and Russian communities led to mass ethno-nationalist mobilizations and the ethnicization of intercommunal tensions. Since then, tensions among the republic's main communities have consistently led to political gridlock over the election and appointment of leaders. In 1999 and 2004, contested elections and interethnic rivalries led to mass demonstrations and riots.[45] However, high levels of ethno-political contestation in Karachai-Cherkessia have largely remained confined to mass protests and have not descended into violence.

In many ways, Karachai-Cherkessia is a mirror image of Kabardino-Balkaria. In Kabardino-Balkaria, the larger of its two titular ethnicities, the Kabardians (currently 57 percent) speak a Circassian language and were not deported during the Second World War, and the titular minority, the Balkars (currently 12.7 percent), speak a Turkic language and were deported. In Karachai-Cherkessia, Karachais form the majority titular nationality (currently 41 percent). The Karachais speak the same Turkic language as the Balkars and consider themselves ethnic brethren of the Balkars. Stalin deported the Karachais along with their Balkar co-ethnics. The Cherkes, Karachai-Cherkessia's minority titular ethnicity (currently 11.9 percent), are Circassians just like the Kabardians with whom they share a common Kabardino-Cherkes language.[46]

Despite their similarities, several key differences between the ethnic makeup of Kabardino-Balkaria and Karachai-Cherkessia have contributed to their divergent levels of ethno-political contestation. Kabardino-Balkaria's population consists of three main communities: Kabardians, Balkars, and Russians (including Cossacks). Of these communities, Kabardino-Balkaria's Russian and Cossack communities are relatively quiescent politically,[47] and ethno-political tensions revolve around the question of Balkar political representation and autonomy in a political system dominated by the Kabardian majority. To be sure, the Cossacks of Kabardino-Balkaria were part of post-Soviet Russia's Cossack revival: they have their own organizations, conduct cultural events, and periodically voice political discontent. In comparison with Cossacks elsewhere, particularly in neighboring Karachai-Cherkessia, Kabardino-Balkaria's Cossacks exhibit low levels of ethno-political mobilization. Their political quiescence is a result of their long-standing acceptance that, as long as Russians are provided relatively proportionate political representation, Kabardino-Balkaria can be led by a representative of the Kabardian majority. In Karachai-Cherkessia, no nationality forms a majority and all the republic's communities have been politically active. Moreover, in addition to the two titular nationalities—Karachai (41 percent) and Cherkes (12 percent)—three other communities have the status of constituent nationalities whose languages have official status in the republic: Russians (31.6 percent), Abazas (7.8 percent), and Nogais (3.3 percent).

Given Karachai-Cherkessia's ethnic diversity, its leadership faces the difficult task of maintaining a mutually acceptable balance of representatives from each of these communities within its political structure. In Karachai-Cherkessia, balancing the political representation of five nationalities has proven far more difficult than balancing the three nationalities in Kabardino-Balkaria. Given the dominant role of ethnicity in post-Soviet politics, particularly in the Caucasus, Karachai-Cherkessia's ethnic makeup has led to ethno-political movements forming informal coalitions during key political contests to defeat candidates whom they see as disrupting the republic's ethnic balance with their policies or platforms. Often this has meant Russians, Cherkeses, and Abazas coming together to prevent Karachai domination. In a testament to the stabilizing effect that authoritarianism often has on multiethnic states, the end of direct elections for governors and heads of republics in Russia since 2004 has helped to decrease the level of political gridlock and ethno-political contestation in Karachai-Cherkessia.[48]

Tensions between Ingush and Ossetians played out differently. Before exploding into violent armed conflict in 1992, tensions had been long brewing between Ossetians and Ingush over Prigorodnyi district. This was an area of compact Ingush settlement located around the North Ossetian capital of Vladikavkaz. After the deportation of the Ingush in 1944, Stalin transferred this district from the dissolved Checheno-Ingush ASSR to the North Ossetian ASSR. The North Ossetian authorities then settled this district with Ossetians from Georgia.[49] Most of this territory was *not* returned to the Ingush after their return. In total, North Ossetia received about one-sixth of the prewar Ingush territory. While many Ingush returned to Prigorodnyi district spontaneously, many more were unable to do so because Ossetians had settled in their former villages.[50] During the last decades of Soviet rule, relations were tense between the North Ossetian government and Ingush elites. Indeed, in 1973, many Ingush took part in protests demanding the return of Prigorodnyi district to the Checheno-Ingush ASSR.[51] In 1981, a similar demonstration held in Ordzhonikidze (Vladikavkaz) turned violent as MVD troops clashed with Ingush demonstrators.[52]

During perestroika, the Ingush and Ossetian national movements, "Niiskho" and "Adaman Tsadish," galvanized around the question of Prigorodnyi district.[53] The Ingush national movement demanded the return of the district and the right-bank side of Vladikavkaz as one of the conditions of their full rehabilitation. The Ossetian national movement opposed any border changes. By 1991, both sides had begun forming paramilitary units, and clashes occurred with increasing frequency.[54] The influx into Prigorodnyi district of thousands of Ossetian refugees from Georgia in the wake of the conflict between Georgia and South Ossetia increased tensions in 1991 and 1992.[55] After an Ossetian armored personnel carrier ran over an Ingush girl in late October 1992, Ossetian-Ingush tensions exploded into five days of violence, leaving 600 dead, thousands wounded, 315 missing, and over 57,000 refugees.[56] The conflict ended when the Russian Army intervened on the side of North Ossetia. The Russian Army intervened on the Ossetian side because Moscow did not want to see any border changes in Prigorodnyi district out of fears that this would set a precedent for territorial revisions elsewhere. After Russian federal forces imposed a cease-fire on October 31, both sides entered years of tense and usually abortive negotiations. Despite both sides reaching agreements on the status of refugees by the early 2000s, Ossetian-Ingush tensions remain, sporadic violence persists, and North Ossetia long remained a target of Ingush terror attacks.

Chechnya's attempt to separate from the Russian Federation after the collapse of the Soviet Union is well known and well researched.[57] Despite the fact that the Chechens and Ingush formed an absolute majority in their autonomous republic (the Checheno-Ingush ASSR), the local Russian-speaking population and the Russian-dominated administration treated Chechens and Ingush as second-class citizens during the last three decades of Soviet rule. After their return of exile, Chechens and Ingush were largely excluded from the republic's industrial and oil-refining sectors and severely underrepresented in administration, education, and the party leadership. By the late 1980s, Chechens and Ingush began to reverse this pattern of interethnic relations and force Russians and other Russian-speaking groups from the republic's political and economic leadership positions. Indeed, the period from 1979 through 1989 witnessed an exodus of Russians from the Checheno-Ingush ASSR.[58] The process of Chechnya's separation from Russia began in the autumn of 1991 when Dzhokhar Dudaev, the leader of the National Congress of the Chechen People, the main opposition movement to the Chechnya's Soviet *nomenklatura*, ousted the Kremlin-backed, Soviet-era government of Doku Zavgaev after it came out in support of the hardline August coup in Moscow. After the results of a controversial referendum in October 1991 showed support for Chechen independence and confirmed Dudaev as president of the new Chechen Republic of Ichkeria, he unilaterally declared the republic's sovereignty and its independence from the Soviet Union.[59] At the same time, Ingushetia declared its sovereignty but as a republic within the Russian Federation. Russia fought two wars with Chechnya, from 1994 to 1996 and from 1999 to 2009, to reestablish control over the breakaway republic. The conflict cost the lives of thousands of Russian soldiers, tens of thousands of Chechens, and created hundreds of thousands of Chechen refugees.[60]

The Causes of Peace and Conflict

Social Structure and Reintegration

The socioeconomic disparities that contributed to the animosities behind many of the region's ethnicized intercommunal conflicts were products of the incomplete reintegration of "punished peoples" after 1957. In his study of nationalist mobilization and ethnic conflict in the Caucasus during the collapse of the Soviet Union, sociologist Georgi Derluguian "attribute[es] . . . the divergent trajectories of the North Caucasus republics . . . to variation in class structure."[61] Derluguian, in line with other scholars of ethnic conflict,[62] views the presence of an ethnically stratified social structure and attendant competition among ethnic communities for positions of power as factors that increase the likelihood of this type of conflict.

Asserting that the Balkars had been reintegrated into society while the Chechens had not, Derluguian employs an ethno-sociological analysis to explain the divergent fates of Kabardino-Balkaria and Chechnya. First, Derluguian argues that "after their return from exile . . . ethnic Balkar representatives had been judiciously incorporated into [the local power] network where they enjoyed the right to occupy the number two positions in every formal office and hierarchy."[63] It is important to add to this correct assessment that on the eve of perestroika, as we will see, there was very little difference in social structure between Kabardians and Balkars. Their similar social structures help explain why Balkar animosities toward Kabardians, despite appearances, were not as elevated as those elsewhere in the region.

Secondly, in explaining the lower level of resistance to and ultimate acceptance of the Soviet-era *nomenklatura* in Kabardino-Balkaria as compared with Chechnya, Derluguian rightly avers that "in Kabardino-Balkaria the Soviet nationality policy really seemed to operate as it was intended insofar as only very few ethnic Russians seem to have held positions of power."[64] As we have seen, after the April 1948 TsK decree "On the Work of the Obkom of the Kabardian ASSR,"[65] the republic's leadership pursued a robust nativization campaign that, by the mid-1950s, led to increases in native representation in traditionally Russian spheres. The nativization and reinvigorated Soviet modernization of the late 1940s and early 1950s created the preconditions for a strong and stable native *nomenklatura* in Kabardino-Balkaria. By the late 1950s and early 1960s, as the Balkars returned, a relatively stable native *nomenklatura* of Kabardians and, thanks to a Balkarization campaign, Balkars came to power in the republic. Indeed, after twelve years of Russian first secretaries, in 1956, Timbora Mal'bakhov, a Kabardian, became first secretary of the Obkom. An example of the stability of national cadres that characterized later decades of Soviet rule,[66] Mal'bakhov would lead Kabardino-Balkaria for nearly thirty years.[67] During the nationalist mobilizations of perestroika, unlike Chechnya where much of the *nomenklatura* was Russian, in Kabardino-Balkaria, as Derluguian points out, "it was more difficult to mobilize the Kabardins against their power elite because too many among the Kabardins were themselves in the establishment or close to its members."[68]

In Kabardino-Balkaria, there was little socioeconomic basis upon which ethnonational entrepreneurs from either side could mobilize their co-ethnics around the idea that they were systematically discriminated against by members of the other ethnicity. As political scientist Donald Horowitz demonstrates, in colonial and postcolonial situations where two ethnic groups were treated relatively similarly by the colonial power, the dichotomy of "backward" versus "advanced" ethnicities that often fuels intercommunal tensions is usually absent.[69]

From the late 1950s through the 1980s, Soviet modernization led to a rapid, if incomplete, cultural transformation among Kabardians and Balkars.[70] Statistical data indicate that, by the late Soviet period, urbanization, industrialization, and attendant social and cultural transformations had affected Kabardians and Balkars in near-equal measure. They also demonstrate that the large socioeconomic gaps that naturally existed between Kabardians and Balkars after the latter's return had been overcome.[71]

Statistics on urbanization and employment illustrate some of the ways in which Kabardians and Balkars experienced near-equal levels of modernization. In 1925, nearly all Kabardians and Balkars were employed in agriculture.[72] By the early 1980s, only about a quarter of Kabardians and Balkars were so employed;[73] in this they approximated the all-union average. In 1925, fewer than 1 percent of Kabardians and Balkars lived in cities.[74] By 1979, about 37 percent of Kabardians and 50 percent of Balkars lived in the republic's urban centers, and by 1989 these figures stood at 43 percent and 59.2 percent, respectively.[75] As we have seen, in 1948 Russians and other nontitulars dominated the republic's *nomenklatura*. By 1990, Kabardians and Balkars, about 58 percent of the population, composed 72 percent of the republic's *nomenklatura* positions.[76] After their return, having been deprived of the benefits of national autonomy for thirteen years and limited in their schooling opportunities, Balkars were acutely underrepresented in the *nomenklatura*. Two decades later, as a result of a Balkarization drive,[77] only about 5 percent more of the Kabardian population than the Balkar population was employed in *nomenklatura* positions.[78] The greatest difference in the social structure between Kabardians and Balkars was among urban workers. Compared with the Kabardians, 11 percent more urban Balkars were employed in unskilled manual labor. Here the exile experience reflected a generational gap, with those who came of age in exile disproportionately represented in unskilled positions.[79] This socioeconomic gap had narrowed by the eve of the Soviet collapse. In terms of education, by 1990, the share of Kabardians and Balkars studying in higher education was higher than their shares of the republic's population (53.3 percent to 48.2 percent and 14.5 percent to 9.4 percent, respectively), while Russians were significantly underrepresented in the republic's higher education network (21.2 percent to 32 percent). Indeed, by the end of the Soviet era, Balkars had slightly higher levels of education than Kabardians.[80]

Karachai-Cherkessia's lack of a strong native ruling elite during the late Soviet era was a key difference that distinguished it from Kabardino-Balkaria. Karachai-Cherkessia's social structure resembled that of Kabardino-Balkaria in that there was little divergence between the republic's titular nationalities, especially in terms of levels of education and urbanization. The principal difference between the two autonomous units lay at the top of the social hierarchy. While Kabardians and Balkars were represented in their republic's Soviet *nomenklatura* in slightly greater proportion to their share in the population, the representation of Cherkeses and especially Karachais among their oblast's *nomenklatura* was well below each community's share in population. Indeed, from 1957 on, in the Karachai-Cherkes AO, the first secretary of the Karachai-Cherkes Obkom was always a Russian.[81] Part of the explanation for the absence of a native first secretary was that Russians, while not forming a majority, were Karachai-Cherkessia's largest community. Moreover, the appointment of Russians from *outside* the oblast as first secretaries in Karachai-Cherkessia was an exception to the unofficial rule (also broken in the Chechen-Ingush case) that non-Russian Republics and autonomous regions be led by a representative of the titular nationality. Karachai underrepresentation was endemic throughout the top leadership and managerial positions of the AO. Karachais made up only about 5 percent of the Obkom and 20 percent of the oblast executive committee. They were also underrepresented at all levels in law enforcement, but particularly at the top where Karachais occupied 11 percent of the leadership positions in the Ministry of Internal Affairs.[82] Even in the main Karachai urban center of Karachaevsk, with its overwhelmingly Karachai population, officials in Moscow and Stavropol (the regional center to which Karachai-Cherkessia was subordinated) consistently appointed Russians to the leadership of the city's Party Committee, police, prosecutor, Justice department, and KGB.[83]

Karachai-Cherkessia's fluid ethno-political situation stands in contrast to the relatively stable ethno-political divisions of power that have characterized Kabardino-Balkaria's transition from Soviet to post-Soviet rule. In the post-Soviet era, Karachai political elites have aggressively sought to redress the political disparities of the Soviet era. While not experiencing armed conflict as in the Chechen and Ossetian-Ingush cases, post-Soviet Karachai-Cherkess Republic experienced sharp reactions on the part of its non-Karachai communities to perceived Karachai political favoritism. These reactions took the form of mass protests, rioting, and political deadlock in the late 1990s and early 2000s. In Kabardino-Balkaria, political contestation on this level was relatively short-lived.

A comparison of the situation in Kabardino-Balkaria to that of Checheno-Ingushetia in the late Soviet period reveals a number of glaring differences: Checheno-Ingushetia's social structure exhibited marked ethnic stratification; Chechens and Ingush had historic animosities with their Russian, Cossack, and Ossetian neighbors; and in terms of demographics and ethno-territorial structure, post-1957 Checheno-Ingushetia looked very different from pre-1944 Checheno-Ingushetia. These differences are indicators of levels of ethnic discrimination and feelings of insecurity and backwardness vis-à-vis neighboring groups absent in the Kabardino-Balkar case and less pronounced in the Karachai-Cherkess case.

Compared with Kabardino-Balkaria, where Kabardians and Balkars were represented relatively evenly throughout the social hierarchy, in Checheno-Ingushetia there was much greater stratification between the titular nationalities at the bottom and the republic's predominantly Russian settler population at the top. Compared with all-Russian averages, the Chechens and Ingush consistently ranked toward the bottom in terms of levels of employment, education, and other indicators of socioeconomic status. Despite the fact that Checheno-Ingushetia had a larger industrial economy than Kabardino-Balkaria, by the 1980s the vast majority (70 percent) of Chechens and Ingush were still employed in agriculture, compared to about 25 percent of Kabardians and Balkars.[84] According to Russian ethnographer Valery Tishkov, "in the period from 1964 through 1991, the Checheno-Ingush economy was divided between two sectors: a 'Russian' economy focused on oil refining, machine construction, and socio-economic infrastructure and a 'native' economy dominated by small commodity agriculture, seasonal labor migration, and construction."[85] For example, of the 50,000 workers in Groznyi's oil industry, only several hundred were Chechens and Ingush. Though Chechens and Ingush had the highest levels of unemployment in the RSFSR and the republic's industrial sector experienced frequent labor shortages, the Russian-dominated leadership of the Checheno-Ingush ASSR did little to attract Chechens and Ingush into industry. With 20 percent employment in white-collar jobs (*umstvennyi trud*), Chechens ranked thirty-fourth among Russia's forty largest nationalities. Accordingly, processes of urbanization affected Chechens and Ingush far less than they did the Kabardians and Balkars. In 1989, 23.5 percent of Chechens and 35.4 percent of Ingush resided in urban centers, compared to 43 percent of Kabardians and 59.2

percent of Balkars.[86] Finally, among the RSFSR's titular nationalities, Chechens had the smallest proportion of academic and scientific specialists.[87]

Checheno-Ingushetia's ethnically stratified social structure was partly a result of low levels of schooling and higher education among Ingush and particularly Chechens. Given the special-settlement regime's restrictions, when the Chechens and Ingush returned from exile in the late 1950s and early 1960s, there was a large discrepancy between their levels of education and those of the republic's mainly Russian settler population.[88] In contrast to the Karachai and Balkar cases, the efforts of Checheno-Ingushetia's leadership to expand education levels among Chechen and Ingush were grossly inadequate. The educational levels among Ingush and particularly Chechens never caught up to all-Russian levels. By 1989, for every 1,000 Chechens and Ingush aged fifteen or older, those with higher education numbered 45 and 60, respectively. This figure stood at 111 for Balkars and 110 for Karachais, just below the all-Russian average of 113. Indeed, Balkar and Karachai levels of higher education were even greater than those of the other titular groups in their regions, groups who were not subjected to forced deportation during the Second World War; these figures stood at 88 for Kabardians and 108 for Cherkeses.[89] Chechen higher education levels were 2.5 times lower than the Russian average and 2.2 times lower than the other deported peoples of the RSFSR. Checheno-Ingushetia had the highest proportion of residents without any middle education of all AOs and republics of the RSFSR.[90] These low levels of schooling and higher education contributed to the socioeconomic gap between the republic's native and settler populations.

Finally, given these figures for education and employment, it should come as little surprise that Chechens and Ingush were poorly represented among their republic's *nomenklatura*. As Chechen historian Musa Ibragimov points out, "all of the key leadership positions were occupied by non-Chechens. No Chechen or Ingush ever held the post of First Secretary of the Obkom, Minister of Internal Affairs, head of the KGB, or Prosecutor."[91] In contrast to other punished peoples, there was no growth in the number of Chechens in leadership positions between 1959 and 1989. At the beginning of the 1980s, despite making up over 60 percent of the republic's population, Chechens and Ingush composed only about 25 percent of the republic's administrative apparatus.[92]

Kabardian-Balkar Relations and the Politics of Rehabilitation

The historical memory of the Stalinist deportations and the experience of exile played a decisive role in Balkars' ethno-political discourse during national mobilizations of the 1990s. Indeed, the idea of full rehabilitation became the issue around which Balkars mobilized during the early 1990s. The ability of Balkar ethno-political entrepreneurs to sustain high levels of mobilization foundered because the Balkars' successful reintegration over the late Soviet period meant that the most pressing and challenging facet of rehabilitation—socioeconomic and ethno-territorial rehabilitation—had been achieved before the Balkars' rehabilitation campaign got off the ground. In paying moderate attention to other aspects of the rehabilitation program for repressed peoples, officials in Moscow and Nalchik disarmed the Balkar ethno-political entrepreneurs' best weapon for mobilization.

The first phase of the rehabilitation of the punished peoples, largely coinciding with the Khrushchev era, was limited to state efforts at the central and republican levels, of varying degrees of success, toward the socioeconomic *reintegration* of the deported peoples' communities back into their homelands and the restoration of their national autonomies. The success or failure of the punished peoples' socioeconomic reintegration was the critical medium-term historical factor structuring intercommunal relations during perestroika. In all cases, however, these first rehabilitation measures were incomplete. Besides socioeconomic reintegration, the Soviet state did not confront other aspects of rehabilitation: the continuing psychological trauma of deportation and the social stigma stemming from the unjust accusations of mass treason; property losses incurred through deportation; and the ways in which discrepancies between pre-deportation and post-return ethno-territorial borders hindered socioeconomic reintegration.

When glasnost allowed for the creation of a more open civil society and released the floodgates of political activity in the Soviet Union, the nascent national movements of the "punished peoples" of the North Caucasus galvanized around the goal of full political, territorial, socioeconomic, and cultural rehabilitation.[93] The national movements of each of the deported peoples placed full rehabilitation at the top of their programs. These movements united their efforts under the Confederation of Repressed Peoples of Russia.[94]

The April 26, 1991, RSFSR Law, "On the Rehabilitation of the Repressed Peoples," included provisions that spoke broadly to the demands of these national movements. These provisions can help explain what these movements meant by "full rehabilitation." Article One called for the "recognition of repressive acts against these peoples as illegal and criminal." In this regard, the law also confirmed recent Supreme Soviet decrees nullifying the Stalin-era decrees on the deportations. Article Three called for the "the reestablishment of [the repressed peoples'] territories and national-state formations . . . as they existed before their anti-constitutional dissolution." Article Four criminalized "agitation and propaganda aimed at the prevention of the rehabilitation of repressed peoples." Article Nine stipulated that "losses incurred by the repressed peoples as a result of state repression must be returned." Article Ten explained that as part of the "social rehabilitation of the repressed peoples," employment during the period of deportation would count triple toward retirement, and those already retired would see an increase in their pensions for each year of work under the special settlement regime. Article Eleven called for the "cultural rehabilitation" of the repressed peoples, including "the return of the former historic names of villages."[95]

The reemergence of the land question in post-Soviet Kabardino-Balkaria, a consequence of the problem of delimiting the borders of the self-proclaimed Kabardian and Balkar Republics, was also directly linked to the question of Balkar rehabilitation. The program of the Balkar national movement called for the "reestablishment of the administrative-territorial districts of Balkaria with the same land reserves that existed on January 1, 1944."[96] When the process of the Balkars' rehabilitation began in 1957, the Kabardino-Balkar government reestablished most Balkar villages but it did not restore the Balkar districts as they existed on the eve of deportation. On January 1, 1944, the Balkars were a majority in all four of their districts of compact settlement. Despite occupying most of their pre-deportation territory after their return, the

Balkars, as a result of redistricting, resided primarily in three districts (Baksanskii, Chegemskii, and Sovetskii) and only formed a majority in *one* of them (Sovetskii). During perestroika, correcting this discrepancy between the Balkars' pre-deportation and post-1957 borders became an important part of the Balkars' platform for full rehabilitation for two reasons: (1) competitive elections meant that the Balkars could only count on being the dominant political bloc in one district; and (2) in order to claim their territorial sovereignty (with an eye toward possible separation from Kabardino-Balkaria), the Balkar elites needed the reconstitution of relatively homogenous Balkar districts. Indeed, the Kabardino-Balkar leadership's unwillingness to restore the January 1944 Balkar districts motivated the First Congress of the Balkar People to proclaim the formation of the Republic of Balkaria in November 1991.[97] However, compared with the territorial grievances of other deported peoples, those of the Balkars were relatively minor, as is evidenced by the peaceful de-escalation of Kabardian-Balkar tensions without fully meeting the territorial aspects of the Balkars' rehabilitation program. Indeed, in his December 1996 address to the people of Kabardino-Balkaria, Beppaev justified his call for Kabardino-Balkaria's continued unity and a de-escalation of tensions by citing the government of Kabardino-Balkaria's recent efforts toward the rehabilitation of the Balkar people.[98]

During perestroika and the immediate post-Soviet years, officials in Moscow and Nalchik made substantial efforts to facilitate the full rehabilitation of the Balkar people. On November 14, 1989, the Supreme Soviet of the USSR issued the "Declaration on the Recognition of Repressive Acts against Peoples Subjected to Forced Deportation as Illegal and Criminal and the Securing of their Rights."[99] After the collapse of the Soviet Union, Boris Yeltsin, representing the Russian Federation, issued formal apologies to the deported peoples of Russia, including the Balkars.[100] Moreover, in 1991 a Russian federal law "On the Rehabilitation of Victims of Political Repression" allocated monetary compensation to victims of the deportations. The Russian government formed commissions to develop a plan for further rehabilitation measures for each deported nationality. In 1996, the Russian government enacted a four-year federal program, "On the Socio-Economic Development and National-Cultural Rebirth of the Balkar People."[101] On the republican level, in addition to a series of important symbolic gestures (official condemnation of the deportations; the designation of March 8 as the Day of Remembrance of the Victims of the Violent Deportation of the Balkar People and March 28 as the Day of the Rebirth of the Balkar People; and the construction of a memorial to the victims of the deportation), the Kabardino-Balkar government allowed Balkar villages to vote on the reconstitution of their pre-deportation districts. Balkars voted in favor of reestablishing Elbrus district according to its January 1944 borders. The Kabardino-Balkar Parliament decreed the formation of Elbrus district on May 5, 1994, giving the Balkars an absolute majority in a second district.[102] In the cases of reestablishing the former Khulam-Bezengi district and changing the borders of Chegem district to match its January 1944 composition, a combination of official governmental opposition and dubious referendum results led to the scraping of these further redistricting changes.[103] In addition to federal compensation for Balkar survivors of the deportation, the government of Kabardino-Balkaria also provided monetary compensation to Balkar families who lost property as a result of the deportation.[104] In placing Sufian Beppaev in charge of his Commission for Human Rights and the Rehabilitation of Victims of Political Repression, President Kokov gave this former leader of the Balkar separatist movement control over the distribution of funds allocated for Balkar compensation and rehabilitation. This position benefited Beppaev symbolically, and also gave him a position from which to distribute state funds widely and build his political patronage networks.[105]

Given the relative socioeconomic equality between Kabardians and Balkars and the lack of major discrepancies between the Balkars' ethno-territorial status in 1944 and 1994, the leaders of the Balkar national movement were unable to sustain heightened levels of mass mobilization on the basis of calls for full rehabilitation. Through the co-opting of Balkar elites and the pursuit of rehabilitation measures, the leadership of the Russian Federation's Kabardino-Balkar Republic managed to stabilize intercommunal relations and marginalize the proponents of Balkar separatism. Balkar grievances, however, are never far from the surface in contemporary Kabardino-Balkaria, and changes or impending changes of officials and patronage networks within the republic's administrative apparatus are frequently accompanied by a resurfacing of the Balkar question.[106]

Post-Soviet rehabilitation measures ostensibly contributed to the easing of Kabardian-Balkar tensions precisely because these tensions had little to do with problems of the Balkars' rehabilitation. Post-Soviet Kabardian-Balkar tensions are based on the difficulties of adapting a system of intercommunal accommodation and symbiosis to Russia's new political and economic realities. Balkar national elites couched their people's legitimate post-Soviet problems in terms of rehabilitation because the discourse of rehabilitation provided a layer of juridical legitimacy (based on Russian laws on the rehabilitation of repressed peoples) and added emotional appeal to their claims. When the first of these post-Soviet challenges to the historic pattern of Kabardian-Balkar relations was overcome with Kabardino-Balkaria's ruling elite's co-optation of Balkar elites, most notably Beppaev, the Balkar elites cited progress toward rehabilitation as their reason for foregoing their confrontation with the Kabardian majority because rehabilitation was the issue on which they had forged the Balkar national movement.

By contrast, post-Soviet rehabilitation measures did little to solve intercommunal conflicts in which the other deported peoples were embroiled. Though highly divergent from each other in their levels of intensity, these conflicts were, at least in part, based on problems associated with their incomplete or failed rehabilitations. In the Karachai, Ingush, and Chechen cases, lingering socioeconomic contradictions and ethno-territorial disputes, associated in part with the inadequacies of these peoples' reintegration after 1957, ran too deep and were too intractable to allow for a peaceful resolution through the co-optation of elites and rehabilitation measures like monetary compensation and symbolic gestures.

Karachai-Cherkessia is the mildest of these three other cases of ethno-political conflict. Nevertheless, tensions here were partially a result of discrepancies between the Karachai people's pre-deportation and post-1957 borders. After a brief experiment with a united Karachai-Cherkes AO from 1922 to 1926, conflicts over political representation led the Soviet state to allow the separation of the Karachais and Cherkes into their own autonomous regions.[107] Therefore, when the Soviet state decided to form a combined Karachai-Cherkes AO in the wake of the return of the Karachais from exile in 1957, this was not a return to the prewar ethno-territorial status quo. The type of border changes implied by the territorial rehabilitation of the Karachai people to their pre-deportation status would entail the breakup of the Karachai-Cherkes Republic, a separatist precedent that Moscow would not want to set. Further complicating matters is the fact that many Karachai now live in parts of Karachai-Cherkessia outside the pre-deportation borders of the Karachai AO.[108]

During the late Soviet period, the fact that Russians, Cherkeses, and others had not, except for a fraught four years in the 1920s, resided in a common administrative unit with the Karachais contributed to a reluctance to integrate the Karachais into positions of power and leadership of Karachai-Cherkessia. Unlike the Balkars in Kabardino-Balkaria, the Karachais were seen as outsiders in their post-1957 autonomy, and the type of economic interdependence that existed between Kabardians and Balkars did not exist among the Karachais and their neighbors. This led to a mistrust of the Karachais and lingering accusations of Karachai treason during the war from the region's dominant Cossack-Russian community. Indeed, the Russian-dominated Karachai-Cherkes Obkom promoted these accusations.[109] For example, in 1979 the first secretary of the Karachai-Cherkes Obkom, Vsevolod Mukharovskii, maliciously legitimizing apocryphal stories of Karachai wartime atrocities, ordered the construction of a monument on the road outside of the popular resort of Lower Teberda to orphan children who were killed by "Karachai Bandits" in August 1942.[110]

The Ingush consider their rehabilitation incomplete because they have not received control over their former lands in North Ossetia's Prigorodnyi district and many Ingush who fled the conflict zone in 1992 are still living as refugees. Ossetian elites, however, buoyed by Kremlin support, are staunch in their refusal to return this land. Unless Ingush demands for full territorial rehabilitation are met, compensation for the victims of deportation and the construction of ornate and expensive memorials, like the "nine towers" complex outside of Nazran, will do little to ease the feeling among the Ingush that the systematic injustice against them at the hands of the Russian state and their loyal Ossetian lackeys continues.

Although Chechens harbored resentment at not being allowed to reestablish many of their mountain *auls* after their return, territorial rehabilitation to their pre-deportation status was not *the* major concern of many Chechens. Here, calls for full political and socioeconomic rehabilitation quickly developed into calls for full sovereignty and independence for the Chechen nation. The inferior socioeconomic and political position of Chechens in their own republic produced in large part by the influx of Russians during the period of Chechen exile became part of a long list of grievances upon which the Chechens built their case for separation.

Structures and Patterns

The divergent ethno-political situations in the North Caucasus in 1990s, between the two extremes of Kabardino-Balkaria and Chechnya, were not simply products of different social structures that had formed since the late 1950s. Nor is the primordialist explanation, offered by one journalist, that "the Chechens are different . . . comparable with no other people in the Caucasus," acceptable.[111] Rather, the divergent post-Soviet fates of the peoples of the North Caucasus reflect, and provide insight into, deeper historical trends and patterns.

The inclusion of the Balkars in the Kabardino-Balkar ASSR's *nomenklatura* after 1957 and, more recently, in the post-Soviet leadership of the Kabardino-Balkar Republic, was the continuation of a long-standing, unofficial power-sharing arrangement that developed during the beginning of the Soviet rule and had its roots in the historic Kabardian-Balkar symbiosis. Though the political parity among Kabardians, Balkars, and Russians envisaged by the 1922 "Conditions for the Unification of Kabarda and Balkaria" proved ephemeral, the reservation for Balkars of key leadership positions in the republic dating back to the 1920s ensured Balkar political quietism within a system in which they were a minority, a system that would always be led by Kabardians.[112] In the post-Soviet period, the prospect of democracy that emerged during perestroika did not bode well for the Balkars.[113] In order to overcome the ethno-political impasse that post-Soviet democratization represented for Kabardino-Balkaria, in 1996 the Kabardian and Balkar elites agreed to continue their long-standing practices of power-sharing and dividing leadership positions in a way that was acceptable for all of the republic's principal nationalities.[114]

However beneficial close economic and political relations with the Kabardians may have been for the Balkars, over the *longue durée* this relationship has never been based on equality or parity of political and economic power. During periods of state collapse, the Balkars have sought to end their subordinate position vis-à-vis the Kabardians. The Kabardian-Balkar symbiosis (based on economic, political, social, and familial ties) means that despite the inequality and subordination when push comes to shove, the choice of both Balkars and Kabardians has been for compromise rather than violence. This choice for compromise in the 1990s—the acceptance of the new political establishment on the condition that the Balkars would retain their traditional levels of political representation and power as the seconds in command in the republic—was just one stage in a long history of compromise and coexistence.

After the collapse of Kabarda under the weight of Ermolov's assault in the 1820s, the Balkars petitioned the tsar and local Russian administrators for permission to resettle in and attain ownership of some of the Kabardian plains lands on which they depended for their winter transhumance. In requesting this land and contesting tributary relations with Kabardian landlords after the introduction of Russian rule, the Balkars wanted to assert their economic independence from the Kabardian feudal elite. The surviving Kabardian landlords used their influence in the Russian administration to prevent Balkar separation from happening, and the Balkars remained locked in the mountain zone. By the late nineteenth century, stability and compromise won out. The tsarist administration allowed some Balkar resettlement in the foothills, and the Kabardians and Balkars had established a system of sharing the mountain pastures in the northwest corner of Nalchik district.

From 1918 through 1922, Balkar elites hoped to use the window of opportunity presented by the collapse of the tsarist state and the reconfiguration of Russia's political and administrative structure to end their land dependence on Kabarda and ensure political independence from their larger Kabardian neighbor. These efforts at economic autarky and political autonomy foundered on the prospect of intractable land disputes and the specter of armed conflict. Compromise reigned during the formation of the Kabardino-Balkar AO in 1922. The Kabardian ruling elites recognized the Balkars' rights to additional, much-needed, land in exchange for the preservation of the territory of both peoples within a unitary Kabardino-Balkaria. The Kabardian and Balkar elites reached a political compromise by which the region's titular nationalities received a mutually acceptable share of political power and influence in the republic. The top leadership position would always go to a Kabardian, and the second most important position would go to a Balkar.

The successful socioeconomic reintegration of the Balkars after 1957, which was important in mitigating conflict during the 1990s, had less to do with Moscow's policies than with the fact that the local Kabardian and Russian populations were largely enthusiastic about the Balkars' return. The cooperation and support with which Kabardians, Russians, and other local communities greeted the Balkars upon their return reflected the long-standing symbiotic relationship that existed among the Kabardino-Balkaria's communities. The Balkars' absence damaged the economy of the Kabardian ASSR.[115] The republic's mountain zone was underutilized, and its stockbreeding never recovered to its prewar level in the Balkars' absence. Moreover, Kabardians' friends and relations were among the Balkars in exile.

Finally, in the early 1990s, the spirit of popular sovereignty and national rebirth that accompanied perestroika led Balkar national elites to use the collapse of Soviet power to end their people's continued participation in a Kabardian-dominated political system. The fact that democratic elections implied a diminution of political power in the republic for a people composing just over 10 percent of the population turned the Balkar elites' impulse toward sovereignty into full-scale nationalist mobilization. Again, compromise spared Kabardino-Balkaria from the ethnicized intercommunal conflict seen elsewhere in the Caucasus.

Compared with the Kabardino-Balkar case, the long-term patterns of power-sharing and symbiosis were absent in the other cases of post-Soviet intercommunal tensions that this chapter has examined. In Karachai-Cherkessia, for example, the Karachais' economy was historically less interdependent with the economies of their Cossack, Cherkes, and Abaza neighbors. The experience of 1922–1926, when perpetual conflict and disagreement among ethno-political blocs in Karachai-Cherkessia's administration impeded effective governance, demonstrated the difficulties of maintaining a combined Karachai-Cherkes AO. Anastas Mikoyan, head of the North Caucasus Regional Party Committee in the 1920s, highlighted the intractable problems that plagued the first Karachai-Cherkes AO:

> The composition of the oblast led to acute national struggle on every petty question and has largely paralyzed the constructive activity of Soviet power in the Karachai-Cherkes oblast. Especially in the first half of 1925, these relations reached such high levels of tension that all three national groups found it impossible to continue to reside together in a united oblast and expressed the necessity of dissolving the united oblast and creating two oblasts independent from each other—Karachai

and Cherkes oblasts—and joining the Russian Cossack districts to Armavir district.[116]

In 1926, the VTsIK decreed the division of the Karachai-Cherkes AO into separate Karachai and Cherkes autonomies.[117] This division would last for over thirty years (for thirteen of which the Karachais were in exile and enjoyed no autonomous status).

The post-Soviet conflict over Prigorodnyi district was not simply a result of the failure to reestablish pre-deportation borders.[118] It was the latest flare up in a long history of territorial disputes dating back to the mid-nineteenth century. The Ossetian-Ingush conflict over Prigorodnyi district has a long prehistory. At the end of the Caucasus War, in 1859 and 1860, the Russian administration decided to reinforce security along the most vulnerable part of the Georgian Military Highway by removing Ingush villages and establishing additional Cossack *stanitsy* around Vladikavkaz in the Tarsk Valley and the upper-Sunzha and Kambileevka rivers, the area now known as Prigorodnyi district. After Cossack colonization, this region was a flashpoint of tensions and conflict for Ossetian, Ingush, and Cossack communities, each of whom had competing claims to the region's land. During the Russian Revolution and Civil War, some of the most intense conflicts in the North Caucasus centered on the relationship among Cossacks, Ingush, and Ossetians, particularly in the territory of the future Prigorodnyi district. Indeed, the infamous cases of deportations of Terek Cossacks occurred precisely in this area. Three of the four *stanitsy* deported by pro-Soviet forces to free up land for Ingush and Chechen settlement in 1918 were located in the future Prigorodnyi district. Ethno-national mobilization and intense disputes over land accompanied the Soviet delimitation of borders between North Ossetia and Ingushetia in 1924. These Ossetian-Ingush disputes focused particularly on Prigorodnyi district and the city of Vladikavkaz.

In the Chechen case, problems between Chechens and Russians had a long history, and long periods of peaceful coexistence were rare. Similar to the Kabardian case, disruptions of Chechen land-tenure practices caused by Cossack colonization along the Terek produced the first conflicts between Chechens and the Russian state already in the late eighteenth century.[119] The Chechens, however, continued to resist long after Ermolov's armies had squelched the Kabardians' resistance. But this difference between the Kabardian and Chechen experiences in the nineteenth century has more to do with differences in social structure, geography, and disease than with national mentalities, to say nothing of a supposed primordial proclivity to resist outside rule. Even after the final capture of Shamil in 1859, Chechens continued to come into conflict with Cossacks over land rights during the late Imperial period and through the Russian Civil War.[120]

The tradition of excluding Chechens from the republic's industrial sector had been established well before the Chechens began their troubled return in 1957. During the late nineteenth and early twentieth centuries, another group of settlers with whom most Chechens would not enjoy friendly relations arrived in the Chechen lands. Russian workers began to settle the old fortress of Groznaia in large numbers as it developed into the oil boomtown of Groznyi and became an island of Russian workers in a sea of Chechen mountaineers.[121] In contrast to the Kabardino-Balkar capital of Nalchik, the Chechen capital, Groznyi, one of the oldest and largest industrial centers in the North Caucasus, had a history of Russian dominance and tensions with surrounding Chechen communities. Indeed, during the first years of Soviet power in the 1920s, the Russian workers of Groznyi refused to join the surrounding Chechen AO, briefly winning a separate autonomous status for their city.[122] Even at the height of Stalin's industrialization push and cultural revolution in the early 1930s, few Chechens entered into their oblast's industrial sector.[123] Nalchik, by contrast, became a city shortly after the formation of the Kabardino-Balkar AO in the early 1920s, and its industrialization and infrastructural development occurred under the auspices of Soviet nationalities policies and as a capital of a national autonomy. Though initially dominated by Russians, by the 1960s Nalchik's modest industrial sector included significant numbers of Kabardians and Balkars.[124]

Cultural Politics and the Transformation of Kabardian-Balkar Tensions

Since the mid-1990s, tensions between Circassians and their Karachai-Balkar neighbors have moved from the streets and squares of Nalchik, Cherkessk, and other cities to the hallowed halls of academia, and especially to the fraught terrain of history. Since the early 1990s, intellectuals throughout the post-Soviet space have been involved in the revision of national histories in response to new forms of ethnopolitics and the legitimating impulses of newly independent nation-states. Even (or perhaps especially) where independence has not resulted from the Soviet collapse, for example in the North Caucasus, the (re)interpretation of history has undergirded strident ethno-nationalisms and attempts to ethnicize intercommunal tensions. While the region's violent conflicts—from Nagorno-Karabakh to Chechnya—have attracted significant attention in the West, the region's "silent conflicts"—those that have fortunately remained nonviolent—have attracted far less attention from academics and journalists alike.[125] These conflicts have often been waged on the pages of history books, journals, and newspapers, and, most recently, online discussion forums, rather than on the region's rugged terrain. National elites have often looked to the region's hazy distant past to articulate exclusivist ethno-national identities, facilitate nationalist mobilization, and justify contemporary claims to disputed territories. Indeed, these Kabardian-Balkar history wars have focused particularly on competing interpretations of the history of intercommunal and land relations in the Central Caucasus. These competing interpretations reveal a desire on the part of Kabardians and Balkars to reclaim their pasts and craft new national narratives capable of consolidating their nations in the making.[126]

While these debates over the region's history have generally been reflective of a more peaceful expression of interethnic animosities and nationalism than street demonstrations, the ethno-historical debates between Kabardian/Circassian and Karachai-Balkar scholars-*cum*-national activists twice led to mass ethno-political mobilization and, on the second occasion, escalated into violence. On September

15, 2008, residents of the Balkar village of Këndelen (as Gundelen was renamed in 1995) blocked the passage through their village of a horseback procession of Kabardian national activists in traditional folk costumes. This ceremonial procession, sponsored by Arsen Konokov, the second president of Kabardino-Balkaria, was part of the commemoration of the 300th anniversary of the Battle of Mount Kanzhal.[127] According to the official interpretations of the Kabardino-Balkar government and the Russian Academy of Sciences, in 1708, after the Kabardians refused the Crimean Khan's demands for tribute, the Kabardian prince Kurgoko Atazhukin led a grossly outnumbered Kabardian army in a night-time battle against the Turkish and Crimean Tatar forces of Khan Kaplan Girey. According to legend, Kabardians forced the Crimean army to flee its encampment on the trans-Malka pastures near Mount Kanzhal by driving in 300 mules with burning hay strapped to their backs. In the ensuing panic, about 7,000 Kabardian horsemen stormed the Crimean forces, inflicting great losses. The remnants of the Crimean Khan's army retreated across the Kuban.[128] The Battle of Mount Kanzhal remained an important component of Kabardian folklore,[129] but there was little documentary evidence to confirm that such a battle ever occurred. Recently, however, Kabardian historians began to write anew about the battle after discovering several textual sources confirming the legend.[130]

In the post-Soviet period, Kabardian national activists have focused most of their historical commemorations on the tragic results of the Circassians' conflict with the Russian state. Given the negative historical role of the Russian state in these commemorations, Kabardino-Balkaria's pro-Kremlin leaders have had to moderate their levels of support for such activities.[131] In 2008, the leadership of Kabardino-Balkaria seized upon the 300th anniversary of this battle as a means of promoting a type of Kabardian patriotism that did not conflict with the larger Russian national project because the Crimean Khanate was a common enemy of Russia and Kabarda. The official interpretation of the Kabardian victory over the Crimean Khan's armies was that it allowed for closer relations between Kabarda and Russia. Balkar elites interpreted the official glorification of the Battle of Mount Kanzhal as another example of the embellishment of Kabardian history and the exaggeration of the power and importance of Kabarda in the history of the North Caucasus. The fact that the battle occurred near Mount Elbrus, one of the symbols of the Karachai-Balkar nation, further upset Balkar elites. In 2008, following a government-sponsored conference and numerous official publications on the Battle of Mount Kanzhal,[132] a group of oppositional Karachai-Balkar scholars, published *The Myth of the Battle of Mount Kanzhal*, a refutation of the scope and significance of the Battle of Mount Kanzhal.[133] This counter-commemoration campaign of the Karachai-Balkar elites found wide resonance among ordinary Balkars, culminating in the standoff outside Këndelen.

This confrontation outside of Këndelen ended peacefully. After two days of tensions, during which republican authorities attempted to break up the roadblock, the Kabardian horsemen ultimately decided to bypass the village and continue their commemorative procession via another route.[134]

During a similar horseback procession commemorating the 310th anniversary of the battle in September 2018, Kabardian-Balkar tensions were not resolved as peacefully as they had been in 2008. After suggesting an alternate route to the Kabardian horsemen, the residents of Këndelen blocked the path of the Kabardian procession. Fighting broke out between the Kabardian-Circassian national activists and Balkar villagers. A contingent of National Guard troops and representatives of the Kabardino-Balkar government rushed to the scene to prevent further violence. The Kabardian activists refused the officials' calls for them to leave the village on buses. Meanwhile, troops sealed off the Balkar village amid reports that Circassian activists were on their way to provide support to the horsemen. Outside Këndelen, clashes ensued between National Guard troops and Circassian activists trying to break through the cordon. The next day, as more Circassian activists attempted to reach Këndelen, clashes broke out at police cordons at other points along the route, with activists hurling rocks at security forces who in turn beat the activists with clubs. The situation de-escalated after Ibragim Iaganov, the organizer of the procession and one of the Circassian national movement's Kabardian leaders, posted a video on Facebook declaring that the procession to Mount Kanzhal had successfully concluded and that "the horses were back in the stable."[135]

The Këndelen events of 2008 and 2018 represent the extremes of ethno-politics in post-Soviet Kabardino-Balkaria. Tensions are never far from the surface here, but actual violence is rare. Indeed, there is persistent struggle in the ethno-cultural sphere between nationalist scholars (joined by armies of pseudo-scholars) over historical narratives. In most cases, these incessant intellectual disputes represent a de-escalation of the type of mass ethno-political mobilization among Kabardians and Balkars witnessed during the early 1990s. The Këndelen affair shows the capacity of these interethnic disputes to move from the academy and the Internet back to the streets. However, the rapid de-escalation of this standoff is also indicative of the ultimately peaceful relations that have prevailed between Kabardians and Balkars in the post-Soviet period. Given the absence of significant socioeconomic differences and the reconfiguration of political power-sharing, ethno-political tensions between Kabardians and Balkars, while certainly not absent, have stabilized since the mid-1990s. In terms of "everyday ethnicity," elite-level ethno-political contention in Kabardino-Balkaria has usually met, and will likely continue to meet, with popular indifference because the everyday concerns of ordinary Kabardians and Balkars are "only occasionally and intermittently interpreted in ethnic terms."[136] As long as Kabardino-Balkaria's social structure is not stratified according to ethnicity and Balkars continue to enjoy an acceptable level of political power in the republic, ethno-political elites will likely be unable to sustain mass mobilizations based on intercommunal contention. As this chapter demonstrates, the long-standing tradition of political compromise between Kabardian and Balkar elites and the continued absence of an ethnically stratified social structure played a significant role in making Kabardino-Balkaria's post-Soviet experience more stable and peaceful than those of its neighbors.

Conclusion

The recent historical discourse on Kabardino-Balkaria is marked by two extremes that reflect the region's transitory post-Soviet political status somewhere between the colonial and postcolonial. On the one hand, official historiography and commemorative discourses ahistorically treat Kabardino-Balkaria as a place that existed for centuries before its creation in 1922.[1] That is, by imposing the modern borders of Kabardino-Balkaria onto a vast expanse of history during which they did not exist, histories of Kabardino-Balkaria naturalize and legitimize the existence of the modern ethno-territorial unit. On the other hand, local Kabardian and Balkar nationalists, opposed to the existence of Kabardino-Balkaria in its present form and rejecting by definition the constructivist theory of nations, argue that Kabardino-Balkaria is an artificial product of Russia's divide-and-rule policies in the Caucasus. Yet their preferred objects of study—Circassia and Karachai-Balkaria—are no less ahistorical and based on contemporary ethno-political projects than that of Kabardino-Balkaria.[2] Far from being the product of Russian policies of divide and rule or, alternatively, an ancient entity, in this study I have tried to use a "situational analysis" to demonstrate how Kabardino-Balkaria (and "Kabardians" and "Balkars") formed out of dynamic interactions among the state, the local societies of the Central Caucasus, and the space they inhabited.[3]

In examining intercommunal and land relations in the Central Caucasus, this book has found that at the core of the enduring, if sometimes troubled, union between Kabardians and Balkars is the symbiotic, though politically and socially unequal, relationship that has linked these two peoples together since the sixteenth century. The Kabardian-Balkar symbiosis in the modern period emerged out of a system of intercommunal relations that connected Central Caucasia's diverse mountaineer communities to Kabarda as a result of the Kabardian elites' control of the region's plains pastures and farmland. Because the Greater Kabardian heartland largely separated the Balkar societies' mountain valleys from the outside world, this symbiosis endured, in continuously evolving forms, long after tsarist conquest and disease destroyed the Kabarda-centered system of intercommunal relations.

Until the social transformations of the early-Soviet period, class or estate categories and confessional affiliations, the latter transcending class and community, held this symbiosis together and had greater meaning in society than ethnic or national ones. Horizontal ties among the region's elites, though undergoing dramatic changes under tsarist rule, lasted through 1917. For example, as we have seen in the case of Lesken, Ossetian Muslims, particularly from elite social strata, remained connected to Kabardian communities through familial relations, religious ties, and land use patterns, long after Kabarda's formal tributary dominance over Ossetian communities had ended.

This book has examined the expansion and evolution of imperial rule and governance over more than two centuries. In the Central Caucasus, as was the case throughout the empire, the Russian state created as much as it destroyed.[4] In transforming the societies of the Central Caucasus—through ethnic cleansing, resettlement, ethicizing borders and territories, educational and missionary activity, and manipulating local politics—Russia brought some communities closer together while separating others and, in promoting colonization of the region by Russian and European peasants, created new types of interactions and exchanges. As we have seen in Russia's security dilemma in the region, the new interactions that the state created in acting as a "bureaucrat-policeman" in pursuit of security and order were often unintended and unwelcome. In some areas, these imperial transformations created long-standing animosities and tensions. For example, Cossack colonization and the attendant resettlement of Ossetians and Ingush created long-standing intercommunal tensions. These tensions have sporadically erupted into violent conflict among Ossetians, Ingush, and Cossacks. In other cases, the consequences of imperial rule produced less conflict. For example, imperial rule reinforced the symbiotic interdependence between the Kabardians and Balkars by linking the two communities administratively and economically through land reforms. In most cases, at least through the late 1920s, the ways in which state policies affected land relations determined much about the larger implications of Russian imperial rule.

One of the most important social transformations wrought by the imperial state was the creation of Kabardians and Balkars as national communities. This process of nation-building began already in the tsarist period with the introduction of ethnic categories for the administration of the region's diverse communities. After 1917, the Bolsheviks' class warfare combined with their institutionalization and territorialization of ethnicity sapped class and estate categories of their significance and gave ethnic and national categories unprecedented meaning in society. From the 1920s on, Soviet policies of nativization, which linked social mobility to nationality and territory, steadily increased the importance of national categories. The Stalinist deportation of nationalities from the North Caucasus during the Second World War, which subjected communities to state violence based on national affiliations, further consolidated ethnic consciousness and reinforced the importance of national categories among the deported communities.

Finally, this book has examined the causes of intercommunal peace and conflict in Kabardino-Balkaria and the North Caucasus more broadly. It finds that over the course of the tsarist and Soviet periods, state policies aimed at achieving both ideological and security goals often produced intercommunal conflict. Population politics of resettlement and deportation disrupted historic land use and ownership regimes and, by shifting demographic balances, disrupted intercommunal symbioses and led to violence. In contrast to communities in other parts of the region, however, Kabardian and Balkar communities, given their demographic patterns, did *not* experience the same acute land pressures as a result of Russian colonization. Kabardian and Balkar communities were able to adapt their symbiotic economic system to include Cossacks, Russian peasants, and other settler communities. In contrast, the imposition of national categories onto the region's peoples and the delimitation of national borders demonstrate how the state's ideological projects also exacerbated intercommunal conflicts. For example, from 1918 to 1926, the Bolsheviks' class warfare and introduction of the national principle led to the ethnicization of intercommunal conflict in the Central Caucasus. The national principle and its instrumentalization by local elites exacerbated tensions by turning feuds between villages over land allotments into conflicts between nations over their national territories.

In addition to the state's role as an unwitting creator of intercommunal conflict, the state also played a crucial role as a mediator of disputes between Kabardians and Balkars (as it did among many other groups in conflict during periods of social and political upheaval). As was often the case, the state steered disputing parties toward a resolution that was most favorable to its policy goals.[5] During periods of state collapse and reconfiguration in the late eighteenth century, the early 1920s, and the 1990s, the relationship between Kabardians and Balkars nearly broke down. In each of these periods, there was a general understanding among Russian officials that the continuation of the close relationship between Kabardians and Balkars would be—in terms of administering the region effectively, maintaining peace and stability, and promoting economic growth—in the state's best interest.

That said, the state was not a puppet master in these intercommunal disputes. In addition to state policies, long-term patterns of intercommunal relations were also at work. Given the historic Kabardian-Balkar symbiosis (based on economic, political, social, and familial ties), the motivations and initiatives for intercommunal accord often came from local elites and the societies on which they depended for support. Indeed, the attitudes of ordinary Kabardians, Balkars, and Russians have been key factors in the preservation of Kabardino-Balkaria as multiethnic republic. As Chapter 6 demonstrates, among the communities of Kabardino-Balkaria, there was little socioeconomic basis for separatism, and the efforts of ethno-political entrepreneurs often met with popular indifference.

This lack of a socioeconomic basis for separatism underscores the importance of modernization as a factor influencing intercommunal conflict over the twentieth century. Kabardian and Balkars ethno-political entrepreneurs were unsuccessful in sustaining their mobilizations and convincing their co-ethnics to take up arms for the creation of separate national territories in large measure because of the relative absence of disparities in modernization levels and general socioeconomic equality between Kabardians and Balkars. As we have seen, ethnicized violence or at least seemingly intractable ethno-political tensions in Karachai-Cherkesia, North Ossetia's Prigorodnyi district, and Chechnya were rooted in long-standing social stratification along ethnic lines. Kabardino-Balkaria stands in marked contrast to these regions.

During my final research trip to Russia for this project in 2012, my host family's location in Vol'nyi Aul, a suburb of the Kabardino-Balkar capital, provided the ideal site to observe everyday life in this multiethnic society. Vol'nyi Aul was founded in 1825 as a settlement for former Kabardian serfs liberated from their anti-Russian feudal lords by General Ermolov. Located just outside the walls of Nalchik Fortress on the right bank of the Nalchik River, this was the only settlement of free peasants in pre-reform-era Kabarda.[6] Historically the nearest Kabardian village to the city of Nalchik, in 1970 this Nalchik suburb and others became part of the growing city.[7] When the Balkars returned to Kabardino-Balkaria in the late 1950s, thousands of them resettled in Nalchik and its suburbs rather than return to their underdeveloped mountain valleys.[8] Over the late Soviet and post-Soviet eras, greater opportunities for employment and education have drawn increasing numbers of Balkars to settle in the Nalchik area, so that today over 44 percent of the entire Balkar population lives within the city limits of Nalchik.[9] While most settled in the Balkar-majority suburbs of Khasan'ia and Belaia Rechka (*Ak Suu*), some settled in Vol'nyi Aul. Today, Balkars make up about 10 percent of Vol'nyi Aul's residents.[10]

While Kabardians and Balkars in Vol'nyi Aul live together amicably and maintain mutual friendships, there are clear Kabardian and Balkar spheres, and there are distinguishing features that mark the two peoples from each other. These spheres are often determined by the historic cultural and economic practices of the two peoples— practices that have peacefully coexisted for centuries. Balkar families brought their traditional cattle-breeding economy to the city. Based on my observations, the few men grazing their cows along the grassy Nalchik riverbank in Vol'nyi Aul were more likely to be Balkars than Kabardians. Indeed, my neighbor was one of these Balkar men. In the mornings, he would bring me and my Kabardian host family fresh ayran, a sour salted yoghurt drink common among Eurasia's Turkic peoples and for which the Balkars are noted locally. The local Balkar elders of Vol'nyi Aul would gather in the evenings on a public bench off Betal Kalmykov Street. Though these Balkar men were friendly and open to discussions and exchanging the standard "*salam aleikum*" with Kabardian passersby, this was clearly a Balkar zone, one of the few in this Kabardian-majority suburb. I would chat with them when I wanted to hear a Balkar take on a particular historical issue. When I asked about the fate and current condition of the Balkar people, these Balkar men placed their historical anger on Lavrenti Beria, Stalin's security chief who organized the deportation of the Balkars during the Second World War. When I asked about the political relationship between Kabardians and Balkars, they replied ironically, with a sentiment perhaps more commonly associated with the feelings of Ukrainians and Georgians toward Russia, that like most small peoples the Balkars had the great fortune of being blessed with a larger neighbor to protect them and with whom they had to live in peace whether they liked it or not.

Notes

Introduction

1 The independent news website Caucasian Knot covered the Balkar protests closely. See, for example, Luiza Orazaeva, *Uchastniki aktsii protesta balkartsev v Moskve vstretiatsia s chlenami obshchestvennoi palaty RF,* last updated December 21, 2010, http://www.kavkaz-uzel.ru/articles/178709.
2 K. I. Kazenin, *Tikhie konflikty na Severnom Kavkaze: Adygeia, Kabardino-Balkariia, Karachaevo-Cherkesiia.* (Moscow: Regnum, 2009), 58.
3 On the Kabardian-Balkar symbiosis, see M. I. Barazbiev, *Etnokul'turnye sviazy balkartsev i karachaevtsev s narodami Kavkaza* (Nalchik: Elbrus, 2000), 5–35.
4 As in Transcaucasia so in the Central Caucasus, before the class warfare and nationalities policy of the Soviet period, "estate and class lines cut across allegiances to nationality for significant groups and even hindered the growth of ethnic nationalism." Ronald Girgor Suny, "Nationalism and Social Class in the Russian Revolution: The Cases of Baku and Tiflis," in *Transcaucasia, Nationalism and Social Change: Essays in the History of Armenia, Azerbaijan, and Georgia,* ed. Ronald Grigor Suny (Ann Arbor: University of Michigan, 1983), 242.
5 In the Russian and Soviet contexts, modernization did not mean the total disappearance of traditional social practices. The Soviet Union and other communist states belie many of the assumptions of modernization theory, particularly in regard to the supposed diminution in importance of personal ties and ascribed status. For a series of essays discussing Russia's particular relationship to modernity, see David L. Hoffman and Yanni Kotsonis, eds., *Russian Modernity: Politics, Practice, Knowledge* (London: MacMillan, 2000). In using the term "modernization," I do not mean, as adherents of modernization theory in the 1950s and 1960s did, a uniform transformational process based on the experience of Western Europe that all societies must go through to be considered modern. Rather, modernization produces different outcomes based on particular historical circumstances. I have in mind specific aspects of modernization: industrialization, urbanization, bureaucratization, mass literacy, and social mobility.
6 Austin Jersild makes this connection between ethnic homogenization and conceptions of governance. See *Orientalism and Empire: North Caucasus Mountaineer peoples and the Georgian Frontier, 1845-1917* (Montreal: McGill-Queen's University Press, 2002), 86.
7 On the Soviet promotion of ethnicity, see Yuri Slezkine, "The USSR as a Communal Apartment, or How a Socialist State Promoted Ethnic Particularism," *Slavic Review* 53, no. 2 (Summer 1994): 414–52.
8 I borrow Theordora Dragostinova's concepts of "national literacy" and "speaking national." Dragostinova expands upon Alexei Yurchak's concept of "ideological literacy"—"a technical skill of reproducing prefabricated 'blocks' of discourse"—for the nation-centered context (the nationalizing Bulgarian state). See Alexei Yurchak,

"Soviet Hegemony of Form: Everything Was Forever, Until It Was No More," *Comparative Studies in Society and History* 45, no. 3 (July 2003): 485–6; Theodora Dragostinova, "Speaking National: Nationalizing the Greeks of Bulgaria, 1900 –1939," *Slavic Review* 67, no. 1 (Spring 2008): 157–8. On "speaking Bolshevik," see Stephen Kotkin, *Magnetic Mountain: Stalinism as a civilization* (Berkeley: University of California Press, 1995), 198–237.

9 Francine Hirsch, *Empire of Nations: Ethnographic Knowledge and the making of the Soviet Union* (Ithaca: Cornell University Press, 2005), 14.
10 Eric Hobsbawm, *Nations and Nationalism since 1780: Programme, Myth, Reality* (Cambridge: Cambridge University Press, 1990), 123.
11 On the achieving and losing of Soviet identity along with an "ethnic" or "traditional" one, see Bruce Grant, *In the Soviet House of Culture: A Century of Perestroikas* (Princeton: Princeton University Press, 1995).
12 Nicholas Breyfogle, "Enduring Imperium: Russia/Soviet Union/Eurasia as Multiethnic, Multiconfessional Space," *Ab Imperio* 9, no. 1 (2008): 77.
13 Ibid., 101, 108, 114.
14 Jane Burbank and Fredrick Cooper highlight the importance of imperial intermediaries in *Empires in World History: Power and the Politics of Difference* (Oxford: Oxford University Press, 2010).
15 Rogers Brubaker, *Ethnicity Without Groups* (Cambridge, MA: Harvard University Press, 2004), 8.
16 Ibid., 12.
17 James Fearon and David Laitin, "Explaining Interethnic Cooperation," *The American Political Science Review* 9, no. 4 (1996): 719.
18 Ibid., 722.
19 For various iterations of this view of "ethnic" violence see Rogers Brubaker and David Laitin, "Ethnic and Nationalist Violence," *Annual Review of Sociology* 24, no. 1 (1998): 444–5; Brubaker, *Ethnicity Without Groups*, 16–17; and James Fearon and David Laitin, "Violence and the Social Construction of Ethnicity," *International Organization* 54, no. 4 (2000): 845–77; and Paul Brass, *Theft of an Idol: Text and Context in the Representation of Collective Violence* (Princeton: Princeton University Press, 1997).
20 Brubaker and Laitin, "Ethnic and Nationalist Violence," 444.
21 Fearon and Laitin, "Violence and the Social Construction of Ethnicity," 846.
22 Brubaker, *Ethnicity without Groups*, 8.
23 Karl Deutsch, *Nationalism and Social Communication: An Inquiry into the Foundations of Nationality*, 2nd ed. (Cambridge, MA: MIT Press, 1966), 123–52; Ernest Gellner makes this connection in his classic *Nations and Nationalism* (Ithaca: Cornell University Press, 1983), 53–62; See also Donald Horowitz's review of theories of ethnicity and modernization in *Ethnic Groups in Conflict* (Berkeley: University of California Press, 1985), 99–105.
24 Ibid., 166–7.
25 Here I draw on the insights of the modernist and constructivist theories of nations and nationalism: Gellner's *Nations and Nationalism* and Benedict Anderson, *Imagined Communities: Reflections on the Origin and Spread of Nationalism* Revised edition (London: Verso, 1991).
26 Ronald Suny, *The Revenge of the Past: Nationalism, Revolution, and the Collapse of the Soviet Union* (Stanford: Stanford University Press, 1993), 87–106; Slezkine, "The USSR as a Communal Apartment"; Terry Martin, *The Affirmative Action Empire: Nations*

and Nationalism in the Soviet Union, 1923-1939 (Ithaca: Cornell University Press, 2001); Hirsch, *Empire of Nations*.

27 Peter Blitstein, "Stalin's Nations: Soviet Nationality Policy between Planning and Primordialism, 1936-1953" (Ph.d. diss., University of California-Berkeley, 1999).

28 Jeremy Smith, "Was There a Soviet Nationalities Policy?," *Europe-Asia Studies* 71, no. 6 (2019): 972–93.

29 Ibid., 972–3.

30 Ibid., 984.

31 Ibid., 978–9.

32 Ibid., 986–7.

33 Jeronim Perović's superb recent account of Russian conquest and colonization uses Chechnya as the basis of most of the case studies included to illustrate broader historical processes in the region and, consequently, devotes significant attention to the role of Islam in resistance to Russia rule. See *From Conquest to Deportation: The North Caucasus under Russian Rule* (New York: Oxford University Press, 2018). Vladimir Bobrovnikov's seminal work on Islam and law in the North Caucasus focuses on Dagestan. See his *Musul'mane Severnogo Kavkaza: obychai, pravo, nasilie: Ocherki po istorii i etnografii prava Nagornogo Dagestana* (Moscow: Vostochnaia literature PAN, 2002). The sources listed in the footnote 34 also demonstrate this focus on the role of Islam in the North Caucasus.

34 For examples of work on the North Caucasus that emphasizes colonial conquest and anti-colonial resistance, see John Baddeley, *The Russian Conquest of the Caucasus* (London: Longmans, Green and Co., 1908); Lesley Blanch, *The Sabres of Paradise* (London: John Murray, 1960); Moshe Gammer, *Muslim Resistance to the Tsar: Shamil and the Conquest of Chechnia and Daghestan* (London: F. Cass, 1994); idem, *The Lone Wolf and the Bear: Three Centuries of Chechen Defiance of Russian Rule* (Pittsburgh: University of Pittsburgh Press, 2006); Anna Zelkina, *In Quest for God and Freedom: Sufi Responses to the Russian Advance in the North Caucasus* (London: Hurst, 2000); Marie Bennigsen Broxup (ed.), *The North Caucasus Barrier: The Russian Advance Toward the Muslim World* (New York: St. Martin's Press, 1992); Anatol Lieven, *Chechnya: Tombstone of Russian Power* (New Haven: Yale University Press, 1994); and Rebecca Gould, *Writers and Rebels: The Literature of Insurgency in the Caucasus* (New Haven: Yale University Press, 2016).

35 For a survey of historiography on the North Caucasus see V. O. Bobrovnikov and I. L. Babich, eds., *Severnyi Kavkaz v sostave Rossiiskoi Imperii* (Moscow: Novoe Literaturnoe Obozrenie, 2007), 18–32. The best English-language overview of the historiography on the North Caucasus, see Perović 's comprehensive account of how tsarist and Soviet policies impacted the region and its peoples from the beginning of Russian rule until the mass deportations of the Second World War, *From Conquest to Deportation*, 3–10.

36 For a sample of this Western scholarship on the North Caucasus, see Perović, *From Conquest to Deportation*; Jersild, *Orientalism and Empire*; Susan Layton, *Russian Literature and Empire: Conquest of the Caucasus from Pushkin to Tolstoy* (Cambridge: Cambridge University Press, 1994); Thomas Barrett, *At the Edge of Empire: The Terek Cossacks and the North Caucasus Frontier, 1700-1860* (Boulder: Westview Press, 1999); Michael Khodarkovsky, *Bitter Choices: Loyalty and Betray in the Russian Conquest of the North Caucasus* (Ithaca: Cornell University Press, 2011); Bruce Grant, *The Captive and the Gift: Cultural Histories of Sovereignty in Russia and the Caucasus* (Ithaca: Cornell University Press, 2009). Charles King's concise survey of the history

of the Caucasus, which focuses particularly on the period from the Russian conquest to the present, while including the standard political and military narratives, also incorporates cultural and social perspectives. See, *The Ghost of Freedom: A History of the Caucasus* (New York: Oxford University Press, 2008).

37 Alexei Miller, "Between Local and Inter-Imperial: Russian Imperial History in Search of Scope and Paradigm," *Kritika: Explorations in Russian and Eurasian History* 5, no. 1 (Winter 2004): 10.
38 See, for example, the following high school textbooks: T. Kh. Kumykov, *Istoriia Kabardino-Balkarii* (Nalchik: Elbrus, 1997) and V. Sh. Nakhusheva *Narody Karachaevo-Cherkesii: istoriia i kul'tura* (Cherkessk: KChRIPKRO, 1998).
39 Miller, "Between Local and Inter-Imperial," 17–18.
40 Ibid., 9.
41 One of the earliest publications in which Balkaria is used to refer to the territory of all five mountaineer societies and Balkar is used to refer to their inhabitants is the Balkar intellectual and educator Misost Abaev's ethnography and history of the Balkars. "Balkariia," *Musul'manin* 4–17 (1911): 586–627.
42 R. M. Begeulov, *Tsentral'nyi Kavkaz v XVII-pervoi chetverti XIX veka: ocherki etnopoliticheskoi istorii* (Karachaevsk: Karachaevo-Cherkesskii Gosudarstvennyi Universitet, 2005), 7.
43 R. A. Buraev and L. Z. Emuzova, *Geografiia Kabardino-Balkarskoi Respubliki* (Nalchik: Kniga, 1998), 13–22.
44 In post-Soviet historiography, Karachai and Balkar historians have questioned the appropriateness of viewing Kabardian-mountaineer relations in terms of a "suzerain-vassal" dichotomy. These terms, while not perfect, most closely approximate the relationship between Kabarda and its neighbors. See for example, Z. B. Kipkeeva, *Severnyi Kavkaz v Rossiiskoi imperii: narody, migratsii, territorii* (Stavropol: Stavropol'skii gosudarstvennyi universitet, 2008); Begeulov, *Tsentral'nyi Kavkaz v XVII-pervoi chetverti XIX veka*; and R. T. Khatuev, "Karachai i Balkariia do vtoroi poloviny XIX v.: vlast' i obshchestvo," in *Karachaevtsy i Balkartsy: etnografiia, istoriia, arkheologiia*, ed. S. A. Arutiunov (Moscow: Rossiiskaia Akademiia Nauk institut etnologii i antropologii, 1999), 5–15.
45 For a discussion of the ethno-political transformations taking place in the North Caucasus between the thirteenth and fifteenth centuries and, particularly, the emergence of Kabarda, see V. V. Gudakov, *Severo-Zapadnyi Kavkaz v sisteme mezhetnicheskikh otnoshenii s drevneishikh vremen do 60-kh godov XIX veka* (St. Petersburg: Izdatel'stvo S.-Peterburgskogo Universiteta, 2007), 112–222; and Zh. V. Kagazezhev, "Etnoterritorial'naia separatsiia adygov v pozdnem srednevekov'e," *Voprosy Istorii*, no. 7 (July 2011): 154–8.
46 Iurii Asanov, *Otkuda est' poshla Zemlia Kabardinskaia. Chto oznachaet nazvanie Kabarda, i kto v nei pervym kniazhil?* (Nalchik: Pechatnyi dvor, 2012), 5–22.
47 K. Kh Unezhev, *Istoriia Kabardy i Balkarii* (Nalchik: El-Fa, 2005), 66–8.
48 G. A. Kokiev, "Raspad Kabardy na bol'shuiu i maluiu i ustanovivshiesia otnosheniia s sosednimi narodami," in *Istoriia Kabardino-Balkarii v trukakh G.A. Kokieva: Sbornik statei i dokumentov*, ed. G. Kh. Mambetov (Nalchik: El-Fa, 2005), 198–206.
49 Idem., "Rol' Temriuka v sblizhenii Kabardy s Moskovskim gosudarstvenom," in ibid., 532–5.
50 Begeulov, *Tsentral'nyi Kavkaz v XVII-pervoi chetverti XIX veka*, 96–134.
51 For descriptions of Kabarda's social structure, see G. A. Kokiev, "Kabardino-Osetinskie Otnosheniia v XVIII v.," in *Istoriia Kabardino-Balkarii v trudakh*, 132–45.

52 T. Kh. Kumykov, *Ekonomicheskoe i kul'turnoe razvitie Kabardy i Balkarii v XIX veke* (Nalchik: Elbrus, 1965), 61.
53 E. N. Kusheva, *Narody Severnogo Kavkaza i ikh sviazi s Rossiei: vtoraia polovina XVI -30-e gody XVII veka* (Moscow: Izdatel'stvo Akademii Nauk SSSR, 1961), 96–103.
54 On Kabardian settlements see Ibid., 94–5, 115; and S. I. Mesiats, *Naselenie i zemlepol'zovanie Kabardy* (Voronezh: Kabardino-Balkarskii Oblastnoi Ispolkom, 1928), 36–8.
55 P. A. Kuz'minov, "Etnodemograficheskaia karta narodov Tereka: razmeshchenie, chislennost' i migratsiia naseleniia v kontse XVIII–pervoi polovine XIX veka," in *Landshaft, etnograficheskie i istoricheskie protsessy na Severnom Kavkaze v XIX— nachale XX veka*, eds. G. V. Novitskii et al. (Nalchik: El-Fa, 2004), 726.
56 See, for example, Stepan Chichagov's 1744 map. T. Kh. Kumykov and E. N. Kushova, eds., *Kabardino-Russkie otnosheniia v XVI-XVIII vv.*, vol. 2 (Moscow: Akademiia Nauk SSSR, 1957), 114–15.
57 The Kabardians and Beslenei Circassians often came into conflict over control of the Tapanta Abaza. See V. P. Nevskaia, *Ocherki istorii Karachaevo-Cherkesii*, vol. 1 (Stavropol: Stavropol'skoe knizhnoe izdatel'stvo, 1967), 139.
58 Kusheva, *Narody Severnogo Kavkaza i ikh sviazi s Rossiei*, 170.
59 As a result of Soviet-inspired impulses toward national consolidation, by the end of the twentieth century, many Karachai and Balkars (always culturally and linguistically related), following the writings of national intellectuals, consider themselves members of a common Karachai-Balkar nation.
60 Bobrovnikov and Babich, *Severnyi Kavkaz v sostave Rossiiskoi Imperii*, 61–70.
61 Begeulov, *Tsentral'nyi Kavkaz v XVII-pervoi chetverti XIX veka*, 29.
62 Ibid., 37.
63 Z. A. Kozhev, "Sistema zemepol'zovaniia v kabardino-gorskikh otnosheniiakh (vtoraia polovina XVIII v)," in *Zemel'nye otnosheniia v Kabarde i Balkarii: Istoriia i Sovremennost'*, eds. Kh. M. Dumanov et al. (Nalchik: Institut gumanitarnykh issledovanii Pravitel'stva KBR i KBNTs RAN, 2005), 28–32; Begeulov, *Tsentral'nyi Kavkaz v XVII-pervoi chetverti XIX veka*, 139.
64 Johann Anton Güldenstädt, *Puteshestvie po kavkazu v 1770-1773 gg.* (St. Petersburg: Peterburgskoe Vostokovedenie, 2002), 225.
65 G. Kh. Mambetov, *Zemel'nyi vopros v tvorchestve obshchestvenno-politicheskikh deiatelei adygov, balkartsev, i karachaevtsev v XIX-nachale XX* (Nalchik: KBNII, 1976), 102–3.
66 G. A. Kokiev, ed., *Materialy po istorii Osetii*, vol. 1 (Ordzhonikidze: Gosudarstvennoe izdatel'stvo Severo-Osetinskoii ASSR, 1934), 197.
67 Güldenstädt, *Puteshestvie po kavkazu v 1770-1773 gg.*, 287.
68 Kokiev, "Raspad Kabardy," 203–4.
69 M. M. Bliev, ed., *Russko-osetinskie otnosheniia v XVIII veke*, vol. 2 (Ordzhonikidze: Ir, 1984), 320.
70 Begeulov, *Tsentral'nyi Kavkaz v XVII-pervoi chetverti XIX veka*, 64.
71 Julius von Klaproth, *Travels in the Caucasus and Georgia Performed in the Years 1807 and 1808 by Command of the Russian Government* (London: British and Foreign Public Library, 1814), 287.
72 Begeulov, *Tsentral'nyi Kavkaz v XVII-pervoi chetverti XIX veka*, 41–4.
73 Julius von Klaproth, *Voyage au mont Caucase et en Géorgie*, vol. 2 (Paris: Charles Gosselin, 1836), 230–1.

74 A. V. Fadeev, *Ocherki istorii balkarskogo naroda* (Nalchik: Kabardino-Balkarskoe knizhnoe izdatel'stvo 1961), 39.
75 Ibid.
76 Begeulov, *Tsentral'nyi Kavkaz v XVII-pervoi chetverti XIX veka*, 62–75.
77 M. I. Barazbiev, "Traditsionnye formy mezhetnicheskikh otnoshenii balkartsev i karachaevtsev s kabardintsami," *Respublika: Al'manakh sotsial'no-politicheskikh i pravovikh issledovanii*, no. 1 (2000): 48–70. On the ties between the Ossetian elites and the neighboring elites of the Central Caucasus, especially the Kabardian aristocracy, see Islam-Bek Temurkanovich Marzoev, *Osetinskaia feodal'naia znat' v sisteme vzaimodeistviia etnicheskikh elit Severnogo Kavkaza (XVIII-nach. XX vv.)* (Vladikavkaz: Severo-Osetinskii institut gumanitarnykh i sotsial'nykh issledovanii, 2008).
78 On the Islamization of Kabarda, see Nadezhda Emel'ianova, *Musul'mane Kabardy* (Moscow: Granitsa, 1999).
79 Bobrovnikov and Babich, *Severnyi Kavkaz v sostave Rossiiskoi Imperii*, 89–91.
80 The Ottoman concession of Kabarda to Russia occurred despite the Ottoman Empire never having ruled over Kabarda.
81 On "invitations to empire," see Sean Pollock, *Empire by Invitation? Russian Empire-Building in the Caucasus in the Reign of Catherine II* (Phd Dissertation, Harvard University, 2006).
82 Hirsch, *Empire of Nations*, 14.
83 I borrow the phrase "punished peoples" from Alexander Nekrich. See *The Punished Peoples: The Deportation and Fate of Soviet Minorities at the End of the Second World War* (New York: Norton, 1978).

Chapter 1

1 Kumykov and Kushova, *Kabardino-Russkie otnosheniia*, vol. 2, 114–15.
2 Nevskaia, *Ocherki istorii Karachaevo-Cherkesii*, 246.
3 On Kabarda's important place in the steppe politics of the sixteenth through eighteenth centuries, see Michael Khodarkovsky, *Russia's Steppe Frontier: The Making of a Colonial Empire, 1500-1800* (Bloomington: Indiana University Press, 2002), 56, 58, 87–8, 199–200.
4 Begeulov, *Tsentral'nyi Kavkaz v XVII-pervoi chetverti XIX veka*, 51–2.
5 M. Polievktov, *Posol'stvo stol'nika Tolchanova i d'iaka Ievleva v Imeretiiu: 1650-1652* (Tiflis: Tiflisskii Universitet, 1926), 119.
6 Ibid., 120.
7 On Russian policies and intercommunal relations in the Baltics, see Edward Thaden and Marianna Foster Thaden, *Russia's Western Borderlands* (Princeton: Princeton University Press, 1984); and Edward Thaden ed., *Russification in the Baltic Provinces and Finland, 1855-1914* (Princeton: Princeton University Press, 1981).
8 Begeulov, *Tsentral'nyi Kavkaz v XVII-pervoi chetverti XIX veka*, 47.
9 Ibid., 45.
10 Artur Tsutsiev, "Ob odnom algoritme krizisnogo pricheneniia na Severnom Kavkaze," *Nauchnye Tetrady Instituta Vostochnoi Evropy*, no. 111 (2009): 168–91.
11 Kokiev, *Materialy po istorii Osetii*, 43.
12 Begeulov, *Tsentral'nyi Kavkaz v XVII-pervoi chetverti XIX veka*, 144.

13 T. Iuzefovich, ed., *Dogovory Rossii s vostokom: politicheskie i torgovye* (Saint Petersburg: Tipografiia O.I. Baksta, 1869), 19.
14 M. M. Bliev, *Russko-osetinskie otnosheniia*, vol. I (Ordzhonikidze: Ir, 1976), 121.
15 This is Zarema Kipkeeva's main point about Kabardino-Russian relations in the second half of the eighteenth century. See Part One of her *Severnyi Kavkaz v Rossiiskoi imperii*, 9–96.
16 Kozhev, "Sistema zemepol'zovaniia v kabardino-gorskikh otnosheniiakh (vtoraia polovina XVIII v)," 29; N. G. Volkova, *Etnicheskii sostav naseleniia severnogo Kavkaza v XVIII—Nachale XX veka* (Moscow: Nauka, 1974), 160.
17 Begeulov, *Tsentral'nyi Kavkaz v XVII-pervoi chetverti XIX veka*, 139.
18 Ibid., 159.
19 Ibid., 51.
20 B. P. Berozov, *Pereselenie osetin s gor na ploskost' v XVIII—XX vekakh* (Ordzhonikidze: Ir, 1980), 40.
21 On Russian missionary activity as a means of expanding Russia's influence in the region, see Firouzeh Mostashari, "Colonial Dilemmas: Russian Policies in the Muslim Caucasus," in *Of Religion and Empire: Missions, Conversion, and Tolerance in Tsarist Russia*, eds. Robert Geraci and Michael Khodarkovsky (Ithaca: Cornell University Press, 2001); Michael Khodarkovsky, "Of Christianity, Enlightenment and Colonialism: Russia in the North Caucasus, 1550-1800," *Journal of Modern History* 71, no. 2 (June 1999): 394–430; and Austin Jersild, "Faith, Custom, and Ritual in the Borderlands: Orthodoxy, Islam and the 'small peoples' of the Middle Volga and North Caucasus," *Russian Review* 59 (October 2000): 512–29.
22 Mostashari, "Colonial Dilemmas," 231.
23 G. A. Kokiev, "Metody kolonial'noi politiki tsarskoi rossii na severnom Kavkaze v XVIII v.," in *Istoriia Kabardino-Balkarii v trudakh*, 91–111.
24 Khodarkovsky, "Of Christianity, Enlightenment and Colonialism," 410.
25 The folk religion of the Circassians (including the Kabardians) was pluriform monotheistic. Circassians worshiped a pantheon of Gods, but they believed in an underlying unity under the supreme God Tkh'a. See A. T. Shortanov, *Adygskie Kul'ty* (Nalchik: Elbrus, 1992).
26 Begeulov, *Tsentral'nyi Kavkaz v XVII-pervoi chetverti XIX veka*, 140.
27 P. G. Butkov, *Materialy dlia novoi istorii Kavkaza s 1722 po 1803 god* (St. Petersburg: Akademiia Nauk, 1869), 441.
28 Kokiev, "Metody kolonial'noi politiki," 107.
29 G. A. Kokiev, ed., *Osetiny vo II polovine XVIII veka po nabliudeniiam puteshestvennika Shtedera*, (Ordzhonikidze: Severo-Osetinskoe gosudarstvennoe izdatel'stvo, 1940), 33.
30 Ia.Ia. Iakubova, *Severnyi Kavkaz v russko-turetskikh otnosheniiakh v 40-70 –e gody XVIII veka* (Nalchik: Elbrus, 1993), 51.
31 Kokiev, "Metody kolonial'noi politiki," 86–99.
32 For a discussion of Konchokin, the establishment of Mozdok, and its larger significance, see Pollock, *Empire by Invitation?*, 71–93.
33 Kumykov and Kushova, *Kabardino-Russkie otnosheniia*, vol. 2, 123.
34 Pollock, *Empire by Invitation?*, 94–106.
35 Volkova, *Etnicheskii sostav naseleniia*, 139.
36 G. A. Kokiev, "Pereselenie kabardinskikh kholopov v Mozdok v XVIII v.," in *Istoriia Kabardino-Balkarii v trudakh*, 228.

37 Ibid.
38 Begeulov, *Tsentral'nyi Kavkaz v XVII-pervoi chetverti XIX veka*, 147.
39 Kokiev, "Metody kolonial'noi politiki," 101.
40 Ibid., 86.
41 Begeulov, *Tsentral'nyi Kavkaz v XVII-pervoi chetverti XIX veka*, 149.
42 Ibid., 151.
43 Safarbi Beituganov, *Ermolov i Kabarda: Ocherki istorii* (Nalchik: Elbrus, 1993), 11.
44 N. A. Smirnov, *Politika Rossii na Kavkaze v XVI-XIX vekakh* (Moscow: Izdatel'stvo sotsial'no-ekonomicheskoi literatury, 1958), 95.
45 Ibid., 84–106.
46 See documents in Kumykov and Kushova, *Kabardino-Russkie Otnosheniia*, vol. 2, 282–6.
47 Michael Herbert Fischer, *Indirect Rule in India: Residents and the Residency System, 1764-1858* (Delhi: Oxford University Press, 1991).
48 For a discussion of Kabarda's internal administration before 1822, see Zh. A. Kalmykov, *Integratsiia Kabardy i Balkarii v Obshcherossiiskuiu sistemu upravleniia (vtoraia polovina XVIII—Nachalo XX veka)* (Nalchik: El-Fa, 2007), 35–48.
49 Kumykov and Kushova, *Kabardino-Russkie otnosheniia*, vol. 2, 299–303.
50 Smirnov, *Politika Rossii na Kavkaze v XVI-XIX vekakh*, 102–3.
51 Ibid., 103–5.
52 Ibid., 104.
53 Iuzefovich, *Dogovory Rossii s vostokom*, 35.
54 Smirnov, *Politika Rossii na Kavkaze v XVI-XIX vekakh*, 109.
55 Begeulov, *Tsentral'nyi Kavkaz v XVII-pervoi chetverti XIX veka*, 151–2.
56 Butkov, *Materialy dlia novoi istorii Kavkaza s 1722 po 1803 god*, 300.
57 Kokiev, "Kabardino-Osetinskie otnosheniia," 173.
58 Kumykov and Kushova, *Kabardino-Russkie otnosheniia*, vol. 2, 308–9.
59 Bliev, *Russko-Osetinskie otnosheniia*, vol. 2, 265.
60 Kipkeeva, *Severnyi Kavkaz v Rossiiskoi imperii*, 82–96.
61 Bobrovnikov and Babich, *Severnyi Kavkaz v sostave Rossiiskoi Imperii*, 50.
62 R. Kh. Gugov, *Kabarda i Balkariia v XVIII veke i ikh vzaimootnosheniia s Rossiei* (Nalchik: El-Fa, 1999), 524.
63 Begeulov, *Tsentral'nyi Kavkaz v XVII-pervoi chetverti XIX veka*, 160–1.
64 Gugov, *Kabarda i Balkariia v XVIII veke*, 527.
65 Begeulov, *Tsentral'nyi Kavkaz v XVII-pervoi chetverti XIX veka*, 161.
66 Ibid.
67 See, for example, V. D. Dzidoev, *Osetiia v sisteme vziamootnoshenii narodov kavkaza v XVII-nach. XX v. (Istoriko-etnologicheskoe issledovanie)* (Vladikavkaz: Izdatel'stvo Severo-Osetinskogo gosudarstvennogo universiteta, 2003), 90–5. On the support of the non-Russian peasantry against the non-Russian nobility, see Andreas Kappeler, *The Russian Empire: A Multiethnic History* (Harlow: Longman-Pearson, 2001), 124–5.
68 Bliev, *Russko-Osetinskie Otnosheniia*, vol. 2, 403.
69 Dzidoev, *Osetiia v sisteme vziamootnoshenii narodov kavkaza*, 90–5.
70 Kozhev, "Sistema zemepol'zovaniia v kabardino-gorskikh otnosheniiakh (vtoraia polovina XVIII v)," 34.
71 Kumykov and Kushova, *Kabardino-Russkie otnosheniia*, vol. 2, 341.
72 L. I. Lavrov, "Karachai i Balkariia do 30-kh godov XIX veka," in *Izbrannye trudy po kul'ture abazin, adygov, karachaevtsev, balkartsev*, eds. B. Kh. Bgazhnokov and A. Kh. Abazov (Nalchik: KBIGI, 2009), 393.

73 Ibid.
74 Begeulov, *Tsentral'nyi Kavkaz v XVII-pervoi chetverti XIX veka*, 166.
75 Kipkeeva, *Severnyi Kavkaz v Rossiiskoi imperii*, 84–94.
76 Volkova, *Etnicheskii sostav naseleniia*, 64.
77 Kipkeeva, *Severnyi Kavkaz v Rossiiskoi imperii*, 31.
78 Ibid., 84–94.
79 V. S. Uarziati, *Kul'tura osetin: sviazi s narodami Kavkaza* (Ordzhonikidze: Ir, 1990), 51–2.
80 Begeulov, *Tsentral'nyi Kavkaz v XVII-pervoi chetverti XIX veka*, 165–8.
81 Kalmykov, *Integratsiia Kabardy i Balkarii*, 48–51.
82 See Begeulov, *Tsentral'nyi Kavkaz v XVII-pervoi chetverti XIX veka*, 184–91.
83 Ibid.
84 Ibid., 183–8.
85 On the history of Islam in this region, see Emel'ianova; A. Kh Mukozhev, "K voprosu o kharaktere islamizatsii kabardintsev," *Vestnik Kabardino-Balkarskogo Instituta Gumanitarnykh Issledovanii*, no. 4 (2003): 51–66; and Zh. A. Kalmykov, "Islam v istorii kabardintsev (XIII-pervaia polovina XIX v.)," *Voprosy kavkazskoi filologii i istorii*, no. 4 (2004): 168–80.
86 E. B. Sattsaev, "Islam v Osetii: istoriia i sovremennost'," in *Problemy konsolidatsii narodov Severnogo Kavkaza: materialy Vserossiiskoi nauchno-prakticheskoi konferentssii "Sovremennye etnopoliticheskie i etnokonfessional'nye protsessy na Severnom Kavkaze: problemy i puti resheniia", (23-27 okt. 2008 g.)* (Nalchik: RIA-KMV, 2008), 377–85.
87 Begeulov, *Tsentral'nyi Kavkaz v XVII-pervoi chetverti XIX veka*, 183–8.
88 A. Kh. Mukozhev, "Islam i adyge khabze," *Istoricheskii vestnik KBIGI*, no. 3 (2006): 426–36.
89 See Edward Thaden, "The Abortive Experiment: Cultural Russification in the Baltic Provinces, 1881-1914," in *Russification in the Baltic Provinces and Finland*, 54–75.
90 On customary law as a means of imperial control in the Caucasus, see Jersild, *Orientalism and Empire*, 89–109; and Bobrovnikov, *Musul'mane Severnogo Kavkaza*, 98–204.
91 Virginia Martin, *Law and Custom in the Steppe: The Kazakhs of the Middle Horde and Russian Colonialism in the Nineteenth Century* (Richmond: Curzon, 2001).
92 Kalmykov, *Integratsiia Kabardy i Balkarii*, 49.
93 On the institutionalization of Islam in the Russian Empire, see Robert Crews, *For Prophet and Tsar: Islam and Empire in Russia and Central Asia* (Cambridge, MA: Harvard University Press, 2006).
94 See ibid., 193–240; and Paul Werth, *The Tsar's Foreign Faiths: Toleration and the Fate of Religious Freedom in Imperial Russia* (Oxford: Oxford University Press, 2014), 47–52.
95 Begeulov, *Tsentral'nyi Kavkaz v XVII-pervoi chetverti XIX veka*, 170, 185. On the history of blood vengeance in the North Caucasus, see Bobrovnikov, *Musul'mane*, 54–60.
96 Begeulov, *Tsentral'nyi Kavkaz v XVII-pervoi chetverti XIX veka*, 185.
97 Berozov, *Pereselenie osetin s gor na ploskost' v XVIII*, 51.
98 Kh. M. Dumanov, ed., *Iz dokumental'noi istorii Kabardino-Russkikh otnoshenii: vtoraia polovina XVIII—pervaia polovina XIX v.* (Nalchik: Elbrus, 2000), 117.
99 T. Kh. Kumykov, "Antikolonial'nye dvizheniia i klassovaia bor'ba v Kabarde i Balkarii v pervoi polovine XIX v.," in *Istoriia Kabardino-Balkarskoi ASSR*, vol. 1, T. Kh. Kumykov et al. (Moscow: Nauka, 1967), 225–6.

100 Kuz'minov, "Etnodemograficheskaia karta," 721.
101 *Akty sobrannie Kavkazskoiu Arkheograficheskoiu Komissieiu* (Tiflis: Tipografiia Kantseliarii glavnonachal'stvuiushchego grazhdanskoi chast'iu na Kavkaze, 1868) [hereafter *AKAK*], 2: 940.
102 Begeulov, *Tsentral'nyi Kavkaz v XVII-pervoi chetverti XIX veka*, 195-200.
103 Ibid., 189.
104 R. T. Khatuev, "Rossiiskoe imperskoe pravo i shariatskii sud na Tsentral'nom Kavkaze: nachal'nyi opyt sushchestvovaniia (konets XVIII—pervaia tret'XIX v.)," *Istoriia gosudarstva i prava*, no. 22 (2010): 27-31.
105 Kumykov, "Antikolonial'naia dvizheniia," 226.
106 Ibid., 226-7.
107 On the resettlement of Kabardians across the Kuban, see T. Kh. Aloev, "Vopros o zakubanskikh territoriiakh Kabardy v kontekste migratsii kabardintsev v pervoi chetverti XIX veka," *Istoricheskii vestnik KBIGI*, no. 3 (2006): 258-70; and "Istoricheskie predposylki vozniknoveniia migratsionnogo dvizheniia v Kabarde vo vtoroi polovine XVIII veka." In ibid., 248-57.
108 A. K. Akiev, S. N. Varshavskii, and P. D. Golubev, "Osnovnye zadachi po izucheniiu faktorov prirodnoi ochagovosti chumy v Tsentral'nom Kavkaze," *Problemy osobo opasnykh* infektsii 2, no. 30 (1974): 5-12; V. I. Efrimenko, *Chernaia smert' i ee ukrotiteli: ocherki istorii chumy na Kavkaze* (Stavropol: Stavropolskaia kraevaia tipografiia, 2000).
109 Begeulov, *Tsentral'nyi Kavkaz v XVII-pervoi chetverti XIX veka*, 171; Kuz'minov, "Etnodemograficheskaia karta," 746, 750.
110 Kumykov, *Ekonomicheskoe i kul'turnoe razvitie*, 56-7; Gugov, *Kabarda i Balkariia v XVIII veke*, 51.
111 Kuz'minov, "Etnodemograficheskaia karta," 739, 741, 748-51.
112 V. A. Fedorov, ed., *Zapiski A.P. Ermolova* (Moscow: Vysshaia Shkola, 1991), 283.
113 Begeulov, *Tsentral'nyi Kavkaz v XVII-pervoi chetverti XIX veka*, 194.
114 Ibid., 203.
115 T. Kh. Kumykov, "Sotsial'no-ekonomicheskie otnosheniia v Kabarde i Balkarii v pervoi polovine XIX v.," in *Istoriia Kabardino-Balkarskoi ASSR*, vol. 1, 196.
116 Gugov, *Kabarda i Balkariia v XVIII veke*, 52.
117 William McNeill, *Plagues and Peoples* (Garden City: Anchor Press, 1976); and S. J. Watts, *Epidemics and History: Disease, Power, and Imperialism* (New Haven: Yale University Press, 1997).
118 Kabardian appeals for access to this land and Russia's refusal are discussed at great length in *AKAK, Tom IV*. See, especially, 845-9.
119 Begeulov, *Tsentral'nyi Kavkaz v XVII-pervoi chetverti XIX veka*, 193-4.
120 Kuz'minov, "Etnodemograficheskaia karta," 751.
121 *AKAK*, 5: 473.
122 Volkova, *Etnicheskii sostav naseleniia*, 53; Kozhev, "Sistema zemepol'zovaniia v kabardino-gorskikh otnosheniiakh (vtoraia polovina XVIII v)," 29.
123 Berozov, *Pereselenie osetin s gor na ploskost' v XVIII*, 41-3; Marzoev, *Osetinskaia feodal'naia znat' v sisteme vzaimodeistviia etnicheskikh elit Severnogo Kavkaza (XVIII-nach. XX vv.)*, 102.
124 Ibid.
125 For an insightful analysis of Ermolov see Khodarkovsky, *Bitter Choices*, 66-81.
126 Ibid., 68-9.
127 Ibid., 66.

128 A. L. Narochnitskii, ed., *Istoriia narodov Severnogo kavkaza*, vol. 2 (Moscow: Nauka, 1988), 30–5.
129 Kh. M. Dumanov, "Zemlevladenie i zemel'no-ierarkhicheskoe pravo v Kabarde v pervoi polovine XIX v.," in *Aktual'nye problemy feodal'noi Kabardy i Balkarii*, ed. K. F. Dzamikhov (Nalchik: Elbrus, 1992), 115–16.
130 Begeulov, *Tsentral'nyi Kavkaz v XVII-pervoi chetverti XIX veka*, 220.
131 Ibid., 232.
132 Kh. M. Dumanov, ed., *Territoriia i rasselenie kabardinstev i balkartsev v XVIII-nachale XX vekov: sbornik dokumentov* (Nalchik: Nart, 1993), 33–81.
133 Dumanov, "Zemlevladenie i zemel'no-ierarkhicheskoe pravo," 115–16.
134 Volkova, *Etnicheskii sostav naseleniia*, 140.
135 Begeulov, *Tsentral'nyi Kavkaz v XVII-pervoi chetverti XIX veka*, 227.
136 Ibid., 237.
137 Barazbiev, "Traditsionnye formy mezhetnicheskikh otnoshenii," 48–71.
138 Vasilii Potto, *Kavkazskaia voina v otdel'nykh ocherkakh, epizodakh, legendakh, i biografiiakh*, vol. 2 (St. Petersburg: Izdanie knizhnogo sklada V.A. Berezovskogo, 1888), 430.
139 Ibid., 398.
140 Beituganov, *Ermolov i Kabarda*, 56.
141 Begeulov, *Tsentral'nyi Kavkaz v XVII-pervoi chetverti XIX veka*, 225.
142 See, Kalmykov, *Integratsiia Kabardy i Balkarii*.
143 On tsarist strategies for colonial control and the position of native elites in the service of the tsar, see Khodarkovsky, *Bitter Choices*; and Sean Pollock, "'As One Russian to Another': Prince Petr Ivanovich Bagration's Assimilation of Russian Ways," *Ab Imperio*, no. 4 (2010): 113–42.
144 Breyfogle, "Enduring Imperium," 114.
145 Begeulov, *Tsentral'nyi Kavkaz v XVII-pervoi chetverti XIX veka*, 238–9.
146 On the Terek Cossacks, see D. I. Savchenko, *Terskoe kazachestvo v istorii prisoedineniia Severnogo Kavkaza k Rossii: XVI-XIX vv.* (Piatigorsk: Tekhnologicheskii universitet, 2005).
147 Breyfogle, "Enduring Imperium," 92–101.
148 Barrett, *At the Edge of Empire*, 6–7.
149 Bobrovnikov and Babich, *Severnyi Kavkaz v sostave Rossiiskoi Imperii*, 70–2.
150 Berozov, *Pereselenie osetin s gor na ploskost' v XVIII*, 112–15.

Chapter 2

1 For a discussion of the emergence of population politics and a comparative examination of it across twentieth-century regimes, see the introduction and the articles in Amir Weiner, ed., *Landscaping the Human Garden: Twentieth-Century Population Management in a Comparative Framework* (Stanford: Stanford University Press, 2003). For a discussion of population politics in Russia and the Soviet Union, including its use in the nineteenth- and twentieth-century North Caucasus, see Peter Holquist, "To Count, to Extract, and to Exterminate: Population Statistics and Population Politics in Late Imperial and Soviet Russia," in *State of Nations: Empire and Nation-Making in the Age of Lenin and Stalin*, eds. Ronald Suny and Terry Martin (New York: Oxford University Press, 2001), 111–44.

2   For a survey of this theme in historiography on Eurasia, see Breyfogle, "Enduring Imperium," 112-13. For a comparative discussion of the perils of social engineering, see James Scott, *Seeing Like a State: How Certain Schemes to Improve Human Condition Have Failed* (New Haven: Yale University Press, 1998).
3   E. S. Tiutiunina, *Grani regional'noi istorii XIX-XX vekov: mnogonatsional'naia Kabardino-Balkariia i ee sosedi (stat'i i dokumenty)* (Nalchik: Izdatel'stvo M. i V. Kotliarovykh, 2008), 38-41.
4   On the coexistence of landownership regimes in Kabarda, see, V. Kh. Kazharov, "K voprosu o dualizme kabardinoskoi sel'skoi obshchiny v predreformennyi period," in *Obshchestvennyi byt adygov i balkartsev*, ed. S. Kh. Mafedzev (Nalchik: Kabardino-Balkarskii institut istorii, filologii i ekonomiki pri Sovete ministrov KBASSR, 1986), 22-45. Valentin Gardanov identified five forms of landownership that coexisted in Kabarda before the Great Reforms. See V. K. Gardanov, *Obshchestvennyi stroi adygskikh narodov (XVIII- pervaia polovina XIX veka)* (Moscow: Nauka, 1967), 146-7.
5   Ekaterina Pravilova discusses a similar situation, whereby opposing conceptions of land tenure coexisted and competed. See her article on property law and Russian agrarian policies in Transcaucasia and Turkestan: "The Property of Empire: Islamic Law and Russian Agrarian Policy in Transcaucasia and Turkestan," *Kritika: Explorations in Russian and Eurasian History* 12, no. 2 (2011): 353-86.
6   For a comparative perspective on this topic, see the essays in *Legal Pluralism and Empires, 1500-1850*, eds. Lauren Benton and Richard J. Ross (New York: New York University Press, 2013). Many works discuss the instrumentalization of pluralistic legal regimes in the Russian Empire. Robert Crews, for example, discusses how ordinary Muslims of the Russian empire circumvented displeasing rulings of Muslim clerics by appealing to imperial legal institutions. See *For Prophet and Tsar*, 24, 107-28. The situation in Kabarda, in which Kabardian nobles utilized Russian concepts of private property (*sobstvennost'*), resembles the land situation in the Ottoman Empire during the Tanzimat reforms. See Huri Islamoglu, "Property as a Contested Domain: A Reevaluation of the Ottoman Land Code of 1858," in *New Perspectives on Property and Land in the Middle East*, ed. Roger Owen (Cambridge, MA: Harvard University Press, 2001), 28.
7   Martin, *Law and Custom in the Steppe*, 3.
8   On the importance of local dynamics to understanding imperial governance in Eurasia, see Breyfogle, "Enduring Imperium," 117-21.
9   P. Kuz'minov and B. Mal'bakhov, Introduction to *Narody Tsentral'nogo Kavkaza v 40-kh—nachale 60-kh godov XIX v.: sbornik dokumental'nykh material'ov v 2-kh tomakh*, eds. P. A. Kuz'minov and B. K. Mal'bakhov (Moscow: Pomatur, 2005), 8-10.
10 On Shamil, the role of Sufism in anti-Russian resistance, and the politics of his Imamate, see, for example, Zelkina, *In Quest for God and Freedom*.
11 Gould, *Writers and Rebels*, 1.
12 On Russia's conquest of the Northwest Caucasus, see, for example, Paul Henze, *Russia's Long Struggle to Subdue the Circassians* (Santa Monica: RAND, 1990).
13 In 1882, there were about 36,000 Circassians remaining in the Northwest Caucasus and about 10,326 Abazas, a community closely related to the Circassians ethnically and linguistically. Walter Richmond, *The Northwest Caucasus: Past, Present, Future* (London: Routledge, 2008), 77-8.
14 For an overview of the Russian conquest of the Northwest Caucasus between 1829 and 1864, see Ibid., 60-80.
15 King, *The Ghost of Freedom*, 96.

16 Arsen Karov, ed., *Administrativno-Territorial'nye preobrazovaniia v Kabardino-Balkarii: istoriia i sovremennost'* (Nalchik: El-Fa, 2000), 14–15.
17 Ibid.
18 B. S. Beslaneev, *Malaia Kabarda (XIII—Nachalo XX Veka)* (Nalchik: Elbrus, 1995), 88–97.
19 Kumykov, *Ekonomicheskoe i kul'turnoe razvitie*, 41.
20 Vladimir Kudashev, *Istoricheskie svedeniia o kabardinskom narode* (1913, Nalchik: Elbrus, 1991), 135.
21 Tiutiunina, *Grani regional'noi istorii XIX-XX vekov*, 24–41.
22 Mesiats, *Naselenie i zemlepol'zovanie Kabardy*, 139–44.
23 E. G. Muratova, *Sotsial'no-politicheskaia istoriia Balkarii XVII-nachala XX v.* (Nalchik: El-Fa, 2007), 173–5.
24 For a history of the Terek Cossacks see Barrett, *At the Edge of Empire*.
25 Barrett, *At the Edge of Empire*, 6.
26 Breyfogle, "Enduring Imperium," 92–3.
27 Bobrovnikov and Babich, *Severnyi Kavkaz v sostave Rossiiskoi Imperii*, 70–2.
28 See David Moon, *The Plough that Broke the Steppes: Agriculture and Environment on Russia's Grasslands, 1700-1914* (Oxford: Oxford University Press, 2013).
29 On cultural-economic exchanges between Kabardians and Cossacks, see R. N. Dzagov, *Vziamodeistvie kul'tur v protsesse formirovaniia mnogonatsional'nogo naseleniia Kabardy* (Nalchik: Kabardino-Balkarskii institut gumanitarnykh issledovanii, 2009), 75–84.
30 Efrimenko, *Chernaia smert' i ee ukrotiteli*, 30.
31 I. Kh. Tkhamokova, *Russkoe i ukrainskoe naselenie Kabardino-Balkarii* (Nalchik: El-Fa, 2000), 27–8.
32 A. S. Dzagalov, "Ukreplenie i kazach'i stanitsy Tsentra Kavkazskoi linii i Vladikavkazskogo voennogo okruga v 30-40-kh godakh XIX v.," *Arkhivy i obshchestvo*, no. 11 (2009): 124.
33 Tkhamokova, *Russkoe i ukrainskoe naselenie Kabardino-Balkarii*, 29.
34 *AKAK*, 9: 281.
35 *AKAK*, 6: 508–9.
36 Z. M. Kesheva, ed., *Dokumenty po istorii adygov 20-50-kh godov XIX v.* (Nalchik: Institut gumanitarnykh issledovanii, 2011), 118–20.
37 Tiutiunina, *Grani regional'noi istorii XIX-XX vekov*, 29–31.
38 Dumanov, *Territoriia i rasselenie*, 101.
39 Beslaneev, *Malaia Kabarda (XIII—Nachalo XX Veka)*, 25.
40 A. B. Mamkhegov, "Kak malokabardintsy utratili zemli kniazei Dzhyliakhstanovykh," *Arkhivy i obshchestvo*, no. 3 (2007): 73–84.
41 Volkova, *Etnicheskii sostav naseleniia severnogo Kavkaza v XVIII*, 159–60.
42 Begeulov, *Tsentral'nyi Kavkaz v XVII-pervoi chetverti XIX veka*, 137.
43 Beslaneev, *Malaia Kabarda (XIII—Nachalo XX Veka)*, 57–63.
44 Ibid., 91.
45 Ibid, 93.
46 P. A. Kuz'minov, "Agrarnye preobrazovaniia u narodov Tsentral'nogo Kavkaza v 50-60-e gody XIX veka," in *Zemel'nye otnosheniia v Kabarde i Balkarii*, 53; See also A. B. Mamkhegov, "Zakat tausultanovykh Kabardy," *Arkhivy i obshchestvo* 5 (2008): 49–51.
47 Beslaneev, *Malaia Kabarda (XIII—Nachalo XX Veka)*, 91–2.

48 A *desiatina* was the preferred unit of land measurement in tsarist Russia. One *desiatina* is approximately 2.702 acres. Hereafter, only the equivalent in acres will be provided.
49 *AKAK*, 6: 474-5.
50 Ibid., 477.
51 Beslaneev, *Malaia Kabarda (XIII—Nachalo XX Veka)*, 73.
52 Volkova, *Etnicheskii sostav naseleniia severnogo Kavkaza v XVIII*, 209.
53 Beslaneev, *Malaia Kabarda (XIII—Nachalo XX Veka)*, 68-74.
54 Mamkhegov, "Kak malokabardintsy utratili zemli," 78.
55 *AKAK*, 6: 474-5.
56 P. A. Kuz'minov, ed., *Agrarnye otnosheniia u narodov severnogo kavkaza v rossiiskoi politike XVIII- nachala XX veka*, vol. 2 (Nalchik: El-Fa, 2008), 258-9.
57 Volkova, *Etnicheskii sostav naseleniia severnogo Kavkaza v XVIII*, 225.
58 See documents in *Agrarnye otnosheniia*, vol. 2, 247-357.
59 Beslaneev, *Malaia Kabarda (XIII—Nachalo XX Veka)*, 73.
60 Ibid., 114.
61 *AKAK*, 8: 667-9.
62 Kuz'minov, *Agrarnye otnosheniia*, vol. 2, 258-61.
63 Ibid., 282-3.
64 Beslaneev, *Malaia Kabarda (XIII—Nachalo XX Veka)*, 120.
65 Kuz'minov and Mal'bakhov, *Narody Tsentral'nogo Kavkaza*, vol. 1, 157.
66 Volkova, *Etnicheskii sostav naseleniia severnogo Kavkaza v XVIII*, 64.
67 Musa Kundukhov, an Ossetian Muslim who had been fully integrated into the tsarist elite as a general in the Russian Army and a trusted colonial official, famously switched sides at the conclusion of the Caucasus War. Fleeing to the Ottoman Empire, Kundukhov helped organize the mass emigration of Chechens and other Muslim peoples from the North Caucasus to Ottoman lands. On Kundukhov, see Perović, *From Conquest to Deportation*, 53-74.
68 Kuz'minov and Mal'bakhov, *Narody Tsentral'nogo Kavkaza*, vol. 1, 191-2.
69 Beslaneev, *Malaia Kabarda (XIII—Nachalo XX Veka)*, 132.
70 Dumanov, *Territoriia i rasselenie*, 102.
71 Volkova, *Etnicheskii sostav naseleniia severnogo Kavkaza v XVIII*, 223.
72 Dumanov, *Territoriia i rasselenie*, 104.
73 Ibid., 110.
74 Kuz'minov, *Agrarnye otnosheniia*, vol. 2, 300-1.
75 G. A. Kokiev, ed., *Krest'ianskaia reforma v Severnoi Osetii* (Ordzhonikidze: Gosudarstvennoe izdatel'stvo Severo-Osetinskoi ASSR, 1940), 179.
76 For a discussion of the Kabarda's mountain pastures and their importance, see Mesiats, *Naselenie i zemlepol'zovanie Kabardy*, 139-48.
77 *AKAK*, 6: 474.
78 Mesiats, *Naselenie i zemlepol'zovanie Kabardy*, 139-48.
79 Dumanov, *Territoriia i rasselenie*, 94.
80 *AKAK*, 7: 863-4.
81 Ibid., 870.
82 Ibid., 863-74.
83 Ibid., 870.
84 Ibid., 866.
85 Dumanov, *Territoriia i rasselenie*, 94.
86 Ibid., 53-4.

87 Ibid., 50.
88 Ibid., 52.
89 N. D. Gaibov, *O pozemel'nom ustroistve gorskikh plemen Terskoi oblasti*, 1905 repr. in *Agrarnye otnosheniia*, vol 2, 5–246, here 66–7.
90 R. U. Tuganov, *Istoriia obshchestvennoi mysli kabardinskogo naroda v pervoi polovine XIX veka* (Nalchik: El-Fa, 1998), 292.
91 Kuz'minov and Mal'bakhov, *Narody Tsentral'nogo Kavkaza*, vol. 1, 204–5.
92 Dumanov, *Territoriia i rasselenie*, 87–8.
93 Nevskaia, *Ocherki istorii Karachaevo-Cherkesii*, 415.
94 Dumanov, *Territoriia i rasselenie*, 88.
95 Kh. M. Dumanov, "Da, byla granitsa!," in *Vymysel i istina*, eds. I. M. Borei, R. K. Dzagulov, and M. F. Kolesnikov (Piatigorsk: RIA-KMV, 2010), 308–9.
96 *AKAK*, 7: 867.
97 E. O. Krikunova, ed., *Dokumenty po istorii Balkarii 40-90 gg. XIX v.* (Nalchik: Kabardino-Balkarskoe knizhnoe izdatel'stvo, 1959), 27.
98 Ibid.
99 Dumanov, *Territoriia i rasselenie*, 83–4.

Chapter 3

1 Kappeler, *The Russian Empire*, 248–82.
2 On the Great Reforms, see, W. Bruce Lincoln, *The Great Reforms: Autocracy, Bureaucracy, and the Politics of Change in Imperial Russia* (Ithaca: Cornell University Press, 1990).
3 On the emancipation in non-Russian regions of the empire, see Willard Sunderland, "The Imperial Emancipations: Ending Non-Russian Serfdoms in Nineteenth-Century Russia," in *Shifting Forms of Continental Colonialism: Unfinished Struggles and Tensions*, eds. Dittmar Schorkowitz, John R Chávez, and Ingo Schröder (Basingstoke: Palgrave Macmillan, 2020), 437–61.
4 These debates resembled ones going in Transcaucasia and Turkestan. See Pravilova, "The Property of Empire," 361–83.
5 For an empire-wide discussion on migration policy, see Charles Steinwedel, "Resettling People, Unsettling the Empire: Migration and the Challenge of Governance, 1861-1917," in *Peopling the Russian Periphery: Borderland Colonization in Eurasian History*, eds. Nicholas B. Breyfogle, Abby M. Schrader, and Willard Sunderland (London: Routledge, 2007), 128–47.
6 Alexei Miller, "Russifikatsiia—klassifitsirovat' i poniat'," *Ab Imperio*, no. 2 (2002): 133–48; Theodore Weeks, "Russification: Word and Practice, 1863–1914," *Proceedings of the American Philosophical Society* 148, no. 4 (2004): 471–89; idem., *Nation and State in Late Imperial Russia. Nationalism and Russification on the Western Frontier, 1863-1917* (DeKalb: University of North Illinois Press, 1960); Robert P. Geraci, *Window on the East: National and Imperial Identities in Late Tsarist Russia* (Ithaca: Cornell University Press, 2001); Darius Staliunas, *Making Russians: Meaning and Practice of Russification in Lithuania and Belarus After 1863* (Amsterdam: Rodopi, 2007); Paul W. Werth, *At the Margins of Orthodoxy: Mission, Governance, and Confessional Politics in Russia's Volga–Kama Region, 1827–1905* (Ithaca: Cornell University Press, 2001).

7 Jersild, *Orientalism and Empire*, 91–2; Jane Burbank, *Russian Peasants go to Court: Legal Culture in the Countryside, 1905-1917* (Bloomington: Indiana University Press, 2004), 5–10.
8 On the multiethnic nature of empire's ruling elite and its implication for how we think about the empire, see Stephen Norris and Willard Sunderland, introduction to idem., eds. *Russia's People of Empire: Life Stories from Eurasia, 1500 to the Present* (Bloomington: Indiana University Press, 2012), 1–15.
9 See Jersild, *Orientalism and Empire*, 147 and *passim*.
10 See, for example, Donald Horowitz's discussions of "the ethnic distribution of colonial opportunity," "colonial policy and the promotion of group disparity," and "colonial evaluations of imputed group character," in *Ethnic Groups in Conflict*, 151–66.
11 See, for example, Pollock, "As One Russian to Another."
12 The concept of governmentality is central to much of Michael Foucault's later work. For a focused discussion of the concept, see Foucault's lectures and interview in *The Foucault Effect: Studies in Governmentality*, eds. Graham Burchell, Colin Gordon, and Peter Miller (Chicago: University of Chicago Press, 1991).
13 Jersild, *Orientalism and Empire*, 84–5.
14 Ibid., 86.
15 Bariatinskii quoted in P. A. Kuz'minov, "Ot voennogo pokoreniia k poisku putei integratsii: zamysly i nachalo osushchestvleniia agrarnykh preobrazovanii u narodov severnogo kavkaza v 60-kh godakh XIX veka," in *Agrarnye otnosheniia*, vol. 1, 429.
16 Kuz'minov and Mal'bakhov, *Narody tsentral'nogo kavkaza*, vol. 2, 151.
17 This was especially the case in Kuban oblast in the Northwest Caucasus, where as much as 90 percent of the indigenous population had emigrated to the Ottoman Empire. See Kuz'minov, "Ot voennogo pokoreniia k poisku putei integratsii," 434–6.
18 This was the case in Lesser Kabarda, where the state set aside a significant amount of land specifically for Russian colonization. See document in Dumanov, *Territoriia i rasselenie*, 113–14.
19 Kumykov, *Ekonomicheskoe i kul'turnoe razvitie*, 59, 207.
20 Breyfogle, "Enduring Imperium," 101.
21 "Izbrannye dokumenty Kavkazskogo komiteta," *Sbornik russkogo istoricheskgo obshchestva* 150, no. 2 (2000): 176–7.
22 Orbeliani discussed the need to avoid creating a rural proletariat in his memo to Miliutin. See ibid.
23 Kokiev, *Krestian'skaia reforma v Severnoi Osetii*, 171–4.
24 On the various committees and their accomplishments, see P. A. Kuz'minov, "Materialy soslovno-pozemel'nykh komissii kak istoricheskii istochnik po istorii narodov Severnogo Kavkaza," in *De die in diem; pamiati A.P. Pronshteina (1919-1998)*, ed. V. V. Chernous (Rostov-na-Donu: Rostovskii gosudarstvennyi universitet, 2004), 122–44.
25 Jersild, *Orientalism and Empire*, 89.
26 Breyfogle, "Enduring Imperium," 108–9. On the "gardening state," see Zygmunt Bauman, *Modernity and the Holocaust* (Ithaca: Cornell University Press, 1989), 13.
27 Quoted in P. A. Kuz'minov, "Agrarnaia i sotsial'naia politika rossiiskogo pravitel'stva v Kabarde i Balkarii v 50-70-e gody XIX veka," in *Agrarnye otnosheniia*, vol. 2, 504.
28 Ibid., 501–6.
29 Bobrovnikov and Babich, *Severnyi Kavkaz v sostave Rossiiskoi Imperii*, 216.

30 M. G. Gonikishvili, "Podgotovka i provedenie krest'ianskoi reformy v kabardinskom okruge," in *Gruzino-Severo-Kavkazskie Vzaimootnosheniia,* ed. G. Togoshvili (Tbilisi: Akademiia Nauk Gruzinskoi SSR, 1981), 136.
31 Kumykov, *Ekonomicheskoe i kul'turnoe razvitie,* 205.
32 "Izbrannye dokumenty," 176-8.
33 M. Kh. Atskanov, *Ekonomicheskie otnosheniia i ekonomicheskie vzgliady v Kabarde i Balkarii (1860-1917 gg.)* (Nalchik: Kabardino-Balkarskoe knizhnoe izdatel'stvo, 1967), 72.
34 Willard Sunderland, *Taming the Wild Field: Colonization and Empire on the Russian Steppe* (Ithaca: Cornell University Press, 2004), 139.
35 Pravilova, "The Property of Empire," 373-4.
36 Ibid., 371.
37 On Loris-Melikov's work in the Caucasus, see Z. Kh. Ibragimova, "M.T. Loris-Melikov," in *Sbornik Statei: Severnyi Kavkaz—vremia peremen (1860-1880),* ed. Z. Kh. Ibragimova (Moscow: Eslan, 2001), 55-79; and P. A. Kuz'minov, "M.T. Loris-Melikov na Kavkaze," *Kavkazskii sbornik* 34, no. 2 (2005): 124-5.
38 Hans Heilbronner, "Alexander III and the Reform Plan of Loris-Melikov," *The Journal of Modern History* 33, no. 4 (1961): 384-97.
39 Loris-Melikov cited in S. A. Ailarova, "D.S. Kodzokov v 30-70 gg. XIX veka: prosvetitel', reformator, khoziaistvennik," *Izvestiia SOIGSI* 40, no. 1 (2007): 88.
40 T. Kh. Kumykov, *Dmitrii Kodzovok* (Nalchik: Izd-vo Elbrus, 1985), 16-17.
41 Tuganov, *Istoriia obshchestvennoi mysli kabardinskogo naroda v pervoi polovine XIX veka,* 122-3.
42 Kumykov, *Dmitrii Kodzokov,* 18-22.
43 See, for example, Layton, *Russian Literature and Empire.*
44 Kumykov, *Dmitrii Kodzokov,* 23-8.
45 Tuganov, *Istoriia obshchestvennoi mysli kabardinskogo naroda v pervoi polovine XIX veka,* 125.
46 Kumykov, *Dmitrii Kodzokov,* 19.
47 On Khomiakov's views in particular, see Peter Christoff, *A.S. Xomjakov* (Princeton: Princeton University Press, 1961); On Slavophiles generally, see Nicholas Riasanovsky, *Russia and the West in the Teaching of the Slavophiles; a Study of Romantic Ideology* (Cambridge, MA: Harvard University Press, 1952).
48 Kodzokov quoted in Ailarova, "D.S. Kodzokov v 30-70 gg. XIX veka: prosvetitel', reformator, khoziaistvennik," 86.
49 Tuganov, *Istoriia obshchestvennoi mysli kabardinskogo naroda v pervoi polovine XIX veka,* 128-9.
50 Kumykov, *Dmitrii Kodzokov,* 56.
51 Ibid., 40-56.
52 Kodzokov quoted in Ailarova, "D.S. Kodzokov v 30-70 gg. XIX veka: prosvetitel', reformator, khoziaistvennik," 89.
53 Ailarova, "D.S. Kodzokov v 30-70 gg. XIX veka: prosvetitel', reformator, khoziaistvennik," 189-91.
54 Kumykov, *Ekonomicheskoe i kul'turnoe razvitie,* 273.
55 Ailarova, "D.S. Kodzokov v 30-70 gg. XIX veka: prosvetitel', reformator, khoziaistvennik," 193.
56 Kodzokov quoted in ibid., 192.
57 On Vorontsov see, L. H. Rhinelander, "Viceroy Vorontsov's Administration of the Caucasus," in *Transcaucasia, Nationalism and Social* Change, 87-104.

58 Kumykov, *Dmitrii Kodzokov*, 56-9.
59 Kudashev, *Istoricheskie svedeniia o kabardinskom narode*, 118.
60 Kumykov, *Ekonomicheskoe i kul'turnoe razvitie*, 214.
61 Kumykov, *Dmitrii Kodzokov*, 58-9.
62 Ibid., 65-6.
63 Tuganov, *Istoriia obshchestvennoi mysli kabardinskogo naroda v pervoi polovine XIX veka*, 134-43.
64 Kumykov, *Dmitrii Kodzokov*, 60-4.
65 Dumanov, *Territoriia i rasselenie*, 88-90.
66 Ibid., 89.
67 On the importance of the map as a tool of colonial control, see Anderson, *Imagined Communities*, 163-85.
68 Ailarova, "D.S. Kodzokov v 30-70 gg. XIX veka: prosvetitel', reformator, khoziaistvennik," 98.
69 T. Kh. Kumykov, *Zhizn' i obshchestvennaia deiatel'nost L.M. Kodzokva* (Nalchik: Kabardino-Balkarskoe knizhnoe izdatel'stvo, 1962), 16-18.
70 "Zapiski o Kavkaze, pisannye N. Beklemishevym v Orenburge v 1849 g.," *Shchukinskii sbornik*, no. 2 (1903): 33.
71 Ibid., 17.
72 Abaev, "Balkariia," 621.
73 Ibid., 622.
74 Kudashev, *Istoricheskie svedeniia o kabardinskom narode*, 203.
75 Karov, *Administrativno-territorial'nye preobrazovaniia*, 23-4.
76 Mesiats, *Naselenie i zemlepol'zovanie Kabardy*, 16.
77 Beslaneev, *Malaia Kabarda (XIII—Nachalo XX Veka)*, 133-4.
78 Dumanov, *Territoriia i rasselenie*, 144.
79 Kokiev, *Krest'ianskaia reforma v Severnoi Osetii*, 181.
80 "Izbrannye dokumenty," 176-7.
81 Zh. Kalmykov, "Cherkesskaia tragediia. Iz istorii nasil'stvennogo vyseleniia adygov v Osmanskyiu imperiiu," in *Cherkesskii vopros: Istoriia, problemy i puti resheniia*, ed. A. Kh. Mukozhev (Nalchik: Koordinatsionnyi sovet adygskikh obshchestvennykh organizatsii, 2012), 60.
82 E. S. "Krepost'nye v Kabarde i ikh osvobozhdeniia," *Sbornik Svedenii o Kavkazskikh Gortsakh*, 1 (1868): 33-4.
83 Quoted in T. Kh. Kumykov, "Zemel'naia reforma v Kabarda v 1863-1869 gg.," *Uchenye zapiski Kabardino-Balkarskogo nauchno-issledovaltel'skogo instituta* 12 (1957): 275.
84 For a contemporaneous description of the tensions in Kabarda on the eve of emancipation, see E. S. "Krepost'nye v Kabarde," 30-8.
85 Dumanov, *Territoriia i rasselenie*, 143.
86 Ibid.
87 Kumykov, *Zhinz' i obshchestvennaia deiatel'nost'*, 16.
88 See Loris-Melikov's criticisms of the Bekovich-Cherkasskii princes in his December 6, 1865, report to the assistant to the commander-in-chief of the Caucasus Army in Dumanov, *Territoriia i rasselenie*, 113-15.
89 For a description and timeline of the Committee's work see the Committee's official report of its activities from 1863 to 1869 in Kokiev, *Kresťianskaia reforma v Severnoi Osetii*, 171-99.
90 Kodzokov quoted in Kumykov, *Zhizn' i obshchestvennaia desiatel'nost'*, 20-1.

91 Kodzokov quoted in Kudashev, *Istoricheskie svedeniia o kabardinskom narode*, 142.
92 Ibid., 143.
93 Kodzokov quoted in Kumykov, *Zhin' i obshchestvennaia desiatel'nost'*, 21.
94 Kodzokov quoted in ibid., 22–3.
95 Ibid., 24.
96 Abaev, "Balkariia," 621.
97 Ibid.
98 David Moon, "Peasant Migration and the Settlement of Russia's Frontiers, 1550-1897," *The Historical Journal* 40, no. 4 (1997): 868–9, 886–8.
99 Sunderland, *Taming the Wild Field*, 146.
100 Ibid., 153.
101 Alex Marshall, *The Caucasus under Soviet Rule* (London: Routledge, 2010), 22.
102 S. A. Khubulova, *Krest'ianskaia sem'ia i dvor v Terskoi oblasti v kontse XIX-nachale XX v.: sotsial'no-ekonomicheskie, etnodemograficheskie i politicheskie aspekty razvitiia* (St. Petersburg: Izd-vo S.-Peterburgskogo universiteta 2002), 60–3.
103 Marshall, *The Caucasus under Soviet Rule*, 22.
104 E. V. Burda, "Sooruzhenie Rostovo-Vladikavkazskoi zheleznoi dorogi i poiavlenie stantsii 'Kotliarevskoi' i pristantsionnogo poselka 'Prishibskogo'," *Arkhivy i obshchestvo*, no. 22 (2012): 55–7.
105 Marshall, *The Caucasus under Soviet Rule*, 23.
106 Z. V. Kanukova, *Staryi Vladikavkaz: istoriko-etnologicheskoe issledovanie* (Vladikavkaz: SOIGSI, 2008).
107 Sunderland, *Taming the Wild Field*, 178–9.
108 G. M. Kashezheva, "Nekotorye voprosy pereselencheskogo dvizheniia v Terskuiu oblast' v poreformennyi period," in *Iz istorii feodal'noi Kabardy i Balkarii*, eds. R. Kh. Gugov and V. N. Sokurov (Nalchik: Institut istorii, filologii i ekonomiki pri Sovete ministrov KBASSR, 1981), 66.
109 Marshall, *The Caucasus under Soviet Rule*, 168–9.
110 See Loris-Melikov's telegram to Grand Prince Mikhail Nikolaevich, informing him that the liberation of Kabarda's serfs had begun in G. A. Kokiev, ed., *Krest'ianskaia reforma v Kabarde: Dokumenty po istorii osvobozhdeniia zavisimykh soslovii v Kabarde v 1867 g.*, repr. in *Istoriia Kabardino-Balkarii v trudakh*, 734–5.
111 Ibid., 732–3.
112 Kuz'minov, "Agrarnaia i sotsial'naia politika," 534.
113 F. P. Troino, "Zemel'naia arenda u gorskikh narodov Severnogo Kavkaza v kontse XIX—nachale XX vekov," *Istoriia gorskykh i kochevykh narodov Severnogo Kavkaza*, Vypusk. 3 (1978): 18
114 Kuz'minov, "Agrarnaia i sotsial'naia politika," 531–2.
115 Quoted in ibid., 536.
116 E. S. "Krepost'nye v Kabarde," 30–8.
117 Kokiev, *Krest'ianskaia reforma v Kabarde*, 773.
118 The amount of property, movable and unmovable, divided between the lords (*taubiis*) and their dependents varied in each society. See Kumykov, *Ekonomicheskoe i kul'turnoe razvitie*, 237–8.
119 "Izbrannye dokumenty," 182.
120 Dumanov, *Territoriia i rasselenie*, 150–1.
121 Quoted in Gaibov, *O pozemel'nom ustroistve gorskikh plemen Terskoi oblasti*, 32.
122 For an overview of the land reform legislation for Kabarda see Kuz'minov, "Agrarnye preobrazovaniia u narodov Tsentral'nogo Kavkaza," 60–7.

123 Gonikishvili, "Podgotovka i provedenie krest'ianskoi reform," 134–68.
124 Troino, "Zemel'naia arenda u gorskikh narodov Severnogo Kavkaza v kontse XIX - nachale XX vekov," 35.
125 Ibid., 16.
126 Evgenii Maksimov, "Kabardintsy: Statistiko-ekonomicheskii ocherk," *Terskii sbornik*, no. 2 (1892): 150–1.
127 Kokiev, *Krest'ianskaia reforma v Severnoi Osetii*, 178–9.
128 Valarie Kivelson has argued that this tendency was already present in the eighteenth and nineteenth centuries in tsarist cartographic practices. See *Cartographies of Tsardom: The Land and Its Meanings in Seventeenth-Century Russia* (Ithaca: Cornell University Press, 2006), 192.
129 See Jersild, *Orientalism and Empire*, 84–6. For example, this view is reflected in Loris-Melikov's December 1865 report on Lesser Kabarda in Dumanov, *Territoriia i rasselenie*, 111–16.
130 Jersild, *Orientalism and Empire*, 85–6.
131 Kokiev, *Krest'ianskaia reforma v Severnoi Osetii*, 178–9.
132 Dumanov, *Territoriia i rasselenie*, 111–16.
133 On the land reforms in Lesser Kabarda, see Gaibov, *O pozemel'nom ustroistve gorskikh plemen Terskoi oblasti*, 53–63.
134 Documents on these land disputes are included in Kuz'minov, *Agrarnye otnosheniia*, vol. 2, 253–358. See also, *AKAK* 8: 654–69.
135 *AKAK* 6: 474–7.
136 In 1860, head of the general staff of the Caucasus Army, Dmitrii Miliutin, first raised the idea of purchasing the Bekovich-Cherkasskii lands to solve Lesser Kabarda's land problems. See Kuz'minov, *Agrarnye otnosheniia*, vol. 2, 266–73.
137 Kokiev, *Krest'ianskaia reforma v Severnoi Osetii*, 179.
138 Ibid.
139 Beslaneev, *Malaia Kabarda (XIII—Nachalo XX Veka)*, 131.
140 See Kodzokov's 1866 report to Loris-Melikov on the purchase of the Bekovich-Cherkesskii lands in Kuz'minov, *Agrarnye otnosheniia*, vol. 2, 334–7.
141 Kokiev, *Krest'ianskaia reforma v Severnoi Osetii*, 178–82.
142 Ibid.
143 See Kodzokov's report to Loris-Melikov on options for where to settle the residents of the Bekovich-Cherkesskii auls in Kuz'minov, *Agrarnye otnosheniia*, vol. 2, 338.
144 See Kate Brown, *Biography of No Place: From Ethnic Borderland to Soviet Heartland* (Cambridge, MA: Harvard University Press, 2004); Pavel Polian, *Against Their Will: The History and Geography of Forced Migrations in the USSR* (Budapest: Central European University Press, 2004). Peter Blitstein, "Cultural Diversity and the Interwar Conjuncture: Soviet Nationality Policy in Its Comparative Context," *Slavic Review* 65, no. 2 (Summer 2006): 273–93; and Francine Hirsch, "Race without the Practice of Racial Politics," *Slavic Review* 61, no. 1 (Spring 2002): 30–43.
145 Dumanov, *Territoriia i rasselenie*, 110–11.
146 Ibid., 111.
147 Kuz'minov, *Agrarnye otnosheniia*, vol. 2, 340.
148 On's Kumyks see Abas Datsiev, *Kizliar-name: istoriia tersko-kumskykh kumykov* (Makhachkala: privately printed, 2004).
149 "Gorskaia letopis'," *Sbornik Svedenii o Kavkazskikh Gortsakh* 1 (1868): 6.
150 Gaibov, *O pozemel'nom ustroistve gorskikh plemen Terskoi oblasti*, 54–5.
151 Ibid.

152 Kuz'minov, "Ot voennogo pokoreniia k poisku putei integratsii," 455.
153 Gaibov, *O pozemel'nom ustroistve gorskikh plemen Terskoi oblasti*, 120–5.
154 Kumykov, *Ekonomicheskoe i kul'turnoe razvtie*, 215, 218.
155 Dumanov, *Territoriia i rasselenie*, 113–15.
156 Gaibov, *O pozemel'nom ustroistve gorskikh plemen Terskoi oblasti*, 55–6.
157 On these factors, see Muratova, *Sotsial'no-politicheskaia istoriia Balkarii XVII-nachala XX v*, 328–34 and I. L. Babich and V. V. Stepanov, *Istoricheskaia dinamika etnicheskoi karty Kabardino-Balkarii* (Moscow: Institut etnologii i antropologii im. Miklukho-Maklaia RAN, 2009), 36–41.
158 Dumanov, Introduction to *Territoriia i rasselenie*, 9.
159 See Peter Sahlins, *Boundaries: The Making of France and Spain in the Pyrenees* (Berkeley: University of California Press, 1989), 1–9 and 155–67.
160 Güldenstädt, *Puteshestvie po kavkazu v 1770-1773 gg.*, 225.
161 Dumanov, *Territoriia i rasselenie*, 26.
162 More specific markers, usually stones or burnt coals, also existed to separate some feudal domains. Kumykov, *Ekonomichsekoe i kul'turnoe razvitie*, 132.
163 Kudashev, *Istoricheskie svedeniia o kabardinskom narode*, 137.
164 Abaev was the first to paint Kodzokov as an anti-Balkar Kabardian nationalist in *Balkaria*, 621–3; Umar Aliev offers the same interpretation in his "Dokladnaia Zapiska" Rossiiskii Gosudarstvennyi Arkhiv Sotsial'no-Politicheskoi Istorii (RGASPI), fond (f.) 558, opis' (op.) 1 delo (d.) 5629, list (l.) 17-18; This type of interpretation was not politique during most of the Soviet period. Post-Soviet Karachai-Balkar historians have attacked Kodzokov's land reform policies for being anti-Balkar with renewed vigor. See, for example, Islam Miziev, "Iz istorii pozemel'nykh sporov mezhdu Balkariei i Kabardoi," *Balkariia* 26, no. 4 (2007): 12–28.
165 See the Committee's report on the delimitation of Kabarda's borders with the five mountaineer societies in Dumanov, *Territoriia i rasselenie*, 91–2.
166 Ibid., 92.
167 M. I. Barazbiev, *Etnokul'turnye sviazi balkartsev i karachaevtsev s narodami kavkaza v XVIII—nachale XX veka* (Nalchik: El'brus, 2000), 24–5; Kiz'minov, "Agrarnye preobrazovaniia u narodov Tsentral'nogo Kavkaza," 63–4; N. P. Tul'chinskii, "Piat' gorskikh obshchestv Kabardy," *Terskii sbornik* 5 (1903): 174–5.
168 Dumanov, *Territoriia i rasselenie*, 83–4.
169 Krikunova, *Dokumenty po istorii Balkarii 40-90 g.g.*, 85–6.
170 Tul'chinskii, "Piat' gorskikh obshchestv Kabardy," 175.
171 The origins or "ethnogenisis" of the Karachais and Balkars have been the subjects of much debate. See, for example, *Materialy nauchnoi sessii po probleme proiskhozhdeniia balkarskogo i karachaevskogo narodov, 22-26 iiunia 1959 g* (Nalchik: Kabardino-Balkarskoe knizhnoe izd-vo, 1960). For a nuanced discussion of how this debate has played into ethno-nationalist political discourse, see Viktor Shnirel'man, *Byt' alanami: intellektualy i politika na Severnom Kavkaze v XX veke* (Moscow: Novoe literaturnoe obozrenie, 2006).
172 Dumanov, *Territoriia i rasselenie*, 85–6.
173 Muratova, *Sotsial'no-politicheskaia istoriia Balkarii XVII-nachala XX v*, 182.
174 Dumanov, *Territoriia i rasselenie*, 92.
175 Ibid., 90–1.
176 Kokiev, *Krest'ianskaia reforma v Severnoi Osetii*, 171.
177 Dumanov, *Territoriia i rasselenie*, 93.

178 Ibid.
179 Ibid.
180 Ibid., 93-4.
181 Mesiats, *Naselenie i zemlepol'zovanie Kabardy*, 143.
182 Dumanov, *Territoriia i rasselenie*, 165-7.
183 Ibid., 263.
184 Ibid., 95-6.
185 Tul'chinskii, "Piat' gorskikh obshchestv Kabardy," 186.
186 See Abaev, "Balkariia," 587; Tul'chinskii, "Piat' gorskikh obshchestv Kabardy," 167, 179-83; and E. O. Krikunova, ed., *Dokumenty po istorii Balkarii; konets XIX-nachalo XX v.* (Nalchik: Kabardino-Balkarskoe knizhnoe izdatel'stvo, 1962), 126-34.
187 Abaev, "Balkariia," 611.
188 Kudashev, *Istoricheskie svedeniia o kabardinskom narode*, 165.
189 Ibid.
190 T. Kh. Kumykov, "K voprosu krest'ianskoi reform v Balkarii v 1867 g." *Sbornik statei po istorii Kabardy i Balkarii* 6 (1957): 105-13.
191 Kokiev, *Krest'ianskaia reforma v Kabarde*, 686.
192 Kumykov, "K voprosu krest'ianskoi reform," 107.
193 Ibid.
194 Muratova, *Sotsial'no-politicheskaia istoriia Balkarii XVII-nachala XX v*, 285; Tul'chinskii, "Piat' gorskikh obshchestv Kabardy," 168-9, 175.
195 Krikunova, *Dokumenty po istorii Balkarii; konets XIX-nachalo XX v.*, 129.
196 Kudashev, *Istoricheskie svedeniia o kabardinskom narode*, 174.
197 Kokiev, *Krest'ianskaia reforma v Severnoi Osetii*, 181-2.
198 Kuz'minov, "Agrarnye preobrazovaniia u narodov Tsentral'nogo Kavkaza," 58-9; Dumanov, *Territoriia i rasselenie*, 178-90; Babich and Stepanov, *Istoricheskaia dinamika etnicheskoi karty Kabardino-Balkarii*, 36-42; K. F. Dzamikhov et al., "Etnoterritorial'naia i administrativno-territorial'naia struktura Kabardino-Balkarii v XVIII.XX vv." in *Vymysel i istina*, 337-8.
199 Babich and Stepanov, *Istoricheskaia dinamika etnicheskoi karty Kabardino-Balkarii*, 36-42.
200 N. P. Gritsenko, "O deiatel'nosti Abramovskoi komissii," *Izvestiia: Stat'i i materialy po istorii Checheno-Ingushetii* 6, no. 1 (1965): 129-71.
201 Ibid., 171.
202 *Trudy komissii po issledovaniiu sovremennogo polozheniia zemlepol'zovaniia i zemlevladeniia v nagornoi polose Terskoi oblasti* (Vladikavkaz, 1908).
203 Gritsenko, "O deiatel'nosti Abramovskoi komissii," 172.
204 Z. Zh. Glasheva, "Proekt Abramovskoi komissii po razresheniiu zemel'nogo voprosa v Balkarii," *Trudy molodykh uchenykh Vladikavkazskogo nauchnogo tsentra RAN*, no. 4 (2010): 147-50.
205 B. B. Temukuev, *Balkarskaia obshchestvennaia kolesnaia doroga* (Nalchik: Izd-vo M. i V. Kotliarovykh, 2008).
206 Kudashev, *Istoricheskie svedeniia o kabardinskom narode*, 172.
207 A. M. Bashiev, "K isotrii obrazovaniia karachaevskogo aula Khasaut," in *Materialy mezhdunarodnoi iubileinoi konferentsii "Rossiia i Kavkaz"; posviashchennoi 235-letiiu prisoedineniia Osetii k Rossii*, ed. Z. V. Kanukova (Vladikavkaz: IPO SOIGSI, 2010), 44-5.
208 Ibid., 46.
209 Ibid., 42-3.

210 R. K. Karmov, "Rod kabardinskikh uorkov Zhereshtievykh," *Arkhivy i Obshchestvo*, no. 8 (2009): 98–101.
211 Safarbi Beituganov, *Kabardinskie familii: Istoki i sud'by* (Nalchik: Elbrus, 1990), 36–7.
212 A. M. Bashiev, "Rod Chipchikovykh v Karachae (na Khasaute)," *Genealogiia narodov Severnogo Kavkaza: Traditsii i sovremennost'*, no. 2 (2010): 66–77.
213 Accounts of the settlement of the upper Malka are found in petitions from Khasaut residents to the Soviet government during the border conflict between Karachai and Kabarda in the early 1920s. These accounts confirm the documentary history. See Gosudarstvennyi Arkhiv Rossiiskoi Federatsii (GARF), f. 5677, op. 3, d. 315, ll. 2–5.
214 Barazbiev, *Etnokul'turnye sviazi balkartsev i karachaevtsev s narodami Kavkaza*, 19–21.
215 Bashiev, "K isotrii obrazovaniia karachaevskogo *aula* Khasaut," 41–6.
216 Quoted in ibid., 45.
217 Ibid.
218 Quoted in ibid.
219 Ibid.
220 Beituganov, *Kabardinskie familii*, 38–40.
221 Dumanov, *Territoriia i rasselenie*, 148.
222 Gaibov, *O pozemel'nom ustroistve gorskikh plemen Terskoi oblasti*, 49–50.
223 Ibid., 50–1.
224 Krikunova, *Dokumenty po istorii Balkarii; konets XIX-nachalo XX v.*, 46.
225 Karov, *Administrativno-territorial'nye preobrazovaniia*, 54.
226 V. P. Nevskaia et al., eds., *Sotsial'no-ekonomicheskoe, politicheskoe i kul'turnoe razvitie narodov Karachaevo-Cherkesii (1790-1917)* (Roston-na-Donu: Izdatel'stvo Rostovskogo universiteta, 1985), 239.
227 Gaibov, *O pozemel'nom ustroistve gorskikh plemen Terskoi oblasti*, 49–53.
228 Berozov, *Pereselenie osetin s gor na ploskost' v XVIII – XX vekakh*, 39.
229 Ibid., 145–54.
230 Marzoev, *Osetinskaia feodal'naia znat' v sisteme vzaimodeistviia etnicheskikh elit Severnogo Kavkaza*, 102.
231 While the other *auls* that Ossetian nobles had formed on Kabardian lands were deemed to have become Ossetian land by right of sale, Kabanovo *aul*, which had a mixed Digora-Ossetian and Balkar population, was considered to be located on lands that were still within Kabardian territory. The resettlement of Kabanovo should be viewed as part of the era's larger *aul* enlargement program. On the resettlement of Kabanovo *aul*, see Safarbi Beituganov, *Kabarda: istoriia i familii* (Nalchik: Elbrus, 2007), 59–67.
232 Gaibov, *O pozemel'nom ustroistve gorskikh plemen Terskoi oblasti*, 133.
233 Mesiats, *Naselenie i zemlepol'zovanie Kabardy*, 12–13.
234 Kuz'minov, "Materialy soslovno-pozemel'nykh komissii," 126–33.
235 Idem, "Agrarnye preobrazovaniia u narodov Tsentral'nogo Kavkaza," 51–3.
236 Berozov, *Pereselenie osetin s gor na ploskost' v XVIII – XX vekakh*, 127–38.
237 Bobrovnikov and Babich, *Istoricheskaia dinamika etnicheskoi karty Kabardino-Balkarii*, 101–6, 262–7; Khodarkovsky, "Of Christianity, Enlightenment, and Colonialism," 394–430.
238 On Islam's role in Kabardian-Ossetian relations, see Marzoev, *Osetinskaia feodal'naia znat' v sisteme vzaimodeistviia etnicheskikh elit Severnogo Kavkaza*, 104–20.
239 Beituganov, *Kabarda: istoriia i familiii*, 71.
240 Berozov, *Pereselenie osetin s gor na ploskost' v XVIII – XX vekakh*, 167–8.
241 A. Besolov, "K 130-letiiu seleniia Lesken." *Severnaia Ossetiia: respublikanskaia ezhednevnaia gazeta*, February 5, 2009; A. B. Mamkhegov, "Dva epizoda iz pereseleniia osetin v Kabardu," *Arkhivy i obshchestvo*, no. 7 (2008): 65–72.

242 Gaibov, *O pozemel'nom ustroistve gorskikh plemen Terskoi oblasti*, 44.
243 RGASPI, f. 65 op. 1 d. 110 l. 90.
244 Mesiats, *Naselenie i zemlepol'zovanie Kabardy*, 12–13.
245 GARF, f. 1235, op. 140, d. 190, l. 45.
246 Tkhamokova, *Russkoe i ukrainskoe naselenie Kabardino-Balkarii*, 37.
247 Troino, "Zemel'naia arenda u gorskikh narodov Severnogo Kavkaza v kontse XIX - nachale XX vekov," 37–47.
248 G. Kh, Mambetov, *Material'naia kul'tura sel'skogo naseleniia Kabardino-Balkarii: (vtoraia polovina XIX-60-e gody XX veka)* (Nalchik: Elbrus, 1971), 12.
249 D. N. Prasolov, "K voprosu zemel'nykh zakhvatakh v kabardinoskoi sel'skoi obshchine poreformennogo perioda," *Vestnik Kabardino-Balkarskogo Instituta Gumannitaynykh Issledovanii*, no. 8 (2001): 60–78.
250 D. N. Prasolov, "Pastbishchnoe i lesnoe obshchinnoe zemlepol'zovanie v Kabarde vo 2-oi polovine 19-nachale 20 v," in *Zemel'nye otnosheniia v Kabarde i Balkarii*, 80–9.
251 Kumykov, *Ekonomicheskoe i kul'turnoe razvtie*, 218.
252 See Ibid., 215; and Kokiev, *Krest'ianskaia reforma v Kabarde*, 753.
253 Dzagov, *Vziamodeistvie kul'tur v protsesse formirovaniia mnogonatsional'nogo naseleniia Kabardy*, 38; Khubulova, *Krest'ianskaia sem'ia i dvor v Terskoi oblasti v kontse XIX-nachale XX v.*, 70.
254 Troino, "Zemel'naia arenda u gorskikh narodov Severnogo Kavkaza v kontse XIX - nachale XX vekov," 72.
255 Mesiats, *Naselenie i zemlepol'zovanie Kabardy*, 68–9; Kashezheva, "Nekotorye voprosy pereselencheskogo dvizheniia v Terskuiu oblast' v poreformennyi period," 70.
256 Tkhamokova, *Russkoe i ukrainskoe naselenie Kabardino-Balkarii*, 34–45.
257 Dzagov, *Vziamodeistvie kul'tur v protsesse formirovaniia mnogonatsional'nogo naseleniia Kabardy*, 38–40.
258 Tkhamokova, *Russkoe i ukrainskoe naselenie Kabardino-Balkarii*, 38–41.
259 M. Z. Sablirov, "Zemledel'cheskaia obshchina tolstovtsev Kabardy i Balkarii," in *Istoriia Severnogo Kavkaza s drevneishikh vremen po nostoiashchee vremia (Tezisy konferentsii 30-31 maia 2000 goda)*, eds. Iu.S. Davydov et al. (Piatigorsk: Izd-vo Piatigorskogo gos. lingvisticheskogo univ, 2000), 203–5.
260 Dzagov, *Vziamodeistvie kul'tur v protsesse formirovaniia mnogonatsional'nogo naseleniia Kabardy*, 43.
261 Mesiats, *Naselenie i zemlepol'zovanie Kabardy*, 86.
262 Tiutiunina, *Grani regional'noi istorii XIX-XX vekov*, 66–70.
263 "Izbrannye dokumenty," 176.
264 *AKAK* 9: 429.
265 A. A. Tsutsiev, *Osetino-Ingushskii konflikt (1992-...): ego predistoriia i faktory razvitie* (Moscow: ROSSPEN, 1998).
266 On these uprisings, see I. F. Muzhev, "Kabarda i Balkariia v period reaktsii i novogo revoliutsionnogo pod"ema (1907-1914)," in *Istoriia Kabardino-Balkarskoi ASSR*, T. I, 391–7.

Chapter 4

1 Kappeler, *The Russian Empire*, 329–40.
2 Marshall, *The Caucasus under Soviet Rule*, 42–3.
3 Kappeler, *The Russian Empire*, 330–1.

Notes 265

4 Narochnitskii, *Istoriia narodov Severnogo kavkaza*, 478–83.
5 Perović, *From Conquest to Deportation*, 122.
6 Ibid., 103, 109.
7 T. N. Litvinova, "Politicheskaia institutsionalizatsiia i bor'ba elit na Severnom Kavkaze v period revoliutsii 1917 goda i grazhdanskoi voiny," *Zhurnal sotsiologii i sotsial'noi antropologii* 20, no. 4 (2017): 155–6.
8 Perović, *From Conquest to Deportation*, 103.
9 O. A. Zhansitov, *Antibol'shevistskoe dvizhenie i denikinskii rezhim v Kabarde i Balkarii, (1917-1920 gg.)* (Nalchik: Institut gumanitarnykh issledovanii Pravitel'stva KBR i KBNTs RAN, 2009), 17.
   Perović, *From Conquest to Deportation*, 103.
10 Ibid., 107.
11 Zhansitov, *Antibol'shevistskoe dvizhenie i denikinskii rezhim v Kabarde i Balkarii*, 17–18.
12 Perović, *From Conquest to Deportation*, 104.
13 Ibid., 115.
14 Marshall, *The Caucasus under Soviet Rule*, 67.
15 Ibid., 63, 65–6.
16 Ibid., 68.
17 Ibid., 69.
18 Zhansitov, *Antibol'shevistskoe dvizhenie i denikinskii rezhim v Kabarde i Balkarii*, 95.
19 Perović, *From Conquest to Deportation*, 123–4, 135.
20 Marshall, *The Caucasus under Soviet Rule*, 69–70.
21 Perović, *From Conquest to Deportation*, 114, 122.
22 Marhsall, *The Caucasus under Soviet Rule*, 71.
23 Perović, *From Conquest to Deportation*, 128.
24 Ibid., 131.
25 Ibid., 133–41.
26 On the transformation of the peasantry's struggle from local to national politics, see Aaron Rettish, *Russia's Peasants in Revolution and Civil War: Citizenship, Identity, and the Creation of the Soviet State, 1914-1922* (Cambridge: Cambridge University Press, 2008), 74–5, *passim*.
27 Sahlins, *Boundaries*, 155–67.
28 Hirsch, *Empire of Nations*, 14.
29 On "speaking Bolshevik," see Kotkin, *Magnetic Mountain*, 224–5. On speaking national, see Dragostinova, "Speaking National," 157–8.
30 On the Civil War in the North Caucasus, see Marshall, *The Caucasus under Soviet Rule*, 51–194; Perović, *From Conquest to Deportation*, 103–44; and Valerii Dzidzoev, *Ot Soiuza obedinennikh gortev Severnogo Kavkaza i Dagestana do Gorskoi ASSR (1917-1924 g.g.): nachal'nyi etep national'no-gosudarstvennogo stroitel'stvo narodov Severnogo Kavkaza v XX veke* (Vladikavkaz: Izd-vo Severo-Osetinskogo gos. Universiteta, 2003)
31 See the Resolution of the Emergency Land Commission in Akim Kazbekovich Dzhanaev, ed., *S'ezdy narodov Tereka*, vol. 1 (Ordzhonikidze: Ir, 1977), 331–2.
32 Peter Holquist, *Making War, Forging Revolution: Russia's Continuum of Crisis, 1914-1921* (Cambridge, MA: Harvard University Press, 2002), 6, 205.
33 A. Kh. Karmov, "Zemel'nye otnosheniia v GASSR," in *Zemel'nye otnosheniia v Kabarde i Balkarii*, 107–9.
34 Zh. A. Kalmykov, *Etnoterritorial'naia i Administrativno-territorial'naia struktora Kabardino-Balkarii i problemy realizatsii v KBR federal'nogo zakona "ob obshchikh*

printsipakh organizatsii mestnogo samoupravleniia v Rossiiskoi federatsii (Nalchik: Respublikanskii poligrafkombinat im. Revoliutsii 1905 g, 2010), 14.
35 Karmov, "Zemel'nye otnosheniia v GASSR," 107.
36 Ibid., 107-8.
37 Ibid.
38 E. F. Zhupikova, "Prichiny politicheskogo banditizma na Severnom Kavkaze v kontse grazhdanskoi voiny," in *Don i Severnyi Kavkaz v period stroitel'stva sotsializma*, ed. N. V. Kiseleva (Rostov-na-Donu: Rostovskii gosudarstvennyi universitet im. M.A. Suslova 1988), 45-7.
39 Islam Khubiev-Karachaily, "Kabardino-Karachaevskii vopros," *Zhizn' natsional'nostei* 133, no. 4 (1922): 1.
40 A. G. Kazharov, "Aliev U.D. i Kabardino-Karachaevskie etnoterritorial'nye otnosheniia v nachale 1920-x g.g.," in *Vymysel i istina*, 276-92.
41 For examples, see RGASPI, f. 64, op. 1, d. 72, l. 13; GARF, f. 5677, op. 2, d. 225, l. 35; and f. 1318, op. 1, d. 231, l. 6.
42 On Stalin's role in the separation of Kabarda from the GASSR, see A. G. Kazharov, "Voprosy zemlevladeniia i zemlepol'zovaniia v usloviiakh stanoleniia i razvitiia gosudarstvennosti Kabardino-Balkarii v 1920-e gg," in *Zemel'nye otnosheniia v Kabarde i Balkarii*, 122-41.
43 P. Kh. Gugov et al. eds., *Za Vlast' Sovetov v Kabarde i Balkarii: Dokumenty i materialy po istorii bor'by za Sovetskuiu vlast' v Kabardino-Balkarskoi Avtonomnoi Oblasti (1917-1922 gg.)* (Nalchik: Kabardino-Balkarskoe Knizhnoe Izdatel'stvo, 1957), 414-15.
44 Ibid., 438.
45 Perović, *From Conquest to Deportation*, 157.
46 Karmov, "Zemel'nye otnosheniia v GASSR," 112.
47 In her discussion of the often-opposing priorities of different state organs charged with border delimitation, Francine Hirsch finds a similar division between ideological and economic motivations. See *Empire of Nations*, 62-100.
48 Karmov, "Zemel'nye otnosheniia v GASSR," 113-20.
49 Babich and Stepanov, 50.
50 Mesiats, *Naselenie i zemlepol'zovanie Kabardy*, 83.
51 Kazharov, "Voprosy zemlevladenie," 124.
52 Ibid.
53 Mesiats, *Naselenie i zemlepol'zovanie Kabardy*, 83.
54 R. Kh. Gugov and B. M. Zumakulov, eds., *Dokumenty po istorii bor'by za Sovetskuiu vlast' obrazovaniia avtonomii Kabardino-Balkarii, 1917-1922 gg.* (Nalchik: Elbrus, 1983), 208-14.
55 Dzhanaev, *S"ezdy narodov Tereka*, vol. 2, 241-2.
56 Dzamikhov et al., "Etnoterritorial'naia i administrativno-territorial'naia struktura Kabardino-Balkarii v XVIII.XX vv.," 342.
57 Gugov, *Za vlast' sovetov*, 364.
58 Karmov, "Zemel'nye otnosheniia v GASSR," 113.
59 GARF, f. 130, op. 5, d. 740, l. 3.
60 Marshall, *The Caucasus under Soviet Rule*, 176-7.
61 Karmov, "Zemel'nye otnosheniia v GASSR," 114.
62 Gugov, *Za vlast' sovetov*, 466.
63 Ibid.
64 Ibid., 414.
65 Ibid., 425.

66 Tsentral'nyi Gosudarstvennyi Arkhiv Kabardino-Balkarskoi Respubliki (TsGA KBR), f. 2, op. 1, d. 2, ll. 18-28.
67 TsGA KBR, f. 2, op. 1, d. 7, ll. 2-5.
68 Ibid., ll. 5-18.
69 TsGA KBR, f. 2, op. 1, d. 2, l. 28.
70 GARF, f. 5677, op. 2, d. 225, ll. 43.
71 TsGA KBR, f. 2, op. 1, d. 7, l. 82.
72 Kazharov, "Voprosy zemlevladenie," 128.
73 Gugov, *Za vlast' sovetov*, 488.
74 GARF, f. 1318, op. 1, d. 10, l. 31.
75 Kazharov, "Voprosy zemlevladenie," 129.
76 GARF, f. 1318, op. 1, d. 432, ll. 3-4.
77 Kazharov, "Voprosy zemlevladenie," 130.
78 Ibid.
79 *Gorskaia Pravda*, December 29, 1921.
80 GARF, f. 1318, op. 1, d. 10, l. 31.
81 Ibid.
82 Kazharov, "Voprosy zemlevladenie," 131.
83 GARF, f. 1318, op. 1, d. 432, ll. 6-7.
84 Gugov, *Za vlast' sovetov*, 488-9.
85 Ibid., 489-90.
86 Ibid.
87 GARF, f. 1318, op. 1, d. 231, ll. 7-8.
88 Ibid., l. 73.
89 Kazharov, "Voprosy zemlevladenie," 137.
90 Gugov, *Za Vlast' Sovetov*, 489-90.
91 GARF, f. 1318, op. 1, d. 16, l. 61.
92 *Krasnaia Kabarda*, August 23, 1922, 1.
93 K. F. Dzamikhov and M. G. Kumakhov, "O stanovlenii Kabardino-Balkarskoi Avtonomnoi Oblast," *Politika i pravo v sfere etnogosudarstvennykh otnoshenii Kabardino-Balkarii*, no. 2 (2001): 261-8.
94 GARF, f. A406, op. 9, d. 526, l. 1-191.
95 Perović, *From Conquest to Deportation*, 3-8.
96 Marshall, *The Caucasus under Soviet Rule*, 22.
97 GARF, f. 5677, op. 2, d. 225, l. 6.
98 Ibid., 7 ob.
99 Ibid., 438.
100 Tiutiunina, *Grani regional'noi istorii XIX-XX vekov*, 101.
101 Quoted in Ibid.
102 Ibid., 109.
103 Ibid., 104.
104 GARF, f. 5677, op. 4, d. 323, l. 4.
105 Ibid.
106 Ibid., 19.
107 Ibid., 17.
108 Ibid., 19.
109 GARF, f. 1318, op. 1, d. 51, l. 54.
110 On the factors that guided Soviet border delimitation, see, for example, Martin, *Affirmative Action Empire*; Hirsch, *Empire of Nations*; Arne Haugen, *Establishment*

of National Republics in Central Asia (Basingstoke: Palgrave Macmillan, 2003); and Jeremy Smith, *The Bolsheviks and the National Question, 1917-23* (New York: St. Martin's Press, 1999).
111 RGASPI, f. 65, op. 1, d. 110, ll. 2-5.
112 GARF, f. 1318, op. 1, d. 148, ll. 36-9.
113 Ibid., ll. 40-3.
114 Ibid., l. 41.
115 Ibid., ll. 32-47.
116 Ibid., l. 38 ob.
117 Ibid., l. 39 ob.
118 For a long list of incidences of disputes between Kabardians and Cossacks in market towns outside Kabardino-Balkaria, see TsGA KBR, f. 2, op. 1, d. 156: ll. 28-31, 61-9, and 83-141.
119 See, for example, a December 14, 1919, report from the White-Army sentry for Kabardian district on fighting between Bolshevik partisans and White forces near the villages of Kaisyn-Anzorovo, Lesken, and Novyi Urukh, in Gugov, *Za vlast' sovetov*, 204-5.
120 GARF, f. 1318, op. 1, d. 51, ll. 268-70.
121 Tsentr Dokumentatsii Noveishei Istorii Kabardino-Balkarskoi Respubliki (TsDNI KBR), f. P-1, op. 1, d. 21, ll. 21-34.
122 GARF, f. 1318, op. 1, d. 51, ll. 268-70.
123 Ibid.
124 GARF, f. 1235, op. 140, d. 190, l. 42.
125 RGASPI, f. 65, op. 1, d. 110, ll. 91-2.
126 GARF, f. 1235, op. 140, d. 190, ll. 41-2.
127 GARF, f. 1318, op. 1, d. 51, l. 270.
128 GARF, f. 1235, op. 99, d. 108, ll. 81-3.
129 Gugov, *Za vlast' sovetov*, 438-9.
130 GARF, f. 5201, op. 2, d. 129, l. 4.
131 Karmov, "Zemel'nye otnosheniia v GASSR," 117.
132 RGASPI, f. 65, op. 1, d. 110, ll. 46-7 and 141.
133 GARF, f. 1235, op. 121, d. 77, l. 139.
134 Ibid., l. 140.
135 TsDNI KBR, f. P-1, op. 1, d. 18, l. 28.
136 GARF, f. 1235, op. 119, d. 36, l. 26.
137 TsDNI KBR, f. P-1, op. 1, d. 12, l. 4.
138 GARF, f. 1235, op. 140/, d. 190, ll. 125-6.
139 Ibid., l. 47.
140 Ibid., l. 29.
141 Ibid., l. 20.
142 Ibid., l. 48.
143 Ibid., l. 52.
144 Ibid., l. 80.
145 Ibid., l. 51.
146 Ibid., l. 72.
147 Ibid., l. 54.
148 Ibid., l. 105.
149 GARF, f. 3316, op. 58, d. 49, l. 68.
150 GARF, f. 1235, op. 140, d. 190, ll. 8, 62.

151 Ibid., l. 3.
152 Ibid., l. 105.
153 Ibid., 106.
154 GARF, f. 1235, op. 104, op. 981, l. 18.
155 The worst clashes were between Balkar and Digoran-Ossetian shepherds over pasturage along the Khazni-Don River. See GARF, f. 1235, op. 119, d. 36, ll. 11–21 and TsDNI KBR, f. P-25, op. 1, d. 85, ll. 28–9.
156 GARF, f. 1235, op. 121, d. 77, l. 42.
157 RGASPI, f. 558, op. 1, d. 5629, l. 30.
158 Dzhanaev, S"ezdy narodov Tereka, vol. 1, 288–90.
159 Ibid., 241.
160 Artur Kazharov, "Administrativno-territorial'noe razmezhivanie Kabardy i Karachaia," Istoricheskii vestnik Kabardino-Balkarskoi Respublikanskoi Instituta Gumanitarnykh Issledovanii, no. 5 (2006): 55.
161 RGASPI, f. 558, op. 1, d. 5629, l. 30.
162 Ibid.
163 Gaibov, O pozemel'nom ustroistve gorskikh plemen Terskoi oblasti, 49–53.
164 Kazharov, "Administrativno-territorial'noe razmezhivanie," 53–5.
165 Quoted in Ibid., 53.
166 Ibid., 55.
167 RGASPI, f. 558, op. 1, d. 5629, l. 30.
168 Gugov and Zumakulov, Dokumenty po istorii bor'by za Sovetskuiu vlast', 623–4.
169 TsGA KBR, f. 2, op. 1, d. 7, ll. 2–3.
170 Ibid., l. 3.
171 Kazharov, "Administrativno-Territorial'noe razmezhivanie," 49–50.
172 GARF, f. 1318, op. 1, d. 114, ll. 106–8.
173 Ibid., l. 113.
174 Khubiev-Karachaily, "Kabardino-Karachaevskii vopros."
175 Ibid.
176 RGASPI, f. 558, op. 1, d. 5629, ll. 15–25.
177 On the Karachai Bolshevik leader, educator, and scholar, see F. V. Abaeva, Umar Aliev: prosvetitel'skaia, pedagogicheskaia i obshchestvennaia deiatel'nost' (Maikop: Adgyeia, 1995).
178 RGASPI, f. 558, op. 1, d. 5629, l. 15.
179 Artur Kazharov argues this in "U.D. Aliev i nekotorye problemy natsional'no-gosudarstvennogo razvitiia narodov severnogo Kavakaza v nachale 1920 gg.," Istoricheskii vestnik Kabardino-Balkarskoi Respublikanskoi Instituta Gumanitarnykh Issledovanii, no. 9 (2010): 82.
180 K. Laipanov and M. Batchaev, Umar Aliev (Cherkessk: Karachai-Cherkesskoe otdelenie Staropol'skogo knizhnogo izdatel'stva, 1986), 148.
181 M., "Kabarda v proshlom i nastoiashchem," Zhinz' natsional'nostei 134, no. 3 (1922): 2.
182 Ibid.
183 Nazarov, "Kabardino-Karachaevskii vopros: po povodu stat'i t. Islama Khubieva (Karachaily) v no. 4 'Zhizn' nats'," Zhinzn' natsional'nostei 136, no. 7 (1922): 3–4.
184 Ibid., 3–4.
185 RGASPI, f. 558, op. 1, d/ 5629, l. 5.
186 Ibid., l. 13.
187 TsDNI KBR, f. P-1, op. 1, d. 1, l. 6.

188 Ibid., l. 7.
189 RGASPI, f. 558, op. 1, op. 5629, l. 6.
190 Ibid., l. 13.
191 RGASPI, f. 65, op. 1, d. 44, l. 105.
192 Ibid., 18.
193 Ibid., 14-15.
194 TsGA KBR, f. 2, op. 1, d. 7, l. 83.
195 TsDNI KBR, f. P-1, op. 1, d. 10, l. 23.
196 GARF, f. A374, op. 27, d. 912, l. 29.
197 Kazharov, "Administrativno-territorial'noe razmezhivanie," 52-3.
198 Ibid., 55-6.
199 GARF, f. 1235, op. 100, d. 140, l. 118.
200 GARF, f. 1235, op. 99, d. 108, ll. 81-2.
201 GARF, f. 1318, op. 1, d. 231 l. 6.
202 Kazharov, "Voprosy zemlevladeniia," 137.
203 TsGA KBR, f. 2, op. 1, d. 70, l. 9.
204 GARF, f. 1235, op. 121, d. 77, ll. 45-7; and GARF, f. 1318, op. 1, d. 231, l. 335.
205 N. F. Bugai, *Severnyi Kavkaz. Gosudarstvennoe stroitel'stvo i federativnye otnosheniia: proshloe v nastoiashchem* (Moscow: Grif i K, 2011), 214, 219.
206 Kazharov, "Administrativno-territorial'noe razmezhivanie," 61.
207 GARF, f. 5677, op. 3, d. 315, ll. 2-3.
208 See, for example, Ibid., l. 4-13; GARF, f. 1318, op. 1, d. 231, ll. 382-3; GARF, f. 1235, op. 99, d. 108, l. 38; GARF, f. 1235, op. 119, d. 36, l. 75; and GARF, f. 1235, op. 119, d. 38, ll. 80-1.
209 GARF, f. 5677, op. 3, d. 315, ll. 12-13, 22.
210 Ibid., l. 13.
211 Kazharov, "Administrativno-territorial'noe razmezhivanie," 58.
212 GARF, f. 1318, op. 1, d. 231, l. 382; and GARF, f. 1235, op. 119, d. 36, l. 72.
213 GARF, f. 1235, op. 119, d. 36, l. 135.
214 Kazharov, "Administrativno-territorial'noe razmezhivanie," 58.
215 Ibid., 54.
216 TsGA KBR, f. 2, op. 1, d. 91, ll. 1-30.
217 Ibid., ll. 7-8.
218 GARF, f. 1235, op. 119, d. 36, l. 73.
219 Ibid., l. 71
220 GARF, f. 1235, op. 73, d. 1144, ll. 9-10.
221 Ibid., l. 61.
222 GARF, f. 1318, op. 1, d. 155, l. 14.
223 Karov, *Administrativno-territorial'nye preobrazovaniia*, 120-1.
224 Ibid.
225 GARF, f. 1235, op. 119, d. 36, l. 115.
226 Ibid., l. 188.
227 A. Kazharov, "Administrativno-territorial'noe razmezhivanie," 64.
228 Quoted in ibid., 66.
229 Mesiats, *Naselenie i zemlepol'zovanie Kabardy*, 88.
230 Karmov, *Administrativno-territorial'nye preobrazovaniia*, 283-6.
231 A. Zh. Shereuzhev, "Administrativno-territorial'nye preobrazovaniia v Kabardino-Balkarskoi Avtonomnoi Oblasti v period prebyvaniia v sostave Severo-Kavkazskogo kraiia (1924-1936)," *Nauchnaia mysl' Kavkaza* 70, no. 1 (2019): 73.

232 "Nashi ocherednye zadachi . . . Rech tov. Kalmykova na 2-om s"ezde kolkhoznikov," *Leninskii put*', March 6, 1932.
233 For the traditional divide-and-rule view, see Richard Pipes, *The Formation of the Soviet Union: Communism and Nationalism, 1917-1923* (Cambridge, MA: Harvard University Press, 1964).
234 See Footnote 85 in this chapter.
235 GARF, f. 1235, op. 121, d. 77, l. 97.
236 Ibid., l. 110.
237 This is an important theme in Kappeler's *The Russian Empire*.
238 Hirsch, "Toward an Empire of Nations: Border-Making and the Formation of Soviet National Identities," in *Empire of Nations: Ethnographic Knowledge and the making of the Soviet Union* (Ithaca: Cornell University Press, 2005), 205.
239 Dragostinova, "Speaking National," 157.
240 Martin discusses the North Caucasus only as an example of the "Kazakh Variant." See *The Affirmative Action Empire*, 59–67. Hirsch gives the delimitation of borders in the North Caucasus brief mention in relation to *raionirovanie*. See *Empire of Nations*, 98. Pipes spends significant time examining the initial Bolshevik rise to power in the North Caucasus, but he spends little time examining border delimitation. See *The Formation of the Soviet Union*, 223–4. Two recent works on the region, Marshall's *The Caucasus Under Soviet Rule* and Perović's *From Conquest to Deportation*, provide nuanced accounts of border delimitation in the North Caucasus.
241 Martin, *The Affirmative Action Empire*, 57.
242 Ibid., 60.
243 Ibid., 69.
244 Breyfogle, "Enduring Imperium," 108–9.
245 On "state-sponsored evolutionism," see Hirsch, *Empire of Nations*, 7.
246 Sahlins, *Boundaries*, 160.
247 Ibid., 159.
248 Rogers Brubaker et al., *Nationalist Politics and Everyday Ethnicity in a Transylvanian Town* (Princeton: Princeton University Press, 2006).

Chapter 5

1 In 1936, the Soviet leadership elevated Kabardino-Balkaria's administrative status from an AO to an autonomous republic.
2 Khadzhi-Murat Sabanchiev, *Byli soslany navechno: deportatsiia i reabilitatsiia balkarskogo naroda* (Nalchik: Elbrus, 2004), 16–23.
3 English-language works on Stalin-era ethnic cleansing are numerous. See, for example, Polian, *Against their Will*; Greta Lynn Uehling, *Beyond Memory: The Crimean Tatars' Deportation and Return* (New York: Palgrave Macmillan, 2004); Norman Naimark, *Stalin's Genocides* (Princeton: Princeton University Press, 2010); Nekrich, *The Punished Peoples*; J. Otto Pohl, "Stalin's Genocide against the 'Repressed Peoples,'" *Journal of Genocide Research* 2, no. 2 (2000): 267–93; Idem., *Ethnic cleansing in the USSR, 1937-1949* (Westport: Greenwood Press, 1999); Robert Conquest, *The Nation Killers: The Soviet Deportation of Nationalities* (London: Macmillan, 1970); and Nikolai Bugai, *The Deportation of Peoples in the Soviet Union* (New York: Nova Science Publishers, 1996).

4 For a description of the rehabilitation program as it stood at the end of the Soviet period, see the 1991 Russian federal law "On the Rehabilitation of Victims of Political Repression." Kh.-M. A. Sabanchiev, ed., *Balkartsy: vyselenie i vozvrashchenie* (Nalchik: Elbrus, 2008), 415–17.
5 Gerhard Simon, *Nationalism and Policy Toward the Nationalities in the Soviet Union: From Totalitarian Dictatorship to Post-Stalinist Society* (Boulder: Westview Press, 1991), 31–42, 138, 150–1; Martin, *The Affirmative Action Empire*, 376–9; Suny, *Revenge of the Past*, 108–9.
6 Blitstein, "Stalin's Nations."
7 On the significant expansion of Kabardino-Balkaria's industrial sector from the late 1950s through the early 1970s, see T. Kh. Khashkhozheva, "Izmemnenie professional'no-kvalifikatsionnyi struktury rabochikh promyshlennosti Kabardino-Balkarskoi ASSR," in *Problemy trudovykh resursov Kabardino-Balkarskoi ASSR*, ed. A. T. Kuantov (Nalchik: Kabardino-Balkarskii nauchno-issledovatel'skii institut pri Sovete ministrov KBASSR, 1975), 29–30. For a general overview of modernization processes in Kabardino-Balkaria during the post-Stalin era, see V. K. Gardanov, ed., *Novoe i traditsionnoe v kul'ture i byte kabardintsev i balkartsev* (Nalchik: El'brus, 1986), 33–40.
8 Artemy Kalinovsky, *Laboratory of Socialist Development: Cold War Politics and Decolonization in Soviet Tajikistan* (Ithaca: Cornell University Press, 2018), 2.
9 Based on the example of Tajikistan, Kalinovsky argues that native elites lobbied Moscow for cultural and economic development in their underdeveloped agrarian republics. Though ultimately disillusioned by the results of Soviet modernization by the late 1980s, these specialists and administrators played a role in shaping the trajectory of modernization in their regions. According to Kalinovsky, native "party leaders, economists, engineers, and architects . . . saw themselves as a vanguard that could define the local variation of Soviet modernity and find the most effective way to implement their vision." Ibid., 12. An examination of the ability of native elites to lobby Moscow and influence the trajectory of Soviet development in Kabardino-Balkaria is beyond the scope of this book. However, a published collection of official correspondence and directives from Timbora Mal'bakhov, the ethnically Kabardian first secretary of the Kabardino-Balkar Obkom from 1956 to 1985, reflects his efforts to do so. See *T.K. Mal'bakhov: Epokha bor'by i sozidaniia: Izbrannye rechi, stat'i, i pis'ma*, ed. B. Kh. Bgazhnokov (Nalchik: Izdatel'stvo M. i V. Kotliarovykh, 2007).
10 O. A. Zhansitov, "Problemy modernizatsii promyshlennoi sfery Kabardino-Balkarskoi respubliki (1960–1980 gg.)," *Bylye gody* 33, no. 3 (2014): 481.
11 Gardanov, *Novoe i traditsionnoe*, 52.
12 See for example, GARF f. 1235, op. 105, d. 450, l. 79.
13 On resistance to see Soviet rule in the North Caucasus, see Perović, *From Conquest to Deportation*, passim.
14 For example, see GARF f. 1250, op. 105, d. 450, ll. 418–21; GARF f. 1250, op. 107, d. 498, l. 496.
15 For example, see GARF f. 1250, op. 121, d. 77, l. 4; GARF f. 1250, op. 140, d. 190, l. 20.
16 M. Kh. Gugova, "Kabardino-Balkariia na kanune i v nachal'nyi period Velikoi Otechestvennoi voiny," *Vestnik KBIGI* 37, no. 2 (2018): 23.
17 Ibid., 25.
18 See Martin, *The Affirmative Action Empire* and Hirsch, *Empire of Nations*.

19 Martin, *The Affirmative Action Empire*, 240-9.
20 Ibid., 361.
21 Ibid., 126.
22 Quoted in ibid., 361.
23 A. Nechiporenko, "V neprimirimoi bor'be s velikoderzhavnym shovenizmom— glavnoi opasnost'iu—i mestnym natsionalizmom," *Baskan-Stroi*, November 28, 1931, 3.
24 With 3,686 workers in 1937, the Baksan Hydroelectric Dam project employed as many industrial workers as were employed in the remainder of Kabardino-Balkaria's industrial sector. See A. T. Kardanov, *Rabochii klass Kabardino-Balkarii v period stroitel'stva sotsializma (1920-1937)* (Nalchik: Elburs, 1976), 87-119.
25 "Baksan GRES dolzhen stroit' kazhdyi trudiashchiisia KBAO," *Leninskii put'*, January 12, 1933, 4.
26 "Pochemu otmalchivaetsia oblsovprof?," *Sotsialisticheskaia Kabardino-Balkariia*, February 2, 1935, 2.
27 See, for example, ibid; "Natsionaly ukhodiat s proizvodstva," *Sotsialisticheskaia Kabardino-Balkariia*, May 22, 1935, 2; "O partiino-organizatsionnoi i politichseki-vospitatel'noi rabote na Baksanstroe," *Sotsialisticheskaia Kabardino-Balkariia*, May 30, 1935, 1; "Na Baksanskoe plokho gotoviat kadry," *Sotsialisticheskaia Kabardino-Balkariia*, March 27, 1935, 2; and Umar Tuganov, "Sozdat' usloviia rabochemu natsionalu," *Leninskii put'*, September 14, 1932, 2.
28 Martin, *The Affirmative Action Empire*, 154.
29 "Istoriia odnogo oproverzheniia," *Leninskii put'*, July 21, 1932, 4.
30 Komsomolets, "Ukratit' shovenista Soldatova," *Leninskii put'*, September 17, 1932, 2.
31 Martin, *The Affirmative Action Empire*, 146.
32 "Ocherednye zadachi oblastnoi partiinoi organizatsii v cel'skom khoziastve: Pech; sekretaria VKP(b) tov. B. Kalmykova na 2-om plenume Obkoma partii 2-go iiulia 1934 goda," *Sotsialisticheskaia Kabardino-Balkariia*, July 17, 1934, 3.
33 "Redaktor gazety 'Sots. Kabardino-Balkarii' sniat s raboty," *Sotsialisticheskaia Kabardino-Balkariia*, November 20, 1937, 1.
34 "Burzhuaznye natsionalisty raspoiasalis," *Pravda*, March 5, 1937, 6.
35 Ibid. and "'Burzhuaznye natsionalisty raspoiasalis': Postanovlenie biuro Kabardino-Balkarskogo Obkoma VKP(b) o korrespondentsii, napechatannoi v 'Pravde' 5 marta 1937," *Pravda*, March 11, 1937, 6.
36 "Burzhuaznye natsionalisty raspoiasalis."
37 Ibid.
38 Ibid.
39 "Reshitel'nyi iskoreniat' burzhuaznykh natsionalistov," *Sotsialisticheskaia Kabardino-Balkariia*, November 21, 1937, 1; "Baksanskii raikom komsomola ne razoblachaet posledstviia burzhuaznykh natsionalistov," *Sotsialisticheskaia Kabardino-Balkariia*, November 28, 1937, 3; "Do kontsa razoblachit' burzhuaznogo natsionalista Sasikova," *Sotsialisticheskaia Kabardino-Balkariia*, Decmber 4, 1937, 4; "Liberal'nichaiut s burzhuaznymi natsionalistami," *Sotsialisticheskaia Kabardino-Balkariia*, December 15, 1937, 4; and "Do kontsa likvidirovat' posledstviia vreditel'stva," *Sotsialisticheskaia Kabardino-Balkariia*, September 2, 1937, 3.
40 "Reshitel'nyi iskoreniat, burzhuaznykh natsionalistov."
41 For an overview of the purges of the Kabardino-Balkar Party organization, see RGASPI, f. 17 op. 21, d. 1238, ll. 21-96.

42 In 1927, leading early Kabardian supporters of Soviet power were purged: "Otkliki 6-go s"ezda sovetov na novyiu vylazku kontrrevoliutsionnoi gruppy oblasti," *Karakhalk*, March 3, 1927, 3.
43 RGASPI 17/21/1238 (1937): 21–4.
44 For data, see GARF, f. 1235 op. 105, d. 450, ll. 12–20; GARF, f. 1235, op. 131, d. 26, ll. 110–11; GARF, f. 1235, op. 141, d. 1024, ll. 30–7; GARF, f. 1235, op. 124, d. 29, ll. 41–6; GARF, f. 1235, op. 124, d. 93, ll. 1–61; GARF, f. A2306, op. 75, d. 2446, l. 53; TsGA KBR, f. 8, op. 2, d. 13, ll. 22–6; TsGA KBR, f. 2, op. 1, d. 634, ll. 83–158; and TsGA KBR, f. 4, op. 1, d. 221, ll. 1–95.
45 In explaining the seeming contradictions in Soviet policies toward its ethnic minorities Terry Martin distinguishes between hard- and soft-line policies and the Soviet institutions that carried them out. *The Affirmative Action Empire*, 21–2.
46 Horowitz, *Ethnic Groups in Conflict*, 99–135.
47 N. S. Lavrova, *Agrarnye preobrazovaniia i razvitie sela v Kabardino-Balkarii v 20-30-e gody XX veka: Avtoreferat kandidatskoi dissertatsii* (Nalchik: Kabardino-Balkarskii Gosudarstvennyi Universitet, 2004), 19.
48 On state-sponsored efforts at the "liberation of the mountaineer woman" (raskreposhchenie gorianki) in Kabardino-Balkaria, see, for example, GARF f. 1235, op. 105, d. 450, ll. 423–4, 470, 472, 477, 538.
49 G. K. Mambetov, "Sotsial'no-ekonomicheskie I politicheskie preobrazovaniia v Kabardino-Balkarii v 1928-1941 godakh," in *Istoriia Kabardino-Balkarii*, eds. T. Kh. Kumykov and I. M. Miziev (Nalchik: El'brus, 1995), 283.
50 Perović makes this argument in *From Conquest to Deportation*, 3.
51 G. K. Dzuev, *Bez prava na obzhalovanie: dokumental'nye ocherki po materialam ChK, GPU, NKVD, KGB, FSB 1920-1940 gg* (Nalchik: Elbrus, 2012), 97–118.
52 On the Baksan Uprising, see Perović, *From Conquest to Deportation*, 230–6.
53 These "*shariatisty*," led by Nazir Katkhanov, were popular Civil War-era pro-Bolshevik intellectuals who advocated blending Islamic law with Marxist-Leninist ideology. On Katkhanov, see Kerim Katkhanov, *Nazyr: Kniga ob ottse* (Nalchik: Elbrus, 2008).
54 G. K. Dzuev, *Krovavoe leto 1928-goda: ocherki* (Nalchik: Elbrus, 1997), 38–9.
55 Ibid., 15.
56 Ibid., 44.
57 G. Kh. Mambetov and Z. G. Mambetov, *Sotsial'nye protivorechiia v Kabardino-Balkarskoe derevne v 20-30-e gody* (Nalchik: Izdatel'stvo KBNTs RAN, 2009), 172–215.
58 Rossiiskii Gosudarstvennyi Arkhiv Noveishei Istorii (RGANI), f. 6, op. 6, d. 1611, ll. 200–9.
59 Rabochaia gruppa Natsional'nogo soveta balkarskogo naroda, "Narod i vremia: problemma Balkarii na fone konseptsii o natsional'no-gosudarstvennom pereustroistve respubliki," *Tere: balkarskii forum*, no. 24, March 1993.
60 "Ob"edinenie Kabardy i Balkarii," *Krasnaia Kabarda*, August 23, 1922, 1.
61 On the purposes of *razukrupnenie* in Kabardino-Balkaria, see GARF, f. 1235, op. 131, d. 26, ll. 112–13.
62 See chapter three in Karov, *Administrativno-territorial'nye preobrazovaniia*, 119–298.
63 On Soviet ethnic cleansing, see Terry Martin, "The Origins of Soviet Ethnic Cleansing," *The Journal of Modern History* 70, no. 4 (1998): 813–61.
64 See Ibid; Holquist, "To Count, to Extract, and to Exterminate," 115–16; and the works referenced in note three of this chapter.

65 Dana Lyn Sherry refers these tsarist-era practices in the region as "social alchemy": the "creat[ion] ... by colonial officials ... of an ideal society ... from scratch" based on "ideas about ethnicity, geography, and the government's goals for the region." See her dissertation, "Imperial Alchemy: Resettlement, Ethnicity, and Governance in the Russian Caucasus, 1828-1865" (Phd diss., University of California-Davis, 2007), 138.
66 Eric Lohr, *Nationalizing the Russian Empire: The Campaign against Enemy Aliens during World War I* (Cambridge, MA: Harvard University Press, 2003).
67 Holquist, *Making War, Forging Revolution*, 166–205.
68 Lynn Viola, *The Unknown Gulag: The Lost World of Stalin's Special Settlements* (Oxford: Oxford University Press, 2007).
69 Martin, *The Affirmative Action Empire*, 327–30.
70 N. F. Bugai and A. M. Gonov, eds., *Po resheniiu pravitel'stva Soiuza SSR (Deportatsiia narodov: dokumenty i materialy)* (Nalchik: El-Fa, 2003), 201–2.
71 Ibid., 135.
72 Ibid., 183–4.
73 Martin, *The Affirmative Action Empire*, 9.
74 Ibid., 315–16.
75 Ibid., 325–8.
76 Alexander Statiev, "Soviet Ethnic Deportations: Intent vs. Outcome," *Journal of Genocide Research* 11, nos. 2–3 (2009): 243–64.
77 Bugai and Gonov, *Po resheniiu pravitsel'stva Soiuza SSR*, 654.
78 Ibid., 358–9.
79 Ibid., 249.
80 Karov, *Administrativno-territorial'noe preobrazovaniia*, 336.
81 Bugai and Gonov, *Po resheniiu pravitel'stva Soiuza SSR*, 613.
82 Martin, *The Affirmative Action Empire*, 321.
83 Joshua Sanborn, *Drafting the Russian Nation: Military Conscription, Total War, and Mass Politics, 1905-1925* (DeKalb: Northern Illinois University Press, 2003), 141.
84 A. M. Bezugol'nyi, *Narody Kavkaza i Krasnaia Armiia, 1918-1945* (Moscow: Veche, 2007), 184, 208.
85 On the historiography on Stalin's national deportations, see Yaacov Ro'i, "The Transformation of Historiography on the 'Punished Peoples,'" *History & Memory* 21, no. 2 (2009): 150–76.
86 Svetlana Alieva, ed., *Tak eto bylo: natsional'nye repressii v SSSR 1919-1952 gody*, vol. 1 (Moscow: Rossiiskii mezhdunarodnyi fond kul'tury, 1993), 258; and Bugai and Gonov, *Po resheniiu pravitel'stva Soiuza SSR*, 500.
87 Sabanchiev, *Balkartsy*, 59.
88 S. I. Lints, *Severnyi Kavkaz nakanune i v period nemetsko-fashistskoi okkupatsii: sostoianie i osobennoisti razvitiia (iiul' 1942 – oktiabr' 1943 gg.)* (Rostov-on-Don: Izd-vo SKBNTs VSh, 2003), 16.
89 Sabanchiev, *Balkartsy*, 46.
90 A. A. Grechko, *Bitva za Kavkaz* (Moscow: Voenizdat, 1967), 200–14.
91 Alieva, *Tak eto bylo*, vol. 1, 258; and Bugai and Gonov, *Po resheniiu pravitel'stva Soiuza SSR*, 500.
92 Sabanchiev, *Balkartsy*, 67–8.
93 Ibid., 74.
94 Ibid., 62–3.
95 I. A. Giliazov, "Pantiurkizm, panturanizm i Germaniia," *Etnograficheskoe obozrenie*, no. 2 (1996): 98.

96 Sabanchiev, *Balkartsy*, 74-7.
97 G. Takoev, "K problemam politiki v SSSR," *Sotsialisticheskii vestnik* 31, no. 3 (1951): 66.
98 Sabanchiev, *Balkartsy*, 88.
99 On the purges in Kabardino-Balkaria see Valerii Khatazhukov, ed. *Politicheskie repressii v Kabardino-Balkarii v 1918-1930-kh godakh (Stat'i i dokumenty)* (Nalchik: Kabardino-Balkarskii Respublikanskii Pravozashchitnyi Tsentr, 2010).
100 RGASPI, f. 17, op. 21, d. 1249, ll. 48-50.
101 RGASPI, f. 17, op. 21, d. 1250, l. 99.
102 A. Kh. Abaev, "Z.D. Kumekhov: Pervyi sekretar' Kabardino-Balkarskogo obkoma VKP(b), 1939-1944 (K stoletiiu so dnia rozhdeniia)," *Arkhivy i obshchestvo*, no. 15 (2010): 200-10.
103 R. Kh. Gugov, "Kul'turnoe stroitel'stvo v Kabardino-Balkarii v pervye gody sotsialisticheskoi rekonstruktsii narodnogo khoziastva SSSR (1926-1929)," *Uchenye Zapiski Kabardino-Balkarskogo Naucho-issledovatel'skogo Instituta*, no. 15 (1959): 109-38.
104 Abaev, "Z.D. Kumekhov," 204.
105 T. Kh. Kumykov, *Istoriia Kabardino-Balkarii* (Nalchik: Elbrus, 1997), 303-4.
106 "Formirovanie 115-i Kabardino-Balkarskoi natsional'noi kavaleriiskoi divizii i ee uchastie v boevykh deistviiakh: normativno-pravovye akty i organizatsionnye raboty partiinykh, sovetskikh i komsomol'skikh organov, vospominaniia i stat'i," *Arkhivy i obshchestvo*, no. 13 (2010): 58-79.
107 Bezugol'nyi, *Narody Kavkaza i Krasnaia Armiia*, 220.
108 Sabanchiev, *Balkartsy*, 62-3.
109 RGANI, f. 6, op. 6, d. 1611, l. 200.
110 Sabanchiev, *Balkarstsy*, 71.
111 RGANI, f. 6, op. 6, d. 1611, ll. 202-7.
112 A. M. Shameev, "Osobennosti i kharakter partizanskogo dvizheniia v Kabardino-Balkarii protiv nemetsko-fashistskikh zakhvatchikov vo vtoroi polovine 1942-nachale 1943 gg," *Arkhivy i obshchestvo*, no. 12 (2010): 207-11.
113 Sabanchiev, *Balkartsy*, 73-4.
114 A. Dirk Moses, ed., *Empire, Colony, Genocide: Conquest, Occupation, and Subaltern Resistance in World History* (New York: Berghahn Books, 2008).
115 Holquist, "To Count, To Extract and To Exterminate," 111-13.
116 TsDNI KBR, f. P-1, op. 53, d. 4, l. 16.
117 K. G. Azamatov et al., *Cherekskaia tragediia* (Nalchik: Elbrus, 1994), 9-10.
118 Ibid.
119 Sabanchiev, *Balkartsy*, 63.
120 Azamatov et al., *Cherekskaia tragediia*, 12.
121 "Podpolkovniku t. Shikinu; 20.00, 30.11.42," in Azamatov et al., *Cherekskaia tragediia*, 155.
122 There are two major works on the Cherek massacre: Azamatov et al. *Cherekskaia tragediia* and B. B. Temukuev, *Sem' dnei odnogo veka: 27 noiabria--5 dekabria 1942 goda: v dokumentakh 1943 g* (Nalchik: Poligrafservis i T, 2004).
123 TsDNI KBR, f. P-1, op. 1, d. 494, l. 4.
124 Sabanchiev, *Balkartsy*, 72; Aslan Borov, "Deportatsiia i reabilitatsiia balkarskogo naroda kak problema obshchestvenno-politicheskoi zhizni Kabardino-Balkarii," *Istoricheskii vestnik Instituta gumanitarnykh issledovanii pravitel'stva Kabardino-Balkarskoi Respubliki*, no. 4 (2006): 295-389, especially, 300.

125 Sabanchiev, *Balkartsy*, 411; N. F. Bugai and A. M. Gonov, *Kavkaz: Narody v eshelonakh (20-60-e gody)* (Moscow: Insan, 1998), 162.
126 Bugai and Gonov, *Po resheniiu pravitel'stva Soiuza SSR*, 485.
127 Ibid., 486-92.
128 Ibid., 490.
129 For example, Sabanchiev argues that Kumekhov was an initiator and willing compiler of such reports. See Sabanchiev, *Byli soslany navechno*, 9-11; Borov and Shabaev argue that Kumekhov had no incentive to provide compromising material on the Balkars and that the NKVD forced him to put his name to falsified reports. See Borov, "Deportatsiia i reabilitatsiia balkarskogo naroda," 302-5 and David Shabaev, *Pravda o vyselenii balkartsev* (Nalchik: "Elbrus", 1994), 7-12.
130 Bugai and Gonov, *Po resheniiu pravitel'stva Soiuza SSR*, 492.
131 TsDNI KBR, f. P-1, op. 1, d. 640, ll. 10-11.
132 Sabanchiev, *Balkartsy*, 93-7.
133 Luk'iaev, "A vy vernetes', ver'te mne . . . Ocherk-vospominanie," in Alieva, *Tak eto bylo*, vol. 3, 29.
134 Sabanchiev, *Balkartsy*, 103-4.
135 Bugai and Gonov, *Po resheniiu pravitel'stva Soiuza SSR*, 495.
136 Ibid., 500.
137 Karov, *Administrativno-territorial'nye preobrazovaniia*, 343; in *Chas ispytanii: deportatsiia, reabilitatsiia i vozrozhdenie balkarskogo naroda (dokumenty i materialy)*, eds. B. M. Zumakulov, A. Kh. Karov, and S. A. Beituganov (Nalchik: Elbrus, 2001), 141.
138 Karov, *Administrativno-territorial'nye preobrazovaniia*, 348-53.
139 See decrees in Section IV Chapter Two of ibid., 344-84.
140 For a testimony of a survivor who was separated from her Kabardian mother during the deportations, see M. A. Kotliarova and V. N. Kotliarov eds., *Balkariia: Deportatsiia. Svidetel'stvuiut ochevidtsy. Vyp. 1* (Nalchik: Poligrafservis i T, 2004), 13-14.
141 Lidiia Zhabelova, "Soslannye navechno: Fragmenty rukopisei knigi Lidii Zhabelovoi o zhizni i deiatel'nosti Mukhtara Kudaeva-osnovopolozhnika professional'noi karachaevo-balkarskoi etnokhoreografii," *Elbrusoid*, last modified March 7, 2008, http://www.elbrusoid.org/articles/karachay-balkar/359202/.
142 See, for example, Kotliarova and Kotliarov, *Balkariia: Deportatsiia. Svidetel'stvuiut ochevidtsy*, vol. 1, 9; vol. 2, 7; Shabaev, *Pravda o vyselenii balkartsev*, 270-3.
143 Sabanchiev, *Balkartsy*, 103.
144 Kotliarova and Kotliarov, *Balkariia: Deportatsiia. Svidetel'stvuiut ochevidtsy*, vol. 1, 9.
145 RGASPI, f. 17, op. 44, d. 391, l. 8.
146 Bugai and Gonov, *Po resheniiu pravitel'stva Soiuza SSR*, 502.
147 Sabanchiev, *Balkartsy*, 73.
148 Bugai and Gonov, *Po resheniiu pravitel'stva Soiuza SSR*, 506-7.
149 Borov, "Deportatsiia i reabilitatsiia balkarskogo naroda," 310-13.
150 Sabanchiev, *Balkartsy*, 117.
151 Zhabelova, "Soslannye navechno."
152 I. I. Maremshaova claims that the Karachais and Balkars (and other deported peoples) experienced a "social death" (*sotsial'naia smert'*) as a result of the deportations. See *Balkariia i Karachai v etnokul'turnom prostranstve Kavkaza* (Nalchik: Elbrus, 2003), 79.
153 Hirsch, *Empire of Nations*, 8-9.

154 That is not to say that individual union republics did not conduct their own nativization campaigns in the later Soviet period, but this was a product of Moscow's of lack of interference in the cultural affairs of some of the republics. See, for example, Suny, *Revenge of the Past*, 108–10, 117–19.
155 Ibid., 11.
156 Ibid., 246–7.
157 RGASPI, f. 17, op. 118, d. 25, l. 19.
158 TsDNI KBR, f. P-1, op. 1, d. 1816, ll. 369–70.
159 Ibid.
160 Ibid.
161 Blitstein, "Stalin's Nations," 196–7, 203.
162 Martin, *Affirmative Action Empire*, 414–24.
163 Ibid., 385.
164 Ibid., 140, 378.
165 On the loss of Kabardian-language literature and textbooks and the problems of rebuilding the republic's cultural and educational infrastructure after the war, see GARF, f. A259, op. 5, d. 435, ll. 3–4.
166 Martin, *Affirmative Action Empire*, 132–9.
167 RGASPI, f. 17, op. 122, d. 304, l. 22.
168 Ibid., ll. 23–24.
169 TsDNI KBR, f. P-1/1/2324: 52.
170 TsGA KBR, f. 686, op. 1, d. 474, ll. 60–7.
171 TsDNI KBR, f. P-112, op. 1, d. 45, l. 22.
172 TsGA KBR, f. 686, op. 1, d. 474, ll. 60–1.
173 See, for example, TsGA KBR, f. 575, op. 1, d. 3, l. 78; TsDNI KBR, f. P-112, op. 1, d. 45, l. 24; TsDNI KBR, f. P-13, op. 1, d. 61, l. 17.
174 TsDNI KBR, f. P-13, op. 1, d. 61, l. 17.
175 TsGA KBR, f. 199, op. 2, d. 18, ll. 45–6.
176 TsDNI KBR, f. P-9, op. 1, d. 57, l. 234.
177 TsGA KBR, f. 574, op. 1, d. 152, l. 23.
178 See, for example, TsDNI KBR, f. P-9, op. 1, d. 57, ll. 234–5; TsDNI KBR, f. P-112, op. 1, d. 45, l. 52; TsDNI KBR, f. P-4, op. 1, d. 120, ll. 17–18; TsDNI KBR, f. P-109, op. 1, d. 83, l. 32.
179 TsGA KBR, f. 574, op. 1/, d. 52, ll. 22–4; TsGA KBR, f. 585, op. 1, d. 36, l. 74; TsGA KBR, f. 199, op. 2, d. 18, ll. 27–8; TsGA KBR, f. 575, op. 1 d. 3, l. 78; TsDNI KBR, f. P-9, op. 1, d. 57, ll. 234–5; TsDNI KBR, f. P-112, op. 1, d. 45, ll. 22–4 and 52; TsDNI KBR, f. P-13, op. 1, d. 61, ll. 17; TsDNI KBR, f. P-4, op. 1, d. 120, ll. 17–18; TsDNI KBR, f. P-78, op. 1, d. 81, ll. 1–2 and 6.
180 TsDNI KBR, f. P-2 op. 1, d. 167, ll. 9.
181 Ibid., l. 3.
182 Ibid., l. 8.
183 Ibid., l. 2.
184 Ibid. ll. 6–7, and TsDNI KBR, f. P-2, op. 1, d. 177, l. 75.
185 TsDNI KBR, f. P-2, op. 1, d. 167, l. 5.
186 Ibid., l. 6.
187 On early work to increase Kabardian representation in industry, see TsDNI KBR, f. P-2, op. 1, d. 177, ll. 1–75.
188 Ibid., 1. 5.
189 Ibid, ll. 5, 9, and 11.

190 See for example, ibid., ll. 3, 6, 24, and 44.
191 Ibid., l. 49.
192 See for example, ibid., ll. 3, 5, 10, 14, and 20; and TsGA KBR, f. 686, op. 1, d. 474, l. 64.
193 TsDNI KBR, f. P-2, op. 1, d. 177, ll. 33, 40, and 44.
194 The entrance of Kabardians into lower-level positions is reflected in the reports contained in ibid. See also, TsDNI KBR, f. P-17, op. 1, d. 65, ll. 6–7, and 14–18; and TsDNI KBR, f. P-4, op. 1, d. 140, l. 100.
195 TsDNI KBR, f. P-1, op. 1, d. 2454, ll. 1–56.
196 TsDNI KBR, f. P-728, op. 1, d. 11, ll. 44, and 412-13; TsDNI KBR, f. P-109, op. 1, d. 83, ll. pp. 32–3; TsDNI KBR, f. P-4, op. 1, d. 140, ll. 97–110; TsDNI KBR, f. P-17, op. 1, d. 65, ll. 2–18; TsDNI KBR, f. P-112, op. 1, d. 50, ll. 12–18, and 44–6; TsDNI KBR, f. P-4, op. 1, d. 160, ll. 36–40; TsDNI KBR, f. P-112, op. 1, d. 65, ll. 55–6.
197 On successful efforts at getting officials to attend Kabardian literacy classes, see TsDNI KBR, f. 1, op. 1, d. 2454, ll. 32. 36, and 38; and TsDNI KBR, f. 112, op. 1, d. 65, l. 55.
198 See for example, TsDNI KBR, f. P-17, op. 1, d. 65, ll. 5–6.
199 TsDNI KBR, f. P-1, op. 1, d. 2324, l. 110.
200 Kh. Sabanchiev, "Sozdanie sovetskoi inteligentsii v Kabarde," *Sbornik statei po istorii Kabardy*, no. 2 (1951): 156.
201 Borov, "Deportatsiia i reabilitatsiia balkarskogo naroda," 330; TsDNI KBR, f. P-1, op. 1, d. 2324, l. 112.
202 N. V. Nartokova, *Sotsial'nye aspekty gosudarstvennoi politiki v Kabardino-Balkarii v 40-kh –nachale 60-kh godov XX veka* (Nalchik: "Elbrus," 2001), 119.
203 For an overview of nativization work from March 1948 through March 1950, see TsDNI KBR, f. P-1, op. 1, d. 2454, ll. 1–56; for a general discussion of the state of nativization in the republic by the end of 1950, see the minutes of the Twentieth Oblast Party Conference: TsDNI KBR, f. P-1, op. 1, d. 2324, ll. 14–15, 20, 23, 27, 29, 35–6, 48, 51–2, 77–9, 82–5, 94–5, 110, 112, and 115–16.
204 TsDNI KBR, f. P-1, op. 1, d. 2324, l. 86.
205 Ibid., l. 51.
206 Martin, *The Affirmative Action Empire*, 373.
207 "Usilit' rabotu po v "Usilit' rabotu po vyrashchivaniiu natsional'nykh kadrov," *Kabardinskaia pravda*, February 6, 1949, 1; "Neustanno rastit' promyshlennye natsoinal'nye kadry," *Kabardinskaia pravda*, January 25, 1952, 1;"Zabotlivo vyrashchivat' natsional'nye kadry v promyshlennosti," June 4, 1952, 2; "Preodolet' otstavanie kabardinskoi dramaturgii," *Kabardinskaia pravda*, June 15, 1952, 3; "Gotovit' natsional'nye kadry sel'skogo khoziaistva," *Kabardinskaia pravda*, September 25, 1952, 3; "Vsemerno uluchshat' podrotovku uchitelei-kabardintsev," *Kabardinskaia pravda*, September 10, 1952, 3.
208 See for example: "Perevod deloproizvodstva na kabardinskii iazyk," *Kabardinskaia pravda*, January 26, 1949, 1; "Prepodavanie russkogo iazyka v podgotovitel'nykh klassakh kabardinskikh shkol," *Kabardinskaia pravda*, February 5, 1952, 3; "Prepodavanie russkogo iazyka v kabardinskoi shkole," *Kabardinskaia pravda*, February 15, 1952, 3. "Za tvorcheskuiu aktivnost' pisatelei Kabardy," *Kabardinskaia pravda*, January 4, 1952, 2; "Natsoinal'nye talanty," *Kabardinskaia pravda*, April 1, 1952, 4; "Za dal'neishee uluchshenie raboty uchrezhdenii iskusstv Kabardy," *Kabardinskaia pravda*, June 29, 1952, 2; "Bol'she vysokoideinykh khudozhestvennykh proizvedennii!," *Kabardinskaia pravda*, March 5, 1949, 1; "Sel'skaia intelligentsia,"

Kabardinskaia pravda, February 15, 1949, 2; "Nasushchnye voprosy razvitiia kabardinskoi literatury," *Kabardinskaia pravda*, January 13, 1955, 3.
209 See for example: Kh. Berbekov, "Progressivnaia rol' russkogo naroda v istorii kabardinskogo naroda," *Kabardinskaia pravda*, August 12, 1952, 2–3; I. Muzhev, "1905 god v Kabarde," *Kabardinskaia pravda*, April 3, 1955, 3–4; T. Kumykov, "Progressivnoe znachenie dobrovol'nogo prisoedineniia Kabardy k Rossii," *Kabardinskaia pravda*, July 13, 1955, 2–3; A. Kasumov, "Proval anglo-turetskikh planov Shamilia v Kabarde," *Kabardinskaia pravda*, July 29, 1955, 2–3; and T. Kumykov, "Sovmestnaia bor'ba russkogo i kabardinskogo narodov protiv inozemnykh i vnutrennykh vragov," *Kabardinskaia pravda*, August 30, 1955, 2–3.
210 See for example, TsDNI KBR, f. 1, op. 1, d. 2324, ll. 85–6 and "V nauchno-issledovatel'skom institute," *Kabardinskaia pravda*, January 1, 1952, 3.
211 P. A. Kuz'minov, *Epokha preobrazovanii 50-70-kh godov XIX veka u narodov severnogo Kavkaza v noveishei istoriografii*. (Nalchik: Pechatnyi dvor, 2011), 68–9.
212 Borov, "Deportatsiia i reabilitatsiia balkarskogo naroda," 330.
213 Sabanchiev, *Byli soslany navechno*, 29.
214 Sabanchiev, *Balkartsy*, 128–9.
215 Sabanchiev, *Byli soslany navechno*, 48–50.
216 Sabanchiev, *Balkartsy*, 130.
217 Aslan Borov, "Kabardino-Balkarii v XX veke: istoriia i etnopolitika," *Voprosy istorii*, no. 6 (2010): 72.
218 Sabanchiev, *Byli soslany navechno*, 37.
219 Sabanchiev, *Balkartsy*, 135–6.
220 Sabanchiev, *Byli soslany navechno*, 55.
221 Ibid., 136, 166–7.
222 Maremshaova, *Balkariia i Karachai v etnokul'turnom prostranstve Kavkaza*, 79–83.
223 Sabanchiev, *Byli soslany navechno*, 74–5.
224 Sabanchiev, *Balkartsy*, 198–9.
225 Greta Uehling makes this case for the Crimean Tatars in *Beyond Memory*, 25–47.
226 Polian, *Against their Will*, 181–216.
227 Sabanchiev, *Balkartsy*, 362–6.
228 Ibid.
229 Ibid., 366.
230 Borov, "Deportatsiia i reabilitatsiia balkarskogo naroda," 316–19.
231 Ibid., 310–13.
232 T. K. Mal'bakhov i A.N. Akhokhov, "O voprosakh, sviazannykh s pereseleniem balkartsev v Kabardinskuiu ASSR: Predlozheniia rukovodstva Kabardinskoi ASSR TsK KPSS; 23 ianvaria 1957 goda," in *T.K. Mal'bakhov: Epokha bor'by i sozidaniia: Izbrannyie rechi, stat'I, pis'ma*, ed. B.Kh. Bgazhnokov (Nalchik: Izdatel'stvo M. i V. Kotliarovykh, 2007), 344.
233 Sabanchiev, *Byli soslany navechno*, 82–3.
234 TsDNI KBR, f. P-1, op. 2, d. 1105, ll. 141–4.
235 Ch. Uianaev, "Neotlozhnye zadachi balkarskhikh kolkhozov," *Kabardino-Balkarskaia pravda*, January 7, 1958, 3.
236 Sabanchiev, *Byli soslany navechno*, 83.
237 A. Sasikov, "Shire razmakh zhilishchnogo stroitel'stva v balkarskikh kolkhozakh," *Kabardino-Balkarskaia pravda*, August 21, 1957, 2; Ch. Uianaev, "Usilit' tempy stroitel'stva v balkarskikh kolkhozakh," *Kabardino-Balkarskaia pravda*, May 16, 1958, 4.

238 TsDNI KBR, f. R-774, op. 2, d. 8, ll. 44–8.
239 Ibid.
240 Borov, "Deportatsiia i reabilitatsiia balkarskogo naroda," 326–39.
241 Nicholas Werth, "The 'Chechen Problem': Handling an Awkward Legacy, 1918-1958," *Contemporary European History* 15, no. 3 (2006): 347–66.
242 Artur Tsutsiev, *Atlas etnopoliticheskoi istorii Kavkaza (1774-2004)* (Moscow: Evropa, 2007), 78–80.
243 Shnirel'man, *Byt' alanami*, 415–569.
244 Tsutsiev, *Osetino-Ingushskii konflikt.*
245 Nekrich, *The Punished Peoples*, 146–66.
246 Sabanchiev, *Byli soslany navechno*, 81.
247 See for example, Sh. Mikheev, "Druzhba bratskikh narodov," *Kabardino-Balkarskaia pravda*, April 22, 1957, 2; "Balkarskie kolkhozy gotoviatsia k vesennemu sevu," *Kabardino-Balkarskaia pravda*, March 22, 1957, 1; I. Kazmakhov, "Bystree vostanovit' ekonomiku i kulturu Balkarii," *Kabardino-Balkarskaia pravda*, April 10, 1957, 2–3; "Trudiashchiesia nashei respubliki gostepriimno vstrechaiut balkarskikh pereselentsev," *Kabardino-Balkarskaia pravda*, October 6, 1957, 1; and RGANI, f. 5, op. 32, d. 108, ll. 139–44.
248 Sabanchiev, *Byli soslany navechno*, 82.
249 RGANI, f. 5, op. 32, d. 108, l. 139.
250 Borov, "Deportatsiia i reabilitatsiia balkarskogo naroda," 310–13.
251 Zumakulov, Karov, and Beituganov, *Chas ispytanii*, 366–78, 413–16, and 467.
252 TsGA KBR, f. 774, op. 2, d. 16, l. 42.
253 Ibid., 329–32.
254 Martin, *The Affirmative Action Empire*, 21–2.
255 Martin, "The Origins of Soviet Ethnic Cleansing," 824–58.

Chapter 6

1 A. I. Tetuev, *Mezhnatsional'nye otnosheniia na Severnom Kavkaze: evoliutsiia, opyt, tendentsii* (Nalchik: El-Fa, 2006), 178–9.
2 Gardanov, *Novoe i traditsionnoe*, 64.
3 On nationalist mobilizations during perestroika, see Mark Beissinger, *Nationalist Mobilization and the Collapse of the Soviet State* (New York: Cambridge University Press, 2002).
4 Miroslav Hroch, *Social Preconditions of National Revival in Europe: A Comparative Analysis of the Social Composition of Patriotic Groups among the Smaller European Nations* (New York: Cambridge University Press, 1985).
5 Tetuev, *Mezhnatsional'nye otnosheniia na Severnom Kavkaze*, 146–52.
6 Hroch, *Social Preconditions of National Revival in Europe*, 22.
7 Georgi M. Derluguian, *Bourdieu's Secret Admirer in the Caucasus: A World-System Biography* (Chicago: University of Chicago Press, 2005), 183.
8 Hroch, *Social Preconditions of National Revival in Europe*, 23.
9 Slezkine, "The USSR as a Communal Apartment, or How a Socialist State Promoted Ethnic Particularism."
10 Shnirel'man, *Byt' alanami*, 415–569.
11 Derluguian, *Bourdieu's Secret Admirer in the Caucasus*, 206–7.

12 When the Abkhaz launched their bid for independence from Georgia, many Kabardians, who share ethnic ties with the Abkhaz, volunteered to fight on the Abkhaz side.
13 Derluguian, *Bourdieu's Secret Admirer in the Caucasus*, 238–42.
14 Hroch, *Social Preconditions of National Revival in Europe*, 23.
15 On the Western borderlands, see Weeks, *Nation and State in Late-Imperial Russia*, 152–71; On Tbilisi, see Ronald Suny, "Tiflis: Crucible of Ethnic Politics, 1860-1905," in *The City in Late Imperial Russia*, ed. Michael F. Hamm (Bloomington: Indiana University Press, 1986), 249–82; on the Nagorno-Karabagh conflict, see Ohannes Geukjian, *Ethnicity, Nationalism and Conflict in the South Caucasus: Nagorno-Karabakh and the Legacy of Soviet Nationalities Policy* (London: Routledge, 2012)
16 S. Akkieva, "Lozung natsional'nogo samoopredelenie i politicheskaia bor'ba v Kabardino-Balkarii. 1989-1996," in *Pravo narodov na samoopredelenie*, ed. A. G. Osipov (Moscow: Zven'ia, 1997), 135–6.
17 Ibid.
18 Borov, "Deportatsiia i reabilitatsiia balkarskogo naroda," 341.
19 I. L. Babich, ed., *Ethnopoliticheskaia situatsiia v Kabardino-Balkarii*, vol. 1 (Moscow: RAN Tsentr po izucheniiu mezhnatsional'nykh otnoshenii, 1994), 59–64; and vol. 2, 143–5.
20 Borov, "Deportatsiia i reabilitatsiia balkarskogo naroda," 346–7.
21 Babich, *Ethnopoliticheskaia situatsiia v Kabardino-Balkarii*, vol. 2, 183.
22 Ibid., 184.
23 Yo'av Karny, *Highlanders: A Journey to the Caucasus in Quest of Memory* (New York: Farrar, Straus and Giroux, 2000), 364.
24 Derluguian, *Bourdieu's Secret Admirer in the Caucasus*, 242; Kazenin, *Tikhie konflikty na Severnom Kavkaze*, 66.
25 Babich, *Ethnopoliticheskaia situatsiia v Kabardino-Balkarii*, vol. 2, 198; Derluguian, *Bourdieu's Secret Admirer in the Caucasus*, 211; Borov, "Deportatsiia i reabilitatsiia balkarskogo naroda," 360.
26 Tetuev, *Mezhnatsional'nye otnosheniia na Severnom Kavkaze*, 176; Babich, *Ethnopoliticheskaia situatsiia v Kabardino-Balkarii*, vol. 2, 13–14.
27 Shnirel'man, *Byt' alanami*, 123–5; Sufian Zhemukhov, "The Birth of Modern Circassian Nationalism," *Nationalities Papers* 40, no. 4 (2012): 503–24.
28 Tetuev, *Mezhnatsional'nye otnosheniia na Severnom Kavkaze*, 176.
29 Khasan Dumanov, "Pravda o granitsakh. Iz etnicheskoi istorii Kabardy i Balkarii XIX-Nach. XX vv.," *Kabardino-Balkarskaia Pravda*, December 10, 1991, 2–3.
30 Khanafi Khutuev, "Byla li granitsa?," *Sovetskaia molodezh*, February 22, 1992, 1.
31 Babich, *Ethnopoliticheskaia situatsiia v Kabardino-Balkarii*, vol. 2, 243–6.
32 See, for example, Borei, Dzagulov, and Kolesnikov, *Vymysel i istina*, 293–32.
33 Tetuev, *Mezhnatsional'nye otnosheniia na Severnom Kavkaze*, 176–7; Derluguian, *Bourdieu's Secret Admirer in the Caucasus*, 210–11.
34 Tetuev, *Mezhnatsional'nye otnosheniia na Severnom Kavkaze*, 176.
35 Ibid., 177.
36 Kazenin, *Tikhie konflikty na Severnom Kavkaze*, 71–2.
37 Tetuev, *Mezhnatsional'nye otnosheniia na Severnom Kavkaze*, 177.
38 Ibid.
39 Ibid., 178–9.
40 *Kabardino-Balkarskaia pravda*, November 23, 1996. Quoted in ibid., 179.

41 Beppaev quoted from the author's personal archive in I. L. Babich, "Severnyi Kavkaz: problema 'gosudarstvennosti' v deiatel'notsi natsional'nykh, islamskikh i politicheskikh dvizhenii," *Tsentral'naia Aziia i Kavkaz* 42, no. 6 (2005): 71.
42 Ibid.
43 Kazenin, *Tikhie konflikty na Severnom Kavkaze*, 75.
44 Shnirel'man, *Byt' alanami*, 144.
45 Kazenin, *Tikhie konflikty na Severnom Kavkaze*, 122–31.
46 Ibid., 116–20.
47 On Kabardino-Balkaria's Cossack movements and their 1990s revival, see, Karny, *Highlanders*, 25–47.
48 Tetuev, *Mezhnatsional'nye otnosheniia na Severnom Kavkaze*, 306.
49 Tsutsiev, *Osetino-Ingushskii konflikt*, 71.
50 Polian, *Against Their Will*, 200.
51 Ibid., 227.
52 Tsutsiev, *Osetino-Ingushskii konflikt*, 80–1.
53 Tetuev, *Mezhnatsional'nye otnosheniia na Severnom Kavkaze*, 148–9.
54 Tsutsiev, *Osetino-Ingushskii konflikt*, 156–61.
55 Shnirel'man, *Byt' alanami*, 122.
56 Polian, *Against Their Will*, 229.
57 For sense of the variety of extant scholarship on the Chechen conflict, see Richard Sakwa, ed., *Chechnya from Past to Future* (London: Anthem Press, 2005).
58 M. M. Ibragimov, "Ob osobennostiakh krizisa v Chechenskoi Respublike v 1990-e gody," in *Chechenskaia Respublika i chechentsy: istoriia i sovremennost'*, eds. Kh. I. Ibragimov et al. (Moscow: Nauka, 2006), 373
59 Derluguian, *Bourdieu's Secret Admirer in the Caucasus*, 248–51.
60 On the humanitarian catastrophes of the Chechen Wars, see Anna Politkovskaya, *A Dirty War: A Russian Reporter in Chechnya* (London: Harvill, 2001) and idem., *A Small Corner of Hell: Dispatches from Chechnya* (Chicago: University of Chicago Press, 2003).
61 Derluguian, *Bourdieu's Secret Admirer in the Caucasus*, 261.
62 Suny focuses on these connections between class and ethnicity. See, *Revenge of the Past*, 29. Donald Horowitz, harkening back to Karl Deutsch, highlights problems of uneven socioeconomic modernization among ethnic groups as a cause of ethnic conflict. Horowitz, *Ethnic Groups in Conflict*, 99–135.
63 Derluguian, *Bourdieu's Secret Admirer in the Caucasus*, 261.
64 Ibid.
65 TsDNI KBR, f. 1, op.1, d. 1816, ll. 369–70.
66 Suny, *Revenge of the Past*, 118–19.
67 Bgazhnokov, *T.K. Mal'bakhov: epokha bor'by i sozidaniia*.
68 Derluguian, *Bourdieu's Secret Admirer in the Caucasus*, 262.
69 Horowitz, *Ethnic Groups in Conflict*, 166–7.
70 Kabardians and Balkars residing in villages retained their traditional social institutions and cultural practices to a far greater extent than those residing in urban areas. See Gardanov, *Novoe i traditsionnoe, passim*.
71 Gardanov, *Novoe i traditsionnoe*.
72 Kabardino-Balkarskoe statisticheskoe biuro, *Kratskii statisticheskii sbornik Kabardino-Balkarskoi Avtonomnoi Oblasti* (Nalchik: Kabardino-Balkarskoe statisticheskii biuro, 1925), 47.
73 Gardanov, *Novoe i traditsionnoe*, 53.

74 Kabardino-Balkarskoe statisticheskoe biuro, 25.
75 Gosudarstvennyi komitet SSSR po statistike, *Itogi vsesoiuznoi perepisi naseleniia 1979 goda.*, vol. 4, section 2 (Moscow: Informatsionno-izdatel'skii tsentr, 1989-1990), 79-82, 113-15; Gosudarstvennyi komitet SSSR po statistike, *Itogi vsesoiuznoi perepisi naseleniia 1989 goda*, vol. 7, section 3, 235, 319. Kabardino-Balkarskoe respublikanskoe upravlenie statistiki, *Narodnoe khoziaistvo KBSSR v 1990 g.* (Nalchik: Kabardino-Balkarskoe respublikanskoe upravlenie statistiki, 1991), 54.
76 Ibid.
77 On the results of the Balkarization campaign from 1957 to 1963, see TsDNI KBR, f. 1, op. 2, d. 1677, ll. 1-12.
78 Gardanov ed., *Novoe i traditsionnoe*, 52.
79 Kabardino-Balkarskoe respublikanskoe upravlenie statistiki, 51.
80 Ibid., 234.
81 S. A. Arutiunov, Ia. S. Smirnova, and G. A. Sergeeva, *Etnokul'turnaia situatsiia v karachaevo-cherkesskoi avtonomnoi oblasti* (Moscow: Institut etnologii i antropologii AN SSSR, 1990), 2.
82 I. M. Shabanov, B. A. Tambieva, and L. O. Abrekova, *Nakazany po natsional'nomu prizaku* (Cherkessk: Karachaevo-Cherkesskii Filial Moskovskogo Otkrytogo Sotsial'nogo Universiteta, 1999), 40-1.
83 Artiunov, Smirnova, and Sergeeva, *Etnokul'turnaia situatsiia*, 9.
84 M. I. Alkhazurov, "Obrazovanie i sotsial'no-ekonoichskoe razvitie ChIASSR," in *Chechenskaia Respublika i chechentsy*, 316.
85 V. A. Tishkov, *Obshchestvo v vooruzhennom konflikte: ethnografiia chechenskoi voiny* (Moscow: Nauka, 2001), 116.
86 Ibragimov, "Ob osobennostiakh krizisa v Chechenskoi Respublike v 1990-e gody," 369-70.
87 M. P. Ovkhadov, "Obrazovatel'nye i iazykovye problem natsional'noi politiki sovetskogo perioda v Chechenskoi Respublike," in *Chechenskaia Respublika i chechentsy*, 354.
88 Statisticheskoe upravelnie Checheno-Ingushskoi ASSR, *Narodnoe khoziastvo Checheno-Ingushskoi ASSR za 1966-1970* (Groznyi: Checheno-Ingushkoe knizhnoe izdatel'stvo, 1971), 92.
89 Gosudarstvennyi komitet SSSR po statistike, *Itogi vsesoiuznoi perepisi naseleniia 1989 goda*, vol. 7, part 3, 235, 319.
90 Ovkhadov, "Obrazovatel'nye i iazykovye," 353-4.
91 Ibragimov, "Ob osobennostiakh krizisa v Chechenskoi Respublike v 1990-e gody," 371.
92 Ibid.
93 Polian, *Against Their Will*, 225-7.
94 Sabanchiev, *Byli soslany navechno*, 96.
95 Sabanchiev, *Balkartsy*, 415-17.
96 Babich, *Etnopoliticheskaia situatsiia v Kabardino-Balkarii*, vol. 2, 175-7.
97 Shnirel'man, *Byt' alanami*, 127-8.
98 Tetuev, *Mezhnatsional'nye otnosheniia na Severnom Kavkaze*, 179-80.
99 Sabanchiev, *Balkartsy*, 410-11.
100 Ibid., 425.
101 Borov, "Deportatsiia i reabilitatsiia," 364; Sabanchiev, *Byli soslany navechno*, 99-101.
102 Karov, *Administrativno-territorial'nye preobrazovaniia*, 556.

103 Kazenin, *Tikhie konflikty na Severnom Kavkaze*, 71.
104 Ibid., 90–104.
105 Ibid., 77.
106 Ibid., 84–97.
107 Bugai, *Severnyi Kavkaz. Gosudarstvennoe stroitel'stvo*, 153–66.
108 Kazenin, *Tikhie konflikty na Severnom Kavkaze*, 116.
109 Shamanov, Tambieva, Abrekova, *Nakazany po natsional'nomu prizaku*, 38–41.
110 Shnirel'man, *Byt' alanami*, 457.
111 Karny, *Highlanders*, 363.
112 Dzamikhov and Kumakhov, "O stanovlenii Kabardino-Balkarskoi Avtonomnoi Oblast," 261–8.
113 Derluguian, *Bourdieu's Secret Admirer in the Caucasus*, 209.
114 Ibid., 211.
115 On the collapse of cattle breeding in the Kabardian ASSR after the Balkar deportations, see TsDNI KBR, f. 1, op. 1, d. 1203, l. 80.
116 Quoted in Bugai, *Severnyi Kavkaz. Gosudarstvennoe stroitel'stvo*, 158–9.
117 Ibid., 161.
118 Tsutsiev, *Osetino-Ingushskii konflikt*, 28–79.
119 B. B. Zakriev, "K istorii rossiisko-chechenskikh otnoshenii poslednei threti XVIII veka," in *Chechenskaia Respublika i chechentsy*, 254–61.
120 Bobrovnikov and Babich, *Severnyi Kavkaz v sostave Rossiiskoi Imperii*, 95–100, 113–23, 143–50.
121 Z. A. Zakhiraev, "Razvitie Groznenskogo neftenosnogo raiona v 1916-1921 godakh," in *Chechenskaia Respublika i chechentsy*, 288–92.
122 Perović, *From Conquest to Deportation*, 185; Marshall, *The Caucasus under Soviet Rule*, 164.
123 T. U. El'buzdukaeva, "Promyshlennoe razvitie Chechni v 20-30-e gody XX veka," in ibid., 295–300.
124 V. K. Gardanov, *Kul'tura i byt narodov Severnogo Kavkaza (1917-1967 goda)* (Moscow: Nauka, 1968), 76–86.
125 Kazenin, *Tikhie konflikty na Severnom Kavkaze*.
126 On Kabardian-Balkar tensions and the historiography on land relations in the Central Caucasus, see my article, "Historiography and the Politics of Land, Identity, and Belonging in the Twentieth-Century North Caucasus," *Nationalities Papers* 44, no. 4 (July 2016): 503–21.
127 Kazenin, *Tikhie konflikty na Severnom Kavkaze*, 99–102.
128 For the official interpretation, see Unezhev, *Istoriia Kabardy i Balkarii*, 147–51.
129 In his 1847 classic *Istoriia adykheiskogo naroda*, which is based on oral histories, Shora Nogmov, the first Kabardian historian, glorifies the Kabardian victory in the Battle of Mount Kanzhal. Sh. B. Nogmov, *Istoriia adykheiskogo naroda, sostavlennaia po predaniiam kabardintsev* (Nalchik: Elbrus, 1994), 146–7.
130 See, for example, B. Kh. Bgazhnokov, ed., *Kanzhal'skaia bitva i politicheskaia istoriia Kabardy pervoi poloviny XVIII veka: issledovaniia i materialy* (Nalchik: Izd. M. i V. Kotliarovykh, 2008).
131 Zhemukhov, "The Birth of Modern Circassian Nationalism," 503–24.
132 B. Kh. Bgazhnokov, "Istoricheskoe znachenie Kanzhal'skoi bitvy," in *Kanzhal'skaia bitva*, 9–50.
133 S. P. Kermenchiev and M. L. Golemba, *Mif o kanzhal'skoi bitve* (Piatigorsk: S. Kermenchiev and M. Golemba, 2008).

134 Kazenin, *Tikhie konflikty na Severnom Kavkaze*, 100.
135 Polina Eremenko, "Kabardintsy i balkartsy possorilis' iz-za bitvy 1708 goda, kotoroi, vozmozhno, ne bylo. Est' zaderzhannye, omonovtsu prolomili golovu." *Meduza*, last modified September 20, 2018, https://meduza.io/feature/2018/09/20/kabardintsy-i-balkartsy-possorilis-iz-za-bitvy-1708-goda-kotoroy-vozmozhno-ne-bylo-est-zaderzhannye-omonovtsu-prolomili-golovu.
136 Brubaker et al., *Nationalist Politics and Everyday Ethnicity*, 168.

Conclusion

1 See, for example, the official high school history textbook approved by the Kabardino-Balkar Ministry of Culture and edited by a duo of the most senior Kabardian and Balkar historians in the republic. T. Kh. Kumykov and I. M. Miziev eds., *Isotriia Kabardino-Balkarii* (Nalchik: Elbrus, 1997).
2 For the historical narrative of the Karachai-Balkar opposition, see the website of the organization "Alan" http://real-alania.narod.ru/; For the pan-Circassian narrative see http://www.aheku.org/.
3 Miller, "Between Local and Inter-Imperial."
4 Breyfogle. "Enduring Imperium," 92–101.
5 Ibid., 74–5.
6 Beituganov, *Kabarda: Istoriia istoriia i familii*, 617–26.
7 Karov, *Administrativno-territorial'nye preobrazovaniia*, 589.
8 T. K. Mal'bakhov, "Ob uveleichenii plana zhilishchnogo stroitel'stva v gorode Nal'chike: Pis'mo v Sovet Ministrov SSSR A.I. Mikoianu, 5 fevralia 1958 goda," in *T.K. Mal'bakhov: Epokha bor'by i sozidaniia*, 344.
9 A. M. Khatukhov and F. Zh. Berova, "Ocobennosti rasselenie naseleniia i stanovleniia sovremennoi etnicheskoi karty KBR," *Izvestiia Kabardino-Balkarskogo nauchnogo tsentra RAN* 86, no. 6 (2018): 191–2.
10 "Sovremennoe rasselenie balkartsev," ASSIA.INFO, Fond "Assiia," 2015, http://assia.info/history/iiau/sovremennoe-rasselenie-balkartsev.html.

Bibliography

Archives

Gosudarstvennyi Arkhiv Rossiiskoi Federatsii (Moscow)

- *Administrativnaia komissiia pri Prezidiume Vserossiiskogo Tsentral'nogo Ispolnitel'nogo Komiteta. (fond 5677)*
- *Sovet Narodnykh Komissarov RSFSR. (fond 130)*
- *Narodnyi komissariat po delam natsionat'nostei RSFSR (fond 1318)*
- *Narodnyi komissariat raboche-krest'ianskoi inspektsii RSFSR (fond A-406)*
- *Vserossiiskii Tsentral'nyi Ispolnitel'nyi Komitet Sovetov Rabochikh, Krest'ianskikh deputatov RSFSR (fond 1235)*
- *Osobaia kollegiia vyshego kontrolia po zemel'nym sporam pri Prezidiume Vserossiiskogo Tsentral'nogo Ispolnitel'nogo Komiteta (fond 5201)*
- *Tsentral'nyi Ispolnitel'nyi Komitet SSSR (fond 3316)*
- *Gosudarstvennyi komitet RSFSR po statistike (fond A-374)*
- *Ministerstvo Prosveshcheniia RSFSR (fond A-2306)*
- *Sovet Ministrov RSFSR (fond A-259)*

Rossiiskii Gosudarstvennyi Arkhiv Noveishei Istorii (Moscow)

- *Apparat TsK KPSS (1949-1991 gg.) (fond 5)*
- *Komitet partniinogo kontrolia pri TsK KPSS (1934-1990 gg.) (fond 6)*

Rossiiskii Gosudarstvennyi Arkhiv Sotsial'no-Politicheskoi Istorii (Moscow)

- *Kavkazskoe biuro TsK RKP(b), 1920-1922 (fond 64)*
- *Iugo-Vostochnoe biuro TsK RKP(b), 1921-1924 (fond 65)*
- *Stalin (nast. Dzhugashvili) Iosif Vissarionovich, 1878-1953 (fond 558)*
- *Tsentral'nyi Komitet KPSS (fond 17)*

Tsentral'nyi Gosudarstvennyi Arkhiv Kabardino-Balkarskoi Respubliki (Nalchik)

- *Ispolnitel'nyi komitet Kabardino-Balkarskogo oblastnogo soveta rabochikh, krest'ianskikh i krasnoarmeiskikh deputatov (fond 2)*
- *Predstavitel'stvo Kabardino-Balkarskoi Avtonomnoi Oblasti pri Narodnom Komissariate po delam Natsional'nostei (fond 8)*
- *Territorial'noe proizvodstvennoe ob''edinenie mestnoi promyshlennosti (fond 686)*

- *Nizhne-Akbashkii sel'skii sovet (fond 575)*
- *Chegemskii raionnyi ispolnitel'nyi komitet (fond 574)*
- *El'brusskii raionnyi ispolnitel'nyi komitet (fond 585)*
- *Nagornyi raionnyi ispolnitel'nyi komitet (fond 199)*
- *Dokumenty po istorii balkarskogo naroda (fond R-774)*

Tsentr Dokumentatsii Noveishei Isotrii Kabardino-Balkarskoi Respubliki (Nalchik)

- *Kabardino-Balkarskii Oblastnoi Komiteta Kommunisticheskoi partii RSFSR, 1921-1991 (fond P-1)*
- *Komissiia po sobiraniiu i izucheniiu materialov po istorii Komunisticheskoi partii i Oktiabr'skoi revoliutsii Kabardino-Balkarskogo obkoma VKP(b) (fond P-25)*
- *Urozhainenskii raionnyi komitet KPSS (fond P-112)*
- *Primalkimskii raionnyi komitet KPSS (fond P-13)*
- *Kubinskii raionnyi komitet KPSS (fond P-9)*
- *Terskii raionnyi komitet KPSS (fond P-4)*
- *Sovetskii raionnyi komitet KPSS (fond P-109)*
- *Baksanskii raionnyi komitet KPSS (fond P-78)*
- *Nalchikskii gorodskoi komitet KPSS (fond P-2)*
- *Nagornyi raionnyi komitet KPSS (fond P-17)*

Newspapers and Periodicals

Baksan-Stroi (Baksan-GES)
Kabardino-Balkarskaia pravda (Nalchik)
Karakhalk (Nalchik)
Krasnaia Kabarda (Nalchik)
Leninskii put' (Nalchik)
Pravda (Moscow)
Sbornik svedenii o kavkazskikh gortsakh (Tiflis)
Sotsialisticheskaia Kabardino-Balkariia (Nalchik)
Sovetskaia molodezh' (Nalchik)
Tëre: Balkarskii forum (Nalchik)
Terskii sbornik (Tiflis)
Zhizn' natsional'nostei (Moscow)

Published Document Collections and Memoirs

Alieva, Svetlana, ed. *Tak eto bylo: natsional'nye repressii v SSSR 1919–1952 gody*. 3 vols. Moscow: Rossiiskii mezhdunarodnyi fond kul'tury, 1993.
Babich, I. L., ed. *Etnopoliticheskaia situatsiia v Kabardino-Balkarii*. 2 vols. Moscow: RAN Tsentr po izucheniiu mezhnatsional'nykh otnoshenii, 1994.
Berzhe, A. P., ed. *Akty sobrannye kavkazskoi arkheograficheskoi kommissiei (AKAK)*. 12 vols. Tiflis, 1866–1904.

Bliev, M. M., ed. *Russko-Osetinskie otnosheniia v XVIII veke.* 2 vols. Ordzhonikidze: Ir, 1984.
Bugai, N. F., and A. M. Gonov. "*Po resheniiu pravitel'stva Soiuza SSR*": *Deportatsiia narodov: dokumenty i materialy.* Nalchik: El-Fa, 2003.
Butkov, P. G. *Materialy dlia novoi istorii Kavkaza s 1722 po 1803 god.* 3 vols. St. Petersburg: Akademiia Nauk, 1869.
Dumanov, Kh. M., ed. *Territoriia i rasselenie kabardinstev i balkartsev v XVIII-nachale XX vekov: sbornik dokumentov.* Nalchik: Nart, 1993.
Dumanov, Kh. M., ed. *Iz dokumental'noi istorii Kabardino-Russkikh otnoshenii: vtoraia polovina XVIII – pervaia polovina XIX v.* Nalchik: Elbrus, 2000.
Dzhanaev, A. K., ed. *S"ezdy narodov Tereka.* 2 vols. Ordzhonikidze: Ir, 1977–1978.
Dzuev, G. K., ed. *Bez prava na obzhalovanie: dokumental'nye ocherki po materialam ChK, GPU, NKVD, KGB, FSB 1920–1940 gg.* Nalchik: Elbrus, 2012.
Fedorov, V. A., ed. *Zapiski A.P. Ermolova.* Moscow: Vysshaia Shkola, 1991.
Gugov, R. Kh., U. A. Uligov, L. B. Tatarokova, D. V. Shabaev, comps., C. R. Babaev, Zh. Zh. Zalikhanov, K. N. Kerefov, E. T. Kesheva, V. P. Krikunov, and T. Kh. Kumykov, eds. *Za vlast' sovetov v Kabarde i Balkarii.* Nalchik: Kabardino-Balkarskoe Knizhnoe Izdatel'stvo, 1957.
Gugov, R. Kh., U. A. Uligov, L. B. Tatarokova, D. V. Shabaev, comps., C. R. Babaev, Zh. Zh. Zalikhanov, K. N. Kerefov, E. T. Kesheva, V. P. Krikunov, T. Kh. Kumykov, and B. M. Zumakulov. *Dokumenty po istorii bor'by za Sovetskuiu vlast' i obrazovaniia avtonomii Kabardino-Balkarii, 1917-1922 gg.* Nalchik: Elbrus, 1983.
Güldenstädt, I. A. *Puteshestvie po kavkazu v 1770–1773 gg.* St. Petersburg: Peterburgskoe Vostokovedenie, 2002.
Iuzefovich, T., ed. *Dogovory Rossii s vostokom: politicheskie i torgovye.* St. Petersburg: Tipografiia O.I. Baksta, 1869.
Karov, A. Kh., ed. *Administrativno-territorial'nye preobrazovaniia v Kabardino-Balkarii: istoriia i sovremennost'.* Nalchik: El-Fa, 2000.
Kesheva, Z. M., ed. *Dokumenty po istorii adygov 20–50-kh godov XIX v.* Nalchik: Institut gumanitarnykh issledovanii, 2011.
Kokiev, G. A., ed. *Krest'ianskaia reforma v Severnoi Osetii.* Ordzhonikidze: Gos. Izdatel'stvo Severo-Osetinskoi ASSR, 1940.
Kotliarova, M. A., and V. N. Kotliarov, eds. *Balkariia: deportatsiia. svidetel'stvuiut ochevidtsy.* 2 vols. Nalchik: Poligrafservis i T, 2004.
Kumykov, T. Kh., and E. N. Kushova, eds. *Kabardino-Russkie otnosheniia v XVI-XVIII vv.* 2 vols. Moscow: Akademiia Nauk SSSR, 1957.
Kuz'minov, P. A., ed. *Agrarnye otnosheniia u narodov severnogo kavkaza v rossiiskoi politike XVIII-nachala XX veka.* 2 vols. Nalchik: El-Fa, 2008.
Kuz'minov, P. A., and B. Mal'bakhov, comps., V. D. Dzidzoev and M. P. Mokhnacheva, eds. *Narody Tsentral'nogo Kavkaza v 40-kh—nachale 60-kh godov XIX v.: sbornik dokumental'nykh material'ov.* 2 vols. Moscow: Pomatur, 2005.
Mambetov, G. Kh., ed. *Istoriia Kabardino-Balkarii v trudakh G.A. Kokieva: Sbornik statei i dokumentov.* Nalchik: El-Fa, 2005.
Nevskaia, V. P., I. M. Shamanov, S. P. Nesmachnaia, comps., P. A. Shatskii, and S. P. Shatskaia eds. *Sotsial'no-ekonomicheskoe, politicheskoe i kul'turnoe razvitie narodov Karachaevo-Cherkesii, 1790–1917: sbornik dokumentov.* Rostov-na-Donu: Izd-vo Rostovskogo universiteta, 1985.
Pallas, Peter Simon. *Travels Through the Southern Provinces of the Russian Empire in the Years 1793 and 1794.* London: Longman and Rees, 1802.

Potto, Vasilii. *Kavkazskaia voina v otdel'nykh ocherkakh, epizodakh, legendakh, i biografiiakh*. 2 vols. St. Petersburg: V.A. Berezovskogo, 1887.
Sabanchiev, Kh.-M. A., ed. *Balkartsy: vyselenie i vozvrashchenie*. Nalchik: Elbrus, 2008.
Temukuev, B. B., ed. *Sem' dnei odnogo veka: 27 noiabria--5 dekabria 1942 goda: v dokumentakh 1943 g*. Nalchik: Poligrafservis i T, 2004.
Tiutiunina, E. S. *Grani regional'noi istorii XIX-XX vekov: mnogonatsional'naia Kabardino-Balkariia i ee sosedi (stat'i i dokumenty)*. Nalchik: Izdatel'stvo M. i V. Kotliarovykh, 2008.
von Klaproth, Julius. *Travels in the Caucasus and Georgia Performed in the Years 1807 and 1808 by Command of the Russian Government*. London: British and Foreign Public Library, 1814.
Zumakulov, B. M., A. Kh. Karov, and S. A. Beituganov, eds. *Chas ispytanii: deportatsiia, reabilitatsiia, i vozrozhdenie balkarskogo naroda (dokumenty, materialy)*. Nalchik: Elbrus, 2001.

Secondary Sources

Abaev, A. Kh. "Z.D. Kumekhov: Pervyi secretar' Kabardino-Balkarskogo obkoma VKP(b), 1939-1944 (k stoletiiu so dnia rozhdeniia)." *Arkhivy i obshchestvo*, no. 15 (2010): 200-10.
Abaev, Misost. "Balkariia." *Musul'manin* 4-17 (1911): 586-627.
Abaeva, F. V. *Umar Aliev: prosvetitel'skaia, pedagogicheskaia i obshchestvennaia deiatel'nost'*. Maikop: Adgyeia, 1995.
Ailarova, S. A. "D.S. Kodzokov v 30-70 gg. XIX veka: prosvetitel', reformator, khoziaistvennik." *Izvestiia SOIGSI* 40, no. 1 (2007): 85-100.
Akiev, A. K., S. N. Varshavskii, and P. D. Golubev. "Osnovnye zadachi po izucheniiu faktorov prirodnoi ochagovosti chumy v Tsentral'nom Kavkaze." *Problemy osobo opasnykh infektsii* 2, no. 30 (1974): 5-12.
Akkieva, S. I. "Lozung natsional'nogo samoopredelenie i politicheskaia bor'ba v Kabardino-Balkarii. 1989-1996." In *Pravo narodov na samoopredelenie*, ed. A. G. Osipov, 130-7. Moscow: Zven'ia, 1997.
Alkhazurov, M. I. "Obrazovanie i sotsial'no-ekonoichskoe razvitie ChIASSR." In *Chechenskaia Respublika i chechentsy: istoriia i sovremennost'*, eds. Kh. I. Ibragimov, A. D. Osmaev, M. Ia. Ustinova, and V. A. Tishkov, 313-17. Moscow: Nauka, 2005.
Aloev, T. Kh. "Istoricheskie predposylki vozniknoveniia migratsionnogo dvizheniia v Kabarde vo vtoroi polovine XVIII veka." *Istoricheskii vestnik KBIGI*, no. 3 (2006): 248-57.
Aloev, T. Kh. "Vopros o zakubanskikh territoriiakh Kabardy v kontekste migratsii kabardintsev v pervoi chetverti XIX veka." *Istoricheskii vestnik KBIGI*, no. 3 (2006): 258-70.
Arutiunov, S. A., Ia. S. Smirnova, and G. A. Sergeeva, *Etnokul'turnaia situatsiia v karachaevo-cherkesskoi avtonomnoi oblasti*. Moscow: Institut etnologii i antropologii AN SSSR, 1990.
Asanov, Iurii. *Otkuda est' poshla Zemlia Kabardinskaia. Chto oznachaet nazvanie Kabarda, i kto v nei pervym kniazhil?* Nalchik: Pechatnyi dvor, 2012.
Atskanov, M. Kh. *Ekonomicheskie otnosheniia i ekonomicheskie vzgliady v Kabarde i Balkarii (1860-1917 gg.)*. Nalchik: Kabardino-Balkarskoe knizhnoe izdatel'stvo, 1967.

Azamatov, K. G., M. O. Termirzhanov, B. B. Temkuev, A. I. Tetuev, and I. M. Chechenov. *Cherekskaia tragediia*. Nalchik: Elbrus, 1994.
Babich, I. L., and V. V. Stepanov. *Istoricheskaia dinamika etnicheskoi karty Kabardino-Balkarii*. Moscow: Institut etnologii i antropologii im. Miklukho-Maklaia RAN, 2009.
Baddeley, John F. *The Russian Conquest of the Caucasus*. London: Longmans, Green and Co., 1908.
Barazbiev, M. I. *Etnokul'turnye sviazi balkartsev i karachaevtsev s narodami kavkaza v XVIII—nachale XX veka*. Nalchik: Elbrus, 2000.
Barazbiev, M. I. "Traditsionnye formy mezhetnicheskikh otnoshenii balkartsev i karachaevtsev s kabardintsami." *Respublika: Al'manakh sotsial'no-politicheskikh i pravovikh issledovanii*, no. 1 (2000): 48–70.
Barrett, Thomas M. *At the Edge of Empire: The Terek Cossacks and the North Caucasus Frontier, 1700–1860*. Boulder: Westview Press, 1999.
Bashiev, A. M. "K isotrii obrazovaniia karachaevskogo *aula* Khasaut." In *Materialy mezhdunarodnoi iubileinoi konferentsii "Rossiia i Kavkaz"; posviashchennoi 235-letiiu prisoedineniia Osetii k Rossii*, ed. Z. V. Kanukova, 40–7. Vladikavkaz: IPO SOIGSI, 2010.
Bashiev, A. M. "Rod Chipchikovykh v Karachae (na Khasaute)." *Genealogiia narodov Severnogo Kavkaza: traditsii i sovremennost*, no. 2 (2010): 66–77.
Bauman, Zygmunt. *Modernity and the Holocaust*. Ithaca: Cornell University Press, 1989.
Begeulov, R. M. *Tsentral'nyi Kavkaz v XVII–pervoi chetverti XIX veka: ocherki etnopoliticheskoi istorii*. Karachaevsk: Karachaevo-Cherkesskii Gosudarstvennyi Universitet, 2005.
Beissinger, Mark. *Nationalist Mobilization and the Collapse of the Soviet State*. New York: Cambridge University Press, 2002.
Beituganov, S. N. *Kabardinskie familii: Istoki i sud'by*. Nalchik: Elbrus, 1990.
Beituganov, S. N. *Ermolov i Kabarda: Ocherki istorii*. Nalchik: Elbrus, 1993.
Beituganov, S. N. *Kabarda: Istoriia i familii*. Nalchik: Elbrus, 2007.
Bennigsen-Broxup, Marie, ed. *The North Caucasus Barrier: The Russian Advance Toward the Muslim World*. New York: St. Martin's Press, 1992.
Benton, Lauren. and Richard J. Ross, eds. *Legal Pluralism and Empires, 1500–1850*. New York: New York University Press, 2013.
Berozov, B. P. *Pereselenie osetin s gor na ploskost' v XVIII – XX vekakh*. Ordzhonikidze: Ir, 1980.
Beslaneev, B. S. *Malaia Kabarda (XIII—Nachalo XX Veka)*. Nalchik: Elbrus, 1995.
Bezugol'nyi, A. M. *Narody Kavkaza i Krasnaia Armiia, 1918–1945*. Moscow: Veche, 2007.
Bgazhnokov, B. Kh., ed. *Kanzhal'skaia bitva i politicheskaia istoriia Kabardy pervoi poloviny XVIII veka: issledovaniia i materialy*. Nalchik: Izd. M. i V. Kotliarovykh, 2008.
Bgazhnokov, B. Kh., ed. *T.K. Mal'bakhov: Epokha bor'by i sozidaniia: Izbrannye rechi, stat'i, i pis'ma*. Nalchik: Izdatel'stvo M. i V. Kotliarovykh, 2007.
Blanch, Lesley. *The Sabres of Paradise*. London: John Murray, 1960.
Blitstein, Peter. "Stalin's Nations: Soviet Nationality Policy between Planning and Primordialism, 1936–1953." Ph.d. diss., University of California-Berkeley, 1999.
Blitstein, Peter. "Cultural Diversity and the Interwar Conjuncture: Soviet Nationality Policy in Its Comparative Context." *Slavic Review* 65, no. 2 (Summer 2006): 273–93.
Bobrovnikov, V. O. *Musul'mane Severnogo Kavkaza: obychai, pravo, nasilie*. Moscow: Vostochnaia literature RAN, 2002.
Bobrovnikov, V. O., and I. L. Babich, eds. *Severnyi Kavkaz v sostave Rossiiskoi Imperii*. Moscow: Novoe Literaturnoe Obozrenie, 2007.
Borei, I. M., R. K. Dzagulov, and M. F. Kolesnikov, eds. *Vymysel i istina*. Piatigorsk: RIA-KMV, 2010.

Borov, A. Kh. "Deportatsiia i reabilitatsiia balkarskogo naroda kak problema obshchestvenno-politicheskoi zhizni Kabardino-Balkarii." *Istoricheskii vestnik Instituta gumanitarnykh issledovanii pravitel'stva Kabardino-Balkarskoi Respubliki*, no. 4 (2006): 295–389.

Borov, A. Kh. "Kabardino-Balkarii v XX veke: istoriia i etnopolitika." *Voprosy istorii*, no. 6 (2010): 65–76.

Brass, Paul. *Theft of an Idol: Text and Context in the Representation of Collective Violence*. Princeton: Princeton University Press, 1997.

Breyfogle, Nicholas . "Enduring Imperium: Russia/Soviet Union/Eurasia as Multiethnic, Multiconfessional Space." *Ab Imperio*, no. 1 (2008): 75–129.

Brower, Daniel R., and Edward J. Lazzerini, eds. *Russia's Orient: Imperial Borderlands and Peoples, 1700–1917*. Bloomington: Indiana University Press, 1997.

Brown, Kate. *Biography of No Place: From Ethnic Borderland to Soviet Heartland*. Cambridge, MA: Harvard University Press, 2004.

Brubaker, Rogers. *Ethnicity Without Groups*. Cambridge, MA: Harvard University Press, 2004.

Brubaker, Rogers, and David D. Laitin. "Ethnic and Nationalist Violence." *Annual Review of Sociology* 24, no. 1 (1998): 423–52.

Brubaker, Rogers, Margit Feischmidt, Jon Fox, and Liana Grancea. *Nationalist Politics and Everyday Ethnicity in a Transylvanian Town*. Princeton: Princeton University Press, 2006.

Bugai, N. F. *The Deportation of Peoples in the Soviet Union*. New York: Nova Science Publishers, 1996.

Bugai, N. F. *Severnyi Kavkaz. Gosudarstvennoe stroitel'stvo i federativnye otnosheniia: proshloe v nastoiashchem*. Moscow: Grif i K, 2011.

Bugai, N. F., and A. M. Gonov. *Kavkaz: Narody v eshelonakh (20–60-e gody)*. Moscow: Insan, 1998.

Buraev, R. A., and L. Z. Emuzova. *Geografiia Kabardino-Balkarskoi Respubliki*. Nalchik: Kniga, 1998.

Burbank, Jane, and Frederick Cooper. *Empires in World History: Power and the Politics of Difference*. Oxford: Oxford University Press, 2010.

Burda, E. V. "Sooruzhenie Rostovo-Vladikavkazskoi zheleznoi dorogi i poiavlenie stantsii 'Kotliarevskoi' i pristantsionnogo poselka 'Prishibskogo.'" *Arkhivy i obshchestvo*, no. 22 (2012): 55–7.

Christoff, Peter K. *A.S. Xomjakov*. Princeton: Princeton University Press, 1961.

Conquest, Robert. *The Nation Killers: The Soviet Deportation of Nationalities*. London: Macmillan, 1970.

Crews, Robert D. *For Prophet and Tsar: Islam and Empire in Russia and Central Asia*. Cambridge, MA: Harvard University Press, 2006.

Datsiev, Abas. *Kizliar-name: istoriia tersko-kumskykh kumykov*. Makhachkala, 2004.

Derluguian, Georgi M. *Bourdieu's Secret Admirer in the Caucasus: A World-System Biography*. Chicago: University of Chicago Press, 2005.

Deutsch, Karl W. *Nationalism and Social Communication: An Inquiry into the Foundations of Nationality*, 2nd ed. Cambridge, MA: MIT Press, 1966.

Dragostinova, Theodora. "Speaking National: Nationalizing the Greeks of Bulgaria, 1900 –1939." *Slavic Review* 67, no. 1 (Spring 2008): 154–81.

Dumanov, Kh. M. "Zemlevladenie i zemel'no-ierarkhicheskoe pravo v Kabarde v pervoi polovine XIX v." In *Aktual'nye problemy feodal'noi Kabardy i Balkarii*, ed. K. F. Dzamikhov, 100–27. Nalchik: Kabardino-Balkarskii NII istorii, filologii i ekonomiki, 1992.

Dumanov, Kh. M. "Da, byla granitsa!" In *Vymysel i istina*, eds. I. M. Borei, R. K. Dzagulov, and M. F. Kolesnikov, 304–12. Piatigorsk: RIA-KMV, 2010.

Dumanov, Kh. M., A. Kh. Borov, V. Kh. Kazharov, and D. N. Prasolov, eds. *Zemel'nye otnosheniia v Kabarde i Balkarii: Istoriia i sovremennost': Materialy nauch.-prakt. konf. (11 avgusta 2005 g.)*. Nalchik: Kabardino-Balkarskii Institut Gumanitarnykh Issledovanii, 2005.

Dzagalov, A. S. "Ukreplenie i kazach'i stanitsy Tsentra Kavkazskoi linii i Vladikavkazskogo voennogo okruga v 30–40-kh godakh XIX v." *Arkhivy i obshchestvo*, no. 11 (2009): 124–9.

Dzagov, R. N. *Vziamodeistvie kul'tur v protsesse formirovaniia mnogonatsional'nogo naseleniia Kabardy*. Nalchik: Kabardino-Balkarskii institut gumanitarnykh issledovanii, 2009.

Dzamikhov, K. F., Kh. M. Dumanov, Zh. A. Kalmykov, and A. G. Kazharov. "Etnoterritorial'naia i administrativno-territorial'naia struktura Kabardino-Balkarii v XVIII.XX vv." In *Vymysel i istina*, eds. I. M. Borei, R. K. Dzagulov, and M. F. Kolesnikov, 337–8. Piatigorsk: RIA-KMV, 2010.

Dzamikhov, K. F., Kh. M. Dumanov, Zh. A. Kalmykov, A. G. Kazharov, and M. G. Kumakhov. "O stanovlenii Kabardino-Balkarskoi Avtonomnoi Oblast." *Politika i pravo v sfere etnogosudarstvennykh otnoshenii Kabardino-Balkarii*, no. 2 (2001): 261–8.

Dzidzoev, V. D. *Osetiia v sisteme vziamootnoshenii narodov kavkaza v XVII-nach. XX v. (Istoriko-etnologicheskoe issledovanie)*. Vladikavkaz: Izdatel'stvo Severo-Osetinskogo gosudarstvennogo universiteta, 2003.

Dzidzoev, V. D. *Ot Soiuza obedinennikh gortev Severnogo Kavkaza i Dagestana do Gorskoi ASSR (1917–1924 g.g.): nachal'nyi etep national'no-gosudarstvennogo stroitel'stvo narodov Severnogo Kavkaza v XX veke*. Vladikavkaz: Izd-vo Severo-Osetinskogo gos. Universiteta, 2003.

Dzuev, G. K. *Krovavoe leto 1928-goda: ocherki*. Nalchik: Elbrus, 1997.

Efrimenko, V. I. *Chernaia smert' i ee ukrotiteli: ocherki istorii chumy na Kavkaze*. Stavropol: Stavropolskaia kraevaia tipografiia, 2000.

El'buzdukaeva, T. U. "Promyshlennoe razvitie Chechni v 20–30-e gody XX veka." In *Chechenskaia Respublika i chechentsy: istoriia i sovremennost'*, eds. Kh. I. Ibragimov, A. D. Osmaev, M. Ia. Ustinova, and V. A. Tishkov, 295–300. Moscow: Nauka, 2005.

Emel'ianova, Nadezhda. *Musul'mane Kabardy*. Moscow: Granitsa, 1999.

Fearon, James D., and David D. Laitin. "Explaining Interethnic Cooperation." *The American Political Science Review* 9, no. 4 (1996): 715–35.

Fearon, James D., and David D. Laitin. "Violence and the Social Construction of Ethnicity." *International Organization* 54, no. 4 (2000): 845–77.

Fischer, Michael H. *Indirect Rule in India: Residents and the Residency System, 1764–1858*. Delhi: Oxford University Press, 1991.

Gaibov, N. D. *O pozemel'nom ustroistve gorskikh plemen Terskoi oblasti*, 1905 repr. in *Agrarnye otnosheniia u narodov severnogo kavkaza v rossiiskoi politike XVIII-nachala XX veka*. Vol. 2, 5–246. Nalchik: El-Fa, 2008.

Gammer, Moshe. *Muslim Resistance to the Tsar: Shamil and the Conquest of Chechnia and Daghestan*. London: F. Cass, 1994.

Gammer, Moshe. *The Lone Wolf and the Bear: Three Centuries of Chechen Defiance of Russian Rule*. Pittsburgh: University of Pittsburgh Press, 2006.

Gardanov, V. K. *Kul'tura i byt narodov Severnogo Kavkaza (1917–1967 goda)*. Moscow: Nauka, 1968.

Gardanov, V. K. *Obshchestvennyi stroi adygskikh narodov (XVIII- pervaia polovina XIX veka)*. Moscow: Nauka, 1967.

Gardanov, V. K., ed. *Novoe i traditsionnoe v kul'ture i byte kabardintsev i balkartsev.* Nalchik: Elbrus, 1986.
Gellner, Ernest. *Nations and Nationalism.* Ithaca: Cornell University Press, 1983.
Geraci, Robert P. *Window on the East. National and Imperial Identities in Late Tsarist Russia.* Ithaca: Cornell University Press, 2001.
Geukjian, Ohannes. *Ethnicity, Nationalism and Conflict in the South Caucasus: Nagorno-Karabakh and the Legacy of Soviet Nationalities Policy.* London: Routledge, 2012.
Giliazov, I. A. "Pantiurkizm, panturanizm i Germaniia." *Etnograficheskoe obozrenie,* no. 2 (1996): 92–103.
Glasheva, Z. Zh. "Proekt Abramovskoi komissii po razresheniu zemel'nogo voprosa v Balkarii." *Trudy molodykh uchenykh Vladikavkazskogo nauchnogo tsentra RAN,* no. 4 (2010): 147–50.
Gonikishvili, M. G. "Podgotovka i provedenie krest'ianskoi reformy v kabardinskom okruge." In *Gruzino-Severo-Kavkazskie Vzaimootnosheniia,* ed. G. Togoshvili, 135–68. Tbilisi: Akademiia Nauk Gruzinskoi SSR, 1981.
Gould, Rebecca. *Writers and Rebels: The Literature of Insurgency in the Caucasus.* New Haven: Yale University Press, 2016.
Grant, Bruce. *In the Soviet House of Culture: A Century of Perestroikas.* Princeton: Princeton University Press, 1995.
Grant, Bruce. *The Captive and the Gift: Cultural Histories of Sovereignty in Russia and the Caucasus.* Ithaca: Cornell University Press, 2009.
Grechko, A. A. *Bitva za Kavkaz.* Moscow: Voenizdat, 1967.
Gritsenko, N. P. "O deiatel'nosti Abramovskoi komissii." *Izvestiia: Stat'i i materialy po istorii Checheno-Ingushetii* 6, no. 1 (1965): 129–71.
Gudakov, V. V. *Severo-Zapadnyi Kavkaz v sisteme mezhetnicheskikh otnoshenii s drevneishikh vremen do 60-kh godov XIX veka.* St. Petersburg: Izdatel'stvo S.-Peterburgskogo Universiteta, 2007.
Gugov, R. Kh. "Kul'turnoe stroitel'stvo v Kabardino-Balkarii v pervye gody sotsialisticheskoi rekonstruktsii narodnogo khoziastva SSSR (1926-1929)." *Uchenye Zapiski Kabardino-Balkarskogo Naucho-issledovatel'skogo Instituta,* no. 15 (1959): 109–38.
Gugov, R. Kh. *Kabarda i Balkariia v XVIII veke i ikh vzaimootnosheniia s Rossiei.* Nalchik: El-Fa, 1999.
Heilbronner, Hans. "Alexander III and the Reform Plan of Loris-Melikov." *The Journal of Modern History* 33, no. 4 (1961): 384–97.
Henze, Paul. *The North Caucasus: Russia's Long Struggle to Subdue the Circassians.* Santa Monica: RAND, 1990.
Hirsch, Francine. "Race without the Practice of Racial Politics." *Slavic Review* 61, no. 1 (Spring 2002): 30–43.
Hirsch, Francine. *Empire of Nations: Ethnographic Knowledge and the making of the Soviet Union.* Ithaca: Cornell University Press, 2005.
Hobsbawm, Eric J. *Nations and Nationalism since 1780: Programme, Myth, Reality.* Cambridge: Cambridge University Press, 1990.
Hoffmann, David L., and Yanni Kotsonis, eds. *Russian Modernity: Politics, Practice, Knowledge.* London: MacMillan, 2000.
Holquist, Peter. "To Count, to Extract, and to Exterminate: Population Statistics and Population Politics in Late Imperial and Soviet Russia." In *A State of Nations,* eds. Ronald Grigor Suny and Terry Martin, 111–44. New York: Oxford University Press, 2001.

Holquist, Peter. *Making War, Forging Revolution: Russia's Continuum of Crisis, 1914-1921.* Cambridge, MA: Harvard University Press, 2003.
Horowitz, Donald L. *Ethnic Groups in Conflict.* Berkeley: University of California Press, 1985.
Hroch, Miroslav. *Social Preconditions of National Revival in Europe: A Comparative Analysis of the Social Composition of Patriotic Groups among the Smaller European Nations.* New York: Cambridge University Press, 1985.
Iakubova, I. I. *Severnyi Kavkaz v russko-turetskikh otnosheniiakh v 40-70 -e gody XVIII veka.* Nalchik: Elbrus, 1993.
Ibragimov, Kh. I., A. D. Osmaev, M. Ia. Ustinova, and V. A. Tishkov, eds. *Chechenskaia Respublika i chechentsy: istoriia i sovremennost'.* Moscow: Nauka, 2005.
Ibragimov, M. M. "Ob osobennostiakh krizisa v Chechenskoi Republike v 1990-e gody." In *Chechenskaia Respublika i chechentsy: istoriia i sovremennost',* eds. Kh. I. Ibragimov, A. D. Osmaev, M. Ia. Ustinova, and V. A. Tishkov, 367-82. Moscow: Nauka, 2005.
Ibragimova, Z. Kh. "M.T. Loris-Melikov." In *Sbornik Statei: Severnyi Kavkaz—vremia peremen (1860-1880),* ed. Z. Kh. Ibragimova, 55-79. Moscow: Eslan, 2001.
Islamoglu, Huri. "Property as a Contested Domain: A Reevaluation of the Ottoman Land Code of 1858." In *New Perspectives on Property and Land in the Middle East,* ed. Roger Owen, 3-62. Cambridge, MA: Harvard University Press, 2001.
Jersild, Austin. "Faith, Custom, and Ritual in the Borderlands: Orthodoxy, Islam and the 'small peoples' of the Middle Volga and North Caucasus." *Russian Review* 59 (October 2000): 512-29.
Jersild, Austin. *Orientalism and Empire: North Caucasus Mountaineer Peoples and the Georgian Frontier,1845-1917.* Montreal: McGill-Queen's University Press, 2002.
Kabardino-Balkarskoe statisticheskoe biuro, *Kratkii statisticheskii sbornik Kabardino-Balkarskoi Avtonomnoi Oblasti.* Nalchik: Kabardino-Balkarskoe statisticheskoe biuro, 1925.
Kagazezhev, Zh. V. "Etnoterritorial'naia separatsiia adygov v pozdnem srednevekov'e." *Voprosy Istorii,* no. 7 (July 2011): 154-8.
Kalinovsky, Artemy. *Laboratory of Socialist Development: Cold War Politics and Decolonization in Soviet Tajikistan.* Ithaca: Cornell University Press, 2018.
Kalmykov, Zh. A. "Islam v istorii kabardintsev (XIII- pervaia polovina XIX v.)." *Voprosy kavkazskoi filologii i istorii,* no. 4 (2004): 168-80.
Kalmykov, Zh. A. *Integratsiia Kabardy i Balkarii v Obshcherossiiskuiu sistemu upravleniia (vtoraia polovina XVIII - Nachalo XX veka).* Nalchik: El-Fa, 2007.
Kalmykov, Zh. A. *Etnoterritorial'naia i Administrativno-territorial'naia struktora Kabardino-Balkarii i problemy realizatsii v KBR federal'nogo zakona "ob obshchikh printsipakh organizatsii mestnogo samoupravleniia v Rossiiskoi federatsii.* Nalchik: Respublikanskii poligrafkombinat im. Revoliutsii 1905 g, 2010.
Kalmykov, Zh. A. "Cherkesskaia tragediia. Iz istorii nasil'stvennogo vyseleniia adygov v Osmanskyiu imperiiu." In *Cherkesskii vopros: Istoriia, problemy i puti resheniia,* ed. A. Kh. Mukozhev, 54-63. Nalchik: Koordinatsionnyi sovet adygskikh obshchestvennykh organizatsii, 2012.
Kanukova, Z. V. *Staryi Vladikavkaz: istoriko-etnologicheskoe issledovanie.* Vladikavkaz: SOIGSI, 2008.
Kappeler, Andreas. *The Russian Empire: A Multiethnic History.* Harlow: Longman-Pearson, 2001.
Kardanov, A. T. *Rabochii klass Kabardino-Balkarii v period stroitel'stva sotsializma (1920-1937).* Nalchik: Elbrus, 1976.
Karmov, A. Kh. "Zemel'nye otnosheniia v GASSR." In *Zemel'nye otnosheniia v Kabarde i Balkarii: Istoriia i sovremennost': Materialy nauch.-prakt. konf. (11 avgusta 2005 g.),* eds.

Kh. M. Dumanov, A. Kh. Borov, V. Kh. Kazharov, and D. N. Prasolov, 107–9. Nalchik: Kabardino-Balkarskii Institut Gumanitarnykh Issledovanii, 2005.

Karmov, R. K. "Rod kabardinskikh uorkov Zhereshtievykh." *Arkhivy i Obshchestvo*, no. 8 (2009): 98–101.

Karny, Yo'av. *Highlanders: A Journey to the Caucasus in Quest of Memory*. New York: Farrar, Straus and Giroux, 2000.

Kashezheva, G. M. "Nekotorye voprosy pereselencheskogo dvizheniia v Terskuiu oblast' v poreformennyi period." In *Iz istorii feodal'noi Kabardy i Balkarii*, eds. R. Kh. Gugov and V. N. Sokurov, 54–73. Nalchik: Institut istorii, filologii i ekonomiki pri Sovete ministrov KBASSR, 1981.

Kasumov, A. Kh. "Proval anglo-turetskikh planov Shamilia v Kabarde." *Kabardinskaia Pravda*, July 29, 1955, 2–3.

Katkhanov, Kerim. *Nazyr: Kniga ob ottse*. Nalchik: El'brus, 2008.

Kazenin, K. I. *Tikhie konflikty na Severnom Kavkaze: Adygeia, Kabardino-Balkariia, Karachaevo-Cherkesiia*. Moscow: Regnum, 2009.

Kazharov, A. G. "Voprosy zemlevladeniia i zemlepol'zovaniia v usloviiakh stanoleniia i razvitiia gosudarstvennosti Kabardino-Balkarii v 1920-e gg." In *Zemel'nye otnosheniia v Kabarde i Balkarii: Istoriia i sovremennost': Materialy nauch.-prakt. konf. (11 avgusta 2005 g.)*, eds. Kh. M. Dumanov, A. Kh. Borov, V. Kh. Kazharov, and D. N. Prasolov, 122–43. Nalchik: Kabardino-Balkarskii Institut Gumanitarnykh Issledovanii, 2005.

Kazharov, A. G. "Administrativno-territorial'noe razmezhivanie Kabardy i Karachaia." *Istoricheskii vestnik Kabardino-Balkarskoi Respublikanskoi Instituta Gumanitarnykh Issledovanii*, no. 5 (2006): 48–70.

Kazharov, A. G. "Aliev U.D. i Kabardino-Karachaevskie etnoterritorial'nye otnosheniia v nachale 1920-x g.g." In *Vymysel i Istina*, eds. Borei, I. M., R. K. Dzagulov, and M. F. Kolesnikov, 276–92. Piatigorsk: RIA-KMV, 2010.

Khan-Girei. *Zapiski o Cherkesii*. Nalchik: El-Fa, 2008.

Kazharov, A. G. "U.D. Aliev i nekotorye problem natsional'no-gosudarstvennogo razvitiia narodov severnogo Kavkaza v nachale 1920 gg." *Istoricheskii vestnik Kabardino-Balkarskoi Respublikanskoi Instituta Gumanitarnykh Issledovanii*, no. 9 (2010): 76–90.

Kazharov, V. Kh. "K voprosu o dualizme kabardinoskoi sel'skoi obshchiny v predreformennyi period." In *Obshchestvennyi byt adygov i balkartsev*, ed. S. Kh. Mafedzev. Nalchik: Kabardino-Balkarskii institut istorii, filologii i ekonomiki pri Sovete ministrov KBASSR, 1986.

Khashkhozheva, T. Kh. "Izmemnenie professional'no-kvalifikatsionnyi struktury rabochikh promyshlennosti Kabardino-Balkarskoi ASSR." In *Problemy trudovykh resursov Kabardino-Balkarskoi ASSR*, ed. A. T. Kuantov, 27–49. Nalchik: Kabardino-Balkarskii nauchno-issledovatel'skii institut pri Sovete ministrov KBASSR, 1975.

Khatazhukov, Valerii, ed. *Politicheskie repressii v Kabardino-Balkarii v 1918–1930-kh godakh (Stat'i i dokumenty)*. Nalchik: Kabardino-Balkarskii Respublikanskii Pravozashchitnyi Tsentr, 2010.

Khatuev, R. T. "Karachai i Balkariia do vtoroi poloviny XIX veka: vlast' i obshchestvo." In *Karachaevtsy i Balkartsy: Etnografiia, Istoriia, Arkheologiia*, ed. S. A. Arutiunov, Moscow: Institut etnologii i antropologii RAN, 1999.

Khatuev, R. T. "Rossiiskoe imperskoe pravo i shariatskii sud na Tsentral'nom Kavkaze: nachal'nyi opyt sushchestvovaniia (konets XVIII – pervaia tret'XIX v.)." *Istoriia gosudarstva i prava*, no. 22 (2010): 27–31.

Khatukhov, A. M., and F. Zh. Berova. "Ocobennosti rasselenie naseleniia i stanovleniia sovremennoi ethnicheskoi karty KBR." *Izvestiia Kabardino-Balkarskogo nauchnogo tsentra RAN* 86, no. 6 (2018): 189–94.

Khodarkovsky, Michael. "Of Christianity, Enlightenment and Colonialism: Russian in the North Caucasus, 1550–1800." *The Journal of Modern History* 71, no. 2 (June 1999): 394–430.

Khodarkovsky, Michael. *Russia's Steppe Frontier: The Making of a Colonial Empire, 1500–1800*. Bloomington: Indiana University Press, 2002.

Khodarkovsky, Michael. *Bitter Choices: Loyalty and Betrayal in the Russian Conquest of the North Caucasus*. Ithaca: Cornell University Press, 2011.

Khubulova, S. A. *Krest'ianskaia sem'ia i dvor v Terskoi oblasti v kontse XIX-nachale XX v.: sotsial'no-ekonomicheskie, etnodemograficheskie i politicheskie aspekty razvitiia*. St. Petersburg: Izd-vo S.-Peterburgskogo universiteta, 2002.

Khutuev, Kh. I. "Byla li granitsa?" *Sovetskaia molodezh*, February 22, 1992, 1.

King, Charles. *The Ghost of Freedom: A History of the Caucasus*. New York: Oxford University Press, 2008.

Kipkeeva, Z. B. *Severnyi Kavkaz v Rossiiskoi Imperii: narody, migratsii, territorii*. Stavropol': Izdatel'stvo Stavropol'skogo gosudarstvennogo universiteta, 2008.

Kivelson, Valerie A. *Cartographies of Tsardom: The Land and Its Meanings in Seventeenth-Century Russia*. Ithaca: Cornell University Press, 2006.

Kokiev, G. A. "Kabardino-Osetinskie otnosheniia v XVIII veke." In *Istoriia Kabardino-Balkarii v trudakh G.A. Kokieva: Sbornik statei i dokumentov*, ed. G. Kh. Mambetov, 122–77. Nalchik: El-Fa, 2005.

Kokiev, G. A. "Metody kolonial'noi politiki tsarskoi rossii na severnom Kavakze v XVIII v." In *Istoriia Kabardino-Balkarii v trudakh G.A. Kokieva: Sbornik statei i dokumentov*, ed. G. Kh. Mambetov, 75–121. Nalchik: El-Fa, 2005.

Kokiev, G. A. "Pereselenie kabardinskikh kholopov v Mozdok v XVIII v." *Istoriia Kabardino-Balkarii v trudakh G.A. Kokieva: Sbornik statei i dokumentov*, ed. G. Kh. Mambetov, 224–31. Nalchik: El-Fa, 2005.

Kokiev, G. A. "Raspad Kabardy na bol'shuiu i maluiu i ustanovivshiesia otnosheniia s sosednimi narodami." In *Istoriia Kabardino-Balkarii v trukakh G.A. Kokieva: Sbornik statei i dokumentov*, ed. G. Kh. Mambetov, 198–206. Nalchik: El-Fa, 2005.

Kokiev, G. A. "Rol' Temriuka v sblizhenii Kabardy s Moskovskim gosudarstvenom." In *Istoriia Kabardino-Balkarii v trukakh G.A. Kokieva: Sbornik statei i dokumentov*, ed. G. Kh. Mambetov, 532–5. Nalchik: El-Fa, 2005.

Kozhev, Z. A. "Sistema zemepol'zovaniia v kabardino-gorskikh otnosheniiakh (vtoraia polovina XVIII v)." In *Zemel'nye otnosheniia v Kabarde i Balkarii: Istoriia i sovremennost': Materialy nauch.-prakt. konf. (11 avgusta 2005 g.)*, eds. Kh. M. Dumanov, A. Kh. Borov, V. Kh. Kazharov, and D. N. Prasolov, 25–38. Nalchik: Kabardino-Balkarskii Institut Gumanitarnykh Issledovanii, 2005.

Kudashev, Vladimir. *Istoricheskie svedeniia o kabardinskom narode* (1913). Nalchik: Elbrus, 1991.

Kumykov, T. Kh. "K voprosu krest'ianskoi reform v Balkarii v 1867 g." *Sbornik statei po istorii Kabardy i Balkarii*, no. 6 (1957): 105–13.

Kumykov, T. Kh. "Zemel'naia reforma v Kabarda v 1863-1869 gg." *Uchenye zapiski Kabardino-Balkarskogo nauchno-issledovaltel'skogo instituta*, no. 12 (1957): 275.

Kumykov, T. Kh. *Zhizn' i obshchestvennaia deiatel'nost L.M. Kodzokva*. Nalchik: Kabardino-Balkarskoe knizhnoe izdatel'stvo, 1962.

Kumykov, T. Kh. *Ekonomicheskoe i kul'turnoe razvitie Kabardy i Balkarii v XIX veke*. Nalchik: Elbrus, 1965.

Kumykov, T. Kh. "Antikolonial'nye dvizheniia i klassovaia bor'ba v Kabarde i Balkarii v pervoi polovine XIX v." In *Istoriia Kabardino-Balkarskoi ASSR*, eds. T. Kh. Kumykov, Z. V. Anchabadze, V. K. Gardanov, A. V. Fadeev, A. Kh. Kasumov, G. Kh. Mambetov, and Kh. I. Khutuev T. I, 219–34. Moscow: Nauka, 1967.

Kumykov, T. Kh. "Sotsial'no-ekonomicheskie otnosheniia v Kabarde i Balkarii v pervoi polovine XIX v." In *Istoriia Kabardino-Balkarskoi ASSR*, eds. T. Kh. Kumykov, Z. V. Anchabadze, V. K. Gardanov, A. V. Fadeev, A. Kh. Kasumov, G. Kh. Mambetov, and Kh. I. Khutuev, T. I, 196–208. Moscow: Nauka, 1967.

Kumykov, T. Kh. *Dmitrii Kodzovok*. Nalchik: Izd-vo El'brus, 1985.

Kumykov, T. Kh., Z. V. Anchabadze, V. K. Gardanov, A. V. Fadeev, A. Kh. Kasumov, G. Kh. Mambetov, and Kh. I. Khutuev, eds. *Istoriia Kabardino-Balkarskoi ASSR*. 2 vols. Moscow: Nauka, 1967.

Kusheva, E. N. *Narody Severnogo Kavkaza i ikh sviazi s Rossiei: vtoraia polovina XVI –30-e gody XVII veka*. Moscow: Izdatel'stvo Akademii Nauk SSSR, 1961.

Kuz'minov, P. A. "Etnodemograficheskaia karta narodov Tereka: razmeshchenie, chislennost' i migratsiia naseleniia v kontse XVIII-pervoi polovine XIX veka." In *Landshaft, etnograficheskie i istoricheskie protsessy na Severnom Kavkaze v XIX-- nachale XX veka*, comp. P. A. Kuz'minov, ed. F. A. Mugutdinova, 641–759. Nalchik: El-Fa, 2004.

Kuz'minov, P. A. "Materialy soslovno-pozemel'nykh komissii kak istoricheskii istochnik po istorii narodov Severnogo Kavkaza." In *De die in diem; pamiati A.P. Pronshteina (1919-1998)*, ed. V. V. Chernous, 122–44. Rostov-na-Donu: Rostovskii gosudarstvennyi universitet, 2004.

Kuz'minov, P. A. "Agrarnye preobrazovaniia u narodov Tsentral'nogo Kavkaza v 50–60-e gody XIX veka." In *Zemel'nye otnosheniia v Kabarde i Balkarii: Istoriia i sovremennost': Materialy nauch.-prakt. konf. (11 avgusta 2005 g.)*, eds. Kh. M. Dumanov, A. Kh. Borov, V. Kh. Kazharov, and D. N. Prasolov, 41–71. Nalchik: Kabardino-Balkarskii Institut Gumanitarnykh Issledovanii, 2005.

Kuz'minov, P. A. "M.T. Loris-Melikov na Kavkaze." *Kavkazskii sbornik* 34, no. 2 (2005): 124–5.

Kuz'minov, P. A. "Agrarnaia i sotsial'naia politika rossiiskogo pravitel'stva v Kabarde i Balkarii v 50–70-e gody XIX veka." In *Agrarnye otnosheniia u narodov severnogo kavkaza v rossiiskoi politike XVIII-nachala XX veka*. Vol. 2, 496–501. Nalchik: El-Fa, 2008.

Kuz'minov, P. A. "Ot voennogo pokoreniia k poisku putei integratsii: zamysly i nachalo osushchestvleniia agrarnykh preobrazovanii u narodov severnogo kavkaza v 60-kh godakh XIX veka." In *Agrarnye otnosheniia u narodov severnogo kavkaza v rossiiskoi politike XVIII-nachala XX veka*. Vol. 1, 419–66. Nalchik: El-Fa, 2008.

Kuz'minov, P. A. *Epokha preobrazovanii 50–70-kh godov XIX veka u narodov severnogo Kavkaza v noveishei istoriografii*. Nalchik: Pechatnyi dvor, 2011.

Laipanov, K., and M. Batchaev. *Umar Aliev*. Cherkessk: Karachai-Cherkesskoe otdelenie Staropol'skogo knizhnogo izdatel'stva, 1986.

Lanzillotti, Ian T. "From Princely Fiefdoms to Soviet Nations: Interethnic Border Conflicts in the North Caucasus and the Village of Lesken." *Central Asian Survey* 31, no. 2 (2012): 209–27.

Lanzillotti, Ian T. "Historiography and the politics of land, identity, and belonging in the twentieth-century North Caucasus." *Nationalities Papers* 44, no. 4 (July 2016): 503–21.

Lanzillotti, Ian T. "Towards an Explanation of Intercommunal Peace in Kabardino-Balkaria: Post-War Nationalities Policy and Late Soviet Society in the North Caucasus." *Europe-Asia Studies* 70 (2018): 942–65.

Lavrov, L. I., "Karachai i Balkariia do 30-kh godov XIX veka." In *Izbrannye trudy po kul'ture abazin, adygov, karachaevtsev, balkartsev*, eds. B. Kh. Bgazhnokov and A. Kh. Abazov, 367–427. Nalchik: KBIGI, 2009.

Layton, Susan. *Russian Literature and Empire: Conquest of the Caucasus from Pushkin to Tolstoy*. Cambridge: Cambridge University Press, 1994.
Lieven, Anatol. *Chechnya: Tombstone of Russian Power*. New Haven: Yale University Press, 1994.
Lints, S. I. *Severnyi Kavkaz nakanune i v period nemetsko-fashistskoi okkupatsii: sostoianie i osobennoisti razvitiia (iiul' 1942 – oktiabr' 1943 gg.)*. Rostov-on-Don: Izd-vo SKNTS VSh, 2003.
Litvinova, T. N. "Politicheskaia institutsionalizatsiia i bor'ba elit na Severnom Kavkaze v period revoliutsii 1917 goda i grazhdanskoi voiny." *Zhurnal sotsiologii i sotsial'noi antropologii* 20, no. 4 (2017): 154–68.
Lohr, Eric. *Nationalizing the Russian Empire: The Campaign against Enemy Aliens during World War I*. Cambridge, MA: Harvard University Press, 2003.
Nekrich, Aleksandr M. *The Punished Peoples: The Deportation and Fate of Soviet Minorities at the End of the Second World War*. Trans. George Saunders. New York: Norton, 1978.
Maksimov, E. "Kabardintsy: Statistiko-ekonomicheskii ocherk." *Terskii sbornik*, no. 2 (1892): 150–1.
Mambetov, G. Kh. *Material'naia kul'tura sel'skogo naseleniia Kabardino-Balkarii: (vtoraia polovina XIX-60-e gody XX veka)*. Nalchik: Elbrus, 1971.
Mambetov, G. Kh. *Zemel'nyi vopros v tvorchestve obshchestvenno-politicheskikh deiatelei adygov, balkartsev, i karachaevtsev v XIX-nachale XX*. Nalchik: KBNII, 1976.
Mambetov, G. Kh., and Z. G. Mambetov. *Sotsial'nye protivorechiia v Kabardino-Balkarskoe derevne v 20–30-e gody*. Nalchik: Izdatel'stvo KBNTs RAN, 2009.
Mambetov, G. Kh., and Z. G. Mambetov, comp., F. A. Mugutdinova, and V. M. Atalikov, eds. *Istoriia Kabardino-Balkarii v trukakh G. A. Kokieva: Sbornik statei i dokumentov*. Nalchik: El-Fa, 2005.
Mamkhegov, A. B. "Kak malokabardintsy utratili zemli kniazei Dzhyliakhstanovykh." *Arkhivy i obshchestvo*, no. 3 (2007): 73–84.
Mamkhegov, A. B. "Zakat tausultanovykh Kabardy." *Arkhivy i obshchestvo* 5 (2008): 49–51.
Maremshaova, I. I. *Balkariia i Karachai v etnokul'turnom prostranstve Kavkaza*. Nalchik: Elbrus, 2003.
Marshall, Alex. *The Caucasus under Soviet Rule*. London: Routeledge, 2010.
Martin, Terry. "The Origins of Soviet Ethnic Cleansing." *Journal of Modern History* 70 (1998): 813–86.
Martin, Terry *The Affirmative Action Empire: Nations and Nationalism in the Soviet Union, 1923–1938*. Ithaca: Cornell University Press, 2001.
Martin, Virginia. *Law and Custom in the Steppe: The Kazakhs of the Middle Horde and Russian Colonialism in the Nineteenth Century*. Richmond: Curzon, 2001.
Marzoev, I.-B. T. *Osetinskaia feodal'naia znat' v sisteme vzaimodeseistviia etnicheskikh elit Severnogo Kavkaza (XVIII – nach. XX vv.)*, 142. Vladikavkaz: IPO SOIGSI, 2008.
McNeill, William H. *Plagues and Peoples*. Garden City: Anchor Press, 1976.
Mesiats, S. I. *Naselenie i zemlepol'zovanie Kabardy*. Voronezh: Kabardino-Balkarskii Oblastnoi Ispolkom, 1928.
Miller, Alexei. "Russifikatsiia—klassifitsirovat' i poniat'." *Ab Imperio*, no. 2 (2002): 133–48.
Miller, Alexei. "Between Local and Inter-Imperial: Russian Imperial History in Search of Scope and Paradigm." *Kritika: Explorations in Russian and Eurasian History* 5, no. 1 (Winter 2004): 7–26.
Miziev, Ismail. "Iz istorii pozemel'nykh sporov mezhdu Balkariei i Kabardoi." *Balkariia* 26, no. 4 (2007): 12–28.
Moon, David. *The Plough that Broke the Steppes: Agriculture and Environment on Russia's Grasslands, 1700–1914*. Oxford: Oxford University Pres, 2013.

Moses, A. Dirk. *Empire, Colony, Genocide: Conquest, Occupation, and Subaltern Resistance in World History*. New York: Berghahn Books, 2008.
Mostashari, Firouzeh. "Colonial Dilemmas: Russian Policies in the Muslim Caucasus." In *Of Religion and Empire: Missions, Conversion, and Tolerance in Tsarist Russia*, eds. Robert Geraci and Michael Khodarkovsky, 229–49. Ithaca: Cornell University Press, 2001.
Mukozhev, A. Kh. "K voprosu o kharaktere islamizatsii kabardintsev." *Vestnik Kabardino-Balkarskogo Instituta Gumanitarnykh Issledovanii*, no. 4 (2003): 51–66.
Mukozhev, A. Kh. "Islam i adyge khabze." *Istoricheskii vestnik KBIGI*, no. 3 (2006): 426–36.
Muratova, E. G. *Sotsial'no-politicheskaia istoriia Balkarii XVII-nachala XX v.* Nalchik: El-Fa, 2007.
Muzhev, I. F. "Kabarda i Balkariia v period reaktsii i novogo revoliutsionnogo pod"ema (1907–1914)." In *Istoriia Kabardino-Balkarskoi ASSR*, eds. T. Kh. Kumykov, Z. V. Anchabadze, V. K. Gardanov, A. V. Fadeev, A. Kh. Kasumov, G. Kh. Mambetov, and Kh. I. Khutuev, Vol. 1, 383–97. Moscow: Nauka, 1967.
Naimark, Norman M. *Stalin's Genocides*. Princeton: Princeton University Press, 2010.
Nakhusheva, V. Sh. *Narody Karachaevo-Cherkesii: istoriia i kul'tura*. Cherkessk: KChRIPKRO, 1998.
Narochnitskii, A. L., ed. *Istoriia narodov Severnogo kavkaza*. Vol. 2. Moscow: Nauka, 1988.
Nartokova, N. V. *Sotsial'nye aspekty gosudarstvennoi politiki v Kabardino-Balkarii v 40-kh – nachale 60-kh godov XX veka*. Nalchik: Elbrus, 2001.
Nevskaia, V. P. *Ocherki Istorii Karachaevo-Cherkesii*. Vol. 1. Stavropol': Stavropol'skoe knizhnoe izdatel'stvo, 1967.
Nogmov, Sh. B. *Istoriia adykheiskogo naroda, sostavlennaia po predaniiam kabardintsev*. Nalchik: Elbrus, 1994.
Norris, Stephen M., and Willard Sunderland, eds. *Russia's People of Empire: Life Stories from Eurasia, 1500 to the Present*. Bloomington: Indiana University Press, 2012.
Ovkhadov, M. P. "Obrazovatel'nye i iazykovye problem natsional'noi politiki sovetskogo perioda v Chechenskoi Respublike." In *Chechenskaia Respublika i chechentsy: istoriia i sovremennost'*, eds. Kh. I. Ibragimov, A. D. Osmaev, M. Ia. Ustinova, and V. A. Tishkov, 352–7. Moscow: Nauka, 2005.
Perović, Jeronim. *From Conquest to Deportation: The North Caucasus Under Russian Rule*. New York: Oxford University Press, 2019.
Pipes, Richard. *The Formation of the Soviet Union: Communism and Nationalism, 1917–1923*. Cambridge, MA: Harvard University Press, 1964.
Pohl, J. Otto. *Ethnic Cleansing in the USSR, 1937–1949*. Westport: Greenwood Press, 1999.
Pohl, J. Otto. "Stalin's Genocide against the 'Repressed Peoples.'" *Journal of Genocide Research* 2, no. 2 (2000): 267–93.
Polian, Pavel. *Against Their Will: The History and Geography of Forced Migrations in the USSR*. Budapest: Central European University Press, 2004.
Polievktov, M. A. *Posol'stvo stol'nika Tolchanova i d'iaka Ievleva v Imeretiiu: 1650–1652*. Tiflis: Tiflisskii Universitet, 1926.
Politkovskaya, Anna. *A Dirty War: a Russian Reporter in Chechnya*. London: Harvill, 2001.
Politkovskaya, Anna *A Small Corner of Hell: Dispatches from Chechnya*. Chicago: University of Chicago Press, 2003.
Pollock, Sean. *Empire by Invitation? Russian Empire-Building in the Caucasus in the Reign of Catherine II*. Ph.d. diss., Harvard University, 2006.
Pollock, Sean. "'As One Russian to Another': Prince Petr Ivanovich Bagration's Assimilation of Russian Ways." *Ab Imperio*, no. 4 (2010): 113–42.
Prasolov, D. N. "K voprosu zemel'nykh zakhvatakh v kabardinoskoi sel'skoi obshchine poreformennogo perioda." *Vestnik Kabardino-Balkarskogo Instituta Gumannitaynykh Issledovanii*, no. 8 (2001): 60–78.

Prasolov, D. N. "Pastbishchnoe i lesnoe obshchinnoe zemlepol'zovanie v Kabarde vo 2-oi polovine 19- nachale 20 v." In *Zemel'nye otnosheniia v Kabarde i Balkarii: Istoriia i sovremennost': Materialy nauch.-prakt. konf. (11 avgusta 2005 g.)*, eds. Kh. M. Dumanov, A. Kh. Borov, V. Kh. Kazharov, and D. N. Prasolov, 80–9. Nalchik: Kabardino-Balkarskii Institut Gumanitarnykh Issledovanii, 2005.

Pravilova, Ekaterina. "The Property of Empire: Islamic Law and Russian Agrarian Policy in Transcaucasia and Turkestan." *Kritika: Explorations in Russian and Eurasian History* 12, no. 2 (2011): 353–86.

Rettish, Aaron B. *Russia's Peasants in Revolution and Civil War: Citizenship, Identity, and the Creation of the Soviet State, 1914–1922*. Cambridge: Cambridge University Press, 2008.

Rhinelander, Anthony L. H. "Viceroy Vorontsov's Administration of the Caucasus." In *Transcaucasia, Nationalism and Social Change: Essays in the History of Armenia, Azerbaijan, and Georgia*, 87–104. Ann Arbor: University of Michigan, 1983.

Riasanovsky, Nicholas. *Russia and the West in the Teaching of the Slavophiles; a Study of Romantic Ideology*. Cambridge, MA: Harvard University Press, 1952.

Richmond, Walter. *The Northwest Caucasus: Past, Present, Future*. London: Routledge, 2008.

Ro'i, Yaacov. "The Transformation of Historiography on the 'Punished Peoples.'" *History & Memory* 21, no. 2 (2009): 150–76.

Sabanchiev, Kh. M. "Sozdanie sovetskoi inteligentsii v Kabarde." *Sbornik statei po istorii Kabardy*, no. 2 (1951): 121–57.

Sabanchiev, Kh.-M. A. *Byli soslany navechno: deportatsiia i reabilitatsiia balkarskogo naroda*. Nalchik: Elbrus, 2004.

Sablirov, M. Z. "Zemledel'cheskaia obshchina tolstovtsev Kabardy i Balkarii." In *Istoriia Severnogo Kavkaza s drevneishikh vremen po nostoiashchee vremia (Tezisy konferentsii 30-31 maia 2000 goda)*, eds. Iu. S. Davydov, N. V. Baryshnikov, V. V. Lazarev, A. I. Perepelitsyn, V. V. Ziuzin, V. P. Ermakov, and S. I. Linets, 203–5. Piatigorsk: Izd-vo Piatigorskogo gos. lingvisticheskogo univ, 2000.

Sahlins, Peter. *Boundaries: The making of France and Spain in the Pyrenees*. Berkeley: University of California Press, 1989.

Sakwa, Richard., ed. *Chechnya from Past to Future*. London: Anthem Press, 2005.

Sanborn, Joshua A. *Drafting the Russian Nation: Military Conscription, Total War, and Mass Politics, 1905–1925*. DeKalb: Northern Illinois University Press, 2003.

Sanford, George. *Katyn and the Soviet Massacre of 1940: Truth, Justice and Memory*. New York: Routledge, 2005.

Sattsaev, E. B. "Islam v Osetii: istoriia i sovremennost'." In *Problemy konsolidatsii narodov Severnogo Kavkaza: materialy Vserossiiskoi nauchno-prakticheskoi konferentssii "Sovremennye etnopoliticheskie i etnokonfessional'nye protsessy na Severnom Kavkaze: problemy i puti resheniia," (23–27 okt. 2008-g.)*, eds. N. F. Bugai, B. Kh. Bgazhnokov, and A. I. Tetuev, 377–85. Nalchik: RIA-KMV, 2008.

Savchenko, D. I. *Terskoe kazachestvo v istorii prisoedineniia Severnogo Kavkaza k Rossii: XVI-XIX vv*. Piatigorsk: Tekhnologicheskii universitet, 2005.

Scott, James C. *Seeing Like a State: How Certain Schemes to Improve Human Condition Have Failed*. New Haven: Yale University Press, 1998.

Shabaev, D. V. *Pravda o vyselenii balkartsev*. Nalchik: Elbrus, 1994.

Shabanov, I. M., B. A. Tambieva, and L. O. Abrekova. *Nakazany po natsional'nomu prizaku*. Cherkessk: Karachaevo-Cherkesskii Filial Moskovskogo Otkrytogo Sotsial'nogo Universiteta, 1999.

Shameev, A. M. "Osobennosti i kharakter partizanskogo dvizheniia v Kabardino-Balkarii protiv nemetsko-fashistskikh zakhvatchikov vo vtoroi polovine 1942-nachale 1943 gg." *Arkhivy i obshchestvo*, no. 12 (2010): 207–11.

Sherry, Dana Lyn. "Imperial Alchemy: Resettlement, Ethnicity, and Governance in the Russian Caucasus, 1828–1865." Phd diss., University of California-Davis, 2007.
Shnirel'man, V. A. *Byt' alanami: intellektualy i politika na Severnom Kavkaze v XX veke*. Moscow: Novoe literaturnoe obozrenie, 2006.
Shortanov, A. T. *Adygskie Kul'ty*. Nalchik: Elbrus, 1992.
Simon, Gerhard. *Nationalism and Policy Toward the Nationalities in the Soviet Union: From Totalitarian Dictatorship to Post-Stalinist Society*. Boulder: Westview Press, 1991.
Slezkine, Yuri. "The USSR as a Communal Apartment, or How a Socialist State Promoted Ethnic Particularism." *Slavic Review* 53, no. 2 (Summer 1994): 414–52.
Smirnov, N. A. *Politika rossii na Kavkaze v XVI-XIX vekakh*. Moscow: Izdatel'stvo sotsial'no-ekonomicheskoi literatury, 1958.
Smith, Jeremy. *The Bolsheviks and the National Question, 1917–23*. London: Macmillan, 1999.
Smith, Jeremy. "Was There a Soviet Nationalities Policy?." *Europe-Asia Studies* 71, no. 6 (2019): 972–93.
Statiev, Alexander. "Soviet Ethnic Deportations: Intent vs. Outcome." *Journal of Genocide Research* 11, nos. 2–3 (2009): 243–64.
Steinwedel, Charles. "Resettling People, Unsettling the Empire: Migration and the Challenge of Governance, 1861–1917." In *Peopling the Russian Periphery: Borderland Colonization in Eurasian History*, eds. Nicholas B. Breyfogle, Abby Schrader, and Willard Sunderland, 128–47. London: Routledge, 2007.
Sunderland, Willard. *Taming the Wild Field: Colonization and Empire on the Russian Steppe*. Ithaca: Cornell University Press, 2004.
Sunderland, Willard. "The Imperial Emancipations: Ending Non-Russian Serfdoms in Nineteenth-Century Russia." In *Shifting Forms of Continental Colonialism: Unfinished Struggles and Tensions*, eds. Dittmar Schorkowitz, John R. Chávez, and Ingo Schröder, 437–61. Basingstoke: Palgrave Macmillan, 2020.
Suny, Ronald Grigor. "Nationalism and Social Class in the Russian Revolution: The Cases of Baku and Tiflis." In *Transcaucasia, Nationalism and Social Change: Essays in the History of Armenia, Azerbaijan, and Georgia*, ed. Ronald Grigor Suny, 239–58. Ann Arbor: University of Michigan, 1983.
Suny, Ronald Grigor. ed. *Transcaucasia, Nationalism and Social Change: Essays in the History of Armenia, Azerbaijan, and Georgia*. Ann Arbor: University of Michigan, 1983.
Suny, Ronald Grigor. "Tiflis: Crucible of Ethnic Politics, 1860–1905." In *The City in Late Imperial Russia*, ed. Michael F. Hamm, 249–82. Bloomington: Indiana University Press, 1986.
Suny, Ronald Grigor. *The Revenge of the Past: Nationalism, Revolution, and the Collapse of the Soviet Union*. Stanford: Stanford University Press, 1993.
Suny, Ronald Grigor, and Terry Martin, eds. *A State of Nations: Empire and Nation-Making in the Age of Lenin and Stalin*. Oxford: Oxford University Press, 2001.
Takoev, G. "K problemam politiki v SSSR." *Sotsialisticheskii vestnik* 31, no. 3 (1951): 66–73
Temukuev, B. B. *Balkarskaia obshchestvennaia kolesnaia doroga*. Nalchik: Izd-vo M. i V. Kotliarovykh, 2008.
Thaden, Edward. "The Abortive Experiment: Cultural Russification in the Baltic Provinces, 1881–1914." In *Russification in the Baltic Provinces and Finland, 1855–1914*, ed. Edward Thaden, 54–75. Princeton: Princeton University Press, 1981.
Thaden, Edward. ed. *Russification in the Baltic Provinces and Finland, 1855–1914*. Princeton: Princeton University Press, 1981.
Thaden, Edward C., and Marianna Foster Thaden, *Russia's Western Borderlands*. Princeton: Princeton University Press, 1984.
Tishkov, V. A. *Obshchestvo v vooruzhennom konflikte: etnografiia chechenskoi voiny*. Moscow: Nauka, 2001.

Tkhamokova, I. Kh. *Russkoe i ukrainskoe naselenie Kabardino-Balkarii.* Nalchik: El-Fa, 2000.
Troino, F. P. "Zemel'naia arenda u gorskikh narodov Severnogo Kavkaza v kontse XIX – nachale XX vekov." *Istoriia gorskykh i kochevykh narodov Severnogo Kavkaza,* Vypusk. 3 (1978): 3–86.
Tsutsiev, A. A. *Osetino-Ingushskii konflikt (1992-...): ego predistoriia i faktory razvitie.* Moscow: ROSSPEN, 1998.
Tsutsiev, A. A. *Atlas etnopoliticheskoi istorii Kavkaza (1774-2004).* Moscow: Evropa 2007.
Tsutsiev, A. A. "Ob odnom algoritme krizisnogo pricheneniia na Severnom Kavkaze." *Nauchnye Tetrady Instituta Vostochnoi Evropy,* no. 111 (2009): 168–91.
Tuganov, R. U. *Istoriia obshchestvennoi mysli kabardinskogo naroda v pervoi polovine XIX veka.* Nalchik: El-Fa, 1998.
Tul'chinskii, N. P. "Piat' gorskikh obshchestv Kabardy." *Terskii sbornik* 5 (1903): 174–5.
Uarziati, V. S. *Kul'tura osetin: sviazi s narodami Kavkaza.* Ordzhonikidze: Ir, 1990.
Uehling, Greta Lynn. *Beyond Memory: The Crimean Tatars' Deportation and Return.* New York: Palgrave Macmillan, 2004.
Unezhev, K. Kh. *Istoriia Kabardy i Balkarii.* Nalchik: El-Fa, 2005.
Viola, Lynne. *The Unknown Gulag: The Lost World of Stalin's Special Settlements.* Oxford: Oxford University Press, 2007.
Volkova, N. G. *Etnicheskii sostav naseleniia severnogo Kavkaza v XVIII – Nachale XX veka.* Moscow: Nauka, 1974.
Watts, Sheldon, J. *Epidemics and History: Disease, Power, and Imperialism.* New Haven: Yale University Press, 1997.
Weeks, Theodore. *Nation and State in Late Imperial Russia: Nationalism and Russification on the Western Frontier, 1863-1917.* DeKalb: University of North Illinois Press, 1996.
Weeks, Theodore. "Russification: Word and Practice, 1863-1914." *Proceedings of the American Philosophical Society* 148, no. 4 (2004): 471–89.
Werth, Nicholas. "The 'Chechen Problem': Handling an Awkward Legacy, 1918-1958." *Contemporary European History* 15, no. 3 (2006): 347–66.
Werth, Paul. *At the Margins of Orthodoxy: Mission, Governance, and Confessional Politics in Russia's Volga-Kama Region, 1827-1905.* Ithaca: Cornell University Press, 2001.
Werth, Paul. *The Tsar's Foreign Faiths: Toleration and the Fate of Religious Freedom in Imperial Russia.* Oxford: Oxford University Press, 2014.
Yurchak, Alexei. "Soviet Hegemony of Form: Everything Was Forever, Until It Was No More." *Comparative Studies in Society and History* 45, no. 3 (July 2003): 480–510.
Zakhiraev, Z. A. "Razvitie Groznenskogo neftenosnogo raiona v 1916-1921 godakh." In *Chechenskaia Respublika i chechentsy: istoriia i sovremennost',* eds. Kh. I. Ibragimov, A. D. Osmaev, M. Ia. Ustinova, and V. A. Tishkov, 288–92. Moscow: Nauka, 2005.
Zakriev, B. B. "K istorii rossiisko-chechenskikh otnoshenii poslednei threti XVIII veka." In *Chechenskaia Respublika i chechentsy: istoriia i sovremennost',* eds. Kh. I. Ibragimov, A. D. Osmaev, M. Ia. Ustinova, and V. A. Tishkov, 254–61. Moscow: Nauka, 2005.
Zelkina, Anna. *In Quest for God and Freedom: Sufi Responses to the Russian Advance in the North Caucasus.* London: Verso, 2000.
Zhansitov, O. A. *Antibol'shevistskoe dvizhenie i denikinskii rezhim v Kabarde i Balkarii, (1917-1920 gg.).* Nalchik: Institut gumanitarnykh issledovanii Pravitel'stva KBR i KBNTs RAN, 2009.
Zhansitov, O. A. "Problemy modernizatsii promyshlennoi sfery Kabardino-Balkarskoi respubliki (1960-1980 gg.)." *Bylye gody* 33, no. 3 (2014): 479–82.
Zhemukhov, Sufian. "The Birth of Modern Circassian Nationalism." *Nationalities Papers* 40, no. 4 (2012): 503–24.

Index

Abaev, Misost 90, 93, 100, 107, 244 n.41, 261 n.164
Abazas 18, 45, 51, 56, 70, 85, 111, 208, 221, 232
  Tapanta Abazas 20, 21, 46, 245 n.57
Abkhazia 216, 218, 282 n.12
Abramov Commission 109–10
Abukov, Iskhak 52
adat. See customary law
Adyge Khasa 215, 217
Adyghe people. *See* Circassians
Ak-Barzoi 69, 100
Akhokhov, Aslanbi 206
aldary (Tagaur-Ossetian nobles) 42
Aleksandrovskaia 140
Alexander I 54
Alexander II 77, 78, 82, 85, 94, 96, 107
Aliev, Umar 129, 153, 154, 261 n.164
Anzorovs (Kabardian noble family) 19, 114, 115
Astrakhan 33
atalyk, practice of 23, 55–6
Atazhukin, Adil'-Girei 48, 49, 52
Atazhukin, Kurgoko 235
Azapshevo 100
Azov-Mozdok Line 43, 65

Baddeley, John 243 n.34
Baev, Mikhail 105
Baksan 180–1
Baksan Hydroelectric Power Station 175, 273 n.24
Baksanskoe 117
Baksan Uprising (1928) 180–1, 274 n.52
Balkar AO 134–5
Balkars 1, 10, 18, 20, 48, 261 n.171
  deportation of 4–5, 8, 10, 26, 169–70, 173, 177, 185–7, 189–95, 203, 204–11, 227–9, 240, 285 n.115
  administrative-territorial changes and 192–4

  experience in exile and 203–5
  Kabardian responses to 193–5
  NKVD culpability for 190–3
  identity of 14
  and Kabardian ASSR in exile 195–205
  national movement 181–2, 215–19, 226–30
  and attempted formation of Republic of Balkaria 217–19, 228
  nobility (*taubiis*) 107–9, 119
  peasant reform and 102–10
  relations with Kabardians 2–5, 42, 45, 46, 58, 60–1, 63, 73, 75, 102–10, 119–20, 131–8, 173–83, 226–30, 234–6
  return and reintegration and 205–10, 227–8
Bariatinskii, Alexander 78, 81, 82
Battle of Mount Kanzhal 39, 235
Begeulov, Rustam 15, 23, 244 n.44
Beketov, Nikita 21
Beklemishev, Nikolai 88, 90
Bekovich-Cherkasskii, Alexander 67
Bekovich-Cherkasskii, Elmurza 67
Bekovich-Cherkasskii, Efim 68
Bekovich-Cherkasskii, Fedor Aleksandrovich 67–8, 99
Bekovich-Cherkasskii lands 67–70, 97, 99–101
Belaia Rechka 109, 194, 240
Beppaev, Sufian 217–19, 229, 283 n.41
Beria, Lavrentii 186, 189–92
Beslaneev, Khabala 161, 163
Bezengi 5, 14, 20, 75, 102, 103, 182
Bezevo 69
Blitstein, Peter 11, 171, 196
Boiar, I.T. 148, 149
border delimitation
  intercommunal conflict and national identity and 126, 130, 132,

133, 157, 266 n.47, 267 n.110, 271 n.240
  land disputes and Soviet nations and   164-8
  during tsarist era   4, 43, 75, 103-6, 110
Brubaker, Rogers   8, 9, 242 n.19
Bulgakov, Sergei Alekseevich   51
Bziava, Konstantin   190, 191

Catherine II   35, 39-41, 77
  Charter of   39
Caucasian war   59-61
  Balkars and   73, 75
  Caucasus Cordon Line and   71-3, 97, 106
  Cossack colonization and intercommunal relations and   63-5
  diversity, displacement, and land disputes in Lesser Kabarda and   65-70
  geopolitical context of   61-2
  land question after Ermolov and   62-3
  pasturage politics and   70-3
Caucasus Bureau of the Communist Party (*Kavbiuro*)   129
Central Caucasus   3, 4, 241 n.4. *See also* Caucasian war; Kabarda; Kabardians
  adat-based Tribal Courts in   49
  after Ermolov   56-8
  ethno-demographic map of   16
  geographic description of   15
  intercommunal relations in   5-6
  Islam in   23-4
  land disputes, border conflicts, and nationality in   127-30
Central Committee (Tsk)   132, 154, 160, 177, 194, 196-8, 200, 202, 205, 206, 209, 223
Chechens   43, 55, 69, 70, 100, 118, 123, 127, 208
  Cossacks and   233
  Ingush and   222, 226
  location in relation to Kabarda   20
Chechnya   12, 24, 54, 57, 60, 61, 63, 180, 186, 218, 222, 243 n.33

Chegem   20, 50, 51, 58,
Cherek   20, 51, 58, 110, 189
Cherek Uprising   119
Cherkesov, Georgii.   219
Chernyshev, Alexander   72
Chichagov, Stepan   29, 245 n.56
Chipchikov, Kurgoko   111
Chirikovo   69
Christianity, conversion to   35-7
Circassians   17, 55, 216
  folk religion of   247 n.25
  national movement of   215-17
  resistance to Russian rule   43, 62
collectivization   164, 170, 173, 179-81, 210
colonization
  Cossack   57, 63-6, 88, 116, 233, 238
  significance of   4, 5, 13, 15, 24, 25, 29, 31, 47-51, 58, 60-2, 76, 165-6, 206, 218, 243 n.33, 256 n.18
colonization and imperial integration
  intercommunal relations and Slavic peasant migration in post-reform Russia and   116-18
  land and the transformation of social relations in Kabarda and   95-102
  land reform and serf emancipation project and   81-5
  Kodzokov and   85-93
  peasant migration to North Caucasus and preconditions and   94-5
  significance of   77-81
communal (*obshchinnaia*) land   84-7, 89, 91, 114, 116, 119, 127
Confederation of Repressed Peoples of Russia   227
Cossacks   37, 39, 42, 56-60, 62, 66, 71, 118, 220
  Chechens and   233
  colonization of Kabarda, and intercommunal relations   63-5
  Kabardians and *inogorodnie* and   138-43
  relations with Kabardians   60, 63-5, 253 n.29, 268 n.118
  stanitsy and   20, 32, 43, 55, 57, 62, 64, 65, 69, 70, 84, 94, 95, 124, 127, 128, 139, 181, 233

Crimean Khanate   18, 29, 31, 33, 38, 40
customary law   47, 49-51, 61, 68, 79,
  82-3, 249 n.90

Dagestan   12, 24, 36, 57, 60, 61, 67, 73,
  82, 243 n.33
Del Pozzo, Ivan   51, 52
Denikin, Anton   125, 127
deportations   12, 59, 165, 275 n.85,
  277 nn.140, 152
  of Balkars   4-5, 8, 10, 26, 169-70,
    173, 177, 185-7, 189-95, 203,
    204-11, 227-9, 240, 285 n.115
  of Chechens   180
  of Cossack *stanitsy*   124, 127, 128,
    132, 143
  Kabardian responses to   193-5
  NKVD culpability for   190-3
  mass   183, 185, 186, 190, 243 n.35
  population politics of   183-4, 238
Dergachev Commission   151, 152
Derluguian, Georgi   222-3
Digora   20, 23, 32, 34, 37, 44, 48, 114,
  145, 269 n.155
Dmitriev Commission   136, 157
Dudaev, Dzhokhar   1, 217, 222
Dzhylakhstanei   17, 66, 68-70, 99, 100.
  See also Kabarda, Lesser

Elbrus   182, 193
Emergency Land Commission of
  the Terek Soviet Republic
  (1918)   128, 131, 150-1
Emmanuel, Georgi   71, 75
Eneev, Magomed   131, 135
Enukidze, Avel   161
Eristov, Georgii   75, 79, 88-9
Ermolov, Aleksei   31, 52, 61, 66-8, 73,
  111, 231, 239
  Central Caucasus after   56-8
  final conquest of Kabarda and   53-6
  land question after   62-3
Eshkakon River   157
ethnic cleansing   11, 25, 26, 238, 271 n.3,
  274 n.63
  intercommunal relations and   170,
    183-5, 189
Etoko pastures   72
Etoko River   71, 89

Filatov, Stepan Ivanovich   191, 192
Fonin, Mikhail   196-7

Gemuev, Ako   178
Georgia   22, 32, 186, 192, 194, 221
  Eastern (Kartli-Kakheti)   42, 45
  Western (Imeretia)   32
Georgian Military Highway   42, 45, 46,
  50, 60, 63, 65-7, 69, 95, 117,
  139, 233
Glazenap, Grigorii 50, 51
Gnadenburg   141, 142, 143
Golaev, Khamzat   150
Golovin, Evgenii   68, 72
Great Reforms   77-8, 101, 255 n.2
Groznyi   95, 123, 139, 150, 208, 233-4
Güldenstädt, Johann Anton   21, 22
Gundelen   109, 111, 112, 159, 194, 195,
  209, 235-6

Hirsch, Francine   7, 126, 266 n.47,
  271 n.240
Hobsbawm, Eric   7
Horowitz, Donald   10, 223, 242 n.23,
  256 n.10, 283 n.62

Iagoda, Genrikh   146
Idarov, Temriuk   17-18
Inarokovo   100
Indarovo   100
Ingush   21, 24, 32, 46, 66, 100, 119, 123,
  127, 208
  Chechens and   222, 226
  conversion to Christianity   36, 42,
    44
  location in relation to Kabarda   20
  Ossetians and   221-2, 230, 233
  relations with Kabardians   41, 44, 45,
    53, 55, 57, 58, 69, 81
  resettling to plains   33, 34
Ingushetia   15, 29, 46, 100, 118, 130, 141,
  145, *162*, 164, 181, 218, 222,
  225-6, 233
inogorodnie   94, 117, 118, 119, 138, 139,
  141, 150
  intercommunal relations   2, 5-6, 9,
    12-13, 23, 24, 26, 137. *See also*
    Caucasian war; colonization and
    imperial integration

Central Caucasus and   30-1, 36, 44, 48, 53, 55-8
Slavic peasant migration in post-reform Russia and   116-18
Soviet nationalities policy and deportation and   170, 173-5, 183, 187, 207, 210
intercommunal relations and ethnic politics   213-15
Chechnya and   222
cultural politics and Kabardian-Balkar tension transformation and   234-6
Ingushetia and   221-2
Kabardino-Balkaria and   215-19
Karachai-Cherkessia and   219-21
peace and conflict cause and   222
Kabardian-Balkar relations and rehabilitation politics   226-30
social structure and reintegration   222-6
structures and patterns of   230-4
Islam   1, 3, 12, 60, 61, 243 n.33, 249 n.85
in Baksan   180
Central Caucasus and   23-4, 35, 37, 57
colonization and   83, 84, 114
institutionalization, in Russian Empire   249 n.93
intercommunal relations and   176, 180, 181, 185
in Kabardian-Ossetian relations   263 n.238
Kabardians and   47, 48, 52
sharia law   48, 49, 61, 83, 184
Islamization   24, 48, 49, 246 n.78

Jersild, Austin   80, 83, 241 n.6, 243 n.36, 247 n.21, 249 n.90, 260 n.129

Kabarda   74, 278 n.165. *See also* Central Caucasus
Baksan party   18
as buffer zone between Ottoman and Russian Empires   29
cultural-linguistic communities of   20
Digora and   32
economy of   19
Ermolov and final conquest of   53-6
etymology of   17
geography of   21, 29
Greater   17, 18, 20, 21, 22, 32, 34, 36-7, 40, 41, 43, 47, 50, 65, 66, 95, 96, 100, 106, 111, 117, 180
Islam and   47-51, 180
Islamization of   246 n.78
Kashkatau Party   18
Kazy   18
land and social relations in, transformation of   95-102
Lesser   15, 17, 18, 21, 22, 29, 32, 34, 36, 40, 41, 43, 47, 50, 53, 57, 58, 60, 62, 63, 65-70, 75, 95, 97-102, 117, 119, 141-3, 256 n.18
map of   30
Ossetian migration to   113-15
peasant reforms in   81-93, 95-102
plague, land, and empire and   51-3
princedoms of   18
Russo-Kabardian tensions and land politics and   42-7
Russo-Ottoman War (1768-74) and   38-41
social hierarchy of   18-19
and tributaries societies, Russia policy towards   31-8
Kabardian Line   65
Kabardian Oblast Party Committee (Obkom)   196, 198
Kabardian Pedagogical Institute   200-2
Kabardian Provisional Court (*Kabardinskii vremennyi sud*)   56
Kabardians   2-3, 250 n.118, 282 n.12
Cossacks and Terek settlers and   138-43
identity of   14
intelligentsia   197, 200, 201, 203
Islamization of   23-4, 48
relations with Balkars   2-5, 42, 45, 46, 58, 60-1, 63, 73, 75, 102-10, 119-20, 131-8, 173-83, 226-30, 234-6
relations with Cossacks   60, 63-5, 253 n.29, 268 n.118
relations with Ingush   41, 44, 45, 53, 55, 57, 58, 69, 81

relations with Karachais   45,
   46, 51, 63, 72–3, 97, 101,
   149–63
relations with mountaineers   3,
   19–23, 32–5, 102
relations with Ossetians   41, 44,
   45, 47, 53, 57, 58, 62, 65, 75,
   81, 105
resettlement, across the
   Kuban   250 n.107
resistance to Russian
   colonization   47–51
responses, to Balkar
   deportation   193–5
Kabardian Scientific Research Institute
   (KNII)   202
Kabardino-Balkaria   130, 163, 213, 223,
   225, 237, 272 n.7, 276 n.99
   creation of   7
   ethno-national mobilization and
      intercommunal tensions
      and   215–19
   geography of   15
   as Kabardian AO   7, 26, 126
   as Kabardian Autonomous
      Soviet Socialist Republic
      (KASSR)   171, 181, 194,
      195–205, 208–9, 211
   as Kabardino-Balkar AO   136,
      142, 145, 148, 167, 182, 209,
      232
   as Kabardino-Balkar Autonomous
      Soviet Socialist Republic
      (KBASSR)   14, 169, 190, 191,
      205–6, 209
   as Kabardino-Balkar Republic   15,
      271 n.1
   nationalities policy in 1930s   174–8
   under Nazi occupation   183–93
Kabardino-Balkar Oblast Committee
   (Obkom)   177, 201
Kabardino-Balkar State
   University   210
Kaisynov, Kaituko   38
Kalmykov, Betal   130, 133, 135, 155, 157,
   160, 161, 163, 176–7, 187
Kalmyks   23
Kambileevka River   21, 52, 66
Karachai-Cherkes AO   208, 224

Karachai-Cherkessia   219–21, 224–5,
   229–30, 232
Karachais   17, 18, 42, 70, 109–13, 133,
   186, 261 n.171, 263 n.213
   place of   20
   relations with Kabardians   45, 46, 51,
      63, 72–3, 97, 101, 149–63
Karadzhaevs (Ossetian noble family)   34,
   44
Karaev, Dris   148
Karasu Treaty (1772)   40
Karaulov, Mikhail   124
Karmovo   109, 133, 135, 159
Kasaev, Devlet   40
Kasaevs (Kabardian princely family)   111
Kashkhatau   109, 194
Katkhanov, Nazir   130, 156
Kazakhstan   165, 169, 203
Kazharov, Artur   134, 266 n.42,
   269 n.179
Këndelen. *See* Gundelen
Keskem   69
Khabaz   109, 133, 135, 159
khabza. *See* customary law
Khamurzin, Atazhuko   48, 49
Khasan'ia   109, 194, 240
Khasaut   110–13, 119, 130, 149, 151–63
Khomiakov, Aleksei   80, 85, 86,
   257 n.47
Khomiakova, Maria   85, 87
Khrushchev, Nikita   169, 205
Khubiev-Karachaily, Islam   153–4
Khulam   5, 14, 20, 75, 102, 103,
   111, 182
Kichmalka River   71, 150, 157
Kirgizia   169, 203
Kirov, Sergei   119
Kislovodsk Line   65, 73, 97
Kizliar   22, 33, 36, 43, 67
Kizliarskoe   101, 141, 142, 143
Klaproth, Julius von   22, 23
Kodzokov, Dmitrii Magometovich
   (Lukman)   79–80, 85–93, 96,
   98, 105–7, 109, 112, 113, 116,
   260 nn.140, 143
Kodzokov Commission. *See* Terek Estate-
   Land Commission
Kogolkins (Kabardian noble family)   114
Kokov, Valerii   218, 219, 229

kolkhozy/kolkhozes (collective farms)   179, 180, 194, 198, 199, 206, 209
Konchokin, Kurgoko   36, 37, 66
Konokov, Arsen   235
Konstantinogorsk   56
Konstantinovskii   67
korenizatsiia (nativization)   11, 171–2, 176–8, 195–202, 209–10, 223, 238, 278 n.154
Kotliarevskaia   95, 140
Kotsev, Pshemakho   123
Kozdemir   68
Krechetnikov, Petr   41
Kuban Oblast   73, 95, 109, 111, 113, 114, 149–51, 256 n.17
Kuban River   15, 20, 38, 40, 46, 55, 62
Kubatievs   (Ossetian noble family)   34
Kudashev, Vladimir   107
Kuibyshev, Nikolai   153, 155
Kuliev, Kaisyn   204
Kuma River   15, 19, 21, 29, 43, 70, 73
Kumekhov, Zuber   187–9, 196, 277 n.129
  NKVD culpability for Balkar deportation and   190–3
Kumykov, T. Kh.   87, 90, 244 n.38, 259 n.118, 261 n.162, 286 n.1
Kumyks   67, 69, 70, 100, 101, 118
Kundukhov, Musa   69, 254 n.67
Kura River   15, 29
Kurdzhiev, Kurman   157
Kurp River   53, 66, 99, 101, 117
Kyzburun 2 (Islamei)   180

Lakhran River   111
Law on the Socialization of Land (1918)   128
legal pluralism   61
Lenin, Vladimir   122
Lesken River   66, 114
Lesken village   115, 119, 164–5
  struggle for   143–9
Little Eshkakon pastures   97, 101
Loris-Melikov, Mikhail   79, 85, 93, 95, 96, 99, 101, 106, 108, 109, 112, 116, 257 n.37, 258 n.88, 259 n.110, 260 nn.140, 143

Magomet-Iurt   68
Magomet-Iurtovskaia   69
Mal'bakhov, Timbora   206, 223, 272 n.9
Malka River   17, 19, 21, 43, 44, 54, 63, 70–2, 150
Mamsurov, Sakhandzherei   142
Mansur, sheikh   47, 49
Martin, Terry   165, 174, 175, 184, 197, 202, 267 n.110, 271 n.240, 274 n.45
Mazin, Nikolai   196–8, 200
Mekhkeme   51, 56
Mikhail Nikolaevich, Grand Duke of Russia   85, 91, 92, 101, 107, 259 n.110
Mikoyan, Anastas   232
Miliutin, Dmitrii   82, 83, 97, 260 n.136
modernization
  significance of   9, 25, 82, 87, 98, 165, 167, 168, 170–1, 173, 178, 179, 200, 213, 239, 241 n.5, 242 nn.23, 25, 272 n.7
  socioeconomic   5, 10, 77, 95, 171, 203, 210, 283 n.62
  Soviet   4, 203, 207, 223, 272 n.9
Mountaineer (*Gorskaia*) Autonomous Soviet Socialist Republic (GASSR)   129–30, 132–4, 139–47, 152, 157
Mountaineer Republic   123–4
mountaineer societies   125–6. *See also individual entries*
  Islam and   48
  Kabardians and   3, 19–23, 32–5, 57–8, 96–7
  religious conversion of   35–7, 48
  serf emancipation in   107–10
  significance of   20–1
Mozdok   22, 36–8, 40, 43, 44, 64, 66, 95, 124
Mudarovs (Kabardian princely family)   17, 18, 22, 66, 67, 68
Muhammad Amin   111
Muromtsev, V.S.   132–5, 153

Nalchik   54, 65, 81, 92, 95, 110, 113, 117, 119, 128, 132, 134, 144, 145, 150, 152, 158, *162*, 189, 192, 201, 206, 226, 231, 234, 240

Narimanov, Nariman   160
Narkomnats (People's Commissariat of Nationality Affairs)   129, 136, 158
Narodnyi kommissariat vnutrennykh del (People's Commissariat for Internal Affairs) (NKVD)   169, 184, 187, 189, 190, 204
   culpability, for Balkar deportation   190–3
Nastuev, Iusuf   131
National Council of the Balkar People (NSBN)   182, 217–19
nativization. *See korenizatsiia*
Nazarov, N.   133, 155
Nazran   69, 100, 119
Nevskii, Vladimir   132
Nevskii Commission   132
Nicholas I   71, 72, 75, 84
Nicholas II   105, 121, 122
Nizhnii Chegem   109
Nogais   18, 22, 43, 62
Nogmov, Shora   285 n.129
North Caucasus   1, 42, 47, 49, 77, 79, 165–6, 243 nn.33–6, 271 n.240
   ethnicity meaning in   3
   geography of   14–15
   historiography of   12–14
   intercommunal conflict in   4
   1905 Revolution and   122
   peasant migration to   94–5, 116–18
   Regional Executive Committee (*Kraiispolkom*)   147
   reintegration politics and   205–10
   religious conversion in   35–6
   Russian Civil War in   123–5
   Russian Revolution (1917) in   123
   Russia's security dilemma in   7
   Stalin-era deportations from   8
North Ossetia   144, 146–9, 164, 192
   Digora in   23, 32, 44, 48, 114, 145, 269 n.155
   Ingush in   208, 221, 222
Novokonstantinovskoe   117
Novopoltavskoe   117
Novyi Urukh   146
Nurid, Aleksandr   91, 92, 96

Odintsov, S.   142, 164–5
Odintsov Commission   130, 142–3, 161
Orbeliani, Grigol   79, 82–4, 91, 118
Ossetian-Ingush conflict   123, 208
Ossetians   17, 46, 66
   Alagirs   20, 44
   conversion to Christianity   36, 42, 48
   Digorans   21, 32, 34, 37, 44, 48, 114, 145
   Ingush and   221–2, 230, 233
   Islam and   12, 48
   Kurtats   20, 44
   migration to Kabarda   113–15
   place of   20
   relations with Kabardians   41, 44, 45, 47, 53, 57, 58, 62, 65, 75, 81, 105
   resettling to plains   33–5
   serfs   44
   Tagaurs   20, 44
   tribute payment to Kabardians   21
Ossetian Spiritual Commission   35, 37, 44
Ottoman Empire   33, 35, 36, 38, 42, 43, 183, 246 n.80, 256 n.17. *See also* Russo-Ottoman Wars
   emigration of Circassians to (*Mukhadzhirstvo*)   62

Paskevich, Ivan   71
Perkhichevo   100
Petrov, Grigorii   177, 178
Piatigor'e   46, 59, 85
Piatigorsk   85, 124, 156
Podkumok River   15, 29, 50
population politics   59, 75, 76, 100, 238
   intercommunal relations and   180, 183–4, 186, 191, 193, 210
   significance of   251 n.1
Potapov, Nikolai   39
Potemkin, Pavel   45, 47
Prigorodnyi district   221, 233
Prishibskaia   140
Prokhladnaia   95
Protopopov, Dmitrii   196
Psedakh   68, 69, 100
Psheapshokov, Kazy.   18
Pshekau   100

Razdol'noe 141, 142, 143
Red Army 125, 127, 144, 149, 153, 181, 185–9
Rostov-on-Don 147, 155, 156, 164
Rostov-Vladikavkaz railway 95
Russian Civil War 123–5
Russian Empire 24, 35
　as bureaucrat-policeman state 7, 82, 92, 138
　ethnicity in 25, 45, 80, 98, 100, 103–4, 112, 119, 183
　imperial governance in 5–8, 29–31, 33, 39, 42, 45, 47, 49, 98, 101–3, 105–9, 112, 119
　Islam and 47–9, 180, 249 n.93
　as landscaper 7, 83
　native elites role in 8
　pluralistic legal regimes in 252 n.6
　presence in Kabarda 47–51
　as referee 7, 57, 83, 105
　Russification in 77, 79, 82, 119, 121
Russian Revolution (1917) 122–4, 127, 167
Russian Soviet Federal Socialist Republic (RSFSR) 171, 196, 206, 226
Russo-Japanese War (1905) 121
Russo-Kabardian tensions and land politics, in late eighteenth century 42–7
Russo-Ottoman Wars
　1735–9　29
　1768–74　38–41
　1787–92　47
　1828–9　62, 86
Rykov, Aleksei 148

Sabanchiev, Khadzhi-Murat 186, 189, 190
Sagopsh 69, 100
Sahlins, Peter 126, 167–8
St. Petersburg 33, 36, 37, 41, 67, 72, 79
Sarmakovo 177
serfs 19, 34, 51, 64, 67, 68
　emancipation of 60, 69, 76, 78–8, 96, 102
　　land reform and 81–93
　　in mountaineer societies 107–10
　fugitive 37, 39
　transition as peasants 78

Shamil 12, 60–2, 72, 73, 88, 252 n.10
sharia law 48, 49, 61, 83, 184
Sleptsovskaia 139
Smirnov Land Commission 130, 141–4, 164
Soldatskaia 140
Soviet Union
　borders and formation of 164–8, 267 n.110
　as bureaucrat-policeman state 167, 186
　collapse of 7, 183–93, 211, 213, 214, 222, 228
　collectivization 164, 170, 173, 179–81, 210
　developmentalism in 195, 202–3, 272 n.9
　ethnic cleansing and 26, 183–5
　industrialization 121, 173, 174, 200–2, 234, 273 n.24
　national intelligentsia and 121, 123, 171, 177, 195–8, 203
　nationalities policy of
　　campaigns against bourgeois nationalism 129, 154, 174–5, 177, 178, 197, 202
　　deportation and 170, 173–5, 183, 187, 207, 210
　　significance of 11, 26, 171, 174–8, 184, 195–205, 234
　　titular 11, 13, 144, 167, 174, 175, 178, 184, 219–20, 226
　as referee 130, 145, 166
special settlers (*spetsposelentsy*) 203–5
Stalin, Joseph 129, 133, 155, 157, 158, 170, 171, 184–7, 190, 192, 196, 220, 266 n.42
Stalinism, Kabardians and Balkars under
　administrative-territorial transformations and 181–3
　Balkars during late-Stalinism 203–5
　collectivization, repression, and resistance and 179–81
　nationalities policy in 1930s Kabardino-Balkaria and 174–8
　nationalities policy in the post-War era 195–203
　significance of 173–4

stanitsy (fortified Cossack
        settlement)   20, 32, 43, 55, 57,
    62, 64, 65, 69, 70, 84, 94, 95, 124,
    127, 128, 139, 181, 233
State Political Directorate (GPU)   146–8
Stolypin, Petr   110
Sufism   24, 252 n.10
Sunzha River   15, 21, 29, 34, 64, 66, 67, 127
Svans   194

Talostanei   17, 66, 69, 70, 99–101. *See
    also* Kabarda, Lesser
Tambukan lake   71
Tashly-Tala   182, 206
Teberda River   20
Temir-Khan-Shura   124
Terek Cossacks   64, 103, 118, 124, 125,
    127, 138–40, 233, 251 n.146,
    253 n.24
Terek-Dagestan government   124
Terek Estate-Land Commission   217
    colonization and imperial integration
        and   85, 89–91, 93, 97–103,
        106, 107, 110, 112, 114, 119
Terek oblast   73, 79, 81, 83, 95, 101, 109,
    113, 114, 119, 123, 127, 149–51
Terek River   15, 17, 20, 21, 29, 32, 36, 43,
    55, 64, 67
Terek Soviet Republic   128, 131
Tiflis (Tbilisi)   71, 88, 91, 101, 129
Tkachenko, Mikhail   152, 156, 161
Toganov, Dmitrii   39
Tormasov, Aleksandr, general   52
Tramovo   56
trans-Malka pastures   96, 101, 106–7,
    112, 182
    border delimitation and
        intercommunal conflict
        and   130, 133, 149, 150, 152,
        155, 157, 159, 160, 163, 168
Treaty of Adrianople (1829)   62
Treaty of Belgrade   29, 33, 35–8
Treaty of Georgievsk (1783)   45
Treaty of Küçük Kaynarca (1774)   24, 40,
    46, 54
Tribal Courts. *See* customary law

Trotsky, Leon   122
Tsitsianov, Pavel, 50, 51
Tuganov, Aslambek   103
Tuganovs (Ossetian noble family)   34,
    114
Turkestan   84
Turkey   187
Tëre   215, 216, 217

Uianaev, Chomai   207
Ul'bashev, Kellet   178
Union of United Mountaineers of
    the North Caucasus and
    Dagestan   123
urbanization   4, 202, 223–5, 241 n.5
Urukh   54
Urusbi   5, 14, 20, 75, 102, 103, 108
Urusbiev, Izmail   108

Vladikavkaz   45, 47, 65, 66, 69, 95, 108,
    123, 124, 140, 221
Vol'nyi Aul   240
Volga Cossacks   71, 72
Volga Tatars   49
von Medem, Johann Friedrich   40, 41
Vorontsov, Mikhail   72, 88, 89, 257 n.57
Vorontsov-Dashkov, Illarion   109, 110
Voroshilov, Kliment   153, 155, 156
vydvizhentsy (promoted workers)   187,
    188

Yeltsin, Boris   220, 228

Zaiukovo   209
Zavadovskii, Nikolai 72
Zavgaev, Doku   222
Zelenchuk River   20
Zhagishevo   100
Zhereshtievs (noble family in Balkaria,
    Kabarda, and Karachai)   111,
    159
Zmeiskaia   140, 141
Zolka pastures   71, 72, 96, 101, 106, 107,
    119, 152, 161, 163
Zolka River   69, 71, 89, 116, 117
Zolka Uprising   119